THE DANCE OF SPICES

THE DANCE OF SPICES

CLASSIC INDIAN COOKING FOR

TODAY'S HOME KITCHEN

LAXMI HIREMATH

JOHN WILEY & SONS, INC.

WILEY

To my husband,

Mahantesh,

& children,

Kailash & Kedar

Published by John Wiley & Sons, Inc., Hoboken, New Jersey

Published simultaneously in Canada

Library of Congress Cataloging-in-Publication Data:

Hiremath, Laxmi, 1958-
  The dance of spices : classic Indian cooking for today's home kitchen / by Laxmi Hiremath.
    p. cm.
  Includes index.
  ISBN 0-471-27273-6 (cloth)
  1. Cookery, Indic. I. Title.
  TX724.5.I4H544 2005
  641.5954--dc22

                    2004029341

Printed in the United States of America

10 9 8 7 6 5 4 3 2 1

CONTENTS

ACKNOWLEDGMENTS   vii

PREFACE   ix

Basics of the Indian Kitchen   1

The Treasures of the Indian Pantry   17

Chapati, Poori, Naan, and Other Fresh Hot Breads   57

Sweet-Scented Basmati: The Fabled Pilafs and Biryanis   91

Chaat: Tantalizing Small Plates and Snacks   127

Pakora, Pappadam, and Other Starters   141

Idli, Dosa, and Other Casual Fare   153

Tongue Teasers: Chutneys and Pickles   171

Cool Yogurt, Refreshing Raitas, and Kachumbers   201

Fresh Paneer: Cheese Panache   219

Bountiful Blossoms: The Vegetable Kingdom   229

Everyday Meat and Poultry Specialties   267

Seafood Paradise   301

The Tastes of Tandoor: Indian Barbecue   335

Dal, Rasam, and Mulligatawny Soups   363

Chill Chasers: Bean and Lentil Sambars and Stews   375

A Sweet Note: Desserts   403

Thirst Quenchers: Cold and Hot Drinks   423

Indian Breath Mints   435

SOURCES   438
INDEX   441

ACKNOWLEDGMENTS

Creating a book like this, with recipes and stories, is a labor of love. It requires patience and effort. This book would never have come into fruition without the encouragement and support of many people.

From the beginning, my husband has critiqued my cooking. Without his involvement and keenness, my cooking wouldn't be nearly so finely honed. His constant editing, proofreading, and cheerleading have made me a better writer and cook. My sons, Kailash and Kedar, have filled my life with joy; their demands, patience, and ready smiles have sustained me. Over the years, they've grown to be adventurous recipe tasters.

I wish to thank my parents for helping to make my life so rich. My mother is a dynamic person. She has been an incredible role model and one of the biggest influences on my life. She encouraged my extracurricular activities. More importantly, she helped me to believe in myself. My father, through his knowledge and wisdom, helped me stay focused and become a better person.

My brother and sister have been my biggest supporters. My sister, Smita, has always proofread my articles, tested my recipes, provided invaluable suggestions, and kept me up-to-date on current food trends in India. Whenever I needed something from India, my brother, Sunil, was just a phone call away. My sister-in-law, Keertilata, has been a source of incredible knowledge about spices. Most southern Indian recipes in this book have been influenced by her suggestions.

My grandmothers have given me happy childhood memories, many of which I've shared in this book. The things I've learned from them extend far beyond these pages. Our cook in India, Gangawwa, was my first teacher. Watching her at work taught me the very basics of Indian cooking. I am grateful to my mother-in-law for her continued support and inspiration.

My literary agent, Jane Dystel, read my outline and a tiny descriptive paragraph and immediately decided to pursue the proposal. I am honored and privileged to be working with such an insightful person. Stacey Glick championed my writing skills, and her support and guidance have been enormous all along the way.

My original editor, Susan Wyler, is truly the pioneer of this work. Without her gentle urging and strength of conviction, I could not have completed this task. A special thanks to Justin Schwartz for editing the book. Many of the recipes received a final endorsement in Justin's kitchen.

The late Barbara Tropp was a small lady with a big heart, and she was ever so helpful. She steered me to Jane Dystel. Emily Luchetti provided further insights and direction.

Thanks also to Sue Dawson of the *Columbus Dispatch* and Michael Bauer, the executive food and wine editor of the *San Francisco Chronicle*. Both have my enduring gratitude for their generosity during my development as a professional writer. I thank Jay Harlow and Elaine Ratner, publishers of *Laxmi's Vegetarian Kitchen*, my first book, for helping me make my debut as an author.

I thank my friends Helen Mehoudar, for reading the introduction, and Shweta Govindarajan, for reviewing the proposal and providing provocative comments. Winery chef Brian Streeter of Cakebread Cellars made sure the wine recommendations were in order.

A few years ago, I started my company, Laxmi's Delights, with product lines of sweet spiced roasted nuts. This is a good time to thank the store buyers and customers for providing encouraging words and telling me often how my products fly off the shelf. I would also like to acknowledge Barbara Anderson of Wood Stove Kitchens for her endless support and valuable input regarding the packaging of my products.

Many thanks to the folks at Morton & Bassett for generously providing fragrant, plump spices for recipe testing. I would like to thank the Hearth Kitchen Company for providing the HearthKit (brick oven) to test the tandoori dishes.

I thank you, fans and students, for the lovely letters over the years. Last but not least, my children's friends, who are too numerous to name—I owe you a great deal.

PREFACE

As a child in India, I had not the slightest interest in learning to cook. During my visits to the kitchen, I sniffed around happily, exclaiming, "Boy, does that smell good!" without ever offering to help or wanting to learn.

Even when I first came to the United States two decades ago, I did not know anything about cooking. My first night in my home in Columbus, Ohio, in unfamiliar surroundings, I rolled up my sleeves and attempted to replicate what I had seen in my mother's kitchen so many years earlier. I made endless blunders, muddling up recipes and burning breads. After presenting my husband with a series of charred *chapati* and odd-tasting vegetable dishes, I decided I had to learn from the beginning. I made a conscious effort to master the basics of Indian cooking. Much to my delight and to my husband's relief, our meals soon improved.

As I learned to cook, I gauged my progress by comparing my creations to my taste memories of the foods prepared by women who had made a difference in my life. My *sambar* had to taste as good as my mother's. My *chapati* had to be as puffy as my grand-mother's. My pilaf had to be as fluffy as my mother-in-law's. My spice paste had to be as fragrant as that of our maid. When I discovered I could duplicate the flavors of my child-hood memories, I rejoiced, once again, in the sensual pleasure of Indian foods, their tex-tures, flavors, and aromas. I came to the realization that cooking good food is a great joy, worthy of intense concentration, careful preparation, and fine discrimination. Learning to prepare great Indian dishes became my top priority.

I had grown up a vegetarian. Over the years, I learned to eat poultry, meat, and fish, but it was a challenge for me to learn to cook them. To do this, I needed the help of some-one whose Indian food memories included meat and seafood dishes. My husband was not a vegetarian, and his astute palate could detect even the slightest mistake, especially when it came to meat and seafood dishes. I took his criticism as the opportunity to perfect my cooking, and success followed. My culinary skills developed to a point where I could understand and enjoy the nuances of each dish I prepared. I was able to take pleasure in my own cooking, and so I came to write this book.

The Dance of Spices is for you. It is designed to be a "hands-on cooking class." I want you to feel as if I am standing by your side in your kitchen, guiding you. Many of the recipes may seem quite demanding and elaborate. Do not be discouraged. The length of a recipe does not indicate that the preparation is long or difficult, only that every nuance and detail of preparation is spelled out to assist you. I have aimed to provide enough clear, in-depth instruction so that every cook, from the beginner to the advanced chef, can achieve success.

The dishes and style of preparation in this book are authentic; they represent the true cuisine of India. Consider this volume a road map. Chapter by chapter and recipe by recipe, you will learn the "whys and wherefores" of this great cuisine. Each chapter is introduced with information about Indian history and social customs, as well as personal anecdotes related to these foods. When you select a recipe, be sure to read the headnote first, to gain a little insight regarding the culture or origin of the dish. A few years ago, the executive chef at the Maurya Sheraton in New Delhi confided to me, "Though Indian cuisine is one of the best in the world, it has not been showcased properly." Here is a complete guide to allow you to create a showcase for Indian foods.

Boasting to former Indian prime minister Indira Gandhi, French president Charles de Gaulle is said to have claimed, "I preside over a country that has 346 cheeses and do a good job," to which Mrs. Gandhi retorted, "You are telling this to someone who rules the country of a thousand spices." In this book, I, Laxmi (pronounced LUCK-shmee), named for the golden-handed goddess of wealth and riches, share with you the great wealth of Indian food. It is an art form that has been passed down by word of mouth through many generations, from *guru* (teacher) to *vidhyarthi* (pupil), from mother to daughter. My native cuisine, the cuisine of India, is intricate, subtle, and richly layered, with an appealing emphasis on spices. It is a bold mosaic of colors and textures, offering a wealth of flavors and aromas.

So start today, maybe even right now. Find your favorite recipes and return to them time and again. As you do, you will discover that your familiarity with Indian food is growing and becoming more gratifying. With this guide, I hope you'll say, "Yes, this is the Indian food I wanted to prepare."

LAXMI HIREMATH
San Ramon, California

BASICS OF THE INDIAN KITCHEN

Hindustani Rasoi ke Aadaab

When I was a child growing up in India, the first thing our cook did each morning was make a curry paste, which served as the flavor base for all her cooking. She gathered up a small bunch of fresh cilantro, three or four garlic cloves, a knob of fresh ginger, a couple of fresh green chilis, and spoonfuls of whole cumin and coriander seeds. I watched intently as she pounded each ingredient thoroughly in a stone mortar before adding the next; she pulverized the cumin, then the coriander, followed by the chilis, ginger, garlic, and cilantro into a thick aromatic paste. She varied the ingredients for different dishes: sprigs of *kari* leaves (see page 28) replaced the cilantro, red chilis were used instead of green ones, or more whole spices were utilized. This was her fragrant "roux" for assorted curries. That was just the beginning of her curry-making. I loved to watch her at work (and I still do, each time I visit India). I was awestruck by mounds of brilliant curry pastes of colorful spices, fresh herbs, robust chilis, onion, ginger, and garlic that could turn any food into a beautiful, aromatic dish. It was a long process, however, and a repetitive one—something that's hard to justify in today's Western lifestyle.

For most Westerners, Indian cooking is synonymous with curry. Many think that all Indian curries are alike, never encountering the distinctive and fascinating local variations. In fact, curry is as diversified as India's people—the multitudes who came, stayed, and slowly became assimilated. Like many cuisines, Indian cooking is a reflection of history and climate, religion, and economics. Dravidian, Aryan, Moghul, British, and Portuguese—all these influences helped shape a cosmopolitan cuisine that evolved into four basic geographic divisions.

A FIRST LESSON IN CURRY MAKING

In my cooking classes, students ask, "What is curry?" So let's begin there. If Americans carry any notion of curry, it's typically of a red one, such as curried potatoes or chicken curry. Also, their first experience is usually in a restaurant, where curries are frequently made with a standard sauce, and often cooked with too much oil and/or butter. Fortunately, that's not all there is to a curry. So what, then, is a curry? A curry is defined as meat, seafood, vegetables, fruit, or legumes cooked in a spiced sauce until the flavors marry and mingle. The sauce can range from barely any (so it clings), to thick and velvety, to thin (soupy) and abundant. To me, curry means a mélange of individual ingredients cooked at a gentle pace with a meticulous balance of flavors, textures, and color. Curries are quite varied. *Korma, kofta* (in the meat and poultry chapter), *rasam, saar, kadhi*, and *dal* (in the soup chapter), seafood curries, vegetable curries, and legume stews all demonstrate the wide spectrum. Wet or dry *masala*, with spices whole or ground, toasted or raw, is the soul of this curry-making craft, creating a core of depth, flavor, and intricacy that is woven into an ornate work of art along with yogurt, nuts, seeds, and herbs.

Indian cooking is enormously varied and complex, and each region has its own perspective on techniques, ingredients, and proportions. Yet certain basic techniques are common to the national cuisine, and understanding or mastering these techniques will make the preparation of curries much easier and more enjoyable. So let's start at ground zero. Remember, there is no set formula for making a curry, and the beauty of curry preparation is that it invites experimentation. Once you understand these simple techniques, you'll be on your way to making Indian cuisine your own.

Step 1: *Tel ya Desi Ghee*, or the Oil or *Desi Ghee*

Always choose a cooking oil with a neutral flavor, because you want to infuse the oil with the tastes of the spices and aromatics that are being used. Flavorless or mild vegetable oils such as canola oil work quite well. (See pages 46–49 for more details on oils.) Traditional, sweetish-nutty *desi ghee*, or clarified butter, has its own distinctive flavor, and because of its high smoking point, it is used for sautéing and stir-frying.

Step 2: *Masala*, or the Spice Mix

What makes each Indian dish so distinctive is the composition of the "dry" *masala*—the blend of whole and/or ground spices. When using spices, it is necessary to be judicious; add too much, and they become overpowering. The sequence in which the spices are added to the oil and the length of time each spice is fried to allow its flavor to release are vital, too. Each spice has its own pattern of releasing flavor with the heat. Let's take the familiar cumin seeds, for example. Since they are delicate, they cook in a few seconds in hot oil, losing their raw taste and becoming crisp and nutty. In a heavy skillet set over moderate heat, the seeds take 3 to 4 minutes to release their toasty characteristics. Cooking lightly crushed cumin seeds takes less time, and the flavor is slightly sharper than with whole seeds. And in powdered form, cumin releases its pungent flavor almost instantly. Remember, spices release flavor in the most potent form in hot oil. Whole spices are added first to the hot oil, followed by powdered ones, because ground spices cook faster than whole, and the goal is to release the volatile oils without burning the spices. Once moisture is added to the spices, they almost stop releasing flavor. Adding spices directly to the liquid makes the spices less flavorful.

Step 3: *Tadka*, or the Dance of Spices

Seasoned oil forms a foundation for the majority of Indian dishes. The three basic spices of Indian cooking are turmeric, mustard seeds, and cumin seeds. Do not mix together all of the spices and dump them into the oil. The mustard and cumin seeds are fried first, then the aromatics (onion, ginger, and garlic) are added. Frying "cooks out" the raw taste of the spices. Do not let the oil smoke, or the delicate spice seeds will char instantly. Once the oil is heated, add the whole spice seeds and continue heating until they sizzle and splutter and release their distinctive bouquet. Wait a few seconds and enjoy this "dance of spices"—the popping of mustard seeds, that is; a few seeds will pop like popcorn. Use a spatter screen or hold a lid over the pan for safety, but do not cover it fully, or the seeds will steam rather than fry. Perfectly toasted mustard seeds look grayish, and cumin seeds turn uniformly reddish brown. The seeds stop popping and start to float after about 30 seconds. You can lower the heat at this point, to avoid burning. Do not cook the seeds too long, or they will turn dark and taste bitter. Add the turmeric; when it sizzles in a few seconds, take the pan off the heat. The flavorful oil that results is the *tadka*. Have all of the ingredients ready before you begin, because the entire process goes very quickly.

Step 4: *Bhoona*, or the Stir-Fry

Bhoona is the Hindi term for browning either dry or moist *masala* (a mixture of aromatics and spices) in hot oil to bring out their natural sweetness and depth, thereby harmonizing the flavors. This is a crucial step in creating pleasing tastes in authentic northern Indian cooking. Chicken Breasts in Korma Sauce (pages 270–271), a most popular dish, provides a good introduction to this simple technique. First, to be sure your ingredients fry properly, heat a heavy dry *kadai* (see page 56), wok, or skillet for a few minutes. Next, add the oil or *desi ghee,* as the recipe directs; it should become very hot. Add the onion and cook, stirring, until it turns a rich brown, as the recipe directs. Add the ginger-garlic paste. Why a paste rather than simply minced? Because the paste cooks more evenly than a mince and melds into the sauce for a smooth finish. Minced ginger and garlic also burn easily. Cook the paste, stirring constantly, in order to smooth out the rough edges and enhance the sweetness. Add the whole spices (they can also be added before the onion), followed by the ground. (Some recipes may call for a wet spice paste, which should be added all at once, as in Konkan Crab Curry; pages 309–310.) The spices must fry in the hot oil to release and develop their flavors. The chemicals in spices break down and restructure into different compounds, with new flavors and aromas, when they come in contact with high heat. Cinnamon sticks unfurl, cardamom pods become plump, and the *masala* takes on a beautiful, orange-red color as the wonderful flavors are released into the oil.

Now add the meat. Sear it well on both sides. This way, the meat is infused with the flavors from the oil. If the meat were browned first, as in other cuisines, the caramelized crust might inhibit the meat from absorbing the lovely flavors. By now, most of the moisture has been cooked out of the ingredients, and the oil has separated and pooled around the meat and the spice paste. This is the secret to a well-made curry. At just about this time, the meat is partially cooked. To prevent burning or scorching, an Indian chef always keeps a bowl of water handy to sprinkle the mixture if it is drying out. It is perfectly okay to sprinkle a dish with water and continue stirring. In fact, the process of adding moisture and scraping the *masala* is repeated two to three times. Once the final moisture—tomatoes, water, or yogurt—is added, the flavors of the spices develop no

A Few Tricks of the Trade for Cooking with Basics

* Reduced tomatoes add a special structure to the dish, so cook down the tomatoes until very soft and give the flavors time to come together, as the recipe proposes, before adding liquid.

* The texture of curries is better with sliced (lengthwise) onion than chopped.

* Whole spices have brighter, more distinct flavors than ground.

* Ground spices are less likely to stick to the pan when cooked quickly.

* Try to work with your nose and palate; smell the properly cooked spices, noting how their acrid flavors transform into lively fragrance and brighten with frying.

* Keep in mind that the flavors get even better the day after curries are made.

further. Note that once the liquid is added, the curry should not simmer for too long, or the brilliant flavor of the spices will fade. I suggest cooking it no more than 45 to 60 minutes.

Step 5: *Gadhapun*, or the Essential Thickener

Finally, a thickener—such as coconut milk, yogurt, yogurt cheese, cream, powdered nuts and seeds (sesame, poppy, melon, pumpkin), pureed lentils, or even fruit—is added to give body and add richness to the curries. Indians rarely use flour for thickening, since it lacks flavor.

Step 6: *Swaad ke Anusar*, or Balancing the Tastes

Even with a reliable recipe, once a dish is finished, it often requires a final touch to balance the taste. Each dish should be a delicate balance of tastes, textures, temperatures, and colors. First, I encourage you to add my suggested quantities of ingredients. Many dishes have a squirt of lime juice or dry mango powder added toward the end of cooking (in some dishes I've suggested passing lime wedges at the table). These flavorings are not intended to make the dish taste sour but to invigorate and bring a subtle harmony to its flavors. Salt is added (even in desserts) to brighten, balance, and focus the flavors. Sugar and jaggery smooth out any tart or rough edges or spicy heat. Cilantro, when properly balanced with other robust flavors, gives an exquisite dimension that adds depth and character to a dish. Taste before serving to determine if any final adjustments are necessary to optimally harmonize the flavors. Indians do not habitually taste food as it is cooking; they rely on visual appeal and their sense of smell. An experienced eye and sensitive nose can gauge whether a dish is prepared harmoniously, and most Indians develop this early on. Also, the daily food is not tasted, because it is offered first to god.

Step 7: *Rang aur Pradarshana*, or Color and Presentation

Aesthetically pleasing, bright color is as important to Indian cooking as the flavors and aromas. Use vibrantly hued spices, ripe tomatoes, brilliant chilis, and fresh young herbs. Serve complementary dishes with contrasting colors.

Presentation is vital to me. I spend a great amount of time on skillful garnishes, as they are the secret to visual charm. An Indian table offers many ways of seasoning and garnishing one's own serving to taste. Various garnishes—chopped herbs, crisp fried onion or garlic slices, julienned fresh ginger, toasted or freshly grated coconut, crunchy potato straws, chickpea flour noodles *(sev)*, chopped bell peppers, nuts, raisins, crumbled *paneer*, spiced oil seasonings, and the list goes on—can be sprinkled over relatively plain dishes to add color and texture, as well as flavor. Sometimes powdered chutneys are sprinkled on foods, much like salt and pepper.

INDIA'S PRIMARY FLAVORS

Most of the world's cuisines combine five primary tastes: sweet, sour, salty, bitter, and pungent. In Indian cuisine, there is a sixth: astringent. (The word *astringent* comes from ancient Indian medicine. Since it has a cooling and drying effect, I like to call it "nippy.") To maintain perfect balance and ensure complete nourishment, Indians include all tastes at every meal. Most curries include all six tastes in abundance. When I was growing up in southwestern India, our meals consisted of *chapati* (flatbread), rice, two vegetable dishes, a legume curry, *raita* (see pages 201–214), chutneys, and pickles. In America, my family's evening meals are composed of similar dishes, and in addition, occasionally I serve poultry, meat, or seafood as a side dish. You need to balance your carbohydrate, protein, and fat intake, and you need to eat these food types together. Eating simple carbohydrates alone causes a rise in blood sugar and makes you feel hungry. Eating in moderation is the key. When I was growing up my father told me, always eat less than your appetite—think of the stomach as a ball. When you eat, fill it half full with food, fill a quarter of the remaining half with water, and leave the remaining quarter empty. In ancient times, the sages removed some food from their plate and set it aside for the birds. The concept was the same, not to eat stomach full. Today, doctors and dieticians recommend eating in moderation and a diet based primarily on vegetables and fruits. The World Health Organization has singled out the cuisine of southwestern India as the most healthful and nutritionally balanced and nominated it as one of the recommended diets.

Though nutritional views have changed over the years, eating a variety of foods, as in Indian cuisine, and moderation are still recommended.

Some examples of primary tastes are:

* Sweet: sugar, rice, butter, milk, meats, and pasta

* Sour: limes, lemons, other sour fruits, aged cheese, tomatoes, and yogurt

* Salt: salt

* Bitter: leafy greens, fenugreek, and turmeric

* Pungent: cayenne and other chilis, ginger, and radishes

* Nippy (astringent): potatoes, eggplant, apples, beans and lentils, and sage

Many recipes in this book may share the same techniques, and even very similar ingredients, yet produce quite different dishes. You can change a dish by varying the proportions of spices and herbs and prepping them differently—for instance, by toasting or not toasting them ahead of time, or by adding whole instead of ground spices or a wet spice paste instead of a dry mix. You can even change the way you use onions in a single recipe for a different result. This infinite variety is part of the splendor of classic Indian cooking.

A LESSON IN TOASTING SPICES

The cooking of India is built on its spices. And it is the careful blending of those spices—subtle gradations of heat and flavor—that makes the regional cuisines of India so distinctive. Toasting, or dry-roasting, spices is the key to good Indian cooking. It adds complexity and a hint of smokiness and makes the spices bright and bold. Heat dries the spices enough to make grinding easier and eliminates any raw aftertaste. Most important, toasting releases the essential oils from the spices and maximizes both flavor and color.

To toast spices, use a heavy nonstick skillet (cast-iron works well). Gather all of the spices you'll need before you begin and make sure there is an even medium heat under your skillet. Heat the pan slightly, then add the spices and toast over moderate heat, stirring frequently, until they have a nice bouquet. You'll hear a faint crackle, and after a few seconds, you'll smell a toasty perfume. Toasting seeds releases their bouquet into the air before they start to brown, so let them cook a little longer after you begin to smell their roasted aromas, until they are uniformly reddish brown and crisp, but not burned. This way the spices are toasted through to the core and not just on the surface. Shake the pan or stir frequently for even toasting, which will take from four to eight minutes, depending on the amount you're roasting. Darkly toasted seeds will permeate a curry with stronger roasted flavors. Do not overtoast, or they will become acrid in taste and make the curry bitter. If they're blackened, they'll impart a burned taste and volatile oils will be lost, defeating the purpose of roasting.

In India, dried chilis are sometimes toasted in a little oil to preserve their freshness. Watch closely. The chilis should directly touch the hot surface. When they crackle, you may even see a faint wisp of smoke. That's okay, but any more will mean burnt chilis.

GRINDING FRESH SPICE BLENDS

Most Indian cooks prefer homemade spice blends, despite the availability of a range of commercial ones. They're fresher and far more aromatic, and many families have their own blends, prized possessions passed from mother to daughter for generations. My favorite, of course, is my mother's recipe, a hauntingly rich and fragrant original mixture containing fifty different spices (see pages 39–40).

Even though the ingredient lists for many spice blends may seem long, they're actually very easy to make ahead in batches and will keep for several months. It doesn't take long to assemble the spices and toast them, and grinding them is a matter of mere seconds in an electric spice grinder or coffee mill (they are easier to powder when the spices are slightly warm). After that, they're as easy to use as powders you've bought in a jar, and far more fragrant. Make no more than you plan to use within two or three months.

MORTAR AND PESTLE VERSUS SPICE GRINDER

I love collecting mortars and pestles. I prefer a medium-size stone mortar and a pestle made of granite, sandstone, marble, or basalt (Mexican *molcajetes*) to crush ginger, garlic, and fresh chilis. I keep a special tiny one exclusively for pulverizing cardamom seeds, which I use in desserts.

Spice Roasting Tips

Each spice is always toasted separately in India, because some are more delicate than others, requiring less time to toast. Occasionally a little oil is added, especially when toasting dried chilis, to preserve freshness. Here are some more pointers:

* Cumin seeds take a little less time to toast fully than coriander seeds, because they are fragile. You may toast them separately.

* Cinnamon, cloves, and peppercorns can be mixed and toasted together.

* Black peppercorns become plump and pop when they are fully toasted.

* Whole cloves also become plump and aromatic after toasting.

* Mustard seeds also start to pop in a dry hot pan when they are completely toasted.

* Fresh herbs, such as *kari* leaves, cilantro, and mint, can be toasted along with spices until they turn crisp and are thoroughly dried.

* Do not toast ground spices such as turmeric and cayenne in oil. Warm ground spices over low heat.

* Solid and powdered asafetida may be toasted in oil to release its strong (unappealing sulfurous) flavor, leaving behind a subtler flavor.

Choose a heavy, smooth-textured mortar, with a surface that looks a little like unpolished granite. To season a brand new stone mortar and pestle, grind a handful of old spices or raw rice grains several times until you've smoothed out the rough edges and the spices no longer look dirty. If you're a beginner with a mortar and pestle, work one ingredient at a time, starting with the dry spices, then working in the softer, juicier stuff. Use a straight pounding motion, as well as a grinding motion, up and down the sides of the mortar. For cleanup, I store a small brush with the mortar to whisk out what I've ground; a kitchen towel works as well.

If hand-grinding, as enjoyable as it is, does not fit into your time schedule or kitchen routine, a spice grinder or coffee mill devoted exclusively to grinding spices works remarkably well. If using a handy coffee mill, grind the spices and then turn the mill upside down, holding it securely closed, and pulse once more; the spice powder slides down into the cap, so it's easy to remove, and cleanup is easier too. After each use, process two teaspoons of raw rice in the spice grinder or coffee mill and discard the grains in order to eliminate the smell of the previous spices. In my recipes, you may use a mortar and pestle, spice grinder, coffee mill, or even a blender, so select the method that is most convenient for you.

INDIAN AROMATICS

In Indian cooking, the magical trio of aromatics is onion, ginger, and garlic. The bulb vegetables of the lily family, onion and garlic, marry and mingle with the ginger to create a wholesome harmony in which the individual parts almost become inseparable. Onion, ginger, and garlic form the heart of Indian cooking. They enrich a dish with a delicate sweetness and add texture and strength.

About Onion

The onion plays a number of roles in Indian cooking, depending on how it is used or combined to achieve texture, taste, color, and flavor. When pureed, it acts as a thickening agent. When fried, it adds color, richness, and sweetness to many dishes. As a rule, cook onions until they are translucent for a lighter-tasting sauce, or until richly browned for heavier sauces, such as those based on yogurt or bound by powdered nuts. For vegetarian dishes, cook onions until they almost begin to turn brown at the edges, just to evaporate out the moisture and set in the sweetness; they should not look raw. For chicken dishes, cook the onion until lightly browned, but not caramelized. For heavier sauces with lamb or red meats, caramelize the onion.

Indian white onions are complex, herbal, and sharp, with a clean, crisp flavor. American yellow onions are a perfect substitute. Sliced onions are preferred in meat dishes. When I refer to sliced onions, I mean onions that are peeled and cut in half lengthwise, then sliced lengthwise into slivers. The finer the onions are slivered, the less time they take to cook or brown. A word of caution: do not add more than the recommended amount, because the assertive onion flavor can drown out the subtler influences of other ingredients.

Indians also serve onions raw. As with lemon or lime wedges, pass sliced onion at the table for each diner to add gusto to a dish, especially with meat, poultry, and *chaat* (small snack plates). Sometimes the raw onion is soaked in water for 20 minutes or so to remove the sharp flavors.

Cooking with Garlic

If you're using a mortar and pestle to make a paste of garlic and ginger, add a sprinkling of kosher salt to make the grinding easier and pull the flavors together. Those who are short on time can press garlic through a garlic press for convenience.

Garlic browns faster than onion, hence it is added after the onion cooks briefly. The acidity of tomatoes will stop the garlic from developing to its full strength. Therefore garlic should be fully cooked before adding tomatoes or other moist ingredients.

About Ginger-Garlic Paste

When cooked, garlic and ginger lose their harshness and take on such a sweet, mild flavor that you can use these aromatics liberally. The role of ginger and garlic, especially in northern India, is an ever-present backdrop to more prevailing flavors.

Freshly minced garlic is always preferred in Indian cooking. The water-filled, minced garlic sold in jars in most supermarkets and some Indian stores is acceptable in a pinch, but dehydrated garlic is not. I buy garlic heads in bulk and store them, uncovered, in a cool place at room temperature in a wicker basket. Garlic heads are smaller in India, but the cloves have more concentrated flavor. They are much more potent than the large heads grown in California. Indians crush garlic cloves and use them whole, using the skins and all, but you should peel the garlic in these recipes. Even when I call for a large garlic clove, do not use "elephant" garlic.

I never peel fresh ginger (it adds fiber to the diet), but you may do so if you wish. Chop the ginger roughly (along the grain and crosswise) and put it in the blender. Add the peeled garlic to the blender, with the required amount of water as called for in the recipe, blend to a smooth, fragrant paste, and use as directed.

About Tomato Puree

Great tomatoes focus flavors with their brightness, and they are a critical ingredient in Indian cooking. Many recipes call for pureed tomatoes. Choose plum tomatoes for a thicker texture and round, juicy tomatoes for a lighter consistency. Plum tomatoes work well in

Keep in Mind While Using This Book

* When recipes call for cilantro, use fresh sprigs, including both the leaves and tender stems.

* Fresh hot green chilis do not need to be seeded. I recommend following the recipes on the number of chilis to use, but you can reduce the number if you or your guests are sensitive to the heat.

* Coconut is always unsweetened unless otherwise indicated. Dried, flaked unsweetened coconut is available at Indian markets, and frozen unsweetened coconut is available at specialty markets and some Asian groceries.

* Lime is always preferable to the weaker-flavored lemon in Indian cooking. To get the most juice out of your limes, either roll them hard on the counter before cutting, or place them in the microwave for 10 seconds.

* When using the oven, always preheat it for 10 to 20 minutes.

* Buy organic, locally grown, seasonal, chemical-free foods whenever possible, especially produce, meat and poultry, and dairy products. Buy high-quality spices, dried legumes, and other ingredients, in stores with high turnaround.

cooked sauces, because they are pulpier and turn rich and thick when cooked. Generally though, juicy (preferably vine-ripened) or hothouse tomatoes will work fine in these recipes. Do go to the extra effort to buy good, ripe tomatoes. At farmer's markets, look for a high-acid tomato for an authentic Indian taste. When high-quality tomatoes are out of season and unavailable, canned tomatoes make an acceptable substitute in most curries. I have specified whenever canned tomatoes may be substituted in the recipes in this book.

DINING, INDIAN STYLE

From an early age, Indian children learn the pleasures and the skills of eating with fingers. For adults as well as children, this way of eating is part of the enjoyment of a meal.

Touching, feeling, sniffing, licking, and savoring the food with the fingers fulfill more than just hunger.

In Vedic tradition, it is believed that eating food with the hands feeds the body, mind and spirit. Hands are our most precious organs of action. Our hands are said to be the conduits of the five elements—space, fire, air, water, and earth. Each one of the five elements flows through each finger. It is believed that the five elements begin to transform food and make it digestible even before it reaches the mouth. This change heightens the senses so that we can smell, taste, and feel the texture of the foods we are eating, and even hear the sounds we make as we eat. All of these sensations help to ready the body, or to awaken the fire *(agni)* within ourselves. This awakening aids digestion, and according to Vedic beliefs, good digestion leads to good thoughts.

AT THE INDIAN TABLE

Traditionally, Indian meals are served on a dinner plate *(thali)*, and the diner sits on a floor mat or low, wooden platform. Today, formal dining tables are quite common, but floor mats are still used for auspicious occasions. I remember my mother folding away the table and using mats during joyous celebrations. I created artwork called *rangoli* around the *thali* with rice flour, grains, and colored lentils. When my American friends visit our home, sometimes I use my artistry to decorate the table, and it makes them feel very special. In India, for gatherings like wedding banquets, where typically more than a hundred people are served lunch or dinner, banana leaves are used for plates and little earthenware cups for bowls, both fully biodegradable.

Whether you dine at the table or on the floor, the same basic rules apply. The dining room should be clean and pleasant. Before sitting at the table, washing both hands is mandatory. The left hand is used only for drinking beverages or to serve oneself (or the hostess will serve). The right hand is only for eating food from the *thali*. It is considered improper to offer food from one's *thali* to others. Placing sticks of incense in a corner of the room creates a sweet fragrance that stimulates the appetite. A lightly colored, delicate floral tablecloth and linen napkins add grace to the table. A pleasant atmosphere and good conversation goes a long way toward making food enjoyable. Indians like to chat and discuss and debate ideas. Soft background music, such as Ravi Shanker's sitar or Zakir Hussain's tabla, completes a perfect setting.

INDIAN PLACE SETTINGS

A typical place setting consists of a dinner plate and three or more small bowls for curry and saucy vegetables. Stainless steel is popular for everyday meals, and silver for special

What about Those Whole Spices?

Many dishes contain whole spices, such as a cinnamon stick, black or green cardamom pods, whole cloves, and star anise, and it is possible that they might wind up in someone's mouth. For the daring, biting on whole spice produces a welcome burst of heat, but for others it may not be an amusing experience. To bypass this problem, before serving, simply pick out any clearly visible whole spices. If you accidentally happen to chew on one, especially when in a restaurant with many people around, politely take it out and place it on the extreme left side of the plate (remember, drier foods are on the left side). I happen to like peppercorns, so I just bite down on them.

occasions. The bowls are arranged in a systematic order around the plate. (Traditionally, the entire meal, from appetizer to dessert, is served all at once on the plate in small portions. The modest servings mean less food is wasted, and one has the choice of asking for more of any dish that is appealing. The tradition is much like today's Western-style buffet.) Thinner curry or *dal* is to the extreme right, where it is easier to dunk or scoop a piece of bread into a bowl and then into the mouth without spilling Moving counterclockwise, thick *dal* and a side dish of meat, seafood, or vegetables come next. *Raita,* chutneys, pickles, and a wedge of lime are to the left of the vegetables, in that order. Rice or bread should be served on the plate in the center. If *pakora* and *papad* are served, they are usually on the extreme left or in the center. You may notice that hot dishes are to the right and cooler dishes to the left. Either bread or rice may be served first, but, except in restaurants, the two are generally not on the plate at the same time. A perfect balance of yin and yang! I have arranged the table of contents in the same manner as well.

HOW TO COMPOSE A DAILY MENU

One has a wide range of choices when it comes to combining Indian dishes or planning a menu. At our home in the United States, our daily dinner is a smorgasbord, a balanced assortment. I prepare one legume curry; one or two contrasting vegetable side dishes, one of them being leafy greens; a *raita, chapati,* and plain rice for a complete meal, all served in small portions. Occasionally I skip the legume and include fish, meat, or poultry as side dish. (Unlike in American cooking, the bread or rice form the main course in Indian cuisine and serve as a neutral background to numerous spicy side dishes.) Chutneys, *papads,* and pickles are not obligatory, though I make them ahead in quantity, so I always have some on hand. Garnishes are vital; for everyday cooking, it may be as simple as chopped fresh cilantro. I pass a pot of *desi ghee* for my family to brush on the *chapati* and drizzle on *dal* and hot rice. Additional plain yogurt is always at the table; my husband likes to spoon a tablespoon over the rice toward the end of the meal to cleanse the palate. Desserts are optional. Occasionally I include Alphonso mango pulp with sliced fresh fruits. Each dish must complement the others in a menu, offer pleasing color contrasts, and provide nutritional balance.

THE TREASURES OF THE INDIAN PANTRY

Kothri Khazaanae

Mention Indian food and a mysteriously exotic cuisine that is colorful, hot, and spicy comes to mind. There are hundreds of tastes and flavors to explore in Indian cooking. Within each region are local favorite ingredients influencing the cuisine. The aromatic barks, flowers, buds, roots, and seeds that make up the spice lexicon, as well as the easy, fragrant homemade spice blends, play an important role in Indian fare. Recipes in this book share a common foundation of spices, herbs, and other basic ingredients. Most of these herbs and spices are available in mainstream supermarkets, natural food stores, specialty stores, and Indian markets. Once you gain knowledge of these staples of Indian cooking, you're well on your way to discovering the succulent flavors of Indian cuisine.

SPICES

The fame of Indian spices is older than is recorded in history books. The search for these exotic treasures not only caused a flotilla of ships to set sail on a wave of treacherous voyages, but also brought about the drawing of the first map of the world. For centuries men sailed the seas and fought wars to procure these flavorful little gems. Indeed, the fascinating history of spices is a story of quest, expedition, invasion, and fierce naval rivalry.

WHAT IS A SPICE?

The term spices refers to aromatic or pungent vegetable substances used for flavoring foods. They stimulate all of the senses and are one of the proud symbols of Indian culture and heritage. They serve three main functions in the subcontinent: as seasoning in cooking, as preservatives, and as remedies in ancient medicine. Once considered a luxury, spices have become an integral part of our daily diet. The characteristic flavors of spices come from the essential oils that are concentrated within them through drying, which helps to preserve their aroma and taste for several months. They have little nutritional value, but besides adding taste and aroma, they stimulate the appetite and help the body produce gastric juices that aid digestion.

SPICE BOUTIQUE

In India, spices continue to be harvested, threshed, and winnowed in ways that have not changed for centuries. Spices reach their full maturity in the hot, sunny, moist climates of the tropical regions and are dried in the hot sun's rays.

I'm so glad spices have spread around the globe and become part of the world's culinary traditions. Without spices, food would be bland and all but tasteless. Besides, spices act as natural antioxidants. Consumers have grown more spice-savvy over the years, and the demand for spices has surely increased. Most of the spices mentioned in this book are widely available in well-stocked supermarkets and specialty stores (or check Sources, page 439). Indian markets sell spices in bulk in a variety of sizes at far more reasonable prices than most supermarkets. Buy spices where the turnover is high for the freshest flavors. Keep in mind that each spice has numerous flavor components that determine the quality; these components dissipate at different rates. Look for fragrant, plump, and unshriveled spices. In supermarkets, buy a top-quality brand; it will be better after a year than a low-quality spice after two months. When in doubt in an Indian market, just smell the spice. If it smells strong and spicy, then buy it. For best results, don't buy spices in quantities larger than you can reasonably use within a few months, and buy whole spices rather than ground, since they keep better. Preground spices oxidize more rapidly, losing their vital volatile oil, resulting in a flat taste. Heat, light, moisture, and air all speed the loss of flavor and color. Store whole spices in tightly covered containers in a cool place at room temperature, away from direct light, for six to eight months, refrigerate up to one year, or freeze for longer storage. The flavor of spices will not be damaged in cold storage, but a cold jar can get the spices wet if left open in a humid kitchen, as condensation will form. Keep smaller quantities in the pantry and freeze or refrigerate backup provisions.

Don't throw away stale spices. Buy dried rose petals and pine cones from the florist, mix them with the spices, and display in bowls as a potpourri for the bedroom or bathroom.

The following list describes the various spices (and other common Indian pantry items) used in this book. Spices and herbs are grouped together, since they are both part of the seasoning process. Once you have been thoroughly acquainted with these seasonings, you can create dishes of your own. The English name is followed by the Hindi name (so that you can order like a pro in an Indian market); the botanical name is also included.

Allspice *(Kababchini), Pimenta officinalis*

This spice has the flavor of cloves, nutmeg, cinnamon, and black pepper all woven into a tiny berry, hence the name. It grows on a bushy evergreen tree, is about 1/4 inch in diameter, and is green when unripe and becomes dark purple to reddish brown when ripe. It is native to the West Indies and cultivated in South America and Kashmir. It has a warm and perfumy aroma, is mildly sweet, and forms the secret ingredient in many northern Indian *biryanis* (see pages 114–125) and curries. Occasionally it is used in tea, spice blends, preserves, and relishes. As a home remedy, it is used to relieve flatulence.

Aniseed *(Pardesi saunf), Pimpinella anisum*

An annual herbaceous plant yields clusters of seeds that are gathered and sun-dried. A close relative of fennel, caraway, and cumin, aniseed is a small, oval seed, 1/8 inch long and sage in color. It has a sharp taste and is aromatic and sweet, changing to bittersweet when dry roasted. Flavored or sugar-coated aniseed is combined with nuts and spices and served as a breath freshener. A sweet-smelling garnish, it is often added to hot oil and used as a seasoning to top meats and vegetables. Ground, it is occasionally used in beverages and desserts. Aniseed tea is sleep-inducing. It is used as a digestive and diuretic, but don't boil the seeds too long in water, or the digestive qualities will be lost.

Ajwain, Carum copticum

A relative of dill, caraway, and cumin and a member of the umbellifer family, *ajwain* is also referred to as *ajowan,* carom seed, lovage (although it is not the same as the European herb of that name), *omam* (in southern India), and bishop's weed. The annual herbaceous plant grows in Iran, Egypt, Afghanistan, and widely in India. The seeds are the size of celery seeds, oval and ridged with fine stalks, and light grayish green in color and possess a sharp thymelike flavor. Chewed on their own, they are bitingly hot, and leave the tongue numb for a while. The flavor mellows upon cooking. *Ajwain* is wonderful with green beans, winter squashes, root vegetables, and legumes that are hard to digest. I like to toss the seeds in any of my flatbread doughs and in tandoori dishes. They are used whole to flavor fried snacks and appetizers, and crushed in pickles. Buy them in small quantities, though they store well in the freezer for up to a year. *Ajwain* was my grandmother's instant remedy (chewed raw) for stomachaches and flatulence. For infants and children with nasal congestion, she crushed *ajwain* seeds, tied them in thin muslin cloth, and placed the packet by the pillow while they slept, as an effective and instant vaporizer. Adults with congestion can boil *ajwain* in water and inhale the steam.

Asafetida (Hing), Ferula asafetida/Asafetida narthex

The dried resin from the rhizomes of a species of *Ferula* yields asafetida. Along with caraway, celery, fennel, parsley, and numerous other herbs and spices, asafetida derives from an umbellifer, that is, a member of the carrot family, or *Umbelliferae*. It grows mainly in Afghanistan and Iran and is cultivated in Kashmir. The stalks of this huge, smelly perennial herb are cut close to the carrotlike roots, and a milky liquid oozes out that dries into resinlike asafetida. This process is repeated many times in the spring to yield about two pounds of resin from each plant. Fresh asafetida is whitish and solid; upon oxidation it turns reddish brown and is sold in solid pieces or in powdered form. I recommend you use the solid pieces, as they are more fragrant, and pulverize them in a mortar until coarsely powdered (if you prefer the powdered variety, ask the grocer for the best brand). When people sniff asafetida for the first time they may find it pungent and unappealing, and the idea of "releasing its full flavor" may seem terrifying. It seems to me that, like Thai fish paste and various other smelly seasonings, it gives off much of its strong sulphurous odor as soon as it is heated, leaving behind a subtler flavor. Still, use it sparingly. To release its full flavor, toast the powder or crushed pieces in hot oil for a few seconds. It has a garlic-like flavor, so a little minced garlic or shallot makes a fine substitute. It is widely used in southern Indian cuisine. It is a strong digestive agent and relieves flatulence by cleansing the intestine and its surroundings. Combined with butter, it was once eaten to soothe the voice and was popular with singers in ancient times.

Basil *(Tulsi), Ocimum santum*

Basil, known as the sacred plant of India, belongs to the mint family. The fresh leaves are rarely used in Indian cooking, but age-old basil tea is popular. Indian basil leaves, brimming with fragrance, are smaller in size and oval in shape; any supermarket variety works well. As a home remedy, basil is valued for treating lung ailments and strengthening nerve tissue.

Bay leaf *(Tej patta), Laurus nobilis/Cinnamon tamala*

Indians use two kinds of bay leaf, fresh or dried: lemony bay laurel, familiar to Americans, and the mellow-tasting Indian bay cassia. The Indian variety comes from an evergreen tree; once the tree matures to ten years, it continues to bear fragrant leaves for many decades. The leaves are 1 to 4 inches long, with a natural depth of flavor and sweet woody aroma. They are slightly pungent, with a hint of cinnamon. Buy whole dried bright green leaves. If you buy fresh ones, treat them like the dried leaves when cooking. Moghuls introduced bay leaves to Indian cooking. In Western cooking, bay leaves are usually added to simmering liquids, but in Indian cuisine they are first toasted in hot oil, as frying releases their sweet perfume. Both types can be used alternately in meats, poultry, pilafs, and vegetable dishes. Always discard the bay leaves before serving. The leaf is a mild digestive stimulant.

Caraway *(Siya jeera), Carum carvi*

The biennial caraway plant, with its fleshy root and slender stems, grows profusely in the northern Himalayas. The seeds are often confused with cumin. Brown caraway seeds are narrow, slightly curved, and ridged—this should help you distinguish them easily from cumin. They are pleasantly aromatic, hence used in spice blends and often in meat dishes. Caraway calms an upset stomach.

Cardamom *(Elaichi), Elettaria cardamomum*

Cardamom, used in India since antiquity, is often called the queen of spices. The botanical name comes from a local word for cardamom seeds, *elattari*. Cardamom, the three-sided seedpod of a plant of the ginger family, grows profusely in the wet hills of southern India, and the Malabar pods are considered the best in the world. Sri Lanka, Guatemala, and Thailand are other major producers. There are three types:

Green (or small) cardamom *(Chota elaichi)* is the second most important spice in India. The smooth, unblemished, unopened, lime-green pod with outer shell has little flavor, but the flavor of the tiny inner seeds is intense. The heady seeds have a refreshing taste and faintly citruslike, sweet aroma. Its delicate flavor is similar to eucalyptus. There are several varieties of green cardamom in India: the two most popular are the dark green, robust, long and round Mysore pods and the light green, angular Malabar pods with closely packed seeds. If you look carefully, you can easily distinguish the two. To determine freshness, pull open the pod. The hard seeds, 10 to 30 per pod, cling together and should be black-brown, plump, and slightly sticky, not wilted or brownish gray. The packaged seeds and ground powder are convenient, but don't keep as well. I suggest you purchase and store whole pods. A quarter teaspoon of seeds is roughly equal to three green cardamom pods. My collection of mortars and pestles includes one set exclusively for cardamom. If you don't own a mortar, an easier way to pulverize the seeds is to spread them on a cutting board and run a rolling pin over them a few times while bearing down on it. For a hint of perfume, the whole pods are used in pilafs, some nonvegetarian dishes, and the famous *chai* (sweetened spice tea). For a more redolent effect, the seeds are removed from the pods and ground, as in desserts and a host of meat and poultry dishes, spice blends, and coolers. Nibbled after meals, green cardamom seeds act as a natural breath freshener. I always carry some in my purse. While brewing coffee you can add crushed seeds; they are believed to detoxify caffeine. Cardamom is the best digestive stimulant; combined with fennel and cooked with water, it makes a soothing tonic for children with upset stomachs.

Black (or large) cardamom *(Barra elaichi),* like the green, is from a herbaceous perennial plant of the *Zingiberaceae* family, native to the eastern Himalayan region. It is also known as Nepal cardamom. Almost twice the size of the green type in length, ovoid, marked with thin ridges, and hairy at one end, it can split readily into three valves enclosing a mass of 20 to 50 seeds. It is found only at Indian markets. Buy plump, fresh, and evenly colored pods. To open the pods easily, it is best to first toast them, especially if you're using large amounts. Black cardamom has a strong, unique smoky flavor and is used only in select spice blends such as *garam masala.* Whole pods are used in northern Indian meat dishes and *biryanis.* Like other spices, it is valued for its medicinal properties.

White cardamom *(Safed elaichi)* is naturally green but often bleached with sulphur dioxide until straw-colored. It is the least flavorful variety of cardamom, so I don't use it.

Chilis (Mirch), *Capsicum annuum/Capsicum frutescens*

India is the largest producer of chilis in the world and a major exporter. Chilis are native to South America, where their cultivation dates back to prehistoric times. The Portuguese introduced chilis to India some 500 years ago, dislodging black pepper from its number-one spot as the hot spice of choice. Chilis are indispensable in an Indian kitchen. Dried or fresh, they are grouped on the basis of their color, shape, and pungency, which ranges from rich and sweet, to volcanic. The level of heat is gauged by the amount of capsaicin present in the skin, veins, and seeds. Capsaicin dilates blood vessels when consumed; this increases circulation and encourages sweating, which in turn cools the body. Dairy products reduce the effect of capsaicin. Consumed in moderation, chilis are digestive and circulatory stimulants and relieve nasal congestion. Here are the chilis that I frequently recommend throughout this book:

Fresh hot green chilis *(Hara mirch)*. Fresh chilis vary in shape and size. In general, chilis with a broad base and rounded tip are moderately hot. Chilis with a narrow base and tapered end are fiery. I have tested all the recipes in the book with serrano chilis. Serranos possess just the right amount of heat for Indian cooking. They are medium-hot, rather than exceedingly hot like Thai chilis, which I don't use. Serrano chilis are 1 1/2 to 2 inches long and slightly tapered at both ends. I personally do not like to seed the chilis, but doing so will temper the heat. You can slit them in half or in fourths, lengthwise, and add them to the dish; that way you can spot them easily and discard them, or leave them in for those who prefer to bite on them. Serranos are available in supermarkets and Mexican and Asian groceries. The widely available and milder jalapeño chilis can also be used if you prefer. Wear gloves while chopping chilis if your hands are sensitive to their piquancy.

Dried red chilis *(Sukhi lal mirch)*. I often call for readily available slim, bright red, three- to five-inch-long cayennes or chiles de arbol in this book. They are similar in heat and flavor. These chilis are ripened on the plant and then sun-dried. Their heat is centered in the seeds. In oil seasoning, they are used broken into rough pieces. In curry pastes, I suggest soaking them in water to soften the skin.

Dried red chilis are roasted until they turn dark red and then ground into cayenne, as it is known to most Americans. Be sure to purchase pure cayenne powder; your best bet is to shop at Indian groceries, where it is sometimes sold as chili powder. The blended "chili powder" sold in supermarkets contains other spices such as cumin, oregano, and garlic, hence it is not appropriate for my recipes; cayenne powder from the supermarket makes an acceptable substitute for the Indian variety; it is rich in vitamin A.

Kashmir *(Deghi mirch)*. This mild-to-sweet, fruity dried red chili laces the valley of Kashmir. It is valued for its extraordinary brilliant color and the gentle heat and sweet taste it contributes to meat curries, spice blends, vegetables, *paneer* dishes, and lentils. The Mexican *guajillo* chili is my new favorite; I use it for its slight heat, smokiness, tanginess, and brilliant color as a substitute for Kashmir chilis, which are not available in the United States. If you can lay your hands on Kashmir chilis, use two whole chilis for every one *guajillo* chili called for in a recipe. Kashmir chilis are sun-dried and ground into a powder called Kashmir *deghi mirch* powder, which can be found in some Indian markets. If unavailable, a little Hungarian sweet paprika works as a substitute.

Cilantro, or fresh coriander leaves *(Hara dhania), Coriandrum sativum*

A member of the umbellifer family, cilantro is an ancient culinary herb and one of the few grown for its seeds, leaves, stems, roots (in Thai curry pastes), and flowers (as garnish). The fragile leaves are fruity, with a hint of ginger. The tender stems are tastier. Cilantro has a delicate aroma and holds a distinct place in Indian cuisine. It is extensively used in chutneys and both nonvegetarian and meatless curries. In other parts of the English-speaking world, it is known as fresh coriander, but in the United States it is identified with Mexican cooking, so it is usually sold under its Spanish name, *cilantro*. For longer storage, chop off the root ends, discard any wilted leaves, and do not wash. Wrap the cilantro loosely in paper towels, letting air circulate freely, and place it in a plastic bag in the refrigerator. It starts to rot easily if too moist. To chop, use a sharp, thin-bladed knife so as not to bruise the delicate leaves. Dried cilantro, the kind in spice jars, is used in some spice blends, but you can dry your own at home. Rinse and pat or spin-dry the leaves and lay them out on a cookie sheet. They should be crisp and crumbly in two to three days. Use a low oven for fast drying. When a recipe calls for cilantro in this book, include the chopped fresh leaves as well as tender stems, unless I specify only the leaves. Cilantro is rich in minerals and vitamins. Freshly squeezed juice from the leaves is a useful remedy for allergies and skin rashes.

Cinnamon *(Dalchini), Cinnamomum verum*

One of the oldest spices, warm, woody, deeply aromatic, and comforting cinnamon is obtained from the young bark of two different trees of the laurel family. Cassia cinnamon sticks come from the bark of the cassia tree and are thick, flat, small, and intensely flavored. On the other hand, pale tan Ceylon or true cinnamon is complex; it has a softer texture and a more delicate flavor, with subtle undertones of citrus, cloves, and ginger. Unlike cassia, it contains eugenol, the chemical compound that gives cloves their distinctive flavor and aroma, so it is also more aromatic. Both are harvested by peeling the bark back from either side of the tender shoots of the trees. Cinnamon strips are allowed to ferment for twenty-four hours, after which the corky outer bark is removed, and the strips of inner bark are curled up together in quills. Cinnamon is chiefly cultivated in the Caribbean islands, Sri Lanka, and west coastal and eastern parts of India. It is usually cassia and not true cinnamon that Americans consume. Both varieties are used in Indian cooking, but the cassia cinnamon is not used in desserts because of its astringency. Sticks of cinnamon are used to flavor pilafs, meats, hot and cold beverages, curries, and spice blends. In olden times, its sweet aromatic flavor was rumored to inspire love. Combined with bay leaf and cardamom in ayurvedic medicine, it aids in digestion. Almost all parts of the cinnamon tree are used for various purposes in India. Cinnamon-leaf oil is used to relieve toothache and muscle tension.

Clove (Lavang), Eugenia caryophyllus

Clove, another most important spice in world trade, is ancient and valuable. Its English name comes from the Latin *clavus* and the French *clou,* both meaning "nail," which describes the shape of the spice. Native to Southeast Asia, the clove is the bud of a highly aromatic, tropical evergreen tree that grows to a height of 36 to 45 feet. The bud has a cylindrical base, crowned by a plump beige ball, which in turn is encircled by a four-toothed calyx. Its unopened pink flower buds are harvested on palm-leaf mats. In the process of drying, the buds lose weight and change color to a reddish brown. Cloves have a powerful pungent and warm aftertaste and are considered a "hot" spice; use the amounts I suggest, because any more will mar the other flavors in the dish. Cloves should be bought whole; look for those that are oily and plump. Good-quality ground cloves should produce a trace of oil when pressed between the fingers. Cloves are used in pickles as a natural preservative, in spice blends, meats, and *biryanis*. Clove is an excellent stimulant, and clove oil is a strong analgesic and soothes toothaches. Its medicinal powers have been acknowledged since 207 BC, when the Han dynasty ruled China. Those who addressed the Chinese emperor were required to hold cloves in their mouths to mask bad breath. Today, clove is used to treat athlete's foot, fungal infections, and respiratory ailments. Clove is also an active ingredient in mouthwashes and a number of over-the-counter toothache pain-relief preparations.

Coriander seed (Sukha dhania), Coriandrum sativum

The seeds of the same plant that gives us cilantro are available in the United States in two varieties. The pale green Indian kind has a taste similar to lemony sage and vaguely like orange peel, with a sweet touch. It makes a pleasant and appealing sauce. The brown or Moroccan variety is less flavorful and makes a dark and dull sauce. Buy only the pale green variety (available at Indian groceries) for recipes in this book. For freshness, lightly toast the spherical whole coriander seeds until crisp before grinding; ground coriander helps thicken curries. Whole seeds are used to flavor snacks; ground seeds are indispensable in the Indian kitchen. Most of the time coriander seed is used in conjunction with cumin; over the years, I have found a ratio of two parts coriander to one part cumin makes a perfect balance of flavors. Together they help to break down carbohydrates in legumes. Coriander seed also works harmoniously with fresh ginger. It has several beneficial properties and makes a perfect treatment for disorders related to the digestive tract. In some regions of Karnataka state, a blend of toasted ground coriander and cumin is stirred into boiling milk and consumed to keep the body warm in the cold season; it is also good for nasal congestion.

Cumin seed *(Jeera), Cuminum cyminum*

Cumin is the seed of a small slender annual herb of the umbellifer family. It is grown extensively in India, Iran, and Morocco. Cumin is a sage-green to brown seed that comes from a fruit. The seeds are elongated, oval, and 1/4 inch long with ridges, resembling fennel and caraway. Cumin seed is a key ingredient, along with mustard and turmeric, in my spice box and common to all regional Indian cuisines. Cumin seeds combine favorably with coriander and fennel as cooling spices. They are used whole, crushed, or ground, toasted or raw; each form is quite different. Its mild, pungent taste works favorably in just about every dish, including meat, seafood, poultry, breads, vegetables, legumes, beverages, spice blends, and salads. A variety available in Indian markets is *kala jeera*, also called black cumin because of the size and shape of the seed. It is sometimes called *shah jeera,* or royal cumin. It is a rare variety that grows along the valley of Kashmir and some parts of Iran. The seed is darker, with a sharp-ridged surface, and easily confused with caraway. Black cumin is prized in Indian cuisine, especially Moghul dishes and spice blends, for its flowery fragrance and sweet mellow taste. Try the seeds in fresh-baked loaves of bread. My grandma's instant home remedy, hot cumin water made by boiling a teaspoon of cumin seeds in 2 cups water, is good for colds, digestion, flatulence, and early-morning nausea.

Fennel seed *(Saunf), Foeniculum vulgare*

Another member of the umbellifer family, these are bright yellowish green, slightly curved, plump, highly aromatic seeds with ridges. They are almost twice the size of cumin. Whole seeds are used in meat dishes, desserts, beverages, some spice blends, fruit chutneys, and in betel leaf for their aniselike flavor. Raw, dry-roasted, or candy-coated fennel seeds are served after meals to aid digestion. The seeds turn mellow after roasting. They act as a natural breath freshener (page 436). I have a little box in my purse that holds a few cardamom pods, cloves, and fennel seeds, which I carry especially on long journeys and chew in place of gum. Fennel is prized as a cooling spice for digestion, flatulence, cramps, and for nursing mothers.

Fenugreek leaf *(Hari methi), Trigonella foenum-graecum*

Leguminous fenugreek is another plant used both for its seeds and its leaves. Fresh fenugreek leaves (a rich source of iron), fragrant and slightly bitter (Indians love the taste and buy it in bunches like cilantro), are used both as an herb and a leafy vegetable. Fenugreek is grown around the Mediterranean, in France, and all over India. Nowadays bunches of fresh leaves can be purchased periodically in spring at farmers' markets in California and are available at some Indian and Middle Eastern groceries. The leaves are used in making salads and cooked like spinach by themselves or with potatoes. It is very easy to grow your own in the garden or in a kitchen window box. Sow the fenugreek seeds, cover with soil, water regularly, and watch it grow. Harvest the tender sprouts at the two-leaf stage for refreshing salads and *raitas* (pages 201–214). Or you can let it grow up to five inches and use the mature greens as you would spinach. (Don't let it grow any taller unless you want to harvest the seeds.) Do not use the hard stems in cooking. Dried fenugreek leaves, known as *sukhi* or *kasoori methi*, are available in Indian markets in packages. You can dry your own and store it, loosely covered, for several months. Dried leaves are crushed or crumbled and used in tandoori dishes, *tikkas* (pages 344–353), kebabs, Butter Chicken (pages 274–275), and most meat dishes. They act as a preservative and allow the meat to remain fresh longer. In dried form, the stems are very tough, so you must discard them. Tender sprouts are a good treatment for indigestion. An infusion of leaves is used as a gargle.

Fenugreek seed *(Methi dana), Trigonella foenum-graecum*

Small, hard, ochre-colored, and cylindrical, with a diagonal groove across them, leguminous fenugreek seeds are used as a spice for their powerful burnt-caramel flavor. The taste is bitter and lingering. To bring out their best essence, toast the seeds. Whole seeds are used in oil seasoning to flavor *kadhi* and *dal* and in pickles as a preservative. The seeds are available in bulk at Middle Eastern, Indian, and specialty supermarkets. In India, powdered seeds are mixed with jaggery (pages 51–52) and given to women to eat after childbirth to strengthen the back. Fenugreek seeds are effective in treating flatulence, the respiratory system, and reproductive ailments. Hippocrates, the father of medicine, is said to have used fenugreek to treat sore throats and colds.

Ginger *(Adrak), Zingiber officinale*

Ginger, one of the major spices of India, is the yellowish brown underground rhizome of an herbaceous three-foot-tall plant with long thin stalks and leaves. The rhizomes are dug up while still tender, if they are to be used fresh. They are harvested when more fibrous and mature and the leaves have dried, if they are to be dried. Both fresh and dried ginger are used in Indian cooking, but remember—the two are not interchangeable. Fresh ginger is bulbous, light fawn in color, with a yellow fibrous interior. Look for young, tender, firm and plump fresh ginger, without mildew and unwrinkled, at supermarkets, Asian markets, and green grocers. A knob should snap off easily, if it is fresh. I do not peel fresh ginger, but simply scrub it clean, rinse it, and use it in cooking, but you can peel it if you wish. Always slice fresh ginger across the grain. You may store ginger in a brown paper or plastic bag in the refrigerator; it keeps fresh for almost three weeks. Fresh ginger has a warm fresh aroma, with a hint of turmeric, which gives a flavorful boost, and is used extensively throughout India in both nonvegetarian and meatless curries, including legumes, pickles, beverages, chutneys, and more. Try fresh, young ginger raw, julienned in salads, in *chaats*, and atop meat dishes. A knob of fresh ginger, crushed, can be used in cooking large, hard-to-digest beans. Ginger and garlic are often pureed together and turned into a paste (page 11), so they meld easily into a curry. Dried ginger, known as *sonth,* is available in small lumps or in powdered form; it is made by dehydrating the fresh rhizome in the sun, then grinding it. It has a sharp, hot aftertaste and is mostly used in meat preparations, spice blends, beverages, and some desserts. In ancient literature, ginger was called *vishwabhesaj,* meaning "the universal medicine," or *maha-aushadhi,* "the great medicine." It is effective in treating digestive and respiratory illnesses, relieves flatulence and cramps, and is also an anti-inflammatory.

Kari leaf or curry leaf *(Kadi patta), Murraya koenigii*

The tropical *kari* plant is a deciduous plant of the *Rutaceae* family that can eventually grow into a hefty, 25-foot-tall tree. It is native to India and Sri Lanka. It is so common, even a small house in southern India will have a curry plant in the yard. The herbal leaves of the plant have dotted glands, are almond-shaped, glossy, and jade-green in color, and measure one to two inches in length. With a character distinctly its own, *kari* leaf is a magical ingredient, imparting an herbal, concentrated, enticing flavor of instant curry with a slight hint of lemon. *Kari* plants are cultivated locally, and groves of them are well established in the hot central valley and southern regions of California and Florida. You can mail order *kari* plants from nurseries (see Sources, page 438) in the United States. You might even find them sold as "curry" plants in some nurseries. Unlike those in India, which can grow quite tall, my American *kari* plant is squat, with large, thick leaves. Though such plants have been cultivated to grow in cooler climates, they are still frost-sensitive and should be protected or moved indoors during the winter.

Small bunches of *kari* leaf sprigs are available in most Indian and some Asian and Middle Eastern markets. Look for a very fresh bunch with unbruised leaves. If you find some moisture in the bag or on the leaves, you might want to dry it off before storing. Fresh leaves will keep in the refrigerator, loosely covered in brown paper or plastic bags, for two to three weeks. *Kari* leaf is absolutely essential to south Indian cooking. The vivid and distinct flavor packs a punch to any dish. When lightly fried in hot oil, they release a characteristic enticing aroma that enhances seafood, meats, lentils, vegetables, and rice dishes. If *kari* leaves are too hard to find (they show up at quite a few Indian grocers in the United States, but not usually in regular supermarkets), omit them from the recipe and substitute with chopped cilantro. Avoid dried leaves, since they have little fragrance and do not make a good substitute for fresh. Rich in iron, calcium, phosphorous, and vitamins A and C, *kari* leaves are used in herbal tonics and as a mild laxative. *Kari* leaf improves the function of the stomach and reduces diabetes and weight problems. When I was little, my grandmother loved to condition my hair with coconut oil and the juice extracted from *kari* leaves, making it soft and shiny.

Mace. See *Nutmeg.*

Mango powder *(Amchur), Mangifera indica*
Hundreds of varieties of mango trees are grown in India; green mangoes that grow wild are used to make this flavoring ingredient. Indians prepare mango (*aam*) powder (*chur*) by peeling, slicing, and sun-drying the tart, raw, hard green mangoes until they are shriveled and look woody and yellowish brown. The slices are then ground into powder or left whole. Both slices and powder are referred to as *amchur* and can be purchased at Indian markets. The fine powder is light brown, with lots of lumps, and crumbles easily. Sour and astringent in flavor, *amchur* powder is preferred, since it melds easily into curries, spice blends, and *chaats*. Add toward the end of cooking for a subtle taste. Leathery, biscuit-colored, dehydrated mango slices are mostly used in meat curries and legume dishes. The slices are simply stirred into the curry sauce for a sour flavor. They keep well for five to six months at room temperature. Lime juice or tamarind makes an acceptable substitute.

Mustard seed *(Rai), Brassica juncea/Sinapsis alba*
The plant that yields mustard greens also produces the vital mustard seeds. The three main varieties are black, brown, and white (or yellow). All varieties grow in India, Argentina, Europe, and America. White or yellow seeds are tan with a smooth, matte finish; to my taste, they are slightly sour, though mild. Black and brown mustard seeds are more popular in Indian cooking, but you can use yellow in the recipes in this book. The more intense black mustard seeds are somewhat larger than the brown and yellow varieties. Tiny round mustard seeds have no smell when raw, but upon cooking they acquire a distinct flavor and slightly bitter taste. Generally, mustard seeds are used in small quantities, whole or crushed. When they are added to hot oil, they sizzle and splutter and

impart a pleasantly nutty taste. They enhance both the taste and appearance of scores of dishes. Besides contributing flavor, they act as a preservative. You can purchase whole mustard seeds at Indian, Middle Eastern, and specialty markets. Mustard seeds are an effective stimulant, increase the appetite, and promote digestion. Mustard sprouts are easy to grow. In Indian religious lore there is a tale of a Brahmin priest who wanted to locate a powerful deity secluded in the state of Orissa. Allowed to travel to the site only if blind-folded, the clever priest dropped mustard seeds along the trail, knowing that when the quickly germinating seeds sprouted, he would be able to retrace the route.

Nigella seed *(Kalonji), Nigella sativa*

A small herb related to the plant known as love-in-a-mist is grown for its jet black seed in Egypt, India, and southern Europe. The beautiful flowers ripen into pods. They are col-lected, dried, and sieved. The 1/8-inch seeds are shaped like tear drops, with five distinct points. They have an elusive flavor. The presence of nigellin makes them taste bitter and faintly peppery. The feather-light seeds are sprinkled on *naan*, salads, and fish and com-bined with other spices to make the famous Bengali *panch puran* (page 50). The seeds are often confused with onion seeds. Nigella seeds are available at Indian and Middle Eastern markets. They are considered a carminative, a diuretic, and a stimulant.

Nutmeg/Mace *(Jaiphal/Javitri), Myristica fragrans*

Nutmeg, one of the old spices, comes from a large evergreen tree with glossy dark leaves and peachlike fruit native to the Moluccas (once known as the Spice Islands). The tree pro-duces two terrific spices known to us. Nutmeg is the kernel of the seed of the fruit; the soft-er, scarlet mace comes from the lacelike filigree covering the nutmeg's outer shell. If you're in the tropics, make it a point to see the fully ripened fruit. It splits open, revealing the fresh, bright red mace and dark large nutmeg. The mace, or aril, is carefully removed, pressed flat, and dried. It becomes slightly brittle and changes in color from brilliant red to a warm orange after drying. Mace blades can be toasted in oil for meats or ground with other spices to make spice blends. They are available in Indian and specialty markets. Ground mace keeps longer than any other spice in ground form. The oval, light-brown nutmeg shrinks upon drying. Nutmeg does not need toasting. Delicate, naturally sweet, with fruity over-tones and a wonderful licorice flavor, it is usually grated on a small-holed grater straight into meat dishes, *biryanis*, desserts, and beverages. Since nutmeg rapidly loses flavor when grat-ed, it is best to buy it whole. In India, shops sell nutmeg still in its outer shell, which makes a convenient container. Mace has a softer flavor than nutmeg, though both are sweet spices. Though they are generally not interchangeable, mace can be substituted for nutmeg if nec-essary. An old belief is that as long as there is a whole nutmeg in the kitchen, the marriage will be sound. Nutmeg in small quantities is valued for its medicinal properties; it increases digestive absorption and is used in treating diarrhea, insomnia, and muscle spasms. A paste of freshly grated nutmeg and milk around the eyes can have a cooling effect.

Peppercorn *(Kali mirch), Piper longum*

Peppercorn is the fruit of a perennial vine that usually grows within fifteen degrees of the equator and is of Southeast Asian origin. The drenching monsoons and warm, humid summers of the Malabar Coast produce the world's finest "king of spices." More than twenty varieties are grown in India. The quality has everything to do with the maturity of the vines. Even on the individual spikes, the peppercorns toward the top tend to get more sunshine and nutrients. The harvesters are ready at all times as pepper matures quickly. As soon as the dark green berries are fully formed, they are ready for harvesting; the entire spike of berries is plucked and sun-dried whole, until their fleshy skin shrinks, turns dark brown, and becomes hard. The berries are threshed, and the larger, more mature corns are separated to be sold as Tellicherry peppercorns. These have a more developed flavor and are considered superior to the so-called Malabar variety, although both come from the same vine. White peppercorns are the result of allowing the berries to ripen more fully on the vine, until yellow and red, then soaking them in water to remove the wrinkled outer skin. This process gives the corns a creamy white color, in addition to a deep, winey, slightly hot flavor. Green peppercorns start out the same way as black but are picked before the berries are mature. Note that pink peppercorns aren't really peppercorns at all. They were given that name because of their size and flavor. Black peppercorns are aromatic and spicy hot; the alkaloid piperine makes them pungent and slightly bitter. Their flavor has universal appeal and readily enhances almost any food. White peppercorns are milder in flavor than black and used in spice blends, herbal tea, and white fish dishes. The green peppercorn has a fresh clean flavor and adds a delicate herbal taste to salads and seafood and vegetable dishes. For best results, purchase whole peppercorns. When I have a cold I like to drink hot milk with two or three crushed white or black peppercorns to ease sinus congestion. Mixed with honey, it is a ready-to-use expectorant and is comforting to sore throats. It is also an excellent digestive stimulant.

Poppy seed *(Khus khus), Papaver somniferum*

India is a major producer of poppy seeds, which come from an annual opium plant (though they contain no narcotic properties) that bears red flowers with a purple center. As the flower withers away, it leaves behind a large oval pod. The dried pods can be cracked open to reveal vertical chambers filled with thousands of seeds. The off-white seeds appear round to the eye but are actually kidney-shaped; they have a pleasant herbal fragrance, crunchy, nutlike flavor and are highly prized in Indian cooking. Soaked in water and ground, or toasted and powdered, they are used in meat dishes, to thicken curries, and in stews in place of flour. White seeds are preferable in Indian cooking and are inexpensive at most Asian markets. Because of their high oil content, the seeds must be refrigerated or frozen, especially in summer. Poppy seeds have been praised since ancient times for their sweet flavor and nutritional and medicinal value.

Pomegranate seeds (Anardana), Punica granatum

The deciduous pomegranate tree, grown throughout the tropics and subtropics, yields scarlet flowers and fruit. When the fruit is cut open, hundreds of angular seeds with translucent red or pink flesh are revealed. In the fall, when fruits are fully ripe in India, the flesh of the seeds is almost shiny ruby-red or burnt red in color. The seeds are separated by hand and sun-dried for a fortnight, then ground to make *anardana* powder. The powder melds easily in curries and is used in much the same way as mango powder *(amchur)*.

Saffron (Kesar), Crocus sativus

Saffron is magnificent—fragrant, sweet, and golden. Saffron is the flavorful red stigma of a fall-flowering perennial bulb that blooms for just two weeks. In Kashmir, the lavender-blue blossoms are plucked at dawn, because they droop after sunrise. Then skillful women carry out the laborious task of delicately removing by hand the three scarlet-yellow stigmas from each flower. To produce one pound, an entire acre of the small flowers—about 70,000 crocuses—must be harvested. The stigmas are spread out and dried in the sun or over an artificial heat source, then carefully packaged. The stigmas are toasted over coal in Spain, another major producer. Due to its dearth, fragility, and splendid flavor, it is one of the most expensive spices. Saffron has a very rich and captivating bouquet and imparts a beautiful golden color to dishes. The flavor is at its best when the saffron is under a year old. Because it's so intense, you don't need much to color and flavor; the better the saffron, the less you need. Do not buy powdered saffron, because it loses flavor quickly. I prefer to buy saffron threads, which I toast over low heat until brittle, cool and crush with the back of a spoon or in a mortar, and then add to hot milk. Saffron is expensive, but it is one of the best stimulants. Young girls in India gulp a pinch of saffron in milk on an empty stomach, a measure presumed to improve the complexion.

Sesame seed (Til), Sesamum indicum

Sesame seeds come from an annual plant that grows to four feet, with pink or white flowers. It is native to India and is grown in the United States, China, and Guatemala as well. Depending on the variety, the seeds can be creamy, red, or black. Sesame is one of the world's most important oil seeds. It has warming qualities and is favored for its sweet nutty taste throughout India as a garnish, as a thickening agent, and in candies. Both white and black seeds add a nice flavor, but white is preferable in Indian cooking. Store sesame seeds in a dry place, as moisture can cause them to clump together. The seeds and oil are thought to be a laxative.

Star anise (Anasphal/Badiyan), *Illicium verum*

Star anise, one of the most beautiful and fragrant spices, is the star-shaped fruit of a small evergreen tree of the magnolia family; it is native to China. The fruits are plucked and dried before they are ripe. The seeds are embedded in six to twelve boat-shaped petals, which form the points of a perfect star; the seeds must be discarded before use. Sweet and highly aromatic, mahogany-colored star anise is not related to aniseed. It is used mainly in *biryanis,* meat dishes, spice blends, and fruit chutneys. You can purchase it in specialty stores and Asian markets. Star anise is prized as an effective stimulant.

Turmeric (Haldi), *Curcuma longa*

Turmeric is the underground root or rhizome of a herbaceous perennial related to ginger. India is the largest producer and exporter of turmeric in the world. The appearance of fresh turmeric is deceptively dull; once the rough brown skin is peeled, the intensely bright, yellow-orange root is revealed. The rhizomes are boiled in water for about an hour for curing. I remember my mother purchasing fresh turmeric roots, boiling them in water, and drying them in the scorching sun for several days until they became light and brittle. The dried roots were cleaned, then sent to the nearest mill to be ground into fresh turmeric powder. The homemade spice is a dazzling golden-orange color. Turmeric is astringent, pungent, dry, and light. It has an earthy, sensual taste that bestows a distinct yellow hue on all the regional cuisines of India. It is almost always used in oil seasoning and fried. The flavor is bittersweet and its aroma slightly musty. Don't allow it to fry too long, or it will turn bitter, and use it in moderation, because it can be overpowering. It is also used extensively with salt as a marinade for seafood. Ground turmeric is inexpensive and widely available in supermarkets. Dried roots are available at Indian and farmers' markets, and with some effort, they can be powdered at home. Never add turmeric while cooking leafy greens, or they will turn bitter and gray. Turmeric is warming, is a powerful preservative, acts as a natural antibiotic and antiseptic, and is an effective home remedy for small cuts and wounds. It is an efficient blood purifier, breaks down the dietary proteins easily (especially legumes), and encourages metabolism. It is also a symbol of prosperity, hence its inclusion in rituals. Women use turmeric on their forehead with *kumkum* (red dot) as a token of friendship and goodwill.

AROMATIC SPICE BLENDS

Khushbudaar Masale

Spice blends are called for in some of the recipes in this book. Homemade spice blends are so much fresher, more aromatic, and more flavorful than the store-bought versions that I recommend you make your own. Some of these recipes may seem long, but the spice mixtures have a long shelf life, so you can prepare a big batch and use it again and again.

TANGY TANDOORI SPICE MIX | Tandoori Chatpata Masala

Think of this mixture as you would salt and pepper, and sprinkle it over finished dishes, particularly tandoori specialties. Many recipes in this book specifically call for this mix, but it may also be used in countless other ways. However, it is best saved for those who prefer spicier flavors. Try sprinkling it on everything from scrambled eggs to barbecued meats.

MAKES ABOUT 1/4 CUP

1 tablespoon cumin seeds

2 teaspoons white peppercorns

1 teaspoon *ajwain* seeds (page 20)

3/4 tablespoon mango powder *(amchur)*, or
    tamarind powder

1 1/2 teaspoons ground ginger

1 teaspoon salt

1. In a small skillet over medium heat, combine the cumin seeds and peppercorns. Toast, stirring regularly, until the seeds are aromatic, about 4 minutes. Add the *ajwain* and continue toasting, stirring regularly, until the seeds darken a shade, about 2 minutes. Transfer to a bowl.

2. Reduce the heat to low and add the mango powder, ginger, and salt to the same skillet. Toast, stirring frequently, until the salt is hot to the touch, about 2 minutes. Remove from the heat and add to the bowl with the spice seeds.

3. Let the spice mixture cool slightly, then transfer to a coffee mill or spice grinder and grind to a fine powder, in batches if necessary. Pour into an airtight glass jar, mix well, and let cool completely. Cover and store at room temperature, away from direct light, for up to 3 months or in the refrigerator for up to 6 months.

HOT AND FRAGRANT CURRY POWDER | Kari Pudi

India has been ruled by many peoples from around the world; the last to leave were the British. During their long stay, they came to enjoy Indian curries, and when they returned to England, they carried home the haunting flavor. They concocted a spice blend they called curry powder to replicate sauces and stews they had eaten in India. (The term curry powder may have derived from the *kari* leaves used in the blend.)

Indians rarely use prepackaged curry powder, preferring freshly ground spice mixtures for every dish. However, the familiar commercial blend does have an approximate counterpart in authentic cooking: *kari pudi*, a deep-brown powdered mixture of lightly roasted *kari* leaves, dried red chilis, and spices. Used occasionally by south Indian cooks, *kari pudi* is a pleasing combination that I occasionally use to flavor meats, vegetables, and legumes. It has a brighter, more concentrated flavor than store-bought curry powder, it's easy to make, and it stores well, too. Most commercial curry powders use too much turmeric for my taste. If you're only familiar with the store-bought version, I strongly suggest that you try this recipe.

MAKES A GENEROUS 1/2 CUP

1/2 cup coriander seeds

2 teaspoons black peppercorns

1 1/2 teaspoons yellow or brown mustard seeds

1 teaspoon cumin seeds

1/2 teaspoon fenugreek seeds

1/2 teaspoon whole cloves

2-inch cinnamon stick, broken

4 green cardamom pods, seeds removed

10 *kari* leaves (page 28) (optional)

1/2 teaspoon vegetable oil

4 small, hot dried red chilis, such as chiles de arbol or cayennes, stemmed

1.   In a large heavy skillet over medium heat, combine the coriander, peppercorns, mustard seeds, cumin seeds, fenugreek seeds, cloves, cinnamon, cardamom, and *kari* leaves, if using. Toast, stirring often, until the seeds are aromatic and darken a shade and the *kari* leaves turn crisp, 5 to 6 minutes. Transfer the mixture to a bowl.

2.   Add the oil to the same skillet set over medium heat. When the oil is hot, add the chilis. Cook, stirring, until the chilis are toasty and turn reddish in places, about 2 minutes. Remove from the heat and transfer to the bowl with the spices.

3.   Let the spice mixture cool slightly, then transfer to a coffee mill or spice grinder and grind to a fine powder, in batches if necessary. Pour into an airtight glass jar, mix well, and let cool completely. Cover and store at room temperature, away from direct light, for up to 3 months or in the refrigerator for up to 6 months.

AROMATIC GARAM MASALA | Garam Masala

Garam means "warm" or "hot"; *masala* means "spice blend," either dry or paste. Although the recipe for *garam masala* varies greatly from region to region, it's a staple of northern Indian cooking.

This homemade version I've put together is highly aromatic. For maximum freshness, I suggest you make only enough to last for a few months. Halve the ingredients if you want to make a smaller batch.

MAKES A GENEROUS 1 1/2 CUPS

20 black cardamom pods

2 1/2 tablespoons green cardamom pods

1/2 cup cumin seeds

1/4 cup coriander seeds

1/4 cup caraway seeds

1 1/2 tablespoons black peppercorns

1 tablespoon whole cloves

4-inch cinnamon stick

1 whole nutmeg

1 tablespoon mace blades

8 bay leaves

1 tablespoon ground ginger

1. In a large skillet over medium heat, toast the black cardamom pods, stirring often, until the pods are very plump, 5 to 6 minutes. Cool slightly, then press each pod between your thumb and forefinger to crack it open. Toasting makes this easier, but you may have to press hard on some stubborn pods. Discard the black husk and place the seeds in a bowl. Add the green cardamom pods to the skillet and toast over medium heat, stirring often, until the pods swell, become plump, and color in spots (some may even crack open), about 4 minutes. Transfer the pods to the bowl containing the black cardamom seeds.

2. In the same skillet over medium heat, combine the cumin seeds, coriander seeds, caraway seeds, peppercorns, cloves, and cinnamon and toast, stirring often, until fragrant, 6 to 8 minutes. Transfer to the same bowl with the cardamom.

3. Wrap the whole nutmeg in a kitchen towel or plastic wrap and, using a heavy pestle or a hammer, break the nutmeg into small rough pieces. Place in the same skillet over low heat, along with the mace and bay leaves, and toast, stirring occasionally, until fragrant and crisp, 4 to 5 minutes. Add to the bowl of spices.

4. Add the ground ginger to the same skillet over low heat. Toast, stirring constantly, until the ginger is toasty and sends a whiff of smoke in the air, about 2 minutes. Transfer to the bowl and mix well. While the spices are still slightly warm, add them in small batches to a spice grinder or coffee mill and grind to a fine powder. Pour into an airtight glass jar, mix well, and let cool completely. Cover and store at room temperature, away from direct light, for up to 3 months or in the refrigerator for up to 6 months. The mixture can also be frozen for up to a year.

SAMBAR POWDER | Sambar Pudi

In this southern Indian spice and chili blend, legumes are used to impart a nutty flavor and velvety texture. *Kari* leaves blended with other spices create a luxuriant flavor foundation that makes *sambars* quite different from the northern curries. Traditionally each ingredient is toasted separately, but I like the ease of combining and toasting most of the spices at the same time; the loss of flavor is minimal.

Once you have this basic spice blend on hand in your kitchen, you can make *sambars* (lentil stews) whenever the urge hits. If you prefer to buy ready-made *sambar* or *rasam* powders, I recommend the MTR brand available at Indian markets.

MAKES A SCANT 1 CUP

1/2 cup coriander seeds

2 tablespoons dried hot red chilis, such as chiles de arbol or cayennes, stemmed and broken into rough pieces

1 medium-large dried *guajillo* chili, stemmed and seeded

1 tablespoon black peppercorns

1 tablespoon cumin seeds

1/2 teaspoon fenugreek seeds

1/2 teaspoon yellow or brown mustard seeds

1/2-inch cinnamon stick, broken

2 tablespoons *chana dal* (split chickpeas)

1 teaspoon *urad dal* (white split gram beans)

30 to 40 *kari* leaves (page 28) (optional)

2 tablespoons dried unsweetened flaked coconut

1. In a large skillet over medium heat, combine all of the ingredients except for the coconut. Toast, stirring frequently, until the seeds are aromatic and darken a shade and the *dals* turn reddish, 5 to 6 minutes. Transfer the mixture to a bowl.

2. Add the coconut to the same skillet and toast over medium heat, stirring frequently, until toasty-smelling and uniformly golden, about 2 minutes. Remove from the heat and add to the bowl.

3. Let the spice mixture cool slightly, then transfer to a spice grinder or coffee mill and grind to a fine powder, in batches if necessary. Pour into an airtight glass jar, mix well, and let cool completely. Cover and store at room temperature, away from direct light, for up to 3 months or in the refrigerator for up to 6 months. The mixture can also be frozen for up to 1 year.

RASAM POWDER | Rasam Pudi

This powder works wonderfully in *rasams* (lentil soups). You may also fold it into soups containing fish or chicken.

MAKES A HEAPING ¹/₂ CUP

1 teaspoon vegetable oil

¹/₂ cup coriander seeds

1 tablespoon cumin seeds

1 tablespoon black peppercorns

1 teaspoon fenugreek seeds

20 *kari* leaves (page 28) (optional)

2 tablespoons dried hot red chilis, such as chiles de arbol or cayennes, stemmed and broken into rough pieces

¹/₄ teaspoon asafetida

1. Heat the oil in a large skillet over medium heat. Add the coriander seeds, cumin seeds, peppercorns, fenugreek seeds, *kari* leaves, if using, and chilis. Toast, stirring frequently, until the seeds are aromatic and darken a shade and the leaves turn crisp, 5 to 6 minutes. Transfer to a bowl.

2. Add the asafetida to the same skillet. Toast over low heat, stirring, until fragrant, about 2 minutes. Add to the bowl and mix well.

3. Let the spice mixture cool slightly, then transfer to a coffee mill or spice grinder and grind to a fine powder, in batches if necessary. Pour into an airtight glass jar, mix well, and let cool completely. Cover and store at room temperature, away from direct light, for up to 3 months or in the refrigerator for up to 6 months. The mixture can also be frozen for up to 1 year.

MY MOTHER'S HEIRLOOM SPICE BLEND | Kala Masala/Kari Khar

In India, spice blends are like family heirlooms, and they are passed on from generation to generation. Amma ("mother"), as we fondly called our maternal grandmother, would make this blend with fifty or more spices. She added two to three varieties of dried chilis to achieve different levels of heat and color. Some of the spices were not available in the United States, so I got some tips from my mother on how to replicate the rich flavors in Amma's *masala* with the ingredients that are available to me. My American friends and neighbors sprinkle this on barbecued meats and even buttered toast. My students use it on steaks, grilled meats and seafood, roasted veggies, legume dishes, croutons, and pilafs. Remove and discard the shiny seeds that are embedded in each of the star anise points before using them.

MAKES 1 CUP

1 1/2 tablespoons white sesame seeds

1 teaspoon poppy seeds, preferably white

1 tablespoon canola or grapeseed oil

4 dried hot red chilis, such as chiles de arbol or cayennes, stemmed

12 green cardamom pods

6 black cardamom pods, seeds removed

3 tablespoons coriander seeds

1 1/2 tablespoons cumin seeds

1 tablespoon yellow or brown mustard seeds

1 teaspoon black cumin seeds *(shah jeera)* (optional)

1 teaspoon whole cloves

1 teaspoon caraway seeds

1/2 teaspoon fenugreek seeds

1/2 teaspoon fennel seeds

1/2 teaspoon mace blades

1/2 teaspoon *ajwain* seeds (page 20)

1/2 teaspoon white peppercorns

1/4 teaspoon black peppercorns

1/4 teaspoon allspice berries

2-inch cinnamon stick, broken

2 whole star anise pods (see headnote)

10 *kari* leaves (page 28) (optional)

1/4 cup loosely packed cilantro leaves

2 bay leaves

1 tablespoon dried unsweetened flaked coconut

1/2 teaspoon ground ginger

1/2 teaspoon garlic powder

1/2 teaspoon sweet paprika

1/2 teaspoon salt

1/4 teaspoon freshly grated nutmeg

1/4 teaspoon asafetida

1/8 teaspoon turmeric

1. In a large skillet over medium heat, combine the sesame and poppy seeds. Toast, stirring frequently, until the seeds are aromatic and become uniformly reddish, about 4 minutes. Transfer the seeds to a medium bowl. Heat the oil in the same skillet over medium heat. Add the chiles, whole spices, and the leaves and toast, stirring frequently, until the seeds are aromatic and darken a shade, the mustard seeds begin to pop, and the leaves turn crisp, 6 to 8 minutes. Transfer to the bowl containing the sesame seeds.

2. Add the coconut to the same skillet and toast over medium heat, stirring frequently, until toasty-smelling and uniformly golden, about 2 minutes. Remove from the heat and add to the bowl. Reduce the heat to low and add the ginger, garlic powder, paprika, salt, nutmeg, asafetida, and turmeric to the skillet. Toast, stirring frequently, until fragrant, about 2 minutes. Add to the bowl and mix well.

3. Let the spice mixture cool slightly, then transfer to a coffee mill or spice grinder and grind to a fine powder, in batches if necessary. Pour into an airtight glass jar, mix well, and let cool completely. Cover and store at room temperature, away from direct light, for up to 3 months or in the refrigerator for up to 6 months. The mixture can also be frozen for up to 1 year.

PUNE-STYLE SESAME-LACED POWDER | Goda Masala

This most popular *masala* from the state of Maharashtra, a staple in my mother-in-law's house in Pune, lends a nutty and slightly sweet taste because of the sesame seeds and coconut. Try it with rice, lentils, and vegetables, or sprinkled over grilled fish.

If you're able to find solid asafetida, which is more fragrant than the powdered form, break it into small pieces first (place the asafetida between plastic sheets and break it with a heavy pestle or a hammer) and toast it in 1/4 teaspoon of oil until aromatic.

MAKES 1 1/2 CUPS

3 tablespoons white sesame seeds

2 teaspoons vegetable oil

15 dried hot red chilis, such as chiles de arbol or cayennes, stemmed

1/2 cup coriander seeds

1/4 cup cumin seeds

1 teaspoon yellow or brown mustard seeds

1/2 teaspoon whole cloves

1/2 teaspoon fenugreek seeds

3-inch cinnamon stick, broken

4 bay leaves

1/2 cup dried unsweetened flaked coconut

1 1/2 teaspoons asafetida

1/2 teaspoon turmeric

1. In a large skillet over medium heat, toast the sesame seeds, stirring frequently, until the seeds are aromatic and become uniformly reddish, about 4 minutes. Transfer the seeds to a bowl. Heat the oil in the same skillet over medium heat. Add the chilis, coriander seeds, cumin seeds, mustard seeds, cloves, fenugreek seeds, cinnamon, and bay leaves. Toast, stirring frequently, until the spices are aromatic and the mustard seeds start to pop, about 4 minutes. Add the coconut and stir until toasty, about 2 minutes more. Transfer the mixture to the bowl containing the sesame seeds.

2. Reduce the heat to low, and add the asafetida and turmeric to the skillet. Toast, stirring frequently, until fragrant, about 2 minutes. Add to the bowl and mix well.

3. Let the spice mixture cool slightly, then transfer to a coffee mill or spice grinder and grind to a fine powder, in batches if necessary. Pour into an airtight glass jar, mix well, and let cool completely. Cover and store at room temperature, away from direct light, for up to 3 months or in the refrigerator for up to 6 months. The mixture can also be frozen for up to 1 year.

CHAAT MASALA

Chaat masala, a tangy mix of spices, adds a wonderful flavor to Indian snack dishes. The blend's distinctive character comes from black salt *(kala namak)*. Black salt is actually neither black nor a salt, but a natural sulfur compound with a pinkish gray color, pleasantly tangy flavor, and smoky aroma. I encourage you to try it; a little goes a long way. If you are unable to find black salt, simply omit it from the recipe. Do not substitute other salt.

This spice blend can also be used for non-Indian foods. Perk up your salads or coleslaw with a sprinkle of *chaat masala*, or mix it with chopped fresh herbs and buttermilk to make a low-calorie dressing. If you're too short on time to make your own, the various brands available at Indian markets will yield favorable results.

MAKES ABOUT 1/2 CUP

1 1/2 tablespoons cumin seeds

1 teaspoon *ajwain* seeds (page 20)

1/4 teaspoon black peppercorns

2 tablespoons dried mint, crushed

1/4 teaspoon freshly grated nutmeg

1 1/2 tablespoons mango powder *(amchur)*

2 teaspoons black salt *(kala namak)* (see headnote)

1/2 teaspoon cayenne

1/4 teaspoon salt

1. In a large skillet over medium heat, combine the cumin seeds, *ajwain* seeds, and peppercorns. Toast, stirring frequently, until the seeds are aromatic and darken a shade, 5 to 6 minutes. Transfer the mixture to a bowl.

2. Reduce the heat to low and add the mint and nutmeg to the same skillet. Toast, stirring frequently, until fragrant, 1 to 2 minutes. Remove from the heat and add to the bowl containing the spice seeds.

3. Let the spice mixture cool slightly, then transfer to a coffee mill or spice grinder and grind to a fine powder, in batches if necessary. Stir in the mango powder, black salt, cayenne, and salt and whirl for few seconds until well mixed. Pour into an airtight glass jar, mix well, and let cool completely. Cover and store at room temperature, away from direct light, for up to 3 months or in the refrigerator for up to 6 months.

LEGUMES

Dal

Listed here are some of the legumes used in the recipes in this book. All can be purchased at Indian markets, and many are available at specialty supermarkets or other ethnic markets. The Indian names for the various legumes tell you not only the variety but in what form it is sold. Split and hulled (without skin) legumes are called *dal*, while those sold whole with skin are called *saabat*. Some legumes, such as black gram beans and mung beans, are sold in three different forms. Buy brightly colored lentils, beans, or peas that are shiny and smooth. I remember my grandmother storing legumes in jars with a few dried red chilis to ward off insects. Freeze them for longer storage.

Note that the listings in the legumes section are organized by the Indian name, because that's how they are most often labeled and sold in Indian markets.

Chana dal (Split chickpeas)

India grows two varieties of chickpeas, the commonly available white variety (see *chole,* next entry) and the less familiar brown or black ones. The black variety (called *kala channa* or *kalé channé*) when split and hulled is known as *chana dal* and sometimes referred to as Bengal gram. Do not confuse *chana dal* with *toovar dal* because of their similar color and shape; *chana dal* is totally different in flavor. These small, thick, bright-yellow, lens-shaped beans are frequently used in thick velvety purees and also as a seasoning in *uppama,* rice dishes, toasted and powdered in spice blends. Compared to other *dals,* they are a little hard to digest, even by Indians who eat legumes frequently, so use in moderation in seasoning and spice blends, as suggested. When *chana dal* is milled, the resulting flour is called *besan* (see chickpea flour, page 46).

Chole (Chickpeas or Garbanzo beans)

Like other legumes, chickpeas grow in pods on a small plant. The pods are harvested in winter, threshed, and sun-dried thoroughly. Also called garbanzo beans or ceci beans, chickpeas have a strong, earthy aroma and a pleasant, nutty flavor. The recipes in this book call for dried or canned chickpeas, which can be bought in supermarkets (I recommend using the widely available canned version, since the dried take too long to cook). Two varieties of garbanzos are available in Indian markets: the common pale yellow kind, called *safed* or *kabuli channa,* and the small dark brown or black variety called *kala channa* or *kalé channé.* Though sold dried, where they grow they are eaten fresh from the pods. The light and dark varieties can be used interchangeably and can be sprouted. High in proteins and minerals, chickpeas are popular in side dishes and stews and are lovely in salads. Just a word of caution: all types of chickpeas are hard to digest, so eat in moderation.

Masoor dal (Pink lentils)

These hulled and split lentils do not require soaking. The color changes after cooking; they cook quickly into a yellowish velvety puree, and are therefore excellent for soups, sauces, and stews. Easy to digest, pink lentils are widely available at ethnic and specialty markets and supermarkets.

Mung dal (Yellow split mung beans)

Golden-yellow, hulled and split, these petite oblong beans are obtained from whole mung beans *(sabaat mung).* Lighter, easier to digest, and relatively quick to cook, they have many uses in Indian cuisine, such as in curries, soups, pilafs, salads, and dumplings. If you've never eaten legumes and want to include them in your diet, then I recommend you start with *mung dal.* They are available in some specialty supermarkets, as well as Indian and other ethnic markets.

Pardesi dal (Split peas)

The common yellow split peas sold in most supermarkets look similar to Indian *toovar dal,* but are slightly thicker. They are not quite as sweet but otherwise make a good alternate.

Rajma (Kidney beans)

Commonly used in American cuisine, red kidney beans are also popular in north Indian cooking. Generally cooked whole, in combination with lentils and vegetables, they have a nutty flavor, toothsome texture, and slightly sweet aftertaste. They are rich in protein and carbohydrates.

Saabat masoor (Brown lentils)

These pale greenish-brown, lens-shaped lentils do not require soaking and are easy to cook. The Indian variety is smaller in size but has the same flavor as the lentils commonly found in supermarkets. The two can be used interchangeably. Brown lentils are cooked with other beans to form a complete protein. They can also be sprouted easily.

Sabaat mung (Mung beans)

Versatile and healthful whole mung beans, native to India, are oval in shape and have aquagreen skins. Their rich, earthy flavor blends well with many foods. Easy to digest, they are a staple in Indian households and often used for sprouts. The beans are milled into flour and used in breads and fritters. There is also a split version with the skin at Indian markets called *mung ki chilke dal;* these can be used interchangeably with whole mung beans. Dried mung beans are available in some supermarkets, as well as specialty, Indian, and other ethnic markets.

Sime avarekai (Lima beans)

Cream to pale green in color, lima beans come in two sizes, small and large. They are similar in shape to kidney beans and have a buttery, mild flavor. They are tasty in pilafs and with meats, vegetables, and side dishes. Available fresh, dried, canned, or frozen in supermarkets, all forms and sizes of lima beans can be used alternately. The tender young lima beans are wonderful in salads or pilafs and are available once in a while in farmers' markets.

Toovar dal, Toor dal, or *Arhar dal* (Yellow lentils)

Also known as pigeon peas, these bright yellow lentils are thin and cook quickly. Their pleasant, subtle, nutty flavor is a natural for *dal* soups, curries, and sweets, or cooked along with rice (in *khichadi*). They are easy to digest. Yellow lentils are available in two forms: plain and oil-coated. Oily lentils have been coated with castor oil to avert insect infestation. They can be washed in several changes of hot water to remove the oil and used interchangeably with the others. I prefer to use the dry type, and all recipes were tested with dry *toovar dal.* These are widely available in Indian and other ethnic markets and some specialty stores.

Urad dal (White split gram beans)

These tiny, hulled and split ivory-white ovals are extensively used in south Indian cooking. One of the ancient beans, *urad dal* is also used as a seasoning in *uppama*, toasted and powdered in spice blends, and used in chutney powders. Rich in proteins and minerals, they are soaked and ground with rice to make the fermented batter of *idli* (steamed cakes) and *dosa* (savory crepes and pancakes). They are also used extensively in making lentil wafers. Whole black gram beans are sold at Indian markets as *saabat urad*, and split with skin as *urad ki chilke dal;* these cannot be substituted for *urad dal*. They are used in making north Indian *makhani dal* (pages 385–386).

FLOURS AND SEMOLINA

My mother would purchase good-quality wheat, clean it, and send it to the nearest mill to turn it into the freshest and purest flour. Even today, it is a norm in India to buy the grains rather than the packaged flour, but fortunately for American cooks, high-quality flours are no farther than the nearest Indian specialty market. In addition to wheat flour, the Indian pantry includes rice and chickpea flours, which are used in a multitude of creations, including savory pancakes, fritters *(pakora),* and desserts; they are thought of much like cornstarch is in the West.

Chapati flour *(Atta)*

Chapati flour is finely ground whole-wheat flour that produces just the right texture for making *chapati* and other flatbreads. The dough is easy to roll, and the breads come out soft and pliable. Although it resembles American whole-wheat pastry flour, it is made from a harder wheat, with a higher ratio of gluten to starch. *Chapati* made entirely with whole-wheat flour from the supermarket will be heavier. There will also be a subtle difference in color; the reddish brown grains of American wheat make darker flatbreads than the cream color of *chapati* flour. It is available at Indian markets.

Chickpea flour *(Besan)*

Chickpea flour is made by finely grinding *chana dal* (yellow chickpeas). The flour is a dull yellow color and somewhat heavy, and its distinctive and pleasant nutty taste blends well into a wide range of Indian dishes. Low in gluten and high in protein, it is used for *pakora* batter, as a thickener in kadhi and toasted and mixed with *desi ghee* in numerous sweets. It keeps well in a cool place; for longer storage, refrigerate in a tightly covered container. Do not use it on a daily basis, as it is a little difficult to digest. It is available at Indian and some specialty markets. *Besan* is used as a body detergent; mixed with cream and turmeric, it leaves the skin soft and silky.

Rice flour *(Chawal ka atta)*

Rice flour, or rice powder, is milled from long-grain white rice. It is rich in starch but has no gluten. A small amount added to breads, crepes, fritters, and pastries makes them crisper. Rice flour is also used to thicken sauces. It is available in specialty and Asian markets. Chinese long-grain rice flour makes a fine substitute, but Chinese glutinous rice flour does not.

Semolina *(Sooji)*

Tiny grains called *sooji* or semolina are made from processed wheat (without the germ). *Sooji* resembles sand, so you'll know what to look for at Indian markets, where it is widely available. It has no aroma and little taste. Therefore, it is well suited to making either desserts or savory snacks. It has a nice smooth texture, comparable to cream of wheat. It almost always has to be toasted first, so it melds easily into the cooking liquid. I recommend you use *sooji* as called for in recipes for authentic taste, but if unavailable, quick-cooking cream of wheat cereal is an alternative. Semolina is usually available in three grades: fine, medium, and coarse (the one used in recipes in this book). Refrigerate *sooji* after purchase for longer shelf life.

DESI GHEE (CLARIFIED BUTTER) AND OILS

Just as a versatile chef keeps several different bottles of oils on hand, an Indian cook has various containers of peanut, corn, sesame, cottonseed, coconut, mustard, and sunflower oils in the pantry. And of course the cherished clarified butter known as *desi ghee* occupies a special place in the cupboard. Pure oils are purchased from the markets in India, while *desi ghee* is almost always made at home, every two to three days, from homemade butter. *Desi ghee* was the primary cooking medium in ancient India, and it remains a staple even today. Besides its use in sautéing and in desserts, it is sprinkled on prepared curries, *dals,* tandoori dishes, and rice and smeared on hot flatbreads before serving.

Desi ghee (Clarified butter)

Desi ghee is regarded as the divine essence of food, since it is butterfat in its purest form and has been mentioned in ancient texts. In olden times it was packaged in leather skins and sold from south India to Rome. It was used by the wealthy, both for cooking and in sacrifices. In prehistoric times, cooks discovered that butter went rancid quickly in tropical weather and looked for ways to preserve it. They tried clarifying it, and *desi ghee* was born.

Traditionally, clotted cream is collected from boiled milk for a number of days; milk and yogurt are added to it, and when it sets, it is churned into butter. The fluffy butter is cooked down into *desi ghee*. Cow's milk *desi ghee* is more intense and bright, but buffalo milk is preferred for its higher fat content.

There is nothing like the wonderful aroma of a pot of *desi ghee* simmering on the stove. To make *desi ghee,* use unsalted sweet cream butter (salted butter produces less yield and forms more sediment). It should be slowly simmered until all of the water evaporates and the protein solids settle at the bottom and harden, leaving the clear butterfat. Do not stir or skim off the foam that rises to the top. Be sure to use a large, heavy pot so it does not spill when it rises. The moisture present in the butter will evaporate away. What is left is pure, concentrated butterfat that can withstand high heat, requires no refrigeration, won't scorch food, and is essentially lactose-free. The browned milk solids account for its distinct aroma and beautiful beige color. It has its own characteristic sweetish-nutty flavor, which enhances curries, tandoori meats, vegetables, *biryanis* and other rice dishes, breads, and sweets. Because of its relatively high smoking point, *desi ghee* can be used for sautéing and stir-frying.

Usli and *kharé ghee* are different terms for *desi ghee,* as opposed to *vanaspati ghee*, which is vegetable shortening. A few companies produce good commercial *desi ghee* (see Sources, page 438); it can be purchased in some specialty and Indian markets in cans or jars, but it is expensive.

MAKING DESI GHEE AT HOME

1 pound butter makes 1²/₃ cups   3 pounds butter makes 5¹/₄ cups

2 pounds butter makes 3¹/₂ cups

1.   Melt unsalted butter in a large, heavy saucepan or Dutch oven over medium to medium-low heat. As the butter starts to melt and simmer, it will be covered with bubbles initially (they will decrease after 15 minutes or so); the butter will spatter for a while, but there is no need to stir. Simmer, uncovered, until the milk solids begin to settle to the bottom and turn lightly brown, 22 to 25 minutes for 1 or 2 pounds, and 30 to 35 minutes for 3 pounds.

You'll also notice the top layer at the edges of the pan begin to brown—this is important to look out for. Turn off the heat while the *desi ghee* is golden or else it will darken—remember that the butter continues to cook for a few more minutes from the retained heat. Cool completely. If by chance your *desi ghee* browns, you may still safely use it; the flavor will be intense, with more of a burnt caramel aroma. Don't turn off the heat any sooner than I've recommended, or it will taste like melted butter.

2. Carefully pour the cooled *desi ghee* through a fine strainer or cheesecloth. (My sister saves the solids from the pan and uses them in *chapati* dough (pages 63–64) to make it soft and pliable.) Pour the clear liquid *(desi ghee)* into a clean jar or stainless steel container. It should have a lovely grainy texture and a beautiful golden color. It becomes semisolid when cool and hardens after refrigeration. Bring to room temperature for use, or melt as called for in recipes.

> MAKE AHEAD Though *desi ghee* can be stored, covered, in a cool dry place for up to 6 months, it's safest to store it in the refrigerator.

VARIATIONS

Flavored desi ghee

While clarifying the butter, my mother adds to the pan whole pods of star anise, *kari* leaf sprigs, or betel leaf (*paan*, available sporadically in Indian and ethnic markets) for added aroma. See the list below for more suggestions. Add to 1 pound of butter during the last 5 minutes of cooking for a delicate perfume. Strain and store as directed above.

You can brush the flavored *desi ghee* on barbecued foods, toasted bread, muffins, and bagels, or drizzle on prepared tandoori meats, steaks, grilled fish, *uppama, idli, dosa,* pilafs, or flatbreads.

1/2 to 1 teaspoon black or white peppercorns, lightly crushed

1/2 to 1 teaspoon cumin seeds, lightly crushed

2-inch piece cinnamon stick

1/2 cup fresh basil leaves, bruised

1/2 cup fresh oregano, coarsely chopped

1 1/2 tablespoons minced ginger

1 tablespoon minced garlic or shallots

1 to 2 fresh hot green chilis, such as serranos or jalapeños, stemmed and minced

Oil *(Tel)*

Indian regional cooking is characterized by the use of different oils.

Northern and central regions use peanut oil; mustard oil is preferred in the eastern and some northern parts; most southerners prefer sesame and coconut oil; and sesame oil, peanut oil, and *desi ghee* are used in the western region. Sunflower and safflower oils are also popular. Walnut and almond oil are used occasionally in the north. Grapeseed oil is neutral and does not lose flavor even when cooked at very high heat; it is wonderful in Indian cooking and my personal favorite. Grapeseed oil is available in specialty supermarkets and some wineries, but unfortunately the cost can be prohibitive. I have tried the recipes in this book with vegetable, canola, and grapeseed oil, all good for high-temperature cooking, and there is no noticeable flavor or aftertaste. Substituting olive oil isn't advised, because the resulting flavors will not be the same.

Amber-colored mustard oil is pressed from the seeds of mustard plants. It has been widely used since olden times in northern and eastern India. In its raw state, the oil has a pungent scent. Therefore, the oil is often brought to the smoking point temporarily; this brief exposure to high heat softens the harsh flavor, making it pleasant, docile, and easy to digest. (Northerners almost always bring mustard oil to smoking, while cooks in Bengal occasionally do prefer it in its raw, *kacccha,* state.) Many chefs use mustard oil in restaurants, and many Indians still prefer the pure stuff. My suggestion would be to use safe brands of oil. Some are labeled "for massage only" or "for external use only." Look for "blended" mustard oil, or to play it safe, go for a light olive, corn, or other neutral oil. Mustard oil is an acquired taste, but you might want to seek it out if you like to explore new flavors.

Coconut oil, extracted from the dried kernel of the coconut, has been used in Indian cooking for hundreds of years, particularly in southern India, where its strong aroma complements coconut-based fish dishes and curries. Like olive oil in Italian cooking, coconut oil is drizzled over finished dishes. It solidifies to a soft mass when cold. Melt it gently in a heavy saucepan over low heat, or place the bottle in hot water for a few minutes; it melts into a pale yellow oil. Coconut oil is available in some specialty markets and Indian groceries.

Indian sesame oil is light and colorless, unlike the dark and aromatic Chinese type, which cannot be substituted.

WHOLE SPICE BENGAL SEASONING | Panch Puran

Panch puran, meaning "land of five rivers," is a colorful blend of five whole spices: cumin seeds, fenugreek seeds, nigella seeds, fennel seeds, and mustard seeds in equal quantities. It is a specialty of Bengal and of neighboring Bangladesh and Orissa. *Panch puran* is always fried in mustard oil or *desi ghee* to release the raw flavors. (See the warnings about purchasing mustard oil above.)

Heat the oil over medium-high heat in a small skillet until smoking. Let it go for a while; you might smell that pungent aroma. At this point, remove the skillet from the heat briefly to avoid scorching the spices. Add the *panch puran* spices, immediately cover with a spatter screen, return the skillet to the heat, and cook until the seeds stop popping and sizzling and start to float, about 1 minute. Remove from the heat. This sizzling oil is delicious when served over stir-fried greens, sautéed shredded cabbage, other vegetables, Bengali *dal* (slightly sweetened, with raisins), and fish. Because of mustard oil's preserving qualities, it is used on seafood pickles as well.

MISCELLANEOUS INGREDIENTS

Here are notes on additional common ingredients that appear in the recipes throughout the book. Salt, sugar, essence, lime, crushed peanuts, pearl tapioca, and tamarind are detailed in this section, along with the increasingly popular *cocum*—used in curries, soups and cocktails to add a tart, fruity kick—and mango, a longtime staple of Indian cooking and the king of tropical fruit.

Cocum, Garcinia indica

Cocum, or *kokum*, has no English name. This slender evergreen tree, bearing the round *cocum* fruit, a cousin to the mangosteen, is native to the western coast of India. The frequent sunshine, adequate rainfall, and rich soil in the Konkan, Malabar, and Karnataka regions make it possible to grow an abundance of *cocum*, also called *amsool*. The fruit is deep purple and contains six to eight large seeds. When the fruits are ripe, the rind is removed, soaked in the juices of the pulp, and sun-dried to make preserved peels. These are dark purple to almost black and somewhat sticky, with curled edges resembling collapsed plum skins. *Cocum* is used just like tamarind in cooking; it imparts a beautiful pinkish-purple color. Though pleasantly fruity, it tastes sour because of the presence of tartaric and malic acids. *Cocum* keeps well at cool room temperature for up to a year and is available in Indian markets. The peels are sold in small packages.

A fruit, somewhat similar to *cocum,* called *kodampuli* or fish tamarind, grows in Kerala. It is shaped a bit like a fish, hence the name. The purple fruit is picked when ripe, and the thick lobes of the fruit are cut, sun-dried, and smoked. It is used in numerous seafood preparations and acts as a preservative in fish.

Essence *(Ruh)*

Indians have perfumed foods with essences from assorted fragrant flowers, bark, and wood for hundreds of years. The two most popular ones are concentrated flavorings extracted from fragrant roses *(gulab)* and screw pine leaves *(kewra)* by steam distillation. Rose essence was first produced in the sixteenth century in India from the strongly perfumed damask rose introduced by the Moghuls. Rare flowers were cultivated in the royal greenhouses for use in perfumes. These days, the damask rose and another variety, the Edward rose, known locally as *baramasi,* are widely cultivated for their scent.

Screw pine, an uncommon shrub with leathery, long leaves, has an entrancing, strong sweet scent; these days, fresh leaves are available in some California farmers' markets. Essences may be diluted and sold as flavored waters; a common one is rose water. Either water or essence can be used in the recipes; use twice as much water as essence, if substituting one for the other. They are used to aromatize *biryanis,* meats, desserts, and beverages, and also as air fresheners in religious and wedding ceremonies. Women in India cherish fresh screw pine petals and use them in braids for fragrance and adornment. Rose and *kewra* water and essences are available in Middle Eastern and Indian markets.

Jaggery *(Gur)*

Sugarcane grows in abundance in tropical India. Jaggery is a byproduct of sugar making. I remember watching the process in my grandmother's fields; it took all night. The sugar cane juice is cooked and stirred continuously in huge containers. As the cane juice boils down and thickens, without further refinement, it is poured into various-size molds—anything from small cones to a bucket—to cool and crystallize. My taste memory of fresh jaggery is divine. It is sweet and caramellike, with a hint of sweet sherry. It is sold in Indian groceries in the Unites States in small pail-like molds that weigh from one to four pounds. Because it's not purified, it may contain bits of agricultural products. It can range in color from light yellowish brown to caramel. You need only small amounts. I find it easiest to break off chunks, usually with a knife, and to let it dissolve in whatever liquid I have in my recipe. It grates very easily on a box grater. Store as is in a dry, tightly covered container at room temperature. I highly recommend you use jaggery in recipes that call for it. It is considered a healthful product. It is used extensively in Indian desserts, tea, and other beverages, serves as a perfect counterbalance for tamarind, and melds beautifully. Occasionally, I make a small piece of jaggery my quick dessert. In most recipes, raw or turbinado sugar is a good substitute.

Raw or turbinado sugar. Most supermarkets now carry boxes of raw or turbinado sugar under the brand name Sugar in the Raw. It is naturally blond and tastes different from brown sugar, because it hasn't been bleached or stripped of the flavor of pure sugar cane. It comes from the initial pressing of sugarcane, which permits some of the natural molasses to remain in the crystals. This gives it its blond color, unique texture, rich taste, and distinct flavor. It makes a good substitute for jaggery. You can also use it in place of granulated sugar. If unavailable, you can substitute light brown sugar, but the flavor may not be the same.

Lime *(Nimbu)*

Although both lime and lemon are native to India, only lime is frequently used in Indian cooking. When Indians refer to lemon, they actually mean lime. Lime is favored because it is more intensely sour; the juice of a lemon is weaker in intensity. Always add lime juice toward the end of cooking if you wish to retain the original tang, because the fresh flavors and sharpness dissipate as it is heated. If fresh limes are unavailable, lemon makes a satisfactory substitute.

Mango *(Aam)*

The mango is an evergreen tree related to the cashew family. Mango has been cultivated in India for more than 6,000 years, and there are hundreds of varieties. On the subcontinent, green mangoes start to appear in late March, gorgeous ripe ones are plentiful in May, and by mid June, at the onset of the monsoon season, they start to disappear from the market. Each healthy tree yields a few hundred mangoes every season. The fruit has a thick, smooth skin, green when young and ripening to a blushing gold. At first, the tender young mango has creamy-white to pale-green flesh, with a delicious fruity tang; when mature it becomes yellow and juicy, with a sweet, delicate flavor much like peaches and pineapples. The most gorgeous mango in India is the brilliant orange-red, fiber-free Alphonso, or *aapoos,* variety, considered to be the finest. The flavor resembles that of nectarine, pineapple, and rose essence all rolled into one. To me, this is *the* mango, the king of tropical fruits. Alphonso mangoes are not available fresh in the West. Mangoes ship well, but imported fruits are usually picked while underripe and treated in a hot-water bath to kill insects, a combination that results in mushy texture and pallid flavor. However, it is worth buying canned Alphonso mango pulp from Indian markets. Ask for Ratna, Gulsitan, or Amrit brand names or order them by phone (see Sources, page 438). Mangoes are an excellent source of vitamin A, have fair amounts of vitamin C, and contain traces of potassium and other minerals.

Selecting ripe mangoes: In the United States, mangoes are available almost year round. To determine ripeness, choose a mango that is firm, with a reddish-orange blush at the end. Don't buy those that are bruised, are overripe, or have soft spots. Gently press the mango; it should give slightly to pressure at the narrow (bottom) end. Smell the mango; it should have a pleasant, sweet aroma. A strong smell indicates overripeness (they often decay near the pit). Store at room temperature for a few days, away from direct sunlight. When fully ripe, or yellow in color, use them in recipes, or refrigerate wrapped in plastic wrap for up to two days.

Selecting green mangoes: Green mangoes are simply unripe regular mangoes. Green mangoes are usually placed separate from the ripe ones in the market and labeled accordingly. Look for them in Indian and Asian specialty produce markets. A green mango should be evenly green in color and so hard that it's almost impossible to dig a fingernail into it. Green mangoes can weigh between six ounces and two pounds, but look for ones that feel heavy for their size. Use in recipes as soon as possible, before the fruit has a chance to ripen, and do not substitute regular, ripe mangoes in any recipes that call specifically for green mangoes.

Peanuts, crushed and roasted *(Daanyacha koot)*

This is a staple in my kitchen, as it is all over Maharashtra state in India. Crushed peanuts are used in stir-fry dishes, stuffed vegetables, *raitas*, and chutneys. I make small batches in a miniblender. Place 1/2 to 1 cup of roasted salted or unsalted peanuts in a miniblender, regular blender, or food processor and pulse until coarsely crushed (the texture should be between coarse and fine, almost like breadcrumbs), 15 to 20 seconds. Store in an airtight glass jar in a cool dry place for up to 2 months.

Pearl tapioca *(Sabudana)*

Pearl tapioca is a starch processed from the trunk of the cassava plant. A groove is cut in the tree trunk at intervals, and the sap that oozes out is collected and strained through special sieves into soft little droplets. Depending on the diameter of the holes in the sieve, different sizes of tapioca are formed, which are dried hard. Pearl tapioca is available in three sizes in Indian and other Asian markets. It is used in puddings and *pappadam*. Pearl tapioca is believed to cool the body system.

Salt *(Namak)*

Salt is one of the six major tastes and is important for balance. Add salt to food when it is cooking so that it dissolves and is absorbed by the food. This makes the salt easier to digest, and you use less than when you add it to the finished dish. I've used kosher salt and flaky sea salt in testing the recipes; both melt faster and better than granular table salt. However, an equal measure of table salt can be substituted if you prefer. Generally, I use salt moderately in cooking, so you can use more (or less) to suite your taste. Remember that potatoes and rice absorb salt, so if a potato or rice dish is made ahead of time, you may have to add more salt to taste before serving.

***Kala namak,* or black salt,** is not really a salt at all. It is available only at Indian markets and is used in making *chaat masala,* beverages, appetizers, and some *chaats* for its earthy taste. It is not black but looks pinkish gray and has a sulfurous flavor. You may not like the aroma at first, but once you start using it in moderation, you might actually become fond of it. If you're unable to find *kala namak* simply omit it. It acts as a digestive.

Silver and gold leaf *(Varq)*

Gold and silver are part of daily life in India. Shimmering in the glass cases of any Indian sweets store are desserts garnished with silver. Fragile and delicate as butterfly wings, silver and gold leaf are used for visually stunning embellishments. They have no taste or aroma but are perfectly edible. *Varq* is made by placing minute silver and gold pellets between sheets of tissue paper enclosed in a leather pouch, then hammering them until they form feather-thin foil. The leaf adheres to one side of the paper and is typically sold in packages of a dozen. Each year, almost twelve tons of silver is converted into edible *varq* in India. It is fragile and often breaks up, so it is a little tricky to use. To use as a garnish, first discard the paper without the leaf. Holding the paper with the leaf facing away from the open palm, invert your hand on the food and carefully press the paper. The silver sticks to the food as you peel away the paper. It is used to adorn sweets, *biryanis,* kebabs, and meat dishes. Relatively inexpensive silver and moderately priced gold leaf are available at gourmet stores, cake-decorating stores, and Indian markets. They keep for several months without tarnishing in the refrigerator.

Tamarind *(Imli), Tamarindus indica*

Tamarind, also known as Indian date, is the fruit of a large evergreen tropical tree that grows in most parts of India. Even the small oval leaves are deliciously sour; as youngsters, my friends and I plucked them from a tree growing at our school. The fruit is a legume-shaped pod enclosed in a grayish brown fragile shell; the fleshy pulp in the pod, held together by a fibrous husk, is dark reddish to brown, with shiny seeds. It is this fruity, sweet-sour pulp that is used as a souring agent in a number of dishes. In south Indian cooking, it forms a perfect hot weather flavoring, since it has a cooling effect on the body. Although it contains sugar, it is intensely sour and imparts piquancy to curries, meats, seafood, chutneys, and relishes. It is available in Asian markets, peeled and pitted, and compressed into blocks of up to a pound, or powdered or concentrated. Though I recommend the readily available concentrate in many recipes, when you have the time, I highly recommend you try using large pods of tamarind (or the compressed form) and extract the pulp for a refreshing, raw, fruitier taste. Tamarind pods are available these days in some farmers' markets and specialty markets. Tamarind packaged as a product of Thailand is sweet and not a good substitute in Indian cooking, as the Indian variety is both tart and sweet. Tamarind leaves are highly antiseptic and astringent, and the fruit is a mild carminative and laxative.

KITCHEN EQUIPMENT

I was carrying some uncommon baggage on the airplane when I came to the United States. In my suitcase, nestled among my dresses and saris were long-handled ladles, an old-fashioned wooden buttermilk churn, a tapered rolling pin, and a little marble mortar and pestle. Fortunately, my baggage was not opened by the customs agents, sparing me from the stares of my fellow passengers at the airport. The buttermilk churn is still in my pantry because it holds sentimental value. The rest of the items are put to good use.

You do not need any special utensils to cook from this book. A standard kitchen is likely to contain everything you'll require. However, some classic Indian utensils have such varied usage, I think they deserve a place in the Western kitchen. Here is a look at some vital ones.

Spice box

A spice box is a beautiful rounded stainless steel container, seven inches or more in diameter, inside of which are several small bowls for individual spices. The box provides the cook convenient, easy access to a whole variety of spices at once, without having to fumble with several little bottles. A typical box contains seven spices. Indian grocery stores carry a wide variety of spice boxes, some with glass tops. To create your own, take a round or square stainless steel or any other metal box. Select seven to nine identical small metal bowls that will fit perfectly in a petal fashion or in rows in the box. Place one or two tiny spoons inside the box. Now you can proudly place it on your counter filled with colorful spices.

Cookware

The most basic utensils in the traditional Indian kitchen are a round-bottomed pan called a *kadai;* a cast-iron griddle called a *tava;* and a rolling pin called a *belan*. These are long-lasting and particularly inexpensive, and they are all available at Indian markets.

The *kadai* resembles a Chinese wok, although it is deeper and smaller in diameter. This pan is used for various cooking purposes: frying, sautéing, braising, and other stovetop cooking. Its rounded bottom and wide top provide a large frying area but require relatively little oil. A wok or a deep iron or heavy-clad stainless steel skillet or sauté pan makes a fine substitute.

The *tava* is the Indian version of an iron griddle and is used in toasting spices and flatbreads. The *chapati tava* is smooth with a concave surface; a little oil drizzled around will gradually drift into the center and moisten the flatbread. If you're making Indian breads often, I encourage you to buy one for perfect results. There is a special flat *tava* for making *dosa*. Be specific and ask for whichever tava you need. A cast-iron griddle or a heavy large skillet makes a good replacement.

An iron *kadai* or *tava,* like any other cast-iron equipment, should be seasoned before use. To season, wash with a dishwashing liquid and wipe dry. Rub the surface with a few drops of vegetable oil. Heat over medium heat until hot, about 6 minutes. Sprinkle with one tablespoon each salt and whole wheat flour; wipe the salt mixture around the interior surface with a paper towel. Continue to cook for 5 minutes more. Turn off the heat. When the pan is cool enough to handle, wash and dry thoroughly with soap and water. Heat for 5 minutes over moderate heat. Now the pan is ready to use. Wash with soap and water to clean after each use.

The *belan*, or rolling pin, is about a foot long, with a long taper from the center toward the ends. This is my favorite for rolling the right thickness of *chapati*. These days, similar but larger French rolling pins are available in department stores and culinary shops. Use one with which you are comfortable.

CHAPATI, POORI, NAAN, AND OTHER FRESH HOT BREADS

Tazi Garm Roti

A lot of my food reminiscences have to do with breads. My childhood memories come rushing back when I make my grandmother's hand-shaped *palak thepla* (Multigrain Flatbread with Spinach, pages 66–67). I remember her cooking these when I visited her village; she would make a spicy, aromatic dough with tender spinach leaves and a mixture of flours—wheat, barley, mung bean, and millet. As I sat watching, she placed a ball of seasoned dough between her palms, then stretched and slapped it back and forth into a perfect round. As she worked, she tended to the fire, blowing on it through a pipe. She then half-roasted the bread on a griddle and completed the cooking by holding the bread directly over the open fire.

I ate these breads hot, brushed with homemade fluffy butter from my grandmother's own cows. To make grandmother's bread these days, I purchase the readily available multigrain flour from a specialty market, prepare the dough using a food processor, and then cook the breads on the griddle. So while grandmother's traditional flat bread was rustic and chewy, mine is soft. In the decades I've lived in the United States, I've learned many ways to streamline my old favorites from home for the contemporary kitchen. The idea is to recreate the subtle, complex flavors of India, while using modern conveniences to cut down on preparation time. It's been easier than I would have thought. The flavors—savory and subtle—aren't lost in this streamlining, and they always take me back to India in the years when I was growing up.

TYPES OF BREAD

Breads have always enjoyed a special place in Indian tradition. Each is prepared from the same key ingredients—milled grains and water—yet these breads have incredibly varying qualities, from pliable and tissue-thin to crackly crisp, moist to chewy, flat to puffy, and sweet to savory.

Chapati

The dough for these daily flatbreads is rolled to a 5- to 7-inch circle almost $1/16$ of an inch thick, and toasted on an ungreased *tava*. The *tava* is a round, single-burner cast-iron griddle with a smooth, concave surface; a little oil drizzled around the edges of a flatbread steadily flows to the interior to coat the entire bottom. A 9- to 10-inch cast-iron griddle or nonstick skillet makes a good alternative to a *tava*. There are dozens of varieties of *chapati*, made from every grain imaginable, including legumes and rice. They are all unleavened and hardly require any preparation. There are more elaborate stuffed ones as well, such as Cardamom-Scented Sweet Dal-Stuffed Flatbread (pages 72–73).

Paratha

Pan-fried *paratha* is yet another Indian favorite, and, not surprisingly, it is nearly as diverse as the subcontinent itself. Leavened or unleavened, *paratha* are slightly thick, and rich with *desi ghee*. They are rolled into layers and pan-fried. Like an expert pastry chef, an Indian cook uses various techniques to fold and roll the *desi ghee*-layered dough to obtain a light, flaky, and puffy texture. Spices and herbs, raw and cooked vegetables, and *paneer* are stuffed in or kneaded into *paratha* dough to make nutritious breads.

Poori

Though popular in restaurants, puffy *pooris* are less popular with home cooks because they are fried, but they are actually easy to prepare. They are usually served at banquets, wedding festivals, and family get-togethers. *Poori* is the simplest variety of fried puffy bread—little balls of *chapati* dough are rolled in small $1/8$-inch-thick circles and slipped into hot oil, where they fill with steam and balloon up instantly. *Poori* crusts are light, thin, and golden brown. There are both plain and more elaborate versions, both sweet and savory. *Bhaturas* (pages 82–83) are a rich, puffed-up delight in which a small amount of yogurt or buttermilk acts as a leavening agent.

Naan

These leavened flatbreads are made today in much the same way they've been for several hundred years. They are leavened with a sourdough starter, commercial yeast, or another agent and are usually round, teardrop-shaped, or oval and about $1/4$ inch thick. *Naan* is best made in a tandoor (pages 335–336). Lined with clay and straw, a tandoor stands vertically, and the charcoal fire on the flat bottom heats the side walls. Watching an expert prepare *naan* is spellbinding. When my husband and I lived in Kashmir, our cook never used a rolling pin; he'd dip his hands in flour, then slap a ball of dough between his palms with astonishing speed and dexterity until it was more or less oval in shape and slightly thick. Then he'd scatter minced garlic and sesame and nigella seeds on one side and moisten the other, and plunge his bare hand into the heated tandoor. Baking on the hot walls of the oven gives the breads a firm, well-browned bottom crust, while the softer tops are cooked by the hot air traveling upward from coals below. To achieve similar results without a tandoor, my first choice is to broil the *naan*. You can also bake directly on a HearthKit (see Sources, page 438). A pizza stone works well too. Another inexpensive option is to line the oven rack with unglazed quarry tiles, available at most hardware or tile stores. Before heading off to the store, measure the rack in your oven, and purchase tiles that will fit side by side to cover the lower rack, leaving a one-inch gap around the sides for the air to circulate.

ABOUT FLOUR

Wheat has been cultivated in northern India for generations. *Atta*, or *chapati* flour, is whole-wheat flour made by milling the whole wheat kernel (that includes the bran, germ, and endosperm). *Atta* is a light-colored, hard, high-gluten, high-protein spring wheat. The harder the wheat, the higher its gluten (protein) to starch ratio; that's what gives the flour its strength and elasticity. This flour makes light-colored, delicate breads that roll and shape easily and cook quickly. The American equivalent, the whole-wheat flour sold in supermarkets, is made from soft red wheat, which is coarse in texture and contains less gluten, resulting in heavier flatbreads. *Atta* resembles pastry flour in appearance and feel, but pastry flour is not a good substitute since it is relatively weak and inelastic. If you can buy *chapati* flour at a specialty store or Indian market (ask the grocer for best brand), I encourage you to use it, because dough made from atta is wonderfully malleable and thoroughly adaptable.

If you can't find *chapati* flour, then I suggest a blend of all-purpose flour, to balance the starch and gluten, and whole-wheat flour; mix 1 1/2 cups whole-wheat flour with 1/2 cup of all-purpose flour for a fuller, high-protein bread, and a ratio of equal parts to make soft breads. You may also try a blend of whole-wheat flour and cake or pastry flour. Proportions of flour are very much a matter of nutrition and personal preference. Once you become familiar with the flavors, textures, and feels of various flours, experiment on your own with varying proportions. If you plan to mix and match with other flours, remember that whole-wheat flour is your gluten source, which helps in binding. Durum wheat, the hardest white wheat, with a protein-loaded endosperm, is ideal for *chapati* making.

MAKING FLATBREADS

Learning to make Indian flatbreads is something like learning to ride a bicycle. The more you practice, the better you get. Here are some useful suggestions to get you started.

* Before you begin, get out a rolling pin, fill a small bowl with flour for dusting, and have melted *desi ghee,* butter, or oil on hand for brushing.

* You can use your food processor fitted with the metal S-blade to make *chapati* dough.

Nifty Ideas for Frying

✳ The deep, bowl-shaped Indian *kadai,* similar in shape to a Chinese wok, is an ideal pan for deep-frying. Both the *kadai* and wok provide a large frying area with a relatively small amount of oil. The rounded sides make turning foods over much easier, and because of the *kadai's* shape, oil seldom spatters outside the pan; the likelihood of grease fire is minimal, as long as the *kadai* is not filled more than two-thirds with oil. Place the *kadai* or wok on the back burner while frying. Avoid using long-handled pans, which tilt easily.

✳ Add oil to a depth of 1½ to 2 inches. If you use less oil, the food will not cook evenly. The oil must be hot enough so that the dough quickly forms a crust and doesn't absorb excess oil. Using a thermometer is the most accurate way to assure the proper heat. You can also drop in a morsel of the food to be fried; if the oil is at the right temperature it will come to the surface immediately, bubbling and sizzling. When you start to see the edges brown, it is time to turn it. It's important to keep the oil as close to 360°F to 375°F as possible. Remember, smoking oil is critically overheated and will give the food a bad taste.

✳ Fry in batches, and do not crowd. If your pan can't comfortably accommodate more than two *pooris,* fry one at a time.

✳ Drain fried foods in a single layer on a cookie sheet lined with brown paper bags or several layers of unbleached paper towel, placing crumpled paper towels on top to remove excess oil. (Bleached paper products can contain residues of dioxin. Foods that come in contact with bleached paper products absorb this toxic substance, so if you use paper towels for draining fried foods, be sure to use the unbleached variety, or, safer yet, use brown paper bags.) If you are making many batches, most fried foods can be kept warm in a low oven up to half an hour. Of course, for the best flavor serve as soon as possible.

✳ One of my favorite oils for deep-frying is canola oil. It is very low in saturated fat and is well suited for Indian cooking.

* Flours differ in the amount of liquid they can absorb. Start by using the smallest amount of liquid and add more in spoonfuls as needed, according to the feel of the dough. You'll have to add a tablespoon or two more water if you're making dough by hand. A pinch of salt added to the flour reduces stickiness and enhances digestion.

* The dough should be medium-soft. If the dough is too soft, you'll have difficulty rolling. Work a little extra flour into the dough if necessary. When the dough is ready, place on a work surface, coat both your hands with oil, and knead well for 6 to 10 minutes. Cover loosely with plastic wrap or a kitchen towel and let rest at least 30 minutes to 1 hour. The kneading helps to develop the gluten and allows the dough to become smooth and elastic. After the resting time, the dough may be wrapped and refrigerated for 2 to 4 days. Bring to room temperature before continuing. Frozen dough needs to be thawed at room temperature; do not thaw in the microwave, because portions of the dough sometimes start to cook, making it lumpy and unusable.

* Your test is in the rolling. Roll very gently from the center outward, without pressing on the dough too firmly; this is the place where you'll need practice, but you can do it. A tapered rolling pin (use the French or Indian style, which is lighter) can be manipulated more easily to achieve this perfection.

* Flours vary with the weather, and what works some days may not on others. Chapati may puff or may not, but they'll still be good to eat and satisfying. If your breads turn out to be tough, the next time try adding a medium cooked, peeled, and mashed potato to the flour to soften the dough. You may also mix 1/2 cup of plain yogurt into the dough to help soften it.

* Indian flatbreads, like any other bread, are best served within 3 or 4 hours. However, rewarming cooled flatbreads can give them new life.

* A tortilla press works quite well for flattening *poori* dough, but not for other types of Indian bread dough.

WHOLE-WHEAT FLATBREAD | Chapati

This recipe and others in this chapter may look long, but that's not because *chapati* making is tricky; *chapati* dough is particularly simple to make and very easy to work with. I simply want to clarify all the details of the procedure so that you can achieve the best results. At first, rolling the dough will feel awkward, but you'll soon become accustomed to the basic motion. To get a good feel for it, try making *chapati* two or three days in a row, or several times in one week; by the end of that time you'll be well on your way to becoming a confident flatbread maker.

In southwestern India, flavorful and nutritious *chapati* are folded and toasted, while in northern and central India, the same dough is simply rolled into a circle, toasted on a griddle, and called *roti*. When cooked over a direct flame, it is known as *phulka*. For your understanding I've included the basic recipes for all of these versions. Prepare them as close to serving time as possible for the most delicious flavor.

MAKES 10 CHAPATIS, SERVES 4 TO 5

2 cups *chapati* flour *(atta)*, or 1¹/2 cups whole wheat flour and ¹/2 cup unbleached all-purpose flour

1 tablespoon vegetable oil, plus extra for brushing and cooking

¹/2 teaspoon salt

³/4 cup plus 2 tablespoons water

1. In a food processor, combine the flour, oil, and salt and pulse until crumbly. With the machine running, gradually add the water through the feed tube in a steady stream and process until the dough comes together into a ball and begins to clean the sides of the bowl. Avoid overprocessing.

2. Place the dough on a work surface. Lightly coat your hands with oil and knead well for 6 to 8 minutes. The dough should be medium-soft, not stiff or sticky, and hold an impression of your fingertips when pressed; it should resemble Play-Doh. Form into a smooth ball, cover loosely with a kitchen towel or plastic wrap, and let rest for 30 minutes to an hour.

3. Place the dough on a lightly floured work surface and knead briefly. Divide the dough into 10 portions and roll each portion between your hands to form a smooth ball. Place the dough balls on a plate and cover with a kitchen towel to prevent drying. Place a piece of dough on a floured work surface and roll it out to a 3-inch circle. Evenly brush the top

surface with oil. Fold in half, forming a semicircle. Brush the top of the semicircle with oil and fold in half once again, forming a triangle. Cover, set aside, and repeat with the remaining balls of dough.

4.   Heat a *tava,* griddle, or skillet over medium-high heat until very hot, about 6 minutes. Temperature is important in getting flatbreads to puff; when you can hold your hand over the pan for only about 5 seconds, then it is ready. Reduce the heat to medium. Flatten one triangle piece gently with your palm, dust with flour, and roll the dough from the center outward into a 7- to 8-inch, 1/16-inch-thick circle (don't worry if the finished shape is somewhere between a triangle and a ragged circle), dusting lightly with flour as necessary. Carefully pick up the flatbread, slap it back and forth to shake off any excess flour, and gently slap it into the pan (make sure there are no creases, or quickly use a spatula to spread it evenly). Cook until it starts to puff in places, then press the unpuffed portions very gently with the back of a spoon, or a kitchen towel compressed into an irregular ball, and guide the air to puff the *chapati.* (This process should not take more than 1 minute.) Drizzle 1 teaspoon of oil around the edges of the *chapati.* Use a spatula to turn it over. The *chapati* should start to balloon gradually; again, press gently and guide the air to the parts that have not puffed so that they fill with steam, about 30 seconds. Make sure the flatbread is fully cooked, with no raw spots, and turn over again to finish cooking, if necessary, until it is lightly speckled brown. A perfect flatbread is one that puffs up all around after the second flip. Repeat with the other triangles, adjusting the heat according to your speed; if you're using a cast-iron pan, the heat will build as you're rolling the next flatbread, so you'll likely have to lower the temperature as you work.

5.   Transfer the finished flatbreads to a cloth-lined basket and serve right away. They're best hot off the griddle. However, they can be stored brushed with *desi ghee* (pages 47–48) or unsalted butter, stacked one on top of the other, covered with foil, and kept in a warm oven if they are to be eaten within an hour or two.

> MAKE AHEAD *Chapati* dough can be stored, covered, in the refrigerator for up to 4 days after the resting time. Bring to room temperature before continuing.
>
> Finished *chapatis* remain fresh in a covered container for a day at room temperature. They can be stored, wrapped in paper towels to absorb moisture and then covered with foil, in the refrigerator for up to 2 days. Or stack them between wax paper, seal them in a plastic bag, and freeze them for up to 1 month. Rewarm in a hot skillet or in the oven; do not use the microwave oven.

Roti

Making *roti* requires some practice; they may or may not puff the first time, but they will still be delicious.

MAKES 12 ROUND ROTIS, SERVES 3 TO 4

Divide the *chapati* dough into 12 portions. Roll each piece into a 6-inch circle, without using too much pressure with the rolling pin; cook the *roti* just like chapati.

Phulka

You can make *phulka* only if you have a gas burner; electric is not suitable. A standard cooking range comes with four burners; usually two are large and the other two are slightly smaller. Use a smaller burner to flame-toast the *phulka*, because very high heat will create burnt spots. *Phulka* is usually smaller in diameter than *roti*, because all of it has to fit on the burner and come in direct contact with the flame to swell like a balloon. For easier dusting and rolling, use rice flour if you have it handy. *Phulkas* are fun to make, and once you become adept (some of my students have learned in just one week), you'll find they are quick and easy.

MAKES 14 ROUND PHULKAS, SERVES 4 TO 5

Divide the *chapati* dough into 14 portions, then roll each piece into a 5-inch circle, without using too much pressure on the rolling pin. Cook on a hot *tava*, griddle, or skillet very briefly, 15 to 20 seconds. Turn over and toast until a couple of air bubbles and light brown spots appear and the *phulka* is fully cooked, about 30 seconds. Turn on a back (small) burner to medium and, using tongs, carefully hold the *phulka* on the burner in direct contact with the flame. Within seconds, the *phulka* will fill with steam and puff like a balloon; remove it from the heat right away. Be sure not to pierce the bread with the edges of the tongs, because if it tears, the *phulka* will not puff. Do not hold the bread on the burner for too long, because its surface tends to burn. Brush the *phulka* with melted *desi ghee* (pages 47–48) or butter. Repeat with the remaining rounds, and serve or store like *chapati*.

MULTIGRAIN FLATBREAD WITH SPINACH | Palak Thepla

This is a variation of *chapati*. With all the fun of shaping, rolling, and flavoring flatbreads, making these is a great way of getting your children involved in the kitchen.

Multigrain flour is available in bulk in specialty and natural food stores. If you can't find it, use *chapati* flour or an even combination of whole-wheat and all-purpose flours. You can improvise with flours from your own pantry, such as rye, barley, millet, or rice flours, but remember that whole-wheat flour must form the base. If you have extra time, make this dough by hand to create lovely streaks of spinach in the bread. Using a food processor will result in green flatbreads, though they're still worth making.

MAKES 8 ROUND FLATBREADS, SERVES 3 TO 4

2 cups packed finely chopped fresh spinach leaves
    and tender stems

1 1/2 cups multigrain flour

1/2 cup cake flour

1 teaspoon salt

1 teaspoon ground coriander

1 teaspoon red pepper flakes

1/4 teaspoon turmeric

1/2 cup water

1. Rinse the spinach and place it in a medium saucepan while still wet (the moisture is enough to cook the spinach). Cover and cook over medium heat, stirring once or twice, until wilted, about 3 minutes. Set aside.

2. In a food processor, combine the multigrain flour, cake flour, salt, coriander, pepper flakes, and turmeric and pulse a few times to mix. Add the wilted spinach and pulse until crumbly. With the machine running, gradually add the water through the feed tube in a steady stream, processing until the dough comes together into a ball and begins to clean the sides of the bowl. Avoid overprocessing.

3. Place the dough on a work surface. Lightly coat your hands with oil and knead well for 6 to 8 minutes. The dough should be medium-soft, not stiff or sticky, and hold an impression of your fingertips when pressed; it should resemble Play-Doh. Form into a smooth ball, cover loosely with a kitchen towel or plastic wrap, and let rest for 30 minutes to an hour.

4. Place the dough on a floured work surface and knead briefly until smooth. Divide the dough into 8 portions and roll each portion between your hands to form a smooth ball. Put the dough balls on a plate and cover with a kitchen towel to prevent drying.

5. Heat a *tava,* griddle, or skillet over medium-high heat until very hot, about 6 minutes. Temperature is important in getting flatbreads to puff; when you can hold your hand over the pan for only about 5 seconds, then it is ready. Reduce the heat to medium.

6. Place a piece of dough on a floured work surface and roll it out into a 5- to 6-inch, 1/8-inch-thick circle, dusting lightly with flour as necessary. Carefully pick up the flatbread, slap it back and forth to shake off any excess flour, then gently slap it into the pan (make sure there are no creases, or quickly use a spatula to spread it evenly). Cook until it starts to puff in places, then press the unpuffed portions very gently with the back of a spoon or a kitchen towel compressed into an irregular ball and guide the air to puff the *thepla.* (This process should not take more than 1 minute.) Use a spatula to turn it over. The *thepla* should start to puff; again, press gently and guide the air to the parts that have not puffed so that they fill with steam, about 30 seconds. Make sure the flatbread is fully cooked, with no raw spots, and turn over again to finish cooking, if necessary, until it is lightly speckled brown. A perfect flatbread is one that puffs up all around. Repeat with the other rounds, adjusting the heat according to your speed; if you're using a cast-iron pan, the heat will build as you're rolling the next flatbread, so you'll likely have to lower the temperature as you work.

7. Transfer the finished flatbreads to a cloth-lined basket and serve right away. They're best hot off the griddle. However, they can be stored brushed with *desi ghee* (pages 47–48) or unsalted butter, stacked one on top of the other, covered with foil, and kept in a warm oven if they are to be eaten within an hour or two.

> MAKE AHEAD *Thepla* dough can be stored, covered, in the refrigerator for up to 3 days after the resting time. Bring to room temperature before continuing.
>
> Finished *thepla* remain fresh in a covered container at room temperature for up to 1 day. They can be stored, wrapped in paper towels to absorb moisture and then covered with foil, in the refrigerator for up to 3 days. Or stack them between wax paper, seal them in a plastic bag, and freeze them for up to 1 month. Rewarm in a hot skillet or in the oven; do not use the microwave oven.

VARIATION

This recipe is very flexible; it can be made with watercress, fenugreek leaves, or mustard green in place of the spinach, or with a combination of greens for very nutritious flatbreads.

KASHMIR ROTI | Kashmiri Roti

Most of the time we have day-old or stale bread, especially those end slices of the loaf. Here is a recipe to make use of them—old bread is soaked in warm milk, tossed in a food processor with other ingredients, and processed to make soft-textured dough. As you finish these *rotis,* collect them in a cloth-lined basket, brush them with *desi ghee,* and serve them right away as snack. They are lovely with lamb dishes, or spread with herb chutneys.

MAKES 8 ROUND FLATBREADS, SERVES 3 TO 4

1 cup unbleached all-purpose flour

1 cup *chapati* flour *(atta),* or 1/2 cup whole-wheat flour and 1/2 cup unbleached all-purpose flour

1 teaspoon sugar

1 teaspoon ground fennel

1/2 teaspoon salt

2 day-old bread slices, soaked in 1/2 cup warm milk

6 tablespoons plain yogurt

Melted *desi ghee* (pages 47–48), or unsalted butter, for brushing

1. In a food processor, combine the all-purpose flour, *chapati* flour, sugar, fennel, and salt and pulse a few times to mix. Add the bread with the milk and pulse until crumbly. With the machine running, gradually add the yogurt through the feed tube in a steady stream. Process until the dough comes together into a ball and begins to clean the sides of the bowl. Avoid overprocessing.

2. Place the dough on a work surface. Lightly coat your hands with oil and knead well for 6 to 8 minutes. The dough should be medium-soft, not stiff or sticky, and hold an impression of your fingertips when pressed; it should resemble Play-Doh. Form into a smooth ball, cover loosely with a kitchen towel or plastic wrap, and let rest for 30 minutes to an hour.

3. Place the dough on a floured work surface and knead briefly until smooth. Divide the dough into 8 portions and roll each portion between your hands to form a smooth ball. Put the dough balls on a plate and cover with a kitchen towel to prevent drying.

4. Heat a *tava,* griddle, or skillet over medium-high heat until very hot, about 6 minutes. Temperature is important in getting flatbreads to puff; when you can hold your hand over the pan for only about 5 seconds, then it is ready. Reduce the heat to medium.

5. Place a piece of dough on a floured work surface and roll it out into a 5- to 6-inch, $1/8$-inch-thick circle, dusting lightly with flour as necessary. Carefully pick up the flatbread, slap it back and forth to shake off any excess flour, then gently slap it into the pan (make sure there are no creases, or quickly use a spatula to spread it evenly). Cook until it starts to puff in places, then press the unpuffed portions very gently with the back of a spoon or a kitchen towel compressed into an irregular ball and guide the air to puff the *roti.* (This process should not take more than 1 minute.) Use a spatula to turn over. The *roti* should start to puff; again, press gently and guide the air to the parts that have not puffed so that they fill with steam, about 30 seconds. Make sure the flatbread is fully cooked, with no raw spots, and turn over again to finish cooking, if necessary. Repeat with the other rounds, adjusting the heat according to your speed; if you're using a cast-iron pan, the heat will build as you're rolling the next flatbread, so you'll likely have to lower the temperature as you work.

6. Transfer the finished flatbreads to a cloth-lined basket. Brush generously with melted *desi ghee* and serve right away.

> MAKE AHEAD *Roti* dough can be stored, covered, in the refrigerator for up to 2 days after the resting time. Bring to room temperature before continuing.
>
> Finished *roti* remain fresh in a covered container for a day at room temperature. They can be stored, wrapped in paper towels to absorb moisture and then covered with foil, in the refrigerator for up to 3 days. Or stack them between wax paper seal them in a plastic bag, and freeze them for up to 1 month. Rewarm in a hot skillet or in the oven; do not use the microwave oven.

RUSTIC PUNJAB CORNMEAL FLATBREAD | Makkai ki Roti

The texture of this flatbread is a little mealier and less smooth than the others, but the aroma when it is toasting is compelling. This robust peasant-style bread is so tasty, I had to share it with you. The bread may look uneven and rustic, and that's how it is supposed to be. Cornmeal does not contain much gluten, and that's why boiling water is added to bind the dough. It's difficult at first to roll these flatbreads, but you'll get better with practice. If one of your guests is allergic to wheat, you can substitute yellow corn flour for the pastry flour. Serve with soft butter or whipped cream cheese, along with *saag* (pages 257–258), the traditional accompaniment in Punjab.

MAKES 6 ROUND ROTIS, SERVES 4 TO 6

1 1/2 cups yellow medium cornmeal

1/2 cup whole-wheat pastry flour

1 teaspoon salt

1 tablespoon vegetable oil

2/3 cup boiling water

Melted *desi ghee* (pages 47–48), or unsalted butter, for brushing

1. In a food processor, combine the cornmeal, pastry flour, and salt and pulse a few times to mix. Add the oil and pulse until crumbly. With the machine running, gradually add the boiling water through the feed tube in a steady stream. Process until the dough comes together into a ball and begins to clean the sides of the bowl. Avoid overprocessing.

2. Place the dough on a work surface. Lightly coat your hands with oil and knead well for 6 to 8 minutes. The dough should be medium-soft, not stiff or sticky. Form into a smooth ball, cover loosely with a kitchen towel or plastic wrap, and let rest for 30 minutes to an hour.

3. Place the dough on a floured work surface and knead briefly until smooth. Divide the dough into 6 portions and roll each portion between your hands to form a smooth ball. Put the dough balls on a plate and cover with a kitchen towel to prevent drying.

4. Heat a *tava,* griddle, or skillet over medium-high heat until very hot, about 6 minutes. Temperature is important in getting flatbreads to puff; when you can hold your hand over the pan for only about 5 seconds, then it is ready. Reduce the heat to medium.

5. Place a piece of dough on a floured work surface and roll it out into a 5- to 6-inch, 1/8-inch-thick circle, dusting lightly with flour as necessary. Carefully pick up the flatbread, slap it back and forth to shake off any excess flour, then gently slap it into the pan (make sure there are no creases, or quickly use a spatula to spread it evenly). Cook until it starts to puff in places, then press the unpuffed portions very gently with the back of a spoon or a kitchen towel compressed into an irregular ball and guide the air to puff the *roti.* (This process should not take more than 1 minute.) Use a spatula to turn it over. The *roti* should start to puff; again, press gently and guide the air to the parts that have not puffed so that they fill with steam, about 30 seconds. Make sure the flatbread is fully cooked, with no raw spots, and turn over again to finish cooking, if necessary. Repeat with the other rounds. (If the dough looks crumbly and is difficult to handle, then reprocess it in food processor with very hot water to get it back to the original texture and reroll.) Adjust the heat according to your speed; if you're using a cast-iron pan, the heat will build as you're rolling the next flatbread, so you'll likely have to lower the temperature as you work.

6. Transfer the finished flatbreads to a cloth-lined basket. Brush generously with melted *desi ghee* and serve right away.

CARDAMOM-SCENTED SWEET DAL-STUFFED FLATBREAD

| Puran Poli/Holige

This traditional recipe is comfort food, my very favorite since childhood. In India it is usually made on festive occasions. I remember each year when we gathered in my grandmother's home for a celebration with all my cousins, twenty-six of us. Grandmother set aside one day for the preparation of *holige*; her's were special, made with very soft dough (soaked in oil), over a foot in diameter, and rolled with plenty of oil instead of flour. So tender, they would melt in the mouth. Because they were so time-consuming to prepare, I hardly made an attempt to learn. But since I loved them so much, I later had no choice but to experiment over the years, devising my own ways to streamline the method, while retaining the classic flavors. The recipe calls for jaggery, which adds to the authenticity, but you can also make it with a combination of raw and brown sugar. Serve with plenty of *desi ghee* alongside.

MAKES 15 FLATBREADS, SERVES 6 TO 8

The Filling

1 cup *chana dal* (split chickpeas)

6 cups water

1 cup jaggery (pages 51–52, also see headnote)

5 green cardamom pods, seeds removed and pulverized

Freshly grated nutmeg

The Dough

1 cup *chapati* flour *(atta),* or 1/2 cup whole-wheat flour and 1/2 cup unbleached all-purpose flour

1 cup unbleached all-purpose flour

3/4 cup plus 2 tablespoons water

Oil, for drizzling

Melted *desi ghee* (pages 47–48), or unsalted butter, for brushing

1. To prepare the filling, in a heavy medium saucepan, combine the *dal* and water, bring to a boil, reduce the heat to medium, and cook, partially covered, until the *dal* is fully cooked (it should mash easily between the fingers), about 50 minutes. Drain the *dal* in a colander and return to the pan. Add the jaggery and cook, stirring regularly, over medium-low heat until the jaggery melts and all of the liquid evaporates, about 20 minutes. Remove from the heat and use a potato masher to blend the mixture well. Return to low heat and continue to cook until the consistency resembles a mass of mashed potatoes, about 10 minutes. (If a spoon stands straight in the filling, that means it is ready—my grandmother's helpful tip.) Add the cardamom to the *dal* mixture, grate a little fresh nutmeg over the top, and mix gently.

2. While the *dal* is cooking, make the dough. In a food processor, combine the *chapati* flour and all-purpose flour with a pinch of salt and pulse a few times to mix. With the machine running, gradually add the water through the feed tube in a steady stream and process until the dough comes together into a ball and begins to clean the sides of the bowl. Avoid overprocessing.

3. Place the dough on a work surface. Lightly coat your hands with oil and knead well for 6 to 8 minutes. The dough should be medium-soft, not stiff or sticky, and hold an impression of your fingertips when pressed; it should resemble Play-Doh. Form into a smooth ball, drizzle with a tablespoon of oil, cover loosely with a plastic wrap, and let rest for 30 minutes to an hour.

4. Place the dough on a floured work surface and knead briefly until smooth. Divide the dough into 15 portions and roll each portion between your hands to form a smooth ball. Put the dough balls on a plate and cover with a kitchen towel to prevent drying. Make 15 portions of the *dal* filling and set aside.

5. Heat a *tava,* griddle, or skillet over medium-high heat until very hot, about 6 minutes. Temperature is important in getting flatbreads to puff; when you can hold your hand over the pan for only about 5 seconds, then it is ready. Reduce the heat to medium.

6. Place a piece of dough on a floured work surface and roll it out into a 2¹/₂- to 3-inch circle, dusting lightly with flour as necessary. Scoop about 1 portion or 1 to 1¹/₂ table-spoons of filling in the center of the circle, bring the edges together, and pinch to seal. Shape into a ball once again. Flatten and place on floured surface and roll gently into a 4- to 5-inch, ¹/₈-inch-thick circle.

7. Carefully pick up the bread and gently slap it into the pan. Cook until it starts to puff in places, about 1 minute, and drizzle a teaspoon of oil around the edges. Use a spatula to carefully turn it over and continue to cook until the bottom is lightly speckled brown. Make sure the flatbread is fully cooked, with no raw spots, but take care when turning to avoid tearing. Repeat with the other rounds, adjusting the heat according to your speed; if you're using a cast-iron pan, the heat will build as you're rolling the next flatbread, so you'll likely have to lower the temperature as you work.

8. Transfer the finished breads onto an attractive platter, brush generously with melted *desi ghee,* and serve right away.

> MAKE AHEAD The dough and filling can be stored separately, covered, in the refrigerator for up to 2 days. Bring to room temperature before continuing; the *holige* are easier to stuff and roll if the filling is slightly warm.

FLAKY CUMIN-SCENTED PARATHA | Sada Paratha

Next to *naan*, *paratha* is one of India's best-known flatbreads. There are three types of *paratha*: flaky and unflavored, like this one; stuffed; or laced with aromatic spices. They are usually pan-fried in hot oil, but I've done away with that process. My secret—brush with *desi ghee*, which makes the dough soft, and sprinkle with rice flour, which gives adequate flakiness. The folding creates natural layers to form delicious and tender *paratha*.

MAKES 8 PARATHAS, SERVES 4

1½ cups *chapati* flour (*atta*), or 1 cup unbleached all-purpose flour and ½ cup whole-wheat flour

½ cup unbleached all-purpose flour

1 teaspoon cumin seeds, lightly crushed

½ teaspoon salt

¼ teaspoon baking soda

2 teaspoons soft *desi ghee* (pages 47–48), or unsalted butter, plus additional for brushing

¾ cup plus 2 tablespoons lukewarm (whole or low-fat) milk

Rice flour, for sprinkling

Oil for drizzling

1. In a food processor, combine the *chapati* flour, all-purpose flour, cumin, salt, and baking soda and pulse a few times to mix. Add the *desi ghee* and pulse until crumbly. With the machine running, gradually add the milk through the feed tube in a steady stream, process until the dough comes together into a ball and begins to clean the sides of the bowl. Avoid overprocessing.

2. Place the dough on a work surface. Lightly coat your hands with oil and knead well for 6 to 8 minutes. The dough should be medium-soft, not stiff or sticky, and hold an impression of your fingertips when pressed; it should resemble Play-Doh. Form into a smooth ball, cover loosely with a kitchen towel or plastic wrap, and let rest for 30 minutes to an hour, until the dough has risen a little in volume.

3. Lightly oil your hands and knead briefly until smooth. Divide the dough into 8 portions and roll each portion between your hands to form a smooth ball. Put the dough balls on a plate and cover with a kitchen towel to prevent drying.

4. Heat a *tava*, griddle, or skillet over medium-high heat until very hot, about 6 minutes. Temperature is important in getting flatbreads to puff; when you can hold your hand over the pan for only about 5 seconds, then it is ready. Reduce the heat to medium.

5. Place a piece of dough on a floured work surface and roll it out into a 3-inch circle. Brush the top surface with melted *desi ghee.* Sprinkle rice flour all over. Now fold in half, forming a semicircle. Repeat the process of brushing *desi ghee,* sprinkling rice flour, and folding, forming a triangle. Flatten this triangle gently with your palm, dust with flour, and roll it out into a 5-inch, 1/8-inch-thick triangle, dusting lightly with flour as necessary.

6. Carefully pick up the flatbread, slap it back and forth to shake off any excess flour, then gently slap it into the pan (make sure there are no creases, or quickly use a spatula to spread it evenly). Cook until it starts to puff in places, then press the unpuffed portions very gently with the back of a spoon or a kitchen towel compressed into an irregular ball and guide the air to puff the *paratha.* (This process should not take more than 1 minute.) Drizzle 1 or 2 teaspoons of oil around the edges of the *paratha.* Use a spatula to turn it over. The *paratha* should start to puff; again, press gently and guide the air to the parts that have not puffed so that they fill with steam, about 30 seconds. Make sure the flatbread is fully cooked, with no raw spots, and turn over again to finish cooking, if necessary, until it is lightly speckled brown. Repeat with the other rounds, adjusting the heat according to your speed; if you're using a cast-iron pan, the heat will build as you're rolling the next flatbread, so you'll likely have to lower the temperature as you work.

7. Transfer the finished flatbreads to a cloth-lined basket and serve right away. They're best hot off the griddle. However, they can be stored brushed with *desi ghee,* stacked one on top of the other, covered with foil, and kept in a warm oven if they are to be eaten within an hour or two.

> MAKE AHEAD *Paratha* dough can be stored, covered, in the refrigerator for up to 2 days after the resting time. Bring to room temperature before continuing.
>
> Finished *paratha* remain fresh in a covered container for a day at room temperature. They can be stored, wrapped in paper towels to absorb moisture and then covered with foil, in the refrigerator for up to 3 days. Or stack them between wax paper, seal them in a plastic bag, and freeze them for up to 1 month. Rewarm in a hot skillet or in the oven; do not use the microwave oven.

FLAKY CILANTRO-LACED PARATHA | Khasta Paratha

This is a richer version of the previous recipe. I've suggested a number of traditional layering methods to make the *paratha* flaky. If you shallow-fry the *paratha* (that is, using 2 to 3 tablespoons oil around the flatbread as it cooks), you'll see the layers much more conspicuously.

MAKES 8 TO 10 PARATHAS, SERVES 4 TO 6

2 cups *chapati* flour *(atta),* or 1 cup whole-wheat flour and 1 cup unbleached all-purpose flour

1 teaspoon baking soda

1 teaspoon salt

6 tablespoons melted *desi ghee* (pages 47–48), or unsalted butter

3/4 cup water

2 tablespoons unbleached all-purpose flour

1 teaspoon ground cumin

1/4 cup finely chopped cilantro or fresh mint leaves

Oil, for drizzling

1. In a food processor, combine the flour, soda, and salt and pulse to mix. Add 4 tablespoons of the *desi ghee* and pulse until crumbly. With the machine running, gradually add the water through the feed tube in a steady stream and process until the dough comes together into a ball and begins to clean the sides of the bowl. Avoid overprocessing.

2. Place the dough on a work surface. Lightly coat your hands with oil and knead well for 6 to 8 minutes. The dough should be medium-soft, not stiff or sticky, and hold an impression of your fingertips when pressed; it should resemble Play-Doh. Form into a smooth ball, cover loosely with a kitchen towel or plastic wrap, and let rest for 30 minutes to an hour, until the dough has risen a little in volume.

3. Fifteen minutes before you plan to roll the *paratha,* in a small bowl, mix together the remaining 2 tablespoons *desi ghee,* the all-purpose flour, cumin, and cilantro.

4. Lightly oil your hands and knead briefly until smooth. Divide the dough into 8 portions and roll each portion between your hands to form a smooth ball. Put the dough balls on a plate and cover with a kitchen towel to prevent drying.

5. Heat a *tava,* griddle, or skillet over medium-high heat until very hot, about 6 minutes. Temperature is important in getting flatbreads to puff; when you can hold your hand over the pan for only about 5 seconds, then it is ready. Reduce the heat to medium.

6. Place a piece of dough on a floured work surface and roll it out into a 6-inch circle. Spread 1 to 2 teaspoons of the herb mixture evenly on top and press gently. Use any of the following methods to make the *paratha.*

Layering method 1: This is the easiest and looks very pretty. Cut a circle of dough length-wise into 1^1/2-inch-wide strips. Stack the strips one on top of another, with the center strip on the bottom, and roll up the stack in jelly-roll fashion. Lay the roll on its side (with the spiral pattern facing up) on a floured surface. Flatten into a circular disc and set aside.

Layering method 2: Make a single cut from the center to the edge of a circle of dough (the radius); start rolling the dough up from the cut edge, ending at the other edge, forming into a cone. Brush with oil and squish the pointy end down to form a circular disc.

Layering method 3: Roll a circle of dough, jelly-roll fashion, into a long rope. Brush the rope with oil. Starting from one end, wind the rope into a spiral to form a coil. Flatten the coil with your fingertips into a circular disc.

Roll each layered portion into a 5- to 6-inch circle, dusting lightly with flour as necessary.

7. Carefully pick up the flatbread, slap it back and forth to shake off any excess flour, then gently slap it into the pan (make sure there are no creases, or quickly use a spatula to spread it evenly). Cook until it starts to puff in places, then press the unpuffed portions very gently with the back of a spoon or a kitchen towel compressed into an irregular ball and guide the air to puff the *paratha*. (This process should not take more than 1 minute.) Drizzle 1 or 2 teaspoons of oil around the edges of the *paratha*. Use a spatula to turn it over. The *paratha* should start to puff; again, press gently and guide the air to the parts that have not puffed so that they fill with steam, about 30 seconds. Make sure the flatbread is fully cooked, with no raw spots, and turn over again to finish cooking, if necessary, until it is lightly speckled brown. Repeat with the other rounds, adjusting the heat according to your speed; if you're using a cast-iron pan, the heat will build as you're rolling the next flat-bread, so you'll likely have to lower the temperature as you work.

8. Transfer the finished flatbreads to a cloth-lined basket and serve hot off the griddle. However, they can be stored brushed with *desi ghee,* stacked one on top of the other, covered with foil, and kept in a warm oven if they are to be eaten within an hour or two.

> MAKE AHEAD *Paratha* dough can be stored, covered, in the refrigerator for up to 2 days after the resting time. Bring to room temperature before continuing.
>
> Finished *paratha* remain fresh in a covered container for a day at room tempera-ture. They can be stored, wrapped in paper towels to absorb moisture and then covered with foil, in the refrigerator for up to 3 days. Or stack them between wax paper, seal them in a plastic bag, and freeze them for up to 1 month. Rewarm in a hot skillet or in the oven; do not use the microwave oven.

POTATO-STUFFED SAVORY PARATHA | Aloo Paratha

You may be familiar with *aloo paratha* from your visits to Indian restaurants. I've devised this method for the home cook; the result is thin and tender, unlike the restaurant version. I've made this stuffed *paratha* even easier by mixing the filling right in with the dough. I like it this way because it is effortless to roll, and there is no loss of flavors. You don't need any water to make the dough, because the moisture from warm mashed potato and cilantro leaves is sufficient.

MAKES 10 ROUNDS, SERVES 4 TO 6

1 medium-large (8-ounce) russet potato

One 2-inch piece fresh ginger, chopped roughly

1 to 2 fresh green serrano or jalapeño chilis, stemmed

1/2 cup packed cilantro

1 teaspoon salt

1 teaspoon ground cumin

1 1/2 cups *chapati* flour *(atta)*, or 1/2 cup whole-wheat flour and 1 cup unbleached all-purpose flour

1. In a medium pot of boiling water, cook the potato until tender, 15 minutes. When the potato is cool enough to handle, peel, dice into large chunks, and set aside.

2. Place the ginger in a food processor and mince finely. Add the chilis and cilantro and mince coarsely. Add the chopped potato, salt, and cumin and process until the mixture forms a thick, coarse paste. Add the flour and process until the dough comes together into a ball and begins to clean the sides of the bowl. Avoid overprocessing.

3. Place the dough on a work surface. Lightly coat your hands with oil and knead well for 5 to 6 minutes. The dough should be medium-soft. Form into a smooth ball, cover loosely with a kitchen towel or plastic wrap, and let rest for 10 minutes.

4. Place the dough on a floured work surface and knead briefly until smooth. If the dough becomes soft, sprinkle it with some flour, or better yet refrigerate the dough. Divide the dough into 10 portions and roll each portion between your hands to form a smooth ball. Put the dough balls on a plate and cover with a kitchen towel to prevent drying.

5. Heat a *tava,* griddle, or skillet over medium-high heat until very hot, about 6 minutes. Temperature is important in getting flatbreads to puff; when you can hold your hand over the pan for only about 5 seconds, then it is ready. Reduce the heat to medium.

6. Place a piece of dough on a floured work surface and roll it out into a 5- to 6-inch, 1/8-inch-thick circle, dusting lightly with flour as necessary. Carefully pick up the flatbread, slap it back and forth to shake off any excess flour, then gently slap it into the pan (make sure there are no creases, or quickly use a spatula to spread it evenly). Cook until it starts to puff in places, then press the unpuffed portions very gently with the back of a spoon or a kitchen towel compressed into an irregular ball and guide the air to puff the *paratha*. (This process should not take more than 1 minute.) Drizzle 1 or 2 teaspoons of oil around the edges of the *paratha*. Use a spatula to turn it over. The *paratha* should start to puff; again, press gently and guide the air to the parts that have not puffed so that they fill with steam, about 30 seconds. Make sure the flatbread is fully cooked, with no raw spots, and turn it over again to finish cooking, if necessary, until it is lightly speckled brown. A perfect flatbread is one that puffs up all around. Repeat with the other rounds, adjusting the heat according to your speed; if you're using a cast-iron pan, the heat will build as you're rolling the next flatbread, so you'll likely have to lower the temperature as you work.

7. Transfer the finished flatbreads to a cloth-lined basket and serve right away. They're best hot off the griddle. However, they can be stored brushed with *desi ghee* (pages 47–48) or unsalted butter, stacked one on top of the other, covered with foil, and kept in a warm oven if they are to be eaten within an hour or two.

MAKE AHEAD *Paratha* dough can be stored, covered, in the refrigerator for up to 2 days after the resting time. Bring to room temperature before continuing.

Finished *paratha* remain fresh in a covered container for a day at room temperature. They can be stored, wrapped in paper towels to absorb moisture and then covered with foil, in the refrigerator for up to 3 days. Or stack them between wax paper, seal them in a plastic bag, and freeze them for up to 1 month. Rewarm in a hot skillet or in the oven; do not use the microwave oven.

PUFFY BREAD | Poori

On leisurely weekends, I find myself tempted to make *poori*, especially because they make a happy accompaniment to Mixed Sprouts Stew (page 399) for brunch. When you entertain, I encourage you to try the variations as well—a multicolored platter of spinach, tomato, yellow bell pepper, or beet *poori* makes an attractive centerpiece. I've added sugar because it helps the *poori* stay puffed longer, though you may omit it if you like. The technique of adding hot oil to the flour is characteristic of southwestern India. Next time you make *poori*, sprinkle them with about a teaspoon of *ajwain* (page 20) or cumin seeds for a unique taste and appearance.

MAKES 18 POORIS, SERVES 6 TO 8

2 tablespoons vegetable oil, plus additional for frying

2 cups *chapati* flour *(atta),* or 1 cup whole-wheat flour and 1 cup unbleached all-purpose flour

1/2 teaspoon sugar

1/2 teaspoon salt

3/4 cup water

1. Heat 2 tablespoons of the oil in a small skillet until hot but not smoking. Remove from the heat.

2. In a food processor, combine the flour, sugar, and salt and pulse a few times to mix. Add the hot oil and pulse until crumbly. With the machine running, gradually add the water through the feed tube in a steady stream. Process until the dough comes together into a ball and begins to clean the sides of the bowl. Avoid overprocessing.

3. Place the dough on a work surface. Lightly coat your hands with oil and knead well for 6 to 8 minutes. The dough should be medium-soft, not stiff or sticky, and hold an impression of your fingertips when pressed; it should resemble Play-Doh. Form into a smooth ball, cover loosely with a kitchen towel or plastic wrap, and let rest for 30 minutes to an hour.

4. Place the dough on a floured work surface and knead briefly until smooth. Divide the dough into 3 portions and roll each portion between your hands to form a long rope. Cut each rope into 6 portions, each about the size of a walnut. Put the dough balls on a plate and cover with a kitchen towel to prevent drying. In a wok or sauté pan, pour oil to a depth of 1 1/2 inches and heat over medium-high heat until very hot, 375°F on a deep-fry thermometer. Temperature is important in getting *poori* to puff. If you do not have a thermometer, slide a tiny piece of the dough in the oil to test; if it comes to the surface imme-

diately, bubbling and sizzling, then the oil is ready. If the dough browns instantly, the oil is too hot; if it stays at the bottom, the oil is not hot enough. You'll likely have to adjust the temperature accordingly.

5. Place a piece of dough on a floured work surface and roll it into a 2 1/2- to 3-inch, 1/8-inch-thick circle, dusting lightly with flour as necessary. You can roll 4 to 6 *pooris* ahead, place them in a single layer on a platter (do not stack), and cover with plastic wrap.

6. Carefully slide 1 to 2 rounds into the hot oil. As the *pooris* rise to the top, use a spoon to bathe them lightly with oil so that they begin to puff. After 20 to 30 seconds, flip the *pooris* and fry until lightly golden, 15 to 20 seconds more. Use a skimmer or slotted spoon to transfer the *pooris* to a tray lined with brown paper bags or unbleached paper towels. Repeat with the other rounds, then roll out and fry the remaining portions of dough.

7. Transfer the finished *pooris* to a cloth-lined basket and serve right away, or place them on a cookie sheet, tent them with foil, and keep them warm in a low oven for up to 30 minutes.

> MAKE AHEAD *Poori* dough can be stored, covered, in the refrigerator for up to 3 days after the resting time. Bring to room temperature before continuing.
>
> Lightly stack *pooris* one on top of the other, double-wrap them in paper towels, then in foil, and store them at room temperature for several hours.

VARIATIONS

In step 4, you may divide the dough into 3 portions and roll each portion into a large 1/8-inch-thick rectangle; then use a 2 1/2-inch cookie cutter to cut out the *poori*.

Spinach Poori (Palak Poori)

Cook 2 cups chopped spinach (or other leafy greens) until wilted and add to the flour. Knead with your hands for pretty streaks of spinach; do not use the food processor or you'll end up with green *poori*. Add 1/3 cup water while kneading, adding more if necessary, according to the feel of the dough. After resting, divide the dough into 2 portions. Roll each portion into a large 1/8-inch-thick rectangle. Using a 3 1/2-inch biscuit cutter, cut out 5 to 6 rounds. Fry each round as directed and repeat with the other portion of dough. You may reknead and roll the trimmings to make a few more rounds.

Tomato and/or Beet Poori

Cut off the stems and roots of 1 medium red beet. Rinse, but do not peel. Cook, covered, in boiling salted water until tender, 45 to 50 minutes. When cool enough to handle, slip the skins off the beet. Dice the beet and 1 small tomato into quarters and combine in a food processor. Add 1/2 teaspoon sweet or hot paprika and process into a puree; then add the other ingredients gradually, omitting the water, and process into a smooth dough. If the dough is soft, add more flour to get the right consistency.

Golden Yellow Beet and/or Yellow Bell Pepper Poori

Prepare as above using a yellow beet and replacing the tomato with 1 yellow bell pepper, cored and cut into quarters.

STREET-STYLE BUTTERMILK BALLOON BREAD | Bhatura

I always look forward to eating these perfumed, soft, slightly sweet, tender balloon breads. Make the dough and side dishes ahead of time, so you can fry the breads as your guests arrive and serve them hot and puffed. This recipe is based on the street-style *bhatura*, which are 10 to 12 inches in diameter and served with garbanzo bean stew in India. You can pair *bhatura* with almost any meal, from a simple snack to special-occasion dinners.

MAKES 18, SERVES 8 TO 10

2 1/2 cups self-rising flour

1/2 teaspoon cumin seeds (optional)

1 teaspoon sugar

1/2 teaspoon salt

2 tablespoons melted *desi ghee* (pages 47–48), or
    unsalted butter

1/2 cup buttermilk

1/2 cup water

Vegetable oil, for frying

1. In a food processor, combine the flour, cumin (if using), sugar, and salt and pulse a few times to mix. Add the *desi ghee* and pulse until crumbly. With the machine running, gradually add the buttermilk, followed by the water, through the feed tube in a steady stream, processing until the dough comes together into a ball and begins to clean the sides of the bowl. Avoid overprocessing.

2. Place the dough on a work surface. Lightly coat your hands with oil and knead well for 6 to 8 minutes. The dough should be medium-soft, not stiff or sticky. Form into a smooth ball, cover loosely with a kitchen towel or plastic wrap, and let rest for 30 minutes to an hour (but no longer than 4 hours), until the dough has risen a little in volume.

3. Place the dough on a floured work surface and knead briefly until smooth. Divide the dough into 3 portions and roll each portion into a long rope between your hands. Cut each rope into 6 portions, each about the size of a golf ball. Form each portion into a smooth ball, put on a plate, and cover with a kitchen towel to prevent drying.

4. Fill a wok or sauté pan with oil to a depth of 2 inches and heat over medium-high heat until very hot, 375°F on a deep-fry thermometer. Temperature is important in getting *bhatura* to puff. If you do not have a thermometer, slide a tiny piece of the dough in the oil to test; if it comes to the surface immediately, bubbling and sizzling, then the oil is ready. If the dough browns instantly, the oil is too hot; if it stays at the bottom, then the oil is not hot enough. You'll likely have to adjust the temperature accordingly.

5. Place a ball of dough on a floured work surface and roll it out into a 3- to 3^1/$_2$-inch circle, a little less than ^{1}/$_4$ inch thick, dusting with flour as necessary. You can roll 4 *bhatura* ahead, place them in single layer on a platter (do not stack), and cover with plastic.

6. Carefully slide 1 round into the hot oil. As the *bhatura* rises to the top, use a spoon to bathe it lightly with oil so that it will begin to puff. After 20 to 30 seconds, flip the *bhatura* and fry until lightly golden, 15 to 20 seconds. Use a skimmer or slotted spoon to transfer the *bhatura* to a tray lined with brown paper bags or unbleached paper towels. Repeat with the other rounds, then the remaining portions of dough.

7. Transfer the finished *bhatura* to a cloth-lined basket and serve right away, or place them on a cookie sheet, tent them with foil, and keep them warm in a low oven for up to 30 minutes.

MAKE AHEAD *Bhatura* dough can be stored, covered, in the refrigerator for up to 4 days after the resting time. Bring to room temperature before continuing.

HOME-STYLE NAAN | Sada Naan

Naan cooked in a tandoor (pages 335–336) is hands-down the best. Don't be discouraged, however; it is possible to prepare it at home, and I encourage you to make your own *naan* occasionally. To get close to the tandoor version, you can, in order of preference: broil; bake directly on a HearthKit (see Sources, page 438), quarry tiles, or pizza stone; or cook on the stovetop using a cast-iron griddle or skillet. For centuries and even today, Indian *tandooriyas* have mastered the art of making *naan:* rhythmically patting flatbreads into discs, pulling on one side to form a teardrop shape, and slapping the *naan* on the tandoor wall with a deft sweep of the hand. For a beginner, or even a practiced hand like me, rolling gently with a rolling pin is a simpler approach, and no less artisanal. That's the way I've written this recipe. Be sure to use active dry yeast and add more yogurt if you choose not to use the egg. Cornmeal provides a slippery surface to assist in sliding the *naan* on and off the peel or baking sheet.

Naan has a lovely chewy texture, making it a quick and easy alternative to pizza crust.

MAKES 12 NAANS, SERVES 4 TO 6

4 cups unbleached all-purpose flour

2 teaspoons baking powder

1 teaspoon sugar

1 teaspoon salt

1 teaspoon active dry yeast

1/2 cup plain yogurt

1 large egg, slightly beaten

3 tablespoons vegetable oil

1/2 cup warm whole or low-fat (2%) milk

6 tablespoons warm water

Sesame, poppy, or nigella seeds, for sprinkling

Cornmeal, for the peel or baking sheet

Melted *desi ghee* (pages 47–48), or unsalted butter, for brushing

1. In a food processor, combine the flour, baking powder, sugar, salt, and yeast and pulse a few times to mix. Add the yogurt, egg, and oil and pulse until crumbly. With the machine running, gradually add the milk, then the water, through the feed tube in a steady stream, processing until the dough comes together into a ball and begins to clean the sides of the bowl. Avoid overprocessing.

2. Place the dough on a work surface. Lightly coat your hands with oil and knead well for 6 to 8 minutes. The dough should be medium-soft, not stiff or sticky. Form into a smooth ball, cover loosely with a kitchen towel or plastic wrap, and let rest in a draft-free spot for 4 to 6 hours, or until the dough doubles in volume. The consistency of the dough is important; after rising, it should not be soft and sticky, or very firm, but should be like medium-soft pizza dough, smooth and slightly elastic.

3. Lightly oil your hands, punch down the dough, place on a floured work surface and knead briefly until smooth. Divide the dough into 12 portions and roll each portion between your hands to form a smooth ball. Place the portions of dough on a baking sheet about 2 inches apart and cover with a kitchen towel; set aside until the dough doubles in volume, about 15 minutes. Place a ball of dough on lightly floured work surface and roll it out into a 5-inch circle or oval shape, a tad more than 1/8 inch thick, dusting lightly with flour as necessary. Carefully pick up the flatbread and pull gently on one side to shape it like a teardrop. Repeat with the remaining dough. Brush the tops of each *naan* with water, oil, or butter. Sprinkle each *naan* with the seeds of your choice and press gently. Cover and set aside.

4. Broiler method: Preheat the broiler for 5 minutes. Place 3 to 4 *naans* on a baking sheet sprinkled with cornmeal. Broil 6 inches away from the heat until lightly speckled brown, 2 to 2 1/2 minutes per side, watching closely to avoid burning. You may have to move each *naan*, depending on the heat distribution of the broiler.

Baking method: Place a HearthKit (see Sources, page 438), pizza stone, or quarry tiles in the oven and preheat it to 500°F (for at least 30 minutes if using the HearthKit). Sprinkle cornmeal on a baker's peel or the backside of a large baking sheet. Place 2 to 3 *naans* on the baker's peel or sheet, brush the tops with water, and slide the *naans* onto the baking surface. Bake 4 or 5 minutes, until lightly speckled brown.

5. Brush the finished *naan* with melted *desi ghee,* transfer to a cloth-lined basket, and serve. *Naan* is at its best when hot.

> MAKE AHEAD *Naan* dough can be stored, covered, in the refrigerator for up to 1 day after the resting time. Bring to room temperature before continuing.

VARIATIONS

Garlic Naan

Mix 2 tablespoons pureed garlic with salt and pepper to taste. In step 3, make a depression in the center of each ball of dough, add a teaspoon of the garlic mixture, shape into a round ball, and continue.

Mint Naan

In a food processor, grind $1/4$ cup finely chopped onion with $1/4$ cup fresh mint leaves and salt and sugar to taste. Add 2 to 3 tablespoons fresh lime juice and mix well. In step 3, make a depression in the center of each ball of dough, add a teaspoon of the mint mixture, shape into a round ball, and continue.

Paneer Naan

Mix $1/2$ cup crumbled Fresh Basic Paneer (pages 221–222), $1/2$ teaspoon crushed yellow or brown mustard or nigella seeds, 2 teaspoons fresh lime juice, and salt and pepper to taste. In step 3, make a depression in the center of each ball of dough, add 2 teaspoons of the *paneer* mixture, shape into a round ball, and continue.

Cilantro-Garlicky Naan

Mix 12 to 15 cloves garlic, minced, with $1/2$ cup chopped cilantro and 3 tablespoons melted *desi ghee*, butter, or olive oil. In step 3, brush the *naan* with water first, spread about 1 tablespoon of the cilantro-garlic mixture all over the *naan,* press gently, and continue with the recipe, omitting the seeds.

Onion–Red Pepper Flakes Naan

Mix 1 cup finely chopped onion with 1 tablespoon red pepper flakes and 2 to 3 tablespoons melted *desi ghee*, butter, or olive oil. In step 3, brush the *naan* with water first, spread about 1 tablespoon of the onion–red pepper mixture all over the *naan,* press gently, and continue with the recipe, omitting the seeds.

Almond-Laced Saffron Naan

Soak 1 teaspoon saffron threads in 2 tablespoons hot milk for 30 minutes; stir in 1 teaspoon of sugar. Add this mixture in step 1 while making the dough. In step 3, after rolling the *naan,* sprinkle with thinly sliced almonds and some raisins, press firmly, and continue with the recipe, omitting the seeds.

NAAN WITH SOURDOUGH STARTER | Khamiri Naan

Khamir is the Indian version of sourdough starter. This classic fermented dough was originally used in making *naan* and its cousins, *kulcha* and tandoori *roti*. *Khamir* is made with a little flour, yogurt, sugar, and salt and kept covered with cheesecloth; the starter ferments at room temperature until a pleasantly sour flavor develops. *Khamir* is always kept on hand; it lasts several days in the refrigerator and can be used with additional leavening in tandoori flatbreads. This *naan* is soft and chewy and tastes slightly different from the previous one. For a special treat, brush *naan* with saffron dissolved in milk, and press in some raisins and chopped cashews or slivered almonds before baking. Garnish the *naan* with silver leaf, cut into wedges, and serve.

MAKES 8 NAANS, SERVES 4 TO 6

2 1/2 cups unbleached all-purpose flour, or 1 1/2 cups unbleached all-purpose flour plus 1 cup *chapati* flour *(atta)*

1/2 cup plus 3 tablespoons plain yogurt

1 teaspoon sugar

1 teaspoon salt

1 teaspoon baking powder

2 tablespoons *desi ghee* (pages 47–48), or unsalted butter, plus extra for brushing

1 large egg, beaten slightly

Cumin or fennel seeds, for sprinkling (optional)

Cornmeal, for the peel or baking sheet

1. The day before you want to make the *naan*, combine 1/2 cup of the flour, the yogurt, sugar, and 1/2 teaspoon of the salt in a small mixing bowl. Mix well and cover with a cheesecloth or lid (do not use plastic; the starter needs to breathe). Set aside to ferment in a warm place, up to 18 hours, preferably overnight. When the starter is ready, you'll see a couple of bubbles at the top, it will smell pleasant, and it will be light and fluffy.

2. In a food processor, combine the remaining 2 cups of flour and 1/2 teaspoon salt, the baking powder, and the *desi ghee* and pulse until crumbly. Add the starter *(khamir)* and egg and process until the dough comes together into a ball and begins to clean the sides of the bowl. Avoid overprocessing.

3. Place the dough on a work surface. Lightly coat your hands with oil and knead well for 6 to 8 minutes. The dough should be medium-soft, not stiff or sticky. Form into a smooth ball, cover loosely with a kitchen towel or plastic wrap, and let rest in a draft-free spot for 3 to 4 hours. The consistency of the dough is important; after rising, it should not be soft and sticky or very firm, but should be like medium-soft pizza dough, smooth and slightly elastic.

4. Lightly oil your hands, punch down the dough, place on a floured work surface, and knead briefly until smooth. Divide the dough into 8 portions (each the size of a small orange), and roll each portion between your hands to form a smooth ball. Place the portions of dough on a baking sheet and cover. Place a ball of dough on a lightly floured work surface and roll it out into a 5-inch circle or oval shape, a tad more than 1/8 inch thick, dusting lightly with flour as necessary. Carefully pick up the flatbread and pull gently on one side to shape it like a teardrop. Repeat with remaining dough. Brush the top of each *naan* with water or oil. Sprinkle each *naan* with the seeds of your choice, if using, and press gently. Cover and set aside.

5. Broiler method: Preheat the broiler for 5 minutes. Place 3 to 4 *naans* on a baking sheet coated with cornmeal. Broil 6 inches away from the heat until lightly speckled brown, 2 to 2 1/2 minutes per side, watching closely to avoid burning. You may have to move each *naan*, depending on the heat distribution of the broiler.

Baking method: Place a HearthKit (see Sources, page 438), pizza stone, or quarry tiles in the oven and preheat it to 500°F (for at least 30 minutes if using the HearthKit). Sprinkle cornmeal on a baker's peel or the backside of a large baking sheet. Place 2 to 3 *naans* on the baker's peel or sheet and slide the *naans* onto the baking surface. Bake for 4 to 5 minutes, until lightly speckled brown.

6. Brush the finished *naan* with melted *desi ghee*, transfer to a cloth-lined basket, and serve. *Naan* is at its best when hot.

> MAKE AHEAD *Naan* dough can be stored, covered, in the refrigerator for up to 2 days after the resting time. Bring to room temperature before continuing.

VARIATION

Nicely developed sourdough starter gives this *naan* a lovely rising power and delicious taste. If you have some in the fridge, go ahead and use it. Substitute 1/2 cup sourdough starter for the mixture in step 1 and reduce the baking powder to 1/2 teaspoon.

ROSE-FLAVORED NAAN WITH SILVER LEAF | Sheer Mal

The rituals of outdoor barbecuing remind me of cooking in a tandoor. We have one, sunken deep next to the barbecue grill, in our backyard; it makes for quite the conversation piece with guests. I remember the very first time I used it to make homemade *naan*; I tried my dexterity at slapping the *naan* onto the walls of the tandoor and pulling them out. Before I became proficient, I lost about six in the burning fuel below.

North Indian *sheer mal* is a rich man's *naan*. Traditionally, a cup of sweet, fudgelike *khoa* (page 404) is added into the dough. The finished *naan* are brushed with milk to soften them and stored. If you use vanilla extract, be sure to add a couple of tablespoons of water for the right consistency. Serve this *naan* with any of the lamb dishes in this book, or use it as a quick pizza crust.

MAKES 8 NAANS, SERVES 4 TO 6

2¹/₂ cups unbleached all-purpose flour, or 1¹/₂ cups unbleached all-purpose flour plus 1 cup *chapati* flour

2 teaspoons sugar

1 teaspoon baking powder

¹/₂ teaspoon active dry yeast

¹/₂ teaspoon salt

6 green cardamom pods, seeds removed and ground

2 tablespoons *desi ghee* (pages 47–48), or unsalted butter, plus extra for brushing

2 tablespoons rose water, *kewra* water (page 51), or 1¹/₂ teaspoons vanilla extract

2 tablespoons heavy cream

³/₄ cup warm whole or low-fat milk

Cornmeal, for the peel or baking sheet

Silver leaf (page 54), for garnish

1. In a food processor, combine the flour, sugar, baking powder, yeast, salt, and cardamom and pulse a few times to mix. Add the *desi ghee*, rose water, and cream and pulse until crumbly. With the machine running, gradually add the milk through the feed tube in a steady stream, processing until the dough comes together into a ball and begins to clean the sides of the bowl. Avoid overprocessing.

2. Place the dough on a work surface. Lightly coat your hands with oil and knead well for 6 to 8 minutes. The dough should be medium-soft, not stiff or sticky. Form into a smooth ball, cover loosely with a kitchen towel or plastic wrap, and let rest in a draft-free spot for 2 to 3 hours. The consistency of the dough is important; after rising it should not be soft and sticky, or very firm, but like medium-soft pizza dough, smooth and slightly elastic.

3.   Lightly oil your hands, punch down the dough, place on a floured work surface and knead briefly until smooth. Divide the dough into 8 portions (each the size of a small orange) and roll each portion between your hands to form a smooth ball. Place the portions of dough on a baking sheet and cover with a kitchen towel. Place a ball of dough on a lightly floured work surface and roll it out into a 5-inch oval shape, a tad more than $1/8$ inch thick, dusting lightly with flour as necessary. Carefully pick up the flatbread and pull gently on one side to shape it like a teardrop. Repeat with remaining dough. Brush the top of each *naan* with milk or water. Cover and set aside.

4.   Broiler method: Preheat the broiler for 5 minutes. Place 3 to 4 *naans* on a baking sheet coated with cornmeal. Broil 6 inches away from the heat until lightly speckled brown, 2 to $2^{1}/2$ minutes per side, watching closely to avoid burning. You may have to move each *naan,* depending on the heat distribution of the broiler.

Baking method: Place a HearthKit (see Sources, page 438), pizza stone, or quarry tiles in the oven and preheat it to 500°F (for at least 30 minutes if using the HearthKit). Sprinkle cornmeal on a baker's peel or the backside of a large baking sheet. Place 2 to 3 *naans* on the baker's peel or sheet, brush the tops with water, and slide the *naans* onto the baking surface. Bake 4 or 5 minutes, until lightly speckled brown.

5.   Brush the finished *naan* with melted *desi ghee* or milk. Garnish with silver leaf (see page 54), transfer to a cloth-lined basket and serve. *Naans* are at their best when hot.

MAKE AHEAD *Naan* dough can be stored, covered, in the refrigerator for up to 2 days after the resting time. Bring to room temperature before continuing.

SWEET-SCENTED BASMATI: THE FABLED PILAFS AND BIRYANIS

Basmati ki Khushbu

Twenty years ago, as a bride, I stood at the doorstep of my new home in India and noticed, over the threshold, a wooden measuring cup piled high with grains of rice. My mother-in-law instructed me to gently kick it. The grains spilled over, scattering into the living room. The ritual, a tradition in India, implied that I was the incarnation of Laxmi, the goddess of wealth, bringing good fortune and fertility, signified by the rice, into the home of my in-laws.

Rice holds a special place in Indian culture. On festive occasions, married women are honored with a coconut, a handful of rice, and a length of fabric and wished a life of fruitfulness. Rice grains are mixed with red powder and a little water to form a thin paste used to paint a red dot on the forehead, and rice is show-ered on bridal couples and guests. It is strewn to form a carpet before the statues of gods and showered on them as an offering.

Beyond these rituals, however, rice plays an important part in Indian cuisine. Every region produces its own variety, which means a staggering array of rices, from inexpen-sive, short-grain red rice, to the world's finest, buttery basmati, to nutty baby basmati. One of the essential talents of a prospective bride is cooking the precious basmati (pro-nounced baas-MA-tee). My mother-in-law was surprised and delighted the first time I cooked it. "Ah!" she exclaimed. "The grains extend like dainty long fingers, and separate from one another, and look like jasmine buds." My secret is simple: purchase aged rice.

Basmati rice, like wine, gets better with age. High-quality packaged basmati is aged up to a year to enhance and intensify its taste, bouquet, and cooking characteristics; under cool, dry conditions, it keeps well for up to ten years. Old rice cooks up fluffy, with sepa-rate grains, while new rice can become sticky.

Basmati—the name means "queen of fragrances"—was brought in 1840 from Afghanistan and planted in the hills of Dehra Dun, at the foot of the Himalayas. There, in northern India, the snow-fed rivers of the majestic mountains water the lush green paddy fields. The soil and atmosphere are unique; this region has growing conditions that are dif-ficult to duplicate elsewhere. No wonder the grains are like no other—delicate, slender, and naturally perfumed.

Rice plays a number of roles in the Indian kitchen. It is casually used as an accom-paniment to many main dishes—legumes, meats, seafood, and vegetables. It takes center stage when combined with legumes (in the form of *idli* and *dosa*) to provide most of the bulk and calories in the southern diet. Along the coast, boiled rice is topped with spiced fish and shellfish to compose fragrant seafood pilafs. *Kitchri* is Indian-style risotto, made with medium-grain rice, lentils, spices, and herbs. In desserts such as Creamy Rice Pudding (page 414), rice is cooked in milk until the mixture condenses and develops mag-nificent flavors.

At formal meals, rice becomes an attractive entrée. Over the centuries, creative Indian cooks have turned rice into many novel dishes using local ingredients. One of the best known is *biryani*, a classic one-pot meal and staple at most north Indian restaurants. Just as a pastry chef expertly layers a cake with different textures, an Indian cook composes a great *biryani* with exquisite tiers of savory rice, spiced meat, and caramelized onions. The dish is then sprinkled with rose water or saffron, covered, and cooked gently over very low heat until the flavors blend. This slow cooking relaxes the basmati rice, allowing it to expand to its fullest, so that each grain enhances the tastes of the meat and seasonings.

A topping of mixed dried fruits and nuts—or even edible gold or silver leaf—completes the presentation. I have devoted a whole section of this chapter to *biryanis* (pages 114–125), since they are some of India's most exquisite preparations.

Despite the elegant reputation of the *biryanis*, rice is also an important staple food. In southern India, there are scores of rice dishes, each one differing in appearance, taste, and texture. Southerners prepare rice with the same veneration that Italians have for their pastas. A superb cook, it is said, can produce a different rice dish for each day of the year. Seasonal fruits and vegetables, coconut milk, legumes, lime juice, and tamarind are used to make aromatic pilafs. You'll find them all in this chapter.

Many supermarkets and most natural food stores are well stocked with basmati rice. If you cannot find basmati rice, other fragrant varieties of rice can be used as alternatives. Some basmati hybrids are cultivated in the United States, including Texmati, Kasmati, and Calmati. Fragrant Thai jasmine rice will also make a fine replacement.

I've discovered wild rice, too. It is biologically not a close relative of cultivated rice, but I love its chewy, slightly gamey flavor and decided to test it in Wild Rice and Chicken Biryani (pages 124–125). Wild rice holds its shape and takes on the spices very gracefully. It has now become a staple in my pantry, alongside basmati.

HOW TO PREPARE PERFECT BASMATI RICE

Basmati is sold under many brand names, including Tilda, Pari, and Dehra Dun—all rich and flavorful. Most bags indicate whether the rice has been aged, preferably for at least one year. Basmati loses moisture as it ages, which increases its capacity to expand when cooked. If the information is not on the label, ask the grocer. I have used basmati rice in all recipes unless specified otherwise.

CLEANING, WASHING, AND SOAKING RICE

To ensure fluffy, tender, and evenly cooked grains, follow these precooking steps:

✳ **Cleaning.** Although most basmati these days is pretty clean, like other grains and legumes, rice may include unhulled rice grains, stones, stems, and tiny travelers. To remove them, spread the rice on a white dinner plate or cookie sheet. Work one small portion of the rice at a time across to the opposite side of the plate, picking out any foreign matter.

* **Washing.** Place the rice in a large bowl and pour in cold tap water to cover. Swish the grains with your fingertips to release the starches and encourage any husks to float to the surface. Pour off the milky water. Wash two or three times until the water runs clear. Use cold water for rinsing and soaking; hot water can wash away valuable vitamins and break the delicate grains.

* **Soaking.** Soak the rice briefly (30 minutes to a few hours; some restaurants soak overnight) before cooking to encourage the grains to relax and absorb moisture. The little bit of water they absorb reduces the tendency for individual grains to stick to each other. This allows the rice to expand into thin, long grains that will not break during cooking. After soaking, drain the rice, saving the soaking water to use as cooking water (this preserves all of the nutrients, such as the water-soluble B vitamins).

GENERAL RICE COOKING TIPS

* **Fluffy texture.** A few drops of oil, butter, or *desi ghee* (pages 47–48) and a teaspoon of fresh lime juice added during cooking help the rice grains to remain separate and light during cooking. Stir-frying the rice in a little oil or *desi ghee* before adding water will also make the grains fluffy and separate.

* **How much water?** The amount of water used will vary, depending upon the strain and age of the rice and the depth and weight of the pan. As a general guideline, decide if you like your rice soft or firm, then gradually adjust the amount of water you use: $1^3/_4$ cups of water to 1 cup of raw basmati rice makes just-tender and fluffy rice—this is how I make rice every day. If you like a very firm texture, add $1^1/_2$ cups water. You may also use chicken, lamb, or vegetable stock in place of water.

* **The right pan.** A heavy, wide cooking pan such as a 3- to 4-quart saucepan with a tight-fitting lid will distribute the heat evenly. I say wide because each basmati grain needs sufficient space to extend its length. If your rice is cooking unevenly (perhaps the top layer is not cooked), then the lid is not fitted tightly enough. Use a kitchen towel as an inside cover; it stops the steam from condensing inside the lid and dripping back into the rice. Also, the towel will absorb the steam and keep the grains separate and fluffy.

* **Don't peek.** Do not stir or disturb the rice as it cooks. Removing the lid will let the steam escape, and the rice will cook unevenly. Let the cooked rice rest, covered, for a few minutes before serving.

Four Basic Rice-Cooking Methods

* **Stovetop.** Clean, rinse, and soak 1 cup basmati rice as described. Drain the rice. Place in a medium-size heavy saucepan and add 1³/₄ cups water. Bring to a boil. Add ¹/₂ teaspoon salt, 1 teaspoon freshly squeezed lime juice, and 1 teaspoon oil, butter, or *desi ghee* (pages 47–48). Reduce the heat to low, cover, and simmer for 15 minutes. Turn off the heat and let the rice rest, covered, for a few minutes before serving. Makes 4 cups rice.

* **Microwave.** Rinse, soak, and drain 1 cup basmati rice. Place in a 3-quart microwave-safe dish with 2¹/₃ cups water and ¹/₂ teaspoon salt. Cook, uncovered, at full power for 12 minutes (in a 750-watt oven). Remove from the oven, stir once, cover, and microwave at full power for 4 minutes more. Remove and let stand, covered, for 5 minutes before fluffing and serving. Makes 4 cups rice.

* **Oven.** Some Indians prefer to cook rice like pasta, boiling it in plenty of salted water until it is partially done. It is then drained, transferred to a baking dish, tightly covered, and baked until tender in a 325°F oven. This method is generally used for *biryanis*.

* **Electric rice cooker.** This appliance is very popular with Indians, because it provides a reliable way to cook perfect rice and can produce a large quantity of rice that does not become mushy. Following the manufacturer's directions, put rice and water in the cooker. Do not add salt. Cover and turn on the cooker. When the rice is done, the cooker will switch to the warm setting automatically, or it will turn off and then on again at intervals to keep the rice hot. Caution: More than an hour of continuous heating will make the rice dry and the bottom crusty, so unplug after 5 to 10 minutes. (If you're using the rice to cook other dishes, such as lemon rice or mint rice, transfer the rice to a platter when it is still hot, so that it will remain fluffy and separate.)

BASIC BASMATI RICE | Sada Chawal

This is the basic method for cooking basmati rice. I follow my grandmother's valuable tips: a sprinkling of fresh lime juice helps the grains remain fluffy and white, and a little oil keeps them separate. You can serve it as is or use it in a variety of other preparations in this chapter. Basmati rice cooks relatively quickly, and as a rule it requires a little less than two parts of water to one part of rice. You can easily double or triple the recipe; just be sure to use a large, wide pan so each grain has enough space to expand. Most basmati these days is pretty clean, but the recipe begins with a cleaning step to rid the rice of any agricultural products. Though the loss is minimal, if you want to preserve all the vitamins, reserve the soaking water and use it for cooking.

MAKES A GENEROUS 8 CUPS

2 cups basmati rice

3 1/2 cups water

2 teaspoons *desi ghee* (pages 47–48), or unsalted
 butter or vegetable oil (optional)

2 teaspoons freshly squeezed lime juice (optional)

1 teaspoon salt

1. Place the rice on a dinner plate. Work a small portion of the rice across to the opposite side of the plate, picking out any stones and unhulled rice grains. Repeat with the remaining rice. Place the rice in a bowl and wash with the tips of your fingers two or three times in cold running tap water. Drain, add water to cover by at least 2 inches, and let soak for 30 minutes or longer.

2. Drain the rice and transfer to a heavy medium saucepan. Add the water, *desi ghee*, if using, lime juice, if using, and salt and stir. Bring to a boil, then reduce the heat to low, cover, and simmer, without peeking, until the rice is tender and all the liquid is absorbed, about 15 minutes. Turn off the heat and let the rice stand, covered, for about 5 minutes. Fluff the rice lightly with a fork before serving.

> MAKE AHEAD Plain rice can be prepared 4 days ahead and kept, covered, in the refrigerator or in the freezer up to 1 month. To reheat, bring to room temperature first, then cook on medium heat or in the microwave until piping hot. Sprinkle it with some water if it looks too dry before reheating.

FRESH MINT RICE | Pudina Bhat

Mint leaves have a strong aroma with a refreshing, sweet flavor and cool aftertaste. I prefer spearmint for its delicate flavor. The lesser-known types of mint—pineapple, lemon, and apple, with fruity overtones—also fare well in this recipe. If using freshly cooked rice, cool thoroughly first. Serve with a refreshing *raita* (see pages 201–214) for a light lunch.

MAKES 4 SERVINGS

3 tablespoons grapeseed or canola oil

1 teaspoon yellow or brown mustard seeds

1 teaspoon cumin seeds

2 tablespoons dried currants or dark raisins

1 cup firmly packed chopped fresh mint leaves, plus beautiful sprigs for garnish

4 cups freshly cooked basmati rice, or jasmine or long grain white rice

1/2 cup coarsely chopped toasted walnuts (page 208)

1. Have a spatter screen ready before you continue. Heat the oil in a small skillet over medium-high heat. Add the mustard and cumin seeds, immediately cover with the spatter screen, and cook until the seeds stop popping, about 30 seconds. Reduce the heat to low, toss in the currants, and cook, stirring, until plump, about 1 minute. Stir in the mint leaves and cook, stirring, until fragrant, 2 to 3 minutes. Remove from the heat.

2. In a large bowl, pour the contents of the skillet over the rice, scraping the pan clean with a spatula. Toss gently. Fold in the walnuts. Transfer to a heated dish. Garnish with mint sprigs and serve warm or at room temperature.

MAKE AHEAD This dish may be assembled several hours ahead and kept covered at room temperature, refrigerated during warmer weather. Cover and reheat on medium flame or in the microwave.

VARIATION

Fresh Fenugreek Rice (Methi Chawal) or Mixed Herb Rice

Fresh fenugreek leaves (page 27) are available at Indian markets and some farmers' markets; try them in place of the mint for a unique taste. You may also substitute other fresh herbs, in greater or smaller amounts, for the mint to suit your personal tastes.

FRAGRANT MIXED VEGETABLE PILAF WITH CASHEWS

| Panchranga Pulao

In this simple yet elegant pilaf, I mix pleasantly crisp-tender vegetables into the rice during the last few minutes of cooking; as a result, they remain crunchy and colorful. Choose your favorites, preferably in a range of colors. You can vary the garnishes as well—add mixed nuts and raisins for a special occasion, or serve it topped with Sweet-Scented Tomato Gravy (page 123).

MAKES 6 TO 8 SERVINGS

2 cups basmati rice

1 tablespoon *desi ghee* (pages 47–48), or unsalted butter

1/2 cup slivered almonds

1/4 cup vegetable oil

1/2 cup carrot sticks (cut in thick, 1-inch-long pieces)

1/2 cup cut green beans (cut diagonally in 1/2-inch pieces)

1/2 cup 1/2-inch cauliflower florets with stems

1/4 cup fresh or frozen peas

12 whole cloves

20 black peppercorns

10 green cardamom pods

4 bay leaves

3 1/2 cups water

1 teaspoon salt

1. Place the rice on a dinner plate. Work a small portion of the rice across to the opposite side of the plate, picking out any stones and unhulled rice grains. Repeat with the remaining rice. Place the rice in a bowl and wash with the tips of your fingers two or three times in cold running tap water. Drain, add water to cover by at least 2 inches, and let soak for 30 minutes or longer. Drain and set aside.

2. Heat the *desi ghee* or unsalted butter in a heavy skillet over medium heat. Add the almonds and cook, stirring, until golden and crunchy, 3 to 4 minutes. Using a slotted spoon, transfer the almonds to a small bowl and set aside. Add 2 tablespoons of the oil to the same skillet and raise the heat to medium-high. Add the carrots, green beans, cauliflower, and fresh peas, if using, and cook, stirring, until the edges of the carrots and cauliflower start to brown, but the vegetables are still crisp, 6 to 8 minutes. Transfer to a plate and cover loosely.

3. Heat the remaining 2 tablespoons of oil in a heavy medium saucepan over medium heat. Add the cloves, peppercorns, cardamom pods, and bay leaves and cook, stirring, until fragrant, about 1 minute. A word of caution: sometimes whole spices become plump and pop out of the pan, so be careful. Add the rice, raise the heat to medium-high, and cook, stirring, until the rice is coated with oil and turns opaque, 4 to 5 minutes. Stir in the water and salt and bring to a boil. Reduce heat to low, cover, and cook for about 12 minutes. Uncover and, using a fork, gently stir in the reserved vegetables. If using frozen peas, add them at this time. Cover and cook for 5 minutes more. Turn off the heat and let the rice stand, covered, for at least 5 minutes.

4. Transfer the pilaf to a warm serving dish and discard the bay leaves, and the other whole spices if you prefer. Sprinkle with the almonds and serve.

VARIATION

Cumin-Scented Rice (Jeera Rice)

In India you'll find a rice accompaniment made with black cumin seeds (*shah jeera*, page 26), which have a smoky aroma and impart a sweet mellow taste. Add about 1 teaspoon of the seeds along with the other spices (you may substitute regular cumin seeds, if *shah jeera* are unavailable) and omit the vegetables. Garnish with crisp fried onions and cashews.

AROMATIC TOMATO RICE | Thakkali Sadam

In recipes like this one, *dal* (dried legumes) is added as a seasoning for the nutty taste it imparts. *Dal* is also favored for contributing a velvety texture and pleasant color. It is quintessential to southern Indian cooking. Top this dish with melted *desi ghee* (page 47–48) for a truly authentic taste.

SERVES 4 AS A LIGHT MAIN DISH, 6 AS A SIDE DISH

1 1/2 cups basmati or jasmine rice

2 3/4 cups water

1 teaspoon salt

4 medium-large tomatoes, or substitute 1 1/2 cups
canned tomato puree

1/4 cup peanut or vegetable oil

1 teaspoon yellow or brown mustard seeds

1/4 cup roasted salted or unsalted peanuts

1/4 teaspoon asafetida (optional)

20 *kari* leaves (page 28) (optional)

1 cup finely chopped yellow onion

6 large cloves garlic, minced

1/3 cup Fragrant Masala Powder (recipe follows),
or 5 to 6 tablespoons Sambar Powder (pages
37–38) or store-bought

1/4 teaspoon cayenne

Several tomato slices, for garnish

1. Place the rice on a dinner plate. Work a small portion of the rice across to the opposite side of the plate, picking out any stones and unhulled rice grains. Repeat with the remaining rice. Place the rice in a bowl and wash with the tips of your fingers two or three times in cold running tap water. Drain, add water to cover by at least 2 inches, and let soak for 30 minutes or longer. Drain and set aside.

2. Place the rice, water, and salt in a heavy medium saucepan. Bring to a boil, then reduce the heat to low, cover, and simmer until the rice is tender and all the liquid is absorbed, about 15 minutes. Turn off the heat and let the rice stand, covered.

3. Coarsely chop the tomatoes, transfer to a blender, and blend to a smooth puree. Press through a medium-mesh strainer into a measuring cup; there should be about 1 1/2 cups of puree. (Skip this step if using canned pureed tomatoes.) Set aside.

4. Have a spatter screen ready before you continue. Heat the oil in a heavy skillet over medium-high heat. Add the mustard seeds, immediately cover with the spatter screen, and cook until the seeds stop popping, about 30 seconds. Add the peanuts and the asafetida and *kari* leaves, if using. After a few seconds, when the leaves are crisp, stir in the onion and garlic and cook, stirring, until the garlic starts to brown, 2 to 3 minutes. Add the tomato puree and cook, stirring occasionally, until medium-thick and the raw smell dissipates, 8 to 10 minutes. Stir in the Fragrant Masala Powder and cayenne. Taste and season with $1/2$ to 1 teaspoon of salt. Add the rice and stir gently to mix. Cover and cook over low heat until heated through. Transfer to a heated serving dish. Garnish with the tomato slices and serve.

FRAGRANT MASALA POWDER

MAKES ABOUT $1/3$ CUP

1 tablespoon plus $1^1/2$ teaspoons coriander seeds

$1/2$ teaspoon fenugreek seeds

2 tablespoons *chana dal* (split chickpeas) (optional)

2 tablespoons dried unsweetened flaked coconut

1. In a small skillet over medium heat, combine the coriander seeds, fenugreek seeds, and *chana dal*. Toast, stirring frequently, until the seeds are aromatic and the *dal* is toasty, about 5 minutes. Add the coconut and toast, stirring frequently, until the coconut is light brown, about 2 minutes more.

2. Let the spice mixture cool slightly, then transfer to a coffee mill or spice grinder and grind to a fine powder, in small batches if necessary. Use immediately, or pour into an airtight glass jar, mix well, and let cool completely. Cover and store at room temperature, away from direct light, for up to 3 months.

KONKAN SHRIMP RICE | Kolmi Bhaat

The Konkan coast, near Mumbai, is known for its abundance of seafood and bountiful produce. The combination of crusty prawns with bracing *masala* is beloved in Konkani cuisine.

For a dressier presentation, scoop individual servings of prepared rice in banana leaves, wrap and secure the leaves with toothpicks, and steam in a steamer until hot. Carry the packets straight to the table and allow the guests to remove the toothpicks and unwrap. As the flavors drift, be ready to accept a round of applause.

SERVES 4 TO 6 AS A LIGHT MAIN DISH

1 pound (22 to 24) large shrimp

1 teaspoon turmeric

1 teaspoon cayenne

2 teaspoons salt

1/2 cup freshly squeezed lime juice

2 1/2 cups basmati rice

1 1/2 tablespoons coriander seeds

2 teaspoons cumin seeds

2 tablespoons sesame seeds

4 bay leaves

8 whole cloves

1/4 cup freshly grated coconut (page 307), or dried unsweetened flaked coconut

2 tablespoons vegetable oil

1 teaspoon yellow or brown mustard seeds

1/4 teaspoon asafetida

12 *kari* leaves (page 28) (optional), or cilantro

4 1/2 cups water

1. Peel the shrimp, leaving the final joint and tail intact. Devein each shrimp by making a shallow incision down the back, exposing the dark intestinal tract, and scraping it out. In a large glass bowl, combine the turmeric, cayenne, 1 teaspoon of the salt, and the lime juice. Add the shrimp and toss to mix. Cover and set aside for 30 minutes in the refrigerator to marinate.

2. Place the rice on a dinner plate. Work a small portion of the rice across to the opposite side of the plate, picking out any stones and unhulled rice grains. Repeat with the remaining rice. Place the rice in a bowl and wash with the tips of your fingers two or three times in cold running tap water. Drain, add water to cover by at least 2 inches, and let soak for 30 minutes or longer. Drain and set aside.

3. Meanwhile, in a medium skillet over medium heat, combine the coriander seeds, cumin seeds, sesame seeds, bay leaves, and cloves. Toast, stirring frequently, until the seeds are aromatic and toasty, about 5 minutes. Add the coconut and toast, stirring frequently, until light brown, about 2 minutes more. Transfer to a spice grinder or coffee mill and grind to a fine powder. Set aside.

4. Have a spatter screen ready before you continue. Heat the oil in a heavy, large saucepan over medium-high heat. Add the mustard seeds, immediately cover with the spatter screen, and cook until the seeds stop popping, about 30 seconds. Add the asafetida and *kari* leaves, if using. After a few seconds, when the leaves are crisp, add the spice mixture and shrimp. Cook, stirring, until fragrant and the shrimp are coated with the spices, about 3 minutes. Add the rice and mix well. Stir in the water and remaining teaspoon of salt. Bring the mixture to a boil. Reduce the heat to low, cover, and simmer until the rice is tender and all the liquid is absorbed, about 15 minutes. Turn off the heat and let the rice stand, covered, for 5 minutes. Transfer the rice to a heated serving dish.

LUSH YOGURT RICE | Dahi Bhaat/Masaru Anna

White rice is the chameleon grain, easily taking on any flavor gracefully. You'll be surprised how delightfully it melds with cool yogurt. Yogurt rice, a southern Indian specialty, is served almost daily, especially in summer months. Cooks make several variations according to the availability of seasonal produce, adding chopped cucumber, green mango, shredded carrots, and peas. Peanuts may be added for extra crunch. I like it best garnished with grapes as well.

Jasmine rice, with its subtle floral scent and smooth, silky texture, may also be used in this recipe.

SERVES 3 OR 4 AS A SIDE DISH

1-inch piece fresh ginger

1 to 2 fresh green serrano or jalapeño chilis, stemmed

1 teaspoon cumin seeds

4 cups cooked basmati rice (page 96) or jasmine or white rice, cooled to room temperature

2 teaspoons sugar

1/2 teaspoon salt (less if you added salt to the cooked rice)

1 tablespoon chopped cilantro

2 cups plain yogurt (preferably whole milk)

1/4 cup milk or buttermilk (optional)

1 1/2 tablespoons vegetable oil

1 teaspoon yellow or brown mustard seeds

2 teaspoons *urad dal* (white split gram beans) (optional)

2 teaspoons *chana dal* (split chickpeas) (optional)

1 good-size banana leaf, optional

2 small clusters seedless red and green grapes, for garnish

1.   In a large mortar and pestle, grind the ginger, chilis, and cumin seeds to a coarse textured paste; the mixture will exude a wonderfully pungent aroma. Pay close attention to breaking up the chilis, and use a spoon, not your fingers, to stir. Alternately, you may finely mince the ginger and chilis and lightly crush the cumin seeds with a rolling pin. Transfer to a large mixing bowl.

2.   Add the rice to the bowl and toss gently to mix. Sprinkle in the sugar, salt, and cilantro and mix well. Fold in the yogurt and milk. The consistency should be like risotto—slightly creamy, but not runny.

3.   Have a spatter screen ready before you continue. Heat the oil in a small skillet over medium-high heat. Add the mustard seeds and *urad dal*, add *chana dal* (if using) immediately cover with the spatter screen. Cook until the seeds stop popping, about 30 seconds. Remove from the heat.

4.   Line a decorative platter with the banana leaf, if using, and spoon yogurt rice in the center. Top with the oil seasoning along with the seeds. Strew some red and green grapes on top just before serving. Serve cold.

> MAKE AHEAD If you're not serving immediately, cover and refrigerate for up to 1 day. If the mixture is too thick, stir in a few tablespoons milk and/or yogurt to get the right consistency.

VARIATION
You may add 1 cup peeled and diced English hothouse cucumber in step 2.

RICE WITH FRENCH GREEN LENTILS | Ven Pongal

In an agricultural country like India, every harvest is very special. The wheat crop is celebrated in the north with folk dances, songs, and food, while in southern states, the "rice bowl of India," this nutritious rice dish is cooked in new earthenware from the rich harvest of grains and offered to Mother Earth as a sign of appreciation. Traditionally, yellow split mung beans *(mung dal)* are added to rice, but I've used French green lentils. They resemble brown lentils but are a little smaller and globular in shape, and can be found in most specialty markets. You may substitute whole mung beans or brown lentils if French lentils are unavailable.

Sprinkled with raisins and cashews, I like to use this pilaf as an out-of-the-ordinary stuffing for turkey.

SERVES 4 AS A MAIN DISH, 6 AS A SIDE DISH

1 cup basmati rice

1/4 cup French green lentils (see headnote)

1 teaspoon coriander seeds

1/2 teaspoon cumin seeds

1/2 teaspoon black peppercorns

1 tablespoon freshly grated coconut (page 307), or dried unsweetened flaked coconut

1 1/2 tablespoons vegetable oil

1/2 teaspoon yellow or brown mustard seeds

2 large cloves garlic, thinly sliced

1-inch piece fresh ginger, minced

1/8 teaspoon turmeric

2 1/4 cups water

1/2 teaspoon salt

Sliced cherry tomatoes for garnish

1. Combine the rice and lentils in a bowl and wash in several changes of water. Add enough water to cover by at least 2 inches and soak for 1 to 2 hours. Drain and set aside.

2. Meanwhile, in a small skillet over medium heat, combine the coriander seeds, cumin seeds, and peppercorns. Toast, stirring frequently, until the seeds are aromatic, about 4 minutes. Add the coconut and toast, stirring frequently, until light brown, about 2 minutes more. Transfer to a spice grinder or coffee mill and grind to a fine powder. Set aside.

3. Have a spatter screen ready before you continue. Heat the oil in a heavy saucepan over medium-high heat. Add the mustard seeds, immediately cover with the spatter screen, and cook until the seeds stop popping, about 30 seconds. Add the garlic, ginger, and turmeric and cook, stirring, until the mixture is aromatic and the garlic starts to brown, about 1 minute. Add the rice and lentils and cook, stirring, until the rice grains are glistening and coated with oil, 4 to 5 minutes. Stir in the water, salt, and ground spice blend. Bring to a boil, reduce the heat to low, cover, and simmer until the lentils are tender and all the water is absorbed, about 20 minutes. (For whole mung beans or brown lentils, add about 2 to 3 tablespoons more water and cook for 30 minutes.) Remove from the heat and let stand, covered, for 5 minutes.

4.   Fluff the rice lightly with a fork and transfer to a warmed serving platter. Garnish with the tomatoes and serve.

VARIATION

Sweet Rice (Chakra Pongal)

A sweet version of this rice dish is served as a dessert in southern India. The rice and *mung dal* are stir-fried in *desi ghee* (pages 47–48) and cooked in milk instead of water (add salt to taste). In the last few minutes of cooking, stir in $1/2$ teaspoon each pulverized green cardamom seeds and freshly grated nutmeg. Soak $1/2$ teaspoon saffron threads in 2 tablespoons warm milk and add to the rice. While the rice is cooking, melt $1/4$ to $1/3$ cup jaggery (pages 51–52) in $1/4$ cup water and simmer for 5 minutes. Make sure the jaggery is clean (straining the syrup if necessary) and add to the rice. Mix gently. Stir-fry 10 whole cashews in 1 tablespoon *desi ghee* and sprinkle over the finished dish.

COCONUT RICE WITH FRESH GREEN CHILIS | Tengai Sadam

Over the years I've grown very fond of the way the sweetness of coconut milk complements the earthiness of rice. This southern Indian dish is one of my favorite rice preparations. For a well-balanced menu, serve it alongside lighter dishes, such as a legume curry like Basic Sambar (pages 388–389), *chapati* (pages 63–64), Skillet-Seared Zesty Zucchini and Eggplant with Pecans (page 233), and Red and Golden Beet Kachumber with Orange (page 216). For a more formal gathering, include Coorg-Style Pork Stew (page 297).

SERVES 4 AS A MAIN DISH, OR 6 AS A SIDE DISH

1¹/2 cups basmati rice

1¹/2 tablespoons mild peanut or vegetable oil

¹/2 teaspoon yellow or brown mustard seeds

1 to 2 fresh green serrano or jalapeño chilis, stemmed and slit lengthwise

10 *kari* leaves (page 28) (optional), or cilantro

2 cups Fresh Coconut Milk (page 308), or canned unsweetened coconut milk

³/4 cup water

³/4 teaspoon salt

2 tablespoons freshly grated coconut (page 307), or dried unsweetened flaked coconut, for garnish

1. Place the rice on a dinner plate. Work a small portion of the rice across to the opposite side of the plate, picking out any stones and unhulled rice grains. Repeat with the remaining rice. Place the rice in a bowl and wash with the tips of your fingers two or three times in cold running tap water. Drain, add water to cover by at least 2 inches, and let soak for 30 minutes or longer. Drain and set aside.

2. Have a spatter screen ready before you continue. Heat the oil in a heavy medium saucepan over medium-high heat. Add the mustard seeds, immediately cover with the spatter screen, and cook until the seeds stop popping, about 30 seconds. Add the chilis and *kari* leaves, if using, and cook, stirring, until the leaves are crisp and chilis are blistered in places, about 30 seconds. Add the rice and cook, stirring, until the rice grains are glistening and coated with oil, about 5 minutes. In a small bowl, mix together the coconut milk and water; add to the rice, sprinkle in the salt, and bring to a boil. Reduce the heat to low, cover, and simmer until the rice is tender and the liquid is absorbed, about 15 minutes. Remove from the heat and let the rice stand, covered, for 5 minutes. Uncover and fluff the rice with a fork. Transfer to a heated serving dish, garnish with the coconut, and serve hot, warm, or at room temperature.

LEMON RICE | Chitranaam

This is a simple yet visually stunning dish. My mother would collect leftover rice and embellish it with a lovely zesty seasoning and lots of fresh lime juice. No one ever minded that it was "recycled" rice. If you don't have leftover cooked rice, it is worth making fresh rice to enjoy this pilaf; that's how I make mine for special meals. Pair it with any of the *raitas* (pages 201–214), warm *paratha* (pages 74–79) and perhaps Konkan Crab Curry (pages 309–310), and you've got a great dinner. (See Lime, page 52.)

SERVES 5 AS A MAIN DISH, 8 AS A SIDE DISH

5 cups day-old cooked basmati rice (page 96)

1 teaspoon salt

1 teaspoon sugar

1/4 cup or more freshly squeezed lemon or lime juice

1/4 cup chopped cilantro, plus additional sprigs for garnish

3 1/2 tablespoons mild peanut or vegetable oil

1 teaspoon yellow or brown mustard seeds

1 teaspoon cumin seeds

1/4 cup roasted salted or unsalted peanuts

1 cup finely chopped onion

2 to 3 fresh green serrano or jalapeño chilis, or fewer to taste, stemmed and chopped

1/4 teaspoon turmeric

1. Place the rice in a large bowl. Sprinkle with the salt, sugar, lime juice, and cilantro. Toss gently to mix. Set aside.

2. Have a spatter screen ready before you continue. Heat the oil in a large heavy sauté pan or Dutch oven over medium-high heat. Add the mustard and cumin seeds, immediately cover with the spatter screen, and cook until the seeds stop popping, about 30 seconds. Add the nuts and cook, stirring, for about 1 minute. Add the onion, chilis, and turmeric and cook, stirring occasionally, until the onion is soft, about 3 minutes. Reduce the heat to low, add the rice, and mix thoroughly until each grain is stained yellow from the turmeric. Cover and cook until very hot, 6 to 8 minutes. Transfer to a heated serving platter. Garnish with sprigs of cilantro and serve hot, warm, or at room temperature.

TAMARIND RICE | Puliyodharai

Here, bland rice gets a rich treatment of nutty *dals*, pungent spices, sweet coconut, and tart tamarind, making it complex and satisfying. If any of the *dal* isn't at the ready for the Fresh Masala Powder, just omit it, and substitute a handful of cilantro for the *kari* leaves. This dish is great with any fish entrée. For a truly authentic touch, serve with melted *desi ghee* (pages 47–48) alongside.

SERVES 6 OR 8 AS A SIDE DISH

3 tablespoons mild peanut or canola oil

1 teaspoon yellow or brown mustard seeds

15 *kari* leaves (page 28) (optional), or cilantro

1/4 cup roasted salted or unsalted peanuts

1/2 teaspoon turmeric

1 tablespoon plus 2 teaspoons tamarind concentrate

3 cups water

2 tablespoons light brown sugar, jaggery (pages 51–52), or raw sugar

3/4 cup Fresh Masala Powder (recipe follows), or 1/4 cup each *sambar* and *rasam* powders (pages 37–38), or store-bought

6 cups cooked basmati rice (page 96)

Have a spatter screen ready before you continue. Heat the oil in a large heavy sauté pan or Dutch oven over medium-high heat. Add the mustard seeds, immediately cover with the spatter screen, and cook until the seeds stop popping, about 30 seconds. Add the *kari* leaves (if using), nuts, and turmeric and cook, stirring for a few seconds until the leaves are crisp. Add the tamarind, water, sugar, and *masala* powder. Cover and cook, stirring occasionally, over medium heat until most of the water evaporates, the oil floats to the top, and the mixture is very thick and reduced to a third of its original volume, 15 to 20 minutes. Stir in the rice and mix well until the rice turns light brown. Cover and simmer until all of the water is absorbed. Turn off the heat and let the rice rest, covered, for 5 minutes. Uncover, lightly fluff with a fork, and transfer to a heated serving platter.

FRESH MASALA POWDER

MAKES ABOUT ³/₄ CUP

2 teaspoons mild peanut or canola oil

6 tablespoons coriander seeds

2 tablespoons *chana dal* (split chickpeas)

2 tablespoons *urad dal* (white split gram beans)

2 dried hot red chilis, such as cayennes or chiles
de arbol, stemmed

2 teaspoons cumin seeds

1 teaspoon black peppercorns

1 teaspoon fenugreek seeds

1 teaspoon yellow or brown mustard seeds

1 tablespoon dried unsweetened flaked coconut

¹/₄ teaspoon asafetida

1. Heat the oil in a small skillet over medium heat. Add the coriander seeds, *chana dal*, *urad dal*, chilis, cumin seeds, peppercorns, fenugreek seeds, and mustard seeds and toast, stirring frequently, until the seeds are aromatic and the *dals* uniformly reddish and toasty, about 5 minutes. Add the coconut and toast, stirring, until light golden, about 2 minutes more. Transfer to a bowl. Add the asafetida to the same skillet over low heat; toast, stirring, for a few seconds, and add to the bowl.

2. Let the spice mixture cool slightly, then transfer to a coffee mill or spice grinder and grind to a fine powder, in small batches if necessary. Use immediately or pour into an airtight glass jar, mix well, and let cool completely. Cover and store at room temperature, away from direct light, for up to 1 month.

SPICY UDUPI-STYLE RISOTTO WITH DAL | Bisi Bele Huli Anna

This was my very favorite spicy rice dish when I was growing up. It's a classic southern Indian preparation, loaded with nutritious ingredients such as lentils, grains, spices, and herbs, and it makes a simple one-pot supper. One of the important ingredients here is the rice itself, which must be a plump, starchy grain. The starch forms a velvety sauce, a marvelous combination of silky and chewy textures. The cooked rice has a thick and creamy, not runny or sticky, consistency and a tender but slightly firm texture.

I like to serve this entrée as a main course accompanied by a big salad and a Rose-Accented Sweet Buttermilk Lassi (page 426).

1 cup long-grain white or Arborio rice

1/2 cup *toovar dal* (yellow lentils) or yellow split peas

5 1/2 cups water

1 1/2 teaspoons salt

2 tablespoons mild peanut or canola oil

1 teaspoon yellow or brown mustard seeds

1/4 teaspoon asafetida

2 tablespoons chopped cilantro

1/4 teaspoon turmeric

1/2 cup thinly sliced onion

1 medium russet or Yukon gold potato, peeled and diced

1 small Japanese eggplant or zucchini, diced

1/4 cup sliced carrots

1/2 small green bell pepper, chopped

1/2 cup cauliflower or broccoli florets, cut in 1-inch pieces

2 tablespoons tamarind concentrate, dissolved in 1/2 cup water

1/2 cup Huli Anna Powder (recipe follows), or 1/4 cup Sambar Powder (pages 37–38) and 3 tablespoons Rasam Powder (page 38), or store-bought

Melted *desi ghee* (pages 47–48), or unsalted butter

Toasted *pappadam* (pages 142–143) (optional)

1. In a bowl, combine the rice and *dal* and wash in several changes of water. Add enough water to cover by at least 2 inches and soak for 30 minutes to 2 hours. Drain.

2. In a heavy, large saucepan, combine the rice and dal, 3 1/2 cups of the water, and 1/2 teaspoon of the salt and bring to a boil. Reduce the heat to low, cover, and simmer until the *dal* is tender, 25 to 30 minutes. Turn off the heat and let the rice and *dal* stand, covered.

3. Have a spatter screen ready before you continue. Heat the oil in a medium skillet over medium-high heat. Add the mustard seeds and asafetida, immediately cover with the spatter screen, and cook until the seeds stop popping, about 30 seconds. Add the cilantro, stir for a few seconds, then add the turmeric, onion, potato, eggplant or zucchini, carrots, bell pepper, and cauliflower or broccoli and cook, stirring, for 2 to 3 minutes. Add the tamarind liquid, cover, and cook until the potato is just tender, 6 to 8 minutes. Season with the remaining 1 teaspoon salt. Add the Huli Anna Powder and remaining 2 cups of water and mix well; pour over the rice and mix gently. Cook over medium heat until most of the water is absorbed, 4 to 5 minutes. Sprinkle the rice with a few tablespoons of *desi ghee*, cover, and let the flavors meld 5 minutes. Turn off the heat and let the rice and *dal* stand, covered, for a few minutes. Serve hot with *pappadam*, if desired.

HULI ANNA POWDER

1 teaspoon mild peanut or canola oil

2 to 4 dried hot red chilis, such as chiles de arbol or cayennes, stemmed

2-inch cinnamon stick

5 green cardamom pods, seeds removed

2 tablespoons *chana dal* (split chickpeas)

2 tablespoons *urad dal* (white split gram beans)

2 tablespoons coriander seeds

2 teaspoons poppy seeds

¹/₄ teaspoon fenugreek seeds

¹/₄ cup freshly grated coconut (page 307), or dried unsweetened flaked coconut

1. Heat the oil in a small skillet over medium heat. Add the chilis, cinnamon, cardamom seeds, *chana dal, urad dal,* coriander seeds, poppy seeds, and fenugreek seeds and toast, stirring frequently, until the seeds are aromatic and the *dals* are toasty, about 5 minutes. Add the coconut and toast, stirring, until light golden, about 2 minutes more.

2. Let the spice mixture cool slightly, then transfer to a coffee mill or spice grinder and grind to a fine powder, in small batches if necessary. Use immediately or pour into an airtight glass jar, mix well, and let cool completely. Cover and store at room temperature, away from direct light, for up to 1 month.

SPICY PILAF WITH VEGETABLES | Masala Bhaat

This is a traditional rice dish from Maharashtra State, made with locally grown vegetables, fresh coconut, and spicy seasonings. Serve it as a main course accompanied with a Salty Lassi with Fresh Mint (pages 426–427). For a special meal, complement this dish with Coastal Kerala Baked Catfish with Tomatoes (pages 321–322) and end with Vermicelli Pudding with Fresh Berries (page 415).

2 cups basmati rice

1/4 cup coriander seeds

1 tablespoon cumin seeds

5 black peppercorns

4 whole cloves

3 dried hot red chilis, such as cayennes or chiles de arbol, or fewer to taste, stemmed

2-inch cinnamon stick

1/4 cup dried unsweetened flaked coconut, plus additional for garnish

2 tablespoons vegetable oil

1/2 teaspoon yellow or brown mustard seeds

1/4 teaspoon turmeric

1/8 teaspoon asafetida

3 tablespoons roasted salted or unsalted peanuts

1 cup cauliflower, cut into 1/2-inch florets

1/2 cup fresh or frozen peas

1/2 cup green beans, cut into 1/2-inch pieces

1 teaspoon salt

1/2 teaspoon sugar

3 3/4 cups water

1 teaspoon *desi ghee* (pages 47–48), or unsalted butter

1.   Place the rice on a dinner plate. Work a small portion of the rice across to the opposite side of the plate, picking out any stones and unhulled rice grains. Repeat with the remaining rice. Place the rice in a bowl and wash with the tips of your fingers two or three times in cold running tap water. Drain, add water to cover by at least 2 inches, and let soak for 30 minutes or longer. Drain and set aside.

2.   In a small skillet over medium heat, add the coriander and cumin seeds, peppercorns, cloves, chilis, and cinnamon and toast, stirring frequently, until the seeds are aromatic, about 5 minutes. Add the coconut and toast, stirring, until light golden, about 2 minutes more. Transfer to a spice grinder or coffee mill, grind to a fine powder, and set aside.

3.   Have a spatter screen ready before you continue. Heat the oil in a large heavy Dutch oven over medium-high heat. Add the mustard seeds, immediately cover with the spatter screen, and cook until the seeds stop popping, about 30 seconds. Add the turmeric, asafetida, peanuts, cauliflower, peas, and green beans and cook, stirring, for 3 to 4 minutes. Add the rice and cook, stirring, until the grains glisten with oil, about 5 minutes. Add the salt, sugar, water, *desi ghee*, and the ground spice mixture. Stir well and bring to a boil. Reduce the heat to low, cover, and cook for 15 minutes. Turn off the heat and let stand at least 5 minutes. Transfer the pilaf into a warm serving dish, sprinkle with coconut, and serve.

Tricks for a Better Biryani

* When you prepare nonvegetarian *biryanis*, make sure the meat and seafood are chunkier than bite-size, since they will shrink by about 30 percent while cooking.

* Marinate meat for at least 3 to 4 hours and chicken for about 2 to 3 hours for an infusion of flavors.

* As always, use fresh spices for full flavor.

* Use only aged basmati; "young" rice will become sticky. The rice must be soaked for at least 30 minutes and cooked partially in vigorous boiling water.

* Avoid cooking in *desi ghee* initially, because the flavors get lost; instead, drizzle with *desi ghee* before baking for wonderful aromas.

* When baking, be sure to tightly seal the baking dish (foil works well) to preserve the flavors. You may also try using a decorative earthenware baking pot; layer first as described, then seal the lid with *naan* dough (pages 84–85), or store-bought frozen puff pastry sheet, and bake.

A BONANZA OF BIRYANIS

Biryani has its origin in the Arab world, where the idea of cooking meat with rice stems from necessity, as the nomads had to cook with a minimum number of pots. This is the food of generations and perhaps centuries, with classics so lavishly delicious, I've devoted a section to them.

Biryani (pronounced bee-r-yaa-ni) is a mixture of rice and spicy meat, arranged in layers in a large pot and sprinkled with aromatic essences, saffron, and *desi ghee*. Traditionally, the ingredients are tightly packed into a stew pot, usually earthen; the lid

The Moghul Influence

Perhaps the greatest and most lasting outside influence on Indian cuisine was that of the Moghuls (from 1526 to 1761), as they introduced opulence to the classic cuisine. In the royal kitchen, the staff worked diligently. They could serve a hundred elaborate dishes at a moment's notice. Various departments had specific duties, such as supervision of drinks, provision of fresh and dried fruits, preparation of food for the palace, and baking and delivery of breads. At the start of each season, cereals, cooking oil, *desi ghee*, birds of various kinds, lamb, and goats were well stocked. The finest basmati rice was brought from the foothills of the Himalayas. Fruits, ducks, and waterfowl were obtained from Kashmir. Livestock was kept separate and properly looked after by the "table attendants." Animals were slaughtered and washed outside the city; individual cuts of meat were sealed in sacks.

The royal kitchen was strictly supervised. No strangers, wanderers, or friends of staff were allowed near the kitchen. When the cooks worked, they covered their mouths and noses with a handkerchief. The chefs and many officers tested the food for poison. Food was transferred in gold or silver containers and wrapped in red cloth; copper and china were cloaked in white fabric. A description of the preparation was written on the red cloth. When the food arrived in the royal dining hall, it was checked against the list for any changes. Condiments like pickles, lemon wedges, fresh ginger julienne, and leafy greens were individually wrapped in small bags. Gorgeous breadbaskets containing *naan*, *roti*, and other paper-thin flatbreads were carefully draped with linens. Even the water, perfumed by the water carriers with special fragrances for different seasons, was preserved until serving time.

is sealed to the pot with *naan* dough, to preserve flavors; and the dish is cooked over very low heat. Hot coals are placed on top of the lid for an even distribution of heat. No steam or flavors escape until the dough is broken and the lid removed when ready to serve. This method of cooking is also termed the *dum* style. *Dum* (see details on page 292) literally means "to breathe in." The result is astonishingly subtle, with a lovely balance of flavors.

Originally, *biryani* was made with lamb or mutton, rice, and spices only. Over time, eggs, chicken, fish, shellfish, *paneer*, and vegetables were added in very creative ways. Over the centuries, the ordinary dish became elaborate and formal; it was elevated to grand status, with flamboyant embellishments such as gold leaf, during the Moghul era, when the emperors entertained guests with extravagant *biryanis*.

MOGHUL LAMB BIRYANI | Mughalai Gosht Biryani

This satisfying one-pot meal originated in the royal kitchens of the Moghuls. It's great for company, because it's best when prepared ahead. If possible, marinate the meat the first day, cook it the next day, and prepare the rice, assemble, and serve on the third day.

SERVES 4 TO 6

8 green cardamom pods

2-inch piece fresh ginger, minced

8 cloves garlic, minced

1 cup finely chopped onion

1 1/2 teaspoons salt

1 teaspoon freshly ground black pepper

1 teaspoon ground cloves

1/2 teaspoon ground cinnamon

1/2 teaspoon ground mace

1/4 teaspoon freshly grated nutmeg

2 cups yogurt cheese (page 205)

6 tablespoons tomato paste

1 1/2 pounds boneless lamb shoulder (or other lamb stew meat), cut into 2-inch cubes

2 cups basmati rice

7 tablespoons grapeseed or canola oil

2 whole pods star anise

4 black cardamom pods (optional)

4-inch cinnamon stick

1/2 cup slivered almonds

1/2 cup dark raisins, or sultanas

2 medium-large yellow onions, peeled, cut in half, and sliced lengthwise

1 to 1 1/2 cups water

3 tablespoons melted *desi ghee* (pages 47–48), or unsalted butter

1 1/2 tablespoons rose water

1 recipe Apricot Yogurt Gravy with Mint (recipe follows)

1. Husk the green cardamom pods. Using a mortar and pestle, pulverize the seeds, and transfer to a blender. Add the ginger, garlic, onion, 1/2 teaspoon of the salt, the pepper, cloves, cinnamon, mace, nutmeg, and 1 cup of the yogurt cheese to the blender and blend to a smooth paste, stopping to scrape down the sides of the bowl a couple of times. Transfer to a glass bowl. Add the remaining 1 cup of yogurt cheese and the tomato paste and mix well. Add the lamb and rub the mixture into the meat. Let the meat marinate for 3 to 4 hours in the refrigerator.

2. Half an hour before you want to cook the *biryani*, place the rice on a dinner plate. Work a small portion of the rice across to the opposite side of the plate, picking out any stones and unhulled rice grains. Repeat with the remaining rice. Place the rice in a bowl and wash with the tips of your fingers two or three times in cold running tap water. Drain, add water to cover by at least 2 inches, and let soak for 30 minutes. Drain and set aside.

3. Bring 6 cups of water to a boil in a large saucepan. Meanwhile, heat 2 tablespoons of the oil in a large, heavy skillet over medium heat. Add the star anise, black cardamom, and cinnamon and cook, stirring, for 30 seconds, then add the rice. Cook, stirring, until the rice grains glisten and are coated with oil, about 5 minutes. Transfer the rice to the boiling water, add the remaining 1 teaspoon salt, and cook uncovered over high heat for 5 minutes. Drain the rice in a colander and set aside.

4. Heat 1 tablespoon of the oil in a heavy large skillet over medium heat. Add the almonds and cook, stirring, until lightly browned, 4 to 5 minutes. Transfer with a slotted spoon to a plate. Add the raisins to the pan and cook, stirring, until plump, about 2 minutes. Transfer to the plate with the nuts. Add 2 tablespoons of the oil to the same skillet, add the onion, and cook, stirring, until deep golden, 10 to 12 minutes. Transfer to a plate.

5. Remove the meat from the marinade. Add 2 tablespoons of the oil to the same skillet. When hot, add the meat cubes and sear until lightly browned, 4 to 5 minutes per side. Add the marinade to the skillet and continue to cook, stirring occasionally, until the oil separates, 6 to 8 minutes. Add the water, cover, and cook until the meat is fork-tender and the liquid is absorbed, 20 to 25 minutes.

6. Meanwhile, position a rack in the center of the oven and preheat to 325°F.

7. To assemble the *biryani*, spread about half of the rice in the bottom of a 4-quart, heat-proof glass baking dish. Layer half of the lamb on top, then sprinkle on half of the fried onion, nuts, and raisins. Add another layer each of the remaining rice and lamb, finishing with a sprinkling of the remaining onion, nuts, and raisins. Sprinkle the *desi ghee* and rose water over the top. Cover tightly with aluminum foil and bake for 20 minutes. Let sit for up to 10 minutes in the warm oven if not serving right away. Remove from the oven and let stand, covered, for 5 minutes before serving. Serve with Apricot Yogurt Gravy with Mint.

VARIATION

In place of the lamb, you may use skinless boneless chicken breasts or beef chuck or sirloin, cut into 2-inch cubes.

APRICOT YOGURT GRAVY WITH MINT | Goshtaba Gravy

This is the ultimate sauce for any lamb entrée. Not only is it lovely with the preceding dish, Moghul Lamb Biryani, you can spoon it over tandoori meat dishes and other *biryanis* as well.

MAKES A GENEROUS 1³/4 CUPS

1/2 cup (about 16) dried apricots

2 tablespoons *desi ghee* (pages 47–48), or unsalted butter

1 cup plain yogurt

2 tablespoons chickpea flour

1/2 teaspoon ground white pepper

2 green cardamom pods, seeds removed and crushed

1 teaspoon salt

1/2 cup water

1 tablespoon chopped fresh mint leaves, for garnish

1. Soak apricots in 1/2 cup of warm water for 30 minutes to an 1 hour. Puree the apricots along with the soaking water in a blender until smooth.

2. Heat the *desi ghee* over medium heat in a heavy medium saucepan. Add the apricot paste to the pan and cook, stirring, until aromatic, about 4 minutes. Meanwhile, in a bowl, whisk together the yogurt, chickpea flour, pepper, cardamom, salt, and water. Add to the pan, stir, and simmer until the gravy is thick, smooth, and velvety, 6 to 8 minutes. Taste it; it should be pleasantly perfumed. Remove from the heat and serve garnished with the mint.

MAKE AHEAD The apricot puree can be prepared through step 1 up to 5 days in advance and stored, covered, in the refrigerator.

SCALLOP BIRYANI SPIKED WITH COCONUT | Marvai Biryani

I tested many traditional *biryani* recipes when I was writing this book, and then gave each my own spin. As the delicate aroma of the basmati fills the kitchen, scallops bathe in a cardamom-scented marinade. The seared and crusted scallops are then arranged on a layer of fluffy basmati, topped with a blanket of caramelized onion, toasted pistachios, and a light drizzle of coconut milk; the flavorful result makes this dish the star of any stylish dinner.

SERVES 6 AS A CASUAL MAIN DISH

2 cups basmati rice

1 teaspoon salt

1/4 teaspoon turmeric

12 green cardamom pods, seeds removed

4 fresh green serrano or jalapeño chilis, or fewer to taste, stemmed

2-inch piece fresh ginger

12 cloves garlic

1/2 teaspoon freshly ground black pepper

1/2 teaspoon ground cinnamon

1/2 cup water

2 pounds bay scallops

6 tablespoons vegetable oil

2 medium yellow onions, cut in half and sliced lengthwise

1/2 cup shelled roasted salted or unsalted pistachios

1/2 cup coconut milk

Several tablespoons freshly grated coconut, or dried unsweetened flaked coconut, for garnish

1. Place the rice on a dinner plate. Work a small portion of the rice across to the opposite side of the plate, picking out any stones and unhulled rice grains. Repeat with the remaining rice. Place the rice in a bowl and wash with the tips of your fingers two or three times in cold running tap water. Drain, add water to cover by at least 2 inches, and let soak for 30 minutes or longer. Drain and set aside.

2. In a medium saucepan, bring 6 cups water to a boil. Add the rice, salt, and turmeric. Cook, uncovered, over high heat for 5 minutes. Drain the rice in a colander and set aside.

3. Position a rack in the center of the oven and preheat to 325°F.

4. Using a mortar and pestle, pulverize the cardamom seeds and transfer to a blender. Add the chilis, ginger, garlic, pepper, cinnamon, and water to the blender and process to a smooth paste, stopping to scrape down the sides of the bowl a couple of times. Transfer to a glass bowl. Add the scallops and toss well. Set aside for 15 minutes, in the refrigerator if the day is warm. Heat 3 tablespoons of the oil in a heavy sauté pan over medium heat. Add the onion and cook, stirring often, until deep golden, 8 to 10 minutes. Transfer to a plate. Add the remaining 3 tablespoons of oil to the pan, and when hot add the scallops with the marinade. Cook, stirring, until the scallops are lightly golden, about 5 minutes per side.

5. To assemble, spread about half of the rice in a 4-quart heat-proof glass baking dish. Spread the scallops over the rice, then top with the onion and pistachios and finish with a layer of the remaining rice. Sprinkle the coconut milk over the top. Cover tightly with foil and bake for 20 minutes. Remove from the oven and let stand, covered, for 5 minutes.

6. While the *biryani* is cooking, toast the coconut in a dry skillet over medium heat, stirring, until toasty and golden, 3 to 4 minutes. Uncover the *biryani*, garnish with the toasted coconut, and serve immediately.

MAHIMAHI BIRYANI | Machchi Biryani

This *biryani* is a stunning variation on Tangy Mahimahi Fillets with Shallots (page 324).

SERVES 6 AS A MAIN DISH

2 cup basmati rice

2 1/2 cups water

1 cup low-fat or whole milk

1 teaspoon black peppercorns

1/2 teaspoon salt

1 recipe Tangy Mahimahi Fillets with Shallots
(page 324)

1/4 cup coarsely crushed peanuts

1. Position a rack in the center of the oven and preheat to 325°F.

2. Place the rice on a dinner plate. Work a small portion of the rice across to the opposite side of the plate, picking out any stones and unhulled rice grains. Repeat with the remaining rice. Place the rice in a bowl and wash with the tips of your fingers two or three times in cold running tap water. Drain, add water to cover by at least 2 inches, and let soak for 30 minutes or longer. Drain and set aside.

3. Bring the water and milk to a boil in a heavy medium saucepan. Add the rice, peppercorns, and salt, reduce the heat to low, cover, and cook until the rice is just tender, about 10 minutes. Set aside.

4. To assemble the *biryani*, spread about half of the rice in the bottom of a 3-quart, 9 x 13–inch heat-proof glass baking dish. Spread the Tangy Mahimahi Fillets with Shallots in a layer over the rice, then top with a layer of the remaining rice. Sprinkle the peanuts over the top. Cover tightly with aluminum foil and bake for 20 minutes. Remove from the oven and let stand, covered, for 5 minutes before serving.

LUCKNOW MIXED VEGETABLE BIRYANI | Lucknowi Tehri Biryani

Lucknow is India's gastronomic mecca, where food is prepared deftly and with a lot of care. This is a straightforward, yet elegant *biryani;* first you cook rice with whole spices, then make a spicy vegetable dish, then combine the two and bake with a sprinkling of saffron. The result is a delicately flavored masterpiece, perfect for special occasions. When in season, use asparagus in place of the peas.

SERVES 6 TO 8 AS A MAIN DISH

2 cups basmati rice

1 teaspoon salt

4-inch cinnamon stick

10 whole cloves

8 green cardamom pods

2-inch piece fresh ginger

10 cloves garlic

3 fresh green serrano or jalapeño chilis, or fewer to taste, stemmed

3 tablespoons water

5 tablespoons vegetable oil

1 1/2 cups sliced yellow onion

8 baby potatoes, cut in half

1 teaspoon *garam masala* (pages 36–37), or store-bought

1/2 teaspoon cayenne

1/4 teaspoon turmeric

1/4 teaspoon asafetida

1 cup cauliflower, cut in 1/2-inch florets

1 cup 1/8-inch diagonally sliced carrots

1/4 cup fresh or frozen peas

3/4 cup plain yogurt

2 tablespoons melted *desi ghee* (pages 47–48), or unsalted butter

1/4 teaspoon saffron threads, dissolved in 2 tablespoons warm milk

1 recipe Sweet-Scented Tomato Gravy (recipe follows)

1. Position a rack in the center of the oven and preheat to 325°F.

2. Place the rice on a dinner plate. Work a small portion of the rice across to the opposite side of the plate, picking out any stones and unhulled rice grains. Repeat with the remaining rice. Place the rice in a bowl and wash with the tips of your fingers two or three times in cold running tap water. Drain, add water to cover by at least 2 inches, and let soak for 30 minutes or longer. Drain and set aside.

3. In a medium saucepan, bring 6 cups water to a boil. Add the rice, salt, cinnamon, 5 of the cloves, and 4 of the cardamom pods. Cook, uncovered, over high heat for 5 minutes. Drain the rice in a colander and set aside.

4. Combine the ginger, garlic, chilis, and water in a blender and process to a smooth puree, stopping to scrape down the sides of the bowl a couple of times. Heat 2 tablespoons of the oil in a large heavy sauté pan over medium heat. Add the onion and cook, stirring frequently, until deep golden, 8 to 10 minutes. Transfer to a plate. Add 1 tablespoon of the oil to the pan, then add the potatoes and cook, stirring, until lightly golden and slightly tender, about 6 minutes. Transfer the potatoes to the plate.

5. Add the remaining 2 tablespoons of oil to the pan, along with the remaining 5 cloves and 4 cardamom pods, and cook, stirring, until aromatic, about 30 seconds. Add the ginger-garlic puree and cook, stirring often, until the raw garlic smell dissipates, 5 to 6 minutes. Add the *garam masala*, cayenne, turmeric, and asafetida and mix well. Add the cauliflower, carrots, and peas, cover, and cook 4 to 5 minutes (if you prefer your vegetables crunchy in the finished dish, you may skip this part). Add the potatoes and fried onion, saving some for garnish. Add the yogurt and cook, stirring often, for 3 to 4 minutes. Taste and season with salt, roughly 1/2 teaspoon; the mixture will taste spicy-hot, and that is how it should be, because plenty of bland rice will be stirred in. Remove from the heat.

6. Gradually add the rice to the pan. Mix gently but thoroughly. The rice should take on a beautiful yellow hue. To assemble the *biryani*, transfer the rice to a 3-quart, 9 x 13–inch glass baking dish. Sprinkle the *desi ghee* and saffron over the top. Garnish with the reserved onion and potatoes. Cover tightly with aluminum foil and bake for 20 minutes. Let sit in the warm oven for up to 10 minutes, if not serving right away. Remove from the oven and let stand, covered, for 5 minutes before serving. Serve topped with the Sweet-Scented Tomato Gravy.

SWEET-SCENTED TOMATO GRAVY | Tamatar Makhani Gravy

Besides serving it with Lucknow Mixed Vegetable Biryani (previous recipe), the uses for this gravy are numerous. Try it as a quick curry sauce to simmer with cooked chicken or meat, or use as a topping for Whole Chicken Breast Stuffed with Apricots and Cranberries (pages 278–279). Be sure to use deep-red, vine-ripened tomatoes; of course, any gravy is best when each ingredient is at its best, but you'll miss the full effect of this sauce if the tomatoes are less than perfect. For a lighter taste, omit the cream.

MAKES A GENEROUS 1 CUP

2 green cardamom pods, seeds removed

2 medium-large tomatoes, or 2 cups canned
    diced tomatoes

1/4 cup whole cashew nuts

1 teaspoon salt

1/4 teaspoon ground cumin

1/8 teaspoon ground cinnamon

1/8 teaspoon freshly grated nutmeg

2 bay leaves

1/2-inch piece fresh ginger, crushed

2 cloves garlic, crushed

1 fresh green serrano or jalapeño chili, stemmed
    and slit in half

2 tablespoons dried fenugreek leaves (optional)

1/3 cup heavy whipping cream

1/2 tablespoon *desi ghee* (pages 47–48), or
    unsalted butter

2 tablespoons honey

1. Using a mortar and pestle, pulverize the cardamom seeds, then transfer to a heavy medium saucepan. Coarsely chop the tomatoes; you should have about 2 generous cups. Add the tomatoes to the saucepan along with the nuts, salt, cumin, cinnamon, nutmeg, bay leaves, ginger, garlic, and chili and bring to a boil. Cook over medium-high heat, uncovered, until thick and nicely reduced but not dry (it should be an easy-to-spoon consistency), about 15 minutes. The taste will be wonderfully piquant and nicely perfumed. Discard the bay leaves. Let the sauce cool, transfer to a blender or food processor, and blend to a smooth puree.

2. Transfer the puree back into the same saucepan and add the fenugreek leaves, cream, and *desi ghee*. Bring to a gentle boil and cook until heated through. Stir in the honey, and it's ready to serve.

MAKE AHEAD The gravy can be prepared through step 1 and refrigerated, covered, for up to 5 days.

WILD RICE AND CHICKEN BIRYANI | Pardesi Murg Biryani

You don't see wild rice *biryani* offered in restaurants in India, though perennial wild rices grow in Assam and other pockets of the subcontinent. Though it is the norm to use the finest basmati rice in *biryanis*, I've taken a contemporary approach and used wild rice instead; the intermingling of main ingredients and trimmings are simply wonderful.

SERVES 4

1 cup wild rice

3 1/2 cups water

1 1/2 teaspoons salt

1/4 teaspoon turmeric

3 tablespoons vegetable oil

1/4 cup cashews

1/4 cup dark raisins, or sultanas

1 yellow onion, finely chopped

2-inch piece fresh ginger, minced

4 cloves garlic, minced

1 teaspoon ground coriander

1/2 teaspoon ground cumin

1/2 teaspoon ground cinnamon

1/2 teaspoon freshly ground black pepper

1/4 teaspoon freshly grated nutmeg

1 pound boneless, skinless chicken breasts, cut into large bite-size pieces

2 small russet potatoes

1/3 cup yogurt cheese (page 205)

1/2 cup fresh or frozen green peas

Sliced tomatoes, for layering

2 tablespoons melted *desi ghee* (pages 47–48), or unsalted butter

1. Wash the rice in 2 or 3 changes of cold water, then place in a bowl, cover with water, and let soak overnight. Drain the rice and place in a saucepan. Add 2 1/2 cups of the water, 1 teaspoon of the salt, and the turmeric and bring to a boil. Reduce the heat, cover, and simmer until the rice is tender, about 30 minutes.

2. Heat the oil in a large heavy saucepan over medium heat. Add the cashews and cook, stirring, until lightly browned, about 4 minutes. Transfer to a plate and set aside. Add the raisins to the pan and cook, stirring, until they plump, about 2 minutes. Remove and place alongside the nuts.

3. Add the onion to the same pan and cook, stirring, until softened, 3 to 4 minutes. Add the ginger and garlic and cook, stirring, until the onion is lightly browned, about 4 minutes. Add the coriander, cumin, cinnamon, pepper, and nutmeg and cook, stirring, until aromatic, about 1 minute. Add the chicken and cook until no longer pink, about 5 minutes per side. While the chicken is cooking, peel and cut the potatoes into cubes; you should have 1 cup. Add the potatoes to the pan, then add the yogurt cheese, the remaining 1 cup of

water, and the remaining 1/2 teaspoon salt. Cover and cook, stirring occasionally, until the chicken is almost tender and the liquid is absorbed, about 15 minutes.

4. Meanwhile, position a rack in the center of the oven and preheat to 325°F.

5. To assemble the *biryani*, spread about half of the rice in a 2-quart heat-proof glass baking dish. Add a layer of half of the chicken, then spread half of the nuts, raisins, peas, and tomato slices on top. Add another layer each of the remaining rice and the remaining chicken. Finish with the remaining nuts, raisins, peas, and tomatoes. Sprinkle with the *desi ghee*, cover tightly with aluminum foil, and bake 20 minutes. Remove from the oven and let stand, covered, for 5 minutes before serving.

VARIATION

You may substitute white basmati for the wild rice. Assemble the *biryani* as described above with basmati rice (cooked, with or without the turmeric, as in step 1); top with layers of fried onion (as in Moghul Lamb Biryani, pages 116–117), in addition to the other ingredients. Toast 1/2 teaspoon saffron threads in a small skillet over low heat, cool, and crush with the back of a spoon. Dissolve the saffron in 2 tablespoons hot milk and sprinkle over the rice. Bake as directed.

CHAAT: TANTALIZING SMALL PLATES AND SNACKS

Chutpata Bhojan

Sometimes my mind races back to childhood summer vacations, my most delicious memories of time spent with my siblings and cousins. When the heat subsided, we'd hit the streets to experience how Mumbai eats. We would walk down to the street corner to see our favorite vendor. Babu was always there behind his cart, singing and smiling as his hand danced above mounds of dry and fresh ingredients. I was dazzled the first time I saw Babu assembling at lightening speed plate after plate of a tempting snack called *bhelpuri* (page 129). It was made with puffed rice cereal as the base, along with chopped tomato, onion, cilantro, peanuts, crushed crisp-fried *pooris* and chickpea flour noodles *(sev)*, perfectly balanced with a hefty dose of sweet and hot chutneys. I would always ask Babu to make my plate *meetha*, then he would sprinkle more of the sweet chutney on top, some of my cousins got theirs *theeka*, that is, with the hot chutney. He'd pile the mixture onto a banana leaf or a paper plate. Sometimes we were lucky enough to get a sprinkling of chopped green mango. He'd give each one of us a round of tiny crisp *poori* to use as a "spoon" to eat the *bhelpuri*. The exhibition was very sensuous, visually seductive, vibrant, and of course mouthwatering.

What an amazing amalgamation of tastes and textures—a profusion of stimulating and exciting flavors. The tastes married flawlessly, enticing the palate and arousing the senses, creating a dish I just couldn't stop eating.

One of his other concoctions was *sev puri* (page 134), a sort of Indian version of taco salad, but with a more flamboyant balance of tastes, textures, temperatures, crunchiness, and colors. Five to six crisp-thin fried *poori* formed the base. The *pooris* were topped with onion, tomato, and chickpea flour noodles, and the whole thing was seductively aromatic, with a gentle afterglow from sweet and hot chutneys. The contrasting flavors were addictive. Babu called these little plates of snacks *chaat*.

Chaat (pronounced *chah-t*) is Indian fast food served on the streets and sidewalks and is as robust and gutsy as street food should be. *Chaat* is a Hindi word meaning "small snack plates." Although *chaat* originated in the regional cooking of Uttar Pradesh, in northern India, these snacks have been eagerly adopted throughout the country for their teasing tastes. *Chaat* flavorings are unique. Though the ingredient lists may seem like quite a mouthful, the result will be a pleasing mélange, full of lively primary tastes and rich textures. *Chaat* preparations involve only a minimal amount of cooking—most of the components are raw and can be tossed together on short notice. And unlike many American snack foods, *chaat* dishes are low in fat. They are usually vegetarian. All of the *chaat* recipes I've provided make attractive party fare, whether served as pass-around appetizers or as part of an elegant buffet.

ROADSIDE COMBO WITH CHUTNEY GARNISHES | Bhelpuri

In this special *bhelpuri* recipe, the balance of crispy (*poori* and chickpea flour noodles), tangy (mango), earthy (potato), and the herb-scented and sweet smells transport you straight to India. The juxtaposition of sweet to savory and tender to crunchy keeps each bite interesting.

If you make a batch of *poori* in advance, the chutney sauces are very simple and quick. This tongue-tingling concoction may be served assembled, or you can let guests create their own versions by setting up a "salad bar" with the ingredients laid out in the order instructed.

After living in the United States for a while, I discovered that plain flat round or triangular tortilla chips can be substituted for the *poori*.

SERVES 4 OR SO AS A SNACK OR INFORMAL APPETIZER

1 large Yukon gold potato

Salt, to taste

1 cup chopped ripe tomatoes

1 cup finely chopped yellow onion

1/2 cup chopped cilantro

12 Crispy Puffy Poori (pages 131–132), broken into 2 to 3 pieces

6 cups store-bought *churmura,* or crisp puffed rice cereal

1/2 cup peeled and finely chopped green mango, or 1/4 cup freshly squeezed lime juice

1/2 cup roasted unsalted peanuts

1 cup or more thin chickpea flour noodles *(sev)*

1/2 cup Sweet Chutney Sauce (recipe follows)

1/2 cup Hot Green Chutney Sauce (recipe follows)

1. Add the potato to a pot of boiling water, add salt, and cook until the potato is tender, about 20 minutes. Drain and let cool. Peel and dice the potato, and place in a large bowl.

2. Add the tomatoes, onion, cilantro, *pooris,* and *churmura* to the bowl; toss gently to mix. Sprinkle the mango, peanuts, and chickpea flour noodles over the mixture, then season with salt, usually about 1 teaspoon, and mix well. Drizzle with the sweet and hot chutney sauces and mix very gently. To serve, spoon the mixture into deep dishes. Alternately, you can use an attractive ring mold, press and mold the *bhelpuri,* and set it on a decorative serving dish. Sprinkle with more noodles, if desired, and serve.

NOTE *Churmura* and *sev* are available at Indian groceries.

SWEET CHUTNEY SAUCE | Meetha Chatni

Use this as a dipping sauce for crudités, onion rings, or fritters. Make a double or triple batch of this sauce and freeze the extra for another *chaat* dish.

MAKES ABOUT 1 CUP

8 pitted dates

2 tablespoons raisins or dried cranberries

1 1/2 teaspoons tamarind concentrate, dissolved in 1/2 cup water

1/4-inch piece fresh ginger

1/2 tablespoon raw sugar, or light brown sugar

1/4 cup water

1 teaspoon ground coriander

3/4 teaspoon salt

1/2 teaspoon ground cumin

In a medium saucepan, combine the dates, raisins, and tamarind liquid and simmer over medium heat until dates are very soft, 6 to 8 minutes. Cool and transfer to a blender or food processor. Add the ginger, sugar, water, coriander, salt, and cumin to the blender. Process to a smooth puree, stopping as necessary to scrape down the sides of the container. Transfer to a serving bowl. Let stand for a few minutes to let the flavors meld. If not using immediately, cover and refrigerate the sauce for up to 1 week.

HOT GREEN CHUTNEY SAUCE | Theeka Chatni

This chutney sauce is great on flat fish; marinate it for half an hour and grill for an herbal flavor. Use as a spread for sandwiches or dollop over charcoal-grilled chicken breasts or fish. Add more chilis if you like a hotter sauce.

MAKES ABOUT 1 1/2 CUPS

2 cups packed cilantro

1 cup packed fresh mint leaves

3 fresh green serrano or jalapeño chilis, or fewer to taste, stemmed

1 teaspoon salt

1 teaspoon sugar

1/4 cup freshly squeezed lime juice

1/4 cup water

Line up the cilantro and mint leaves on a cutting board and chop coarsely. Using a large mortar and pestle, grind the chilis, salt, and sugar to a coarsely textured paste, paying close attention to breaking up the chilis—the mixture will exude a wonderfully pungent aroma. Add the chopped cilantro and mint, a little at a time, gradually incorporating the herbs into the mixture. Add a splash of the lime juice and water. Continue grinding, stirring from time to time and adding more lime juice and water as needed, until you have a fairly smooth-textured chutney. (Alternately, you may combine all of the ingredients in a blender and process until smoothly pureed, stopping from time to time to scrape down the sides of the container.) Transfer to a serving bowl and let stand for a few minutes to let the flavors meld. If not using immediately, cover and refrigerate for up to 3 days.

CRISPY PUFFY POORI | Gol Gappa

Traditionally, this recipe is made with a fine Indian semolina called *sooji* so the *pooris* can remain crisp and puffed for several months at room temperature. I have used readily available semolina pasta flour, which also works well. These *pooris* are used only in *chaat* dishes and are not to be confused with the *poori* recipe in the bread chapter. They are made in advance and kept handy to make instant snacks for guests or family.

When you fry *pooris*, some will puff and others may not; use the puffed ones for making *pani puri* (pages 132–133) and the flat ones in other recipes in this chapter. Adding lime juice and placing the finished *pooris* in a hot oven ensures crispness. I do not add salt, because it makes the *poori* soft.

MAKES 60 POORIS

2 tablespoons vegetable oil, plus more for frying

1 1/2 cups semolina pasta flour, or fine Indian semolina *(sooji)*

1/2 teaspoon baking powder

1 tablespoon freshly squeezed lime juice

1/2 cup hot water

1. Heat the 2 tablespoons of oil in a large skillet until hot but not smoking. Remove from the heat and set aside.

2. In a food processor, combine the pasta flour and baking powder and pulse a few times to mix. Add the hot oil and lime juice and pulse until crumbly. With the machine running, gradually add the water through the feed tube in a steady stream, processing until the dough comes together into a ball and just begins to clean the sides of the bowl. Avoid overprocessing.

3. Turn the dough out on a work surface and lightly oil your hands. Form the dough into a smooth ball and knead well for 6 to 8 minutes. The dough should be medium-soft, not stiff or sticky; it should resemble Play-Doh. Cover and let rest for 30 to 60 minutes.

4. Place the dough on a floured work surface (use only semolina pasta flour for kneading and rolling) and knead briefly until smooth. Divide the dough into 3 portions and roll each portion between your hands to form a smooth ball. Put the dough balls on a plate and cover to prevent drying. Place a piece of dough on the floured work surface and roll it out to 1/8 inch thick. Using a 2-inch biscuit cutter, cut out 15 rounds.

5. Fill a wok or sauté pan with oil to a depth of 1 1/2 inches and heat over medium-high heat until very hot, 365°F to 375°F on a deep-fry thermometer (temperature is important in getting the *poori* to puff). Carefully slide 4 to 6 rounds into the hot oil. As the *pooris* rise to the top, use a long-handled spoon to lightly bathe them with oil so that they begin to puff. After 20 to 30 seconds, turn the *pooris* over and fry until lightly golden, 15 to 20 seconds more. Use a skimmer or slotted spoon to transfer the cooked *pooris* to a tray lined with brown paper bags or unbleached paper towels.

6. Reduce the heat slightly to maintain the oil temperature while you roll out and cut another batch of dough rounds. Repeat with the third piece of dough, then reknead and reroll the trimmings, and cut out and fry a few more rounds.

7. Cool the *pooris* completely. Sort the puffy ones from unpuffed, flat *pooris* (see headnote), cover, and store in airtight containers for up to 1 month.

CRISPY PUFFY POORI FILLED WITH ZESTY TAMARIND SAUCE
| Pani Puri

In this classic recipe, puffy *pooris* are popped open at the top and filled with beans and tamarind sauce. As with all *chaat* dishes, *pani puri* are informal morsels intended to be prepared and eaten on the spot. Diners are instructed to down the snack all in one bite. The rich and tangy shot of flavor is tempered with just a hint of citrus.

Pani literally means water; the runny tamarind sauce filling, called *jal jeera*, aids in digestion. It is sometimes served by itself as an appetizer or as a refreshing beverage. In this recipe, I recommend using large pods of tamarind and extracting the pulp for a refreshing, raw taste, or using the packaged tamarind pulp (not the Thai variety) sold in Indian markets.

SERVES 6 TO 8 AS A SNACK OR INFORMAL APPETIZER

1/2 cup dried whole mung beans, or one 15-ounce can chickpeas

2 cups water

1/8 teaspoon turmeric

1 1/2 teaspoons salt

1 cup peeled and seeded tamarind pods, soaked in 4 cups water for 2 to 4 hours

1/2 cup loosely packed fresh mint leaves

2 fresh green serrano or jalapeño chilis, stemmed

1/4-inch piece fresh ginger

4 whole cloves

1 tablespoon raw sugar, or light brown sugar

1 teaspoon cumin seeds

1/4 teaspoon black peppercorns

1 tablespoon freshly squeezed lime juice

50 to 60 Crispy Puffy Poori (pages 131–132, puffed ones are best)

1. In a medium saucepan, combine the dried mung beans and the water and set over medium-high heat. Add the turmeric, bring to a boil, then reduce the heat to medium and simmer, partially covered, until the beans are tender but still hold their shape, 30 to 40 minutes. There should be barely any water left. (If using canned chickpeas, rinse and drain well.) Season the beans with 1/2 teaspoon of the salt and cool to room temperature. Transfer to a serving dish.

2. Squeeze and strain the tamarind pulp to extract as much liquid as possible. Discard the fibers and pods. Transfer about half the tamarind water to a blender, reserving the rest of the tamarind water in a bowl. Add the mint, chilis, ginger, cloves, sugar, cumin, peppercorns, lime juice, and remaining 1 teaspoon salt and process to a smooth puree. Stir the puree into the remaining tamarind water. Transfer the tamarind sauce to a decorative bowl.

3. The moment you are ready to serve, arrange 6 to 8 *pooris* on a serving plate and break the top of the *pooris* slightly or make a small hole with your fingertip. Spoon a generous tablespoon of beans into each *poori* and drizzle with about 1 tablespoon or more of the tamarind sauce to fill the *poori*. Serve at once, since they lose their texture quickly.

CLASSIC POORI CANAPÉ WITH SAVORY TOPPING | Sev Puri

Once you taste these sweet-hot mouthfuls, *sev puri* will become one of your treasured recipes. As with all *chaat*, *sev puri* are unfussy and meant to be eaten right away.

SERVES 6 AS A FIRST COURSE

1 large Yukon gold potato

Salt, to taste

30 to 40 Crispy Puffy Poori (pages 131–132, flat ones are best)

1 large yellow onion, finely chopped

1 large ripe tomato, finely chopped (optional)

1 cup thin chickpea flour noodles *(sev)*

1/2 cup chopped cilantro

1/2 cup Sweet Chutney Sauce (page 130)

1/2 cup Hot Green Chutney Sauce (page 130)

1. Add the potato to a pot of boiling water, add salt, and cook until the potato is tender, about 20 minutes. Drain and let cool. Peel the potato, finely dice with a fork, and set aside.

2. When ready to serve, arrange 6 to 8 *pooris* on each serving plates. Assemble one plate at a time, spooning a portion of potato, onion, and tomato, if using, over the *poori*. Sprinkle each serving with some of the chickpea flour noodles, cilantro, and chutney sauces.

CLASSIC POORI CANAPÉ CROWNED WITH YOGURT TOPPING

| Dahi Batata Puri

This starts off with soft potato on crispy *poori*, topped with onion and a dollop of cool yogurt. When guests spoon down to the bottom, they'll find an explosion of sweet date, velvety chutney, and spicy herb chutney.

SERVES 6 AS A FIRST COURSE

1 large Yukon gold or boiling potato

Salt, to taste

1 cup plain yogurt

1/2 teaspoon sugar

30 to 40 Crispy Puffy Poori (pages 131–132, flat ones are best)

1 large yellow onion, finely chopped

1 cup thin chickpea flour noodles *(sev)*

1/2 cup chopped cilantro

1/2 cup Sweet Chutney Sauce (page 130)

1/2 cup Hot Green Chutney Sauce (page 130)

1.   Add the potato to a pot of boiling water, add salt, and cook until the potato is tender, about 20 minutes. Drain and let cool. Peel the potato, mash with a fork, and set aside.

2.   In a medium bowl, whisk the yogurt. Season with the sugar and salt to taste.

3.   When ready to serve, arrange 6 to 8 *pooris* on each plate. Assemble one plate at a time, spooning a portion of potato, onion, and a tablespoon of yogurt over the *poori*. Sprinkle each serving with some of the chickpea flour noodles, cilantro, and chutney sauces.

VARIATION

Papdi Chaat

Substitute one recipe of Savory Yogurt Sauce (page 137) for the yogurt mixture prepared in step 2. Arrange and top as instructed above, then sprinkle with some *chaat masala* (pages 41–42), if desired, and serve.

DUMPLINGS BATHED IN SAVORY YOGURT SAUCE

| Dahi Bhalla / Dahi Wada

Indians season yogurt in many different ways to suit different dishes. Here it is sweet, a little smoky, and a tad spicy.

MAKES 4 TO 6 SERVINGS

1 cup *urad dal* (white split gram beans)

1 cup water

1 teaspoon salt, or to taste

Vegetable oil, for frying

Savory Yogurt Sauce (recipe follows)

1/2 cup Sweet Chutney Sauce (page 130), or more to taste

1/2 cup chopped cilantro

1 tablespoon shredded fresh ginger

1.   Rinse the beans thoroughly, place in a medium bowl with water to cover, and soak for 4 hours. Drain the beans. Using a blender and working in 2 batches, process the beans with 1 cup of water (the batter should be very thick—do not add any more water than recommended) until pureed and silky smooth, about 5 minutes. To test, put a teaspoon of the *urad dal* paste into a cup of water; it should float. If it settles, blend for 2 to 3 minutes more. Season the batter with the salt and set aside in a warm place to ferment for about 6 hours.

2.   Fill a wok or sauté pan with oil to a depth of 2 inches and heat over medium-high heat until very hot but not smoking, 350°F on a deep-fry thermometer. Scoop roughly 2 tablespoons of the batter at a time into the hot oil, working in batches to avoid overcrowding. Fry the dumplings, stirring occasionally, until golden brown, 2 to 3 minutes. Use a skimmer or slotted spoon to remove the dumplings, leaving as much oil as possible behind, then drop them into a bowl of cold water. Allow them to soak in water for 5 minutes. Meanwhile, prepare the remaining dumplings. Remove the dumplings from the water and squeeze very gently to remove any excess water, taking care not to break them, and transfer to the chilled Savory Yogurt Sauce. Let the dumplings absorb the flavors for 8 to 10 minutes. Do not add all the dumplings at once to the yogurt; this is best done a few at a time.

3. Arrange 3 to 4 dumplings per serving in soup plates. Spoon some yogurt sauce on top, add 1 to 2 tablespoons of Sweet Chutney, and sprinkle with cilantro. Top with some shredded ginger and serve right away.

> MAKE AHEAD You can fry the dumplings, soak them in water, and remove to a plate in step 2, up to several hours in advance. Store, covered, in the refrigerator. Just before serving, transfer the dumplings to the yogurt sauce and finish the assembly.

SAVORY YOGURT SAUCE

The yogurt sauce can be prepared up to 2 to 3 days in advance and stored, covered, in the refrigerator.

MAKES 4 CUPS

4 cups plain yogurt

2 teaspoons sugar

1 teaspoon salt

3/4 teaspoon Indian black salt *(kala namak)* (optional)

1 teaspoon ground cumin

1 teaspoon cayenne

In a mixing bowl, combine the yogurt, sugar, salt, black salt (if using), cumin, and cayenne and beat lightly with a fork to mix. Taste and adjust the seasonings. Refrigerate for at least 30 minutes or until required.

GUJARAT STUFFED PASTRY WITH SAVORY TOPPING

| Khasta Kachori

In this recipe, pastry dough is stuffed with spicy mung *dal* and rolled in the same fashion as *poori*. You can serve these snacks the way the Gujaratis would—break the top off the pastries, fill them with chickpeas, onion, cilantro, and chickpea flour noodles, then top them liberally with chutney sauces. This dish is like *pani puri* (pages 131–132), meant to be filled and eaten on the spot, though it is more substantial.

SERVES 12 AS AN APPETIZER

1/4 cup vegetable oil, plus additional oil for frying

11/2 cups unbleached all-purpose flour

1/2 cup whole-wheat pastry flour

1/2 teaspoon salt

1/2 cup plus 1 tablespoon water

1 recipe Savory Mung Dal (recipe follows)

2 cups cooked chickpeas (pages 42–43), or canned, drained

1 large yellow onion, finely chopped

1/2 cup chopped cilantro

1 cup Sweet Chutney Sauce (page 130)

1 cup Hot Green Chutney Sauce (page 130)

1 cup thin chickpea flour noodles *(sev)*

1. Heat the 1/4 cup of oil in a small skillet until hot but not smoking. Set aside.

2. In a food processor, combine the all-purpose flour, pastry flour, and salt and pulse a few times to mix. Add the hot oil and pulse until crumbly. With the machine running, gradually add the water through the feed tube in a steady stream, processing until the dough comes together into a ball and begins to clean the sides of the bowl. Avoid over-processing.

3. Place the dough on a work surface and lightly coat your hands with oil. Knead the dough well for 6 to 8 minutes. Form the dough into a smooth ball. Cover and let rest for 30 to 60 minutes.

4. Place the dough on a floured work surface and knead briefly. Divide into 2 portions and roll each portion into a long rope. Cut each rope into 12 pieces and put on a plate. Roll each piece between your palms to make a smooth ball and cover with a kitchen towel to prevent drying.

5. Fill a large wok or sauté pan with oil to a depth of 11/2 inches and heat over medium-high heat until very hot, 365°F to 375°F on a deep-fry thermometer.

6. Place a ball of dough on a floured work surface and roll it out into a 2-inch circle, dusting lightly with flour as necessary. Scoop 1 to 1½ tablespoons of the Savory Mung Dal filling in the center of the dough circle, bring the edges together, and pinch to seal. Shape into a ball once again. Flatten and place on a floured surface and gently roll into a 3-inch, ⅛-inch-thick circle.

7. Carefully slide 2 to 4 rounds at a time in a single layer into the hot oil. As the pastries rise to the top, use a spoon to lightly bathe them with oil so that they begin to puff. After 20 to 30 seconds, turn the pastry and fry until lightly golden, 15 to 20 seconds more. Use a skimmer or long-handled slotted spoon to transfer the pastry to a tray lined with brown paper bags or unbleached paper towels. Repeat with the remaining portions of dough.

8. Place the pastries on a large platter. Set up a self-serve buffet or serve them individually, one or two per plate at a time. Break open the top of the pastry slightly or make a small hole with your fingers, add a generous tablespoon of chickpeas, and fill liberally with onion and cilantro. Add a generous portion of the sweet and hot chutney sauces and chickpea flour noodles. Serve immediately.

MAKE AHEAD The pastries can be stored, covered, at cool room temperature for up to 3 days.

SAVORY MUNG DAL

This stuffing mixture is wonderful in all types of flatbreads. You can also mix this filling with a variety of fresh vegetables and use it as a stuffing for turkey.

½ cup mung *dal* (yellow split mung beans)	¼ teaspoon turmeric
1½ tablespoons vegetable oil	1 teaspoon salt
2 teaspoons ground coriander	½ cup water
1 teaspoon ground cumin	½ teaspoon coarsely crushed fennel seeds
½ teaspoon cayenne	

1. Sort the mung *dal* and remove any debris. Using a strainer, rinse in several changes of cold water. Transfer to a bowl and add enough water to cover by at least 2 inches. Soak for 2 to 4 hours. Drain well.

2. Heat the oil in a heavy medium skillet over medium heat. Add the coriander, cumin, cayenne, and turmeric and stir for a few seconds until aromatic. Add the mung *dal*, salt, and water and bring to a boil. Reduce the heat, cover, and simmer until the mung *dal* is soft and all the water is absorbed, about 25 minutes. Stir in the fennel seeds and remove from the heat. Cool slightly and use as directed or store, covered, in the refrigerator for up to 3 days.

PAPAYA-KIWI CHAAT WITH PISTACHIOS | Phal Chaat

Serve this as a first course, as a light salad, or over toasted minibagels or crackers for a delectable and novel hors d'oeuvre. In the summer, use a mélange of seasonal fruits to make this mixed spicy fruit *chaat* and offer it as a cool side dish. Instead of the *chaat masala,* you can also use toasted ground cumin seeds with salt to taste.

MAKES 8 APPETIZER SERVINGS

2 1/2 cups peeled and diced (3/4 inch) firm-ripe papaya

2 1/2 cups peeled and diced (3/4 inch) firm-ripe kiwi

1/2 cup finely chopped red onion

3 tablespoons finely chopped fresh mint leaves

1 to 2 fresh green serrano or jalapeño chilis, stemmed and slivered

1/2 cup freshly squeezed orange juice

1/4 cup freshly squeezed lime juice

1/3 cup coarsely chopped toasted pistachios, or almonds (page 208)

1 to 2 teaspoons *chaat masala* (pages 41–42), or store-bought

1/3 cup thin chickpea flour noodles *(sev)*

1. In a wide serving bowl, combine the papaya, kiwi, onion, mint, and chilis and mix well. At this stage, you may cover and chill for up to 2 hours.

2. Gently stir in the orange and lime juices. Cover and let stand at cool room temperature for about 10 minutes to let the flavors blend.

3. Just before serving, fold in the nuts and sprinkle with the *chaat masala*. Divide the mixture onto serving plates, sprinkle with chickpea flour noodles, and serve immediately.

PAKORA, PAPPADAM, AND OTHER STARTERS

Shaandar Shuruaat

As a child, I used to take part in the *pappadam*-making marathon during summer break. My mother would promise me a nice vacation for my help in the kitchen. Friends and neighbors also participated in the rolling process. It was a perfect forum for gathering, chatting, and laughing—an annual tradition, full of fun. They would bring their rolling pins and boards, roll portions of dough made from *urad dal* flour, which was kneaded and pounded for hours ahead of time. The terrace of our house was cleaned, and white sheets were laid out. My sister and I would carry the rolled *pappadam* on trays, spread them on the sheets in a single layer to dry, and cover them with plastic. After they were completely dried in the scorching heat, my mother made gift packs for her friends, and the rest were kept airtight in a cool place. We would have almost a year's supply of flavorful *pappadam* or *papad* of assorted colors, shapes, and sizes. Mother would also frequently offer to help her friends in *papad* making. Every family would share some of their varieties.

Although as a youngster I enjoyed making *pappadam*, today, I am glad they are available ready-made in the package in Indian markets, as well as in some American supermarkets. Nowadays, cottage industries in India make good quality, inexpensive handmade ones by the thousands and ship them all over the world. If you have never bought a package of sun-dried, paper-thin *papad* then you are in for a pleasant surprise. They are quick, easy, and fun to prepare.

Americans are drawn to Indian cuisine for its warm and convivial casualness. Don't limit yourselves to chips and salsa for snacks. In addition to the recipes in this chapter, there are ideas for exotic starters and snacks throughout this book, and I encourage you to broaden your repertoire.

CRISPY PAPPADAM | Pappadam

Pappadam should be familiar to most people as the complimentary, crispy crackers that are served upon seating in most Indian restaurants. Prepackaged *papad*, as they are known in northern India, or *pappadam*, as they are known in the south, are available nowadays in Indian markets and some supermarkets. I encourage you to try making them, since they are a snap to fix. Plain or flavored, *pappadam* come in various sizes and shapes—round, square, or oval, and from 1 to 8 inches in diameter. At the Indian markets, you might even come across colored ones—red, orange, green, and yellow—tinted with food coloring. They are most commonly made of a pliable dough based on *urad dal* (white split gram bean) flour. The dough is seasoned with salt and other flavorings, such as pepper, cumin, cayenne, minced garlic, and chilis.

Here, I provide a recipe for toasting 5-inch *pappadam*. I recommend using Lijjat, a common brand. Fresh, thin *pappadam* contain more moisture, which means they do not break as easily and take less time to toast, while the dried, thick ones are brittle and take a few seconds longer. Toasting and deep-frying are the two basic methods of preparing *pappadam*. The toasted variety makes a healthy alternative to potato chips and other fried finger foods. Pass around a platter of *pappadam* with bowls of Fresh Mint Chutney with Garlic (page 176), Sweet Chutney Sauce (page 130), and Hot Green Chutney Sauce (page 130), and enjoy with a glass of Johannisberg Riesling.

YIELDS 15 PAPPADAMS PER PACKET

1 packet Lijjat *pappadam*

Stovetop Method: Set your burner (gas or electric) on medium-high heat. Place a flame-tamer, if you have one. Hold one *pappadam* delicately with tongs on the tamer or directly over the burner, and rotate constantly until light in color and evenly flecked with light brown spots, about 30 seconds, then turn and cook on the other side until crisp, about 30 seconds more. Repeat with as many *pappadam* you want toasted.

Baking Method: You may bake the *pappadam* in a preheated 400°F oven. Place the *pappadam* in a single layer on cookie sheets. Bake until cream-colored and covered with little blisters, 2 1/2 to 3 minutes.

Deep-Fry Method: Fill a heavy large wok or sauté pan with oil to a depth of 1 inch and heat over medium-high heat. Slide one *pappadam* at a time into the oil. The *pappadam* will instantly change color and texture and expand in size. Immediately lift it out with a pair of tongs, check to make sure it is cooked all around the edges, and drain on brown paper bags or unbleached paper towels.

> MAKE AHEAD *Pappadam* will stay crisp for 2 to 4 hours at cool room temperature. If they get limp because of humidity, stack them together and retoast them in a low oven until crisp, 1 1/2 to 2 minutes. If you are not serving them immediately, as soon as they are cool, store them in a tightly covered container for up to 1 week.

VARIATION

Masala Papad

On a serving plate, top 8 crispy, toasted *pappadams* with 1/2 cup minced yellow onion and 1/4 cup minced cilantro, sprinkle with a tablespoon of toasted cumin seeds, and drizzle with 1 1/2 tablespoons good-quality olive oil. Serve right away.

CRISPY PAKORA | Pakora

My mother had a box labeled *"pakora* mix" in her pantry. She toasted *chana dal* and raw rice, mixed it with a handful of toasted red chilis and cumin seeds, and sent the mixture to a mill to turn into flour. This toasty blend came in especially handy when guests visited unannounced. She combined it with water to make a batter, plucked vegetables from her garden, and voilà! *Pakora* in an instant. This recipe is a loose adaptation of my mother's, with my own contemporary spin. I like *pakora* lightly batter-coated and crispy. (That's why I add rice flour; when you use all chickpea flour the way some books suggest, the batter tends to be on the heavier side.) The coating crackles, releasing steamy waves of flavor.

Pass around a platter of mixed *pakoras* with bowls of tantalizing chutneys—tamarind, mint, and cilantro are typical, but even ketchup works well. Though beer makes a nice accompaniment for these flavors, when served as hors d'oeuvres at a formal meal, *pakoras* can be paired with white wines like sauvignon blanc, fume blanc, pinot gris, or champagne.

MAKES 50 TO 60 SMALL PAKORAS, SERVES 10 TO 12 AS A FIRST COURSE

1¹/₂ cups chickpea flour

¹/₂ cup rice flour

2 teaspoons ground cumin

1 teaspoon cayenne

1 teaspoon *ajwain* seeds (page 20)

2 teaspoons salt

¹/₄ teaspoon baking soda

¹/₄ cup chopped cilantro, plus additional sprigs
    for garnish

1¹/₂ cups water

2 small Japanese eggplants

2 medium new or russet potatoes

2 medium yellow onions

Vegetable oil, for frying

Sweet Chutney Sauce (page 130), Hot Green
    Chutney Sauce (page 130), and Fresh
    Cilantro Chutney with Peanuts (page 174),
    for serving

1. In a large bowl, combine the chickpea flour, rice flour, cumin, cayenne, *ajwain* seeds, salt, baking soda, and cilantro and stir. Gradually add the water, stirring to form a very smooth, thick batter, the consistency of thick ketchup. Cover and set aside for 10 to 15 minutes.

2. While the batter is resting, rinse the eggplants, scrub the potatoes, and peel the onions. Slice the eggplants and potatoes a tad more than ¹/₈ inch thick. Cut the onions lengthwise in half. Slice each onion half lengthwise into slivers. Loosen and separate the onion crescents and set aside.

3. Fill a large wok or heavy sauté pan with oil to a depth of 1½ to 2 inches and heat over medium-high heat until very hot but not smoking, 375°F on a deep-fry thermometer. If you do not have a thermometer, add a teaspoon of the batter to the oil to test; if it comes to the surface immediately, bubbling and sizzling, the oil is ready. If it browns instantly, the oil is too hot; if it stays at the bottom, then the oil is not hot enough. Adjust the heat accordingly. Working quickly with groups of 6 to 10 slices at a time so the wok won't get crowded, toss eggplant and potatoes into the batter. Stir to coat the slices evenly. Lift one slice at a time out of the batter with your fingers (it's easiest if you hold it at one end), then slide it into the hot oil. Fry for 1 to 2 minutes, then use a long-handled spoon to lightly bathe the slices with the hot oil (this will help set the batter on top). As soon as they're golden underneath, turn them over. Fry on the other side (no need to baste this time) until lightly golden, about 1 minute. Use a skimmer or slotted spoon to remove the *pakoras* to a baking sheet or a plate lined with several layers of brown paper bags or unbleached paper towels. After frying all the eggplant and potato slices, add the onions to the remaining batter and mix well. With a spoon, scoop roughly 1 to 2 tablespoons at a time into the hot oil. Fry as described above until crispy and golden. Remove and drain on brown paper bags or paper towels. Keep the fried *pakoras* in a low oven until done.

4. Set assorted bowls of chutney at the table. Arrange the *pakoras* on a warm serving platter, decorate with sprigs of cilantro, and serve immediately.

VARIATIONS

Other vegetables: Green beans, yams, okra, broccoli, and summer squashes such as zucchini, pattypan, crookneck, or Indian bottle gourd can be used interchangeably. Select firm vegetables and cut them into manageable bite-size pieces. Be sure to cut winter squashes into thinner slices and cook a little longer. Tomatoes have a lot of moisture, which spatters in the oil; sliced green tomatoes work better. Cauliflower *pakora* is very popular: cut into 1-inch florets and add julienned fresh ginger to the batter. For okra, keeping the stem end intact, slit in half lengthwise, sprinkle with ground coriander and cumin, dip in the batter, and deep fry. Ripe banana *pakora* is popular in western India.

Mix and match the following ingredients to make colorful, flavorful *pakora* platters:

Leafy Greens Pakora: Unbruised large fresh spinach leaves (1 bunch) with stems are commonly used. Thin the *pakora* batter with 1 or 2 tablespoons water so it spreads easily into the grooves of the irregularly shaped leaves and season with 1 teaspoon whole coriander seeds. Dip leaves in the batter, coating both sides completely.

Chili Pakora: Slit fresh jalapeño and/or Anaheim chilis (25 to 35 total) lengthwise, leaving the stems intact; if you prefer spicy-hot, leave the seeds inside. Add a tablespoon of lime juice or 2 teaspoons mango powder *(amchur)* to the batter. Dip the chilis in the batter to coat the outsides well. Remove from the batter, holding the stems straight up, then slide into the hot oil.

Fragrant Mashed Potato Balls (*batata wada* or *aloo bonda*): Mash 1/2 recipe of Yukon Gold Potatoes with Zesty Seasoning (pages 236–237). Shape into walnut-size balls, dip in the batter, and fry.

Paneer Pakora: Use large squares or wedges of *paneer* (2 recipes, pages 221–222, or 1 pound store-bought). For an innovative approach, slit each piece on one side, stuff with Cilantro Chutney with Peanuts (page 174), dip in the batter, and deep-fry. You may flavor the batter with Chaat Masala (pages 41–42) or Garam Masala (pages 36–37), if desired.

Mixed Nuts Pakora: Use large, plump nuts such as cashews, almonds, pecans, walnuts, and Brazil nuts. Add about 1/4 cup more water to the batter to thin it. Adjust the salt and other seasonings to your taste. Add apprixamately 2 cups of mixed nuts to the batter, scoop with a spoon, and deep-fry. Cook until the coating becomes crispy and crackly like parchment.

Mixed Meat Pakora: Meat and poultry must be sliced thinly and uniformly and cut into bite-size pieces to ensure complete cooking. Add 1 teaspoon each of whole coriander and cumin seeds to the batter. Use 1 1/2 to 2 pounds of boneless, skinless meat such as chicken breasts or boneless lamb shoulder, cut into small pieces. You can also cook the meat ahead, coat it with the batter, and fry to avoid any risk of undercooking or to use up leftovers.

Mixed Seafood Pakora: Calamari and shrimp can be batter-coated and fried until crispy and golden. Use the same batter as for Mixed Meat *Pakora*, or for variation, add dried unsweetened coconut to the batter. Catfish, salmon, and other white-fleshed fish fillets work well too.

Mixed Shellfish Pakora: Select 60 to 80 plump freshly shucked oysters, mussels, or clams; dip in *pakora* batter and fry.

CRISP OKRA WITH CHAAT MASALA | Bhendi Kurkure/Tali Hui Bhindi

This is a simple but stunning hors d'oeuvre, best made just before serving time. Make sure the okra is very fresh and tender, so there is sufficient moisture when it is sliced and an adequate amount of spice mix adheres to it. Fry gently until crisp. This way the okra will remain crunchy for a few hours. If leftovers get limp because of moisture, bake them in the oven on low heat for about 20 minutes until crispy. The crisp okra strips can double as croutons and are delicious over light soups.

SERVES 6 OR SO AS A SNACK OR INFORMAL APPETIZER

1 pound okra

2 tablespoons chickpea flour

1 1/2 teaspoons salt

1/2 teaspoon cayenne

1/2 teaspoon mango powder *(amchur)*, or
    tamarind powder

1/2 teaspoon ground cumin

1/2 teaspoon *chaat masala* (pages 41–42), or
    store-bought (optional)

Vegetable oil, for deep frying

Sweet Chutney Sauce (page 130), for serving

1. Rinse the okra and pat it dry; snip off both ends. Using a sharp paring knife, slice each okra pod lengthwise into 4 thin slices. Place in a medium bowl.

2. In a small bowl, combine the chickpea flour, salt, cayenne, mango powder, cumin, and *chaat masala*, if using, and mix well. Sprinkle the spice mixture over on the okra and toss to coat.

3. Fill a large wok or heavy saucepan with oil to a depth of 1 1/2 inches and heat over medium-high heat until very hot, 375°F on a deep-fry thermometer. If you do not have a thermometer, add a small piece of okra to the oil to test; if it comes to the surface immediately, bubbling and sizzling, the oil is ready. If the okra browns instantly, the oil is too hot; if it stays at the bottom, then the oil is not hot enough. Adjust heat accordingly. Using a slotted spoon, carefully add the okra, in small batches without crowding, to the hot oil. Reduce the heat to medium and deep-fry slowly, separating each piece with a fork; do not allow slices to stick to each other. Cook until crisp and lightly golden, turning once, for 3 to 4 minutes. Use a skimmer or slotted spoon to transfer the okra to a tray lined with brown paper bags or unbleached paper towels. Repeat with the remaining okra. Transfer to a warm serving platter and serve immediately with Sweet Chutney Sauce.

FRAGRANT LAMB SAMOSA | Samosa

These triangular pastries have been popular since olden times. Around 1350, the pastry called *samusak* was first filled with minced meat, pistachios, walnuts, almonds, onion, and spices and fried in *desi ghee*. During the Mughal period, the stuffing was enriched to cater to royal tastes, and the pastry was termed *kutub* and *sanbusa*. At the Jaipur Palace in Rajasthan, one memorable snack was *samosa*. The master chefs at the maharaja's palace showed off their talents with enterprising entrées. This pastry was deep-fried gently over low heat, with a live bird and other stuffing inside. At the table, when the maharaja "opened" the *samosa*, the bird flew out the window!

These days, *samosas* are filled with potatoes and peas or spicy ground lamb and served as snacks during afternoon tea. The pastries are lively party food. You can also make them the centerpiece of an informal meal, served with bowls of colorful chutneys.

MAKES 24 SAMOSAS

1/4 cup vegetable oil, plus extra for frying

2 cups self-rising flour, plus additional for dusting

1/2 teaspoon salt

2/3 cup water

1 recipe Hyderabad Fragrant Ground Lamb (pages 289–290), cooled

Tamarind Chutney with Banana (page 182), Sweet Chutney Sauce (page 130), Hot Green Chutney Sauce (page 130), or Fresh Cilantro-Mint-Onion Chutney Dip (page 177), for serving

1. Heat the 1/4 cup of oil in a small skillet until hot but not smoking. Set aside.

2. In a food processor, combine the flour and salt and pulse twice to mix. Add the hot oil and pulse until crumbly. With the machine running, gradually add the water through the feed tube in a steady stream, processing until the dough comes together into a ball and begins to clean the sides of the bowl. Avoid overprocessing. Form the dough into a smooth ball, cover, and let rest for 30 to 60 minutes.

3. Place the dough on a floured work surface and lightly coat your hands with oil. Knead the dough well for 5 to 6 minutes. Divide into 12 portions and roll each portion between your hands to form a smooth ball. Put the dough balls on a plate and cover to prevent drying. Place a piece of dough on a floured work surface and roll it out into a 4-inch, 1/8-inch-thick circle. Cut in half to form two semicircles. Form each semicircle into a cone by folding half of the straight edge over the second half and pinch the seam to seal. Hold the cone facing up and stuff with 1 1/2 to 2 tablespoons of the Hyderabad Fragrant Ground Lamb. Pinch the open sides together to enclose the filling; if necessary, moisten the edges with a little water to seal them. Shape the remaining pastries and cover with a kitchen towel.

4. Fill a large wok or heavy saucepan with oil to a depth of about 2 1/2 inches and heat over medium-high heat until very hot, 375°F on a deep-fry thermometer. If you do not have a thermometer, slide a tiny piece of the dough in oil to test; if it comes to the surface immediately, bubbling and sizzling, the oil is ready. If the dough browns instantly, the oil is too hot; if it stays at the bottom, then the oil is not hot enough. Adjust heat accordingly. Carefully slide 4 to 6 *samosas* into the hot oil in a single layer without crowding. As the *samosas* rise to the top, use a spoon to lightly bathe them with oil. The *samosa* pastry puffs rather unevenly, unlike puff pastry, giving the crust its characteristic bubbles and bumps in places. After they turn light brown, 20 to 30 seconds, turn the *samosas* and fry until lightly golden, 15 to 20 seconds more. Use a skimmer or slotted spoon to transfer the *samosas* to a tray lined with brown paper bags or unbleached paper towels. Repeat with the remaining pastries. Place the *samosas* on a cookie sheet and keep warm in a low oven for up to 15 minutes. Transfer to a warm serving platter and serve hot, warm, or at room temperature with any of the suggested chutneys.

MAKE AHEAD After the resting time in step 2, the dough can stored, covered, in the refrigerator for up to 2 days. Bring to room temperature before continuing.

VARIATIONS

Spiced Potato Samosa

Substitute 1 recipe Yukon Gold Potatoes with Zesty Seasoning (pages 236–237) for the filling instead of the lamb mixture to make vegetarian pastries.

Cocktail Samosa

To make tiny, 1 1/2- to 2-inch *samosas*, in step 3, divide the dough into about 25 walnut-size portions, roll each portion into a 2-inch circle, and continue with the recipe. Makes approximately 50 cocktail *samosas*.

INSTANT STEAMED DHOKLA BREAD | Dhokla

This lovely, soft, light, and porous quick bread made with chickpea flour and buttermilk is a Gujarat specialty that resembles cornbread. *Dhokla* is commonly steamed and cut into squares; the yellow-hued spongy cubes are finished with a zesty mustard-and-sesame-laced oil seasoning. I have tried substituting fresh lime juice, but the spongy texture is better with the pure citric acid.

SERVES 4 OR SO AS A SNACK OR INFORMAL APPETIZER

1 cup chickpea flour

1 teaspoon sugar

1/2 cup buttermilk

1/4 cup water

1/2 teaspoon citric acid (available in the baking section of some supermarkets, pharmacies, and Indian markets)

1 teaspoon grated fresh ginger

1 or 2 fresh green serrano or jalapeño chilis, stemmed and finely chopped

1/2 teaspoon salt

1/4 teaspoon baking soda

1 tablespoon vegetable oil

1/2 teaspoon yellow or brown mustard seeds

1/2 teaspoon sesame seeds

2 tablespoons chopped cilantro

1. In a medium bowl, combine the chickpea flour, sugar, buttermilk, water, and citric acid. Mix thoroughly with a large spoon until smooth. Cover and let the batter rest for 15 to 30 minutes.

2. Add the ginger and chilis to the batter, mix, and set aside. Brush an 8-inch round cake pan with a little oil or cooking spray. Fill a steaming pot, large enough to hold the cake pan, with water to a depth of 1 inch and bring to a boil. Stir the salt and baking soda into the batter. Pour into the prepared cake pan.

3. Place the cake pan on the steaming rack, cover, and steam until a knife inserted in the middle comes out clean, 12 to 14 minutes. Turn off the heat and let the *dhokla* rest in the steamer for 10 minutes.

4. Have a spatter screen ready before you continue. While the *dhokla* is resting, heat the oil in a small heavy skillet over medium-high heat. Add the mustard seeds, immediately cover with the spatter screen, and cook until the seeds stop popping, about 30 seconds. Toss in the sesame seeds and stir for a few seconds until the seeds are lightly golden. Remove from the heat.

5. Cut the *dhokla* into 1-inch diamonds and transfer to a bowl. Pour the seasoning oil with the seeds over the *dhokla*. Sprinkle on the cilantro and toss gently to mix. Mound on an attractive heated serving platter and serve warm or at room temperature.

> MAKE AHEAD The prepared *dhokla* can be stored, covered, at room temperature for several hours.

ZESTY PUFFED RICE NIBBLE WITH DRIED FRUITS AND NUTS
| Chivda

Indian markets sell all kinds of spicy snack mixes made from corn flakes, beaten rice, fried legumes, and *boondi* (chickpea pearls). This snack made with cereal has been my favorite since childhood. It can be served anytime, anywhere and makes an excellent traveling companion. It welcomes just about any main ingredient—use popcorn or fried potato straws, or add your own touches to create a new version for your next casual party.

SERVES 8 TO 10

2 tablespoons vegetable oil

2 tablespoons vegetable shortening

1 tablespoon yellow or brown mustard seeds

1 tablespoon cumin seeds

12 large cloves garlic, thinly sliced

2 to 4 fresh green serrano or jalapeño chilis, or fewer to taste, stemmed and minced

1 teaspoon turmeric

1/4 cup roasted salted or unsalted peanuts

1/4 cup whole roasted salted or unsalted cashews

1/4 cup dark raisins

2 tablespoons sesame seeds

2 tablespoons dried unsweetened flaked coconut

1 tablespoon sugar

1 tablespoon salt

6 cups crisp puffed rice cereal or *churmura* (available at Indian markets)

1.   Have a spatter screen ready before you continue. Heat the oil and shortening in a large sauté pan over medium-high heat. When the oil is hot but not smoking, add the mustard and cumin seeds, immediately cover with a spatter screen, and cook until the seeds stop popping, about 30 seconds. Add the garlic and chilis and cook, stirring, until the garlic is light golden brown, 2 to 3 minutes. Add the turmeric, peanuts, cashews, and raisins, reduce the heat to medium-low, and cook, stirring, for 2 minutes. Add the sesame seeds, coconut, sugar, and salt and cook, stirring, until pleasantly perfumed, 3 to 4 minutes. Add the cereal and mix thoroughly until the *churmura* is well coated with the seasoning and crisp, 4 to 5 minutes. Serve warm or cool completely and store in an airtight container for up to 2 weeks.

IDLI, DOSA, AND OTHER CASUAL FARE

Lazeez Lawaazmaat

In India, my mother had a large, handmade, chiseled-out stone grinder, much like a mortar and pestle, which she displayed proudly in the kitchen. The stone was used exclusively for wet-grinding grains to create a fluffy batter for southern Indian specialties such as steamed *idli* cakes and thin *dosa*. The batter expanded to almost four times its original quantity and became absolutely silky to the touch. Very few cooks these days (in India or beyond) use hand-carved stone. On my last visit, I saw a smaller version of this grinding stone, trimly installed in a stainless steel container. This appliance, called an Ultra Grinder, is electrically operated. The next best thing is to use a blender, which is far better than a food processor because its blades go faster and can grind even the smallest grains. But not all blenders are created equal, and choosing the right blender is important. Some plastic models don't have near the pureeing capabilities of, say, a commercial Waring blender, or the oh-so-powerful Vita-Mix. All of the recipes in this book have been tested using a regular, home-style Osterizer blender.

I remember that each week my mother made large amounts of batter out of rice and *urad dal,* an important grain-legume combination. She'd soak the rice and *dal* until soft, then grind them and let the mixture ferment into an airy batter. From this basic batter, she made a variety of dishes, each with a distinct taste, appearance, and texture. Steamed in special *idli* molds, the batter would become *idli,* to be served with *sambar.* Sometimes she flavored the batter with coconut shavings and chilis and fried them like dumplings. The following day, she thinned the batter with more water and cooked it on a flat griddle to make various kinds of thin and thick pancakes known as *dosa* and *uttappam.* A good south Indian cook is known for dexterously altering the consistency and flavor of the batter.

My American friends often ask what is served for breakfast in India. Besides the *idli* and *dosa,* lightly spiced healthful breakfasts are made with flaky beaten rice (*poha*) and cream of wheat laced with nuts, spices, onion, potatoes, tomato, peas, carrots, and cilantro. These nutritious dishes don't take much time to prepare.

More Ideas for Successful Idli and Dosa Batter

* Use long-grain white rice, such as the California variety, not basmati or jasmine rice to make the *idli* or *dosa* batter.

* Grind the ingredients in small batches, about 1 cup at a time, with a little water, for 4 to 5 minutes. If the mixture won't move through the blades of your blender, pulse several times, stopping and moving the mixture around with a spoon. Don't add any more liquid than suggested. The pureeing capabilities of the blender are much reduced when too much liquid is added.

* Do not stir the batter while it is fermenting. When the batter is ready, the texture will be light, almost like a mousse.

* A well-seasoned cast-iron griddle will yield an ideal, crispy and feather-light interior for *dosa*. A nonstick skillet also works well, though it yields a slightly softer crust. Preheat the griddle or skillet over medium-high heat for at least 5 minutes.

* *Idlis* are traditionally steam-cooked in special *idli* molds or in an *idli* stand. The stand and steamer are available at Indian markets. The stand consists of anywhere from 3 to 8 plates, spaced apart on a central rod. Each plate has 4 depressions or molds, usually round but sometimes square, about 3 inches in diameter, 1 inch deep in the center, and tapered at the edges. The molds have tiny holes that allow a properly prepared batter to "breathe" freely. If the batter is runny or not well fermented, however, it will drip through the holes. The entire stand goes inside a large steamer filled with 1 inch of water. It is then covered and steamed. Depending on the size of the pot and the stand, anywhere from 12 to 32 *idlis* can be steamed at once. You can also improvise with equipment from your own kitchen. Small metal cups set in Chinese steamer baskets work perfectly fine. Round cake pans can also be used to make large *idli* to be cut into wedges.

STEAMED IDLI CAKE | Idli

The northern Indians who migrated to the Unites States during the late 1950s brought with them dishes such as tandoori chicken and *naan*. More recently, a new generation of southern Indians have come to America and helped popularize *idli* and *dosa*. In the 1990s, southern Indian restaurants sprouted all over the Bay Area in California and in New York City as well. I encourage you to make these rice-legume, steamed, spongy white cakes. Only the soaking and fermenting takes extra time; once you become proficient at handling the batter, you can make double the quantity in the same amount of time. Feel free to fold chopped cashews, cumin seeds, and whole black peppercorns into the batter just before steaming.

In India, various sizes of *idli*—from 1-inch (cocktail *idli*) to 6-inch rounds—are prepared in special molds. My aunt in Bangalore lines the molds with banana or turmeric leaves for a distinctive taste. The molds are also lined with damp linen so the *idli* come off easily. For a perfect balance of flavors, the bland *idlis* are served with sambar and chutney for dipping.

MAKES 36 TO 40 MEDIUM-SIZE IDLI

3 cups long-grain white rice

1 cup converted, parboiled long-grain rice such as Uncle Ben's

1 cup *urad dal* (white split gram beans)

2 cups water

2 teaspoons salt

Vegetable oil for brushing, or cooking spray

Banana leaves, for lining the platter (optional)

Basic Sambar (pages 388–389) or Pearl Onion Mysore Sambar (pages 390–391), for serving

Coconut Chutney with Zesty Oil Seasoning (page 179), for serving

1. Two days before you plan to make the *idli*, place the long-grain rice and converted rice together in a large bowl. Place the *urad dal* in a separate bowl. Rinse both the rice and *dal* in several changes of water. Add water to both the rice and *dal* to cover by at least 2 inches. Soak separately for 6 to 8 hours or overnight. The *urad dal* will swell to almost double the size, and the rice will look pleasantly white.

2. Drain the rice and *dal*. Place about a third of the rice in a blender with a little of the water (use the water sparingly—you shouldn't need more than 1 cup for blending all of the rice) and blend to a thick, smooth to slightly grainy paste. Transfer the rice paste to a

4- to 5-quart glass or metal bowl, scraping the sides of the blender well. The rice and *dal* expand when fermenting, so be sure to use a bowl large enough to accommodate the expansion. Repeat the process with the rest of the rice and add to the bowl. Repeat the process with the *dal*, but be sure to blend it until silky smooth. You should not need more than 1 cup of water to blend all of the *dal*. Add the *dal* paste to the bowl with the rice mixture. Add the salt to the batter and mix thoroughly.

3. Set the batter aside, covered, in a warm place (about 75°F) for 12 to 15 hours. The batter is ready when it has expanded to almost double in volume and some bubbles and cracks appear on the surface. The batter should be thick but light and airy as mousse, with a pleasantly fermented, slightly sour smell. In cold and humid conditions, 24 hours will be needed for the batter to ferment, but do not leave the batter for more than 30 hours. Stir very gently in one direction for about 5 minutes.

4. Lightly coat four *idli* plates with the oil or cooking spray. Fill a large stockpot or Dutch oven (wide enough to hold the *idli* stand) with water to a depth of 1 inch and bring to a boil over high heat. Spoon the batter into the *idli* molds, filling halfway. Stack the *idli* plates on the central rod of the *idli* stand. Transfer the tiered stand to the pot. Cover securely and steam until the *idlis* are puffed and a toothpick inserted in the center comes out clean, 10 to 12 minutes. Turn off the heat, replace the cover loosely, and let the *idlis* rest for 5 minutes. Properly steamed *idli* will have a soft, well-rounded surface. Uncover the steaming pot, lift out the stand, and disassemble the plates. Ease the *idlis* out with a butter knife dipped in hot water. Keep warm in a napkin-lined basket. Repeat the steaming process with the remaining batter.

5. Arrange the *idlis* on a platter lined with banana leaves, if desired, and serve right away with the *sambar* and chutney.

> MAKE AHEAD In step 3, after the fermentation, the batter can be refrigerated, covered, for up to 3 days. Bring to room temperature before continuing.

VARIATION

Across India, in restaurants, leftover *idlis* are deep-fried in oil until golden and served in steaming bowls of *sambar* (see headnote). In homes, leftover *idlis* are crumbled and tossed with spiced oil seasoning and sprinkled with Dal-Rice Chutney Powder (page 191).

STEAMED CREAM-OF-WHEAT IDLI CAKES | Rava Idli

Each southern Indian state has its own version of instant steamed cakes. If you've visited Kerala you may have tasted *puttu*, made of coarse rice flour moistened with water and *desi ghee*, mixed with freshly grated coconut and steamed in a special cylindrical colander that is placed flush on the lip of a pot of boiling water. When you're in hurry and want *idli* in an instant, these mellow cream-of-wheat cakes from Chennai (formerly Madras), laced with buttermilk, literally melt in your mouth. For a quick snack I like to spread these with melted *desi ghee* (pages 47–48) and Fresh Cilantro Chutney with Peanuts (page 174).

MAKES 24 MEDIUM-SIZE IDLI

2 cups quick-cooking cream of wheat, or Indian semolina (*sooji*, page 46)

2¹/4 cups buttermilk

2 tablespoons vegetable or peanut oil

1 teaspoon yellow or brown mustard seeds

1 teaspoon cumin seeds

1 teaspoon salt

¹/2 teaspoon baking soda

¹/2 cup finely chopped yellow onion

¹/4 cup chopped cilantro

2 to 3 fresh green serrano or jalapeño chilis, stemmed and chopped

Vegetable oil for brushing, or cooking spray

Assorted chutneys such as Fresh Cilantro-Mint-Onion Chutney Dip (page 177) and Green Tomato–Sesame Chutney (page 183), for serving

1.   Combine the cream of wheat and 2 cups of the buttermilk in a medium glass bowl. Mix well, cover, and set aside for 1 to 2 hours. (If you're using Indian *sooji*, it need not be toasted here.)

2.   Have a spatter screen ready before you continue. Heat the oil in a small skillet over medium-high heat. Add the mustard and cumin seeds, immediately cover with the spatter screen, and cook until the seeds stop popping, about 30 seconds. Remove from the heat, cool slightly, and pour over the cream-of-wheat mixture, scraping the pan. Stir in the salt, baking soda, onion, cilantro, chilis, and remaining ¹/4 cup of buttermilk. Mix well and set aside.

3.   Lightly coat four *idli* plates with the oil or cooking spray. Fill a large stockpot or Dutch oven (wide enough to hold the *idli* stand) with water to a depth of 1 inch and bring to a boil

over high heat. Spoon the batter into the *idli* molds, filling halfway. Stack the *idli* plates on the central rod of the *idli* stand. Transfer the tiered stand to the pot. Cover securely and steam until puffed and a toothpick inserted in the center comes out clean, 10 to 12 minutes. Turn off the heat, replace the cover loosely, and let the *idlis* rest for 5 minutes. Properly steamed *idli* will have a soft, well-rounded surface. Uncover the steaming pot, lift out the stand, and disassemble the plates. Ease the *idlis* out with a butter knife dipped in hot water. Keep warm in a napkin-lined basket. Repeat the steaming process with the remaining batter.

4. Arrange the *idlis* on a platter lined with banana leaves, if desired. Set bowls of the chutneys at the table. Let guests spoon chutney on individual plates to eat with the *idli*.

PAPER-THIN CRISPY RICE CREPES | Udupi Dosa

These pancakes from the small town of Udupi have become popular all around the world. My auntie Prema, who hails from Udupi, shared this recipe with me. The batter may sound exotic, but there is nothing difficult about making the crepes. With a little practice you'll be well on your way to creating and enjoying *dosa*. You can be inventive and use any filling to make *masala dosa*, the most common of which is a spicy potato filling. As with *idli*, serve *dosa* with *sambar* and chutney.

MAKES 18 CREPES, SERVES 6 TO 8

3 cups long-grain white rice

3/4 cup *urad dal* (white split gram beans)

1/4 cup *mung dal* (yellow split mung beans)

1 tablespoon fenugreek seeds

1 3/4 cups plus 2 tablespoons water

1/2 tablespoon salt

Vegetable oil, for brushing and cooking

Yukon Gold Potatoes with Zesty Seasoning (pages 236–237), for filling

Basic Sambar (pages 388–389) or Pearl Onion Mysore Sambar (pages 390–391), for serving

Coconut Chutney with Zesty Oil Seasoning (page 179), for serving

1. Two days before you'd like to make the *dosa*, in a large bowl, combine the rice, *urad dal*, *mung dal*, and fenugreek and rinse in several changes of water. Add water to cover by at least 2 inches and soak for 6 hours or overnight. Drain and set aside.

2. Place the rice-*dal* mixture in a blender and process in portions, dividing the water among the batches (but do not use any more water than the amount called for). Blend each batch until smooth and transfer to a 4-quart glass bowl, scraping the sides of the blender. When all of the mixture is ground, add the salt and mix well. Set the batter aside, covered, in a warm place (about 75°F) for at least 15 hours. The batter is ready when it has slightly risen in volume and smells slightly sour and pleasantly fermented.

3. Preheat a 12-inch or larger griddle or skillet over medium-high heat for 4 minutes. Brush a little oil on the griddle and wipe off the excess with a paper towel. (The batter will not spread if there is too much oil.) Stir the batter thoroughly. Pour 1/2 cup in the center of the griddle and, using the bottom of a large spoon, immediately lightly spread the batter outward in a continuous spiral motion, thinning the edge, to an 8-inch circle. Drizzle 1/2 to 1 teaspoon of oil around the edge of the circle. Cook only one side until the bottom is crispy and golden, about 2 minutes. Fold the *dosa* in half and transfer to a plate. Repeat with the remaining batter, adjusting the heat according to your speed of preparation.

4. For *masala dosa,* place 1/4 cup of Yukon Gold Potatoes with Zesty Seasoning on one half of each *dosa* when the *dosa* is ready and starts to curl slightly at the edges, then flip the other half over the filling. Transfer to a heated plate and serve immediately.

MAKE AHEAD The batter can be prepared through step 2 and refrigerated, covered, for up to 3 days.

PINEAPPLE-SPECKLED CRUSTY PANCAKES | Pineapple Uttappam

Here's my take on the traditional *uthappam*. Studded all over with tangy tropical pineapple, it offers a wonderful balance of flavors. Since it is substantial, serve this pancake all by itself topped with chutney and melted butter or *desi ghee* if you wish. Keep in mind that it takes two days to prepare the *dosa* batter.

MAKES 12 PANCAKES, SERVES 4 TO 6

1/2 cup thinly sliced yellow onion

4 fresh green serrano or jalapeño chilis, stemmed and finely chopped (optional)

1 cup pineapple chunks (1/2 inch pieces)

1 cup chopped cilantro

1 recipe Paper-Thin Crispy Rice Crepes *(dosa)* batter (pages 159–160)

Vegetable oil, for brushing and cooking

Dal-Rice Chutney Powder (page 191), for serving (optional)

Melted *desi ghee* (pages 47–48), or unsalted butter, for serving (optional)

1. In a bowl, combine the onion, chilis, if desired, pineapple, and cilantro, mix gently, and set aside.

2. Preheat a heavy 12-inch or larger griddle or skillet over medium-high heat for 4 minutes. Reduce the heat to medium and brush a little of the oil on the griddle. Stir the batter thoroughly. Pour 1/3 cup of the batter in the center of the griddle and, using the bottom of a large spoon, lightly spread the batter outward to a 5- to 6-inch, 1/4-inch-thick circle. Do not thin the edges. Sprinkle 2 to 3 tablespoons of the pineapple mixture on top, drizzle 1/2 to 1 teaspoon of oil around the edge, cover with a lid, and cook until the bottom is lightly browned, 4 to 5 minutes. Flip the pancake and cook, uncovered, until the fruit is slightly caramelized, about 2 minutes more. Transfer to a serving plate, with the pineapple side on top. Repeat with the remaining batter and pineapple mixture. Cut into neat wedges and serve hot with the chutney powder and *desi ghee*.

VARIATION

In place of the pineapple, add a mixture of any combination of chopped onion, tomato, bell peppers, and shredded cabbage.

QUICK SEMOLINA CREPES | Rava Dosa

These crepes are subtle, somewhat crispy, and exceptionally tasty. Don't worry if you can't get the lacy pattern right on your first attempt; even I needed a little practice. Serve as an afternoon snack, along with fruit chutney for children.

MAKES 18 CREPES, SERVES 6 TO 8

1 cup quick-cooking cream of wheat, or Indian semolina (*sooji*, page 46)

1 cup rice flour

1 cup unbleached all-purpose flour

2 teaspoons salt

1 cup buttermilk

$2^1/2$ to 3 cups water

2 to 4 fresh green serrano or jalapeño chilis, or less to taste, stemmed and finely chopped

$1/2$ cup finely chopped cilantro

Vegetable oil, for brushing and cooking

1. In a large bowl, combine the cream of wheat, rice flour, all-purpose flour, and salt and mix. Whisk in the buttermilk, followed by the water, until very smooth. Make sure there are no lumps. Stir in the chilis and cilantro. Cover and set aside at room temperature for at least 3 hours.

2. Preheat a heavy 12-inch or larger griddle or skillet on medium-high heat for 4 minutes. Brush a little oil on the griddle. Stir the batter thoroughly and pour, from a height of 4 to 6 inches, about $1/2$ cup per *dosa,* starting near the outer edge of the griddle and continuing to pour inward, using a circular motion, to create a lacy pattern with irregular, tiny holes. Drizzle $1/2$ to 1 teaspoon of oil around the edge of the circle. Cook only one side, until the bottom is crispy and golden, about 2 minutes. Fold in half and transfer to a plate. Repeat with the remaining batter, adjusting the heat as necessary.

VARIATION

Rava Masala Dosa

Place $1/4$ cup of Yukon Gold Potatoes with Zesty Seasoning (pages 236–237) on one half of the crepe when the crepe is ready and fold in half. Transfer to a heated plate and serve immediately.

MAKE AHEAD The batter can be prepared through step 1 and refrigerated, covered, for up to 4 days.

EASY POTATO CREPE | Aalu Gedde Dosa

A typical *dosa* made with rice and legumes is rich, complex, and satisfying, but on a recent trip to India, I was amazed with this easy potato crepe that my sister makes so often. Pass Hot and Sweet Cranberry-Tangerine Chutney (page 189) or Sweet Spiced Mango Chutney with Pecans (page 185) at the table if desired.

MAKES 10 CREPES, SERVES 4 TO 6

1 pound (about 3 medium) russet potatoes

1 cup rice flour

1/2 cup plain yogurt

2 teaspoons salt

1/2 teaspoon ground white pepper

1/4 cup finely chopped cilantro

2 cups water

Vegetable oil, for brushing and cooking

1. Rinse potatoes and place in a large pot. Add water to cover and boil until tender, 15 to 20 minutes. Cool until easy to handle, peel, and mash the potatoes in a ricer. Transfer to a mixing bowl.

2. Add the flour and yogurt to the bowl and mix well. Add the salt, pepper, cilantro, and water and stir until smooth. Cover and set aside for about 30 minutes at room temperature.

3. Preheat a heavy 12-inch or larger griddle or skillet over medium-high heat for 5 minutes. Brush a little oil on the griddle and wipe off the excess with a paper towel. Stir the batter thoroughly. Pour 1/2 cup in the center of the griddle and, using the bottom of a large spoon, immediately lightly spread the batter outward into a 6-inch circle, thinning the edge. Drizzle 1/2 to 1 teaspoon of oil around the edge of the circle. Cook until the bottom is crispy and golden, about 2 minutes. Flip the pancake over and cook for 1 to 2 minutes more. Fold in half and transfer to a plate. Repeat with the remaining batter and serve hot.

MAKE AHEAD The batter can be prepared through step 2 and refrigerated, covered, for up to 3 days.

SAVORY MIXED-FLOUR CREPE | Ghirdi

If you like the crisp texture and flavors of *dosa* but can't spend all that time rinsing, soaking, grinding, and fermenting, then this quick mixed-flour crepe may entice you. The ingredients for this healthy, supple crepe may already be in your pantry. You can make it as nutritious as you wish by adding 1/4 cup of soy or multigrain flour for some of the millet flour. You can also substitute tomato juice for half the water for color and flavor. Serve topped with melted butter and a large salad on the side for a quick and substantial meal.

MAKES 12 CREPES, SERVES 6

2 cups whole-wheat flour

1 cup rice flour

1/2 cup millet flour or cornmeal

1/2 cup unbleached all-purpose flour

2 teaspoons salt

1 teaspoon cumin seeds

3 1/2 cups water

Vegetable oil, for brushing and cooking

1 cup finely chopped yellow onion

4 to 6 fresh green serrano or jalapeño chilis, stemmed and chopped, or to taste

1/4 cup chopped cilantro

1. In a large mixing bowl, combine the whole-wheat flour, rice flour, millet flour, all-purpose flour, salt, and cumin seeds and stir. Gradually add the water and stir until smooth. Set aside.

2. Heat a heavy 8- to 10-inch griddle or skillet over medium heat. Brush lightly with oil. Stir the batter. Pour 1/3 cup into the pan, spreading with the back of a large spoon into a 6-inch, 1/8-inch-thick circle (or lift and tilt the pan so that the batter spreads and forms a 6-inch circle). Sprinkle a little chopped onion, chilis, and cilantro on top, as desired. Cook until the bottom is lightly browned, 3 to 4 minutes. Turn, add 1/2 teaspoon of oil around the edges of the crepe, if needed, and cook the other side for about 2 minutes more. Transfer to a heated serving plate. Remember, it's not crisp like *dosa*. Repeat with the remaining batter, onion, chilis, and cilantro and serve immediately.

MAKE AHEAD The batter can be prepared through step 1 and refrigerated, covered, for up to 3 days. Finish step 2 just before serving.

TOASTY MYSORE CREAM OF WHEAT WITH CARROTS AND BEANS

| Uppuma/Khara Bhat

Uppuma (pronounced oop-mah) is somewhat like couscous. For an authentic taste, don't skip the optional *dal*, and use *sooji*. This is a light, balanced dish to serve for a weekend breakfast or brunch, along with hash browns and Mango Lassi (page 425), for an all-vegetarian meal; for an afternoon lunch, accompany with Warm Chickpea and Green Mango Kachumber (page 215). Without *desi ghee*, this flavor-packed, low-calorie dish is sure to please calorie counters.

SERVES 4

2 tablespoons vegetable or peanut oil

1 teaspoon *urad dal* (white split gram beans) (optional)

1 teaspoon *chana dal* (split chickpeas) (optional)

1/4 teaspoon yellow or brown mustard seeds

1/4 teaspoon cumin seeds

2 tablespoons roasted salted or unsalted peanuts or cashews

10 *kari* leaves (page 28) (optional), or cilantro

1/2 cup chopped yellow onion

1 fresh green serrano or jalapeño chili, stemmed and chopped

1/4 cup carrot sticks (1/2 inch long and 1/4 inch thick)

1/4 cup green beans, cut 1/2 inch diagonally

1 cup Indian semolina (*sooji*, page 46), or quick cooking Cream of Wheat

2 1/4 cups water

1 teaspoon salt

1 teaspoon sugar

Juice of 1/2 lime

1 1/2 tablespoons *desi ghee* (pages 47–48), or unsalted butter

Tomato slices or wedges, for garnish

Fresh chopped cilantro, for garnish

1. Have a spatter screen ready before you continue. Heat the oil in a heavy large skillet over medium-high heat. Add the *urad* and *chana dals*, if using, the mustard seeds, and the cumin seeds, immediately cover with the spatter screen, and cook until the seeds stop popping, about 30 seconds. Add the peanuts and *kari* leaves, if using, and cook, stirring, for 1 to 2 minutes. Add the onion, chili, carrots, and green beans and cook, stirring occasionally, until the onion is softened but not browned, about 3 minutes. Add the semolina, reduce the heat to medium, and cook, stirring frequently and taking care not to brown, until you begin to smell the nutty flavor, 10 to 12 minutes. (If using Cream of Wheat, cook for just 5 to 6 minutes.) Transfer to a bowl and set aside.

2. Add the water to the same skillet and bring to a boil. Add the salt and sugar, reduce the heat to medium, and gradually stir in the semolina mixture. (Water is critical here: the rule of thumb is twice the amount of grain, but I prefer a tad more, which helps the grains to soak and plump.) Stir constantly in one motion until all the water is absorbed, and be careful, because the mixture will start to spatter; reduce the heat to low at this time. Sprinkle in the lime juice and mix gently. Add the *desi ghee*, cover, and cook, without peeking, until the grains are fluffy and plump and the flavors meld, about 5 minutes. Let rest, covered, for 5 minutes.

3. Just before serving, spoon the *uppuma* into individual custard cups or a decorative mold. For an attractive arrangement, place a warmed serving plate upside down on top of the decorative mold, invert the mold over the plate, holding both securely, and let the *uppuma* slide down onto the serving plate. Top each serving with tomato slices or wedges and serve hot, sprinkled with fresh cilantro. I like this *uppuma* best when it is warm; as it cools, it looses its fluffy texture.

> MAKE AHEAD The *uppama* can be stored, covered, at room temperature for several hours. Just before serving, sprinkle with a little water and reheat over medium heat or in a microwave oven.

VARIATIONS

Add 1 teaspoon of freshly grated ginger with the vegetables. For color, you may also add 1/4 teaspoon turmeric along with the onion.

Cabbage Rolls Stuffed with Uppuma

Stuff leftover *uppuma* in cabbage leaves. Place in a baking dish, top with Sweet-Scented Tomato Gravy (page 123), and bake at 375°F for 20 minutes. Serve topped with a dollop of sour cream.

NUTRITIOUS MUMBAI BREAKFAST WITH BEATEN RICE

| Poha / Pohe / Avalaki

Once you've made *poha* once or twice, you'll find the process is easy. Crunchy nuts and onion, along with tangy tomatoes and lime, provide a nice contrast of flavors and textures, yet the finished dish is in total harmony. This traditional, healthful breakfast is popular in Maharashtra and Karnataka states. Have all the ingredients ready, because once you start, the preparation goes quickly. *Poha* keeps well for several hours at room temperature; I've taken it to many potluck parties, and it is great for a buffet. For variety, add a small cooked, peeled, and diced potato or some green peas along with the tomato. For a dressier presentation, top with freshly grated coconut. Note that two varieties of *poha*, thick and thin, are available at Indian groceries. Select the thick type for this recipe, because it holds its shape when rinsed (the thin type disintegrates and gets mushy and is mainly used in making trail mix).

SERVES 4

2 cups Indian beaten rice (thick-type *poha*, see headnote)

$2^1/_2$ tablespoons vegetable oil

1 teaspoon yellow or brown mustard seeds

$^1/_2$ teaspoon cumin seeds

2 tablespoons roasted salted or unsalted peanuts

$^1/_2$ cup finely chopped yellow onion

2 or 3 fresh green serrano or jalapeño chilis, or less to taste, stemmed and chopped

$^1/_4$ teaspoon turmeric

$^1/_2$ cup finely chopped ripe tomato, or canned diced tomatoes

1 teaspoon salt

$^1/_2$ teaspoon sugar

2 tablespoons freshly squeezed lime juice

Chopped cilantro, for garnish

1. Sort through the *poha* grains and remove any foreign matter. Place the *poha* in a colander and rinse under cold running water, swishing it to make sure every grain is soaked. Set aside to drain.

2. Have a spatter screen ready before you continue. Heat the oil in a heavy medium skillet over medium-high heat. Add the mustard and cumin seeds, immediately cover with the spatter screen, and cook until the seeds stop popping, about 30 seconds. Add the peanuts and cook, stirring, for 1 to 2 minutes. Add the onion, chilis, and turmeric and cook, stirring occasionally, until the onion is softened, about 3 minutes. Add the tomato and cook, stirring, until barely softened, about 4 minutes more.

3. Meanwhile, fluff the *poha* gently with your fingers to separate the grains. Add to the skillet. Reduce the heat to low, sprinkle the *poha* with salt, sugar, and lime juice, and mix gently. The delicate *poha* grains will take on the beautiful hue of the turmeric; make sure every grain is coated. Cover and cook until the grains are heated through, about 5 minutes, sprinkling with a little water toward the end of the cooking, if necessary, to keep the dish soft. Finished *poha* should resemble cooked orzo pasta. Let the *poha* rest, covered, for 3 to 4 minutes. Serve on individual warmed plates, with a sprinkling of cilantro.

> MAKE AHEAD The *poha* can be stored, covered, at room temperature for several hours. Reheat in the oven or over medium heat, stirring occasionally; do not use the microwave oven, because the *poha* grains will get hard. As with rice, if the top layer of grains looks dry, sprinkle with a little water and reheat.

CLASSIC PEARL TAPIOCA PILAF | Saboodana Khichdi

Khichdi, savory pearl tapioca, is a specialty from the state of Maharashtra. I stir in carrot, cauliflower, and peas to add more flavor, color, and nutritional value. Three sizes of pearl tapioca are available at Indian and other Asian markets. The large is usually deep-fried and turned into snack mix; the midsize variety, the kind found in tapioca pudding, is used in this recipe; and the tiny kind is used in making *pappadam*.

MAKES 4 TO 6 SERVINGS

1¹/2 cups medium pearl tapioca, cleaned

³/4 cup water

³/4 cup roasted salted or unsalted peanuts

1 medium russet potato

¹/4 cup vegetable oil

1¹/4 teaspoons yellow or brown mustard seeds

2 to 3 fresh green serrano or jalapeño chilis, or fewer to taste, stemmed and chopped

1 teaspoon salt

1 teaspoon sugar

1/4 cup chopped fresh cilantro

Juice of 1 lime

2 tablespoons *desi ghee* (pages 47–48), or unsalted butter

Freshly grated coconut (page 307), or defrosted frozen unsweetened coconut

1.   Rinse the tapioca in several changes of water and drain thoroughly. Place in a bowl with the water (be sure to use the recommended amount of water, because too much will make it mushy). Cover and let soak for 6 hours.

2.   Place the peanuts in a food processor or blender and process until coarsely crushed. Set aside. Scrub, peel, rinse, and quarter the potato. Slice 1/8 inch thick and place in water to cover. When you're ready to cook the potato, drain it and pat it dry.

3.   Have a spatter screen ready before you continue. Heat the oil in a heavy medium skillet over medium-high heat. Add the mustard seeds, immediately cover with the spatter screen, and cook until the seeds stop popping, about 30 seconds. Add the potato and chilis, cover, and cook, stirring occasionally, until the potato is tender, about 5 minutes.

4.   While the potato is cooking, in a bowl, mix the tapioca with the crushed peanuts, salt, and sugar. Add to the skillet. Cook, stirring constantly, until thoroughly mixed, about 3 minutes. Reduce the heat to low, cover, and cook until very hot, about 4 minutes. Sprinkle with the cilantro, lime juice, and *desi ghee*, mix gently, cover, and cook 5 minutes more. Turn off the heat and let the tapioca rest, covered, for 5 minutes. Serve in individual warmed plates, with a generous sprinkling of fresh grated coconut.

MAKE AHEAD The tapioca can be presoaked as in step 1 and stored, covered, in the refrigerator for up to 3 days. Sprinkle with a little water if it looks dry.

VARIATION

Pearl Tapioca Cakes (Sago Vadai)

Mix the leftovers with a couple of cooked, peeled, and mashed potatoes. Season with salt and chopped cilantro and form the mixture into a soft dough. You can also sprinkle the dough with a little chickpea flour or corn flour for binding, if desired. Using a small ice cream scoop or your hands, scoop the mixture into balls. Brush your hands with oil and press each ball between your palms to shape into a patty. Fry a few at a time in a skillet with a little oil over medium-high heat, until golden brown on both sides, 3 to 4 minutes per side. You can also deep-fry them; of course, they taste even better. Serve with Fresh Mint Chutney with Garlic (page 176).

TONGUE TEASERS: CHUTNEYS AND PICKLES

Zubaan ki Khwahish

Peanut chutney powder has always graced our dinner table. When I mix it with melted *desi ghee* as a spread for hot flatbreads, it's a favorite with my sons as well as their peanut butter–loving American friends. When I packed flatbreads spread with chunky fruit chutney for my young son's school lunch, his American friends eagerly traded their turkey sandwiches. So I always made a point of sending him to school with extras in his lunchbox. Indian pickles are astoundingly ingenious. They stay fresh at room temperature, keep their color beautifully, and continue to taste delicious days after they are made. You'll find more about pickles along with recipes (including a kids-friendly Indian pickle recipe) following the section on chutneys.

CHUTNEYS

Chutneys, those piquant relishes and palate teasers, are as diverse as the languages spoken in India. Like maharajas' palaces, chutneys are opulent and elaborate and no two are the same. They all add a lively note to any meal, from breakfast to supper to a late-night snack. They boost the appetite and aid in digestion.

Chutneys originated in India. The word *chutney* was coined during British colonial rule. It's the anglicized spelling and pronunciation of *chatni*, a noun derived from an ancient Indian language, Sanskrit, and it comes from the verb *chatna*, meaning "to lick." The word *chutney* entered the Oxford English Dictionary in the nineteenth century. It is believed that Indian spices and piquant chutneys reached such popularity in Europe, particularly around the seventeenth century, that their prices rivaled those of gold.

American cooks are most familiar with the viscous, spicy-sweet mango preserves sold at supermarkets, but the parade of Indian chutneys does not end with Major Grey's bottled condiment. India's rich tapestry of vibrant flavors and its world-class cuisine have given rise to a multitude of these relishes, from tart to sweet and from mellow to spicy hot. The simplest are smooth, saucelike, uncooked herb chutneys, which resemble American dip, or pesto without the oil. Another type is relishlike and has more texture, similar to Mexican salsa or corn relish. A third type is cooked chutney, which is chunky, mild, and sweet. Lastly, dry chutney powder focuses on toasted ground nuts and lentils, mixed with aromatic spices. All are highly flavored, eaten cool or at room temperature, and play more than a supporting role. Most require very little work to make, since the process is just one step.

REFRESHING, RAW CHUTNEYS

Anyone who has visited an Indian restaurant is familiar with those green, yellow, and red dipping sauces accompanying *pappadam* and *pakora*. These delightful chutneys are a snap to create. In most Indian households, they are made fresh daily. With a blender or food processor, they can be made effortlessly in minutes. The ingredients—aromatic fresh herbs, ginger, garlic, onion, green chilis, lime juice, yogurt—add essential vitamins and minerals to the diet. Preserving ingredients such as salt, sweeteners, and lime juice are used sparingly, so these chutneys are meant to be consumed within a week. These uncooked chutneys make a wonderful dipping sauce for fritters or pastries. They also make a lovely addition to grilled fish or meat and offer a low-calorie alternative to mayonnaise in sandwiches and snacks. For extra protein, just add ground-up nuts, which will also thicken the chutneys.

RELISHLIKE CHUTNEYS

These are made with farm-fresh vegetables and fruits and are cooked for a short time. They keep longer in the refrigerator than raw chutneys. Preserving ingredients are used in moderation. Ingredients like ginger, garlic, and chilis not only contribute to the flavoring, but act as digestive stimulants. Tamarind Chutney with Banana (page 182), for example, is moderately laced with heat and spices, and it gets texture and natural sweetness from pieces of dates and slices of banana. One of my favorites is the aromatic and spicy Green Tomato–Sesame Chutney (page 183), which can be used as a spread on warm buttered rolls. All of these relishes make nice accompaniments to tandoori dishes, roasts, and kebabs.

COOKED FRUIT CHUTNEYS

Then there are the tempting, mellow, chunky preserved chutneys, the chutneys of Major Grey fame. Major Grey, a British army officer stationed in India during the late 1800s, enjoyed cooking and popularized the pairing of mango chutney with Indian curries. His recipe soon became a favorite among Anglo-Indians.

Cooked chutneys are made with fresh and dried fruits, a touch of spice, sugar, and vinegar for accent and preservation. They remain fresh for months, to be enjoyed year round (either bottled and sealed, or frozen), and the flavors mellow and mature over time. In India such chutneys are served on holidays and on wedding, festival, and banquet menus. They also go well with grilled lamb chops, roast turkey, or just about any other dish in Western cuisine. Soft, pulpy fruit chutneys are a natural with spicy curries, and you can even serve them on pancakes, as sundae toppings, or as pie fillings.

DRY CHUTNEY POWDER

The array of dry chutneys, made with toasted, crushed nuts, flaked coconut, and *dals,* mixed with spices, are extremely popular in my native southwestern India. They are not well known outside of India. The ingredients are ground to a coarse powder, resulting in an unusual combination of textures, to make a dry seasoning that resembles a rustic spice blend. Traditionally these chutneys are served alongside any southern Indian meal or spread on *dosa.* Sprinkled over rice, grilled meat, or steamed fish, they add an exotic touch. Mixed with plain yogurt or melted *desi ghee,* they make instant dip or a spread for any type of bread.

Chutney Choices

❋ Select bunches of fragrant herbs from the farmers' market or supermarkets or harvest them from your herb garden. Use tender sprigs, stems, and leaves of fresh cilantro and mint leaves. Discard the tough stems.

❋ Quantities of herbs and spices may be increased or decreased to suit your own taste. Be sure to use fresh spices. Choose a bright red (not dark) cayenne or chili powder for the chutneys and pickles to attain a brilliant orange-red color. Your best bet is to shop at an Indian or specialty market where the turnover is high.

❋ Use juicy, tree-ripened preferably organic fruit from farmers' markets, roadside stands, or your own garden.

❋ Cold-storage fruits from most supermarkets will not yield such flavorful results. Fruit must be firm and ripe, without any blemishes or soft spots. The more luscious the fruit, the more glorious the chutney will be.

❋ Heavy-bottomed nonaluminum pans reduce the risk of the thick mixtures sticking or burning.

FRESH CILANTRO CHUTNEY WITH PEANUTS | Hara Dhania Chatni

Handmade chutney prepared with a mortar and pestle has a delightful coarseness, rustic appeal, and a lack of uniformity—that's what makes it so special. When time permits I use the mortar to get the wonderful taste and texture of this traditional chutney the way it should be made, by hand. I won't ask you to forgo the ease and speed of a food processor or blender; choose the process that best suits your frame of mind. Either way, the chutney will certainly be worth making.

MAKES ABOUT 1¹/₂ CUPS

3 cups packed fresh cilantro leaves with tender stems, plus a little additional for garnish

1 to 2 fresh green serrano or jalapeño chilis, stemmed

1 teaspoon cumin seeds

1 teaspoon salt

1/4 cup roasted salted or unsalted peanuts

1/4 cup freshly squeezed lime juice

1/2 teaspoon sugar

1/4 cup water

In a blender, combine the cilantro leaves and stems, chilis, cumin seeds, salt, peanuts, lime juice, sugar, and water. Process until smoothly pureed, stopping from time to time to scrape down the sides of the container. Transfer to a bowl. Let stand for a few minutes to let the flavors meld. Serve in a decorative bowl, garnished with fresh cilantro leaves.

MAKE AHEAD This chutney can be refrigerated, covered, for up to 3 days, but it is never better than the minute it is made, as the color darkens and the flavor changes.

VARIATIONS

Lemony Green Garlic–Cilantro Chutney

I love green garlic, so I grow it in my backyard, or I buy several bunches at a nearby farmer's market. Should some come your way, add 1 cup coarsely chopped green garlic, using both the white part and the pale-green tender shaft, and use 2 cups of cilantro instead of 3. If the outer layer of the shaft feels tough, remove it. Because it's so moist, green garlic is much more perishable than dried bulb garlic. Treat it like a flower: leave the roots on, stand the shoots up in a glass of water in the refrigerator, and cover with plastic bag. Or keep it in a plastic bag in the vegetable bin with a damp paper towel in the bag. It should last for at least a week.

Fresh Cilantro Chutney with Coconut

Cilantro chutney is really best made with peanuts, but coconut can be substituted for a different taste. Try replacing the peanuts with 1/2 cup freshly grated coconut (page 307) or store-bought, frozen defrosted coconut.

Making Chutneys with a Mortar and Pestle

Traditionally, chutneys are prepared using a mortar and pestle. For ease and convenience, I've written the directions for using a blender. If you'd like to make your chutney the old-fashioned way, here's how: Line up the cilantro leaves and sprigs on a cutting board and chop coarsely. In a large mortar, use the pestle to grind the chili, cumin seeds, and salt to a coarsely textured paste; it will exude a wonderfully pungent aroma. Pay close attention to breaking up the chili, and use a spoon to stir; do not use your fingers. Add the peanuts and continue to combine with the pestle until the nuts are ground. Add the chopped cilantro a little at a time, gradually incorporating it into the mixture. Add a splash of lime juice and continue grinding. Stir from time to time, if necessary. Add the sugar and grind until you have a coarsely textured chutney. Transfer to a bowl and stir in water to achieve the desired consistency. Let stand for a few minutes to let the flavors meld. Garnish with cilantro.

FRESH MINT CHUTNEY WITH GARLIC | Pudina Chatni

In India, when little kids fight, they often say to one another, "I'll make a chutney of you," which literally means, "I'll pound you to a pulp." Ah, chutney!

The aroma of a bunch of mint, cloves of garlic, and fresh chili should motivate you to dig out the mortar and pestle you stashed away in the pantry, but the blender works just as well for this lively chutney. Serve this fragrant, pastel-colored condiment of fresh mint and cool yogurt with an assortment of crackers or crudités, slathered on buttered toast, smeared on fish or steak, or thinned with buttermilk to make a refreshing salad dressing; the possibilities are endless.

MAKES 1 CUP

2 cups fresh mint leaves with tender stems

1 fresh green serrano or jalapeño chili, stemmed
   and chopped

2 large cloves garlic

1/2 teaspoon salt

1/4 cup water

1/4 cup plain yogurt

In a blender, combine the mint leaves and stems, chili, garlic, salt, and water. Process until smoothly pureed, stopping from time to time to scrape down the sides of the container. Transfer to a serving bowl. Whisk in the yogurt. Let stand a few minutes to let the flavors meld, and serve.

> MAKE AHEAD This chutney can be refrigerated, covered, for up to 3 days, but it is never better than the minute it is made, as the color darkens and the flavor changes.

FRESH CILANTRO-MINT-ONION CHUTNEY/DIP | Pudina Chatni

For the best texture and brilliant flavors, make this chutney within an hour of serving time. The robust onion flavor makes it perfect for serving with onion rings, french fries, and *pappadams*, or spread on baguettes or grilled garlic bread. It also makes a refreshing marinade for white-fleshed fish and scallops.

MAKES 1 1/2 CUPS

2 cups lightly packed fresh mint leaves with tender stems, plus a little additional for garnish

1 cup lightly packed cilantro

1 to 2 fresh green serrano or jalapeño chilis, stemmed

1/2-inch piece fresh ginger

1/2 teaspoon cumin seeds

1/2 teaspoon salt

1/2 teaspoon sugar

1 small yellow onion, coarsely chopped

1/3 cup freshly squeezed lime juice

1/4 cup water

In a blender, combine the mint, cilantro, chilis, ginger, cumin seeds, salt, sugar, onion, lime juice, and water. Process until smoothly pureed, stopping from time to time to scrape down the sides of the container. Transfer to a serving bowl and let stand for a few minutes to let the flavors meld. Garnish with mint leaves.

> MAKE AHEAD This chutney can be refrigerated, covered, for up to 3 days, but it is never better than the minute it is made, as the color darkens and the flavor changes.

Tamarind-Cilantro-Mint Chutney

Substitute dried red chiles de arbol for the green chilis and 1/2 to 1 teaspoon of tamarind concentrate for the lime juice.

Chutney Rice

This is becoming popular in restaurants across India; it is simple to assemble and quite refreshing in summer. Stir 1/4 cup of the chutney into 1 cup cooked plain long-grain white rice and serve right away.

Potato-Chutney-Cheese Bake

This was my son Kedar's idea, a casserole of sliced potatoes and cheese topped with green chutney and sprinkled with onion. Thinly slice 1 medium onion and cook, stirring often, with 1 1/2 tablespoons of oil in a heavy large skillet over medium heat, until deep golden, 8 to 10 minutes. Peel and thinly slice 2 medium-large russet potatoes, then wash and pat dry. Position a rack in the center of the oven and preheat to 375°F. Place one layer of potato rounds, slightly overlapping, in a 2-quart glass baking dish and season with salt. Add a layer of fried onion and sprinkle with a couple of tablespoons of the chutney. Repeat the layering until the remaining potato, onion, and chutney are used. Top with grated cheddar cheese. Bake uncovered for 30 minutes, or until the potatoes are tender. Before serving, run the dish under the broiler for a minute to turn the top golden. Serves 4 as a side dish.

COCONUT CHUTNEY WITH ZESTY OIL SEASONING | Khobri Chatni

Just as Americans grind fresh coffee in stores, Indians grate their own fluffy coconut from the machines installed in supermarkets in the cities of southern India. Believe me, the light, airy coconut meat is simply divine. I encourage you to use freshly grated coconut (page 307); if you prepare the chutney with a mortar and pestle, the aromatics will be distinctly fuller and richer, and the texture of the coconut will be delightfully pureed. Serve this chutney alongside *idli* and *dosa* (page 153). It also works well as a garnish for shrimp, shellfish, and salmon.

MAKES ABOUT 1 CUP

1 cup fresh grated coconut (page xxx), or dried unsweetened flaked coconut

1 to 2 fresh green serrano or jalapeño chilis, stemmed and chopped

2 large cloves garlic, peeled

1/4 cup cilantro

1/2 teaspoon cumin seeds

1/2 teaspoon salt

1/2 cup water

1 tablespoon canola or vegetable oil (optional)

1/2 teaspoon yellow or brown mustard seeds (optional)

2 dried hot red chilis, such as cayennes or chiles de arbol, stemmed and broken (optional)

10 *kari* leaves (page 28) (optional)

1. In a blender, combine the coconut, green chilis, garlic, cilantro, cumin seeds, salt, and water. Process until smoothly pureed, stopping from time to time to scrape down the sides of the container. Transfer to a serving bowl. At this point, you can serve the chutney as is or top with the following oil seasoning.

2. Have a spatter screen ready before you continue. Heat the oil in a small skillet over medium-high heat. Add the mustard seeds, immediately cover with the spatter screen and cook until the seeds stop popping, about 30 seconds. Add the chilis and *kari* leaves, if using, and cook, stirring, for a few seconds until the chilis darken a shade and even send up a slight wisp of smoke. (The aroma will fill the kitchen and might make you sneeze.) Remove from the heat and cool slightly. Pour the oil and seasonings over the chutney and mix gently.

MAKE AHEAD Refrigerate, with or without the oil seasoning, covered, for up to 3 days, or freeze for up to 3 months. If frozen, bring to room temperature and refresh with a new batch of oil seasoning before serving. If the chutney is too thick, stir in some water to reach the desired consistency.

RUBY-RED TOMATO–CARROT CHUTNEY | Tarkari Chatni

My chemistry background has helped me a great deal in creating recipes with well-balanced tastes and harmonious flavors; this recipe is one I put together when I had a bounty of carrots in my garden. This classic chutney displays the most beautiful shades of red you've ever seen. Infused with a combination of ginger, garlic, tomato, and carrot, it has bright flavors as well. Spoon on sandwiches and salad greens.

MAKES 1 GENEROUS CUP

1 pound ripe tomatoes

2 small carrots

4 large cloves garlic, minced

1/2-inch piece fresh ginger, minced

1/2 cup sugar

2 black cardamom pods (optional)

3 dried hot red chilis, such as cayennes or chiles de arbol, or fewer to taste, stemmed and broken into rough pieces

5 whole cloves

3/4 teaspoon salt

1/2 teaspoon cayenne

1/4 teaspoon black peppercorns

1/8 teaspoon freshly grated nutmeg

3 tablespoons freshly squeezed lime juice

1. Bring a pot of water to a boil, add the tomatoes, and cook for about 1 minute to loosen the skin. Let cool briefly, peel, and chop coarsely. Transfer to a nonaluminum medium saucepan. Peel and finely chop the carrots; measure a heaping 1/2 cup and add to the pan.

2. Add the garlic, ginger, sugar, cardamom, chilis, cloves, salt, cayenne, and peppercorns to the pan. Bring the mixture to a boil and cook over medium heat, stirring occasionally, until the chutney is thick and nicely glazed, 30 minutes. Remove from the heat, cool slightly, and stir in the nutmeg and lime juice. Transfer to a serving bowl.

MAKE AHEAD Refrigerate, covered, for up to 1 week.

PASCHIM ZESTY APPLE RELISH WITH JAGGERY | Panchamrit

Having a jar of this chunky, medium-spicy, relish made from toasted sesame, tangy tamarind, astringent apples, sweet coconut, and jaggery will inspire you to create more delicacies than any bottled condiment. Perk up your bland grilled steaks or fish with this popular accompaniment from Paschim, the western region of India. Mix a little of it with skillet-roasted shrimp or scallops, or smear it on toast for a quick snack. My sister-in-law in Pune makes this with guava. I've used the apples that are ubiquitous here, and it's lovely with pears too. I recommend using jaggery for an authentic taste. It is also necessary to use the number of fresh chilis I've recommended to balance the sweet flavors.

MAKES 1 CUP

2 tablespoons sesame seeds

1 tablespoon vegetable oil

1 teaspoon cumin seeds

1/4 teaspoon turmeric

1/8 teaspoon asafetida

4 fresh green serrano or jalapeño chilis, stemmed and finely chopped

2 tablespoons dried unsweetened flaked coconut

2 tablespoons coarsely crushed roasted salted or unsalted peanuts

1 teaspoon *goda masala* (pages 40–41), or store-bought

1/2 teaspoon salt

1 teaspoon tamarind concentrate, dissolved in 1/2 cup water

1/4 heaping cup jaggery (pages 51–52), or raw sugar or light brown sugar

1 cup thinly diced (1/4-inch pieces) apple, pear, or guava

1. Toast the sesame seeds in a heavy small skillet over medium heat, stirring frequently, until the seeds are uniformly reddish brown and aromatic, 3 to 4 minutes. Cool slightly. Transfer to a coffee mill or spice grinder and grind to a powder.

2. Heat the oil in a heavy medium saucepan over medium heat. Add the cumin seeds. When the seeds are uniformly colored and start to float, about 30 seconds, add the turmeric, asafetida, and chilis and cook, stirring, for 1 minute. Add the coconut and cook, stirring, until toasty, about 2 minutes. Add the ground sesame seeds, peanuts, *Goda Masala*, salt, tamarind liquid, jaggery, and apple. Bring to a boil. Reduce the heat, cover, and simmer until the relish is pleasantly sweet-and-sour and thick, 8 to 10 minutes. Cool to room temperature before serving.

MAKE AHEAD Refrigerate, covered, for up to 3 days.

TAMARIND CHUTNEY WITH BANANA | Imli Chatni

My mother hosted outstanding *chaat* parties. She'd make an array of condiments and organize them in a neat constellation of small colorful pots so guests had many to choose from. She made this wonderfully balanced, sweet-sour tamarind chutney; it looked exceptional with chopped dates, banana, and some green garlic snipped on top. She served baskets of Crispy Puffy Poori (pages 131–132) for dipping.

Thai tamarind pods are sweetish compared to the tart Indian ones; choose the latter. If you buy tamarind pods, be sure to remove the brittle, crackly light-brown shell first and then weigh. At Indian markets, tamarind pulp is sold in cellophane-wrapped blocks. I call for the pulp or pods and not the concentrate, because of their superior, fruitier taste.

MAKES ABOUT 1 1/2 CUPS

4 ounces fresh tamarind pods or Indian tamarind pulp, cut into rough pieces (see headnote)

2 cups hot tap water

1/2-inch piece fresh ginger, crushed

1/4 cup light-brown sugar or raw sugar

1/2 teaspoon ground coriander

1/3 teaspoon crushed hot pepper flakes

1/4 teaspoon salt

2 tablespoons chopped dates or raisins

1 ripe banana

Snipped chives, for garnish

1. In a glass bowl, combine the tamarind and hot water. Let stand, covered, for 1 hour. Break up the tamarind pulp with a spoon or your fingers. Strain through a sieve into a non-aluminum saucepan, pressing on the solids with the back of a spoon to extract as much tamarind puree as possible. You should have about 1 1/2 cups of puree. Discard the seeds, pods, and fibers.

2. Add the ginger, sugar, coriander, pepper flakes, and salt to the saucepan. Cook over medium heat, stirring regularly, until the mixture is thick, 12 to 15 minutes. Taste and season with salt and sugar to your liking—salt to liven up the flavors and sugar to smooth any tart or rough edges. At this point you can cool, cover, and refrigerate. Bring to room temperature before continuing with the next step.

3. Just before serving, stir in the dates or raisins; peel and thinly slice the banana. Add the fruit to the chutney, garnish with chives, and serve in an attractive bowl.

MAKE AHEAD Store, without the fruit added in step 3, covered, in the refrigerator for up to 1 week. Freeze for up to 3 months.

GREEN TOMATO–SESAME CHUTNEY | Hara Tamatar Chatni

A mouthful of this chutney, with its fresh flavors and nutty taste, transports me straight to my mother's organic garden. When I was growing up, green tomato chutney was a staple in my mother's home.

Step four is not obligatory, but a little asafetida stirred into the oil seasoning gives the chutney a distinctive aroma. If you're using unsweetened coconut, add sugar to taste, roughly half a teaspoon.

MAKES 1 CUP

2 tablespoons sesame seeds

1/2 teaspoon cumin seeds

2 tablespoons sweetened flaked coconut

1 1/2 tablespoons sesame or canola oil

1 pound (4 medium) green tomatoes, roughly chopped

2 fresh green serrano or jalapeño chilis, stemmed and chopped

1/2 teaspoon salt

1/2 teaspoon yellow or brown mustard seeds

Pinch asafetida (optional)

1. Combine the sesame and cumin seeds in a small heavy skillet over medium heat. Toast, stirring frequently, until the seeds are aromatic, 3 to 4 minutes. Add the coconut and cook, stirring, until toasty, 2 to 3 minutes more. Cool the mixture slightly, then transfer to a coffee mill or spice grinder and grind to a fine powder.

2. Heat 1 tablespoon of the oil in a heavy large skillet over medium-high heat. Add the tomatoes and chilis and cook, stirring, until the tomatoes are soft and blackened in spots, about 15 minutes.

3. Transfer the tomato mixture and any accumulated juices to a food processor or blender. Add the sesame-coconut mixture and salt. Pulse the machine until everything is thick and relatively smooth. Transfer to a decorative bowl, cover, and let stand for a few minutes to let the flavors meld.

4. Meanwhile, have a spatter screen ready before you continue. Heat the remaining 1/2 tablespoon of oil in a small skillet or *kadai* over medium-high heat. Add the mustard seeds, immediately cover with the spatter screen, and cook until the seeds stop popping, about 30 seconds. Add the asafetida, if using. Let it sizzle (it gives off much of its strong odor as soon as it is heated, leaving behind a subtler flavor) for a few seconds. Remove from heat and pour the oil seasoning and seeds over the chutney. Mix gently and serve.

MAKE AHEAD Refrigerate, covered, for up to 1 week. Freeze for up to 3 months. If frozen, bring to room temperature and refresh with a new batch of oil seasoning before serving.

Green Tomato–Tomatillo Chutney

Though I want you to appreciate the unique flavor of green tomatoes by making this chutney, a few tomatillos in the mix adds a tangier, more citrusy flavor. Adjust the seasonings to your taste.

ZUCCHINI CHUTNEY WITH FRESH DILL | Lauki Chatni

Certainly one of the beauties of Indian chutneys is that they marry endlessly well with Western dishes. Try topping tortellini, fettuccine, or linguine with this refreshing chutney. I like its genteel flavors with seafood, too. It also makes a healthful dip for fritters or onion rings.

MAKES 1 CUP

1 tablespoon vegetable oil

1/2 teaspoon cumin seeds

2 fresh green serrano or jalapeño chilis, stemmed

1/2 pound (2 medium) zucchini, ends trimmed and diced in 1-inch pieces

2 tablespoons chopped fresh dill, plus a little additional for garnish

1/2 teaspoon tamarind concentrate, dissolved in 1/2 cup water

3/4 teaspoon salt

1.   Heat the oil in a medium saucepan over medium heat. Add the cumin seeds and chilis and cook, stirring, until aromatic, about 30 seconds. Add the zucchini and cook, stirring, until the zucchini is softened, 8 to 10 minutes. Set aside to cool completely.

2.   Add the zucchini mixture to a blender or food processor, along with the dill, tamarind liquid, and salt. Pulse the machine until everything is thick and relatively smooth. Transfer to a decorative bowl, cover, and let stand for a few minutes to allow the flavors to meld. Serve sprinkled with a little fresh dill.

MAKE AHEAD Refrigerate, covered, for up to 3 days. Freeze for up to 3 months.

SWEET SPICED MANGO CHUTNEY WITH PECANS | Aam Chatni

Not too sweet, and counterbalanced with a hint of spices and farm-fresh mangoes, the brilliant and sassy flavors of this chutney will entice you to create batch after batch. Delicious with duck, lamb, or Cornish hens, this chunky chutney also goes well with robust curries, smeared over chicken before grilling, slathered on pork before roasting, or as a filling in a piecrust.

MAKES ABOUT 1 1/2 CUPS

1 pound (4 medium) firm, ripe mangoes

1 teaspoon grated fresh ginger

10 whole cloves

1 teaspoon ground coriander

1/2 teaspoon ground cinnamon

1/2 teaspoon hot pepper flakes

1/2 teaspoon salt

3/4 cup sugar

1 tablespoon dried red or black currants

1/2 cup plus 2 tablespoons distilled white vinegar

1/4 cup coarsely chopped pecans, toasted (page 208)

1. Using a sharp knife, slice the mangoes lengthwise on either side into 2 pieces about 1/2 inch thick. Cut the flesh of each half, making a fine crisscross pattern. Turn each half inside out and scoop with a spoon or cut the fruit from skin. Peel the remaining skin from the pit and cut the fruit in chunks.

2. In a heavy nonaluminum medium saucepan, combine the mango with the ginger, cloves, coriander, cinnamon, pepper flakes, salt, sugar, currants, and vinegar. Bring to a gentle boil, reduce the heat, and simmer, stirring occasionally, until the chutney is nicely reduced, chunky, and glossy, 20 to 25 minutes. It should be an easy-to-spoon consistency and nicely perfumed. Add salt and/or sugar to your taste.

3. Stir the pecans into the chutney. Cool slightly and serve. Depending on the accompaniments, sometimes I like my chutneys warm. If not serving immediately, cover and let the chutney ripen for a day at room temperature. The flavors improve and the chutney tastes better the next day.

MAKE AHEAD Refrigerate, covered, for up to 2 weeks.

BANANA AND PEACH CHUTNEY | Ardoo ki Chatni

Cooking the peaches in two stages makes this chutney a bit more complicated than most, but it ensures the best color, flavor, and texture. The bananas disintegrate into the chutney without browning, and the peaches remain distinct and fruity. Try this healthful, fruit-filled chutney with any lamb curry in the meat and poultry chapter. It's also good with Skillet Egg Masala (pages 299–300), flatbreads, and a pilaf, for a substantial meal. For dessert, try it as a sundae topping, served with scones, or as a filling for pastries and piecrusts.

MAKES 2 CUPS

1 pound (5 small) ripe but firm peaches

1/2 cup distilled white vinegar

2 medium ripe bananas

5 green cardamom pods, seeds removed and ground

1 teaspoon yellow or brown mustard seeds, lightly crushed

1/2 teaspoon salt

1/2 teaspoon ground coriander

1/4 teaspoon ground cinnamon

1/8 teaspoon freshly grated nutmeg

3/4 cup sugar

1. Bring a pot of water to a boil, add the peaches, and blanch for 3 to 4 minutes. Transfer to a bowl of cold water. When cool enough to handle, pull off the peels. Halve the peaches, remove the pits, and cut into 1/2-inch wedges.

2. Combine the peaches and vinegar in a nonaluminum medium saucepan. Bring to a boil, reduce the heat to medium, and cook until the peaches are just tender, about 5 minutes. Remove the peaches with a slotted spoon and set aside.

3. Slice the bananas into the saucepan and add the cardamom, mustard seeds, salt, coriander, cinnamon, nutmeg, and sugar. Cook gently over low heat, stirring, until the bananas disintegrate and the chutney starts to thicken, about 5 minutes. Return the peaches to the pan, cover, and cook, stirring occasionally, until the chutney is thick and glazed, 5 minutes more. Remove from the heat. Cool slightly and serve.

MAKE AHEAD Refrigerate, covered, for up to 2 weeks.

PEAR-APRICOT CHUTNEY WITH ALMONDS | Jardalu Chatni

My husband's colleague presented us with a large basket of pears from his tree. I combined the pears with other fruits I had on hand, stirred in some spices and seasonings, and this soft, spicy, wonderfully textured condiment was born. The following day, I sent some chutney with the recipe and an assortment of crackers with my husband to his workplace. Now all of his friends make this chutney regularly. Serve this delicate chutney with *kofta* curries and lamb or pork dishes.

MAKES ABOUT 2 1/2 CUPS

1 pound (3 medium) Bartlett, Bosc, or Seckel pears

1/4 pound (2 or 3 small) fresh apricots

1/4 pound (1 or 2 medium) nectarines

1/4 cup orange juice

2 tablespoons freshly squeezed lime juice

1/4 cup chopped yellow onion

1/2 tablespoon grated fresh ginger

1/2 tablespoon grated lime or lemon zest

3/4 teaspoon salt

1/2 teaspoon crushed red pepper flakes

1/4 teaspoon whole cloves

1/8 teaspoon ground cinnamon

1/8 teaspoon freshly ground black pepper

2 tablespoons light-brown sugar, or raw sugar

1/4 cup chopped almonds, toasted (page 208)

1. Wash the fruits and wipe them dry. Cut each pear in half lengthwise, then cut each half into 6 wedges. Remove and discard any seeds. Cut the apricots and nectarines in half, discard the pits, and cut into neat wedges.

2. In a heavy large nonaluminum saucepan, combine the fruits with the orange juice, lime juice, onion, ginger, zest, salt, red pepper, cloves, cinnamon, black pepper, and sugar. Bring to a gentle boil, reduce the heat to low, and cook, stirring occasionally, until the chutney is nicely reduced, thick, and glazed, 20 to 25 minutes. It should be an easy-to-spoon consistency and nicely perfumed. Add salt and/or sugar to your taste.

3. Stir the almonds into the chutney. Cool slightly and serve. Depending on the accompaniments, sometimes I like my chutneys warm. If not serving immediately, cover and let the chutney ripen for a day at room temperature. The flavors improve and the chutney tastes better the next day.

MAKE AHEAD Refrigerate, covered, for up to 2 weeks.

SPICY-SWEET KUMQUAT CHUTNEY WITH FIGS | Aamtekai Chatni

Early in the morning in India, whenever the crow settled on our fence or porch and cawed its "musical notes," my superstitious grandmother would be convinced we would have some visitors, and she would straightaway plan an elaborate menu. She made the chutney using *aamtekai*, subtropical fruit that resemble loquats. I was inspired to create this from a bumper crop of bright and glistening, sweet-tart kumquats from my own backyard, even without the call of the crow.

MAKES ABOUT 2 1/2 CUPS

1 pound kumquats

1 cup freshly squeezed orange juice

1/2 cup sliced Mission figs, or dark raisins

1/2 cup finely chopped yellow onion

2 teaspoons finely chopped garlic

1 teaspoon grated fresh ginger

1 cup sugar

1/2 teaspoon ground star anise

1/3 teaspoon salt

1/3 teaspoon freshly ground black pepper

1/4 teaspoon fennel seeds, lightly crushed

1/8 teaspoon freshly grated nutmeg

1.   Rinse and wipe the kumquats. Using a small sharp paring knife, first cut off the little green stem and discard, then cut the fruit in half lengthwise; quarter any larger ones. Remove the seeds and discard, if you prefer. You should have about 3 1/2 cups of kumquats.

2.   In a heavy medium nonaluminum saucepan, combine the kumquats with the orange juice, figs, onion, garlic, ginger, sugar, star anise, salt, pepper, fennel seeds, and nutmeg. Bring to a gentle boil, reduce the heat to low, and cook, stirring occasionally, until the chutney is nicely reduced, thick, and glossy, and the skins of the kumquats are tender, 15 to 20 minutes. It should be an easy-to-spoon consistency and nicely perfumed. Add salt and/or sugar to your taste. For the best flavor, allow the chutney to sit, covered, at room temperature, for a day before serving.

MAKE AHEAD Refrigerate, covered, for up to 1 week.

HOT AND SWEET CRANBERRY-TANGERINE CHUTNEY

| Karonda Chatni

I like this chutney because it is such a breeze to make. Toasted walnuts add a chunky crunch to the otherwise velvety texture. It makes an ideal holiday gift; write the recipe on small cards and tie them to each bottle with a piece of plaid fabric for an elegant homemade present. Serve this chutney with your Thanksgiving turkey or lamb chops.

MAKES 3 CUPS

2 small tangerines

1 bag (12 ounces) fresh cranberries, stemmed and washed

1/4 cup chopped yellow onion

1 tablespoon grated fresh ginger

3/4 cup sugar

4 green cardamom pods, seeds removed and ground

1/2 teaspoon cayenne

1/3 teaspoon salt

1/4 teaspoon ground cinnamon

1/4 cup chopped walnuts, toasted (page 208)

1. Halve the tangerines crosswise without peeling. Remove the seeds and cut into 1/2-inch wedges.

2. In a heavy nonaluminum medium saucepan, combine the tangerines with the cranberries, onion, ginger, sugar, cardamom, cayenne, salt, and cinnamon. Bring to a gentle boil, reduce the heat to low, and cook, stirring regularly, until the sugar dissolves and the tangerine rind is slightly softened, 12 to 14 minutes. The chutney should be nicely reduced, thick and glossy, and adequately perfumed. Stir in the nuts. For the best flavor, allow the chutney to sit, covered, at room temperature, for a day before serving.

MAKE AHEAD Refrigerate, covered, for up to 2 weeks.

PECAN-PEANUT CHUTNEY POWDER | Shenga Chatni

A range of chutneys adorns the dining table in Indian homes, just as ketchup, salt, and pepper do in the West. You may be surprised that this dry chutney powder is one of the most popular chutneys in my home. When it's fondly handmade, it makes a gift that is unparalleled. My great aunt, who lived for over a hundred years and made the best *shenga chatni*, ground the nuts with a whole head of garlic in a mortar until they exuded their rich oils, then gradually worked in the spices for additional zest. You can mix this with melted *desi ghee* or butter, then spread it on flatbreads and roll and serve as a snack, or combine it with yogurt and slather it on buttered toast or crusty bread.

MAKES 1 CUP

4 large cloves garlic, peeled

1/2 cup pecans, toasted (page 208)

1/2 cup roasted salted or unsalted peanuts

1/2 teaspoon cayenne, or more to taste

1/2 teaspoon cumin seeds

1/2 teaspoon salt

1/2 teaspoon sugar

1 tablespoon chopped cilantro (optional)

Add the garlic to a food processor and pulse until coarsely minced. Add the pecans, peanuts, cayenne, cumin seeds, salt, sugar, and cilantro and process until the nuts are finely powdered and the seasonings are thoroughly incorporated, about 1 1/2 minutes. It should resemble a coarse, moist spice blend. Make sure you don't overprocess it and turn it into spicy peanut butter. Cool and store in an attractive jar.

MAKE AHEAD Store, covered, at cool room temperature for up to 1 month, or in the refrigerator for up to 6 months.

DAL-RICE CHUTNEY POWDER | Karnataka Chatni Pudi

Also known as *idli* chutney or *milagai pudi*, this is traditionally used as a topping for *dosa, idli,* and plain steam-cooked rice. I sprinkle it on pancakes, crepes, and pasta as well, and my American friends love it. This southern Indian, fragrant, nutty, and versatile condiment can even be sprinkled on sautéed vegetables, grilled fish, and light meats. Serve it in moderation; a teaspoon or less should be plenty. I call for toasting the *dals* and rice first, then the sesame, and finally the chilis, because they all cook at different rates.

MAKES 1 CUP

1/4 cup *chana dal* (split chickpeas)

2 tablespoons *urad dal* (white split gram beans)

1 heaping tablespoon raw long-grain white rice

2 teaspoons coriander seeds

1 teaspoon cumin seeds

2 tablespoons sesame seeds

2 tablespoons dried unsweetened flaked coconut

2 tablespoons packed *kari* leaves (page 28) (optional), or cilantro

3 to 4 dried hot red chilis, such as cayennes or chiles de arbol, stemmed and broken into rough pieces

1 teaspoon tamarind powder

1/2 teaspoon salt

1/4 teaspoon asafetida

1. Combine the *dals,* rice, coriander seeds, and cumin seeds in a small dry skillet over medium heat. Toast, stirring frequently, until the *dals* start to darken a shade, the rice turns opaque, and the seeds are aromatic, about 5 minutes. Transfer to a coffee mill or spice grinder and grind to a fine powder, in small batches if necessary. Transfer to a small bowl.

2. Add the sesame seeds to the same skillet and toast, stirring, for about 2 minutes; add the coconut and continue toasting, stirring, until the coconut smells toasty and starts to brown, about 2 minutes. Transfer to the coffee mill, grind to a fine powder, and add to the bowl.

3. Add the *kari* leaves, if using, and chilis to the same skillet and toast over medium heat, stirring, until the leaves are crisp, about 3 minutes. Reduce the heat to low, push the leaves and chilis to one side of the skillet, and add the tamarind powder, salt, and asafetida. Toast, stirring, until hot, about 1 minute. Transfer to the spice grinder and grind to a fine powder. Add to the bowl and mix well. Cool and store in an attractive jar.

MAKE AHEAD Store, covered, at cool room temperature for up to 4 months, or in the refrigerator for up to 1 year.

PICKLES

Pickles are the soul of the Indian kitchen, and when they are lovingly handmade, and passed from generation to generation like family heirlooms, they are a perfect gift to the culinary world. Sometimes, it's really the small things that make a big difference. Humble pickles—be they lime, green mango, vegetable, or seafood—can enhance and even glorify a meal. If you think pickles are something only your grandmother would make and that they're hard to prepare, then the recipes in this section will prove otherwise.

A meal in India is never complete without pickles. Their place is on the side, just for "licking." They are eaten in tiny amounts because they are well seasoned, just the way pickles should be. In other words, several intense elements come together in a single bite. They are almost essential in the tropics, because the hot weather slows physical activity, and as a result the flow of the digestive juices is inhibited. Like chutneys, pickles stimulate the appetite and promote digestion.

Pickles are regional, each recipe reflecting the cuisine of a particular state. Spices not only make pickles tasty, but prevent rancidity and act as antioxidants. You'll find quite a mind-boggling assortment: hot and spicy, acidic and oily, sharp and pungent, sweet and relishlike. Lime and mango are most common, since they are acidic and naturally keep well.

Pickles are made in the summer in India, because that is when the best and juiciest produce is available, and to take advantage of the sun's intense tropical heat. Crocks containing freshly made pickles are set outside at dawn and left out until sunset, then brought back in. The pickles are aged in natural heat daily for a couple of weeks or more, depending on the type. The sunlight initiates an antiseptic reaction and speeds the fermentation. The appearance and taste of pickles ripened in the sun's rays are absolutely marvelous.

Some authentic recipes in this section are made on the stove top, and others require no cooking at all. If you're craving pickles, here are some refreshing ones. You can serve them as garnishes, enjoy them as relish over sandwiches, or serve them alongside any seafood or meat.

MY MOTHER'S HEIRLOOM PICKLED LIMES | Limbekai Upinkai

This wonderful treasure captures the freshness of classic Indian home-style cooking. This oil-free and straightforward preparation is my mother's fifty-year-old recipe. She makes it every summer for family, friends, and neighbors. The preparation of pickles used to be an elaborate process. I can recall mother purchasing five hundred plump, juicy limes, carefully screening each one for blemishes. The limes were meticulously rinsed and wiped with linen. Large earthenware crocks were cleaned and dried in the sun. Plump, fragrant spices were hand-picked and sun-dried as well. The choice of chili powder (cayenne) was very important. It was always freshly pounded; mother would combine three or four different varieties of dried chilis to achieve a deep ruby-red color, so the finished pickle could attain a beautiful hue. The pickling process was carried out only on a bright sunny day to avoid moisture from the atmosphere. The care and love that went into the preparation was worth the time and effort, since these pickles kept well for almost two years. Although I make these myself in late spring or early summer when limes are large and juicy, each time I visit India I stock up on my mother's handmade pickles. These are lovely with vegetarian, as well as fish and meat, dishes.

MAKES ABOUT 3 CUPS

2 pounds (10 large) limes

1 1/2 teaspoons fenugreek seeds

1 1/2 teaspoons cumin seeds

1 tablespoon yellow or brown mustard seeds

1/2 teaspoon turmeric

1/8 teaspoon asafetida

1/2 cup sugar

1/2 cup salt

2 1/2 tablespoons cayenne

1/4 cup freshly squeezed lime juice

1. Wash the limes in cold water and wipe them dry. Cut each lime in half crosswise, then cut each half into 4 wedges. Remove and discard any seeds, or leave them in for rustic appeal. Place the limes in a large mixing bowl.

2. In a small skillet, combine the fenugreek, cumin, and mustard seeds. Toast over medium heat, stirring frequently, until they are aromatic and the mustard seeds start to pop, about 5 minutes. Cool and transfer to a coffee mill or spice grinder and grind to a fine powder. Transfer to a small bowl. Add the turmeric and asafetida to the same skillet and warm over low heat for 1 minute. Add to the bowl. Add the sugar, salt, and cayenne to the bowl and mix thoroughly. Sprinkle the spice mixture over the limes and mix throughly Place the limes in a crock. Pour the fresh lime juice on top. Cover with the lid and store in a cool dry place. Let the pickles cure for 3 to 4 days before serving. Give them a shake occasionally to move everything around. Cover and refrigerate. (I recommend refrigeration, to be on the safe side, though traditionally this pickle is kept at cool room temperature.)

MAKE AHEAD Refrigerate, covered, for up to 3 months.

VARIATION

Chile-Lime Pickles

If you prefer, slit 10 to 15 long, slender fresh hot green chilis such as serranos or jalapeños (do not stem), sprinkle some of the pickling *masala* in to the slits, and toss into the crock.

NOTE The amounts of sugar, salt and cayenne may seem too much. Remember, this is a pickle recipe. I encourage you to try making this flavorsome pickle at least once.

CASHEW-LIME SWEET PICKLE | Tokku

I can almost pass this pickle off as a stylish, sweet-spiced lime chutney. This recipe is a good choice for those trying Indian pickles for the first time. Adults as well as children like it; in fact, my sister-in-law, Keertilata, introduced this to my children. Choose good-quality, smooth, thin-skinned limes that are free of any blemishes or soft spots. Lemons give a similar flavor but don't keep as well as the limes unless they are preserved in oil. Use jaggery for an authentic taste. The dried mixed fruits that are usually available during the holiday season are perfect here.

MAKES A GENEROUS 1 1/2 CUPS

3/4 pound (4 large) limes

1/2 teaspoon cumin seeds

1 1/2 teaspoons coriander seeds

1 1/2 teaspoons cayenne

1/2 teaspoon salt

1/2 teaspoon black peppercorns

2 fresh green serrano or jalapeño chilis, stemmed and slit into fourths

1/2 cup dried mixed fruits (pineapple, cherries, and apple)

1 scant cup jaggery (pages 51–52), or light-brown sugar or raw sugar

3 tablespoons distilled white vinegar

12 whole cashews

1. Wash the limes in cold water and wipe dry. Cut each lime in half crosswise, then cut each half into 4 wedges. Discard any seeds. Place the lime pieces in a heavy medium non-aluminum saucepan.

2. In a small skillet over medium heat, combine the cumin and coriander seeds. Toast, stirring frequently, until the seeds are aromatic, about 5 minutes. Transfer to a coffee mill or spice grinder and grind to a fine powder.

3. Add the ground spices to the pan containing the lime pieces. Add the cayenne, salt, peppercorns, chiles, dried fruits, jaggery, vinegar, and nuts. Bring mixture to a gentle boil over medium heat. Cook, stirring occasionally, until the lime rind is a dull olive green and the mixture is thick and syrupy, 25 to 30 minutes. The pickle should be nicely glazed and perfumed. For best flavor, allow the pickle to sit for a day at room temperature before serving. Then cover and refrigerate.

MAKE AHEAD Refrigerate, covered, for up to 6 months.

CRANBERRY-STUDDED PICKLED PINEAPPLE | Ananas Upinkai

This is one of my favorites, a symphony of sweet, pungent, hot, and cool. Spread it on toast or use it as a flavorful topping for grilled meat or fish. Whisk some yogurt and mix it together with this chutney, and you'll have a lovely, fruity, low-calorie salad dressing.

MAKES A GENEROUS 1 1/2 CUPS

2 pounds (1 medium) pineapple

1 teaspoon salt

1/4 cup distilled white vinegar

1/3 cup sugar

1/2 teaspoon black peppercorns

1/2-inch cinnamon stick

8 whole cloves

2 to 4 dried hot red chilis, such as cayennes or chiles de arbol, stemmed and broken into two

1/2-inch piece fresh ginger, julienned

2 tablespoons dried cranberries

1. Using a large, sharp knife, slice off the bottom end and the green top of the pineapple. Stand the pineapple on one end and slice off the skin in wide strips, from top to bottom. To remove the eyes, cut diagonally around the fruit, following the pattern of the eyes and making narrow groves in the pineapple. Cut away as little of the meat as possible. Chop the pineapple meat away from the core; discard the core. Cut the fruit into a 1/2-inch dice and scoop into a large bowl. Measure 2 cups. Sprinkle with the salt and set aside.

2. In a heavy medium nonaluminum saucepan, combine the vinegar and sugar. Bring to a gentle boil, reduce the heat to medium-low, and cook, stirring regularly, until the sugar dissolves, about 6 minutes. Add the pineapple, peppercorns, cinnamon, cloves, chilis, ginger, and cranberries. Cook over medium heat, stirring regularly, until most of the liquid has evaporated, about 22 minutes. The pickle should be nicely glazed and perfumed. For the best flavor, allow the pickle to sit for a day at room temperature before serving. Then cover and refrigerate.

MAKE AHEAD Refrigerate, covered, for up to 6 weeks.

SHORTCUT Use a 20-ounce can of pineapple chunks, drained, and skip step 1.

SPICY-SWEET GREEN MANGO RELISH | Chundo

India is the abode of hundreds of varieties of magnificent mangoes. There is an astounding selection of just-green pickling mangoes that vary in tartness, shape, and size, from one to twelve inches in length. My childhood memories come rushing back when I make anything with green mango. Before my mother would start the pickling process, we would eat some of the raw slices, dipping them first in a heap of salt. I can still recall the taste. Buy an actual "green" mango (so hard and unripe, it's almost impossible to dig a fingernail into it), available in Indian and specialty markets and some supermarkets, usually placed separate from the ripe ones.

MAKES A GENEROUS 1 CUP

1 pound (1 large) green mango

1 1/2 tablespoons sesame or vegetable oil

5 whole cloves

3-inch cinnamon stick, broken into rough pieces

1/8 teaspoon asafetida

1/2 cup sugar

2 teaspoons cayenne

1 teaspoon salt

1. Wash and wipe the mango thoroughly. Peel the mango with a vegetable peeler. Using a hand grater (the fine holes of a hand grater result in a fine, fluffy texture, which I prefer), grate about 1/2 inch of the mango on all sides, then grate the remaining fruit carefully, avoiding the large flat pit. Measure 1 1/4 cups and set aside. (Don't throw the pit away; add it to *sambars* or *rasams* while cooking to increase the sour taste.)

2. Heat the oil in a heavy medium nonaluminum skillet over medium heat. Add the cloves, cinnamon, and asafetida. When the spices swell and turn aromatic, about 30 seconds, add the grated mango. Cook, stirring, until the moisture just evaporates, 4 to 5 minutes. Add the sugar, cayenne, and salt and mix well. Cook, stirring occasionally, until the relish is nice and thick and attains a beautiful orange-red color, about 15 minutes. Set aside to cool, scoop the relish into a decorative bowl, and serve.

MAKE AHEAD Store, covered (I suggest a small jar), at room temperature for 2 to 3 days, or in the refrigerator for up to 6 months.

PICKLED COASTAL SHRIMP | Prawn Balchao

When I presented several jars of this bright orange-red pickle to my neighbors, they used it as a gorgeous garnish for cold pasta, in garden salads, and even on open-faced sandwiches. *Balchao* is a special pickle from Goa, nestled on the west coast of the Indian subcontinent. Goa has its own wonderful cuisine that combines Indian and Portuguese influences. *Balchao*, tangy and mildly spicy, can be made in a number of ways; you can vary this traditional condiment each time you make it. In the first step, you may grind the shrimp to a paste or chop them into pieces (I prefer to leave them whole), or substitute dried shrimp for the fresh ones; *kari* leaves may be added in the final step for a distinctive taste; a mixture of tamarind and lime juice can replace the vinegar used for cooking the shrimp and making the spice paste.

MAKES ABOUT 2 CUPS

1/2 pound (12 to 14) jumbo shrimp

2 1/2 cups distilled white vinegar

1 teaspoon cumin seeds

4 dried red chilis, such as cayennes or chiles de arbol, stemmed and softened (microwave for 30 seconds in 1/4 cup water, then discard water)

1/2-inch piece fresh ginger

3 large cloves garlic

1/4 teaspoon turmeric

3 tablespoons peanut or canola oil

1 cup finely chopped yellow onion

2 medium ripe tomatoes, or 1 cup canned diced tomatoes

1/2 teaspoon black peppercorns

1/2 teaspoon salt

1. Peel the shrimp, leaving the final joint and tail intact. Devein each shrimp by making a shallow incision down the back, exposing the dark intestinal tract, and scraping it out. Thoroughly rinse the shrimp in 2 cups of the vinegar. Discard the vinegar. In a medium nonaluminum saucepan, combine the shrimp and 1/4 cup of the vinegar and cook over medium heat for about 6 minutes. At this point, you may make a paste of the shrimp using a blender, or cut the shrimp into 1/2-inch pieces, and add them back to the vinegar.

2. Using a mortar and pestle, lightly crush the cumin seeds, then transfer to a blender. Add the chilis, ginger, garlic, turmeric, and remaining 1/4 cup of vinegar to the blender and blend to a smooth puree, stopping to scrape down the sides of the bowl a couple of times. Transfer to a bowl.

3. In another heavy medium nonaluminum saucepan, heat the oil over medium heat. Add the onion and cook, stirring occasionally, until the onion is very soft and the edges start to brown, 6 to 8 minutes.

4. Meanwhile, bring a pot of water to a boil, add the tomatoes, and cook for about a minute to loosen the skins. Cool briefly, peel, and chop finely, collecting the juices. Measure 1 cup and set aside. (Skip this step if using canned tomatoes.)

5. Add the peppercorns and spice paste to the onion and cook, stirring, for 3 to 4 minutes. Add the tomatoes and salt and bring the mixture to a boil. Add the shrimp along with the vinegar and cook, stirring gently, until the mixture is thick and you begin to see oil at the top, 15 to 20 minutes. It will be shiny on top when perfectly reduced. Season to taste, if necessary. Serve at room temperature.

MAKE AHEAD Refrigerate, covered, for up to 5 days.

PICKLED VEGETABLES WITH ZESTY SEASONING | Tarkari Upinkai

A galaxy of bright, colorful, and crunchy veggies are bathed in a smoky, mildly spicy, sweet-sour seasoning. This simple but scrumptious preparation displays the seasonal bounty of the late summer garden. You can be creative in selecting the combination of vegetables; add some of your favorites to the list, or make up a list of your own. Eggplant, daikon, brussels sprouts, chayote, turnip, bitter melon, and banana squash all work with favorable results. Oil is added to give shine, smoothness, and flavor. Don't use any garlic that is bruised or sprouting. This pickle can be made far in advance, and the vegetables will stay crunchy and full-flavored for several weeks. Serve with meatless dishes or with meats, including pot roast and steak.

MAKES A GENEROUS 2 1/2 CUPS

1/2 cup peeled and cubed (1-inch pieces) cucumber

1/2 cup sliced carrot

1 cup chopped (1/2-inch pieces) cauliflower florets

1/2 cup trimmed and chopped (1-inch pieces) green beans

4 pearl onions, peeled

1 1/2 tablespoons sesame or mustard oil (see notes, page 49)

5 large cloves garlic, sliced

1-inch piece fresh ginger, julienned

1/8 teaspoon asafetida (optional)

3 dried hot red chilis, such as cayennes or chiles de arbol, stemmed and broken into rough pieces

5 tablespoons distilled white vinegar

2 1/2 tablespoons raw sugar, or light-brown sugar

1/4 teaspoon fenugreek seeds

3 green cardamom pods, seeds removed and ground

1 teaspoons yellow or brown mustard seeds, lightly crushed

1/2 teaspoon salt

1/4 teaspoon ground cumin

1/8 teaspoon ground cinnamon

1/8 teaspoon freshly ground black pepper

1. In a large shallow dish, combine the cucumber, carrot, cauliflower, green beans, and pearl onions. Bring 2 quarts of water to a rolling boil; pour over the vegetables and let sit for 5 minutes. Drain in a colander, spread the vegetables on a cookie sheet lined with clean kitchen towels or paper towels and pat dry thoroughly. Loosely pack the blanched vegetables into a clean 2-quart crock or jar.

2. Heat the oil in a small skillet over medium heat. Add the garlic, ginger, and asafetida and cook, stirring, until aromatic and the garlic starts to brown at the edges, about 3 minutes. Stir in the chilis and cook, stirring, until the chilis darken a shade and even send up a slight wisp of smoke, about 30 seconds. Remove from the heat and set aside.

3. In a small saucepan, combine the vinegar and sugar and bring to a boil. Reduce the heat and simmer until slightly thick, about 10 minutes. Meanwhile, toast the fenugreek seeds in a small skillet over medium heat, stirring, until the seeds start to darken, about 2 minutes. Transfer to a coffee mill or spice grinder and grind to a fine powder.

4. Add the ground fenugreek, cardamom, mustard seeds, salt, cumin, cinnamon, and pepper to the vinegar mixture; stir until the salt dissolves and remove from the heat. Stir in the ginger-garlic oil seasoning and mix well. Pour over the vegetables. Shake the jar so that the vegetables are well coated. Taste; it might be a little intense at first, but it will mellow by the following day. Cover and, for the best flavor, set aside to cure at cool room temperature for a day.

MAKE AHEAD Refrigerate, covered, for up to 2 weeks.

COOL YOGURT, REFRESHING RAITAS, AND KACHUMBERS

Bagiche ki Peshkash

As a youngster, I used to wonder why my grandmother would toss a couple of potatoes, yams, and sometimes even squashes or eggplants into the dying embers of the clay oven after the cooking was done. The next day, she would collect the veggies, wipe away the ash, peel off the skins, and mix the butter-soft pulp with cool, spiced yogurt and garnish with spice-infused oil seasoning and cilantro. While my grandmother's *raitas* were a bit elaborate, my mother's were simple. She would mix diced or shredded raw vegetables with plain yogurt and fold in crushed peanuts. When I visited my aunts in Mumbai, theirs were even simpler; they would mix prepackaged crisp fried *boondi* (seasoned chickpea flour pearls) with yogurt, or fold yogurt into bowl of mixed fruit. I learned early on that there are many ways to prepare healthful, refreshing *raita*.

Taking a cue from them, I always make a point of including some sort of raw vegetable dish with dinner. It may be as simple as sliced onions sprinkled with coarse salt; diced cucumber dolloped with yogurt; sliced tomatoes drizzled with toasted crushed cumin; or shredded carrot squirted with fresh lime juice. Or it may be more elaborate, such as a mélange of finely chopped fruits or vegetables folded into silky yogurt. The most intricate of these dishes, called *raitas*, are embellished with aromatic, spice-infused oils, fresh herbs, and roasted, crushed nuts. Another lesser-known style of Indian salads, called *kachumber*, relies on chopped, crisp vegetables moistened with oil-based dressings, rather than yogurt flavored with spices. Both *raitas* and *kachumbers* can be made from raw or cooked fruits and vegetables, standing alone or in combination.

RAITAS

Although many Indian restaurants rely on cucumber or tomato *raitas*, you can make *raitas* from a dazzling array of fruits or vegetables—just about whatever the summer garden or produce market has to offer. Cauliflower, carrot, daikon, radish, potato, spinach, eggplant, and okra all make strikingly beautiful compositions. I also use avocado, kiwi, zucchini, colorful bell peppers, fresh corn, and even purple potatoes. Yogurt is a common ingredient in all regions of the Indian subcontinent, and in southern India it is a staple. Hundreds of years ago, *raita,* or *pachadi,* as it is called in the south, began as a way to use leftover yogurt before it turned sour in the tropical climate. Radish tops were probably the first addition. Yogurt was also folded into leftover side-dish vegetables like okra and smoky eggplant. These creations traveled to Gujarat in western India, where the cooks flavored them with generous amounts of *rai,* or mustard seeds, which led to the name *raita*.

Raita also caught the fancy of cooks in northern India, who flavored the mixture with toasted, crushed cumin seeds. Combining both traditions, today's *raitas* can be topped with mustard- and cumin-infused oils to enhance their look and flavor. Cooks from southern India also add fresh green chilis along with the oil. I like to add crushed nuts for a contrasting crisp texture, a technique popular in southwestern India.

Which Yogurt?

I have tried all *raitas* with store-bought plain yogurt. *Raitas* are best made with whole milk yogurt. In some recipes, I recommend adding sour cream to low-fat or nonfat yogurt to approximate the creamy texture of Indian yogurt. This texture is especially important in *raitas* made from high-moisture vegetables like cucumber and tomato; the extra butterfat keeps the *raita* from getting thin and watery as it stands. If you are watching calories, you can exclude the sour cream; assemble the *raita* just before serving so it will maintain its body.

In Indian cuisine, *raita* is served as a cooling accompaniment to balance spicy meat dishes and curries, and for a moist counterpoint to breads and pilafs. But *raita* can be used in all sorts of cuisines, as a filling for warm tortillas or pita breads and as an accompaniment to grilled meat and seafood dishes.

KACHUMBERS

Compared to *raitas, kachumbers* are not well known outside India. In texture, *kachumber* resembles coleslaw, but contains no mayonnaise. A light coating of spice-infused oil seasoning takes the place of vinaigrette. It is added to give shine, smoothness, and flavor. Most *kachumbers* use one or two grated or shredded vegetables, either raw or cooked, with a flavorful boost from the zesty spice-infused oil, a touch of fresh herbs, and a sprinkle of lime juice. Whether the salads use vegetables that are raw or blanched, sliced or shredded, they are meant to be refreshing contrasts to the accompanying dishes.

HOMEMADE YOGURT | Dahi

Yogurt—so literally a gift of nature—is a culinary catalyst to all of India's many regional cuisines. It is enjoyed for its tangy, tart flavor and accompanies every meal in one form or another. It acts as a natural antacid and helps to relieve flatulence, hence it has been valued since ancient times as a staple as well as a health aid.

Commercial yogurt tends to be slightly sour (compared to homemade), and contains thickeners like gelatin and pectin that mask its natural delicate flavor. Most households in India make their own yogurt every other day. In the tropics, it sets naturally in two to three hours. Buffalo milk is preferred over cow milk because the yield is sweeter, richer, and creamier in consistency. I make yogurt once a week; it is very easy, and you don't need any special gadgets or an elaborate yogurt maker. Begin with milk and a starter. The starter is nothing more than commercial plain yogurt that is a "live culture." Any milk—whole, low-fat, or nonfat—can be used, or mix any of these according to your preference. Whole milk makes firm, sweet yogurt, and low-fat has a very thick consistency, while the nonfat produces a thin-textured yogurt.

Temperature is vital to every step of making yogurt. First the milk must reach boiling point, then it is cooled until warm to touch before adding the starter. If you add starter to hot milk, the live bacteria will die, and if the milk is cold, the bacteria will take a longer time to multiply, and may not grow at all. Make sure the starter is fresh, or the yogurt may not set. After the starter is added, the milk mixture needs to sit in a warm place, undisturbed.

MAKES 4 CUPS

4 cups whole or low-fat (2%) milk (use whole milk for a creamier texture)

2 tablespoons plain yogurt, homemade or store-bought

1. In a heavy medium saucepan over medium-high heat, bring the milk to a boil. Remove from the heat and let the milk cool until warm, 110°F to 115°F. A thin layer of clotted cream will form at the top; you may leave as is or remove it with a slotted spoon. I place mine on toast and sprinkle with chutney powder (pages 190 or 191). Transfer the milk into a ceramic container. (Ceramic bowls are good for setting yogurt, but any Pyrex or Corningware dish is a good choice.)

2. Place the yogurt in a cup. Add 2 or 3 tablespoons of the warmed milk and stir to mix. Pour into the milk and stir to mix. Cover the container with a dinner plate or a lid. Do not use an airtight cover, because bacteria need to breathe. Cover and set the container in a warm place (70°F to 100°F) until the yogurt is set—the texture resembles flan or cheesecake. It has a watery wheylike liquid at the top, after anywhere from 6 to 12 hours, depending on the temperature and the quality of the starter. Transfer to the refrigerator, cover tightly, and use within 4 days.

VARIATION

Yogurt Cheese (Dahi ka Channa)

Line a deep mixing bowl with a double layer of cheesecloth. Spoon the plain yogurt onto the cheesecloth. Gather the ends of the cheesecloth and knot them around the handle of a wooden spoon. Rest the spoon across the top of the bowl so the bundle of yogurt is suspended about two inches above the bottom; if the bowl isn't deep enough, use a pot or a large jar instead.

Cover the bowl with plastic wrap and refrigerate for 12 hours. The whey will drain out of the yogurt, leaving thick, creamy yogurt cheese, which has a fresh, tangy taste. An alternative is to place the yogurt in a strainer or colander lined with muslin (or two layers of cheesecloth) and set it in a larger bowl, elevating the colander at least 1 inch from the bottom of the bowl; refrigerate for a few hours or overnight. One cup of yogurt yields 1/3 cup yogurt cheese if set for 8 hours. If you set it for 3 to 4 hours, the yield is 3/4 cup.

MANGO-MACADAMIA RAITA | Aam Raita

This incredibly fresh *raita* is marvelous for a stylish dinner. Traditionally it is prepared with bananas, but I like it best with mangoes. Select mangoes that are firm, with a reddish-orange blush at the stem end. Close your eyes and sniff the ripe fruit: it should have a pleasant, sweet aroma, and smell floral and fruity at the stem end. A strong smell indicates it is overripe. It should give slightly when pressed, like a peach. When fully ripe or yellow in color, use in recipes.

SERVES 6 AS AN ACCOMPANIMENT

2 large (1 1/2 to 2 pounds total) ripe mangoes

1 cup plain yogurt

1/4 cup coarsely crushed roasted macadamia nuts

1/2 teaspoon ground cumin

1/4 teaspoon salt

2 teaspoons grapeseed or vegetable oil

1/2 teaspoon yellow or brown mustard seeds

1 fresh green serrano or jalapeño chili, stemmed and cut in half

12 *kari* leaves (page 28) (optional), or cilantro leaves

1. Rinse and wipe the mangoes thoroughly. Cut off the stem end of each mango. Using a sharp knife, slice the mangoes lengthwise on either side of the flat pit, into 2 pieces, each about 1/2 inch thick. Cut the flesh of each half, making a fine crisscross pattern. Turn each half inside out and cut the fruit from the skin. Peel the remaining skin and cut the fruit into chunks. Transfer to a serving dish. Mash some chunks with a fork, saving the prettier ones. You should have about 2 cups of mashed mango.

2. Fold the yogurt and nuts into the mango. Sprinkle with cumin and salt and mix gently. Transfer to an attractive serving dish. Top with the pretty mango chunks. Set aside.

3. Have a spatter screen ready before you continue. Heat the oil in a small skillet over medium-high heat. Add the mustard seeds, immediately cover with the spatter screen, and cook until the seeds stop popping, about 30 seconds. Add the chili and *kari* leaves, if using. Stir and cook for a few seconds until the chili skins blister and the leaves are crisp. Remove from the heat and cool slightly. Pour the seasoned oil along with the seeds over the mango mixture and serve.

CUCUMBER AND RADISH RAITA | Sowthekai Pachadi

Here, the soft ripe tomatoes, the crunch of raw onion and cucumber, and the heat of green chilis are well balanced by cool yogurt and aromatic cilantro.

SERVES 6 TO 8 AS AN ACCOMPANIMENT

2 medium ripe tomatoes

2 medium cucumbers, such as English, pickling (about 6), or regular

4 small red radishes

1 small white or red onion

2 tablespoons chopped cilantro

2 cups plain yogurt

$1/4$ cup sour cream, or crème fraîche

1 teaspoon salt

1 teaspoon sugar

$1/4$ cup crushed roasted salted or unsalted peanuts

Several romaine lettuce leaves, for lining your serving bowl (optional)

Fresh green or red chilis, such as serrano or jalapeño, stemmed and slivered, for garnish (optional)

Tomato slices or wedges, for garnish (optional)

1. Core the tomatoes, chop finely, and transfer to a large mixing bowl. Peel and seed the cucumber, cut into $1/2$-inch cubes, and transfer to the bowl. Finely slice the radishes, then stack and julienne the slices; transfer to the bowl. Peel and quarter the onion and slice thinly lengthwise; transfer to the bowl. Sprinkle with the cilantro.

2. Just before serving, in a bowl, combine the yogurt, sour cream, salt, sugar, and peanuts. Beat with a fork until smooth. Fold into the prepared vegetables. Taste and adjust the salt and sugar according to the tartness of the yogurt. For a decorative presentation, if desired, line a serving dish with the lettuce leaves and mound the *raita* in the center; arrange the slivered chilis in petal fashion, and garnish with the tomato slices. Serve.

MAKE AHEAD The chopped vegetables in the bowl and the yogurt mixture can be prepared separately up to a few hours in advance, but do not combine the vegetables and yogurt mixture until shortly before serving.

VARIATION

This recipe can be made with just cucumbers or just tomatoes; finely chopped young raw bell peppers make a lovely addition, as do finely sliced white or purple radishes, daikon, or button mushrooms.

CARROT RAITA WITH TOASTED WALNUTS | Gajar Raita

This *Raita*, made without chilis, is particularly popular with children. Sesame seeds are not traditional, but they add a pleasant nutty flavor. I would serve this at a casual dinner or with Stewed Kabocha Squash with Mung Beans (page 400), *chapati* (pages 63–64), and Fresh Mint Rice (page 97) for a healthy meatless meal. If you must include a meat dish, try for the Goa Chicken Xacuti (pages 281–282) or Kerala-Style Aromatic Lamb (page 291).

SERVES 4 AS AN ACCOMPANIMENT

1/2 pound (3 medium) carrots

1/2 teaspoon salt

2 teaspoons freshly squeezed lime juice

1 cup plain yogurt

2 tablespoons dark raisins

2 teaspoons peanut or grapeseed oil

1/4 teaspoon yellow or brown mustard seeds

1/4 teaspoon cumin seeds

1/4 teaspoon sesame seeds

Chopped cilantro, for garnish

Coarsely chopped walnuts, toasted (see sidebar)

1. Wash and peel the carrots. Using a hand grater (the fine holes of a hand grater result in a fine, fluffy texture, which I prefer; the larger holes create a coarse texture), grate the carrots. Measure a generous 1 1/2 cups and place in a bowl.

2. Sprinkle the salt and lime juice over the carrots. Fold in the yogurt and raisins.

3. Have a spatter screen ready before you continue. Heat the oil in a small skillet over medium-high heat. Add the mustard seeds, cumin seeds, and sesame seeds, immediately cover with the spatter screen, and cook until the seeds stop popping, about 30 seconds. Remove from the heat and cool slightly.

4. Transfer the *raita* to a pretty serving dish. Pour the seasoned oil and seeds over the *raita* and mix gently. Garnish with cilantro and walnuts, if using, and serve.

MAKE AHEAD The *raita* will hold well for up to 2 hours at cool room temperature, or in the refrigerator, covered, for up to 1 day.

Toasting Nuts

To toast nuts, place in a medium skillet over medium heat. Cook, stirring, until the nuts are toasty and start to brown, 3 to 4 minutes.

CORN-ZUCCHINI RAITA | Makkai-Lauki Raita

Some of my students like this salad so much, they eat it for breakfast. Make your *raita* within an hour or so of serving for great texture and vibrant flavors. If you're not using the sour cream, be sure to replace it with equal amounts of yogurt.

SERVES 6 TO 8 AS AN ACCOMPANIMENT

2 ears corn

2 small zucchini

1 1/2 cups plain yogurt

2 to 3 tablespoons sour cream, or crème fraîche (optional)

1/2 teaspoon salt

1 tablespoon vegetable oil

1/4 teaspoon yellow or brown mustard seeds

1/4 teaspoon cumin seeds

1 to 2 fresh green serrano or jalapeño chilis, stemmed and slit lengthwise

1/4 cup finely chopped red bell pepper, for garnish

Chopped chives, for garnish

1. Husk the corn and, using a sharp knife, cut the kernels from the cobs and measure 1 1/2 cups. Trim the zucchini ends and cut into 1/2-inch cubes. Place the corn kernels and zucchini in a steamer basket over boiling water. Cover and steam until tender, about 4 minutes. Let cool to room temperature.

2. Transfer the vegetables to a bowl. Fold in the yogurt and sour cream, if using. Add the salt, taste, and add more if you prefer.

3. Have a spatter screen ready before you continue. Heat the oil in a small skillet over medium-high heat. Add the mustard seeds and cumin seeds, immediately cover with the spatter screen, and cook until the seeds stop popping, about 30 seconds. Add the chilis, stir, and cook for a few seconds, until the chili skins blister. Remove from the heat and cool slightly.

4. Transfer the *raita* to a pretty serving bowl. Pour the seasoned oil along with the seeds over the *raita* and mix gently. Garnish with the bell peppers and chives and serve.

SHORTCUT You can make this in the winter using canned or frozen corn; there is no need to steam canned corn.

YAM-POTATO RAITA | Aloo Raita

When I visited my grandmother's farmhouse as a youngster, I remember, she often tossed a handful of potatoes into the slow embers of her wood-burning clay oven. They cooked slowly for hours, until smoky and butter-soft inside. Then she used them in a number of creative ways. This quick *raita* is one of my favorites. If you're baking potatoes for another purpose, you might as well bake a few extra and keep some handy to make this dish. Think of it as a low-calorie, zesty "potato salad" without the mayonnaise.

SERVES 4 AS AN ACCOMPANIMENT

1 medium (6 ounces) sweet potato

1 medium (6 ounces) Yukon gold potato

1/2 teaspoon cumin seeds

1/4 teaspoon black peppercorns

1/8 teaspoon cayenne

1/2 teaspoon salt, or to taste

1 1/2 cups plain yogurt

4 good-size lettuce leaves

1/4 teaspoon sweet or hot paprika, or *chaat masala* (pages 41–42)

Minced fresh mint leaves

2 tablespoons shelled, roasted, salted or unsalted, coarsely chopped pistachios

1. In a pot of boiling salted water, cook the sweet potato and Yukon gold potato, covered, until tender, 20 to 25 minutes. Drain and cool to room temperature. Peel and cube into 1/2-inch dice.

2. While the potatoes are cooking, combine the cumin seeds and peppercorns in a small skillet over medium heat. Toast, stirring frequently, until the seeds are aromatic, about 5 minutes. Transfer to a coffee mill or spice grinder and grind to a coarse powder. Transfer to a mixing bowl.

3. Add cayenne and salt to the mixing bowl. Add the yogurt and whisk to mix. Fold in the diced potatoes. Cover and chill for 2 to 4 hours, if you prefer cold *raita*. Taste and adjust the salt, but remember that potatoes absorb salt when kept for some time.

4. Line a beautiful serving dish with lettuce leaves and scoop in the *raita*. Sprinkle the paprika over the top. Garnish with the mint and pistachios and serve.

MAKE AHEAD The *raita* can be prepared through step 3 and refrigerated, covered, for up to 1 day. The *raita* firms as it cools, so you may have to add at least 1/4 cup of yogurt to get the right consistency.

Any variety of potatoes—baby potatoes, red potatoes, and even blue and purple potatoes—can be substituted to make a multicolored raita.

GARLIC RAITA | Bellulli Pachadi

Garlic has five of the six tastes identified by the Ayurveda—sweet, salty, pungent, bitter, and astringent. Hailed as the "bulb of life," it is renowned for its numerous healthful attributes and medicinal properties. Eaten in moderation it is an effective stimulant, regulates blood circulation, aids respiratory problems, lowers cholesterol, and rejuvenates and detoxifies. My father taught me to eat two raw garlic cloves every day at dinnertime. To tempt my family, I concocted this recipe, which I'm sure even Gilroy Garlic Festival enthusiasts would approve of. Lately, it has become my favorite to serve alongside fish and meat dishes. Leftovers can serve as a salad dressing.

SERVES 3 TO 4 AS AN ACCOMPANIMENT

1 cup plain yogurt

1/2 teaspoon salt

1/2 teaspoon sugar

1/4 teaspoon ground white pepper

1 1/2 tablespoons vegetable oil

1/4 teaspoon yellow or brown mustard seeds

1/4 teaspoon cumin seeds

8 large cloves garlic, chopped

Sweet paprika, for garnish

1/4 cup finely chopped red bell pepper, for garnish

1. Place the yogurt in a bowl and whisk until smooth. Season with the salt, sugar, and pepper and mix well.

2. Have a spatter screen ready before you continue. Heat the oil in a small skillet over medium-high heat. Add the mustard seeds and cumin seeds, immediately cover with a spatter screen, and cook until the seeds stop popping, about 30 seconds. Add the garlic and cook, stirring, until lightly browned, 3 to 4 minutes. Remove from the heat and cool slightly.

3. Transfer the yogurt to a pretty serving bowl. Pour the seasoned oil along with the garlic and seeds over the yogurt and mix gently. Sprinkle the paprika over the top, garnish with the bell pepper, and serve.

ROASTED ZUCCHINI RAITA | Pachadi

Roasted zucchini becomes a cooling *raita* here. Serve as a dip or spread on small toast rounds.

SERVES 4 TO 6 AS AN ACCOMPANIMENT

1 pound (2 medium) yellow zucchini

1/2 cup plain yogurt

1/2 teaspoon salt

1/2 teaspoon sugar

1/4 teaspoon cayenne

2 tablespoons coarsely crushed, roasted salted or unsalted peanuts

1 tablespoon *desi ghee* (pages 47–48), or unsalted butter

1/4 teaspoon yellow or brown mustard seeds

1/4 teaspoon cumin seeds

1/2 pound large spinach leaves, stemmed, rinsed, and dried, for serving

Sliced ripe tomatoes, for garnish

Chopped cilantro, for garnish

1. Brush each zucchini with 1/2 teaspoon oil. Preheat the broiler. Roast the zucchini, turning occasionally, until the skin is completely charred and the pulp is soft, about 20 minutes. Let cool briefly, slit in half, and scoop out the soft pulp. Discard the charred skin. You should have about 1 cup of pulp. Coarsely chop the pulp.

2. In a bowl, combine the yogurt, salt, sugar, and cayenne and whisk until very smooth. Fold in the peanuts and zucchini.

3. Have a spatter screen ready before you continue. Heat the *desi ghee* in a small skillet over medium-high heat. Add the mustard and cumin seeds, immediately cover with the spatter screen, and cook until the seeds stop popping, about 30 seconds. Remove from the heat and cool slightly.

4. Just before serving, arrange the spinach leaves on a decorative serving dish. Scoop the *raita* into the center. Pour the seasoned oil along with the seeds over the *raita*. Garnish with the slices of tomato and cilantro and serve.

> MAKE AHEAD You can make the zucchini pulp (step 1) and store it, covered, in the refrigerator for up to 3 days. The *raita* can be prepared through step 2 and stored in the refrigerator, covered, up to 1 day in advance. The *raita* firms as it cools, so add more yogurt to achieve the desired consistency.

SCALLION-SPINACH RAITA WITH SESAME SEEDS | Palak Raita

This *raita* gets its kick from mustard seeds and dried red chilis. Cumin and sesame seeds add crunch and a nutty flavor, while the cooling yogurt brings it all together. Serve as an accompaniment to meat dishes and pilafs. You can strip this recipe down to a minimum and serve the spinach alone if you like, with the yogurt and seasoning.

SERVES 4 AS AN ACCOMPANIMENT

2 cups packed chopped fresh spinach leaves

1 tablespoon *desi ghee* (pages 47–48), or unsalted butter

1/4 cup finely chopped scallions (use both green and white parts)

1/4 cup grated carrot

1 cup plain yogurt

1/2 teaspoon salt

1 tablespoon vegetable oil

1/2 teaspoon yellow or brown mustard seeds

1/4 teaspoon cumin seeds

1/3 teaspoon black or white sesame seeds

2 dried red chilis, such as cayennes or chiles de arbol, stemmed and broken into rough pieces

1. Bring a pot of water to a boil. Place the spinach in a steamer basket, set over the boiling water, cover, and steam until tender, about 4 minutes. Immediately plunge the spinach into a bowl of ice-water to stop the cooking. When the spinach is cool enough to handle, drain and gently squeeze out the excess water and set aside.

2. Heat the *desi ghee* in a small skillet over medium heat. Add the scallions and carrot and cook, stirring, until the carrot is just tender, 3 to 4 minutes.

3. Transfer the spinach, carrot, and scallion to an attractive serving dish and fold in the yogurt. Season with the salt.

4. Have a spatter screen ready before you continue. Heat the oil in a small skillet over medium-high heat. Add the mustard seeds, cumin seeds, and sesame seeds, immediately cover with the spatter screen, and cook until the seeds stop popping, about 30 seconds. Toss in the chilis. Cook for a few seconds, until crisp and lightly browned. Remove from the heat and cool slightly.

5. Pour the seasoned oil along with the seeds over the spinach-yogurt mixture. Just before serving, stir once or twice to create swirls of oil.

VARIATION

The spinach may be replaced with amaranth, watercress, Swiss chard, kale, or collard greens.

PUNJAB BOONDI RAITA | Boondi Raita

You must have come across this *raita* as a side order at north Indian restaurants. Seasoned chick-pea flour batter is pressed through a special strainer and deep-fried to make pearls or *boondi*. Inexpensive packages of crisp-fried *boondi* are available at Indian groceries (see Sources, page 439); the easiest option is to buy a few packets (usually placed with chickpea flour noodles, *sev*, and other hot snack mixes) to keep on hand so that you can prepare this recipe on short notice.

SERVES 4 TO 6 AS AN ACCOMPANIMENT

4 cups *boondi* (see headnote)

1 1/2 teaspoon cumin seeds

2 cups plain yogurt

1 teaspoon sugar

1 teaspoon salt

1/2 teaspoon cayenne

Chopped cilantro, for garnish

1. Soak the *boondi* in a bowl of hot water for a few minutes until they swell. Gently squeeze the *boondi* between your palms, without mashing, to remove excess water. Transfer to a bowl.

2. In a small skillet over medium heat, toast the cumin seeds, stirring frequently, until the seeds are aromatic and darken a shade, about 5 minutes. Cool slightly, then transfer to a spice grinder or coffee mill and grind to a fine powder.

3. Transfer the yogurt to a pretty bowl and whisk with a fork until smooth. Add the sugar, salt, and cayenne and mix well. Gently stir in the *boondi*. Sprinkle the toasted cumin on top. Garnish with cilantro and serve.

WARM CHICKPEA AND GREEN MANGO KACHUMBER

| Kairi Koshimbir

In India, green mangoes are not only used in pickles but utilized like a vegetable as well. Green mango is really white inside, resembling daikon, jícama, or green papaya. Its juicy tart flavor is a natural bonus to a creative cook. I've partnered it with bland chickpeas (also known as garbanzo beans) and contrasting sweet coconut. The result is a warm, inviting salad with a wonderful hint of tanginess. Your grocer can probably find a very green mango from his stock, if you ask. Green mangoes are also available at Asian markets. If you have leftover cooked chicken or lamb in your refrigerator, by all means use some in this salad.

SERVES 4 TO 6 AS AN ACCOMPANIMENT

1 medium green mango

1 tablespoon vegetable oil

1/2 teaspoon yellow or brown mustard seeds

2 dried red chilis, such as cayennes or chiles de arbol, stemmed, seeded, and broken into rough pieces

2 cups cooked chickpeas (freshly cooked or canned, drained)

2 tablespoons freshly grated coconut (page 307), or defrosted frozen unsweetened coconut

1/2 teaspoon salt

Several lettuce leaves, for serving

1 small avocado

1. Wash and wipe the mango thoroughly. Peel the mango with a vegetable peeler. Using a hand grater (the fine holes of a hand grater result in a fine, fluffy texture, which I prefer; the larger holes create a coarse texture), grate about 1/2 inch of the mango on all sides, then grate the remaining fruit, carefully avoiding the large flat pit. Measure 1 cup and set aside.

2. Have a spatter screen ready before you continue. Heat the oil in a medium skillet over medium-high heat. Add the mustard seeds, immediately cover with the spatter screen, and cook until the seeds stop popping, about 30 seconds. Toss in the chilis and cook for a few seconds until crisp and lightly browned in spots. Add the mango, chickpeas, coconut, and salt and cook, stirring, until heated through, 5 to 6 minutes.

3. Just before serving, arrange the lettuce leaves in a decorative deep dish. Mound the salad in the center. Peel, pit, and dice the avocado, sprinkle it over the top of the salad, and serve right away.

RED AND GOLDEN BEET KACHUMBER WITH ORANGE

| Beets Kachumber

This is a variation on a salad I tasted several years ago at the Culinary Institute of America in St. Helena. Here the golden and red beets combine with tangy green mango. Save the graceful beet greens for making *saag* (pages 257–258).

SERVES 4 AS AN ACCOMPANIMENT

1 large red beet

2 medium yellow beets

1 small orange, separated into sections and white pith removed

1 small green mango, peeled and grated (see instructions in step 1 of previous recipe)

1/4 cup freshly squeezed lime juice

1/4 cup coarsely chopped almonds, toasted (page 208)

2 tablespoons *desi ghee* (pages 47–48), or unsalted butter

1 teaspoon yellow or brown mustard seeds

12 *kari* leaves (page 28) (optional), or 1/4 cup chopped cilantro

1.   To prepare the beets, cut off all but 1 inch of the stems and roots. Rinse, but do not peel. Cook, covered, in boiling salted water until crisp-tender, 40 to 50 minutes. When cool enough to handle, slip the skins off the beets.

2.   Dice the beets into 1/8-inch-thick wedges. Transfer to a decorative serving bowl. Add the orange segments and grated mango. Drizzle with the lime juice. Top with chopped almonds and toss to mix.

3.   Have a spatter screen ready before you continue. Heat the *desi ghee* in a small skillet over medium-high heat. Add the mustard seeds, immediately cover with the spatter screen, and cook until the seeds stop popping, about 30 seconds. Toss in the *kari* leaves and cook for a few seconds until crisp. Cool slightly and pour the seasoned oil along with the seeds and *kari* leaves over the *kachumber*. Serve right away.

CELERY ROOT KACHUMBER WITH FRESH DILL | Celery Root Kachumber

Sometimes labeled celeriac, celery root has a wonderfully pungent celery taste and aroma. The round knobby root has an intimidating, rough, hairy brown skin, which needs to be cut away, revealing the pristine white flesh. Select a root firm to the touch, with stiff, unmottled stalks and a healthy intact beard. The crisp, pungent root makes a delicious flavor combination with the exotic oil seasoning. Crunchy nuts add a lovely contrasting texture.

SERVES 8 AS AN ACCOMPANIMENT

1 medium celery root

5 to 6 radishes (red, white, purple, or a mixed bunch)

1 small bunch fresh dill

1/4 cup freshly squeezed lime juice

2 tablespoons vegetable oil

1/2 teaspoon yellow or brown mustard seeds

1/2 teaspoon cumin seeds

2 teaspoons *urad dal* (white split gram beans) (optional)

1/8 teaspoon asafetida

2 dried red chilis, such as cayennes or chiles de arbol, stemmed, seeded, and broken into rough pieces

1 teaspoon salt, or to taste

1/2 cup coarsely chopped salted or unsalted peanuts

Radish roses, for garnish (optional)

1. Peel the celery root (a small knife works best for the knobs and whorls). Briefly immerse in cold water acidulated with lemon or lime juice to prevent discoloration, drain, and grate using a food processor or the medium side of a box grater. Transfer to a large mixing bowl. Finely slice the radishes, then stack and julienne the slices; add to the bowl. Using a sharp knife, shave off the fronds of the dill (I like a rough chop), measure 1 cup, and transfer to the bowl. Add the lime juice and toss to mix.

2. Have a spatter screen ready before you continue. Heat the oil in a small skillet over medium-high heat. Add the mustard seeds, cumin seeds, and *dal*, immediately cover with the spatter screen, and cook until the seeds stop popping, about 30 seconds. Toss in the asafetida and chilis and cook for a few seconds, until crisp and lightly browned. Remove from heat and cool slightly.

3. While the seasoning cools, add the salt to the *kachumber*. Add the nuts and stir. Transfer the *kachumber* to a pretty deep dish. Pour the seasoned oil along with the seeds over the *kachumber* and mix gently. Garnish with the radish roses, if using, and serve.

QUICK CABBAGE KACHUMBER WITH PEAS | Cabbage Koshimbir

In this atypical salad, cabbage is cooked briefly so it retains its color, crisp texture, and sweetness. Warm salads are not part of Indian cooking—most vegetables are served either raw or fully cooked. I prefer crunchy vegetables, so I created this dish.

SERVES 6 AS AN ACCOMPANIMENT

1 medium (about 1 pound) green cabbage

2 tablespoons peanut or canola oil

$1/2$ teaspoon yellow or brown mustard seeds

$1/2$ teaspoon cumin seeds

2 fresh green serrano or jalapeño chilis, stemmed and slit lengthwise

$1/2$ cup fresh or frozen peas

$1/2$ teaspoon freshly ground black pepper

$1/2$ teaspoon salt

1 tablespoon freshly squeezed lime juice

Chopped cilantro, for garnish

1. Using a sharp knife, cut the cabbage in half crosswise. Starting at one end, finely shred the cabbage, preferably with the knife rather than a grater. Measure 4 cups, cover, and set aside.

2. Have a spatter screen ready before you continue. Heat the oil in a large skillet over medium-high heat. Add the mustard seeds and cumin seeds, immediately cover with the spatter screen, and cook until the seeds stop popping, about 30 seconds. Toss in the chilis and cook for a few seconds until the chilis are blistered. Add the cabbage, peas, and pepper and cook, stirring, until the vegetables are well coated with oil but still crunchy to bite, 3 to 4 minutes. Remove from heat and season with salt. Sprinkle with the lime juice and toss to mix. Transfer the *kachumber* to an attractive shallow dish, sprinkle with cilantro, and serve.

VARIATION

Cauliflower, carrot, beet, and mashed potato work in this *kachumber* as well.

FRESH PANEER: CHEESE PANACHE

Swadisht Paneer Nagme

There are many stories about how *paneer* came to be. My grand-mother's version tells of a daughter-in-law who accidentally dropped a wedge of lime into the milk she was heating. To her dismay, the milk curdled. Fearing the wrath of her mother-in-law, the woman tied the curd into a piece of cloth torn from her *sari* and hung it in a corner; later, she hid it under a heavy object. The mother-in-law found it anyway and, happily for all, was captivated by the taste. Another ancient legend attributes its discovery to an Arab, who was carrying his milk supply across the desert in a pouch made from a sheep's stomach hung around the neck of his camel. When he stopped to quench his thirst, he discovered that most of the milk had turned into a semisolid mass of curdled milk. The bobbing of the camel's head and the heat of the day had so shaken the milk that it was transformed into cheese. Whichever story we believe, it's safe to say that cheese was developed shortly after the domestication of the cow.

Like all cheeses, *paneer* started as a way to preserve fresh milk. Now it's a favorite food in its own right. The milk of choice for authentic *paneer*—a fresh, white, velvety, mellow farmers' cheese—comes from the water buffalo, the most common source of dairy products in India. Fortunately, *paneer* is easy to make at home with whole or low-fat (2%) milk.

Paneer's cooking characteristics distinguish it from other types of cheese. It has enough body to be sautéed or deep-fried without crumbling or melting. Even after prolonged cooking, *paneer* maintains its shape, texture, and flavor. I've devised a new technique that involves broiling *paneer* wedges for couple of minutes per side, until they're lightly speckled all over. Broiled *paneer* looks elegant and is flavorful. A softer, moister relative of *paneer*, called *channa*, is used in desserts, dips, sauces, and *koftas* (page 222).

If you are short on time, good quality *paneer* is available these days at most Indian groceries. Although tofu (bean curd) does not have the same lovely taste and texture as *paneer*, it makes an acceptable replacement. Either the firm or the extra-firm can be used. Cut or slice the tofu as suggested in the recipe, place the cut pieces between several layers of paper towels, and press lightly to remove excess moisture. Broil, sauté, or fry, if needed, or simply dice and use as recommended in the recipes.

If your local Indian market doesn't carry *paneer*, don't worry. India's beloved and versatile cheese is as close as your kitchen cupboard. In fact, there is really no need to buy *paneer*, because it can be made at home from ingredients you probably already have on hand.

FRESH BASIC PANEER | Sada Paneer

For this recipe, I like to use the readily-available low-fat buttermilk, which has mild acid flavor and still contains sufficient lactic acid to curdle the milk. The resulting *paneer* is very mellow-tasting, with a silky texture. Do not use nonfat milk. It sticks to the bottom of the pan and burns easily. Be sure to use a large heavy pan to avoid burning.

MAKES 8 OUNCES

6 cups whole or 2% low-fat milk   1¹/2 cups buttermilk

1.   In a large heavy saucepan over medium to medium-high heat, bring the milk to a boil, stirring occasionally. Add the buttermilk and reduce the heat to medium. Let the mixture return to a boil, stirring gently, until the milk curdles and separates from the whey (the pale green transparent liquid), 6 to 8 minutes. Turn off the heat and let stand, uncovered, to cool for about 15 minutes.

2.   Line a colander with a double thickness of cheesecloth. If you want to reserve the whey for cooking, or for future batches of cheese, place the colander over a bowl. Gently pour the contents of the pan into the colander. Gather the four corners of the cheesecloth and twist them together. Tie the corners with twine and hang the cheese from a faucet to drain into the sink for 3 hours.

3.   Place an inverted (upside-down) salad plate on top of a dinner plate (to catch the excess whey). Place the cheese in its cheesecloth on the inverted plate. Place a baking pan on top of the cheese. Fill an empty 1-gallon plastic milk container with water (or use another heavy container) and stand it in the pan for 2 to 3 hours while the cheese drains. The weight will form the cheese into a 4-inch roughly circular disc. Unwrap the *paneer* and place it on a cutting board. Using a sharp, thin-bladed knife, cut the *paneer* into 8 wedges, 2-inch cubes, or other desired shapes. If not using the cheese immediately, store it whole in a tightly covered container in the refrigerator for up to 3 days.

In place of the buttermilk, you may use other coagulating agents, such as 3 to 4 table-spoons distilled white vinegar; 3/4 cup plain yogurt (be sure to use yogurt made without gelatin, which could affect the texture); 1/4 cup or more freshly squeezed lime or lemon juice; or 2 cups of the *paneer* whey from a previous batch of cheese. When you are using any one of these agents, add it gradually; sometimes the curd forms before all of the coagulant is added. Once the curd forms, do not add any more of the coagulant—it might harden and toughen the delicate cheese. If, on the other hand, you've added all the cur-dling agent and curds have not formed sufficiently, add more of the agent (a teaspoon or two at a time) until the whey separates. Each of these starters gives the curd a different body, taste, and texture. Yogurt yields slightly sour *paneer*. Lemon juice adds a citruslike aroma. *Paneer* made with vinegar has a strong tangy flavor. If the *paneer* is too sour, hold the undrained cheese, still wrapped in the cheesecloth, under cold running water and rinse for 5 minutes to reduce the acidity, and finish the *paneer* as suggested. You can also use balsamic or rice vinegar, but the taste will be different.

Soft Curd Cheese *(Channa):* In addition to *paneer*, Indian cooks make a softer, moister rel-ative called *channa*. *Channa* is simply *paneer* that has been pressed for less time, so it retains more moisture and has a soft, spreadable texture.

To make *channa*, use the same process as for Fresh Basic Paneer, but reduce the draining time in step 2 to 2 hours and the pressing time in step 3 to 30 to 45 minutes. Transfer the soft cheese to a container and refrigerate until ready to use, up to 3 days.

Whisk *channa* with fresh herbs, minced garlic, and cracked pepper to make a zesty dipping sauce. Add crumbled *channa* to guacamole, dip, or salad dressings for a tangy fla-vor boost. Use as a spread on toasts. *Channa* is used frequently in Bengali desserts.

DELICATE MANGO SAUCE CROWNED WITH PANEER
| Paneer Mastani

Mangoes sold in American markets are disappointing compared with those of my homeland. When cooking, I use Alphonso mango pulp. I love creating recipes with mangoes, and I envi-sioned white, velvety, speckled *paneer* in a dazzling deep-orange mango sauce. Voilà! This recipe turned out delicious the first time I made it. It's sweet-smelling and as stunning in appearance as it is in taste. A bottle of lovely late-harvest chenin blanc is a heavenly match. For a shortcut, and of course extraordinary taste, use Alphonso mango pulp (pages 52–53) in place of fresh mangoes.

SERVES 4 AS A SIDE DISH

2 large ripe mangoes

2 1/2 tablespoons melted *desi ghee* (pages 47–48), or unsalted butter

1 recipe Fresh Basic Paneer (page 221), or 8 ounces store-bought

1 cup finely chopped yellow onion

1 teaspoon ground coriander

1/2 teaspoon ground cumin

1/2 teaspoon cayenne

1/4 teaspoon ground cinnamon

1/8 teaspoon turmeric

3 tablespoons freshly squeezed lime juice

1/2 teaspoon salt

Minced cilantro for garnish

1.   Wash and wipe the mangoes thoroughly. Working with 1 mango at a time, cut off the stem end of each mango. Using a sharp knife, slice the mango lengthwise on either side of the flat pit, into 2 pieces about 1/2 inch thick. Cut the flesh of each half, making a fine crisscross pattern. Turn each half inside out and cut the fruit from the skin. Peel the remaining skin and cut the fruit into chunks. Transfer to a blender or food processor and process to a smooth puree. Transfer to a measuring cup; there should be about 1 1/2 cups of puree. Set aside.

2.   Preheat the broiler. Cut the *paneer* into 8 chunky wedges. Brush the wedges with about 1/2 tablespoon of the melted *desi ghee*. Place on a lightly buttered broiler pan, 4 to 6 inches away from the heat source and broil until speckled with light-brown spots, 2 to 2 1/2 minutes. Cover loosely with foil and set aside.

3.   Heat the remaining 2 tablespoons *desi ghee* in a heavy medium saucepan over medium heat. Add the onion and cook, stirring, until the onion is very soft and starts to brown at the edges, about 5 minutes. Add the coriander, cumin, cayenne, cinnamon, and turmeric and stir for a few seconds until fragrant. Stir in the mango puree and bring to a gentle boil, stirring. Stir in the lime juice and salt. Cook until the sauce is very hot, 3 to 4 minutes.

4.   Spoon the mango sauce into a heated decorative deep dish. Arrange the *paneer* wedges, speckled surface facing up, in petal fashion. (You may also add the *paneer* wedges to the pan and cook a few minutes so that the *paneer* absorbs the flavors.) Garnish with cilantro and serve.

PAN-FRIED PANEER AND CHICKEN WITH KHADA MASALA

| Paneer Murg Khada Masala

This is a quick and tasty dish; the chicken and *paneer* are tossed together with coarsely crushed spices *(khada masala)* and tomatoes.

SERVES 4 AS A LIGHT MAIN COURSE

2 tablespoons *desi ghee* (pages 47–48), or unsalted butter

1/2 teaspoon salt

1/4 teaspoon turmeric

1 1/2 pounds boneless, skinless chicken breasts, cut into 2-inch pieces

2 teaspoons coriander seeds

1 teaspoon cumin seeds

1 teaspoon caraway seeds

1/2 teaspoon black peppercorns

4 green cardamom pods, seeds removed

1 cup thinly sliced yellow onion

2 teaspoons julienned fresh ginger

4 large cloves garlic, thinly sliced

1 fresh green serrano or jalapeño chili, stemmed and slivered

1 cup chopped ripe tomatoes

1 recipe Fresh Basic Paneer (page 221), or 8 ounces store-bought, cut into wedges

Chopped cilantro, for garnish

1. Heat 1 tablespoon of the *desi ghee* in a heavy large skillet over medium heat. Add the salt and turmeric and stir for a few seconds. Add the chicken and cook until tender, 5 to 6 minutes per side. Transfer to a plate.

2. While the chicken is cooking, combine the coriander seeds, cumin seeds, caraway seeds, peppercorns, and cardamom seeds in a coffee mill. Pulse a few times until the spices are coarsely crushed or to your liking. Set aside.

3. Heat the remaining 1 tablespoon of *desi ghee* in the same skillet over medium heat. Add the onion and cook, stirring, until very soft, about 4 minutes. Add the ginger, garlic, and chili and cook, stirring, until the onion starts to brown, 4 to 5 minutes. Add the ground spices and stir until fragrant, about 30 seconds. Add the tomatoes, *paneer*, and chicken. Cook, uncovered, stirring gently, until the tomato is soft and the chicken is nicely coated with spices, 5 to 6 minutes. Scoop into a warm serving dish, garnish with cilantro, and serve.

ROASTED PANEER IN FRAGRANT SPINACH SAUCE | Palak Paneer

Greens are a significant part of the Indian diet. You'll find them in robust stews and spicy sauces, as well as blanched and stir-fried with garlic and simmered with *paneer*, as in this delectable entrée. Broiling *paneer* and folding it into a creamy spinach sauce creates a dish rich in protein, iron, and flavor. Restaurants add cream; you may do so toward the end of cooking—about half a cup is sufficient.

MAKES 6 SIDE DISH SERVINGS

2 recipes Fresh Basic Paneer (page 221) or 16 ounces store-bought

1/4 cup melted *desi ghee* (pages 47–48), or unsalted butter

6 cups (1 1/2 pounds total) packed chopped fresh spinach

1/2-inch piece fresh ginger

6 large cloves garlic

2 to 4 fresh green serrano or jalapeño chilis, or less to taste, stemmed and roughly chopped

1 cup water

1/2 cup grated yellow onion

1 teaspoon ground cumin

1/2 teaspoon turmeric

1/2 teaspoon freshly ground black pepper

1 teaspoon salt

1/4 cup shelled roasted salted or unsalted pistachios

1. Preheat the broiler. Cut the *paneer* into 2 x 1/2 x 1/4–inch strips or into 16 wedges. Brush with about 1/2 tablespoon of the melted *desi ghee*. Place on a lightly buttered broiler pan 4 to 6 inches away from the heat source and broil until speckled with light-brown spots, 2 to 2 1/2 minutes; watch closely, as it burns quickly. Cover loosely with foil and set aside.

2. Place the spinach with 1/4 cup of water in a pot, cover, and cook over medium heat, stirring occasionally, until wilted, about 6 minutes. Immediately transfer the spinach to a bowl of ice water to stop the cooking and preserve its color. Let the spinach sit in the water for at least 5 minutes. Squeeze the spinach gently and transfer to a blender. Add the ginger, garlic, chilis, and 1/2 cup of the water. Process to a very smooth and velvety puree (adding a little more water if needed to keep the mixture moving). Cover and set aside.

3. Heat the remaining 3¹/₂ tablespoons of *desi ghee* in a heavy medium saucepan over medium heat. Add the onion and cook, stirring, until it starts to brown, about 6 minutes. Add the cumin, turmeric, and pepper and stir for a few seconds. Add the spinach puree, remaining ¹/₂ cup water, and the salt. Bring to a gentle boil, reduce the heat, and simmer until piping hot, about 5 minutes. Taste and adjust the seasonings, if necessary. Add the *paneer,* mix gently, and cook until the cheese is heated through. Transfer to a heated decorative serving dish, strew some pistachios over the top, and serve.

VARIATIONS

Occasionally, I vary from the traditional and add broccoli florets. Cook the broccoli with the spinach and puree together.

Kingfish in Spinach Gravy (Tarlleli Surmai)

Seafood can easily replace the *paneer* here. Coat about 1 pound of kingfish fillets with a mixture of 1¹/₂ tablespoons ginger-garlic paste (page 11), 1 tablespoon lime juice, salt, and cayenne and set aside for 15 minutes. Fry the fish in 1¹/₂ tablespoons of oil on both sides before simmering in the sauce. Use white cod or snapper if kingfish is not available.

GLAZED SKILLET PANEER WITH MUSHROOM AND BELL PEPPER

| Kadai Paneer

Paneer and vegetables are cooked together with *masala* until any sauciness becomes a beautiful, fragrant glaze. If you prefer, you may broil the *paneer* as in previous recipes such as Roasted Paneer in Fragrant Spinach Sauce (pages 225–226).

MAKES 6 TO 8 SIDE DISH SERVINGS

2 tablespoon vegetable oil

1/4 cup *desi ghee* (pages 47–48), or unsalted butter

2 large yellow onions, grated

2 tablespoon fresh grated ginger

8 large cloves garlic, minced

1 cup diced green or yellow bell pepper

10 white button mushrooms, quartered

3 1/2 cups chopped tomato

2 teaspoons *garam masala* (pages 36–57), or store-bought

2 teaspoons sugar

1 teaspoon salt

1 recipe Fresh Basic Paneer (page 221), or 8 ounces store-bought, cut into 1/4-inch wide strips

Chopped cilantro, for garnish

1. Heat the oil and *desi ghee* in a heavy large skillet over medium-high heat. Add the onion and cook, stirring, until softened, about 4 minutes. Add the ginger and garlic and cook, stirring constantly, until the onion is lightly browned, 8 to 10 minutes.

2. Add the bell pepper, mushrooms, tomato, *garam masala,* sugar, and salt to the pan. Reduce the heat to medium and cook, stirring occasionally, until the raw tomato smell dissipates and the vegetables are soft, 8 to 10 minutes. Add the *paneer* wedges and stir gently to mix. Turn off the heat, cover, and set aside a few minutes to let the flavors blend. Garnish with cilantro and serve straight from the pan.

PANEER STEAKS WITH HONEY SAUCE AND CASHEW

| Shahed aur Kaju Paneer

This is a contemporary-style dish I created for one of my son's birthday parties. When the teenagers applauded the flavors, I decided to include it in the book. The seared *paneer* brings richness to this elegant dish, and sesame seeds and nuts stud the rich sauce. This is a breeze to fix if you have *paneer* ready, or you can buy thick slabs of *paneer* at your local Indian market.

SERVES 4 AS A MAIN DISH, OR 8 AS A SIDE DISH

2 recipes Fresh Basic Paneer (page 221), or 16 ounces store-bought

1/4 cup vegetable oil

1 teaspoon salt

1/2 teaspoon cayenne

1/4 cup whole roasted salted or unsalted cashews

1 1/2 cups finely chopped yellow onion

4 large cloves garlic, minced

1 teaspoon ground cumin

1 1/2 cups chopped ripe tomatoes, or canned diced tomatoes

1/4 cup tomato ketchup

2 teaspoons honey

Chopped cilantro, plus additional sprigs for garnish

Sesame seeds

1. Using a sharp paring knife, slice each circular *paneer* disc crosswise, to get 4 circles of *paneer*. Heat 2 tablespoons of the oil in a heavy large skillet over medium to medium-high heat. Add the *paneer* discs in a single layer, and sprinkle with a little of the salt and cayenne. Sear both sides until lightly golden, 3 to 4 minutes per side. Sprinkle the second side with more salt and cayenne, if you prefer. Turn off the heat and set aside.

2. Heat 1/2 tablespoon of the oil in a heavy medium skillet over medium heat. Add the cashews and toast, stirring regularly, until light golden, 3 to 4 minutes; transfer to a plate and set aside. Add the remaining 1 1/2 tablespoons of oil to the skillet. Add the onion and cook, stirring, until soft, about 4 minutes. Add the garlic and cook, stirring, 3 to 4 minutes more. Add the cumin and stir until fragrant, about 30 seconds. Add the tomato and cook, stirring occasionally, until soft, 6 minutes. Add about 1/4 teaspoon salt, or to taste. Stir in the ketchup and cook 2 minutes more to let the flavors meld. Remove from the heat and stir in the honey. (Do not cook after adding the honey.) Add 1 to 2 tablespoons chopped cilantro and mix gently.

3. Turn on the oven to its lowest setting and warm four plates in it. Just before serving, place one circular *paneer* steak on each plate. Spoon a couple of tablespoons of honey sauce on top of each steak. Sprinkle with sesame seeds and the toasted cashews. Garnish each plate with cilantro sprigs and serve right away.

BOUNTIFUL BLOSSOMS:
THE VEGETABLE KINGDOM

Sabziown ki Bahaar

When I work in the garden, weeding and planting, my mind occasionally drifts back to India, to my mother's large, lush garden. Mother had a meticulous layout—roses at the entrance, followed by ornamental plants, a small hill in a corner covered with varieties of cacti and rocks, and a cascading water fountain in the center surrounded with blue, white, and pink lotuses.

The adjoining kitchen garden received special attention. It was filled with patches of green beans, assorted eggplants, onions, peppers, and squash of various shapes and colors. Rows of lush leafy greens veiled the herbs—basil, dill, cilantro, and mint. Peppercorn vines crept onto nearby arches and trellises, and cardamom stalks reached as high as 15 feet. The *kari*-leaf plant was almost as large as a full-grown tree.

Mother also planted "basmati leaf," which resembled scallion tops. She would add this herb to rice to impart a basmatilike fragrance. Groves of finger-size bananas, guavas, mangoes, and papayas were planted far from the house, and golden corn, sugarcane, and coconut trees lined the fence. The wide-spreading tamarind tree in the corner shaded almost a quarter of the yard. The cool trees were home to tropical parrots and parakeets. I learned that nothing was more gratifying than planting a seed and watching it grow into a mature plant. By touching and feeling the young plants, my mother said we were "talking" to them. Flowers, fruits, and vegetables were dearly loved and treated with respect.

When I came to the United States, I brought with me this love for the fresh bounty of the garden, and I also inherited my mother's passion for gardening.

VEGETABLE COOKING TECHNIQUES

Besides being economical and healthful, the dishes in this chapter are all relatively easy to prepare. The recipes are arranged by cooking technique.

Sautéed and Stir-Fry Dishes

Evenly cut pieces—julienned, chopped, or diced—are cooked over medium-high heat and gently lifted and turned and dressed in spice-infused oil until bright, crisp, and shiny. Stir-frying brings out the rich, deep flavors of vegetables, and the quick cooking helps them retain their valuable nutrients. Stir-fried dishes are at their best when served immediately. They can be served as side dishes or combined with other foods. Toss them with cooked pasta or leftover rice for a light meal. The traditional pan for stir-frying is the large, deep Indian *kadai*. The high, sloped sides of the *kadai* make it easier to sauté and toss the food. The similarly shaped Chinese wok makes an excellent substitute, and a heavy, large skillet will work just as well for any recipe in this chapter.

Seasoned Cooked Vegetables

With this technique, cooked vegetables are combined with seasoned oils. First, the vegetables are precooked to near tenderness—roasted, boiled, or blanched. Then, they are seasoned with spices, herbs, and other seasonings, and briskly cooked to give the resulting dish a feisty punch. This style of dish is not too saucy and has a moist texture.

A Food Fable

Once, God invited all the families in the vegetable kingdom to gather in the heavenly garden. He told them to pick and choose their appearance, color, flavor, and height as a reward. There was a huge turnout. Beets, beans, carrots, cucumbers, chilis, peas, potatoes, pumpkins, radishes, turnips, tomatoes, onions, and okra were all present. All the denizens of the vegetable kingdom gathered around the stage, and one by one, they made their requests.

Tomato walked up to the podium and bowed and said, "I would like to be red and luscious. I will contribute my bit by adding color to a dish, providing the thickness, and helping my fellow ingredients to soften when added with me into a dish." Eggplant, another lovely member of the nightshade family, asked for glossy purple and white skin and a voluptuous figure. Miss Okra looked resplendent as she walked up the steps onto the stage. Looking shy and nervous, she hesitantly began, "I am here to represent the female population of the vegetable kingdom. I promise to bring them recognition. Therefore, make me resemble long, beautiful ladies' fingers." There was a thunderous applause from the audience.

Bitter Gourd wanted to be different from the others, and so she chose to have a bitter taste. On the other hand, cucumber wanted to be cool and without any spikes. Pumpkin dispensed with the formalities. She began at once, "My Lord, make me into varied shapes and sizes. I want to be tiny like a decorative ornament that fits into a human hand. But at other times, make me enormous, so that no one can carry me. I would also like graceful arms—ummmm—leaves that creep onto nearby arches, and spill from trellises and trees." Potato's requests were more humble, however. He agreed to grow hidden beneath the soil, and requested a simple, earthy flavor. Although Carrot also chose to grow underground, she wanted a rich, vibrant color and hoped to be loved by both humans and animals. Then it was Chili's turn. With her sharp tongue, she proudly remarked, "I want to be the spice of life and save food from blandness. Without me no dish shall taste as good, and my fellow ingredients will be unable to achieve much without my help. Make me the undisputed queen." Onion, however, looked sad, and he said with dejection, "I will merely be cut and thrown into the pot. Please, Master, give me another day to think of my request, and I will return." As Onion walked home, he came across a group of people who were sobbing. Upon inquiring as to the reason, he learned that one of their relatives had met with an untimely demise and that they were overcome with sadness.

The next day, all the vegetables gathered before God for one last time. Onion returned to the podium. First, he thanked God for the extension that had been granted to him. "My Lord," he said respectfully, "I want to hold all the ingredients together. I will put my heart and soul into a dish, and because I will be slashed and tossed into the pot, I want everyone to shed some tears for me."

And so, we all cry for the onion. I loved to hear this story over and over again, and Mother always made it special.

Poriyals

These are southern Indian vegetable dishes with no sauce. The vegetables are covered and cooked gently over low heat. Sometimes they are steamed or cooked in very little water or their own natural juices. This aids in preserving the basic freshness of the vegetables. These dishes are wonderfully balanced, with subtle seasonings.

Kootu, Korma, and Shukto

Kootu, from the south, *korma*, from the north, and *shukto*, of Bengal in the east, are somewhere in between a dry curry and a thick stew. These classic dishes have a velvety sauce to be eaten with bread and rice. All three have yogurt as their basic ingredient. An assortment of vegetables is steeped in a soothing yogurt sauce.

Stuffed Vegetables

Brimming with flavor, stuffed vegetables raise simple ingredients to luscious new heights. Richly colorful and sensuous in form and texture, fresh vegetables are nature's "bowls of plenty," all but begging to be cut open, carved out, and filled with creative mixtures of your own making. All it takes is the clever use of ingredients and seasonings. Be inventive with regard to the vegetables you use, but take care and make sure they are sturdy enough to contain the filling without collapsing or leaking. Also, remember to pair vegetables with filling that complement one another in terms of flavor and color. More importantly, adjust the amount of filling according to the length and width of the vegetables. The recipes I've included go beyond the traditional Western bread or rice-based stuffing by using such ingredients as roasted peanuts, almonds, cashews, sesame seeds, fresh coconut, chilis, caramelized onions, garlic, mashed potatoes, and split peas with fragrant herbs and spices.

Kofta Curries

These are the crowning glory of Indian cuisine. The word *kofta* means meatball, a preparation found in various forms from India to the Middle East (see, for example, Kandahar Chicken Kofta in Ruby Red Grapefruit Juice, pages 276–277). Indian cooks have skillfully developed a similar cooking technique for vegetarian cuisine. A variety of vegetables—carrots, potatoes, leafy greens, radishes, cabbage, and squash—are combined with nuts, raisins, fresh herbs, and seasonings. A little chickpea flour or cornstarch is used to bind the ingredients. *Koftas* by themselves make lovely hors d'oeuvres; floating in a sauce, they make an attractive, hearty entree.

SKILLET-SEARED ZESTY ZUCCHINI AND EGGPLANT WITH PECANS

| Tavai Baingan

Our maid in India often cooked a tasty dish using large chunks of cauliflower and potatoes, turning and frying them until tender without adding a trace of water. Another of her specialties was deep-fried eggplant slices served with a sprinkling of chili powder and turmeric. I like to simply sear the eggplant, combine it with zucchini, and embellish it further with pecans and sesame seeds. For a complete meal, begin with Kerala Mussel Chowder (page 366), accompanied with Puffy Bread (pages 80–81), and almost any rice dish. Finish with Cakey Balls in Rose-Scented Warm Syrup (pages 412–413) for a special meal.

SERVES 4

1/2 pound (1 medium) eggplant, or substitute 3 Japanese eggplant

1/2 pound (3 medium) zucchini

4 teaspoons salt

1/4 cup pecans

1/4 cup vegetable oil

1 teaspoon sesame seeds

1/2 teaspoon cayenne

1/4 teaspoon turmeric

1/4 teaspoon sugar

1 tablespoon freshly squeezed lime juice

Chopped cilantro, for garnish

1.   Slice the eggplant and zucchini 1/8 inch thick. Place the slices in a colander in the sink or over a bowl, sprinkle with the salt, and toss to coat. Set aside for 10 minutes. Rinse thoroughly and pat dry.

2.   In a small skillet over medium heat, toast the pecans until lightly browned, 4 to 5 minutes. Chop coarsely and set aside.

3.   Heat 1 tablespoon of the oil in a nonstick 12-inch skillet over medium heat, rotating the pan so that the oil coats the bottom and the sides. Add as many eggplant and zucchini slices as will fit in a single layer in the pan. Cover and cook until the bottoms are lightly golden in places, 3 to 4 minutes. Turn and cook on the other side for 2 to 3 minutes. Transfer to a platter, set aside, and repeat with the remaining oil, eggplant, and zucchini in 2 or 3 more batches.

4.   Return all of the cooked eggplant and zucchini slices to the pan. Sprinkle in the sesame seeds, cayenne, turmeric, sugar, and lime juice and toss very gently. Cover and cook until heated through. Transfer to a warmed serving platter. Sprinkle with the pecans and garnish with the cilantro.

PEPPERY BRUSSELS SPROUT STIR-FRY WITH SESAME

| Tavai Tilwala Pattagobi

In 1498 Portuguese voyager Vasco da Gama stepped onto Indian soil and called out, "for Christ and for spices!" He paved the way for other Europeans to reach the spice world in India. In those days, not nearly enough black pepper was available to satisfy the enormous demand. Fortunately for us, modern production and transportation methods have made it affordable and easy to acquire. Pepper is one of my favorite spices, and in this recipe I use it liberally. Glistening brussels sprouts are stunning with crushed peppercorns and sesame seeds. For some added spice, sprinkle with Hot and Fragrant Curry Powder (page 35) during the last few minutes of cooking. This dish makes a great topping for freshly cooked brown or wild rice.

SERVES 6 AS A SIDE DISH

2 tablespoons sesame seeds

3 tablespoons vegetable oil

1 teaspoon yellow or brown mustard seeds

1 cup sliced yellow onion

3 fresh green serrano or jalapeño chilis, or fewer to taste, stemmed and chopped

1 teaspoon black peppercorns, lightly crushed

2 pounds brussels sprouts, trimmed of outer leaves and quartered

1 teaspoon salt

Dried unsweetened flaked coconut, or freshly grated coconut (page 307) (optional)

1. In a small skillet over medium heat, toast the sesame seeds until the seeds are aromatic and uniformly reddish in color, about 4 minutes. Cool thoroughly. Transfer to a coffee mill or spice grinder and grind coarsely. Set aside.

2. Have a spatter screen ready before you continue. Heat the oil in a large skillet over medium-high heat. Add the mustard seeds, immediately cover with the spatter screen, and cook until the seeds stop popping, about 30 seconds. Add the onion and chilis and cook until the onion is very soft and just beginning to turn brown at the edges, about 4 minutes. Add the pepper and sesame seeds and stir for a few seconds. Add the brussels sprouts and cook, stirring, until the sprouts are coated. Sprinkle with salt and reduce the heat to low. Cover and cook until the sprouts are crisp-tender, 10 to 12 minutes. Transfer to an attractive heated serving dish. Garnish with the coconut, if desired, and serve.

SWEET-SPICED SQUASH WITH GARLIC | Kumbala Palya

Squash is one of the most prized vegetables in Indian cooking. It's nutritious and simple to prepare. The chunks of squash in this colorful side dish melt on your tongue.

If you can't find banana squash in your market, you can substitute pumpkin or other hard winter squashes. Acorn and Hubbard are lighter, with a soft texture, and butternut squash offers a dense texture and rich taste. And though acorn and Hubbard squash must be peeled first, I prefer not to peel banana squash, because it gives the dish a nice texture.

SERVES 6

1 1/2 pounds medium wedge banana squash (see headnote)

2 tablespoons vegetable oil

1/2 teaspoon yellow or brown mustard seeds

1/2 teaspoon cumin seeds

1 teaspoon *urad dal* (white split gram beans) (optional)

3 large cloves garlic, minced

2 to 3 fresh green serrano or jalapeño chilis, or fewer to taste, stemmed and chopped

1/4 teaspoon turmeric

1 1/4 cups water

1 teaspoon light-brown sugar, jaggery (pages 51–52), or raw sugar

1/2 teaspoon salt

2 teaspoons freshly squeezed lime juice (optional)

Cilantro sprigs, for garnish

Freshly grated coconut (page 307), or defrosted frozen unsweetened coconut, for garnish

1. Wash the wedge of squash and pat dry. Do not peel. Using a large sharp knife, dice into 1-inch cubes to make approximately 4 cups. Cover and set aside.

2. Have a spatter screen ready before you continue. Heat the oil in a heavy medium skillet over medium-high heat. Add the mustard seeds, cumin seeds, and *dal*, if using, immediately cover with the spatter screen, and cook until the seeds stop popping, about 30 seconds. Toss in the garlic and chilis and cook until the chili skins blister and the garlic starts to brown, about 2 minutes. Add the squash cubes and turmeric and cook, stirring, for 2 to 3 minutes. Stir in the water, sugar, and salt. Bring to a boil, then reduce the heat, cover, and simmer until most of the water has evaporated and the squash is tender but not mushy, 12 to 15 minutes. Add the lime juice and remove from the heat. Let stand for about 5 minutes before serving to allow the flavors to blend.

3. Transfer the squash to a heated serving dish. Garnish with the cilantro sprigs and coconut.

YUKON GOLD POTATOES WITH ZESTY SEASONING | Aalu Gedde Palya

This simple dish is common to all regions of India and has many uses; served wrapped in *dosa*, stuffed in *samosa*, batter-coated and deep-fried as *bonda* or *wada*, and as a filling for sandwiches. It is also served as an accompaniment with puffy *poori* for brunch.

Some of the heat of the chilis will leach into the potato, making them less hot, but those who prefer a less spicy meal may chop the chilis in larger pieces to make them easier to pick out.

SERVES 8 TO 10 AS A SIDE DISH

2 pounds (6 medium) Yukon gold potatoes

1/4 cup vegetable oil

1/2 teaspoon yellow or brown mustard seeds

1/2 teaspoon cumin seeds

2 tablespoons dark raisins

1/4 cup roasted salted or unsalted cashews

1 cup finely chopped yellow onion

3 to 4 fresh green serrano or jalapeño chilis, or
fewer to taste, stemmed and chopped

1/2 teaspoon turmeric

1 1/2 teaspoons salt, or to taste

1/2 teaspoon sugar

1/2 lime, juiced

Chopped fresh cilantro, plus additional sprigs for
garnish

1.   Wash and scrub the potatoes and place them in a large pot. Add water to cover and bring to a boil. Boil until just tender, about 15 minutes. Let the potatoes sit until cool enough to handle, then peel and dice them into 1-inch pieces. Set aside.

2.   Have a spatter screen ready before you continue. Heat the oil in a heavy large skillet over medium-high heat. Add the mustard and cumin seeds, immediately cover with the spatter screen, and cook until the seeds stop popping, about 30 seconds. Toss in the raisins and cashews and cook, stirring, until the raisins are plump, about 1 minute. Add the onion, chilis, and turmeric and cook, stirring, until the onion is very soft, about 3 minutes. Reduce the heat to low. Stir in the potatoes. Sprinkle with the salt and sugar and mix thoroughly. If this is to be used as a filling, at this time the potatoes should be mashed while stirring. Otherwise, you can gently stir until thoroughly mixed. Cover and cook until heated through. Sprinkle with the lime juice and cilantro. Just before serving, adjust the salt to taste—remember, this is a potato dish, and potato absorbs salt as it sits.

Lush White Wines

Some nice choices for pairing white wines with Indian food include Riesling, chenin blanc, and Gewürztraminer. Gewürztraminer is often described as having a spicy flavor, which complements the spices used in Indian cooking. For more full-bodied whites like chardonnay or viognier, look for wines with good balance, that don't seem overly oaky or buttery, so that the applelike, tropical fruit flavors of the chardonnay or the floral, fruity qualities of the viognier shine through. The steely acidity in sauvignon blanc and fumé blanc match perfectly with the tartness of tamarind. Sparkling wines and off-dry whites such as Riesling, Napa gamay, and Gewürztraminer are good choices with my vegetarian dishes because they balance their natural sweetness. Rosés possess the fruitiness of a red and the refreshing crispness and body of a white wine, so they pair nicely with many recipes in this book. On the bitter end of the spectrum, drier whites like pinot grigio match well with a dish like Home-Style Bitter Melon (page 250) in the vegetable chapter.

Scoop the prepared potatoes into an attractive heated serving dish. Garnish with the cilantro sprigs and serve.

MAKE AHEAD This dish can be refrigerated, covered, for up to 5 days.

VARIATION

You can of course make this dish with other potatoes. Russet are very good all around and offer a mealy texture, while red new potatoes are firm, with a smooth texture. Toss in 1/2 cup fresh or frozen, thawed peas along with the raisins.

CHILI- AND GARLIC-STUFFED ROASTED EGGPLANT WITH MASALA

| Baingan Bharata

I've altered this classic dish by stuffing the eggplant with chilis and garlic for additional gusto. Like potatoes, eggplant is a principal vegetable and native to India. There are several varieties of eggplant, including Japanese or Asian, Italian, and white. Choose a strikingly shiny, firm and heavy, tight-skinned eggplant with a green stem. When gently squeezed, it should spring back, and it should sound hollow when tapped. A soft, spongy consistency is a sign that the vegetable is no longer at its peak.

Use the stalk as a "handle" while roasting the eggplant over an open flame. If you have a large quantity of eggplants to roast, you can use a charcoal grill or the broiler to save time. Once roasted and peeled, eggplant pulp can be stored for several days in the refrigerator.

SERVES 6 AS A SIDE DISH

1 1/2 pounds (1 medium-large) eggplant, stem intact

3 large cloves garlic, peeled and crushed

2 fresh green serrano or jalapeño chilis, stemmed and slit lengthwise

1/2 teaspoon plus 2 tablespoons vegetable oil

1/2 teaspoon yellow or brown mustard seeds

1/2 teaspoon cumin seeds

3/4 cup finely chopped yellow onion

1/4 teaspoon turmeric

1 cup chopped ripe tomatoes, or canned diced tomatoes

1/2 teaspoon *garam masala* (pages 36–37), or store-bought

1/2 cup fresh or frozen green peas (optional)

1 teaspoon salt, or to taste

1/2 teaspoon sugar

Chopped fresh cilantro, plus additional sprigs for garnish

1. For stove-top roasting, line a stove-top burner (electric and gas both work well) with foil (to catch the drippings). Alternately, you may preheat the broiler or prepare a charcoal grill to roast the eggplant.

2. Rinse and wipe the eggplant. Using a sharp knife, make a 2-inch slit in the middle of eggplant. Stuff the garlic and chilis deep inside and gently press closed. Brush the eggplant on all sides with the 1/2 teaspoon of oil. Place the eggplant stem-side up directly on the burner, roast over medium-high heat for about 5 minutes, and then lay it on its side. Turn the eggplant every few minutes, using the stem as a handle or using tongs, until the outside skin is completely charred and the pulp is butter-soft, 25 to 30 minutes. Place in a bowl and cover to trap the steam, which helps loosen the skin.

3. After about 20 minutes, the eggplant should be cool enough to handle. Hold the stem with one hand and peel off the charred skin with the other. Dip your hand in a bowl of cold water every now and then so that any skin sticking to your fingers will slip off in the water. (Alternately, you may slit the eggplant in half and scoop out the soft pulp. You may rinse the pulp in cold running water to wash away any remaining bits of skin, but if you do this, some roasted flavor will leach out; bits of skin are not a problem.) Place on a cutting board and cut off and discard the stem end, plus any tough, stringy parts. Chop the pulp coarsely along with the garlic and chilis. You should have 1 1/2 to 2 cups of pulp.

4. Have a spatter screen ready before you continue. Heat the remaining 2 tablespoons of oil in a heavy medium skillet over medium-high heat. Add the mustard and cumin seeds, immediately cover with the spatter screen, and cook until the seeds stop popping, about 30 seconds. Add the onion and turmeric and cook, stirring, until the onion is softened, 2 to 3 minutes. Add the tomato and cook, stirring, for another 3 minutes. Stir in the eggplant, *Garam Masala*, and peas, if using. Reduce the heat to low, cover, and cook, stirring occasionally, until piping hot, 8 to 10 minutes. Season with salt and sugar. Transfer to a warm serving dish. Garnish with the cilantro and serve.

VARIATIONS

Roasted Zucchini Masala (Zucchini Bharata)

Roasted zucchini tastes even better than eggplant. Roast zucchini as described in step 1 for 15 to 20 minutes, and proceed with the remaining steps. You'll need 6 to 8 medium zucchini.

Roasted Green Tomato Masala (Hara Tamatar Bharata)

Roast tomatoes as described in step 1 for 15 to 20 minutes, and proceed with the remaining steps. You'll need 5 to 6 large tomatoes. Substitute *goda masala* (pages 40–41) for the *garam masala*.

GREEN BEANS PORIYAL | Beans Poriyal

I prefer green beans that have been cooked until they are just firm around the edges and tender inside, tossed in a rich, southern-style seasoning and nestled under sweet fresh coconut. This dish is visually appealing and delicious beneath a roasted quail, grilled fish, or Cornish hen.

As with tomatoes and other hot-weather vegetables, there's nothing as good as a green bean fresh-picked and warm from the sun. Select lively, tender pods that have good color, are stiff rather than flaccid, and small rather than large.

SERVES 4

1/2 pound green beans, trimmed

2 tablespoons vegetable oil

1/2 teaspoon yellow or brown mustard seeds

1/2 teaspoon cumin seeds

2 teaspoons *urad dal* (white split gram beans) (optional)

1/8 teaspoon turmeric

1/8 teaspoon asafetida

1 to 2 fresh red or green serrano or jalapeño chilis, stemmed and chopped

1/4 cup water

1 teaspoon salt

2 tablespoons freshly grated coconut (page 307), or defrosted frozen unsweetened coconut

1. Cut the green beans diagonally into 1/2-inch pieces. Cover and set aside.

2. Have a spatter screen ready before you continue. Heat the oil in a heavy medium skillet over medium-high heat. Add the mustard and cumin seeds and *urad dal,* immediately cover with the spatter screen, and cook until the seeds stop popping, about 30 seconds. Add the turmeric, asafetida, and chilis and cook, stirring, for a few seconds. Add the beans and cook, stirring, for about 3 minutes more. Add the water and salt. Reduce the heat to low and cook uncovered (so the beans retain their original green color) until the beans are just tender and slightly crunchy, 10 to 12 minutes. Transfer the beans to a heated serving dish. Garnish with the coconut and serve.

MAKE AHEAD This dish can be refrigerated, covered, for up to 5 days.

VARIATIONS

This recipe can be made with a combination of yellow and green beans. The highly prized, tender French haricots verts make an interesting addition. Or substitute 2 medium diced rutabagas for the green beans. Half a teaspoon of *ajwain* seeds (page 20) adds a nice flavor dimension as well.

BELL PEPPER PORIYAL | Kuda Milagai Poriyal

Brightly hued, glossy, crisp-textured peppers merge splendidly with the meticulous Indian seasoning in this dish. The *masala* paste is made with nuts, seeds, and coconut—the sweetness perfectly balanced with piquant chili. For an informal meal, serve this dish with Flaky Cilantro-Laced Paratha (pages 76–77), Lamb Korma (page 288), and any of the *raitas* on pages 201 to 214.

SERVES 6 AS A SIDE DISH

1 tablespoon poppy seeds, preferably white

1/2 cup freshly grated coconut (page 307), dried unsweetened flaked coconut, or defrosted frozen unsweetened coconut

1/4 cup salted or unsalted roasted cashews

2 fresh green serrano or jalapeño chilis, stemmed and roughly chopped

1/2 cup water

1 teaspoon salt

4 medium bell peppers (green, red, yellow, and/or orange)

2 tablespoons vegetable oil

1. Coarsely grind the poppy seeds in a coffee mill or spice grinder (or coarsely crush on a flat surface with a rolling pin). Transfer the poppy seeds to a blender. Add the coconut, cashews, chilis, and water and whirl until smooth. Add the salt and pulse once to combine.

2. Rinse and wipe the peppers. Using a sharp paring knife, core the peppers and cut in 1-inch dice. Set aside.

3. Heat the oil in a heavy skillet over medium-high heat. Add the diced peppers and cook, stirring, until the edges start to brown, 4 to 5 minutes. Reduce the heat to medium-low and add the spice mixture. Stir and cook, uncovered, until the moisture evaporates and the peppers are tender and coated with the cashew mixture, 6 to 8 minutes.

PLANTAIN BRAISED WITH TAMARIND | Arati Kai Koora

Plantains are enjoyed as a starchy vegetable in southern India. Don't overlook this recipe just because you've never cooked with plantains before. The harmonious pairing of plantain with tamarind is further enhanced by the spiced oil, a lovely, contrasting note. Supermarkets sell plantains in various stages of ripeness—for this recipe you should buy them green, when their sugar is lowest and starch is highest. The easiest way to peel a plantain is to cut off the ends, make a slit lengthwise in the skin with a sharp knife, and peel the skin from the sides.

Serve this not-too-saucy dish hot, warm, or at room temperature. For a variation, try it with couscous or pasta.

SERVES 6 AS A SIDE DISH

2¹/4 pounds (3 medium-large) plantains

³/4 teaspoon tamarind concentrate dissolved in
¹/4 cup water

¹/2 cup water

³/4 teaspoon salt

¹/4 teaspoon turmeric

3 tablespoons vegetable oil

3 teaspoons *chana dal* (split chickpeas) (optional)

³/4 teaspoon yellow or brown mustard seeds

3 fresh green serrano or jalapeño chilis, or fewer
to taste, stemmed and chopped

¹/4 teaspoon asafetida

15 *kari* leaves (page 28) (optional), or cilantro

1¹/2 teaspoons light-brown sugar, jaggery (pages
51–52), or raw sugar

1. Peel the plantains, cut them lengthwise into quarters, and dice into 1-inch pieces. Transfer to a large saucepan. Add the tamarind liquid, water, salt, and turmeric. Bring to a boil. Reduce the heat to medium-low, cover, and cook until the water is absorbed and the plantains are tender, 6 to 8 minutes. Turn off the heat and set aside.

2. Have a spatter screen ready before you continue. Heat the oil in a heavy medium saucepan over medium-high heat. Add the *chana dal*, if using, and the mustard seeds, immediately cover with the spatter screen, and cook until the seeds stop popping, about 30 seconds. Add the chilis, asafetida, *kari* leaves, if using, and sugar. Cook, stirring, until the chili skins blister, about 1 minute. Add the plantains and cook until heated through, 3 to 4 minutes. Transfer to an attractive warm serving dish and serve.

RUTABAGA IN SILKEN YOGURT | Rutabaga Kootu

Rutabaga is not available in India, but I was pleasantly surprised when I first tried preparing it using this southern technique. I introduced it to some of my cooking students. Though it sounded unappealing to some, when they tried it, the students were amazed. One of them quipped, "It makes me look at the lowly rutabaga with the same admiration I usually save for truffles or heirloom tomatoes." Once you make this recipe, I'm sure you too will be hooked.

SERVES 4 AS A SIDE DISH

1¹/₄ pounds (4 medium) rutabagas

¹/₂ cup plain yogurt

3 tablespoons vegetable oil

1 teaspoon yellow or brown mustard seeds

1 teaspoon cumin seeds

¹/₂ teaspoon turmeric

¹/₂ teaspoon cayenne

¹/₂ cup water

1 teaspoon salt

Freshly grated coconut (page 307), or defrosted frozen unsweetened coconut, for garnish

1. Wash and cut the ends of the rutabagas. Peel and cut into ¹/₂-inch dice. Transfer to a large bowl. Add the yogurt and toss well. Set aside to marinate at room temperature for 15 to 20 minutes.

2. Have a spatter screen ready before you continue. Heat the oil in a heavy medium skillet over medium-high heat. Add the mustard and cumin seeds, immediately cover with the spatter screen, and cook until the seeds stop popping, about 30 seconds. Add the turmeric and cayenne and stir for a few seconds until fragrant. Add the water and salt, stir well, and bring to a boil. Reduce the heat to low and stir in the rutabaga along with the marinating yogurt. Cover and cook, stirring occasionally, until the rutabagas are tender and the sauce thickens to the consistency of ketchup, 15 to 20 minutes. Transfer to a heated serving dish. Garnish with coconut and serve.

MAKE AHEAD This dish can be refrigerated, covered, for up to 5 days. Rewarm over low heat.

QUICK AND EASY YAMS IN HERB SAUCE | Gedde Kootu

Though the ingredients may sound similar to those in the previous recipe, the technique for preparing these yams is quite different, with refreshing herbal flavors. Plantains are also lovely cooked in this way. This *kootu* makes an attractive light main course to serve with Flaky Cumin-Scented Paratha (pages 74–75), over pasta, with roast poultry, or as a filling for soft tacos.

SERVES 4 AS A SIDE DISH

1¼ pounds (2 large) yams

1 to 2 fresh green serrano or jalapeño chilis, stemmed

1 cup plain yogurt

¼ cup lightly packed cilantro

¼ teaspoon cumin seeds, lightly crushed

⅛ teaspoon turmeric

¼ teaspoon salt

2 tablespoons vegetable oil

1 teaspoon yellow or brown mustard seeds

2 dried red chilis, such as cayennes or chiles de arbol, stemmed and broken into rough pieces

Pinch of asafetida

1. Wash the yams and place in a large pot with salted water to cover. Bring to a boil and boil until just tender, about 15 minutes. When cool enough to handle, peel and cut into ½-inch pieces. Transfer to a skillet.

2. Combine the fresh chilis, ½ cup of the yogurt, and the cilantro in a blender. Process until finely pureed and as smooth as possible. Pour over the yams in the skillet. Add the remaining ½ cup of yogurt, the cumin seeds, turmeric, and salt and toss well. Bring the mixture to a gentle boil and simmer for 6 to 8 minutes to let the flavors meld. Scoop into a warm serving dish.

3. Have a spatter screen ready before you continue. Heat the oil in a small skillet over medium-high heat. Add the mustard seeds, immediately cover with the spatter screen, and cook until the seeds stop popping, about 30 seconds. Add the dried chilis and asafetida and cook for a few seconds until crisp and lightly browned. Remove from the heat and cool slightly. Pour the seasoned oil, along with the seeds, over the yams. Serve right away.

> MAKE AHEAD This dish can be prepared through step 2 and refrigerated, covered, for up to 2 days. Before serving, rewarm over low heat and pour the freshly prepared oil seasoning over the dish.

MIXED VEGETABLE KOOTU | Moru Kootu

Don't be afraid to use yogurt in cooking—lower the heat first and add a little yogurt at a time. You'll be treated to a voluptuously creamy texture, without the cream. If you do not have plantains, three half-ripe bananas are an acceptable substitute. Serve this mélange bathed in mild, nutty yogurt sauce with Kerala-Style Aromatic Lamb (page 291) and Fresh Mint Rice (page 97) for a casual meal.

SERVES 8 AS A COMPLIMENTARY DISH

1 teaspoon vegetable oil

4 dried red chilis, such as cayennes or chiles de arbol, or fewer to taste, stemmed, seeded, and broken into rough pieces

2 tablespoons *chana dal* (split chickpeas)

1 tablespoon coriander seeds

1 teaspoon fenugreek seeds

1/4 cup dried unsweetened flaked coconut

1 cup plain yogurt

1/2 pound (2 large) Japanese eggplant

1 pound (2 medium) plantains

3 tablespoons *desi ghee* (pages 47–48), or unsalted butter

1 teaspoon yellow or brown mustard seeds

20 *kari* leaves (page 28) (optional) or cilantro

2 cups 1-inch cauliflower florets with stems

1/4 teaspoon turmeric

1 cup water

1 teaspoon salt

1. Heat the oil in a small skillet over medium heat. Add the chilis, *chana dal*, and coriander and fenugreek seeds and toast, shaking the pan frequently, until toasty smelling and the seeds have darkened a bit, 3 to 4 minutes. Add the coconut and toast for 2 minutes more. Cool slightly. Transfer to a spice grinder or coffee mill and grind to a fine powder. Transfer to a mixing bowl and whisk in the yogurt. Set aside.

2. Dice the eggplants; you should have 2 cups. Peel the plantains (or half-ripe bananas); you should have 2 cups.

3. Have a spatter screen ready before you continue. Heat the *desi ghee* in a heavy skillet over medium-high heat. Add the mustard seeds, immediately cover with the spatter screen, and cook until the seeds stop popping, about 30 seconds. Reduce the heat to medium. Add the *kari* leaves, if using. After a few seconds, when the leaves are crisp, add the diced eggplant, plantains, and cauliflower along with the turmeric and cook, stirring, for 2 to 3 minutes. Stir in the water and salt. Bring to a gentle boil, cover, and cook until the eggplant is just tender, about 5 minutes. Stir in the yogurt mixture. Simmer until the vegetables are heated through and the flavors meld, 5 to 6 minutes more.

YAMS AND GREEN BEANS IN AN AROMATIC VELVETY SAUCE

| Tarkari Kari

This recipe makes use of one large onion in two different ways. One half is used for the paste, and the other half is cooked along with the vegetables, providing a unique texture. Cauliflower, broccoli, or carrots can be utilized here to make this dish different each time you prepare it.

SERVES 4 AS A SIDE DISH

1 large yellow onion

2 dried red chilis, such as cayennes or chiles de arbol, stemmed, seeded and broken into rough pieces

2 teaspoons coriander seeds

3 whole cloves

1/4 teaspoon black peppercorns

1/2-inch cinnamon stick

2 tablespoons dried unsweetened flaked coconut

1 1/2 cups water

2 tablespoons vegetable oil

1/4 teaspoon yellow or brown mustard seeds

1/4 teaspoon cumin seeds

1/8 teaspoon turmeric

1 bay leaf

2 cups peeled and diced (1-inch pieces) yams

3/4 teaspoon salt

1/2 cup chopped (1/2-inch pieces) green beans

1.   Peel the onion and cut it in half lengthwise. Slice one half of the onion lengthwise, and finely chop the other half.

2.   In a small skillet, combine the chilis, coriander seeds, cloves, peppercorns, and cinnamon stick. Toast over medium heat, shaking the pan frequently, until toasty smelling and the seeds have darkened a bit, 3 to 4 minutes. Add the coconut and toast 2 minutes more. Cool slightly. Transfer to a spice grinder or coffee mill and grind to a fine powder. Transfer to a blender. Add the sliced onion and 1/2 cup of the water and process until smooth

3.   Have a spatter screen ready before you continue. Heat the oil in a heavy saucepan over medium-high heat. Add the mustard and cumin seeds, immediately cover with the spatter screen, and cook until the seeds stop popping, about 30 seconds. Add the chopped onion, turmeric, and bay leaf and cook until the onion starts to brown at the edges, about 4 minutes. Stir in the pureed spice mixture. Cook, stirring, until the raw onion smell dissipates, 8 to 10 minutes. Add the yams, and stir to mix. Add the remaining 1 cup water and the salt, and bring the mixture to a boil. Reduce the heat to low, cover, and cook for 10 minutes. Stir in the green beans, and cook, covered, until the yam is tender, about 15 minutes. Transfer to a warm deep dish and serve hot.

CHETTINAD CORN SIMMERED WITH TANGY TAMARIND

| Mokka Jonna Kulambu

Every region in the Indian Subcontinent boasts its own version of vegetable curry. Of late, Chettinad cuisine from southern India has become popular. In this home-style Chettinad dish, I've decided to use corn on the cob instead of native squash. The southern Indian flavors of tamarind, coconut, and fenugreek blend beautifully with corn's sweet taste, making this a wondrously complex dish.

Serve with Lucknow Mixed Vegetable Biryani (pages 121–122), a creamy *raita*, Flaky Cilantro-Laced Paratha (pages 76–77), and limeade for a complete meatless meal.

SERVES 4 TO 6

4 tender corn cobs, husks removed

2 to 4 dried red chilis, such as cayennes or chiles de arbol, or fewer to taste, stemmed, seeded, and broken into rough pieces

1 teaspoon fenugreek seeds

2 teaspoons coriander seeds

1/2 teaspoon plus 2 tablespoons vegetable oil

1 cup freshly grated coconut (page 307), or defrosted frozen unsweetened coconut

2 teaspoons tamarind concentrate dissolved in 1/4 cup water

2 cups water

2 teaspoons light-brown sugar, jaggery (pages 51–52), or raw sugar

1 teaspoon salt

1/2 teaspoon turmeric

1 teaspoon yellow or brown mustard seeds

10 *kari* leaves (pages 28) (optional) or cilantro

Cilantro sprigs, for garnish

1. Cook the corn in a large pot of boiling salted water until the kernels are just tender, about 10 minutes. When the cobs are cool enough to handle, cut each in 2-inch pieces.

2. In a small skillet over medium heat, combine the chilis and fenugreek and coriander seeds with the 1/2 teaspoon of oil. Toast, shaking the pan frequently, until aromatic and the seeds start to darken, 3 to 4 minutes. Let cool slightly. Transfer to a coffee mill or spice grinder and grind to a fine powder. Transfer to a blender. Add the coconut and tamarind liquid. Process until finely pureed and as smooth as possible.

3. Transfer the coconut mixture to a heavy saucepan and add the water, sugar, salt, turmeric, and corn. Bring to a boil, then reduce the heat and simmer until the sauce thickens, 10 to 12 minutes.

4. Have a spatter screen ready before you continue. Heat the remaining 2 tablespoons of oil in a small skillet over medium-high heat. Add the mustard seeds, immediately cover with the spatter screen, and cook until the seeds stop popping, about 30 seconds. Add the *kari* leaves, if using. After few seconds, when the leaves are crisp, remove from the heat. With a slotted spoon, transfer the corn to a warm serving dish, then ladle the sauce over it. Pour the oil seasoning along with the seeds over the corn. Decorate with cilantro sprigs and serve.

MAKE AHEAD This dish can be prepared through step 3 and refrigerated, covered, for up to 5 days. Thin with a little water if necessary, and adjust the salt before serving.

QUEEN'S MANGO AND KUMQUAT WITH SUBTLE CITRUS-CURRY SAUCE | Sasam

While writing this book, I have drawn inspiration from a little-known Indian heroine, a brave queen of my Indian home state, Karnataka. Rani Channamma, the queen of Kittur, is an icon for many people in the independence movement in southwestern India. Her example set in motion the freedom struggle that eventually rid the subcontinent of its colonial rulers. When Rani's husband died young, she almost immediately assumed control of the small kingdom. She was an able administrator, a shrewd politician, and a staunch defender of freedom. A gallant leader, she fought single-handedly against the British. In her gentler moments, she encouraged the culinary arts and poetry and enjoyed her own botanical garden. To honor courageous Rani, I have created this special recipe with sesame and fruits.

My family history ties me to this heroic woman. My great-grandfather, Gurshidappa, was the commander-in-chief of her army. When the British army attacked Kittur, the queen was defended by several hundred of her brave personal warriors. The fierce battle lasted for several days, and in the end, Rani succumbed to injuries. Gurshidappa, my great-grandfather, killed British general Thackeray on the battlefield, for which he was awarded the highest honor. Each time my family visits India, I take my sons to the museum where my great-grandfather's sword, shield, and armor are on display, donated by my grandmother.

1 heaping tablespoon sesame seeds

1 teaspoon fenugreek seeds

2 tablespoons dried unsweetened flaked coconut

3 pounds (4 large) ripe mangoes

1/2 cup kumquats

1 cup orange juice

1/2 cup freshly squeezed lime juice

1 teaspoon cayenne

1 teaspoon light-brown sugar, jaggery (pages 51–52), or raw sugar

1 teaspoon salt

1/2 teaspoon turmeric

2 tablespoons vegetable oil

1 teaspoon yellow or brown mustard seeds

1. In a small heavy skillet over medium heat, combine the sesame and fenugreek seeds. Toast, stirring occasionally, until the seeds are aromatic and darken one or two shades, 4 to 5 minutes. Add the coconut and cook, stirring, until toasty, about 2 minutes. Transfer to a coffee mill or spice grinder and grind to a fine powder. Set aside.

2. Rinse and wipe the mangoes thoroughly. Cut off the stem end of each mango. Using a sharp knife, slice the mangoes lengthwise on either side of the flat pit, into 2 pieces about 1/2 inch thick. Cut the flesh of each half, making a fine crisscross pattern. Turn each half inside out and cut the fruit from the skin. Peel the remaining skin and cut the fruit into chunks. You should have about 4 cups of mango. Rinse and wipe the kumquats. Using a small, sharp paring knife, cut off the little green stems and discard, then cut the fruits in half lengthwise. Larger kumquats may be quartered. Remove the seeds and discard. Or leave them whole if you like, skin, seeds, and all.

3. In a heavy saucepan, combine the mangoes, kumquats, orange and lime juices, cayenne, sugar, salt, turmeric, and sesame powder. Bring to a boil. Reduce the heat, cover partially, and simmer, stirring occasionally, until slightly thick, about 5 minutes. Adjust salt and sugar to taste.

4. Have a spatter screen ready before you continue. Heat the oil over medium-high heat in a small skillet. Add the mustard seeds, immediately cover with the spatter screen, and cook until the seeds stop popping, about 30 seconds. Remove from the heat. Transfer the mango-kumquat curry to a warm serving dish. Pour the oil seasoning along with the seeds on top and serve hot.

MAKE AHEAD This dish may be refrigerated, covered, for up to 4 days. Rewarm over medium heat or in a microwave oven. If the curry is too thick, thin it with 1 to 2 tablespoons of orange juice.

HOME-STYLE BITTER MELON | Pawakkai Kari

The beauty of Indian-style vegetables is that even such humble ingredients as the "bitter" melon turn delicious with skillful cooking. There is a saying in India: At least once a year, eat bitter melon to cleanse your system. If you've never cooked with this vegetable before, I recommend you make this recipe your first foray. Here the bitter melon is first soaked in water, then cooked with tamarind and turmeric to remove some bitterness, and finally combined with appropriate seasonings for a harmonious blend.

SERVES 6 AS A SIDE DISH

1 1/2 pounds (8 to 10 small) bitter melons

1 1/4 cups water

1/2 teaspoon tamarind concentrate

1/4 teaspoon turmeric

1 teaspoon salt

2 tablespoons vegetable oil

2 tablespoons *chana dal* (split chickpeas)

4 to 6 dried red chilis, such as cayennes or chiles de arbol, or fewer to taste, stemmed and broken into rough pieces

1 cup roughly chopped yellow onion, or 10 to 12 pearl onions, peeled

6 cloves garlic, minced

2 tablespoons dried unsweetened flaked coconut

3 teaspoons light-brown sugar, jaggery (pages 51–52), or raw sugar

Chopped cilantro, for garnish

1. Rinse the melons and cut off the ends. Cut the melons in half lengthwise. Using a spoon, scoop out the seeds and chop into 1-inch pieces. You should have about 4 cups total. In a large bowl, soak the melon in water for 30 minutes to remove the bitterness. Drain well and transfer to a saucepan. Add 1 cup of the water, the tamarind concentrate, turmeric, and salt. Bring the mixture to a boil. Cover and boil until the melon is just tender and most of the water has evaporated, about 10 minutes. Set aside.

2. Heat the oil in a small skillet over medium heat. Add the *chana dal* and chilis and cook for a few seconds, stirring, until the chilis darken a shade and send up a slight wisp of smoke. Add the onion and garlic and cook, stirring regularly, until the onion starts to brown and the garlic is blotchy in places, about 5 minutes. Add the coconut and cook, stirring, until toasty, about 2 minutes. Remove from the heat. Let cool and transfer the contents to a blender. Add the remaining 1/4 cup of water and blend to a smooth paste.

3. Transfer the paste to the saucepan containing the bitter melon. Add the sugar, cover, and cook over low heat until the flavors meld, about 5 minutes. Sprinkle with 2 to 3 tablespoons of water if the curry starts to stick to the pan. Transfer to a warm deep dish and serve garnished with cilantro.

BROCCOLI-CAULIFLOWER MANGALORE CURRY | Cauliflower Ghassi

When I give my husband a shopping list for groceries, he invariably forgets a few things, but he always brings home cauliflower, a large head of cauliflower. Send him back two days later and there's another cauliflower! Out of that abundance was born this curry, based on a Mangalore dish from southern India.

One reason many cooks shy away from Indian cooking is the long ingredients lists, like the one in this recipe. One rule of thumb is to stock your pantry with staples such as mustard seed, cumin seed, turmeric, and other basic spices, tamarind concentrate, and a few varieties of *dal* (dried beans and peas), which these days are available at mainstream markets. Then you don't need to make so many trips to Indian grocery stores. That's the beauty of Indian cooking.

MAKES 4 TO 6 SERVINGS

3 tablespoons vegetable oil

1 cup finely chopped yellow onion

1 teaspoon ground coriander

1/2 teaspoon black peppercorns

1/2 teaspoon ground cumin

1/2 teaspoon ground cinnamon

1/4 teaspoon ground fenugreek

1/2 teaspoon tamarind concentrate, dissolved in 1 cup water

1/2-inch piece fresh ginger, minced

1 large clove garlic, minced

1/8 teaspoon turmeric

1 teaspoon sweet paprika

1 cup Fresh Coconut Milk (page 308), or canned unsweetened coconut milk

1 cup 1-inch broccoli florets with stems

1 1/2 cups 1-inch cauliflower florets with stems

1 teaspoon salt

1. Heat 2 tablespoons of the oil in a small skillet over medium heat. Add the onion and cook, stirring, until the edges start to brown, about 6 minutes. Stir in the coriander, peppercorns, cumin, cinnamon, and fenugreek. Cook, stirring, until aromatic, about 1 minute. Transfer to a blender. Add the tamarind liquid and process into a thick puree. Set aside.

2. Heat the remaining 1 tablespoon of oil in a large heavy skillet over medium heat. Add the ginger, garlic, and turmeric and cook, stirring, until aromatic, about 1 minute. Add the paprika and the tamarind puree and cook, stirring, for 4 to 5 minutes. Add the coconut milk and cook over low heat, stirring occasionally, for 5 minutes more. Add the broccoli, cauliflower, and salt and cook, uncovered and stirring occasionally, until the sauce is thick and the cauliflower is tender, 8 to 10 minutes. Transfer to a warm serving dish and serve.

SAUTÉED OKRA IN TURMERIC-TINTED YOGURT

| Vendakkai Mor Thalippu

You'll be surprised by the flavor of this simple dish, not to mention the beautiful hue. Fresh okra is most plentiful from July through September. Look for small, crisp, brightly colored pods without blemishes. Traditionally, half a tablespoon of coconut oil is drizzled on the finished dish before serving, but you can use olive oil if you prefer.

For a special meal, start off with Chicken Mulligatawny with Mixed Vegetables (page 368), accompany the okra with Scallop Biryani Spiked with Coconut (pages 118–119) and Banana and Peach Chutney (page 186), and finish with Vermicelli Pudding with Fresh Berries (page 415).

SERVES 8 AS A SIDE DISH

1 pound okra

1 large yellow onion

6 tablespoons vegetable oil

1 teaspoon yellow or brown mustard seeds

1 teaspoon fenugreek seeds

20 to 30 *kari* leaves (page 28) (optional) or cilantro

4 to 6 dried red chilis, such as cayennes or chiles de arbol, or fewer to taste, stemmed and broken into rough pieces

1 teaspoon turmeric

3 cups plain yogurt

1 teaspoon salt

1/2 teaspoon sugar

1. Wash the okra and cut off the stems. Slit the smaller okra lengthwise and cut the remaining okra into 1/2-inch-thick slices. Peel the onion, cut it lengthwise, and thinly slice each half. You should have about 2 cups of onions.

2. Have a spatter screen ready before you continue. Heat the oil over medium-high heat in a heavy skillet. Add the mustard and fenugreek seeds, immediately cover with the spatter screen, and cook until the seeds stop popping, about 30 seconds. Add the *kari* leaves, if using, and chilis. After few seconds, when the leaves crisp, add the okra, onion, and turmeric. Cook, stirring frequently, until the okra is crisp-tender, the slimy juices have disappeared, and the okra start to brown at the edges, about 8 to 10 minutes.

3. Reduce the heat to low, and stir in the yogurt, salt, and sugar. Simmer until the yogurt takes on a nice curry flavor, 4 to 5 minutes. Taste and season with salt and sugar—salt to brighten and focus the flavors, sugar to smooth any tart or rough edges in the yogurt. Remove from the heat. Transfer to a warm dish and serve hot.

KASHMIR MUSHROOMS BRAISED IN TOMATO SAUCE

| Rogani Dhingri

Highly prized for their woodsy flavor, both wild (the trumpet-shaped chanterelle, called *dhingri*, and the precious cone-shaped morel, known as *guchhi*) and commercial (the familiar button-shaped agaricus, called *khumbi*) mushrooms are popular in northern India. Fresh morels are a rare delicacy in spring in Jammu and Kashmir, where they grow at high elevations in the forest. This simple, light curry is made with roasted ginger, garlic, onion, tomatoes, and chunky mushrooms, and it is perfumed with fragrant spices. It works wonderfully with cultivated mushrooms, but try to get wild ones. For a summer backyard party, try serving this dish with Lush Yogurt Rice with Grapes (pages 103–104), a big chef's salad, and Sweet-Scented Hyderabad Ground Lamb (pages 289–290). Serve with store-bought *naan*.

SERVES 4

2^1/$_2$ tablespoons vegetable oil

1 cup coarsely chopped yellow onion

^{1}/$_2$-inch piece fresh ginger, crushed

4 cloves garlic, crushed

2 medium-large ripe tomatoes, or 2 cups canned
    diced tomatoes

4 bay leaves

8 green cardamom pods

4 whole cloves

1-inch cinnamon stick

^{1}/$_2$ cup water

1/3 cup plain yogurt

1 teaspoon salt

1 teaspoon ground coriander

^{1}/$_2$ teaspoon ground cumin

^{1}/$_2$ teaspoon cayenne

^{1}/$_4$ teaspoon turmeric

10 ounces white button mushrooms

Chopped cilantro, for garnish

1. Heat 1^1/$_2$ tablespoons of the oil in a heavy medium skillet over medium heat. Add the onion and cook, stirring often, until softened, 4 to 5 minutes. Add the ginger and garlic and continue to cook, stirring, until the onion is deep golden, 3 to 4 minutes. Transfer to a blender. Coarsely chop the tomatoes and add to the blender. Blend to a smooth puree and set aside.

2. Heat the remaining 1 tablespoon of oil in the same skillet over medium heat. Add the bay leaves, cardamom, cloves, and cinnamon and cook, stirring, until fragrant, about 1 minute. Add the tomato-onion puree and cook, stirring occasionally, until the raw tomato smell dissipates, about 10 minutes. Stir the water and yogurt together and add to the pan. Cook, stirring, for 2 minutes, then add the salt, coriander, cumin, cayenne, turmeric, and mushrooms. Cook, stirring, until piping hot, 6 to 8 minutes. Transfer to a warm serving dish and garnish with cilantro.

VARIATION

Fresh morels are available March through May in farmers' markets, specialty stores, and some supermarkets. Dried morels are available year round. To prepare dried morels, soak them in warm water to cover for 30 minutes. Drain and rinse under cold water, then scrub gently with a stiff brush to remove any grit. Pat dry with paper towels. Discard any tough stems and use as instructed.

GRANDMA'S TAMARIND-LACED POTATO CURRY | Aalu Gedde Rassa

Occasionally, when I indulge in traditional cooking, memories will surface, taking me home to India. One such childhood remembrance is of the annual summer visits to my grandmother's farmhouse. On one of my stays there, the village was recovering from famine. The usual lush tropical produce was missing from her kitchen, but she had sacks of potatoes—baby potatoes, russet-like potatoes, red new potatoes, and sweet potatoes. She called the homely tubers "famine food," because they had survived the drought, but she would soon turn them into culinary jewels. With her fragile but magical hands, with joy and care, she produced a vast array of potato creations, and I marveled at how versatile potatoes could be. She served them in various guises—a different way at every meal.

Mornings, I would wake up to the delicious aromas of beaten rice with potatoes. For lunch, she made this curry with a handful of baby potatoes, simmering in a spicy tamarind sauce. She sometimes cooked them in bold, flavorful coconut milk or a creamy yogurt sauce. Occasionally, she presented them in an elegant spiced cream sauce.

She made potato *koftas* and simmered them in a fragrant herb sauce. She flavored mashed sweet potatoes with cinnamon and sugar and stuffed them into dough to make sweet puffy breads. Tea-time snacks included finely crafted potato cutlets, potato *pakora* (pages 144–146), and seasoned fried potato wedges. For dessert, a smooth and satisfying dollop of sweetened mashed potato, perfumed with rose water and cardamom, epitomized culinary comfort. Grandmother's bounty of potato recipes was never ending. Even for my journey home, she packed delicious wraps of zesty potatoes studded with raisins and cashews, neatly rolled into *chapatis*.

On the train going home, I always cried. Grandmother filled my life with sweet memories. Here's what she taught me.

SERVES 4 AS A SIDE DISH

1¹/2 pounds Yukon gold, russet, or new potatoes

2 tablespoons vegetable oil

1 teaspoon yellow or brown mustard seeds

1 cup finely chopped yellow onion

¹/2 teaspoon turmeric

1 teaspoon tamarind concentrate, dissolved in 1 cup water

1 heaping tablespoon light-brown sugar, jaggery (pages 51–52), or raw sugar

1 teaspoon salt

1 teaspoon ground coriander

¹/2 teaspoon cayenne

Cilantro sprigs, for garnish

1. Scrub the potatoes and place them in a large pot. Boil until just tender, 15 minutes. Let cool until easy to handle, then peel the potatoes and dice them into 1-inch pieces. Set aside.

2. Have a spatter screen ready before you continue. Heat the oil in a heavy large skillet over medium-high heat. Add the mustard seeds, immediately cover with the spatter screen, and cook until the seeds stop popping, about 30 seconds. Add the onion and turmeric and cook until the onion is very soft and starts to brown on the edges, about 3 minutes. Add the potatoes and cook, stirring, for 2 to 3 minutes more. Add the tamarind liquid and stir. Reduce the heat to low and sprinkle with sugar, salt, coriander, and cayenne and mix gently but thoroughly. Cover and simmer until the sauce is very thick and tastes pleasantly sweet-and-sour, 8 to 10 minutes. Garnish with several sprigs of cilantro. Taste and adjust the salt, if necessary, before transferring to a warm serving dish.

APRICOTS AND FIGS IN A DELICATE NUTTY SAUCE

| Badam-Jodambe Kari

This recipe makes me think of a royal banquet, so I've put together a menu just for that purpose. Serve this dish with Butter Chicken (pages 274–275), Fragrant Lamb Maharaja with Almonds and Caramelized Onion (pages 350–351), Mahimahi Biryani (page 120), and Celery Root Kachumber with Fresh Dill (page 217). Serve hot *naan* alongside, and enjoy a lush, fruity red wine. Zinfandel provides a wonderful brightness. It will be an unforgettable feast. For an informal meatless dinner, try this dish with Tamarind Rice (page 109), a variety of whole-wheat flat breads, and cool Cucumber and Radish Raita (page 207). Bake a few dozen Full Moon Cookies (page 421) ahead for dessert.

Look for sultanas in Indian or Middle Eastern markets.

SERVES 4 TO 6

2 tablespoons vegetable oil

1 cup chopped yellow onion

2 cloves garlic, sliced

1/2-inch piece fresh ginger, sliced

1 fresh green serrano or jalapeño chili, stemmed and chopped

2 teaspoons ground coriander

1 teaspoon ground cumin

1/2 teaspoon ground cinnamon

1/4 teaspoon ground white pepper

1/8 teaspoon freshly grated nutmeg

2 cups chopped ripe tomatoes, or canned diced tomatoes

3/4 cups roasted mixed nuts (almonds, cashews, pistachios, and macadamia nuts)

1 cup plain yogurt

1 1/2 cups water

1 1/2 tablespoons *desi ghee* (pages 47–48), or unsalted butter

4 dried apricots, chopped

4 dried figs, chopped

1/2 cup sultanas, or dark raisins

1 teaspoon salt

2 squares silver or gold leaf (page 54)

Fresh cherries, for garnish

1. Heat the oil in a heavy skillet over medium heat. Add the onion and cook, stirring, until deep golden, about 8 minutes. Add the garlic, ginger, and chilis and cook, stirring, for 3 to 4 minutes more. Add the coriander, cumin, cinnamon, pepper, and nutmeg and cook, stirring, until aromatic, about 1 minute. Stir in the tomatoes and cook, stirring, until softened, about 5 minutes. Remove from the heat and transfer to a blender. Add 1/4 cup of the mixed nuts and process as smoothly as possible. Set aside. In a mixing bowl, whisk together the yogurt and water and set aside.

2. Heat the *desi ghee* in the same skillet over medium heat. Add the remaining 1/2 cup of nuts and toast, stirring occasionally, for 2 to 3 minutes. Add the apricots, figs, and sultanas and cook, stirring, for 1 minute. Add the spice-onion puree and cook, stirring, for 2 to 3 minutes. Stir in the yogurt mixture and salt, cover, and simmer until the sauce is thick and takes on a pleasant curry taste, 8 to 10 minutes more. Transfer to a heated decorative serving dish. Garnish with gold leaf and cherries. Serve hot.

MIXED GREENS WITH TOASTED PECANS | Saag

The preparation of glistening *saag*, a great-tasting and nutritious side dish, is simple. Traditionally, *saag* is made with spinach. I like to add other greens, including pumpkin greens. Indian cooks use pumpkins—and their greens—with particular creativity. Pumpkins are used for breads, side dishes, and fritters. In this dish, I've added green Swiss chard, but you can substitute almost any greens, including collards, beet greens, red Swiss chard, sorrel, chicory, kale, or turnip greens, though each has a slightly different cooking time.

The addition of orange juice and pecans is my contemporary twist on this classic dish. Don't be alarmed if the pan looks too full. The greens will wilt considerably during cooking. Serve this alongside meats and seafood; for a variation, serve over cooked pasta. This dish is traditionally served with soft butter. Add cream (and cook for a few minutes) if you prefer *saag* the way it is served in Indian restaurants, and omit the juice.

2 tablespoons peanut or vegetable oil

1 teaspoon coarsely crushed cumin seeds

1 teaspoon sesame seeds (optional)

5 large cloves garlic, minced

2 fresh green serrano or jalapeño chilis, stemmed and chopped

2 cups chopped green Swiss chard leaves (see headnote)

4 cups chopped fresh spinach leaves, with tender stems

1 teaspoon salt

2 tablespoons coarsely chopped pecans, toasted (page 208)

Yellow pear tomatoes, cut into wedges

2 tablespoons fresh orange juice

1.   Heat the oil in a large wok or sauté pan over medium heat. Add the cumin and sesame seeds, if using, and cook, stirring, until aromatic, about 30 seconds. Add the garlic and chilis and cook, stirring, until the garlic starts to brown, about 2 minutes. Add the Swiss chard and spinach leaves and cook, stirring occasionally, until the greens are wilted, about 2 minutes. Cover and cook 6 to 8 minutes. Add the salt and mix gently. Remove from the heat. Transfer into a heated serving dish. Toss in the pecans. Garnish with pear tomatoes. Sprinkle with the orange juice and serve right away.

VARIATIONS

Omit the pecans and garnish with deep-fried peanuts, elevating this dish to party fare. You may also add a few diced potatoes for a change in texture. For a spicier version, sprinkle with 1/2 to 1 teaspoon of Hot and Fragrant Curry Powder (page 35) or My Mother's Heirloom Spice Blend (pages 39–40) during the last few minutes of cooking.

GOLDEN PANEER KOFTA IN AROMATIC SPINACH SAUCE
| Makhmale Kofte

There are many versions of special-occasion *kofta* curries in India. My current favorite is this one—spinach, garlic, sweet tomato sauce, and spices, with a flotilla of golden velvety *paneer* balls. Be sure to make plenty of *koftas*. When you pop one in your mouth and experience the gush of creaminess, you'll want more.

This full-flavored dish is a great accompaniment to Chili- and Garlic-stuffed Roasted Eggplant (pages 238–239), steamed basmati rice, and *roti* (page 65), for an all-vegetarian dinner.

SERVES 6 AS A MAIN COURSE

Paneer Kofta

3/4 pound (2 medium) russet potatoes, boiled, peeled, and mashed

1 recipe Fresh Basic Paneer (page 221), or 8 ounces store-bought, crumbled

2 teaspoons salt

1/4 teaspoon ground white pepper

2 tablespoons chickpea flour, or corn flour

Vegetable oil for frying

Spinach Sauce

1 1/2 pounds (2 bunches) spinach, with tender stems

2 tablespoons vegetable oil

1 tablespoon minced garlic

1 teaspoon ground coriander

1/2 teaspoon cayenne

1/4 teaspoon turmeric

1 1/2 cups tomato puree

2 teaspoons salt

1 cup water

1 teaspoon *garam masala* (pages 36–37), or store-bought

1. To prepare the *paneer kofta:* In a mixing bowl, combine the potatoes, *paneer,* salt, pepper, and chickpea flour. Mix well; the consistency should resemble very soft dough. Shape into walnut-size balls and set aside. Heat 2 inches of oil in a deep-fryer or wok to 365°F to 375°F. Fry a few *koftas* at a time, in a single uncrowded layer, until lightly browned on all sides, 3 to 4 minutes; after you add the *koftas* to the oil, do not turn them for at least half a minute or they may break apart. Transfer to paper towels to drain. Fry the remaining *koftas.* Keep the *koftas* in a serving bowl tented with foil while you prepare the sauce.

2. To prepare the spinach sauce: Rinse and coarsely chop the spinach. Place the spinach in a large skillet, cover, and cook over medium heat until wilted, about 3 minutes. Plunge the spinach in ice water to retain the color. Squeeze gently, transfer to a blender or food processor, and blend to a smooth puree.

3. Heat the oil in the same skillet over moderate heat. Add the garlic and cook, stirring, until lightly browned, 3 to 4 minutes. Add the coriander, cayenne, and turmeric and cook, stirring, until aromatic, about 30 seconds. Add the tomato puree and cook until the raw tomato smell disappears, 6 to 8 minutes. Add the salt, water, and spinach puree. Cook, stirring, until piping hot. Stir in the *garam masala* and *koftas* and cook until heated through. Transfer to a warm shallow serving dish.

MAKE AHEAD The sauce may be stored, covered, in the refrigerator for up to 2 days.

MIXED VEGETABLE KOFTA IN CREAM SAUCE | Sabji Malai Kofta

Once you try it, this luscious entrée will be ingrained in your memory. The creamy curry creates a harmonious and richly flavored base to welcome the *koftas,* laced with spices and studded with raisins. Bite-size *koftas* make tempting cocktail hors d'oeuvres. Serve on toothpicks with an assortment of chutneys and/or dips. Use the curry sauce by itself to dress cooked meat.

These *koftas* can be served with the sauce spooned over them or simmered for a while in the sauce so that they soften and absorb the flavors. This dish is perfect served with Fresh Mint Rice (page 97) and Spicy-Sweet Green Mango Relish (page 197). A full sauvignon blanc or viognier is a good match to the richness of the sauce.

SERVES 4 OR 5 AS MAIN COURSE

Vegetable Kofta

1 pound (2 large) russet potatoes, boiled, peeled, and mashed

1/4 cup fresh or thawed frozen peas

1/4 cup shredded carrot

1/4 cup shredded zucchini

1/4 cup shredded cheddar cheese

1 to 2 fresh green serrano or jalapeño chilis, chopped

1 1/2 teaspoons salt

1 teaspoon ground coriander

1/2 teaspoon ground cumin

1/4 cup coarsely chopped cashews

1 tablespoon dark raisins

3/4 cup chickpea flour, or corn flour

1/2 cup water

Vegetable oil for frying

Sauce

10 whole roasted unsalted cashews

1/4 teaspoon ground cloves

1/4 teaspoon ground cinnamon

1/8 teaspoon freshly grated nutmeg

2 large cloves garlic, peeled

2 tablespoons *desi ghee* (pages 47–48), or unsalted butter

1 large yellow onion, grated

2 teaspoons sweet paprika

1 teaspoon salt

1/2 teaspoon cayenne

1/2 teaspoon ground coriander

1/4 teaspoon turmeric

1 cup water

2 cups heavy whipping cream

2 tablespoons chopped cilantro

1. To prepare the vegetable *kofta:* In a mixing bowl, combine the potatoes, peas, carrot, zucchini, cheese, chilis, 1 teaspoon of the salt, the coriander, cumin, chopped cashews, and raisins and mix well. Shape into walnut-size balls.

2. In a mixing bowl, stir together the chickpea flour and water to make a batter; season with the remaining 1/2 teaspoon of salt. Heat 2 inches of oil in a deep-fryer or wok to 365°F to 375°F. Working with one at a time, dip the *koftas* into the batter to coat completely. Fry a few *koftas* at a time in a single uncrowded layer until lightly browned on all sides, 3 to 4 minutes; after you add the *koftas* to the oil, do not turn them for at least half a minute or they may break apart. When browned, transfer to paper towels to drain. Continue frying the remaining *koftas.* Keep the *koftas* in a serving bowl tented with foil while you prepare the sauce.

3. To prepare the sauce: In a blender, combine the whole cashews, cloves, cinnamon, nutmeg, and garlic with 1 to 2 tablespoons water. Process until smooth.

4. Heat the *desi ghee* in a large heavy saucepan over medium-high heat. Add the onion and cook, stirring, until lightly browned, 4 to 5 minutes. Reduce the heat to medium and add the cashew mixture. Cook, stirring, until fragrant, about 4 minutes. Add the paprika, salt, cayenne, coriander, and turmeric and cook, stirring, until aromatic, about 1 minute. Add the water, bring to a boil, reduce the heat, cover, and simmer until sauce is slightly thick, 10 minutes. Stir the cream and *koftas* into the sauce. Cook until heated through. Transfer to a heated shallow serving dish. Garnish with cilantro.

> Make Ahead: The sauce may be made without the cream and stored, covered, in the refrigerator for up to 2 days. Add the cream and heat through just before serving.

VARIATION

Malai Kofta

These *koftas* are so lovely, they barely hit the table before they are devoured. Substitute 1/3 cup crumbled Fresh Basic Paneer (page 221) for the carrot, zucchini, and cheddar cheese, and continue with the rest of the recipe.

PEANUT-STUFFED OLD-FASHIONED EGGPLANT | Yenkai Badnekai

Here, onion is slowly sautéed and cooked further with crushed peanuts, coconut, fresh herbs, and my mother's heirloom spice blend. The filling is then stuffed into slits in the already delicious eggplant and slowly cooked to create a delectable, homey dish.

MAKES 4 TO 6 SERVINGS

1¹/2 pounds (about 12 small) Japanese eggplants, stems intact

5 tablespoons peanut or vegetable oil

1 cup finely chopped yellow onion

¹/4 teaspoon turmeric

¹/2 cup dried unsweetened flaked coconut, or freshly grated coconut (page 307)

³/4 cup crushed roasted salted or unsalted peanuts

1 to 1¹/2 tablespoons My Mother's Heirloom Spice Blend (pages 39–40) or Hot and Fragrant Curry Powder (page 35), or store-bought curry powder

2 teaspoons sugar

2 teaspoons salt

¹/2 teaspoon cayenne

¹/4 cup packed finely chopped cilantro

1. Rinse the eggplants and slit them, making 2 perpendicular cuts (an X), keeping the stem end intact. Place them in a bowl of ice cold water for 10 to 20 minutes to open them up slightly and prevent discoloration.

2. Meanwhile, heat 2¹/2 tablespoons of the oil in a small heavy skillet over medium heat. Add the onion and cook, stirring, until the onion is soft and starts to brown at the edges, about 6 minutes. Add the turmeric, coconut, and peanuts and cook, stirring, for 4 minutes more. Add the heirloom spice blend, sugar, salt, cayenne, and cilantro and cook, stirring occasionally, until the spices are incorporated and pleasantly aromatic, 3 to 4 minutes. Remove from the heat and set aside until the mixture is cool enough to handle.

3. Remove the eggplants from the water and pat dry. Stuff each eggplant with a table-spoon or more of the filling mixture by gently opening the slits. Press together to enclose the filling and set aside. Heat a large nonstick skillet over medium heat. Add 2 tablespoons of the oil; when the oil is hot, rotate the pan to coat the bottom evenly with oil. Transfer the stuffed eggplants to the skillet (you may have to do this in batches or in 2 skillets if your pan isn't large enough). Drizzle the remaining ¹/2 tablespoon of oil over the egg-plants. Cover and cook until lightly browned on one side, 6 to 8 minutes. Uncover and turn the eggplants gently, reduce the heat to low, cover, and cook until tender, 8 to 10 minutes. Transfer to a heated decorative platter and serve hot.

SQUASH BOATS FILLED WITH LENTILS | Padolkai Doni

One of the easiest and most flavorful ways to dress up your favorite squashes is to halve them and toss them on the griddle to sear, and then top them with humble cooked lentils and fresh dill. The sizzling heat and delicious aromas in this attractive, low-calorie dish is perfect for a cool autumn night.

MAKES 8 SIDE DISH SERVINGS

3 tablespoons peanut or vegetable oil

1 teaspoon cumin seeds

3 medium shallots, finely chopped

1/4 teaspoon turmeric

2 fresh green serrano or jalapeño chilis, stemmed and chopped

1 cup lightly packed chopped fresh dill, plus additional for garnish

1 cup *toovar dal* (yellow lentils), or yellow split peas, cleaned, rinsed, and drained

2 cups water

3/4 teaspoon salt

1 1/2 pounds (about 12) baby crookneck or patty-pan squash

1. Heat 1 tablespoon of the oil in a heavy medium skillet over medium to medium-high heat. Add the cumin seeds and sizzle until the seeds darken a shade, about 30 seconds. Add the shallots and cook, stirring, until soft but not browned, about 2 minutes. Stir in the turmeric and chilis and cook, stirring, for 30 seconds. Add the dill and cook, stirring constantly, until fragrant, about 2 minutes. Add the *dal,* water, and salt and stir to combine. Bring to a boil, reduce the heat to low, cover, and simmer until the *dal* is tender but still holds its shape, 25 to 30 minutes. Let stand, covered, for 5 minutes.

2. While the lentils are cooking, cut each squash in half lengthwise and scoop out a little of the seeds, leaving an indentation to fill. In a large skillet, heat the remaining 2 tablespoons of the oil over medium-high heat. Place the halved squash in the skillet, cut-side down in a single layer, without overcrowding, and cook in 2 to 3 batches, if necessary. Sear the squash until the edges turn golden brown, 4 to 5 minutes. Turn over and cook until tender, 1 to 2 minutes more. Repeat until all of the squash is cooked (adding more oil if needed).

3. Sprinkle salt over the squash, if desired, and place on a heated serving platter, skin-side down. Spoon the lentils into the squash boats. Garnish with dill and serve immediately.

My mother used to make this with ridge gourds, also known as *loofah,* or Chinese okra. This gourd couldn't be simpler to deal with, so don't be put off by its curious name. Look for ridge gourds at Asian markets, farmers' markets, or specialty produce stores. The best gourds are relatively small, about 12 inches in length, hard, and heavy for their size.

Baby zucchini and even young Japanese eggplants are attractive alternatives for entertaining.

ALMOND-STUFFED PASILLA CHILIS | Tumbidu Mensinkai

Across central and southern India, fresh hot chilis stuffed with spices and soaked in buttermilk are sun-dried until crisp (like *pappadam*). Fried to golden perfection, they show up on tables to offer a spicy accent. Such creations are typically served as a side dish to a meal. My own concoction of almonds perfumed with delicate spices and citrus, an unexpected but perfectly balanced mix, fills these little wonders. This dish is perfect with lamb or duck. Use a coffee mill or blender to grind the almonds to a powder.

SERVES 4 TO 6 AS A SIDE DISH

8 large fresh pasilla chilis, stems intact

1/4 cup vegetable oil

2 cups finely chopped yellow onion

1/2 cup powdered toasted almonds (page 208, see headnote)

1 tablespoon ground coriander

1 1/2 teaspoons ground cumin

2 teaspoons sugar

1 teaspoon salt

1/2 cup lightly packed chopped fresh cilantro

5 tablespoons freshly squeezed lime juice

1. Rinse the chilis and slit lengthwise, keeping the stem end intact. Place them in a bowl of cold water for 10 to 15 minutes to open them up slightly.

2. Heat 2 tablespoons of the oil in a heavy medium skillet over medium to medium-high heat. Add the onion and cook, stirring occasionally, until it starts to brown, about 4 minutes. Reduce the heat to medium and add the powdered almonds, coriander, and cumin and cook, stirring, until fragrant, about 2 minutes. Stir in the sugar, salt, cilantro, and lime juice. Mix well. Remove from the heat.

3. Stuff each chili with a tablespoon or more of the filling mixture by gently opening the slits and pressing and molding them roughly into their original shape. Heat a nonstick skillet large enough to hold all the chilis in a single layer over medium heat. Add 1 tablespoon of the remaining oil; when the oil is hot, rotate the pan to coat the bottom evenly with oil. Transfer the stuffed chilis to the skillet, drizzle them with the remaining 1 tablespoon of oil, cover, and cook until lightly browned on one side, 8 to 10 minutes. Uncover, turn the chilis gently, reduce the heat to low, cover, and cook until tender, 6 to 8 minutes. Transfer to a heated platter and serve hot.

VARIATIONS

If pasilla chilis are hard to find, use 6 good-size poblanos, 12 to 14 jalapeños, or 4 to 6 8-inch long Anaheim chilis.

EVERYDAY MEAT AND POULTRY SPECIALTIES

Lazeez Maausaahari Zaayeqae

In this chapter, I want to open my heart and share with you a little secret: how I first learned to cook with chicken. Thirty years ago, my culinary education began in my mother's kitchen in India. Since my father was a strict vegetarian, almost all of our food was meatless. While he was at work, my mother occasionally made omelets and scrambled eggs for my brother, sister, and me. She had separate pans, hidden away in the pantry, for cooking eggs. But cooking poultry and meat at home was out of the question.

Still, we did learn to eat chicken. We had heard stories that in Europe and America only nonvegetarian food was available. If we were to go abroad, Mother reasoned, we might have to eat chicken and other meat. To get us used to meat, she sneaked us into local restaurants to try some chicken dishes. I started out with *murg makhani*—butter chicken—relishing the sauce, but not the meat. On another occasion, I tried a small piece of tandoori chicken. I literally had to gulp it down with a big glass of water. On another visit, my brother suggested I try chicken *tikka masala*, and assured me that the meat tasted like *paneer.*

After that, I took professional cooking lessons to learn to prepare chicken, but they weren't too successful. Then, for my sixteenth birthday, my aunt surprised me with a Pomeranian puppy. My sister and I were thrilled, but we were in a dilemma, because the little dog ate only cooked chicken.

Once again, Mother came to our rescue. With the help of our maid we were able to cook chicken, but only in the backyard so as not to upset our father. We huddled behind the maid's quarters while she placed three large rocks in a semicircle to form a makeshift stove, heated by charcoal or firewood. My first success, with our maid's help, was poached chicken. Soon after, I learned to sauté and braise the bird. It was all done in secret.

Then one day my father caught us. "Your favorite pet prefers early dinner, I guess," he said. My sister and I looked at each other and smiled.

When I got married, I wanted to show off my cooking expertise to my husband. I remembered a few ingredients that went into making Chicken Breasts in Korma Sauce (page 270–271). It turned out delicious. Now, every time I cook chicken, my husband recalls that first recipe as one of the best.

When we moved to the United States, I was inspired by the availability of all sorts of cuts of meat and poultry, and I was delighted to find out how versatile chicken is. Chicken has become a staple back home in India, too. Years ago, royal kitchens served lavish chicken dishes that took hours to prepare—poultry was expensive and considered a delicacy— but now simple chicken preparations are eaten every day.

My favorite meat dishes are those seasoned with the ingredients I know best—chilis, coconut, coriander, cumin, cinnamon, ginger, garlic, and lots of onions. Chicken has turned out to be wonderfully adaptable to Indian seasonings. It may not fit with all the traditions of Indian cooking, but for learning to use Indian seasonings, there's no better place to begin. I almost always remove the skin, so the marinade and spices can permeate and tenderize the chicken. Depending on whether I want the mild flavor of chicken breasts or the more robust-tasting dark meat, I can vary the mixture of spices, and even add fruit, vegetables, and legumes. These dishes are fairly quick to make.

During one of my regular tours visiting family in India, my father gave me some magazine clippings that he had saved. As I leafed through them on my return flight, I saw that one of the sheets had my father's handwriting. For all that secret cooking, it read: "Heard this is a great chicken recipe. Try it."

YESTERDAY AND TODAY

The Indians of the past were avid hunters. The many meat and poultry dishes from the northern and western regions owe their existence to this passion. Master chefs marinated lamb with ten-year-old mango preserves, and basted fowl with twenty-year-old *desi ghee*. They sprinkled partridges with the essence of musk and grilled them to mouthwatering crispness over fragrant sandalwood. Succulent wild boar was spit-roasted to melting tenderness. Cockscomb was used as a coloring agent, and the whole chicken was covered with wet clay and baked in stone-lined pits. The royal court hunted peacocks, deer, pheasants, quails, and antelopes, which royal cooks turned into spicy, fragrant curries and stews.

Today, even with all of the authentically inspired Indian food available in the United States, many Westerners aren't aware of the diversity that abounds in Indian cuisine. The cooking of the north has been influenced by climate and occupations. The classic Moghul cuisine is the richest and most lavish, known for charcoal-roasted meats in creamy, yogurt-based, velvety sauces. To help fend off the cold, these curries incorporate lightly roasted, warm seasoning—*garam masala*. Ground nuts—almonds, cashews, and pistachios—and dried fruits are generously used.

The most phenomenal culinary tapestry is found in the south. From Goa come countless *vindaloo* dishes. In *vindaloo* curry, the spices and herbs are ground in vinegar to make a paste that lends an appealing, offbeat sweet-sour taste. Near the equator, the cooking of Chennai (formerly Madras) is known for its versatility; lamb and chicken are cooked in a variety of ways. Farther south, in the lands of swaying palms along the Kerala coastline, creamy coconut milk appears in an astonishing variety of combinations; the results are smooth and slightly sweet meat and poultry curries. My recipe for Kerala Chicken Stew with Summer Vegetables (page 280) demonstrates this regional style.

India's tropical east coast features curries seasoned with freshly ground "wet" *masala*—a red spice mix containing fresh hot red chilis, or a yellow one with mustard seed paste and turmeric—and cooked in smoking mustard oil. Sauces are sometimes seasoned with Whole Spice Bengal Seasoning (page 50), which is fried in *desi ghee* or mustard oil to release the aromas. Sometimes, mustard paste, which imparts an herbal fragrance, is added to thicken the sauces. The west's vast stretches of desert sand and blistering sunshine have made growing vegetables difficult, so the classical cuisine in this region is centered on meats. In olden days game meats were soused in spices, encased in dough, and buried in hot desert sand for roasting. These days, traditional game has been replaced with lamb and chicken.

CHICKEN BREASTS IN KORMA SAUCE | Murg Korma

This classic rich, spicy northern Indian dish, featuring onion, chicken, and tomatoes, intrigues the palate and will soothe even the most hesitant dinner guest. The yogurt adds a pleasant tartness to the delicate sauce. If you've invited friends, simmer a pot of Warm Mango Soup (pages 364–365), toss together Carrot Raita with Toasted Walnuts (pages 208–209), and prepare a rich dessert like Creamy Rice Pudding (page 414). Buy frozen *naan* or make your own (pages 84–85). A soft, lush, aromatic red is just the kind of wine you'd want to enjoy with this dish.

SERVES 4

1¹/2-inch piece fresh ginger

5 large cloves garlic

2 tablespoons vegetable or grapeseed oil

1¹/2 cups thinly sliced yellow onion

2 tablespoons *desi ghee* (pages 47–48), or unsalted butter

2-inch cinnamon stick

10 whole cloves

8 green cardamom pods

2 teaspoons ground coriander

1 teaspoon Kashmir *deghi mirch* powder (pages 23–24), or sweet paprika

1 scant teaspoon ground fennel

1/2 teaspoon cayenne

1/2 teaspoon turmeric

2 pounds boneless, skinless chicken breasts

2 cups finely chopped ripe tomatoes with their juices, or canned diced tomatoes

1/4 cup roasted unsalted cashews

1 cup plain yogurt

1 teaspoon salt

Beautiful sprigs of cilantro, for garnish

1.   Combine the ginger and garlic with 3 to 4 tablespoons water in a blender. Blend to a smooth paste, stopping to scrape down the sides of the bowl a couple of times. Set aside.

2.   Heat the oil in a heavy large sauté pan over medium heat. Add the onion and cook, stirring often, until deep golden, 8 to 10 minutes. Transfer to a plate. Add the *desi ghee* to the pan, and when hot add the ginger-garlic paste. Cook, stirring, until the mixture is fragrant and light brown, 3 to 4 minutes. Add the cinnamon, cloves, and cardamom pods and stir for a few seconds. Add the coriander, *deghi mirch* powder, fennel, cayenne, and turmeric and cook, stirring, until the mixture takes on a beautiful orange-red color and becomes fragrant, about 30 seconds. Add the chicken and sear until light golden and no longer pink, about 3 minutes per side. Add the tomato with juices and cook, stirring occasionally, until the tomato is very soft, 6 to 8 minutes.

Boosting Flavor

* For authentic Indian flavor, use free-range chicken, which develops the right chewiness and richness.

* The onion must be cooked to a rich brown to bring out its sweetness. Plain sweating does not add flavor to chicken and meat dishes. For red meats, the onion must be caramelized.

* If you can find Kashmiri red chili powder, called Kashmir *deghi mirch* powder (pages 23–24) at Indian markets, use it in recipes as I've suggested for brilliant color and flavor. If unavailable, sweet paprika makes a good substitute.

3. While the tomatoes are cooking, combine the cashews with 2 tablespoons water in the blender and blend to a smooth paste. Add to the chicken. Whisk the yogurt and stir it into the pan. Add the reserved onion and salt and mix well. Bring to a gentle boil, cover, and simmer until the chicken is tender, 20 to 25 minutes. With a slotted spoon, transfer the chicken to a warm serving dish, then ladle the sauce over it, decorate with cilantro sprigs, and serve.

VARIATION

Fruit and Vegetable Navratna Korma

In place of the chicken, stir in a mélange (4 cups total) of fresh produce in step 2. There is no need to sear the vegetables. A combination of cauliflower, broccoli, bell peppers, potatoes, carrots, pineapple, cherries, and orange sections is wonderful in this *korma*. Add 1/2 cup heavy whipping cream along with the other ingredients in step 3, and cook until the veggies are just tender. Taste and adjust the salt. Serve garnished with cherries.

CHICKEN TIKKA MASALA | Murg Tikka Masala

Indian restaurants have made this dish, my son's favorite, so popular that it probably doesn't need much explanation. The stunning, deep rusty-red color and absolutely pleasing flavor of *tikka masala* are worth the extra effort it takes to prepare it. If you have leftover Tandoori Chicken (pages 340–341) or Seared Chicken Tikka (pages 344–345), you can skip the marinade steps and go directly to preparing the sauce. A two-step marinade adds complexity to the chicken, but you can skip the first marinade if you're short on time. You may grill the *tikka,* as I've suggested, or sear it (5 minutes per side) to an almost mahogany hue in a sauté pan without oil, and cook down the marinade along with the chicken until the chicken is thoroughly cooked and almost dry.

Try serving this dish with Rose-Flavored Naan with Silver Leaf (pages 89–90), Celery Root Kachumber with Fresh Dill (page 217), and steamed basmati rice, and you've got a wonderful dinner.

SERVES 4 TO 6

Chicken Tikka

2 to 2¹/₂ pounds boneless, skinless chicken breasts, cut into 2-inch pieces

1 teaspoon sweet paprika

6 tablespoons freshly squeezed lime juice

1-inch piece fresh ginger

6 large cloves garlic

¹/₂ cup plain yogurt

1 teaspoon salt

1 teaspoon *garam masala* (pages 36–37), or store-bought

1 teaspoon ground coriander

¹/₂ teaspoon ground cumin

¹/₄ cup heavy whipping cream

To Finish the Recipe

16 whole roasted unsalted cashews

1-inch piece fresh ginger

6 large cloves garlic

8 to 10 medium ripe tomatoes (choose plum tomatoes for a thicker texture), or 4 cups canned pureed tomatoes

2 tablespoons vegetable oil

2 tablespoons butter, preferably unsalted

2 bay leaves

1 teaspoon Kashmir *deghi mirch* powder (pages 23–24), or 1 teaspoon sweet paprika

¹/₂ teaspoon cayenne

1 teaspoon light-brown sugar, jaggery (pages 51–52), or raw sugar

¹/₂ cup whole or low-fat (2%) milk

¹/₄ cup heavy whipping cream

¹/₂ cup water

2 teaspoons *garam masala,* or store-bought

¹/₂ teaspoon salt

Beautiful cilantro sprigs, for garnish

1.   To prepare the chicken *tikka*: At least a day before you plan to serve, rinse the chicken pieces and pat them dry. Place in a casserole or glass bowl. For the first marinade, combine the paprika and 2 tablespoons of the lime juice in a small bowl and stir to mix. Pour over the chicken. Rub the mixture thoroughly onto the chicken. Cover and set aside at cool room temperature, or refrigerate, for 30 minutes.

2.   While the chicken is marinating, prepare the second marinade. Combine the ginger and garlic with 1/4 cup of the yogurt in a blender. Blend to a smooth puree. Transfer to a bowl. Add the remaining 1/4 cup of yogurt, the salt, *garam masala,* coriander, cumin, and cream. Stir in the remaining 4 tablespoons of lime juice and whisk until well blended. Pour over the chicken and rub into the meat, turning several times to coat the pieces evenly. Cover and refrigerate overnight, turning the chicken pieces occasionally in the marinade.

3.   Preheat the oven to 450°F. Thread the chicken pieces on 4 to 6 skewers. Grill, broil, or roast the chicken on a baking sheet until tender, 15 to 20 minutes, basting once. Check once or twice to ensure that it is not browning too quickly. Use tongs to transfer the chicken to a dish. Cover loosely and set aside.

4.   To finish the recipe: Soak the cashews in 1/4 cup hot tap water for 15 to 30 minutes. While the nuts are soaking, combine the ginger and garlic with 3 tablespoons of water in a blender and blend to a puree, stopping to scrape down the sides of the bowl a couple of times. Transfer to a small bowl. Add the cashews with their soaking liquid to the blender and grind to a smooth paste. Transfer to another bowl and set aside.

5.   Blanch the tomatoes in a pot of boiling water for about 1 minute to loosen their skin. Transfer to a bowl of ice water to cool. Peel, core, and chop coarsely. Transfer to a blender and blend to make 4 cups of puree. (Skip this step if using canned pureed tomatoes.)

6.   Heat the oil and butter in a heavy large sauté pan over medium heat. Add the bay leaves and stir for 1 minute. Add the ginger-garlic paste and cook, stirring, until the mixture is fragrant and light brown, 4 to 5 minutes. Add the tomato puree and cook, stirring, until most of the moisture is absorbed and the sauce is thick, 15 to 20 minutes. Add the *deghi mirch* powder, cayenne, and sugar and cook, stirring, for 1 minute. Add the cashew paste and stir to mix. Reduce the heat to low. Combine the milk and cream and add to the pan, stirring. (It may look curdled at first, but don't worry about it.) Add the water and bring the mixture to a boil over medium heat. Add the chicken *tikka, garam masala,* and salt, cover, and simmer until the flavors meld and the sauce achieves a beautiful orange-red color, 10 to 12 minutes. Discard the bay leaves. Scoop into a warm deep serving dish. Garnish with cilantro and serve hot.

For a contemporary touch, simmer the chicken with $1/2$ cup diced red or green bell peppers, 4 or 5 halved baby pear tomatoes, and 1 or 2 peeled and quartered pearl onions.

BUTTER CHICKEN | Murg Makhani

Murg makhani was born in the 1950s and became an instant hit with customers of the popular New Delhi restaurant Moti Mahal. The restaurant would sell hundreds of servings of tandoori chicken every day. Once, the chef tampered with the leftovers by adding butter and reduced tomatoes to the pan juices. Voilà! Ever since then, this recipe has topped the menu at every Indian restaurant. Do not use *desi ghee* here, as it is the butter that makes the sauce so good.

SERVES 4 TO 6

1 recipe chicken *tikka* (use recipe from Chicken Tikka Masala, pages 272–274)

Butter Sauce

8 to 10 medium ripe tomatoes (choose plum tomatoes for a thicker texture), or 4 cups canned pureed tomatoes

1 tablespoon tomato paste

1 cup water

2 teaspoons light-brown sugar, jaggery (pages 51–52), or raw sugar

$1^1/2$ teaspoons salt

1 teaspoon cayenne

1 teaspoon *garam masala* (pages 36–37), or store-bought

$1/2$ teaspoon ground ginger

6 tablespoons chilled butter, preferably unsalted

1 cup heavy whipping cream

$1/4$ cup lightly packed dried fenugreek leaves, or cilantro or any other mild-flavored fresh herb

Pinch freshly grated nutmeg

Sliced almonds, for garnish

1. Starting at least a day before you plan to serve, to allow for the marinating time, prepare the chicken *tikka*.

A World of Red Wines

Red wines marry well with the depth and complexity of Indian food. Bright acidity is the key to pairing wines with spicy foods. Look for wines with ripe, lush fruit flavors. I find good acidity and intensity in Syrahs and pinot noirs. Syrah has great depth—it is broad and balanced, spicy and round at the same time, so all the varied flavors can be accommodated. Spicy wines bursting with flavors complement the liveliness of my cuisine. Zinfandel is another of my favorite matches. Remember, spicy foods do not match well with high tannin or toasty oak. The spices in Indian cooking will only accentuate the tannins and alcohol in full-bodied red wines and make them seem unbalanced. A great choice would be cabernet franc; it offers the complexity of cabernet sauvignon or merlot, but is usually less tannic and often has bright raspberry fruit characteristics.

2. To prepare the butter sauce: While the chicken is roasting, blanch the tomatoes in boiling water for about 1 minute to loosen the skin. Transfer to a bowl of ice water to cool. Peel, core, and chop coarsely. Transfer to a blender and blend to make 4 cups of puree. (Skip this step if using canned pureed tomatoes.)

3. Combine the tomato puree, tomato paste, and water in a heavy large sauté pan over medium-high heat. Cook, stirring occasionally, until most of the moisture is absorbed and the sauce is very thick, about 25 minutes. Add the sugar, salt, cayenne, *garam masala,* and ginger and mix well. Cut the butter in chunks, add it to the pan, and stir until it just melts into the sauce, about 1 minute. Stir in the cream, Chicken *Tikka,* and fenugreek leaves. Cover and cook until the flavors blend, 8 to 10 minutes. Sprinkle with a generous grating of nutmeg, stir for a few seconds, and then taste and adjust the seasonings, as necessary. Transfer to a heated serving dish, garnish with almonds, and serve hot.

KANDAHAR CHICKEN KOFTA IN RUBY-RED GRAPEFRUIT JUICE

| Murg Kandahari Kofte

Here is my twist on chicken *kofta* curry, a specialty of the northwestern frontier. The original includes *garam masala* and pomegranate juice, but this one is more delicate, with subtle spices and a hint of heat to balance the sweetness of ruby-red grapefruit juice. I think you'll like the overall harmony. The sauce is so delicious, you can use it with just about anything; it makes a grand topping for Tandoori Lamb Rolls with Lentils (pages 356–357). Toss sautéed vegetables into the sauce to make a vegetarian delicacy. Add hard-cooked eggs to make egg curry. To make meat *kofta,* substitute minced lamb for the ground chicken. Have some Kashmir Roti (pages 68–69) on hand, prepare Warm Chickpea and Green Mango Kachumber (page 215), and make Coconut Rice with Fresh Green Chilis (page 107), and you'll have a delicious, multihued spread.

SERVES 4

For the Kofta

1 pound ground chicken

1/2 teaspoon ground cinnamon

1/2 teaspoon salt

1 cup good chicken stock, or water

For the Sauce

8 large cloves garlic

2/3 cup cashew pieces

2 medium ripe tomatoes, or 2/3 cup canned
   pureed tomatoes

1/4 cup vegetable oil

1 teaspoon cayenne

1 cup water

1 teaspoon salt

1 cup ruby-red grapefruit juice, preferably fresh

1 cup heavy whipping cream

Pinch of freshly grated nutmeg

Chopped chives, for garnish

1. To prepare the *kofta:* Place the ground chicken in a bowl. Separate the clumps of meat with a fork. Add the cinnamon and salt and mix thoroughly. Using a small ice cream scoop for even size, scoop about a tablespoon of the meat mixture at a time and shape into a smooth 1-inch ball with your fingers. You should have about 24 *koftas.* Place the *koftas* in a heavy skillet. Add the stock and bring to a boil. Cover and simmer, turning once, until *koftas* are tender, about 15 minutes.

2. To prepare the sauce: While the chicken is cooking, place the garlic in a blender with 3 to 4 tablespoons water and grind to a smooth paste. Transfer to a bowl. Add the cashews to the blender with about $1/2$ cup of water, process to a smooth paste, and transfer to a bowl. Blanch the tomatoes in a pot of boiling water for about 1 minute to loosen the skin. Transfer to a bowl of ice water to cool. Peel, core, and chop coarsely. Transfer to a blender and process to make $2/3$ to 1 cup of puree. (Skip this step if using canned pureed tomatoes.)

3. Heat the oil in a large heavy sauté pan over medium heat. Add the garlic paste and cook, stirring, until it's fragrant and starts to brown, 2 to 3 minutes. Add the cayenne and stir for a few seconds. Add the cashew paste and cook, stirring, until well blended and the oil starts to separate, about 5 minutes. Add the tomato puree, water, and salt, bring to a boil, and cook, stirring, until the sauce is thickened and takes on a beautiful reddish hue, 8 to 10 minutes. Stir in the grapefruit juice, stir, and cook for 2 minutes. Add the cream, the *koftas* along with their cooking stock, and the nutmeg. Cook, stirring gently, until heated through, about 4 minutes. Transfer to a serving dish, top with the chives, and serve hot.

VARIATION

Plum-Stuffed Kofta (Alu Bukhara Kofte)

This preparation is a Kashmir specialty. Before rolling the minced meat into *kofta* in step 1, place a dried pitted plum or a plum and a blanched almond, in the center. Form into a smooth round ball. In addition to the sauce from this recipe, you may also serve the *koftas* with Sweet-Scented Tomato Gravy (page 123) or the spinach sauce of Golden Paneer Kofta in Aromatic Spinach Sauce (pages 258–259).

CHICKEN BREAST STUFFED WITH APRICOTS AND CRANBERRIES
| Murg Daraanpur

I stayed away from this time-honored recipe for years because it takes so long to prepare. One day my sister walked me through it while visiting me; now I am a convert. This stylish entrée is worth the effort. Ask your butcher to butterfly the whole chicken breast and open it up to allow for stuffing. The elegant filling provides a lot of flavor—a symphony of sweet, pungent, hot, cool, and crunchy flavors and textures.

For a complete menu, serve it with Fresh Mint Rice (page 97), and Scallion-Spinach Raita with Sesame Seeds (page 213). Uncork a bottle of cabernet franc, with its bright raspberry flavors. And prepare Vermicelli Pudding with Fresh Berries (page 415) for dessert.

SERVES 4 TO 6

2 to 2¹/₂ pounds (1 pound each) boneless, skinless whole chicken breasts, butterflied (see headnote)

¹/₂ teaspoon fenugreek seeds

¹/₂-inch piece fresh ginger

2 large cloves garlic

3¹/₂ tablespoons white vinegar

1 teaspoon ground cumin

1¹/₄ teaspoons salt

³/₄ teaspoon ground white pepper

¹/₄ teaspoon cayenne

¹/₈ teaspoon turmeric

2 teaspoons vegetable oil, plus additional for frying

3 dried apricots, finely chopped

2 tablespoons dried cranberries or dark raisins, chopped

3 tablespoons chopped cashews

2 tablespoons minced cilantro

2 fresh green serrano or jalapeño chilis, stemmed and minced

1 tablespoon unbleached all purpose flour

1 large egg, beaten

Lettuce leaves, rinsed and thoroughly dried, for serving

1. Rinse the chicken breasts well, then pat dry. Cover the butterflied chicken with clear plastic wrap. Working from the center outward, gently pound the poultry until it is flattened to ¹/₂ inch thick. Try to get both about the same thickness. Make about ¹/₄-inch-deep incisions every few inches over the breasts. Place in a single layer in a glass baking dish.

2. Heat a small skillet over medium heat. Add the fenugreek seeds and toast, shaking the pan frequently, until toasty smelling and colored a bit, 3 to 4 minutes. Let cool slightly. Transfer to a spice grinder and grind to a fine powder. Combine the ginger, garlic, and 2 tablespoons of the vinegar in a blender and process to a coarse, wet paste. Transfer to a bowl. Add the ground fenugreek, cumin, salt, 1/2 teaspoon of the pepper, the cayenne, turmeric, and 2 teaspoons of oil. Mix well. Smear the chicken breasts with the spice paste, cover, and set aside.

3. To prepare the filling, combine the apricots, cranberries, cashews, cilantro, and chilis in a small bowl. Place half of the mixture on one half of a butterflied chicken breast, fold the other half of the breast over, and tuck. Repeat with the other chicken breast and remaining filling.

4. To make the batter, in a medium bowl, mix together the remaining 1/4 teaspoon of pepper, 1/4 teaspoon of salt, 1 1/2 tablespoons of vinegar, flour, and egg. Whisk until smooth. Fill a large saucepan or skillet with oil to a depth of 1 inch and heat over medium-high heat until hot but not smoking, 365°F on a deep-fry thermometer. Carefully dip the stuffed chicken breasts, one at a time, in the batter and coat evenly. Fry in the oil, turning once, to an appetizing and crusty, rich golden brown, 10 to 12 minutes per side. Drain on paper towels. Cut each chicken piece in half diagonally. Serve on a bed of lettuce on a warmed platter.

KERALA CHICKEN STEW WITH SUMMER VEGETABLES

| Kaikari Ishtew

The word *ishtew* may have come from the British raj, as colonists tried to teach local cooks their version of Irish stew. You'll find many variations of this meaty stew, as well as a vegetarian version, in Kerala. Add a salad, a pilaf, and some multigrain bread for an unfussy dinner.

SERVES 4 TO 6 GENEROUSLY

2 cups sliced yellow onions

1-inch piece fresh ginger

2 to 4 fresh green serrano or jalapeño chilis, or fewer to taste, stemmed

1 teaspoon black peppercorns

1/2 teaspoon turmeric

3 tablespoons vegetable oil

1 teaspoon yellow or brown mustard seeds

4 bay leaves

2 large cloves garlic, sliced

1-inch cinnamon stick

6 green cardamom pods

20 *kari* leaves (page 28) (optional), or cilantro

2 1/2 pounds chicken thighs (or other bone-in chicken parts), skin removed

1/2 pound (about 5 small or baby potatoes) Yukon gold or new potatoes, cut in half

2 medium carrots, cut in 1-inch sticks

1 cup 1-inch cauliflower florets with stems

4 pattypan squash, quartered

1 1/2 cups water

2 teaspoons salt

3 cups Fresh Coconut Milk (page 308), or canned unsweetened coconut milk

1. Combine the onion, ginger, chilis, peppercorns, turmeric, and 2 tablespoons of the oil in a blender. Blend to a smooth puree, stopping to scrape down the sides of the bowl a couple of times.

2. Have a spatter screen ready before you continue. Heat the remaining 1 tablespoon of oil in a medium skillet over medium-high heat. Add the mustard seeds, immediately cover with the spatter screen, and cook until the seeds stop popping, about 30 seconds. Add the bay leaves, garlic, cinnamon, cardamom, and the *kari* leaves, if using, and cook, stirring, until fragrant, about 1 minute. Add the onion-ginger puree and cook, stirring occasionally, for about 5 minutes. Add the chicken and sear until browned on both sides, 3 to 4 minutes per side, spreading the curry paste onto the chicken. Add the potatoes, carrot, cauliflower, pattypan squash, water, and salt, and bring to a boil. Reduce the heat and gradually stir in the coconut milk. Cook, stirring occasionally, until the chicken and the potatoes are tender, 20 to 25 minutes, and serve.

GOA CHICKEN XACUTI | Xacuti

Xacuti (pronounced "shakuti") was originally a vegetarian dish; *sha* is Konkani for "vegetable," and *kotee* means "cut into small pieces." This spicy yet fragrant preparation—with poppy seeds, star anise, and nutmeg—was meant to rejuvenate the weary rice planters. The dish is trendy in Goa these days; chicken, shark, and wild boar preparations are often simmered in *xacuti* sauce.

The smoky, slow cooking gives the meat succulence, with alluring aromas that perfume the air. Dish up Chicken *Xacuti* with steaming basmati rice, Ruby-Red Tomato-Carrot Chutney (page 180), and Mango Mousse (pages 405–406) for dessert.

SERVES 4 TO 6 AS A SIDE DISH

2 pounds boneless, skinless chicken-breast halves, cut into 2-inch pieces

1 teaspoon salt

2 teaspoons white poppy seeds

2 tablespoons coriander seeds

1¹/₂ teaspoons fennel seeds

1 tablespoon cumin seeds

1 whole pod star anise, seeds removed and broken into rough pieces

2 dried hot red chilis, such as cayennes or chiles de arbol, stemmed

¹/₂ cup dried unsweetened flaked coconut

3¹/₂ tablespoons vegetable oil

2 cups sliced yellow onion

2 fresh green serrano or jalapeño chilis, stemmed and chopped

¹/₄ teaspoon turmeric

¹/₂ teaspoon tamarind concentrate dissolved in 1 cup water

Pinch freshly grated nutmeg

Cilantro sprigs for garnish

1. Rinse the chicken and pat it dry. Sprinkle with the salt and set aside for 15 to 30 minutes at cool room temperature, or in the refrigerator during warm weather.

2. In a small skillet over medium heat, toast the poppy seeds, stirring occasionally, for 3 to 4 minutes. Transfer to a medium bowl and let cool. Meanwhile, in the same skillet, toast the coriander seeds, fennel seeds, cumin seeds, star anise, and chilis, stirring occasionally, until aromatic, about 4 minutes. Add the coconut and toast until fragrant and golden, 2 to 3 minutes more. Turn off the heat. Transfer the poppy seeds to a coffee mill or spice grinder and grind to a powder. Return to the bowl. Add the coconut-spice mixture to the coffee mill and process to a fine powder, in batches if necessary. Mix with the ground poppy and set aside.

3. Heat 1¹/₂ tablespoons of the oil in a heavy large sauté pan over medium heat. Add the onion and cook, stirring frequently, until rich brown, 10 to 12 minutes. Transfer to a blender. Add ¹/₄ cup of water and blend to a smooth paste. Heat the remaining 2 tablespoons of the oil over medium heat in the same sauté pan. Add the chilis and cook, stirring, for 1 minute. Add the turmeric, the spice mixture, and the chicken. Mix well until the meat is coated with the spices and cook, stirring, for 3 to 4 minutes. Add the onion paste, tamarind liquid, and nutmeg and bring to a boil. Cover and simmer until the chicken is tender and the sauce is thick, 25 to 30 minutes. With a slotted spoon, transfer the meat to a warm deep dish, then ladle the sauce over it. Garnish with cilantro and serve.

MANGALORE CHICKEN WITH SWEET, TOASTY GARLIC | Kori Ghassi

The palm-fringed coastal town of Mangalore, in Karnataka State, is situated between Goa and Kerala. Besides its wonderful fish dishes, Mangalore has its own authentic chicken creations. *Ghassi* is a Mangalorean sauce—a unified, cherry-red beauty, thickly textured and very fragrant. The toasty *masala* ingredients are ground along with coconut milk. I have substituted *guajillo* chilis for the traditional Indian varieties; they offer bright color and slight heat. The coconut milk balances out the natural pungency of the chilis. If you have tidbits of meat left over after a party, they can be put to good use in this sauce. Occasionally I'll serve it with potatoes, plantains, and bitter melon to make vegetarian curries.

You can find *guajillo* chilis in markets that specialize in Mexican ingredients. If unavailable, substitute a combination of 3 teaspoons sweet paprika and ¹/₂ teaspoon cayenne.

2 teaspoons plus 2 tablespoons vegetable oil

10 cloves garlic, crushed

2 medium-large dried *guajillo* chilis, stemmed and broken into large pieces

2 tablespoons coriander seeds

2 teaspoons cumin seeds

1 teaspoon black peppercorns

1/2 teaspoon fenugreek seeds

1/4 cup freshly grated coconut (page 307), or defrosted frozen unsweetened coconut

2 cups Fresh Coconut Milk (page 308), or canned unsweetened coconut milk

1 cup water

2 cups sliced yellow onion

2 1/4 pounds boneless, skinless chicken breasts

2 teaspoons salt

A few *kari* leaves (page 28) plus a beautiful sprig for garnish (optional), or cilantro

Juice of 1 lime

1. Heat 2 teaspoons of the oil in a large heavy skillet over medium heat. Add the garlic and cook, stirring, until lightly browned in spots, about 3 minutes. Add the chilis, coriander, cumin, peppercorns, and fenugreek seeds and toast, stirring, until the seeds are aromatic, about 4 minutes. Add the coconut and cook, stirring, until toasty and golden, about 2 minutes more. Transfer the mixture to a blender. Add 1/2 cup of the coconut milk and 1/2 cup of the water to the blender. Blend to a smooth paste, stopping to scrape down the sides of the bowl a couple of times. Transfer to a bowl and set aside.

2. Heat the remaining 2 tablespoons of the oil in a large heavy sauté pan over medium heat. Add the onion and cook, stirring regularly, until deep golden, 8 to 10 minutes. Stir in the spice mixture and cook, stirring, for 2 minutes. Add the chicken and sear on both sides until coated with the paste and no longer pink, about 4 minutes per side. Add the remaining 1/2 cup of water and the salt and bring to a boil. Reduce the heat and stir in the remaining 1 1/2 cups of coconut milk and *kari* leaves, if using. Cover and simmer until the chicken is tender and the sauce takes on a beautiful red color, about 25 minutes. Add the lime juice and remove from the heat. With a slotted spoon, transfer the chicken to a warm serving dish, ladle the sauce over it, decorate with a *kari* leaf sprig, and serve.

PAN-ROASTED CILANTRO-MINT MARINATED CHICKEN

| Kadai Murg Pasandey

This nonsaucy chicken is best cooked shortly before serving, though it will keep in a low oven for about half an hour. Tender lamb ribs or loin can replace the chicken. This makes a wonderful starter served before Mixed Vegetable Kofta in Cream Sauce (pages 260–261), Warm Chickpea and Green Mango Kachumber (page 215), and Flaky Cumin-Scented Paratha (pages 74–75).

SERVES 4 TO 6 AS AN APPETIZER

1¹/4 pounds boneless, skinless chicken breasts, cut into 2-inch pieces

1-inch piece fresh ginger

3 large cloves garlic

1 teaspoon salt

1/2 cup cilantro

1/4 cup fresh mint leaves

1/2 cup plain yogurt

1/4 teaspoon ground cinnamon

1/8 teaspoon ground white pepper

3 whole cloves

4 green cardamom pods, seeds removed

1 teaspoon coriander seeds

1/2 teaspoon cumin or caraway seeds

2¹/2 tablespoons vegetable oil

1/4 cup sliced almonds

1 cup sliced yellow onion

1/2 teaspoon cayenne

1. Place the chicken in a glass baking dish or bowl. In a blender, combine the ginger, garlic, salt, cilantro, mint, yogurt, cinnamon, white pepper, cloves, cardamom seeds, coriander seeds, and cumin or caraway seeds. Blend to a smooth paste, stopping to scrape down the sides of the bowl a couple of times. Pour the paste over the chicken pieces and marinate for at least 2 hours but no longer than 8.

2. Heat the oil in a large heavy skillet over medium heat. Add the almonds and cook, stirring, until lightly browned, 3 to 4 minutes. Transfer to a plate with a slotted spoon. Add the onion and cook, stirring, until very soft and beginning to color, 6 to 8 minutes. Add the cayenne and stir for 30 seconds; when it turns deep red, add the chicken along with the marinade. Cook, uncovered, stirring occasionally, for 12 to 15 minutes. Turn the chicken and cook until tender, 6 to 8 minutes more. Transfer to a heated decorative platter, garnish with almonds, and serve immediately.

VARIATION

Dip the leftover chicken into *pakora* batter (pages 144–145) to make chicken fritters; serve with Chicken Tikka Masala Sauce (pages 272–274) or Korma Sauce (pages 270–271).

LAMB CHOPS IN GOLDEN APRICOT SAUCE | Jardaloo Ma Gosht

This simple preparation of Persian origin has a lovely sweet-and-sour balance to it. It traditionally calls for dried Hunza or Afghan apricots with winelike overtones and a hint of lemon, but you can use Mediterranean or any other dried apricots. Make this dish and invite some friends over; since it has sweet tones, I'd serve it with Crispy Pappadam (pages 142–143) Lemon Rice (page 108), Pickled Vegetables with Zesty Seasoning (pages 199–200), and Velvety Pistachio and Chayote Pudding (page 416).

SERVES 4 TO 6

1/2 cup (about 16) dried apricots, plus additional for garnish

3 tablespoons vegetable oil

1 cup finely chopped yellow onion

1/2-inch piece fresh ginger, minced

2 large cloves garlic, minced

1-inch cinnamon stick

5 green cardamom pods

1/2 teaspoon ground cumin

1/2 teaspoon cayenne

1/8 teaspoon freshly ground black pepper

2 pounds lamb chops (6 to 8), trimmed of all fat

1 cup chopped ripe tomatoes, or canned diced tomatoes

1/2 teaspoon *garam masala* (pages 36–37), or store-bought

1 teaspoon salt

1/2 teaspoon sugar

2 teaspoons freshly squeezed lime juice

1. Soak the apricots in 1/2 cup of warm water for 30 minutes to 1 hour. Puree the apricots along with the soaking water in a blender until smooth.

2. Heat the oil in a heavy large skillet over medium heat. Add the onion and cook, stirring, until lightly browned, 6 to 8 minutes. Add ginger and garlic and cook, stirring, until the onion is caramelized, about 5 minutes more. Add cinnamon and cardamom and stir until fragrant, 1 minute. Stir in the cumin, cayenne, and pepper and stir for 30 seconds. Add the lamb chops and sear for 4 to 5 minutes per side. Add the tomatoes and cook, stirring occasionally, until soft, about 5 minutes. Add the apricot puree, *garam masala,* salt, and sugar. Cover and cook over low heat until the lamb is tender, 30 to 35 minutes. Check once or twice; if the sauce is too dry and threatens to burn, stir in 1/4 to 1/2 cup of water, but remember that this preparation is not too saucy.

3. Add the lime juice and mix gently. Remove from the heat. Taste and add salt and sugar if necessary. Transfer to a heated deep dish and serve garnished with additional apricots.

FENNEL-SCENTED KASHMIR LAMB | Rogan Josh

Kashmiri cuisine is a blend of the best elements of Indian, Iranian, Afghan, and Central Asian haute cuisine. The exotic flavors, which are distinct from those of other regions in India, can be credited to a few spices: local cherry-red chilis (Kashmir *deghi mirch*, pages 23–24) with fleshy, flavorsome, gentle heat; ground ginger; fennel seeds; and *praan*, a garlicky Kashmiri shallot. The large black cardamom is another heat-producing spice that you'll find included in many Kashmiri dishes.

The natives make *rogan josh*, which means "red" (as in red color), in many different ways, but the coloring agent is always cockscomb, a purplish red flower that grows in profusion in spring and summer and is sun-dried, powdered, and kept for the specific purpose of making this dish. Here I substitute paprika.

Zinfandel and Australian cabernets, with fruity overtones and hints of eucalyptus and mint, are a good match for this dish.

SERVES 4

1 pound boneless lamb shoulder (or other lamb stew meat), cut into 1¹/2-inch cubes

4 large cloves garlic, crushed

3 tablespoons *desi ghee* (pages 47–48), or unsalted butter

8 medium shallots, chopped

4 bay leaves

2-inch cinnamon stick

4 whole cloves

4 green cardamom pods

4 black cardamom pods

¹/2 teaspoon mace blades (see page 30)

2 teaspoons Kashmir *deghi mirch* powder (pages 23–24), or sweet paprika

1 teaspoon ground fennel

1 teaspoon ground coriander

1 teaspoon ground ginger

¹/4 teaspoon turmeric

1 teaspoon cayenne

¹/2 cup plain yogurt

2 cups water

1 teaspoon salt

1. Rinse the lamb pieces and place them in a large skillet. Add the garlic and about 1¹/2 cups of water. Bring to a gentle boil, cover partially, and cook over medium heat until the lamb is just starting to become tender but is still chewy, 15 to 20 minutes.

2. Heat the *desi ghee* in a heavy large sauté pan over medium heat. Add the shallots and cook, stirring often, until richly browned, 8 to 10 minutes. Add the bay leaves, cinnamon, cloves, green and black cardamom pods, and mace. Cook, stirring, until the spices swell and are fragrant, about 1 minute. Add the *deghi mirch* powder, fennel, coriander, ginger, turmeric, and cayenne and stir for few seconds, until the mixture turns deep red. Add 1 to 2 tablespoons of water and mix well. Add the lamb along with the garlic (discarding the water) and mix well until the meat is coated with the spices. Cook, stirring, for 4 to 5 minutes. Whisk the yogurt and add to the pan. Mix gently, then add the water and salt. Bring to a gentle boil, cover, reduce the heat, and simmer until the lamb is tender and the flavors meld thoroughly, about 20 to 30 minutes. Discard the bay leaves before serving.

VARIATION

Potato Rogan Josh

For a vegetarian version, substitute 1 1/2 pounds of potatoes and 1/2 cup fresh or frozen peas for the lamb. There is no need to cook the potatoes ahead; start with step 2, and decrease the final simmering time to about 15 minutes, or until the flavors have melded well.

LAMB KORMA | Martsawangan Korma

Kashmiri cuisine is essentially meat-based. Lamb, goat meat, and chicken form the basis of many a famous dish, such as this showstopper. It is delicately flavored with Kashmiri chili powder (*deghi mirch* powder), which is not too spicy but imparts a rich red color to the food. Modern Kashmiri cuisine can be traced back to the fifteenth-century invasion of India by the Mongol conqueror Timur and the migration of skilled woodcarvers, weavers, architects, calligraphers, and cooks from Samarkand to the valley of Kashmir. The descendants of these cooks, called *wazas*, are the master chefs of Kashmir. The classic formal banquet in Kashmir is the royal *wazwan*. It includes thirty-six courses, primarily meat preparations, cooked overnight by the master chef, *vasta waza*, and his retinue of *wazas*. The meal begins with a ritual washing of hands at an intricately engraved copper sink embellished with a soap dish, called the *tash-t-nari*, which is carried around by attendants. Guests are seated in groups of four and share the meal out of a large, beautifully carved copper platter called the *trami*. As the guests eat, each empty *trami* is replaced with a new one promptly. This *korma* dish and Fennel-Scented Kashmir Lamb (pages 286–287) are two of the most popular dishes of the feast. Kashmiris eagerly look forward to *wazwan* at special occasions.

This dish is somewhat similar to Chicken Breasts in Korma Sauce (pages 270–271); the difference here is that the meat is cooked with the spices ahead of time until almost tender, then bathed in a well-balanced creamy yogurt sauce.

SERVES 4 TO 6

2 pounds boneless lamb shoulder (or other lamb stew meat), cut into bite-size cubes

2-inch cinnamon stick

10 whole cloves

8 green cardamom pods

1/2 teaspoon salt

3/4 cup water

1 1/2-inch piece fresh ginger

5 large cloves garlic

2 tablespoons vegetable oil

2 cups thinly sliced yellow onion

2 tablespoons *desi ghee* (pages 47–48), or unsalted butter

2 teaspoons ground coriander

1 teaspoon Kashmir *deghi mirch* powder (pages 23–24), or sweet paprika

1 teaspoon cayenne

1 teaspoon ground fennel

1/2 teaspoon turmeric

2 cups finely chopped ripe tomatoes with juices, or canned diced tomatoes

1/2 cup roasted unsalted cashews

1 cup plain yogurt

Beautiful sprigs of cilantro, for garnish

Lime wedges, for serving (optional)

1. Rinse the lamb pieces and place in a large skillet. Add the cinnamon, cloves, cardamom, salt, and water. Bring to a gentle boil, cover partially, and cook over medium heat until the lamb is just starting to become tender but is still chewy, 15 to 20 minutes.

2. Combine the ginger and garlic with 3 to 4 tablespoons water in a blender. Blend to a smooth puree, stopping to scrape down the sides of the bowl a couple of times. Set aside.

3. Heat the oil in a heavy large sauté pan over medium heat. Add the onion and cook, stirring often, until the onion is a rich golden color and caramelized, 12 to 15 minutes. Transfer to a plate. Add the *desi ghee,* and when hot, add the ginger-garlic paste. Cook, stirring, until the mixture is fragrant and turns light brown, 4 to 5 minutes. Add the coriander, *deghi mirch* powder, cayenne, fennel, and turmeric and stir well; the *masala* will take on a beautiful orange-red color at this point. Add the tomato with juices and cook, stirring occasionally, until very soft, about 6 minutes.

4. Meanwhile, combine the cashews with 1/4 cup of water in the blender and blend to as smooth a paste as possible. Add to the pan. Whisk the yogurt and stir into the pan; the sauce will look curdled at first, but don't worry about it. Add the reserved onion and the cooked lamb with the spices (discard the water or save for use in soups) and mix well. Taste and season with salt, usually 1/2 teaspoon. Bring to a gentle boil, cover, and simmer until the lamb is tender and the flavors blend thoroughly, about 30 to 40 minutes. With a slotted spoon, transfer the lamb to a warm serving dish, then ladle the sauce over it and decorate it with cilantro sprigs. Serve wedges of lime to squirt on the lamb, if desired.

SWEET-SCENTED HYDERABAD GROUND LAMB | Hyderabadi Kheema

Kheema—Indian chili without the beans—is a dry, spicy dish made of minced lamb or beef that is considered a delicacy among Indian Muslims. It is wonderfully complex, with all the seasonings toasted one by one, a classic technique that translates into deep, rich flavor. Cinnamon provides a lovely aroma and a distinct warmth. For variety, try adding fresh peas in the final step. Keep in mind that if you use ground turkey meat, it gives off a lot of moisture when cooked and you might have to drain a bit off before adding the tomatoes.

I have served this dish many times at northern California cricket matches, and it's always a hit with players and fans. They spread *kheema* on *naan* or *chapati*, rolled them like wrappers, and devoured them. *Kheema* is also great stuffed in warm pita bread or used as a topping for spaghetti.

SERVES 6

1-inch piece fresh ginger

4 large cloves garlic

1 to 2 fresh green serrano or jalapeño chilis, stemmed

1/4 cup vegetable oil

1 1/2 cups finely chopped yellow onion

4-inch cinnamon stick

4 whole cloves

2 black cardamom pods

2 green cardamom pods

1 teaspoon cumin seeds

1 teaspoon ground coriander

1 teaspoon *garam masala* (pages 36–37), or store-bought

1/4 teaspoon turmeric

1 pound lean ground lamb, beef, or turkey, rinsed well

2 cups finely diced ripe tomatoes, or canned diced tomatoes

1 1/4 cups chicken or vegetable stock, or water

1 1/2 teaspoons salt

1/2 cup loosely packed chopped cilantro, plus additional for garnish

1. In a blender, combine the ginger, garlic, and chilis with 1/3 cup of water. Blend to a smooth puree, stopping to scrape down the sides of the bowl if necessary. Transfer to a small bowl and set aside.

2. Heat the oil in a heavy large sauté pan over medium heat. Add the onion and cook, stirring, until lightly browned, about 8 minutes. Add the ginger-garlic paste and cook, stirring frequently, until fragrant and the raw garlic smell dissipates, about 5 minutes. Add the cinnamon, cloves, and black and green cardamom pods and stir until the spices are plump, about 1 minute. Add the cumin, coriander, *garam masala,* and turmeric and stir for a few seconds until aromatic. Add the ground meat and cook, stirring regularly, until the meat is no longer pink and the seasonings are incorporated, 6 to 8 minutes. Stir in the tomatoes and cook, stirring, until soft, about 6 minutes. Add the stock, salt, and cilantro and bring to a boil. Reduce the heat and simmer, covered, until the meat is tender and all the liquid is absorbed so that the mixture looks almost dry, 25 to 30 minutes. If there is any water remaining, cook uncovered, stirring, until it evaporates. Let the meat rest, covered, for 5 minutes. Transfer to a warmed serving dish, garnish with cilantro, and serve hot.

KERALA-STYLE AROMATIC LAMB | Eratchi Ularthiyathu

This is a lovely, dry curry in which the fragrant *masala* clings to chunks of tender lamb. The *masala* in this dish is very versatile; I once replaced the lamb with squash for a vegetarian friend. It works beautifully with jumbo shrimp as well.

SERVES 4

1 pound boneless lamb shoulder (or other lamb stew meat), cut into bite-size cubes

3 tablespoons vegetable oil

2 cups sliced yellow onion

1-inch piece fresh ginger

4 large cloves garlic

2 to 4 dried hot red chilis, such as cayennes or chiles de arbol, or fewer to taste, stemmed and softened (microwave for 1 minute in 1/4 cup water)

20 *kari* leaves (page 28) (optional), or cilantro

1 tablespoon ground coriander

1/4 teaspoon freshly ground black pepper

2 cups finely chopped ripe tomatoes with juices, or canned diced tomatoes

2 tablespoons dried unsweetened flaked coconut

1 teaspoon ground fennel

1 teaspoon salt

1/2 cup water

1. Rinse the lamb pieces and place them in a medium skillet. Add about 1 1/2 cups of water. Bring to a boil, cover partially, and cook over medium heat until the lamb is just starting to become tender but is still chewy, 15 to 20 minutes. Remove from the heat.

2. Meanwhile, heat the oil in a heavy large sauté pan over medium heat. Add the onion and cook, stirring, until richly browned, 10 to 12 minutes. While the onion is cooking, combine the ginger and garlic with 3 to 4 tablespoons water in a blender. Blend to a smooth puree, stopping to scrape down the sides of the bowl if necessary. Add to the pan and cook, stirring, until the puree is fragrant and starts to brown, about 4 minutes. Add the chilis and their soaking liquid to the blender and blend into a smooth puree. Add to the pan. Add the *kari* leaves, if using, and stir until fragrant, about 30 seconds.

3. Add the coriander and pepper and stir for a few seconds. Add the tomatoes with juices and cook, stirring occasionally, until the tomato is very soft and the mixture starts to dry out, 6 to 8 minutes. Add the lamb, discarding the cooking water, and coconut and stir until the meat is well coated with the *masala*. Add the fennel, salt, and water and bring to a boil. Reduce the heat and simmer, stirring occasionally, until all of the liquid is absorbed and the lamb is tender, 30 to 35 minutes, adding a little water if necessary to prevent the lamb from drying out. Transfer to a warm serving dish and serve hot.

FRAGRANT DUM-STYLE LAMB WITH MUSHROOMS

| Handi Gosht Khusk Purdah

Loosely translated, *dum* means "stewing pot." In this recipe, partially cooked ingredients are neatly packed into an earthenware or copper stewing pot, and the lid is sealed with bread dough. Very little or no liquid is added at this stage, and the juices and seasonings from the various ingredients are "breathed into" the stew, creating a quick meal. No steam or flavors escape until the seal is broken. The result is a highly aromatic, comforting dish, which caught the attention of the nawab (sultan) of Oudh in 1784, at a time when there was a famine in the region. The nawab had commanded the construction of a vast edifice to keep his starving subjects employed. He had food distributed to all the workers. The laborers filled enormous cauldrons with assorted vegetables, rice, spices, and meat and sealed the lids with bread dough. Red-hot coals were piled on top of the secured containers, and the mixture was slowly cooked all night over a fire. The intertwining aromas permeated the neighborhoods, drawing people to the cooking fires. It was the opening of one of these cooking pots that attracted royal attention. Captivated by the enticing flavors, the nawab ordered his chefs to recreate them in the imperial kitchens. Eventually, the *dum* method was adopted by royal chefs and considered the food of the emperors.

Here a full-flavored stew of lamb, mushrooms, and cauliflower is draped with a "purdah" (curtain) of puff pastry and finished in the oven. When you "crack" the pastry open at the table, the aromas entice the dinner guests, making this dish a good choice for any party.

SERVES 4

1-inch piece fresh ginger

3 large cloves garlic

1/4 cup vegetable oil

1 large yellow onion, sliced

4-inch cinnamon stick

10 whole cloves

1/2 teaspoon mace blades (page 30)

4 allspice berries

6 green cardamom pods

1 teaspoon *garam masala* (pages 36–37), or store-bought

1 teaspoon ground coriander

1/2 teaspoon turmeric

1/2 teaspoon cayenne

1 pound boneless lamb shoulder, cut into 2-inch pieces

1 cup pureed ripe tomatoes, or canned tomato puree

10 white button mushrooms

1/2 cup green beans, sliced into 1-inch diagonal pieces

1/4 cup sliced carrots

1/4 cup plain yogurt

1/2 cup water

2 teaspoons salt

1 teaspoon sugar

1/2 cup whole roasted unsalted cashews

1 sheet thawed frozen puff pastry, or 1/4 recipe *naan* dough (pages 84–85)

1. In a blender, combine the ginger and garlic with 2 to 3 tablespoons of water. Blend to a smooth puree, stopping to scrape down the sides of the bowl if necessary. Set aside.

2. Heat 2 tablespoons of the oil in a heavy large sauté pan over medium heat. Add the onion and cook, stirring often, until the onion is a rich golden color and caramelized, 12 to 15 minutes. Transfer the onion to a blender, blend to a paste, and set aside. Heat the remaining 2 tablespoons of oil in the same pan. Add the ginger-garlic paste and cook, stirring, until the paste is fragrant and starts to brown, about 3 minutes.

3. Add the cinnamon, cloves, mace, allspice, and cardamom to the pan and cook, stirring, until the spices are plump and fragrant, about 1 minute. Add the *garam masala*, coriander, turmeric, and cayenne and cook, stirring, until the spices are aromatic, about 30 seconds. Add the lamb and onion paste and mix well until the meat is coated with the spices. Cook, stirring, for 5 to 6 minutes. Add the pureed tomatoes and cook, stirring, until the raw tomato smell disappears, 6 to 8 minutes. Add the mushrooms, green beans, and carrots and cook, stirring, for 1 minute. Reduce the heat to low and stir in the yogurt, followed by the water, salt, sugar, and cashews. Mix well. Simmer until the lamb is tender and the sauce is thick, 30 to 35 minutes.

4. Meanwhile, preheat the oven to 375°F. Transfer the meat mixture into an earthenware or copper pot or a baking dish. Cover the top with the pastry sheet and cut away the excess around the edges. Bake until the pastry sheet is nicely golden, about 20 minutes.

KASHMIR DUCK BREAST WITH CRUSTY TURNIP AND RUTABAGA

| Gogji Bathak

Moist and tender duck breasts with a deep, rich, and intensely flavored sauce are perfectly complemented by crunchy winter vegetables. Kashmiris preserve turnips and other winter produce in holes dug deep in snow or dry them and suspend them on walls. Traditionally, Kashmiris prepare a spice blend made with shallots and garlic or asafetida and store it in a cake form called *vari masala*. The cake is highly fragrant and vibrant with saffron, cockscomb flower heads, Indian black cumin *(shahi jeera)*, betel leaves, and areca nut (which contains enzymes that help break down the muscle fibers of protein in meat). The *masala* cakes are made in large quantities and sun-dried and stored for several months for use in winter. Chunks of cake are broken and added just like any spice blend to flavor local dishes.

Australian cabernet sauvignons tend to be more fruity and less oaky than other cabernets, making them a good match for this spicy dish. Alongside freshly cooked basmati rice and Mango-Macadamia Raita (page 206) or any fruit chutney in this book, duck seems just right.

SERVES 6 TO 8

1 medium turnip

1 medium rutabaga, peeled

2¹/2 teaspoons salt

5 tablespoons vegetable oil

2 cups sliced yellow onion

1-inch piece fresh ginger

4 large cloves garlic

4 bay leaves

4 whole cloves

¹/4 teaspoon turmeric

2 teaspoons ground coriander

2 black cardamom pods, seeds removed and crushed

1 teaspoon ground fennel

1 teaspoon cayenne

1 teaspoon Kashmir *deghi mirch* powder (pages 23–24), or sweet paprika

Two 1-pound boneless Muscovy or Moulard duck breast halves, skin left on

1 cup water

1. Cut off the ends of the turnip and rutabaga and slice into wedges slightly less than ¹/4 inch thick. Transfer to a colander in the sink. Sprinkle with 2 teaspoons of the salt (to remove some of the bitterness) and set aside for 15 minutes to drain; rinse and pat dry.

Heat 2 tablespoons of the oil over medium heat in a large skillet. Place vegetables in a single layer and cook until crusty, about 5 minutes per side. You may have to do this in batches. Transfer to a plate.

2.   Heat the remaining 3 tablespoons of oil in a large sauté pan over medium heat. Add the onion and cook, stirring often, until deep golden, about 8 minutes. While the onion is cooking, combine the ginger and garlic with 3 to 4 tablespoons of water in a blender. Blend to a smooth puree, stopping to scrape down the sides of the bowl if necessary. Add to the pan and cook, stirring, until the puree is fragrant and starts to brown, about 4 minutes. Add the bay leaves and cloves and stir until fragrant, about 1 minute. Add the turmeric, followed by the coriander, cardamom, fennel, cayenne, and *deghi mirch* powder; stir for 30 seconds. Place the duck, skin-side down, in the pan. Cook until seared, about 5 minutes per side. Add the water and remaining 1/2 teaspoon of salt, cover, and cook until the meat is tender, 20 to 25 minutes.

3.   Stir in the reserved vegetables, cover, and cook until the flavors blend, 3 to 4 minutes more. Serve hot.

DUCK LEGS WITH SUBTLE SPINACH SAUCE | Palak Bathak

Duck is available from many specialty markets nowadays. The sauce here is a bit subtler than the previous recipe, great for anyone who prefers a milder flavor. I like to cook the duck with the flavorful skin.

Alongside this relatively simple duck dish, I like to serve fragrant Rhubarb Rasam Soup (page 369), hot *chapati* (pages 63–64), Red and Golden Beet Kachumber with Orange (page 216), and plain rice. Vanilla ice cream with Indian-Style Baked Flaky Doughnuts (page 420) makes for a perfect ending.

1-inch piece fresh ginger

3 large cloves garlic

1 to 2 fresh green serrano or jalapeño chilis, stemmed

1/4 cup plain yogurt

3/4 teaspoon ground cumin

1/2 teaspoon ground coriander

1 1/2 pounds Muscovy duck legs, with skin on

2 1/2 cups packed chopped fresh spinach

3/4 cup water

1 1/2 tablespoons vegetable oil

1 cup finely chopped yellow onion

2-inch cinnamon stick

2 black cardamom pods

1 whole pod star anise

1/2 cup chopped ripe tomatoes, or canned diced tomatoes

2 tablespoons tomato paste

1/2 teaspoon salt

1. Combine the ginger, garlic, and chilis with 2 tablespoons of water in a blender. Blend to a smooth puree, stopping to scrape down the sides of the bowl if necessary. Transfer to a medium bowl. Add the yogurt, 1/4 teaspoon of the cumin, and the coriander to the bowl and whisk with a fork to mix. Rinse the duck legs, pat them dry, and place them in a glass or nonaluminum pan. Prick the duck skin with fork tines in a few places. Coat the duck with the marinade and set aside for 1 to 2 hours at cool room temperature, but do not leave any longer.

2. In a saucepan over medium heat, combine the spinach and 1/2 cup of the water and cook, covered, until wilted, 3 to 4 minutes. Cool slightly and puree in a blender. Set aside.

3. Heat the oil in a medium sauté pan over medium heat. Add the onion and cook, stirring, until the edges start to brown, about 6 minutes. Add the cinnamon, cardamom, and star anise and cook, stirring, until fragrant, about 1 minute. Add the remaining 1/2 teaspoon cumin and stir for a few seconds. Add the meat, marinade and all, to the pan. Sear skin side for about 6 minutes, then turn the meat and cook 6 more minutes, until the yogurt melds away and oil pools around the meat. Add the tomatoes and tomato paste, stir, and cook until the tomatoes are soft, about 5 minutes. (You can skim off some of the fat and discard it, if you prefer.) Add the salt and remaining 1/4 cup of water, cover, and cook until the meat is chewy, 10 to 12 minutes (the way I prefer it), or until tender, about 5 minutes more.

4. Stir in the spinach puree and cook, covered, until the flavors meld, about 5 minutes. Transfer to an attractive heated serving dish and serve.

COORG-STYLE PORK STEW | Codwa Pandi Kari

One place particularly dear to me in Karnataka State is Coorg; it reminds me of northern California. Coorg is an environmentalist's delight: lush greenery, beautiful mountains draped with fog at dawn, numerous waterfalls, and free-roaming wildlife. Large crops of rice, oranges, pepper, cardamom, and more than a quarter of India's coffee plantations can be found here. Coorgis are tall and beautiful, with warm, graceful manners that belie a long martial tradition. They hunt and fish avidly, unlike most southerners. In olden days they hunted wild boar. Nowadays hunting is banned, so domestic pork is used in this absolutely gorgeous hot-and-sour, almost picklelike stew. This dish uses many unusual ingredients, such as *sambar* onions and *kachipalli* (brown tamarindlike pulp), and is served with dainty steamed rice balls, made with rice flour.

SERVES 4 TO 6

1-inch piece fresh ginger

6 large cloves garlic

1 teaspoon cayenne

1 teaspoon pepper

1/2 teaspoon turmeric

2 tablespoons vegetable oil

6 pearl onions or shallots, peeled and sliced 1/8 inch thick

1 1/2 pounds boneless pork loin, well trimmed and

cut into 1-inch chunks

1 cup water, or chicken stock

1 teaspoon salt

1/2 teaspoon ground cumin

1/4 teaspoon ground cinnamon

2 green cardamom pods, seeds removed and pulverized

2 tablespoons freshly squeezed lime juice

1. In a blender, combine the ginger and garlic with 1/4 cup of water. Blend to a smooth puree, stopping to scrape down the sides of the bowl if necessary. Transfer to a small bowl and set aside. In another small bowl, combine the cayenne, pepper, and turmeric with 2 tablespoons of water to make a paste. Set aside.

2. Heat the oil in a heavy large sauté pan over medium heat. Add the pearl onions and cook, stirring often, until the onions start to brown, about 4 minutes. Add the ginger-garlic paste and cook, stirring, until the paste is fragrant and starts to brown, about 2 minutes. Add the cayenne paste to the pan and cook, stirring, until fragrant and the liquid evaporates, about 1 minute. Add the pork and sear for 5 minutes per side. Add the water and salt, stir, and cook until the pork is tender and the sauce very thick, almost like ketchup, about 35 minutes. Add the cumin, cinnamon, and cardamom and stir well. Add the lime juice, stir, and remove from the heat. Serve hot with white rice on the side, if desired.

CLASSIC PORK VINDALOO | Pork Vindalho

Vindaloo is an amalgamation of two Portuguese words, *vinho*, which means "wine" (or vinegar) and *alho*, which means "garlic." It sums up the dish quite well. Coconut *feni* (locally made alcohol) is used here; my aunt thinks there is no substitute for the distinct sweet-sour flavor and light effervescence of the Goan alcohol. I agree, but I've used tamarind pulp for a fruitier taste and velvety thickness. Traditionally this dish is very hot, but you can control the intensity. Use *guajillo* chilis for color and slight heat. Skip the dried hot chilis, if desired, and add cayenne to the paste in step 2; about 1 1/2 teaspoons is just right. Complement *vindaloo* with a wide variety of *naan* (pages 84–90) and a fruity rosé to quench the spicy heat.

SERVES 6 TO 8 AS A SIDE DISH

3 to 4 medium dried *guajillo* chilis, stemmed and broken into large pieces

6 tablespoons white or cider vinegar

1 1/2 teaspoons cumin seeds

2-inch cinnamon stick, broken

10 whole cloves

1/2 heaping teaspoon black peppercorns

1 whole pod star anise, seeds removed from the points

6 to 10 dried hot red chilis, such as cayennes or chiles de arbol, or fewer to taste (see head-note), stemmed

2 teaspoons poppy seeds, preferably white

3-inch piece fresh ginger

12 large cloves garlic

1 teaspoon light-brown sugar, jaggery (pages 51–52), or raw sugar

2 pounds boneless pork loin, well trimmed and cut into 2-inch pieces

1/4 cup vegetable oil

2 cups finely chopped yellow onion

3 tablespoons tamarind pulp (pages 54–55)

2 teaspoons salt

2 cups water

Beautiful sprigs of cilantro, for garnish (optional)

1. Soak the *guajillo* chilis in the vinegar for 1 hour. (For quick soaking, if you're short on time, microwave the mixture for 30 seconds.)

2. In a skillet over medium heat, combine the cumin, cinnamon, cloves, peppercorns, star anise, and chilis and toast, stirring frequently, until the seeds are aromatic, about 4 minutes. Add the poppy seeds to the skillet and cook, stirring, until toasty, about 2 minutes more. Cool slightly. Transfer to a coffee mill and grind to a fine powder. Transfer the spice blend to a blender. Add the ginger, garlic, sugar, and soaking *guajillo* chilis along with the vinegar. Blend to a smooth paste, stopping to scrape down the sides of the bowl a couple of times. Add 1 or 2 tablespoons of water to facilitate blending, if needed.

3. Transfer the *vindaloo* paste to a shallow glass dish. Add the meat pieces and rub the paste thoroughly onto the pork, coating the pieces evenly. Cover and set aside at cool room temperature for 1 to 2 hours, or refrigerate for up to 4 hours.

4. Heat the oil in a large heavy sauté pan over medium heat. Add the onion and cook, stirring regularly, until deep golden, 8 to 10 minutes. Add the pork, reserving the marinade, and sear the meat for 5 to 6 minutes per side. Add the marinade, tamarind pulp, salt, and water and bring to a boil. Reduce the heat, cover, and simmer until the pork is tender, the sauce takes on a brilliant deep red color, and the flavors come together, about 30 minutes. With a slotted spoon, transfer the meat to a warm serving dish, then ladle the sauce over it. Garnish with cilantro, if desired, and serve.

SKILLET EGG MASALA | Kadai Ande

Every region in India has its own egg curry; the sauce ranges from a soupy chowder consistency to almost dry, as in the following recipe. Egg curry is very traditional and considered an important part of Indian cuisine, and it's especially popular with children. My neighbors tasted many of my creations while I was testing recipes for this book; Mike and Dorothy wrote their feedback on note cards and left them at my doorstep each morning. For this recipe the card reads, "Nice combination with eggs, a different experience than usual deviled eggs, a more flavorful tasty treat with a wealth of spices, yet mild."

Eggs are considered nonvegetarian in India; that's why this "meatless" dish is in this chapter. You can serve this *masala* over steamed or roasted vegetables or any firm white fish steaks.

SERVES 4 AS A SIDE DISH

8 large eggs

4 green cardamom pods, seeds removed

6 whole cloves

1-inch cinnamon stick

3 teaspoons coriander seeds

1 teaspoon fennel seeds

1 teaspoon black peppercorns

1 teaspoon cayenne

1/4 cup vegetable or canola oil

2 cups thinly sliced yellow onion

1 cup finely chopped ripe tomatoes, or canned diced tomatoes

1/2 cup water

1 teaspoon salt

1. Place the eggs in a single layer in a saucepan. Add enough cold water to come 1 inch above the eggs and bring to a boil over high heat. Reduce the heat, cover, and simmer for 15 minutes; drain. Place the eggs in cold water until cool enough to handle; drain. Gently tap each egg on the countertop and peel off the eggshell, starting at the large end. Cut the eggs in half lengthwise.

2. While the eggs are cooking, combine the cardamom seeds, cloves, cinnamon, coriander seeds, fennel seeds, peppercorns, and cayenne in a spice grinder or coffee mill and grind to a fine powder. Set aside.

3. Heat the oil in a heavy medium skillet over medium heat. Add the onion and cook, stirring often, until deep golden, 8 to 10 minutes. Add the ground spice powder and stir until fragrant, about 30 seconds. Add the tomato and cook, stirring occasionally, until soft, about 6 minutes. Add the water and salt (you may add the halved eggs now if you want them to absorb more curry flavor); cook the sauce for 2 minutes more and remove from the heat. If you haven't added them yet, place the eggs neatly on a warm serving platter, top each half with the curry sauce, and serve.

VARIATION

Add 1/2 cup crumbled Fresh Basic Paneer (page 221) in step 3 along with the tomatoes and continue with the recipe.

SEAFOOD PARADISE

Samundar ki Gulnaar

This chapter will take you on a special culinary journey through India's seafood paradise. India boasts more than 4,000 miles of exotic coastline, from Karwar in the west to Kolkata in the east—along the Arabian Sea, Indian Ocean, and Bay of Bengal. The country also has numerous inland lakes and rivers. Almost 180 varieties of fish, from Kashmir in the north to Kerala in the south, are relished and turned into hundreds of fish recipes, with countless local variations. To Western tastes, the resulting dishes are nearly always haunting and exotic. Many are the creations of the fishermen and boatmen themselves—sometimes simple and mild, sometimes recklessly pungent. Before you cook, let's sail!

A SEAFOOD TOUR OF INDIA

KASHMIR

As we kick off our expedition, floating in the *shikaras* (houseboats) of Kashmir, you'll see a landscape of abundant beauty, gardens of water lilies, orchards of apples and walnuts, sweet snow-water falls along the foothills of the Himalayas, cool, clear deep lakes, and of course, copious fish. Surrounded with a ring of snow-capped, majestic mountain ranges, Kashmir is often referred to as "an emerald set in pearls." Water has definitely influenced the cuisine of Kashmir. Favorites among both boat dwellers and locals who live on shore are seasonal freshwater fish, as well as smelt, baby catfish, mackerel, carp, lobster, and shrimp; trout is a new addition introduced by the British, found in numerous streams. In Kashmir curries, the seafood is blended harmoniously with root vegetables, squashes, and leafy greens. Fish is often sun-dried and smoked for use in winter.

MUMBAI (FORMERLY BOMBAY)

Near the city of Mumbai, the Gateway of India, numerous fishing communities (called *koli*), each with its own atmosphere, dot the coast of the Arabian Sea. Let's start with Bombay "duck." Of course, it is not a duck at all. It is a small fish, *bommaloe machchi,* that likely got its Anglicized name because its Indian name was too hard for the British to pronounce. Dried in the sun on wide bamboo frames, it ends up resembling crispy bacon. More mainstream is pomfret, a saltwater flatfish with a firm texture that's a coastal favorite. I like it stuffed with fresh coconut and herbs, then slowly steamed in banana leaves. The bright green packets make an attractive presentation at the table served with salsalike Quick Mango-Cucumber Chaat (page 332).

MALVAN

As we move along the western Konkan trail, we arrive at a coastal area called Malvan, known for its coconut-based, delicious seafood curries. I remember a family friend from the Malvan region saying, "I've eaten so much fish in all my life, even if my body is thrown into the sea after my death, it will not cleanse me fully." This region is so gifted with outstanding seafood, a story comes to mind: Hundreds of years ago, a boy named Saraswat was taking lessons in Vedas (ancient Hindu scriptures) along with other students. A severe drought fell on the land. All the other pupils left the place, but Saraswat sat meditating, unaware of the drought. Overcome by his strength of mind, God granted Saraswat a blessing and advised him to eat fish from the sea for sustenance. In this way a fish-eating Brahmin community evolved. Since then Saraswat Brahmins have always enjoyed their seafood.

Goa

Farther down the emerald coast is the state of Goa, a tiny peninsula lush with jungles, beaches, palm groves, mesmeric sunsets, and cashew coppice, not to mention a remarkable cuisine that draws from Indian and Portuguese influences. Fish is the staple diet of the Goans, with an abundance of kingfish, pomfret, mackerels, sardines, squid, shark, prawns, and mussels. Fishing, both inshore with small boats, canoes, and hand nets, and offshore with modern trawlers, is a main source of income for Goans. Scarlet-hued vindaloo curries are typical of this state, made with liberal quantities of vinegar, spices, and chilis. Throughout the centuries, Goa has been a cauldron in which many cultures have melded to form a formidable cuisine, a treat for taste buds.

Karwar

Navigating the turbulent waters of the Arabian Sea, we now reach Karwar, a port in Karnataka State. Coconut palms and lush paddy fields sway to the strong gusts of wind from the Arabian Sea. Gurgling streams crisscross the winding roads and undulating hills and valleys of the Western Ghats. Arab traders once sailed this region and called it "bay of safety." Dates, coconut palms, and rice fields hug the lush coastal strip. Small fish such as smelt, catfish, mackerel, oysters, and prawns are cooked in a variety of combinations here, with vegetables and spices that include pepper, turmeric, chilis, coriander, and fenugreek seeds. Fish heads are cooked with legumes to enhance flavors. One of the essential talents of a prospective bride is that of cleaning and cutting fish.

MANGALORE

We now slowly drift along the southwestern coast to the city of Mangalore in Karnataka State. The seaside is scalloped with palm, mango, and jackfruit trees. Fish is abundant and much favored by nonvegetarians. Shellfish such as mussels and prawns are available year-round; mackerel, sardines, and even small sharks are dried for off-season use. One of my favorite memories is of my aunt preparing a robust prawn curry. First the prawns were cleaned and salted. Then she would methodically pick a handful of aromatics—garlic, chilis, coriander seeds, white peppercorns, onion, and a bunch of cilantro—and grind them together on a grinding stone until the paste was smooth and silky. As she gently rubbed the herbal paste over the plump prawns and cooked them in coconut oil, she would tell me an old tale about a fisherwoman who was visiting her sister in Mysore, a fragrant city known for jasmine, incense, and sandalwood. After a while, however, the fisherwoman got so tired of the local scents that she slept with her fish basket over her face. We would laugh, and my aunt's curries were always wonderful.

KERALA

Still farther south, where the Arabian Sea meets the Indian Ocean, is the Kerala (literally, the land of coconuts) coastline. India's richest seafood treasures are found here. The sea forms a fascinating network of lagoons, canals, and rivers called the backwaters. They are graced with swaying palms, cashew nut trees, clusters of banana trees, mango and sweet jackfruit groves, lush rice fields, and thatched huts—in short, this is everyone's storybook tropical Indian Subcontinent. Fish curries are enlivened with sweet-sour fruits, aromatic spices, incendiary chilis, and milky white coconut cream. Every evening just at sunset, fishermen set out large circular nets; at high tide, a school of fish swims into the nets, letting the fishermen get their catch to market just before dawn. The waters—salty, fresh, and brackish—yield herring, fish roe, mackerel, bass, pomfret, sardines, shrimp, small crabs, whitebait, and small sharks of unsurpassed delectability. An old Kerala saying, "Better give her a big fish," perhaps best signifies the dexterity of local cooks.

KOLKATA (CAPITAL OF WEST BENGAL, FORMERLY CALCUTTA)

The silver and sapphire Bay of Bengal is bordered by a lush coastline, studded with date and coconut palms, rice paddies, and mustard fields. River fish are especially abundant here. Fish is considered to be very auspicious, second only to rice as an essential in the diet. Bengalis are famed for their long, black tresses and beautiful eyes, which are attributed to the fish in their diet. Wedding feasts include numerous fish entrees. Traditionally, the bride's family sends the finest fish possible to the groom's home with great pomp. As is the custom, the fish will show up at the wedding "dressed" in fine attire, with flower garlands around the gill, and sometimes a precious stone in its nose, a gorgeous silk scarf around its head, or perhaps a cigarette in its mouth! Along with the fish, fresh spices and oil are provided. The fish is turned into a rich delicacy by the groom's family. No one enjoys fish more than the Bengalis. They cook it in a variety of styles, from marinating it in spices, to cooking it in mustard paste or yogurt.

COCONUT, THE TREE OF LIFE—MOTHER NATURE'S SUSTENANCE PACKAGE

Coconut and coconut milk form an integral part of many fish dishes. That's why I have placed the directions for preparing coconut in this chapter. The coconut is aptly called *shrifal,* or "fruit of the gods." The coconut tree is called the *kalpavriksha,* or "tree that grants boons," because in India it is believed that a single coconut tree takes care of an individual human existence. Besides the fluffy freshly grated coconut and creamy coconut milk it provides, every part of the tree is a precious gift from nature. For instance, the tender blossoms of coconut trees store fragrant nectar, which is tapped, made into natural sugar, and used as a sweetener in desserts. If allowed to ferment longer, the nectar turns into rich palm wine, enjoyed by peasants and villagers. New tender palm leaflets are chopped and cooked with vegetables to impart a unique flavor. Young green coconuts are prized for their refreshing water. The coconut meat is desiccated and turned into coconut oil for cooking; perfumed, it is used as hair oil. The hard coconut shells are carved into kitchen utensils, such as ladles, bowls, cups, and spatulas. They make fine decorative household items, jewelry, and musical instruments as well. When I was in grade school, I always used coconut shells for art projects. Coconut husk is used as fuel in the kitchen. It is also used as a scouring pad for cookware; believe me, it works—vessels come out sparkling clean. The versatile fiber of the husk, known as *coir,* is spun into heavy-duty twine. The long mature fronds are used for thatching material, while plaited leaflets make beautifully crafted, sturdy baskets, hats, and mats. The stripped ribs of the leaflets bundled together make sturdy brooms. The dried leaves, coconut shells, and tree trunk are used as firewood. The decay-resistant trunk is also used for building homes and making furniture.

Coconuts are eaten in different stages of ripeness. When young and green, the clear water inside is sweet and refreshing. I always look forward to green coconuts when I visit my parent's home in India, as they are naturally fragrant, with a delicate hint of flowers. Green coconut water is not only a good thirst quencher but restores energy. In ayurvedic medicine, coconut water is recommended for reducing fevers and strengthening the heart. Fresh coconut milk is a popular gargle for mouth inflammation, as it is soothing and healing. The coconut meat starts out gelatinous, growing thicker as the fruit matures. When the coconut is green, you can easily spoon the tender meat out and eat its creamy and lightly sweet center. It has a pleasant, refreshing taste as it moves smoothly down the throat. I remember when my brother roasted young coconuts in their husks. The clear water turned even sweeter, with a subtle smoked aroma, and the meat became richer.

Nearly all coconut palms are grown for their mature fruit, which yield shredded coconut and milk. In the West, coconut is best known in its sweetened, shredded form, used to make desserts and piña coladas. As a little girl, I loved to watch when my mother made coconut milk. She added boiling water to the freshly grated coconut. The coconut was steeped for awhile and then strained. When it was cool enough to handle, she gathered the pulp a fistful at a time and squeezed it until all the "milk" was pressed. She termed this heavy coconut cream. She added more hot water to the pulp and repeated the procedure. The second pressing yielded a more pallid liquid that she called light coconut milk. The "thin milk" from the third pressing resembled skim milk. Freshly pressed milk was flavorful, delightfully nutty, and naturally sweet. She kept all three types of coconut milk on hand for use in different dishes and to add at various stages of cooking. The gradations are simply degrees of dilution. The pulp was strewn in the garden or used to make compost.

In the following recipes, freshly grated coconut (used as a flavoring and garnish in this book) and coconut milk are frequently used. Both the meat and milk are available in prepared form, but for incomparable flavor and texture, try preparing them yourself from fresh coconuts.

TO CRACK AND GRATE FRESH COCONUT

Coconuts are delicate and do not store well once the husk is removed. When buying fresh coconuts, look for ones without mold (check the eyes) or cracks. Choose coconuts that are heavy for their size—a sign that they contain plenty of liquid—which keeps the meat from drying out. The thin, clear liquid, or "coconut water," can be used in soups, for making bread dough, or for cooking rice. You can also drink it as is. If it tastes sweet, the coconut is fresh; if it tastes oily, the coconut is rancid and should be discarded.

A quick and easy way to crack a coconut is to use a cleaver or hammer. Holding it with one hand so that the midriff rests in the middle of your palm, with the tip on one end and the eyes on the other, whack the coconut with the back of a cleaver or a hammer a few times all around the center until it cracks open cleanly into two nearly equal halves. Do this over a bowl to catch the water as it drains. The white flesh can be scraped out using a small implement with a row of sharp teeth called a grater, available from Indian and Southeast Asian markets. Here is an easier oven method to crack and grate a coconut for fresh-tasting meat.

MAKES ABOUT 2 1/2 CUPS

1 fresh coconut

Preheat the oven to 400°F. Pierce the softest eye of the coconut with a metal skewer or screwdriver and drain the liquid into a bowl to sample; if it tastes oily, the coconut should be discarded. (The outer husk, covered in coarse, stiff brown fiber, has three small indentations known as eyes, which suggest a monkey's face; hence *cocos*, which is Portuguese for "grinning face.") Bake the coconut for 15 minutes. The heat from the oven will loosen the meat inside from the shell. Do not leave the coconut in the oven too long, because it will cook the meat; cooked meat will not yield fresh-tasting coconut milk. Let cool briefly; then, with a hammer or the back of a heavy cleaver, break the shell. With the point of a strong knife, remove the meat, levering it out carefully. Remove the brown membrane with a sharp paring knife or vegetable peeler. Grate the coconut as needed against the small teardrop-shaped holes of a 4-sided grater or in a food processor. Freshly grated coconut keeps, frozen, in an airtight container, for up to 3 months.

If you do not wish to grate coconut, which is tedious, freshly grated coconut is available frozen in some Asian, Indian, Middle Eastern, and specialty food stores. It makes a perfect substitute. Flaked (dried) unsweetened coconut is inexpensive, widely available at Indian groceries and some specialty supermarkets, and makes a good substitute for fresh.

FRESH COCONUT MILK

If you do not wish to go through the trouble of making fresh coconut milk, then there are several brands of canned coconut milk available in supermarkets and Indian, Middle Eastern, and Southeast Asian markets. Some brands taste better than others; over the years my cooking students and I have enjoyed and successfully used Chaokoh and Mae Ploy brands. These are the best, with a rich, thick texture and pleasant coconut taste. Avoid buying "light" coconut milk, which has too thin a texture and poor flavor, and is often thickened with flour or cornstarch. For thick coconut milk, shake the can and use as is. For a thinner consistency, remove some of the cream or dilute with half as much water. Unlike fresh coconut milk, canned milk can curdle when cooked over very high heat, or when it is simmered covered for a long period. Take care not to boil or simmer it for very long; heat it just enough to warm. If you must cook coconut milk longer, then do so at a moderate temperature in an uncovered pan.

MAKES ABOUT 2 CUPS

2 cups water   4 cups freshly grated coconut (page 307)

In a medium saucepan, bring the water to a boil and add the coconut. Cook the coconut over medium-high heat for 2 minutes and remove the pan from the heat. Let the mixture stand, covered, for 10 minutes. In a food processor or blender, blend the coconut mixture until very thick. In a fine sieve set over a bowl, strain the coconut mixture, pressing hard on the solids. Working over the bowl, squeeze small handfuls of the solids to extract as much milk as possible. The coconut milk keeps, covered, in the refrigerator for up to 3 days, or frozen in an airtight container for up to 6 months. If you prefer a thinner coconut milk, add 1/4 cup boiling water to the coconut residue and squeeze it again. Use separately, or add to the thick coconut milk above.

KONKAN CRAB CURRY | Kurli Masala

The Konkan coast, a verdant, lush strip along the western state of Maharashtra, is known, like the San Francisco Bay area, for its pleasant weather and a cornucopia of bounty, including top-class mangoes, coconut, jackfruit, guava, rice, and plentiful sweet, delicate seafood. Seafaring traders, fishermen, farmers, and folk artists have made Konkan colorful and rich. A varied cuisine has evolved because of the integration of local and itinerant cultures. A community of people called Konkani Saraswat live along the coast; their cuisine is fragrant and superbly balanced, with texture and flavor.

Dungeness crab is native to the Bay Area and is one of San Francisco's culinary icons. When crab season opens, it kicks off the holiday season. Indigenous to the Pacific Coast, Dungeness crabs were first caught commercially in the area just before the Gold Rush. Some Bay Area denizens contend that the local crabs are sweeter than their out-of-state relatives; warmer water makes for a sweeter crustacean.

Freshness in crab is easy to determine—look for heavy crabs with hard shells, and creamy, not stark white or yellow, bellies. Always cook live crab the day you buy it, with a pinch of turmeric, and for this recipe, have the staff at the fish counter cook the crab for you. Mixed with all the zesty goodness of India, this is a dish for classy dinners. It's a mess to eat, but it's fabulously tasty. With plain basmati rice to serve alongside the fish, you'll have the perfect spring meal. The ocean sweetness of the crab is well suited to a creamy, buttery, full-bodied chardonnay, or even a viognier.

SERVES 4

2 teaspoons poppy seeds, preferably white

8 dried hot red chilis, such as cayennes or chiles de arbol, stemmed and softened (microwave for 30 seconds in 1/4 cup water and do not drain)

1 cup sliced yellow onion

1 cup coarsely chopped red bell pepper, plus additional for garnish

1-inch piece fresh ginger

6 large cloves garlic

1 tablespoon coriander seeds

2 teaspoons cumin seeds

1/2 teaspoon turmeric

2 tablespoons vegetable oil

1 teaspoon tamarind concentrate, dissolved in 1 cup water

Two 1 1/4-pound whole cooked Dungeness crabs, or rock, stone, king or other crabs, broken into pieces

2 teaspoons salt

2 cups Fresh Coconut Milk (page 308), or canned unsweetened coconut milk

1. Spread the poppy seeds on a work surface and crush coarsely with a rolling pin. (Alternately, use a coffee mill or mortar and pestle.) Transfer to a blender. Add the chilis with soaking water, onion, bell pepper, ginger, garlic, coriander seeds, cumin seeds, and turmeric to the blender. Process as smoothly as possible.

2. Heat the oil in a large heavy skillet over medium heat. Add the spice paste and cook, stirring occasionally, until fragrant and the raw smell dissipates, 10 to 12 minutes. Add the tamarind liquid and cook, stirring, for about 6 minutes more. Add the crab and salt and bring to a boil. Reduce the heat, stir in the coconut milk, and bring to a simmer. Cook, uncovered, until the sauce is thickened, 10 to 12 minutes. Transfer the crab to a heated deep dish and spoon the sauce over the crab. Garnish with slices of bell pepper.

VARIATION

Try substituting lobster, shrimp, or any whole white-fleshed fish for the crab, adjusting the cooking time as necessary.

BOATMAN'S CRAB CURRY | Denji Kari

Whenever fishermen go away on trawlers to fish in turbulent seas, the women live under a cloud of insecurity till the men return safely. A recipe in their name deserves a mention. This curry is styled after the ones folks in fishing villages cook for themselves. It incorporates many ingredients from their kitchen: black peppercorns, fiery red chilis, mustard seeds, and the omnipresent coconut.

SERVES 6

1¹/2 pounds jumbo lump crab meat

2 tablespoons vegetable or canola oil

1 teaspoon yellow or brown mustard seeds

1 cup finely chopped yellow onion

3 large cloves garlic, minced

1-inch piece fresh ginger, minced

2 dried hot red chilis, such as cayennes or chiles de arbol, stemmed

¹/2 teaspoon black peppercorns

2 teaspoons ground coriander

1 teaspoon ground cumin

¹/2 teaspoon turmeric

¹/4 cup packed cilantro

1¹/2 cups Fresh Coconut Milk (page 308), or canned unsweetened coconut milk

1¹/2 teaspoons salt

Sliced scallion greens, for garnish

1. Pick over crabmeat to remove any bits of shell and cartilage.

2. Have a spatter screen ready before you continue. Heat the oil over medium-high heat in a heavy large sauté pan or saucepan. Add the mustard seeds, immediately cover with the spatter screen, and cook until the seeds stop popping, about 30 seconds. Add the onion and cook, stirring, until softened, 3 to 4 minutes. Add the garlic, ginger, chilis, and peppercorns and cook, stirring, until the garlic starts to brown, about 3 minutes. Stir in the coriander, cumin, and turmeric and cook, stirring, until aromatic, about 1 minute. Add the crab and cook, gently stirring occasionally (to avoid breaking up crab), for about 4 minutes.

3. While crab mixture is cooking, chop the cilantro. Stir the cilantro into the crab mixture with the coconut milk and salt and simmer until slightly thickened, 6 to 8 minutes. Transfer to a heated dish. Garnish with scallion greens and serve.

PARSEE SHRIMP IN SWEET-HOT-SOUR CURRY

| Dhan Dar Ne Colmi No Patio

From the tenth century onward, groups of Zoroastrians migrated to India from Iran—mainly from the province of Fars, and hence they were known as Parsees. They settled on the west coast and assimilated with the local population, and yet maintained their identity. The Parsee palate is a little fastidious, and their taste in food is esoteric. Traditionally this *patio*, sweet-hot-sour curry, is served for a family gathering along with rice *(dhan)* and legumes *(dar)*. It is important that you cook the curry in stages as I've recommended; this adept method develops the distinctive depth, striking shade, and meticulously combined tastes of Parsee cuisine. Pair this dish with a dry chenin blanc, Riesling, or Gewürztraminer.

SERVES 4 AS A SIDE DISH

1 pound (22 to 24) jumbo shrimp

6 tablespoons vegetable oil

2 to 4 fresh green serrano or jalapeño chilis, or less to taste, stemmed

6 large cloves garlic

2 teaspoons ground cumin

2 cups finely chopped yellow onion

2¹/2 teaspoons *garam masala* (pages 36–37), or store-bought

¹/2 teaspoon cayenne

¹/4 teaspoon turmeric

2 cups diced ripe tomatoes, or canned diced tomatoes

1¹/2 tablespoons light-brown sugar, jaggery (pages 51–52), or raw sugar

2 teaspoons salt

2 teaspoons tamarind concentrate, dissolved in ¹/4 cup water

1 cup water

2 tablespoons chopped cilantro

1. Peel the shrimp, leaving the final joint and tail intact, and devein. Set aside in a bowl.

2. In a blender or food processor, combine 3 tablespoons of the oil, the chilis, garlic, and cumin. Blend to a smooth puree, stopping to scrape down the sides of the bowl a couple of times. Transfer to a glass bowl.

3. Heat the remaining 3 tablespoons of oil in a heavy large sauté pan over medium heat. Add the onion and cook, stirring often, until softened, 6 to 8 minutes. Add the chili-garlic paste and cook, stirring, until the onion is deep golden, 3 to 4 minutes. Add the *Garam Masala*, cayenne, and turmeric and stir until aromatic, 30 seconds. Add the tomatoes and cook, stirring, until sauce is almost dry, 6 to 8 minutes. Add the sugar and salt and stir to mix. Add the tamarind liquid and water and cook, stirring occasionally, until the raw tamarind smell dissipates, 8 to 10 minutes.

4. Taste; it should be pleasantly sweet, sour, and hot. Adjust the seasonings if necessary. Add the cilantro and shrimp and cook, stirring occasionally, until the shrimp are pink and curl slightly, 5 to 6 minutes. Transfer to a warm serving dish and serve.

VARIATION

Substitute an equal weight of scallops for the shrimp. Or try substituting wide strips or 2-inch squares of a substantial fish such as halibut, tuna, salmon, or snapper; they'll take a few minutes longer to cook.

FRAGRANT STEAMED GOA CLAMS | Tisryo

Among the bewildering variety of Goan seafood curries, this is a lovely variation on vindaloo, with lime juice replacing the vinegar. It features steamed clams with sautéed onion, ginger, spices, and creamy coconut milk. The clams are then tossed with grated coconut, cilantro, and a squirt of lime juice and are typically accompanied with *pao*, a soft, warm roll (a Portuguese contribution) for sopping up the juices. I have called for small (less than 2 inches in diameter), hard-shelled clams such as littlenecks, but this recipe is equally good with oysters.

I suggest matching this delicate dish, with its dominant flavors of coconut milk and lime, with an Italian wine, such as Gavi, from the Piedmont region. California's Wente Livermore Valley Sauvignon Blanc, a classic, crisp, citrus wine, works well here too.

SERVES 4 AS A FIRST COURSE

2 pounds (about 2 dozen) small, hard-shelled, tightly closed clams or fresh mussels

1 1/2 tablespoons vegetable or coconut oil

1 cup finely chopped yellow onion

1 tablespoon grated fresh ginger

2 teaspoons sweet paprika

1 teaspoon ground coriander

1/2 teaspoon ground cumin

1/2 teaspoon salt

1/4 teaspoon cayenne

1/2 cup Fresh Coconut Milk (page 308), or canned unsweetened coconut milk

1 tablespoon freshly squeezed lime juice, for serving

2 tablespoons chopped cilantro, for garnish

Freshly grated coconut (page 307), or defrosted frozen unsweetened coconut, for garnish

1.   Scrub the clams well. If using mussels, remove any stringy "beards" trailing from between the shells.

2.   Heat the oil in a heavy large sauté pan over medium heat. Add the onion and ginger and cook, stirring occasionally, until lightly browned, 5 to 8 minutes. Add the paprika, coriander, cumin, salt, and cayenne and cook, stirring, until aromatic, about 1 minute. Add the coconut milk and bring to a gentle boil. Add the clams, cover, and boil gently, stirring occasionally, until the clams have opened, 6 to 8 minutes. (Discard any unopened clams). Serve the clams in bowls with the cooking liquid and sprinkled with lime juice, cilantro, and grated coconut.

VARIATION

Try adding thinly sliced baby potatoes (about 4 is plenty) along with the onion. Adjust the salt before serving.

MALABAR SCALLOPS ROASTED IN BANANA LEAF
| Malabar Karimeen Pollichathu

Here's an easy and elegant entrée for you to show your creativity with when you have guests coming and you want to serve something exceptional. The fish is cooked gently with a sprinkling of turmeric, pepper, coriander, cayenne, green chili, lime juice, and *kari* leaves. A local Kerala fish, known as pearlspot *(karimeen)*, with firm and tender flesh, is typically used for this dish, but I've used scallops; they are even better.

SERVES 4

1 pound sea or bay scallops

1/2 teaspoon salt

1/2 teaspoon freshly ground black pepper

1/4 teaspoon turmeric

2 tablespoons vegetable oil

1/4 teaspoon yellow or brown mustard seeds

1/2 cup sliced yellow onion

5 cloves garlic

2 fresh green serrano or jalapeño chilis, stemmed

10 *kari* leaves (page 28) (optional), or cilantro

1 teaspoon ground coriander

1/4 teaspoon cayenne

Juice of 1 lime

4 untreated fresh or thawed frozen banana leaves, or large Swiss chard leaves

Fresh Cilantro-Mint-Onion Chutney/Dip (page 177), for serving (optional)

Crunchy potato straws, for serving (optional)

1. Rinse the scallops and pat them dry. Place in a medium glass bowl. In a small bowl, combine the salt, pepper, and turmeric and sprinkle over the scallops. Cover and marinate for 30 minutes at cool room temperature, or refrigerate.

2. Have a spatter screen ready before you continue. Heat the oil in a heavy large skillet over medium heat. Add the mustard seeds, immediately cover with the spatter screen, and cook until the seeds stop popping, about 30 seconds. Add the onion and cook, stirring, until lightly golden, about 6 minutes. While the onion is cooking, pulverize the garlic and chilis to a coarse paste with a mortar and pestle (or mince finely). Add to the skillet with the *kari* leaves and cook, stirring, until fragrant, about 2 minutes. Remove the onion mixture to a plate. Add the scallops and sear for 2 minutes per side. Add the coriander and cayenne, the onion mixture, and the lime juice and stir. Simmer until the sauce is thickened, 5 to 6 minutes. At this point you may cook a few more minutes and serve, or continue with steps 3 and 4 for a more dramatic finish.

3. Preheat the oven to 350°F.

4. If using banana leaves, cut away the ribs. Soften the leaves in a large bowl of hot water for about 1 minute, to help keep them from splitting. Cut four 10-inch squares from the leaves. On a work surface, arrange 1 leaf square and pat it dry; place 4 or 5 scallops (or about 1/2 cup if using bay scallops) on each banana leaf. Fold the top and bottom edges of the leaf over the scallops, enclosing them. Make 3 more packets in the same manner. Tie each packet with kitchen twine, if desired. Arrange the packets, seam-side down, in a baking dish and bake for 15 minutes. Remove from the oven and let stand a few minutes. Serve the packets as is, or unwrap them and dress up the scallops in a pool of luscious Fresh Cilantro-Mint-Onion Chutney/Dip and strew with the crunchy potato straws, if desired.

VARIATION

Pompano fillets or shrimp make good substitutes for the scallops.

KARWAR OYSTER SKILLET ROAST | Sukke Kalwas

You can pick up these crusty, spice-and-herb-coated oysters with your fingers and enjoy them one by one as an appetizer, or serve them in clusters as a side dish. In the rain forests of western India, contorted trees produce *tirphal*, hollow, split flower buds that are dark brown when dried. They are woody, with a pungent taste and slight bitter aftertaste. Since *tirphal* is only available sporadically, I suggest using *ajwain* seeds instead. If you can find the indigenous *tirphal*, by all means crush and sprinkle it on top of the oysters.

SERVES 4 AS A SIDE DISH

1 teaspoon salt

1/2 teaspoon turmeric

20 shucked Kumamoto oysters, or any variety of local oysters

1-inch piece fresh ginger

3 cloves garlic

2 teaspoons ground coriander

1/2 teaspoon red pepper flakes

1 cup lightly packed coarsely chopped cilantro

1/2 cup freshly grated coconut (page 307), or defrosted frozen unsweetened coconut

2 tablespoons vegetable or coconut oil

1/2 teaspoon *ajwain* seeds (page 20), lightly crushed

2 limes, thinly sliced

1. In a medium bowl, combine the salt and turmeric. Add the oysters and toss to coat evenly. Cover and set aside for 10 minutes.

2. In a small food processor, combine the ginger, garlic, coriander, and red pepper and process to a coarse paste; this will exude a wonderful aroma. Add the chopped cilantro and the coconut a little at a time, gradually processing them into the mixture, and adding 2 to 3 tablespoons of water to keep the mixture moving through the blades. Process until you have a coarsely textured paste. Mix well with a spoon and add to the bowl containing the oysters. Toss the oysters gently to coat with the paste.

3. Heat 1 1/2 tablespoons of the oil in a heavy large skillet or sauté pan over medium heat, rotating the pan so that the oil coats the bottom. Add the oysters in a single layer. Sprinkle the *ajwain* seeds all over the oysters. Top the oysters with a layer of lime slices, squeezing a few as you place them. Sprinkle the remaining 1/2 tablespoon of oil on top. Cover and cook over medium heat until the flavors meld and the oysters are crusty on the bottom, 6 to 8 minutes. Serve straight from the skillet, discarding the lime slices, if desired.

COCHIN LOBSTER AND CALAMARI BATHED IN AROMATICS
| Konju Koonthal Ularthiyathu

A few years ago on a trip to Kerala State, I stayed at the Taj Malabar, an elegant colonial structure; it has a private garden and a jetty with a spectacular view of the harbor. As I sat enjoying
a glass of wine, all day an endless procession of boats passed by the window—ferry boats,
snake-shaped boats, tug boats, and fishing boats. Taj Malabar's seafood restaurant is actually
located on a rice boat. It was there that I was introduced to a dish like this, and I couldn't wait
to get home and try my own variation.

The sweet, plump, succulent, and firm-textured white lobster meat and the firm, white, mild
calamari meat take on the flavor of shallots, ginger, garlic, *kari* leaves, and tamarind delightfully
when cooked together. Coconut oil is prized in the state of Kerala for its delicate flavor; I
encourage you to try it occasionally. Tamarind pods can be found in Indian and specialty markets in America, but if you find very tart *cocum* (pages 50–51) at your local Indian market, then
add 4 or 5 rinds to the cooking liquid instead of the tamarind.

Pair this special entrée with Lemon Rice (page 108). If you love wine, try chenin blanc or
Riesling. And pass around a plate of Nankhatai (page 421) for dessert.

SERVES 3 TO 4 GENEROUSLY

3 tablespoons fresh tamarind pods	1/2 pound lobster tails
3/4 cup water	1/2 pound fresh calamari rings
5 shallots, peeled and halved	3/4 teaspoon salt
1 1/2-inch piece fresh ginger	20 *kari* leaves (page 28) (optional), or cilantro
5 large cloves garlic	2 1/2 tablespoons coconut or vegetable oil
1 teaspoon ground coriander	1 teaspoon yellow or brown mustard seeds
1/2 teaspoon cayenne	1/4 teaspoon turmeric
1/4 teaspoon ground white pepper	1 lime, cut into wedges, for serving

1. In a glass bowl, combine the tamarind pods and 1/4 cup of the water. Let stand, covered, for 2 hours. Break up the tamarind pulp with a spoon or your fingers. Strain through
a sieve into a nonaluminum saucepan, pressing on the solids with the back of a spoon to
extract as much tamarind puree as possible. You should have about 3 tablespoons puree.
Discard the seeds, pods, and fibers.

2.   In a blender or food processor, combine the shallots, ginger, garlic, coriander, cayenne, pepper, and 1/4 cup of the water. Blend to a smooth paste, stopping to scrape down the sides of the container a couple of times. Transfer to a heavy large sauté pan. Add the remaining 1/4 cup of water, the tamarind puree, lobster tails, calamari, salt, and 10 of the *kari* leaves and stir to mix. Bring the mixture to a boil, then reduce the heat to medium and cook, stirring occasionally, until all the liquid evaporates, the raw shallot and garlic smell dissipates, and the lobster meat is tender, 15 to 20 minutes.

3.   Have a spatter screen ready before you continue. Heat the oil in a medium skillet over medium-high heat. Add the mustard seeds, immediately cover with the spatter screen, and cook until the seeds stop popping, about 30 seconds. Add the turmeric and remaining 10 *kari* leaves. After a few seconds, when the leaves are crisp, stir into the cooked seafood. Stir gently until the seafood is well coated with the oil seasoning. Transfer to an attractive warm serving dish and serve hot. Pass the lime wedges for everyone to squeeze at the table.

HOT-SOUR GOA CALAMARI | Amotik

I've given directions for making the paste using a mortar and pestle. No mortar and pestle? Then feel free to use a blender with very little liquid, as called for in many other recipes, but be sure to cook down the paste until almost dry. This quick dish seems just right served with red or a brown rice. Try *rasam* to start and Vermicelli Pudding with Fresh Berries (page 415) for dessert.

SERVES 4

1 1/2 pounds fresh calamari rings	1/4 teaspoon freshly ground black pepper
1 teaspoon salt	1/8 teaspoon ground cinnamon
8 large cloves garlic	2 tablespoons vegetable oil
2 teaspoons ground cumin	1 cup thinly sliced yellow onion
1 teaspoon red pepper flakes	2 tablespoons red or white wine vinegar
1/4 teaspoon turmeric	Cilantro sprigs, for garnish

1.   Place the calamari in a shallow glass dish. Sprinkle the salt over the calamari and toss to mix. Cover and set aside for 15 minutes at cool room temperature, or refrigerate.

2.   Using a large mortar and pestle, crush the garlic. Add the cumin, red pepper flakes, turmeric, black pepper, and cinnamon and grind until you have a coarse-textured paste (using a spoon to stir together). It will exude a wonderfully pungent aroma.

3.   Heat the oil in a heavy medium sauté pan over medium heat. Add the onion and cook, stirring often, until deep golden, 8 to 10 minutes. Add the garlic paste and cook, stirring, until fragrant, 2 to 3 minutes. Add the calamari and stir to coat well. Add the vinegar and mix again. Cover and cook until the flavors are well blended, about 5 minutes. Transfer to a warm serving dish, garnish with cilantro sprigs, and serve.

DAKSHIN FENUGREEK-MARINATED SALMON BRAISED IN COCONUT MILK | Dakshini Meen Kari

Southern (dakshin) Indian food is as much of a misnomer as northern Indian food. Each state in the south—Karnataka, Tamil Nadu, Kerala, Andhra Pradesh—has its own distinctive flavor. And within each state, each region flaunts its individuality. Although much of the south is vegetarian, there are significant nonvegetarian pockets, and the coastal regions have found distinctive ways of cooking fish that are just delicious.

Here, marinated salmon is seared with aromatic spices and simply cooked in a curry sauce that is enriched with coconut milk; there are no complex techniques involved. I've used sautéed colorful bell peppers as a garnish. For an elegant presentation, try topping with salmon roe. Pair it with some Rice with French Green Lentils (pages 105–106), Mango-Macadamia Raita (page 206), and warm paratha, and you are ready to celebrate a stylish dinner. Try serving with a Robert Mondavi chardonnay.

2 teaspoons ground coriander

1 teaspoon ground cumin

1/2 teaspoon ground fenugreek

1/2 teaspoon cayenne

1/4 teaspoon turmeric

2 tablespoons red or white wine vinegar

1 1/2 pounds salmon fillets, skin removed

1/4 cup vegetable oil

1 cup thinly sliced yellow onions

15 *kari* leaves (page 28) (optional), or cilantro

4 large cloves garlic, finely chopped

1 tablespoon grated fresh ginger

2 cups Fresh Coconut Milk (page 308), or canned unsweetened coconut milk

1 teaspoon salt

3 small bell peppers (preferably different colors), cut into thin strips

1.   In a small bowl, combine the coriander, cumin, fenugreek, cayenne, turmeric, and wine vinegar and mix until smooth. Place the fish in a shallow glass baking dish and, if you wish, use tweezers to pull out any white pin bones. Smear the spice paste over both sides of each fillet. Cover and marinate at cool room temperature 30 minutes, or refrigerate for 1 to 2 hours (but not more than 4).

2.   Heat 1 1/2 tablespoons of the oil in a heavy large skillet over medium-high heat. Lay the salmon fillets in a single layer and do not crowd. Cook until the fillets are crusty and brown underneath, 4 to 5 minutes, then use a thin-bladed metal spatula to carefully flip them over. Cook until the salmon is golden on the other side and done to your liking, 4 to 5 minutes. (I like mine a tad translucent in the center.) Transfer the salmon to a plate.

3.   In the same skillet, heat 1 1/2 tablespoons of the oil over medium-high heat. Add the onion, kari leaves, garlic, and ginger and cook, stirring occasionally, until the onion just begins to brown, about 4 minutes. Reduce the heat to medium, stir in the coconut milk and salt, and bring the sauce to a boil, stirring. Add the salmon fillets to the sauce and gently simmer until the fish begins to flake easily and the sauce is slightly thickened, 5 to 6 minutes.

4.   Meanwhile, in another skillet, heat the remaining 1 tablespoon of oil over medium-high heat. Add the peppers and cook, stirring, until crisp-tender and beginning to brown in places, 5 to 6 minutes. Season with salt if necessary. Transfer the fish to a heated deep dish and spoon the sauce over the fish. Garnish with the peppers and serve.

COASTAL KERALA BAKED CATFISH WITH TOMATOES | Fish Molee

Even the kids can make this classic dish. Arranging layers of aromatics and fish in a casserole is as easy as assembling lasagna. Yet it's also a very appealing, delicately flavored, and attractive entrée, appropriate even for formal dinner tables. It has a velvety texture and practically melts in your mouth.

This stove-top dish is traditionally cooked in an earthenware pot called a *meen chatti*, exclusively used for cooking fish in Kerala. I've devised an oven method to achieve the same classic taste. Onions baked in sweet coconut remain nice and crunchy.

If someone in your family is new to eating fish, I suggest preparing it with catfish; a similar small, plump, fleshy fish in India is *kane*, or ladyfish. It has a clean, pleasant, nonfishy taste. Use salmon for a colorful preparation.

SERVES 4

1 medium yellow onion

20 *kari* leaves (page 28) (optional), or cilantro

1 cup sliced ripe tomatoes

1 tablespoon julienned fresh ginger

4 large cloves garlic, finely sliced

2 to 3 fresh green serrano or jalapeño chilis, or fewer to taste, stemmed and chopped

1 pound skinless fish fillets, such as catfish, petrale sole, salmon, tilapia, or trout

2 tablespoons freshly squeezed lime juice

1 teaspoon salt

1/2 teaspoon turmeric

3/4 cup Fresh Coconut Milk (page 308), or canned unsweetened coconut milk

1 1/2 tablespoons coconut or olive oil

1/2 teaspoon yellow or brown mustard seeds

1 lime, cut into wedges, for serving (optional)

1. Preheat the oven to 450°F.

2. Peel the onion and cut it lengthwise. Slice thinly and cut the slices into thirds. Measure 1 cup and set aside.

3. Lay 10 of the *kari* leaves, if using, at the bottom of a 2-quart, 8 x 11–inch baking dish. Lay the onion in the dish in a single layer and top with the tomato slices. Sprinkle with the ginger, garlic, and chilis, one by one. Lay out the fish fillets, without crowding them. In a small bowl, combine the lime juice, salt, and turmeric and stir to mix. Spoon evenly over the fish fillets. Pour the coconut milk over the fish and place remaining 10 *kari* leaves, if using, over the top. Bake until the fish just flakes when pressed firmly and the sauce is reduced to a medium thickness, 20 to 25 minutes.

4. Have a spatter screen ready before you continue. Heat the oil in a small skillet over medium-high heat. Add the mustard seeds, immediately cover with the spatter screen, and cook until the seeds stop popping, about 30 seconds. Remove from the heat and pour over the fish, scraping with a spatula. Serve immediately with a plate of lime wedges, if using, for everyone to squeeze to taste.

VARIATION

Kashmir Dum-Style Baked Fish

To make a Kashmir version, combine the ginger and garlic, along with 1 teaspoon coriander, $1/2$ teaspoon cumin, $1/2$ teaspoon cayenne, $1/4$ teaspoon turmeric, $1/4$ teaspoon whole cloves, the seeds from 3 green cardamom pods, and 2 tablespoons oil, in a blender. Process to a very smooth paste, adding a little water if needed to keep the mixture moving through the blades. Place the fish in a shallow baking dish, then smear the spice paste over both sides of each fillet. Cover and marinate at cool room temperature for 30 minutes, or refrigerate for 1 to 2 hours (but not more than 4).

Lay the onion in a single layer at the bottom of the baking dish and top with the tomato slices. Lay out the fish fillets without crowding, cover the dish tightly with foil, and bake until the fish is crisp and just flakes when pressed firmly, 30 to 35 minutes.

MALVAN HALIBUT SIMMERED IN GREEN SAUCE | Hirvi Malvani Kalvan

Here, the fragrant sauce is gently seasoned; if you like, add more dried red chilis to taste, or serve with Spicy Pilaf with Vegetables (pages 112–113) instead of plain rice. Finish with Banana Fudge Halvah (page 419).

2 teaspoons salt

2 teaspoons cayenne

$1/2$ teaspoon turmeric

Juice of 2 limes

2 pounds (about 4) halibut, pompano, kingfish, or
    mackerel steaks

2 tablespoons poppy seeds, preferably white

1 teaspoon cumin seeds

2 teaspoons coriander seeds

2 large cloves garlic

1 cup lightly packed cilantro

$1/4$ cup lightly packed fresh mint leaves (optional)

2 teaspoons tamarind concentrate, dissolved in
    $1/4$ cup water

1 cup freshly grated coconut (page 307), or
    defrosted frozen unsweetened coconut

2 cups water

3 tablespoons coconut or vegetable oil

1 teaspoon yellow or brown mustard seeds

1 cup thinly sliced yellow onion

1. In a small bowl, combine the salt, cayenne, turmeric, and lime juice and mix until smooth. Place the fish in a shallow glass dish. If you wish, use tweezers to pull out any white pin bones. Rub the marinade over both sides of each steak, cover, and marinate at cool room temperature 30 minutes, or refrigerate for 1 to 2 hours (but not more than 4).

2. While the fish is marinating, in a small skillet over medium heat, toast the poppy seeds, stirring occasionally, until toasty (some seeds even pop) but not brown, 3 to 4 minutes. Transfer to a coffee mill or spice grinder, grind to a coarse powder, and transfer to a blender or food processor. Add the cumin and coriander to the skillet and toast, stirring occasionally, until they darken a shade, 4 to 5 minutes. Transfer the cumin and coriander to the coffee mill or spice grinder, grind to a fine powder, and add to the blender. Add the garlic, cilantro, mint, if using, tamarind liquid, coconut, and $3/4$ cup of the water to the blender. Blend to a smooth paste, stopping to scrape down the sides of the container a couple of times. Set aside.

3. Have a spatter screen ready before you continue. Heat the oil in a large sauté pan or skillet over medium-high heat. Add the mustard seeds, immediately cover with the spatter screen, and cook until the seeds stop popping, about 30 seconds. Add the onion and cook, stirring, until it starts to brown at the edges, about 4 minutes. Add the coconut paste and cook, stirring regularly, until fragrant and almost dry, 8 to 10 minutes. Add the remaining $1 1/4$ cups water and bring the mixture to a boil. Add the fish steaks to the sauce and gently simmer, turning once or twice, until they are just cooked through and begin to flake easily and the sauce is thickened, 6 to 8 minutes. Transfer to an attractive warm serving dish and serve hot.

TANGY MAHIMAHI FILLETS WITH SHALLOTS | Meen Vevichathu

Many fish dishes, especially the southern recipes, use *kari* leaves for authentic flavor; should they come your way through an Indian or farmers' market, be sure to stock up. They last several weeks in the refrigerator in a plastic bag.

SERVES 4 AS A SIDE DISH

1/4 teaspoon fenugreek seeds

2-inch piece fresh ginger

10 large cloves garlic

1 1/2 teaspoons cayenne

1/4 teaspoon turmeric

1/4 cup vegetable oil

1 teaspoon yellow or brown mustard seeds

20 kari leaves (page 28), plus additional sprigs for garnish (optional), or cilantro

2/3 cup peeled and thinly sliced shallots

1 teaspoon tamarind concentrate, dissolved in 2 cups of water

1 teaspoon salt

1 pound mahimahi, orange roughy, or tilapia fillets, with or without skin

1. Using a coffee mill or spice grinder, grind the fenugreek seeds to a fine powder and transfer to a blender. Add half of the ginger, 5 of the garlic cloves, the cayenne, and the turmeric to the container and blend to a smooth paste, stopping to scrape down the sides of the bowl a couple of times; add a few tablespoons of water if necessary to keep the mixture moving through the blades. Set aside. Mince the remaining ginger and garlic and set aside.

2. Have a spatter screen ready before you continue. Heat 2 tablespoons of the oil in a heavy large sauté pan over medium-high heat. Add the mustard seeds, immediately cover with the spatter screen, and cook until the seeds stop popping, about 30 seconds. Stir in the *kari* leaves, if using, the shallots, and the minced ginger and garlic and cook, stirring, until the shallots are very soft, 5 to 6 minutes. Using a slotted spoon, transfer to a plate. Add the remaining 2 tablespoons of oil to the pan over medium heat. When the oil is hot, stir in the spice paste and cook, stirring, until the paste is fragrant and starts to dry, about 6 minutes. Add the tamarind liquid and stir. Add the salt and simmer, uncovered, until the raw tamarind smell disappears and the sauce is thick, 6 to 8 minutes. Add the mahimahi fillets and fried shallot mixture and simmer gently until the fillets are just cooked through and begin to flake easily and the sauce is slightly thickened, 6 to 8 minutes. Transfer the fish to a heated deep serving dish and spoon the sauce over the fish. Garnish with sprigs of *kari* leaves, if desired, and serve.

SEARED BENGAL FISH IN TANGY MUSTARD SAUCE

| Shorshay Baata Maach

The contrasting tastes of this straightforward fish are irresistible. Beyond the mustardy notes, the traditional Bengal flavors are spicy and clean. The Bay of Bengal is renowned for its abundance of fresh and saltwater fish. Even vegetarians are known to eat this "fruit of the sea."

I have experimented with this recipe using readily available mustard paste, but the preservatives mar the flavor, so I like to make it authentically using mustard seeds. Mustard is energetic; it has the capacity to soothe the mind, create a peaceful temperament, and sharpen brainpower.

Serve with Rhubarb Rasam Soup (page 369) to start, steamed basmati rice alongside, and a soothing Beet Pudding (page 417) to finish. For wine, I would recommend a minerally Riesling to complement the mustard seed.

SERVES 4 AS A SIDE DISH

2 tablespoons yellow or brown mustard seeds

1 3/4 teaspoons salt

1/2 teaspoon turmeric

1 1/2 pounds skinless fillets of sole, carp, trout, catfish, or other white firm fish

1 tablespoon poppy seeds, preferably white

1/4 cup dried unsweetened flaked coconut

8 large cloves garlic

4 fresh green serrano or jalapeño chilis, or fewer to taste, stemmed

1 cup coarsely chopped yellow onion

1 1/2 cups water

2 1/2 tablespoons mustard oil (see notes, page 49), or vegetable oil

Juice of 1/2 lime

Beautiful cilantro sprigs, for garnish

1. Soak the mustard seeds and 1/4 teaspoon of the salt in 1/2 cup of water for 4 hours or overnight. Transfer to a blender and blend to a smooth paste. Strain into a cup, pressing on the solids to extract as much liquid as possible; you should get a lovely yellow, smooth-textured, slightly liquid 4 tablespoons of mustard paste. Set aside.

2. In a small bowl, combine the remaining 1 1/2 teaspoons of salt and 1/4 teaspoon of the turmeric and sprinkle over both sides of the fish fillets. Set aside for 15 to 30 minutes at cool room temperature, or refrigerate.

3. In a small skillet over medium heat, toast the poppy seeds until toasty (some seeds even pop) but not brown, 3 to 4 minutes. Transfer to a coffee mill or spice grinder and grind to a powder; transfer to a blender or food processor. Add the coconut, garlic, chilis, onion, 1/2 cup of the water, and the mustard paste. Blend to a smooth puree.

4. Heat 2 tablespoons of the oil in a heavy large skillet over medium heat until very hot. Lay the fish fillets in a single layer in the skillet; do not crowd. Cook until the fish is crusty and brown underneath, 4 to 5 minutes. Use a thin-bladed metal spatula to carefully flip the fish over, and sear it until golden on the other side and done to your liking, 2 to 3 minutes more. Transfer the fillets to a plate.

5. Add the remaining $1/2$ tablespoon of oil, $1/4$ teaspoon of turmeric, and the pureed onion mixture to the skillet and cook, stirring, until the raw onion smell dissipates, about 6 minutes. Add the remaining 1 cup of water and bring to a boil. Cook until thick, 3 to 4 minutes. Add the fillets to the sauce and simmer gently until they are just cooked through and begin to flake easily, 4 to 5 minutes. Add the lime juice and turn off the heat. Transfer the fish to a heated deep serving dish and spoon the sauce over the fish. Garnish with cilantro sprigs and serve hot.

FRAGRANT FISH FRY | Ayala Porichathu / Tareli Tava Machchi

Once you've tasted this lightly coated, home-fried fish, I'm sure it will be high on your list of favorite fish dishes. Fried fish is a universal food, something you never tire of. It is popular all over the subcontinent. In southern-style fried fish, *ayala porichathu,* mustard seeds are used, and in the northern style, *tareli tava machchi,* ground cumin is the key ingredient.

Fried fish makes a very appetizing starter. The spice paste works well on any kind of fish, and can even be used on a whole fish; be sure to make several gashes on both sides if you use whole fish. Serve with condiments such as Fresh Mint Chutney with Garlic (page 176) or Tamarind Chutney with Banana (page 182), or pass lime wedges for your guests to squeeze at the table. For a quick condiment, fried fish even pairs well with ketchup.

1 teaspoon yellow or brown mustard seeds

12 shallots, peeled

1-inch piece fresh ginger

8 large cloves garlic

1 teaspoon salt

1/2 teaspoon freshly ground pepper

1/2 teaspoon cayenne

1 pound boneless, skinless fish fillets, such as petrale sole, mackerel, rock cod, lingcod, sand dab, sea bass, or halibut

Vegetable oil, for frying

Rice flour, for dredging

1. Using a coffee mill or spice grinder, grind the mustard seeds to a fine powder and transfer to a blender. Add the shallots, ginger, garlic, salt, pepper, and cayenne to the blender and blend to a smooth paste, stopping to scrape down the sides of the container a couple of times; add 1 to 2 tablespoons water if needed to keep the mixture moving through the blades. It should form a paste rather than a liquidy puree. Place the fish in a shallow glass dish, then smear the spice paste over both sides of each fillet. Cover and marinate at cool room temperature for 30 minutes or refrigerate for 1 to 2 hours, but not more than 4.

2. Fill a large wok or sauté pan with oil to a depth of 1 inch and heat over medium-high heat until hot and sizzling but not smoking, 365°F to 375°F on a deep-fry thermometer. Working with one piece of fish at a time, place the fillets on the rice flour and turn to coat evenly. Shake off any excess flour and carefully slip the fish into the hot oil. Fry in two or more batches (without crowding), turning each piece only once, until crusty and rich golden brown, about 2 minutes per side. As each piece of fish is done, transfer it to brown paper or paper towels to drain briefly. Transfer to an attractive warm platter and serve right away.

VARIATIONS

For a crisper coating, dredge the fish in equal amounts of rice flour and medium- or fine-ground cornmeal, instead of the rice flour alone.

Serve the fish topped with Apricot Yogurt Gravy with Mint (page 118), and you've got a dish that truly captures the imagination.

GOA FISH IN FRAGRANT COCONUT SAUCE | Goan Pomfret Caldeen

This traditional Goan dish is made with a local, trout-size, white-fleshed flat fish called pomfret. Pomfret is available along the coast of Florida and in Asian markets in California as pompano. Some specialty supermarkets will also take special orders. I've used scrod, a lovely North Atlantic cod; it cooks in a few minutes and looks beautiful in this dazzling orange-red curry. A fresh citrus marinade gives this fish a delicate tang. Lemon Rice (page 108), Banana and Peach Chutney (page 186), and a bottle of Taj Mahal beer will complement this dish.

MAKES 4 TO 6 SERVINGS

2 tablespoons freshly squeezed lime juice

2 teaspoons salt

1 teaspoon turmeric

1 1/2 pounds skinless scrod fillets, or one 1 1/2- to 2-pound whole fish such as red snapper, grouper, bass, or pompano, gutted and scaled

6 dried hot red chilis, such as cayennes or chiles de arbol, or fewer to taste, stemmed and softened (microwave for 30 seconds in 1/4 cup water, then discard water)

3 teaspoons coriander seeds

1 teaspoon cumin seeds

1 cup freshly grated coconut (page 307), or defrosted frozen unsweetened coconut

2 cups sliced yellow onion

4 large cloves garlic

2 teaspoons tamarind concentrate, dissolved in 1/2 cup water

1 1/2 cups water

2 tablespoons vegetable oil

1 teaspoon sweet paprika

1 cup pureed ripe tomatoes, or canned pureed tomatoes

Chopped chives, for garnish

1. In a small bowl, combine the lime juice, 1/2 teaspoon of the salt, and 1/2 teaspoon of the turmeric and mix until smooth. In a shallow glass baking dish, rub the scrod all over with the marinade. Marinate the scrod, covered, at cool room temperature for 30 minutes (refrigerate in the summer). Remove the fish from the juice and dry thoroughly with paper towels.

2. In a blender, combine the chilis, coriander seeds, cumin seeds, coconut, 1 cup of the sliced onion, the garlic, tamarind liquid, remaining 1/2 teaspoon of turmeric, and 1/2 cup of the water. Process to a very smooth and satiny puree, adding a little more water if needed to keep the mixture moving through the blades.

3. In a medium heavy skillet, heat the oil over medium heat. Add the remaining 1 cup sliced onion and cook, stirring occasionally, until deep golden, 6 to 8 minutes. Add the coconut puree and cook, stirring occasionally, until the raw onion smell disappears, 8 to 10 minutes. Add the paprika, pureed tomatoes, remaining 1 cup of water, and remaining 1¹/₂ teaspoons of salt and cook, stirring occasionally, until fragrant, about 8 minutes. Add the scrod and gently simmer, turning once or twice, until the fish is just cooked through and the sauce is thickened, 6 to 8 minutes. Transfer the fish to a heated deep dish and spoon the sauce over the fish. Garnish with chives and serve.

MAKE AHEAD The curry paste in step 2 can be refrigerated, covered, for up to 5 days.

KASHMIR-STYLE STURGEON FILLET WITH KOHLRABI | Monji Gada

If you've picked up a bunch of turnips, parsnips, or kohlrabis at the market and you're wondering what to do with them, this is a good preparation to try. Kashmiris add lightly sautéed vegetables such as radishes, mushrooms, kohlrabi, and lotus stems to their fish. Saffron flowers, native to Kashmir, are also often used in this dish. You'll find the technique for cooking these ingredients quite distinctive. Seared fish, vegetables, and spices are immersed in water, and hot sizzling oil is poured on top; asafetida and cayenne are fried briefly and then added, creating a distinctive appearance and taste.

SERVES 4

3¹/₂ tablespoons mustard oil (see notes, page 49), or vegetable oil

1¹/₂ pounds fresh sturgeon or carp fillets

2 small kohlrabi, peeled and diced in 1-inch pieces

¹/₄ teaspoon saffron threads

³/₄ cup water

1 teaspoon salt

1 teaspoon ground fennel

1 teaspoon black cumin (*shah jeera*, page 26), or regular cumin seeds, lightly crushed

¹/₂ teaspoon ground ginger

¹/₄ teaspoon ground cinnamon

¹/₄ teaspoon turmeric

8 black peppercorns, lightly crushed

1 teaspoon cayenne

¹/₄ teaspoon asafetida

1. Heat 2 tablespoons of the oil in a large heavy skillet over medium to medium-high heat. Lay the fish fillets in the pan in a single layer; do not crowd. When the pieces of fish are crusty and brown underneath, in 4 to 5 minutes, use a thin-bladed metal spatula to carefully flip them over and sear them on the other side until golden, 3 to 4 minutes longer, or until the fish is done to your liking. Transfer the fish to a plate. Add 1/2 tablespoon of oil to the pan. Add the kohlrabi and cook, stirring, until crisp-tender and lightly browned, 6 to 8 minutes. Turn off the heat.

2. In a small skillet over low heat, toast the saffron threads. Cool slightly, then crush with the back of a large spoon and set aside.

3. Heat the water in a medium saucepan over medium heat. Add the kohlrabi, fish, saffron, salt, fennel, cumin, ginger, cinnamon, and turmeric. While the fish is cooking, heat the remaining 1 tablespoon of oil in a small skillet until very hot. Turn off the heat, stir in the cayenne and asafetida, and immediately pour the hot spiced oil over the fish. Cover the pan to let the flavors meld, about 2 minutes; the fish will take on a beautiful orange-red hue. Bring to a simmer and cook until the fish flakes easily and the sauce is slightly thick, 5 to 6 minutes. Transfer the fish to a heated deep dish, spoon the sauce over the fish, and serve right away.

VARIATION

Try making this dish with other vegetables, such as parsnips, radishes, lotus stems, and jícama.

MUMBAI FISH STEAMED IN BANANA LEAVES | Patrani Machchi

Any white-fleshed whole fish or fillet will do well here: sand dab, halibut, sole, deep-water rock cod, or lingcod, not to mention chicken breast halves. In my favorite seafood preparations, the fish is smeared with an herb paste and steamed in a banana leaf. The leaf lends a unique fragrance and makes an attractive presentation at any table, but should not be eaten. This dish is commonly served at Parsee weddings.

Occasionally, I grill the packets over a charcoal fire (for about 10 minutes). Soften the leaves in hot water before using to prevent burning, though the leaves will crisp to some degree. To turn this into a delicious vegetarian dish, substitute thick squares of *paneer* (page 221) or tofu for the fish.

3 large cloves garlic

1 to 2 fresh green serrano or jalapeño chilis, stemmed

1/2 cup freshly grated coconut (page 307), or defrosted frozen unsweetened coconut

1 cup packed cilantro

1/2 cup fresh mint leaves

1/4 cup freshly squeezed lime juice

1/4 cup water

1 teaspoon ground cumin

1/2 teaspoon salt

6 untreated fresh or thawed frozen banana leaves, or large Swiss chard leaves

Six 5-ounce halibut, salmon, or haddock fillets, with or without skin

2 tablespoons red wine vinegar

Lemon Rice (page 108), for serving

Quick Mango-Cucumber Chaat (recipe follows), for serving

1. In a blender or food processor, combine the garlic, chilis, coconut, cilantro, mint, lime juice, water, cumin, and salt. Blend to a smooth puree, stopping to scrape down the sides of the bowl a couple of times. Transfer to a glass bowl.

2. If using banana leaves, cut away the ribs and soften the leaves in a large bowl of hot water for 1 minute to help keep them from splitting. Cut the leaves into six 8-inch squares. On a work surface, place 1 leaf square and pat it dry. Spread 1 to 2 teaspoons of the herb paste down the middle of the square to equal the length of a piece of fish. Arrange a piece of fish, skin-side down, on the paste. Spread 1 tablespoon of the paste over the fish. Fold the top and bottom edges of the leaf over the fish, enclosing it. Make 5 more packets in the same manner.

3. Arrange the packets, seam-side down, in a bamboo steamer or on a large steamer rack. Add the red wine vinegar to the steaming water and bring to a boil. Steam the packets over the boiling water, covered, until the fish is just cooked through, about 8 minutes. Using a spatula, transfer the packets to a warmed decorative platter.

4. To serve the fish, you have two choices: Carefully open the packets and fold the leaves back and under, creating a little nest for the fish, and serve each person a packet. Or remove the fish from the packages and serve immediately on individual plates with Lemon Rice and Quick Mango-Cucumber Chaat.

VARIATION

You may also panfry the packets in hot oil for 5 minutes per side. Replace the garlic with shallots, the cumin with fennel seeds, and the lime with vinegar for another flavor combination.

QUICK MANGO-CUCUMBER CHAAT

MAKES 3 CUPS

2 cups peeled, pitted, and diced ripe mango

1 small hot-house cucumber, peeled, seeded, and diced

1 fresh green serrano or jalapeño chili, stemmed and chopped

2 teaspoons grated fresh ginger

1/4 cup coarsely chopped cilantro sprigs

1 tablespoon light-brown sugar, jaggery (pages 51–52), or raw sugar

1/2 teaspoon salt

1/2 teaspoon freshly ground black pepper

Juice of 1 lime

In a bowl, combine the diced mango, cucumber, chili, ginger, and cilantro and toss lightly to combine. Sprinkle the sugar, salt, and pepper over the mixture and toss again. Drizzle the lime juice over the mixture and stir gently. Let stand at room temperature for 30 minutes before serving. Stir again just before bringing to the table. Refrigerate any leftovers.

PAN-ROASTED BENGAL FISH WITH RAISINS | Doi Maach

For this dish, turmeric root is traditionally soaked in water overnight, cut into smaller pieces, and blended into a smooth paste with water to make a golden marinade for the fish. If the root is easily available (a two- to three-inch piece is plenty here), I more than welcome you to use it for its pristine taste. Fish is considered very special in Bengal and in nearby Bangladesh. In fact, villagers are so fond of fish that many of them spawn their own *rahu* (carp), *kaatol*, and *mrigal* in ponds in the vicinity of their homes. Yogurt *(doi)* is more frequently used in fish dishes in Bengal than in other regions of India.

Choosing seafood is as simple as selecting cut flowers. Let your eyes, nose, hands, and ears be the judge. Imagine a fresh ocean breeze; the fish must smell just like it. In the same way, what you look for in a flower is its heady scent. Fish should be firm to the touch, as sprightly as a fresh-cut flower. If the fish is whole, the eye should be bright, the scales ought to replicate light, and the gills should be red, just as flowers should be brilliant, with no bruised petals.

To make the mustard paste, see step 1 of the directions for Seared Bengal Fish in Tangy Mustard Sauce, pages 325–326.

1 teaspoon salt

1/2 teaspoon turmeric

1 1/2 pounds carp, haddock, or cod steaks or fillets

1 cup coarsely chopped yellow onion

1-inch piece fresh ginger

1/4 cup mustard oil (see notes, page 49), or vegetable oil

2 bay leaves

1-inch stick cinnamon

6 green cardamom pods

4 whole cloves

1/4 teaspoon fenugreek seeds

2 teaspoons ground coriander

1 teaspoon cayenne

1 teaspoon ground cumin

2 teaspoons mustard paste (see headnote)

1 cup plain yogurt

1/2 cup water

1/2 teaspoon sugar

2 tablespoons golden raisins or sultanas

1.　In a small bowl, combine the salt and turmeric. Place the fish in a shallow glass dish, and sprinkle the salt mixture over both sides. Cover and marinate at cool room temperature for 15 to 30 minutes, or refrigerate for 1 to 2 hours (but not more than 4).

2.　In a blender or food processor, combine the onion and ginger with 2 to 3 tablespoons water and blend to a smooth paste, stopping to scrape down the sides of the bowl a couple of times. Set aside.

3.　Heat the oil in a heavy large skillet over medium heat. Add the fish and sear until golden, 3 to 4 minutes per side. Transfer to a plate. Add the bay leaves, cinnamon, cardamom, cloves, and fenugreek seeds to the pan, and stir for a few seconds until aromatic. Add the onion paste and cook, stirring occasionally, until the mixture is lightly colored and the raw smell dissipates, 4 to 5 minutes. Add the coriander, cayenne, cumin, and mustard paste, stir for a few seconds, and reduce the heat to low. Whisk together the yogurt and water, add to the pan, and stir. Stir in the sugar and raisins and mix thoroughly. Add the fish, cover, and cook until the fish flakes easily, 5 to 6 minutes. Taste and adjust the seasonings. (Sugar is added to balance out the flavors, not to make the sauce taste sweet.) Discard the bay leaves before serving.

THE TASTES OF TANDOOR: INDIAN BARBECUE

Tandoori Zaayeqae

When my children were growing up, summer to me meant the height of Little League season. I was on call to head the outdoor cooking team. And during the course of my involvement, I discovered that parents, coaches, and even kids liked the spicy flavors of my native India, especially anything grilled. So tandoori sirloin steaks, tandoori leg of lamb, tandoori fish, and of course tandoori chicken were always on the menu for team parties. For me, warm memories of fire and smoke, sizzle and scent are part of the pleasure of informal outdoor dining.

Over several centuries, tandoori cooking has grown in popularity and stature around the world. But many fans don't know its special history, or its central place in Indian cuisine. Tandoori cooking originated in ancient India, most likely in the region that is now Pakistan. In those days, when animals were sacrificed, they were skewed on spears and spit-roasted; historical documents also reveal that the old jungle fowl *gallus gallus*, the forebear of the modern chicken, was bred by the Indus Valley civilization. Ancient traders took their culinary techniques, including the building of tandoor, or clay ovens, with them as they journeyed to other parts of the world. And when the emperors traveled, the royal chefs carried relatively light, metal versions of the tandoor by camel, using them to prepare fresh, hot breads and savory roasted meats and fowl.

In the sixteenth century, Guru Nanak, founder of the Sikh religion, urged the people to share communal clay tandoors. Not only would sharing conserve fuel, but, he hoped, it would also work to eliminate the caste system by bringing people together to cook and eat and talk. Today, we know this wondrous oven as a great contribution to the culinary world.

The tandoor, lined with clay and straw, stands vertically. The charcoal fire on the flat bottom heats the oven to 800°F to 900°F. In tandoori cooking, food cooks over indirect, very high heat within minutes, so that it sears on the outside and retains juiciness inside. I have also used the HearthKit brick oven (see Sources, page 438) and pizza stones quite successfully for tandoori dishes; set the roasting pan directly onto the HearthKit or pizza stone and bake in the oven. Remember, the HearthKit brick oven takes a little longer than the kitchen range to preheat to the desired temperature.

The rituals of almost any barbecue remind me of tandoor cooking. We have a tandoor sunken deep in our backyard, next to the barbecue grill, and it serves to bring friends and company together. You probably won't have a real tandoor to work with, so I've written these tandoori-style recipes so that much of their authentic flavor comes from the marinades. All can be easily grilled or broiled.

NATURAL TENDERIZERS

In a conventional oven, tandoori dishes take twice as long to roast. To overcome this, I suggest treating them with tenderizers. Tenderizing and marinating is in part a kind of cooking process—just think of ceviche, where the fish "cooks" in acidic lime juice. In Indian cuisine, the tenderizers and marinades serve much the same function, allowing you to do the actual cooking at a higher temperature in a shorter time.

Cuts of Meat in My Tandoori Kitchen

In India, chickens roam the poultry yard, so they have plenty of muscle. Choose plump, free-range chicken for a more authentic Indian flavor and texture. Unless suggested otherwise, the meat or poultry is always skinless. Cooking time is determined by the type of cut you're using and not by the size or weight of the meat, poultry, or fish. There are four main cuts used in tandoori cooking: whole chicken, fish, or leg of lamb; large pieces, such as steaks, chops, or cut-up chicken; *tikka*, small tender cuts, such as 2-inch cubes of boneless chicken breast or legs, kebabs, or other chunks of meat; and minced or ground meats for kebabs.

The most commonly used tenderizers in Indian cooking are yogurt, raw papaya, acid fruits such as pomegranate, lime, and tamarind, and sometimes vinegar. Often many tenderizers are used in combination. Here's how they work:

Yogurt: Helps to break down meat fibers and make the meat soft and succulent.

Lime: Not only softens meat but provides a special tangy finishing touch.

Green papaya: Contains a protein-digesting enzyme, papain, that helps in tenderizing meat. Buy an actual green papaya at an Asian market. It should have a pale, celadon-green interior and hard crunchy texture. Use it skin and all to make the paste: Chop $1/2$ cup raw papaya in chunks and puree in blender with a couple of tablespoons of water. Yields $1/4$ cup papaya paste.

Raw pineapple: The acid and active tenderizing enzyme bromalein in raw pineapple is very pungent and acts like papain (from papaya). Most greengrocers pick the fruit at the green-ripe stage; buy the least-ripe, hardest ones you can find. You can also ask the produce department to save you the green ones. Peel and chop $1/2$ cup raw fruit in chunks and puree in a blender with a couple of tablespoons of water. Yields about $1/4$ cup of pineapple paste.

Tamarind: Contains tartaric and citric acids, which provide its characteristic sour taste and its tenderizing qualities. These days, fresh tamarind pods are available in some specialty markets and supermarkets.

Vinegar: Its acetic acid acts as a softener.

MARINADES

Whether you use a conventional oven, a tandoor, a hibachi perched on a picnic table, or the finest gas grill, the secret to a classic tandoori dish is the marinade. It should enhance the taste of what you're cooking, not overwhelm it. Remember, the marinade should be a thick paste, and not thin, watery, or lumpy. Most of the time, Indian cooks purchase ginger and garlic paste or use a mortar and pestle to make their own. To expedite the process, I have suggested the use of a regular blender with minimal liquid to obtain a smooth paste. A well-made paste will adhere nicely through the marinating process and remain on the meat after roasting.

The marinade—a mixture of natural tenderizers, spices, and herbs—fosters a moist texture and sweetens the smoky flavor. Sometimes nuts and dried fruits are ground and used to enhance the flavors. I prefer to use the traditional method of marinating in two stages. I don't use salt in the first stage, especially for red meats, because it releases juices from the meat, making it stringy. I first coat the meat with "harsher" ingredients such as ginger and garlic. Then, in the second stage, I use delicate spices, salt, and yogurt. (For white meats and vegetables, salt can be used in the first stage.)

To help the marinade flavors penetrate the meat, score it by making shallow slashes in its outer surface. While marinating, occasionally rub the marinade into the slits you've made; this massage enriches the flavor. Once the meat is in the marinade, it can be kept in the refrigerator for up to 24 hours in a glass or other nonreactive container. Bring the meat to room temperature before roasting or grilling.

Hints for Outdoor Grilling

You may or may not own a tandoor, but you likely own a kettle-type grill. Think of your kettle grill as an outdoor tandoor. The smoky chamber of this grill is well suited to tandoori foods. The high heat circulates around the food, searing in flavor and juices in much the same way as it does with a tandoor. Here are some ways to make sure that your tandoori-style foods are juicy and smoky:

* Layer the fuel (coals) evenly and carefully in the barbecue. I like mixing equal amounts of mesquite and regular charcoal briquettes to get an even heat.

* Keep an eye on temperature and smoke levels. Check the coals every half-hour or so. To keep the temperature constant, add two or three fresh briquettes as needed.

* One of the best ways to prevent foods from sticking to the grill is to equalize temperatures as much as possible. Bring the food up to room temperature, and preheat the grate over the fire before you start to cook.

* With smaller items, you'll need skewers to support the food; use long-handled, sturdy skewers. If you are using bamboo skewers, soak them in water first so they won't burn. You can improvise with wrappers, cooking meat or fish in banana, mustard, cabbage, or other edible leaves for distinctive flavors. *Desi ghee* or oil should be applied to the clean metal skewers before threading. Do not push meat straight onto the skewer; instead, "weave" it using an up and down motion. This ensures that the meat will not slip off easily.

TANDOORI CHICKEN | Tandoori Murg

This is my favorite approach to making tandoori chicken. The classic technique of marinating in two stages might appear time-consuming if you haven't done it before, but when you taste the seductive contrasts—hot, tender, and seared outside, with the gush of juicy liquid inside—you'll be inspired to try it again until the process becomes second nature.

To finish the entrée, all you need is a good-looking serving platter. Fragrant basmati rice and Spicy-Sweet Kumquat Chutney with Figs (page 188) or a *raita*, as well as a soothing dessert like Beet Pudding (page 417), makes a nice meal.

SERVES 4 TO 6

One 3 1/2-pound chicken, skinned and cut into 6 to 8 pieces

2 1/2-inch piece fresh ginger

12 large cloves garlic

1/4 cup freshly squeezed lime juice

2 medium yellow onions, sliced

3 tablespoons vegetable oil

2 teaspoons salt

2 teaspoons ground cumin

1 1/2 teaspoons sweet paprika

1/2 teaspoon cayenne

1/2 teaspoon ground mace

1/2 teaspoon ground cinnamon

12 green cardamom pods, seeds removed and ground

1/4 teaspoon ground cloves

1 cup plain yogurt

2 tablespoons melted *desi ghee* (pages 47–48), or unsalted butter

A beautiful bunch of cilantro, for garnish

1 large red onion, thinly sliced, for garnish

Several wedges of lime, for squeezing

1. Several hours or the day before you plan to serve, rinse the chicken pieces well and pat them dry. Score the meat by making a few slashes in each piece. Place in a large glass bowl.

2. In a blender, combine the ginger, garlic, and lime juice. Puree until the paste is as smooth as you can get it, stopping to scrape down the sides of the bowl a couple of times. Pour this mixture over the chicken and rub thoroughly, pushing the marinade into the incisions and coating evenly. Cover and set aside at cool room temperature for 1 hour, or refrigerate for up to 2 hours.

3. In a blender, combine the onions and oil and puree until smooth. You may have to pulse several times, stopping and scraping down the sides of the bowl, if necessary. Transfer to a medium glass bowl. Add the salt, cumin, paprika, cayenne, mace, cinnamon, cardamom, and cloves and mix. Gradually whisk in the yogurt. Pour this onion-spice mixture over the chicken and rub it in thoroughly. Cover and refrigerate for at least 6 hours or overnight, up to a maximum of 24 hours, turning the chicken pieces occasionally in the marinade.

4. To cook the chicken on a barbecue grill, prepare a charcoal fire, letting the coals burn until they are covered with a gray ash and are medium-hot. Position the rack about 8 inches above the coals and lightly coat with oil. Lay the chicken pieces on the hottest portion of the grill, cover, and cook for about 12 minutes on one side. Then turn and cook on the other side until tender, 8 to 12 minutes more. Alternatively, to cook the chicken in a conventional oven, preheat the oven to 550°F. Lay the chicken pieces in a single layer in a shallow roasting pan. Roast the chicken until it is tender and still juicy, with no trace of pink near the bone, basting with the *desi ghee* and turning once, 25 to 30 minutes.

5. Use tongs to transfer chicken to a heated decorative platter. Arrange big tufts of cilantro around the chicken. Strew some of the red onion around and garnish with wedges of lime to squirt on the chicken. Serve right away.

SPINACH-CRUSTED TANDOORI CHICKEN | Palak Tangdi

This is easily my favorite twist on tandoori chicken—a little green, rather than red, and a little more suave because the raw onion is caramelized. The marinade is a beautiful spring-green color. Infused with a unique combination of leafy greens, cilantro, and green chilis, this simple roast has delightful flavors. You'll see that here, as well as in most recipes that follow, I've added chickpea flour to the marinade; it acts as a thickener and helps the seasonings adhere to the poultry, meats, and vegetables. Place the platter of tandoori chicken on the table, have *naan* (pages 84–85) or other bread handy, and serve with any refreshing *raita* or *kachumber* (pages 201–218).

SERVES 4 TO 6

4 pounds chicken parts, skinned

1/2-inch piece fresh ginger

6 large cloves garlic

1/2 cup chopped cilantro

1/4 cup papaya or pineapple paste (page 337), or 2 tablespoons freshly squeezed lime juice

1/4 teaspoon turmeric

2 1/2 tablespoons vegetable oil

1 cup plain yogurt

1/2 cup sliced yellow onion

1 fresh green serrano or jalapeño chili, stemmed and chopped

1 teaspoon ground coriander

2 cups chopped fresh spinach, with tender stems

1 cup chopped fresh Swiss chard, with tender stems

1 tablespoon chickpea flour, or corn starch

1 teaspoon salt

2 tablespoons melted *desi ghee* (pages 47–48), or unsalted butter, for basting

Beautiful sprigs of watercress, for garnish

Yellow pear tomatoes and red tomatoes, thickly sliced, for garnish

Tangy Tandoori Spice Mix (page 34) (optional)

1. Several hours or the day before you plan to serve, rinse the chicken pieces well and pat them dry. Score the meat by making a few slashes in each piece. Place in a large glass bowl.

2. In a blender, combine the ginger, garlic, cilantro, papaya or pineapple paste, turmeric, 2 tablespoons of the oil, and 1/2 cup of the yogurt. Process until the paste is pureed and as smooth as you can get it. Transfer to a medium glass bowl and whisk in the remaining 1/2 cup of yogurt. Pour this mixture over the chicken and rub thoroughly, pushing the marinade into the incisions and coating evenly. Cover and set aside at cool room temperature for 1 hour, or refrigerate for up to 2 hours.

3. Heat the remaining 1/2 tablespoon of oil in a heavy medium skillet over medium heat. Add the onion and cook, stirring, until it turns a rich brown, 10 to 12 minutes. Add the chili, coriander, spinach, and Swiss chard and cook, stirring, for 1 minute. Cover and cook, stirring occasionally, until the greens are wilted, about 4 minutes. Transfer to a blender. Add the chickpea flour and salt and blend to a smooth puree. Pour the spinach mixture over the chicken and rub it in thoroughly. Cover and refrigerate for at least 5 hours or overnight, up to a maximum of 24 hours, turning the chicken pieces occasionally in the marinade.

4. To cook the chicken on a barbecue grill, prepare a charcoal fire, letting the coals burn until they are covered with a gray ash and are medium-hot. Position the rack about 8 inches above the coals and lightly coat with oil. Lay the chicken pieces on the hottest portion of the grill, cover, and cook for about 12 minutes on one side. Then turn and cook on the other side until tender, basting with the *desi ghee*, 10 to 12 minutes more. Alternatively, to cook the chicken in a conventional oven, preheat the oven to 550°F. Lay the chicken in a single layer in a shallow roasting pan. Roast the chicken until it is tender and still juicy, with no trace of pink near the bone, basting with the *desi ghee* and turning once, 30 to 35 minutes.

5. Line a warm serving platter with the sprigs of watercress and surround with the sliced tomatoes. Use tongs to transfer the chicken to the platter and serve. Pass the Tangy Tandoori Spice Mix on the side for your guests to sprinkle on the chicken, if desired.

SEARED CHICKEN TIKKA | Tandoori Tikka

You can savor the sizzle in every bite of this classic dish. The chicken has a crackling exterior, a moist interior, and an herb-scented, rich, complex flavor that's truly delectable. I suggest you freeze the chicken, marinade and all, for 15 minutes before roasting, so the creamy marinade can harden slightly, which helps it adhere to the meat while roasting. For a stylish party menu first course, serve a few *tikkas* on a bed of lightly dressed baby greens, sprinkled with Tangy Tandoori Spice Mix (page 34).

SERVES 6

2 to 2 1/2 pounds boneless, skinless chicken breasts, cut into bite-size pieces

1/2 cup sliced raw pineapple, or papaya

1-inch piece fresh ginger

4 large cloves garlic

1/4 cup freshly squeezed lime juice

10 green cardamom pods, seeds removed and ground

1 teaspoon ground white pepper

1/2 teaspoon ground cinnamon

2 tablespoons chickpea flour, or corn starch

1/2 cup minced yellow onion

1 to 2 fresh green serrano or jalapeño chilis, stemmed and minced

1/4 cup minced cilantro

2 tablespoons vegetable oil

1/4 cup heavy whipping cream

1 cup plain yogurt

1 teaspoon salt

Big beautiful cilantro sprigs, for garnish

1. Several hours or the day before you plan to serve, rinse the chicken pieces well and pat them dry. Place in a large glass bowl.

2. In a blender, combine the pineapple, ginger, garlic, and lime juice. Blend to a smooth paste and pour over the chicken. Rub the mixture thoroughly onto the chicken. Cover and set aside at cool room temperature for 30 minutes or refrigerate for up to 1 hour.

3. In a medium bowl, combine the cardamom, pepper, cinnamon, chickpea flour, onion, chilis, cilantro, oil, cream, yogurt, and salt in a medium bowl. Whisk until well blended. Pour this mixture over the chicken and rub thoroughly, turning several times to coat evenly. Cover and refrigerate for at least 5 hours or overnight, up to a maximum of 12 hours, turning the chicken pieces occasionally in the marinade.

4. To cook the chicken on a barbecue grill, prepare a charcoal fire, letting the coals burn until they are covered with a gray ash and are medium-hot. Position the rack 6 to 8 inches above the coals and lightly coat with oil. Thread the chicken pieces on metal skewers. Lay the skewers on the hottest portion of the grill and cook for 6 to 8 minutes. Turn the skewers and cook until tender, 5 to 6 minutes more. Alternatively, to cook the chicken in a conventional oven, preheat the broiler for 5 minutes. Place the skewers on a broiler pan and broil 6 inches away from the heat source for 6 to 8 minutes. Turn and cook until tender and still juicy, 6 to 8 minutes more.

5. Transfer the skewers to a heated serving platter, garnish with cilantro, and serve.

VARIATION

Leftover Seared Chicken Tikka can be used in preparing Chicken Tikka Masala (pages 272–274) or Butter Chicken (pages 274–275).

TANDOORI CORNISH GAME HEN STUFFED WITH MANGO
| Aam Bhareli Murg

Tandoori dishes have been very popular in the West since Indian cuisine was first introduced. However, other than the ubiquitous chicken and lamb, not many tandoori recipes show up in cookbooks or restaurant menus. I like the texture and flavor of Cornish game hen, and it takes on the aromatics gracefully. The stuffing, with mango and pistachios, emits the distinctive perfume of cardamom. Ever since I created this recipe, I've been serving it regularly for entertaining.

Here the mango does not have to be fully ripe; mangoes that are still slightly green on the outside and yellow inside hold well as they cook.

2 medium (1 1/4 pounds each) Cornish game hens, skinned

2-inch piece fresh ginger

10 large cloves garlic

1/4 cup papaya paste (page 337), or 2 table-spoons freshly squeezed lime juice

1/4 cup vegetable oil

2 1/2 teaspoons salt

1 teaspoon cayenne

1 1/2 cups plain yogurt

1/2 cup shelled, roasted salted or unsalted pista-chios

4 green cardamom pods, seeds removed and ground

2 tablespoons chickpea flour, or corn starch

1/4 cup dried cranberries, or dark raisins

1 cup diced semi-ripe mango

6 tablespoons melted *desi ghee* (pages 47–48), or unsalted butter, for basting

Banana leaves, lemon leaves, or lettuce leaves, for lining the platter

1. Several hours or the day before you plan to serve, rinse the Cornish game hens well and pat them dry. Place them in a large casserole or similar container.

2. In a blender, combine the ginger, garlic, papaya paste, and oil and blend to a smooth puree. You may have to pulse several times, stopping and scraping down the sides, if necessary. Transfer to a small bowl. Add two teaspoons of the salt, the cayenne, and 1/2 cup of the yogurt and mix well. Pour over the Cornish game hens and rub the mixture thoroughly into the meat, turning several times to coat evenly. Cover and refrigerate for 8 to 12 hours.

3. Fifteen minutes before you are ready to roast, place the pistachios in a food processor or blender and process until finely powdered. Transfer to a small bowl. Add the cardamom, chickpea flour, cranberries, mango, and remaining 1 cup of yogurt and season with the remaining 1/2 teaspoon of salt. Mix well and spoon half of the stuffing mixture into the neck and body cavity of each Cornish game hen. Tie the legs together loosely with kitchen twine.

4. Preheat the oven to 550°F. Place the Cornish game hens on a large roasting pan or foil-lined baking sheet and bake until tender and still juicy, with no trace of pink near the bone, 35 to 40 minutes, basting with the *desi ghee* from time to time.

5. Arrange the hens on a warm platter that's lined or decorated with leaves. Spoon any accumulated juices and stuffing on top and serve.

TANDOORI QUAIL WITH TROPICAL FRUITS | Tandoori Bater

This is the easiest tandoori bird dish I've created, and it works well with everything from quail to goose to partridge. Tender and juicy, farm-raised quails are available in specialty markets. I keep these tiny, mild-flavored game birds on hand in the freezer, because they make easy, unusual meals in no time. They are best cooked just before serving. The garnish is a sweet and spicy, salsa-like mélange of bright, tropical and California-grown fruits with a dusting of cumin. The quail is served atop baby greens seasoned with minced onion, walnut oil, and sherry vinegar.

SERVES 4

8 good-sized whole quail (I prefer ones that are 4 or 5 ounces each)

2 to 3 teaspoons *garam masala* (pages 36–37), or store-bought

1 teaspoon salt

2-inch piece fresh ginger

6 large cloves garlic

1/2 cup plain yogurt

5 cups loosely packed baby greens

1/4 cup finely chopped red or white onion

4 cherry tomatoes, halved

2 tablespoons sherry vinegar

1 to 2 tablespoons walnut oil, or olive oil

1 small ripe pineapple, peeled, cored, and cut into chunks

1 ripe mango, peeled, pitted, and chopped

1 orange, peeled, halved, sliced, and seeded

1/2 cup sliced strawberries

1/2 cup seedless green or red grapes

2 teaspoons ground cumin, or *chaat masala* (pages 41–42)

1. Using poultry shears or a sharp knife, cut out the backbone of each quail. Flatten each quail with the palm of your hand so it will lie flat. Place the birds in a large glass dish.

2. In a blender, combine the *garam masala*, salt, ginger, garlic, and 1/4 cup of the yogurt and blend to a smooth puree, stopping to scrape down the sides of the bowl a couple of times. Transfer to a bowl and whisk in the remaining 1/4 cup of yogurt. Pour the mixture over the birds and rub the marinade into all sides. Cover and marinate in the refrigerator for at least 2 hours or overnight.

3. A few hours before you're ready to grill, combine the greens, onion, tomatoes, vinegar, and oil in a bowl. Mix well and set aside. In another bowl, combine the pineapple, mango, orange, strawberries, and grapes. In a heavy small skillet over medium heat, toast the cumin seeds, stirring regularly, for 3 to 4 minutes. Cool slightly, transfer to a coffee mill or spice grinder, and grind to a fine powder. Sprinkle the cumin over the fruit and toss gently to mix. Set aside for 30 minutes to marinate.

4. To cook the quail on a barbecue grill, prepare a charcoal fire, letting the coals burn until they are covered with a gray ash and are medium-hot. Position the rack about 8 inches above the coals and lightly coat with oil. While the grill heats, lay the quail on a baking sheet. Tie the legs together with kitchen twine, then brush both sides with some of the remaining marinade. Lay the quail, breast-side down, on the hottest portion of the grill, cover, and cook for about 8 minutes. Turn the quail over. Cover and continue grilling until the leg meat will separate from the bone quite easily when you squeeze a leg between two fingers, 4 to 6 minutes more. Alternatively, to cook the quail in a conventional oven, preheat the broiler. Place the quail on a broiler pan and broil 6 inches away from the heat source for about 4 to 5 minutes on each side for medium-rare. Remove to a platter and let rest for about 5 minutes while you set up your plates.

5. Divide the greens among 4 warm dinner plates. Set 2 quail over the salad on each plate and garnish with generous spoonfuls of the fruit mélange.

TANDOORI TURKEY WITH POMEGRANATE JUICE | Tandoori Teetar

At the request of loyal students, I've included my recipe for tandoori turkey. This sweet-spicy masterpiece offers an unusual spin on the traditional holiday bird. A whole turkey marinates in pomegranate juice, yogurt, and spices for several hours, making the flesh very tender. Just before roasting the turkey, you can pack sprigs of herbs, green beans, carrots, celery, and leeks into the cavity to turn the roast into a complete meal. You can substitute 2 cups store-bought pomegranate juice, which is available in Middle Eastern markets and many supermarkets.

SERVES 12 TO 14 GENEROUSLY

One 12- to 14-pound turkey, preferably free-range

5-inch piece fresh ginger

26 large cloves garlic (approximately 2 large garlic heads)

2 large yellow onions, coarsely chopped

2 tablespoons ground coriander

2 tablespoons green cardamom pods, seeds removed and ground

1 tablespoon ground cumin

1 tablespoon salt

2 teaspoons ground cloves

1 teaspoon cayenne

2 cups plain yogurt

4 large pomegranates

1/4 cup melted *desi ghee* (pages 47–48), or unsalted butter, for basting

Banana leaves, or lemon leaves, for lining the platter

2 large red bell peppers, seeded, deribbed, and sliced, for garnish

2 large yellow bell peppers, seeded, deribbed, and sliced, for garnish

2 large ripe tomatoes, sliced, for garnish

4 lemons or limes, cut into wedges, for garnish and squeezing

1. The day before you plan to serve, rinse the turkey well and pat it dry. Using a sharp, thin-bladed knife, at regular intervals, make deep incisions in the turkey, penetrating to the bone. Place in a nonreactive pan large enough to hold the turkey.

2. In a blender, combine the ginger, garlic, onions, coriander, cardamom, cumin, salt, cloves, cayenne, and 1 cup of the yogurt. Process until the paste is pureed and as smooth as you can get it. Transfer to a medium glass bowl and whisk in the remaining 1 cup of yogurt. Rub the marinade all over the turkey and into the cavity, turning several times, pushing the marinade into the incisions, and coating evenly.

3. Cut the pomegranates in half crosswise. Use a large citrus juicer to extract the juice. One large pomegranate yields about 1/2 cup, and you'll need 2 cups of juice in total. Pour the juice over the turkey and rub gently. Cover and refrigerate for at least 12 hours or up to 24 hours, rubbing the marinade into the turkey from time to time.

4. Preheat the oven to 450°F. Truss the turkey with string. Place the turkey on a rack set in a large heavy roasting pan, reserving any extra marinade, and roast for 30 minutes. Reduce the oven temperature to 325°F. Brush the turkey with the marinade and roast until a meat thermometer inserted in the thickest part of a thigh registers 175°F, 3 to 3 3/4 hours total roasting time. Baste occasionally with pan juices and melted *desi ghee*, or unsalted butter. Let rest for 10 minutes before carving.

5. Arrange the bird on a warm platter that's lined or decorated with leaves. Garnish the platter with the peppers, tomatoes, and lime wedges and serve.

VARIATION

Kandahari Chicken Tikka

The regions of Kabul and Kandahar in Afghanistan are well known for tandoori dishes too. Dried sour grape powder and pomegranate juice are traditional tenderizers. Cut the marinade recipe by a third and use about 3/4 cup pomegranate juice for 2 pounds of chicken or lamb *tikka*.

FRAGRANT LAMB MAHARAJA WITH ALMONDS AND CARAMELIZED ONION | Ran Maharaja

Lamb, with a crusty, caramelized exterior and rosy-rare meat, is one of the simplest Indian roasts for American cooks to become skilled at, since most are familiar with grilling and barbecuing. Mixing gently browned onion paste into the marinade, an age-old technique, adds rich taste. In royal kitchens, dried rose petals were used in the marinade to impart a unique fragrance, and the finished dish was adorned with stunning gold leaf. For a richer taste yet, baste with saffron threads soaked in hot milk. Full-bodied Australian shiraz and zinfandel stand up well to this hearty fare.

SERVES 4 TO 6 GENEROUSLY

2 pounds leg of lamb, trimmed of all fat

2 tablespoons vegetable oil

1 large yellow onion, coarsely chopped

1 tablespoon coriander seeds

1/2 tablespoon cumin seeds

2-inch piece fresh ginger, crushed

5 cloves garlic, crushed

2 tablespoons raw papaya paste (page 337)

1 teaspoon sweet paprika

1/2 teaspoon cayenne

1/4 teaspoon ground cinnamon

1/4 cup freshly squeezed lime juice

1/4 cup cilantro

20 fresh mint leaves, plus extra sprigs for garnish

10 whole blanched almonds

1/2 cup yogurt cheese (page 205)

2 teaspoons salt

1/4 cup melted *desi ghee* (pages 47–48), or unsalted butter, for basting

1. The day before you want to serve, rinse the lamb well and pat it dry. Using a sharp, thin-bladed knife, make 4 deep incisions in the lamb, penetrating to the bone. Place in a large bowl.

2. Heat the oil in a heavy medium skillet over medium heat. Add the onion and cook, stirring often, until richly browned, 10 to 12 minutes. Add the coriander seeds and cumin seeds and cook, stirring, until fragrant, 1 to 2 minutes. Cool slightly and transfer to a blender. Add the ginger, garlic, papaya paste, paprika, cayenne, cinnamon, lime juice, cilantro, mint, almonds, and 1/4 cup of the yogurt cheese. Blend to a smooth paste, stopping to scrape down the sides of the bowl a couple of times. Transfer to a small bowl and whisk in the remaining yogurt cheese. Rub the mixture onto the lamb, pushing the marinade into the incisions and coating evenly. Cover and refrigerate for 10 to 12 hours or overnight, turning the lamb and rubbing with the marinade from time to time.

3. Prepare a charcoal fire. Meanwhile, season the lamb with the salt and set aside for 15 minutes. When the coals are covered with gray ash and are medium-hot, move them to the perimeter of the grill rack and position a drip pan in the center (optional). Lightly coat the grill rack with oil and place the lamb on the rack, directly over the drip pan. Cover the grill and cook until the lamb reaches 130° to 140°F (rare to medium-rare) on an instant-read thermometer. Figure on about 15 to 20 minutes per pound, and cook until it is tender and still juicy, turning the leg and basting with the *desi ghee* from time to time. Grill an additional 10 to 15 minutes until well done, with no trace of pink near the bone. Add more coals if necessary to maintain the heat.

4. Let the lamb rest for 10 minutes before carving, then slice it about 1/4 inch thick. Arrange the slices on a warm, decorative serving platter. Garnish with mint sprigs and serve.

TANDOORI LAMB TIKKA WITH SAFFRON SAUCE

| Reshmi Mamsa / Boti Kabab

Imagine delicate morsels of lamb marinated in creamy nuts, yogurt, and spices and roasted to golden perfection. In this recipe, the marinade is cooked with saffron to create an exclusive dipping sauce. Accompany with *naan* (pages 84–85), Pear-Apricot Chutney with Almonds (page 187), Garlicky Dal Stew (page 383), and Mahimahi Biryani (page 120).

SERVES 4 AS AN APPETIZER, WITH ABOUT 1 CUP DIPPING SAUCE

1 pound boneless lamb shoulder, cut into 2-inch pieces

1/4 cup shelled, roasted unsalted pistachios

10 whole roasted unsalted cashews

3 tablespoons chickpea flour, or corn starch

1-inch piece fresh ginger

6 large cloves garlic

2 tablespoons freshly squeezed lime juice

1 tablespoon *garam masala* (pages 47–48), or store-bought

1 teaspoon ground cumin

1/2 teaspoon cayenne

3 tablespoons vegetable oil

1 cup plain yogurt

1 teaspoon salt

1/2 teaspoon saffron threads

Big beautiful mint sprigs, for garnish

1. Several hours or the day before you plan to serve, rinse the lamb pieces well and pat them dry. Place in a bowl.

2. In a blender, combine the pistachios and cashews and process until finely powdered. Add the chickpea flour, ginger, garlic, lime juice, *garam masala,* cumin, cayenne, oil, and 1/2 cup of the yogurt. Blend to a smooth paste, stopping to scrape down the sides of the bowl a couple of times. Transfer to a small bowl, whisk in the remaining 1/2 cup of yogurt, and mix well. Pour over the lamb, then rub into the meat, turning several times to coat the pieces evenly. Cover and refrigerate for 6 to 12 hours, turning the lamb pieces occasionally in the marinade.

3. To cook the lamb on a barbecue grill, prepare a charcoal fire. Remove the lamb from the marinade, reserving the marinade to make the sauce. Season the lamb with the salt; set aside for 15 minutes before roasting. When the coals are covered with gray ash and are

Kakori is a small hamlet on the outskirts of Lucknow. At this little known place, during the freedom struggle, a group of freedom fighters looted a train carrying the British government treasury money, an episode that was later dubbed the Kakori Case. It was customary for the nawabs to entertain British officers and offer them the finest hospitality. At one such social gathering, a British officer complained of the coarseness of kebabs. The nawab Syed Mohammad Haider Kazmi immediately convened his cooks and asked them to create a novel delicacy. After days of incessant reworking and refining, *khoa* (page 404) was substituted for the animal fat, white pepper was used in place of black, and the minced meat was ground dexterously to create a silky smooth texture. During the marinating process, the clever royal chefs placed a hot coal in a small bowl and poured few tablespoons of *desi ghee* on top. The bowl was placed in the center of the lamb mixture, and the whole dish was covered tightly for about 15 minutes. (You too can try this in step 1; I do for special meals.) The resulting flavors were divine, and of course the British officer was captivated by the new tastes. Since then, every Lucknowi has been proud of the area's skillfully executed kebabs.

medium-hot, position the rack about 8 inches above the coals and lightly coat with oil. Lay the lamb pieces on the hottest portion of the grill, cover, and cook for 6 to 8 minutes on one side. Then turn and finish cooking on the other side until tender, 6 to 8 minutes more. Alternatively, to cook the lamb in a conventional oven, preheat the broiler for 5 minutes. Place the lamb pieces on a broiler pan and broil 6 inches away from the heat source for 6 to 8 minutes. Turn and cook until tender and still juicy, 6 to 8 minutes more.

4. While the lamb is cooking, soak the saffron in 2 tablespoons of hot tap water and set aside. In a small saucepan, simmer the marinade over low heat, stirring occasionally, until the raw meat flavor dissipates, 6 to 8 minutes. If the marinade starts to stick to the bottom of the pan during cooking, add couple of tablespoons of water to avoid scorching. Add the saffron to the sauce, cover, and cook, stirring occasionally, until the sauce is thickened and the flavors have melded, about 5 minutes. Ladle the sauce into a pretty bowl and place on a heated platter. Surround with the lamb. Decorate with sprigs of mint and serve.

OUDH-STYLE TENDER TANDOORI LAMB KEBABS | Kakori Kabab

A variety of kebabs originated in Oudh (now Lucknow), a historic region of northern India that is currently part of the state of Uttar Pradesh. Initially, the Moghuls prepared these kebabs with beef, but later influences and innovations led to the use of minced lamb, prized for its soft texture and better flavor. Since lamb is tougher than chicken, I treat it a little differently—that is, I add richer and more robust ingredients. I have stir-fried the chickpea flour until aromatic to enhance the taste. A citrusy sauvignon blanc tastes great with this dish.

MAKES 16 TO 20 PATTIES, SERVES 6 TO 8

1/2-inch piece fresh ginger

6 large cloves garlic

6 tablespoons freshly squeezed lime juice

1 teaspoon ground white pepper

1/2 teaspoon ground mace

1 pound lean ground lamb

2 tablespoons vegetable oil

1/4 cup chickpea flour, or corn starch

1 cup plain breadcrumbs

2 large egg yolks, slightly beaten

1/2 cup coarsely chopped cilantro

1 teaspoon salt

8 green cardamom pods, seeds removed and ground, plus more for garnish

1 teaspoon ground coriander

1/4 cup melted *desi ghee* (pages 47–48), or unsalted butter, for basting and serving

A few drops of *kewra* essence (page 51) (optional), for serving

Fresh Mint Chutney with Garlic (page 176), for serving

1. In a blender, combine the ginger, garlic, and lime juice and blend to a smooth paste. You may have to pulse several times, stopping and scraping down the sides, if necessary. Transfer to a medium glass bowl. Add the pepper, mace, and ground meat and mix thoroughly. Cover and refrigerate for 3 to 4 hours. Bring the meat to room temperature (if you're using a hot coal to enhance the smoky flavors, then do so at this time). Traditionally, the meat is ground to a paste before continuing, which you can do using a food processor or blender. If you prefer a coarser texture, you may skip this step.

2. Heat the oil in a small skillet over medium heat. Add the chickpea flour and cook, stirring regularly, until toasty smelling, about 4 minutes. Cool slightly and add to the lamb.

Add the breadcrumbs, egg yolks, cilantro, salt, cardamom, and coriander and mix thoroughly. The mixture should feel soft to the touch and should be easy to shape; if the mixture is too soft, then add a little more chickpea flour or refrigerate until firm. Shape the lamb mixture into 1 1/2-inch patties. (You can also shape the mixture into 4-inch long cylindrical logs around thick metal or several bamboo skewers.) With a brush, daub some melted *desi ghee*, or unsalted butter, on all sides to prevent sticking.

3. To cook the lamb on a barbecue grill, start a charcoal fire, letting the coals burn until they are covered with a gray ash and are medium-hot. Position the rack about 8 inches above the coals and coat the rack lightly with oil. Grill the patties, turning once and basting with *desi ghee*, until lightly browned, 8 to 12 minutes total cooking time. Alternatively, to cook the lamb in a conventional oven, place a HearthKit (see Sources, page 440) or pizza stone in the oven, if using, and preheat the oven to 500°F. Lay the patties directly on the HearthKit or pizza stone, or a baking sheet, and cook, turning once and basting with the *desi ghee*, until lightly browned and tender, 15 to 20 minutes.

4. Transfer the patties to a warmed platter and serve sprinkled with cardamom and a few drops of the *kewra* essence, if using. Traditionally, melted *desi ghee* is also sprinkled on the kebabs before serving. Serve with a big bowl of the Fresh Mint Chutney with Garlic.

VARIATION

Spicy Indian Lamb Burger

For a special treat, place a patty or two on toasted burger buns. Top with Sweet-Spiced Mango Chutney with Pecans (page 185), slices of onion and tomato, and tender sprouts.

TANDOORI LAMB ROLLS WITH LENTILS | Shami Kabab

Here is another take on the previous recipe, made with India's beloved lentils. You can use the same approach, replacing the lentils with mung bean sprouts. I suggest you discard most of the whole spices after the cooking process, but I like peppercorns, so I prefer to leave them in. *Cabob,* or *kebab,* is the Persian term for roasted or grilled meat specialties. *Kebachis* are chefs who specialize in the preparation of *tikkas,* kebabs, and shish kebabs. This typical tandoori dish is listed on quite a few restaurant menus.

SERVES 6 TO 8 AS AN APPETIZER

2 pounds lean ground lamb or beef

1/4 cup pink lentils, or *toovar dal* (yellow lentils), cleaned and rinsed

1/4 teaspoon black peppercorns

3 green cardamom pods

3 black cardamom pods (optional)

4-inch cinnamon stick

2 bay leaves

4 whole cloves

2 1/2 cups water

2 to 3 fresh green serrano or jalapeño chilis, stemmed and minced

1/4 cup chopped cilantro

1/4 cup finely chopped yellow onion

1 tablespoon minced fresh ginger

1 tablespoon *garam masala* (pages 36–37), or store-bought

2 large egg yolks, slightly beaten

2 teaspoons salt

3 tablespoons melted *desi ghee* (pages 47–48), or unsalted butter

Fresh Cilantro-Mint-Onion Chutney/Dip (page 177), for serving

1. In a large skillet, combine the lamb, lentils, peppercorns, green and black cardamom pods, cinnamon, bay leaves, cloves, and water and stir. Bring the mixture to a gentle boil over medium heat. Cover partially, reduce the heat, and simmer until the lamb is tender and the water has evaporated, 25 to 35 minutes. If there is any liquid left, cook, uncovered, and stir until it evaporates. Remove from the heat and cool thoroughly. Discard the whole spices. Transfer the meat mixture to a food process or blender and grind to a thick, silky paste. Transfer to a large bowl.

2. Add the chilis, cilantro, onion, ginger, *garam masala*, egg yolks, and salt to the lamb and mix thoroughly. The mixture should feel soft to the touch and be easy to shape; if it is too soft, then add a couple of tablespoons of chickpea flour or cornstarch, or refrigerate until firm.

3. Start a charcoal fire, letting the coals burn until they are covered with gray ash and are medium-hot. Position the rack 4 to 6 inches above the coals and lightly coat with oil. Shape the lamb mixture into 4-inch-long cylindrical logs around 6 to 8 thick skewers. With a brush, daub some melted *desi ghee*, or unsalted butter, on all sides before roasting to prevent from sticking. (You can also shape the lamb mixture into 1 1/2-inch patties) Grill the skewers, turning occasionally, until lightly browned in places, 8 to 12 minutes.

4. Transfer the kebabs to a cutting board and cut into 2-inch logs. Arrange on a heated decorative platter with toothpicks. Serve with Fresh Cilantro-Mint-Onion Chutney/Dip for dipping.

VARIATIONS

Alternatively, you can panfry the patties in a skillet with a little oil over medium heat for 4 to 6 minutes per side, or deep-fry in oil until golden brown.

Tandoori Lamb Rolls with Paneer (Shikampuri Kabab)

Substitute 1/2 cup crumbled *paneer* for the lentils. Follow the first step without the lentils, and in step 2, mix in the crumbled *paneer* along with the other ingredients and proceed with the recipe.

AJWAIN-MARINATED WHOLE TANDOORI FISH | Ajwaini Machchi

The delicate flavor of fish is enhanced by the addition of *ajwain* seeds, an Indian spice with a subtle thymelike taste. Once you learn about *ajwain's* strength, you'll rank it as a kitchen staple. Serve the fish sizzling hot on a bed of julienned onions, which will be bathed with the juices of the fish. Begin with Crispy Pakora (pages 144–145), followed by Fragrant Mixed Vegetable Pilaf (pages 98–99) and Mango-Macadamia Raita (page 206), and end with a plate of fresh fruits. A full sauvignon blanc is my favorite accompaniment. If you choose to use whole salmon, a light red wine such as pinot noir is a great match.

Two 1- to 1¹/4-pound whole fish (such as snapper, salmon, catfish, halibut, mackerel, or
   pompano), gutted and scaled

1-inch piece fresh ginger

6 large cloves garlic

2 tablespoons chickpea flour, or corn starch

1 tablespoon sweet paprika

2 teaspoons ground cumin

1 teaspoon ground white pepper

1 teaspoon cayenne

1 teaspoon *ajwain* seeds (page 20)

1 teaspoon salt

¹/2 teaspoon turmeric

¹/4 cup heavy whipping cream

1 tablespoon mango powder *(amchur)*, (page 29)
   or 2 tablespoons freshly squeezed lime juice

1 large egg yolk, slightly beaten

³/4 cup yogurt cheese (page 205)

¹/4 cup melted *desi ghee* (pages 47–48), or
   unsalted butter, for basting

Large banana leaf, for serving (optional)

Tangy Tandoori Spice Mix (page 34), for serving
   (optional)

1. Rinse the fish well and pat it dry. Place in a nonreactive pan or baking dish large enough to hold both fish. With sharp scissors, trim off all fins and cut out the gills from both fish, then make three diagonal slashes, penetrating to the bone, on each side of the fish.

2. In a blender, combine the ginger, garlic, chickpea flour, paprika, cumin, pepper, cayenne, *ajwain,* salt, turmeric, cream, and mango powder and process to a smooth paste. Transfer to a medium glass bowl. Whisk in the egg yolk and yogurt cheese. Smear the mixture over both sides of each fish. Cover and refrigerate for 3 to 4 hours, but not more than 6.

3. To cook the fish on a barbecue grill, start a charcoal fire, letting the coals burn until they are covered with gray ash and are medium-hot. Position the rack 6 to 8 inches above the coals and lightly coat with oil. Grill the fish, turning once, until crusty and lightly browned, basting with the *desi ghee,* for 10 minutes per inch of thickness at the thickest point. Check for doneness by pulling the meat away from the collar of the fish; it should pull away, but hesitantly, and appear moist. Alternatively, to cook the fish in a convention-al oven, preheat to 450°F. Lay the fish in a baking dish and roast until crusty and brown underneath and just beginning to flake, 20 to 25 minutes, or until the fish are done to your liking.

4. Use 2 metal spatulas to carefully transfer the fish to a platter lined with banana leaf, if using, and serve with the Tangy Tandoori Spice Mix, if desired.

TANDOORI-STYLE JUMBO BENGAL SHRIMP | Jhinge ka Tikka

Try these crusty-coated, spicy, gingery, smoky shrimp as a starter. The flavorful seasonings are locked in by the crisp batter. Serve a platter sprinkled with lime juice, melted *desi ghee,* and chopped cilantro. I've substituted lobster tails in this recipe quite successfully.

SERVES 6 TO 8 AS AN APPETIZER

1 pound (20 to 24) jumbo shrimp

1/2-inch piece fresh ginger

3 shallots, peeled

2 teaspoons *garam masala* (pages 36–37), or store-bought

1/2 cup loosely packed cilantro

1/4 cup loosely packed fresh mint leaves

1/4 cup freshly squeezed lime juice

1/4 cup vegetable oil

1 teaspoon salt

3/4 cup yogurt cheese (page 205)

2 tablespoon heavy whipping cream

2 teaspoons chickpea flour, or corn starch

1 large egg yolk, lightly beaten

1. Peel the shrimp, leaving the final joint and tail intact. Devein each shrimp by making a shallow incision down the back, exposing the dark intestinal tract, and scraping it out. Set aside.

2. In a blender, combine the ginger, shallots, *garam masala,* cilantro, mint, lime juice, oil, and salt. Blend to a smooth puree, stopping to scrape down the sides of the bowl a couple of times. Transfer to a large glass bowl and whisk in the yogurt cheese. Add the shrimp and rub the mixture gently over them. Cover and refrigerate for 2 to 3 hours.

3. In a small bowl, combine the cream, chickpea flour, and egg yolk and whisk until smooth. Season with a pinch of salt. Dip the shrimp one at a time in the batter to coat evenly. Coat 4 to 6 thick metal skewers with a little oil. Thread the shrimp onto the skewers at regular intervals, so they will stay flat when you turn them on the grill.

4. To cook the shrimp on a barbecue grill, prepare a charcoal fire, letting the coals burn until they are covered with gray ash and are medium-hot. Place the rack about 4 to 6 inches above the coals and lightly coat with oil. Grill the shrimp for 2 to 3 minutes on each side. Alternatively, to cook the shrimp in a conventional oven, preheat the broiler. Broil the shrimp on a lightly oiled broiling pan about 4 inches away from the heat, for 2 to 3 minutes on each side. Serve immediately on warm plates.

FISH SEEKH WITH ZUCCHINI | Machchi Seekh

1/2 pound boneless, skinless fish fillets (such as sea bass, cod, mackerel, or halibut)

1/2 pound (2 medium) zucchini

1 teaspoon minced fresh ginger

1 fresh green serrano or jalapeño chili, stemmed and minced

2 tablespoons minced cilantro

1 teaspoon ground coriander

1 teaspoon salt

1/2 teaspoon tamarind concentrate, dissolved in 1 tablespoon water

1/2 teaspoon ground cumin

1/4 teaspoon turmeric

1 large egg yolk, beaten slightly

2 tablespoons chickpea flour, or corn starch

3 tablespoons melted *desi ghee* (pages 47–48), or unsalted butter

Cilantro sprigs, for garnish

Coconut Chutney with Zesty Oil Seasoning (page 179), for serving

4 lemons or limes cut into wedges, for serving

1. Place the fillets in a steamer basket, cover, and steam over boiling water until the fish begins to flake easily, 6 to 9 minutes per 1/2-inch thickness. Set aside. Cut off the ends of the zucchini and dice into 1/4-inch-thick slices; steam until crisp-tender, 4 to 6 minutes.

2. When cool enough to handle, in a medium glass bowl, mash the zucchini and fish together with a fork. Add the ginger, chili, cilantro, coriander, salt, tamarind liquid, cumin, and turmeric and mix thoroughly with your fingers until well incorporated. Cover and set aside at cool room temperature for 30 minutes or refrigerate for up to 60 minutes.

3. Add the egg yolk and chickpea flour to the fish mixture and mix thoroughly. The mixture should feel soft to the touch and be easy to shape. If it's too soft, mix in a little extra flour, or chill in the refrigerator. Shape the fish mixture into 4-inch-long cylindrical logs around 2 thick metal or several bamboo skewers. With a brush, daub some melted *desi ghee*, or unsalted butter, on all sides before roasting to prevent sticking. (You can also shape the mixture into 1 1/2-inch patties.)

4. Start a charcoal fire, letting the coals burn until they are covered with gray ash and are medium-hot. Place the rack 4 to 6 inches above the coals and lightly coat with oil. Grill, turning and basting occasionally with *desi ghee,* until the kebabs start to brown, 6 to 8 minutes total cooking time.

5. Loosen the kebabs and slide them onto a heated decorative platter. Arrange them neatly, decorate with cilantro sprigs, and serve with the Coconut Chutney and wedges of lime.

TANDOORI CAULIFLOWER AND BROCCOLI | Tandoori Masala Gobi

These gingery, roasty, batter-coated florets are a great snack, because they're light and filled with bracing flavors.

SERVES 4 TO 6 AS AN APPETIZER OR CASUAL SIDE DISH

1 medium head cauliflower (about 1 pound)

1 small head broccoli with stalk (about 1/2 pound)

2 teaspoons ground coriander

1 teaspoon ground cumin

1 teaspoon sweet paprika

2-inch piece fresh ginger

6 large cloves garlic

1 tablespoon vegetable oil

1/2 cup plain yogurt

2 tablespoons chickpea flour, or corn starch

1 teaspoon salt

1/2 teaspoon caraway seeds (optional)

Several lettuce leaves for lining the platter (optional)

Lime wedges, for serving

Tamarind Chutney with Banana (page 182), for serving

Fresh Cilantro Chutney with Peanuts (page 174), for serving

1.   Trim the cauliflower and broccoli and cut into 1-inch florets, leaving 1/2-inch-long stalks for skewering. Gently prick the florets with a fork and set aside.

2.   In a blender, combine the coriander, cumin, paprika, ginger, garlic, oil, and yogurt and blend into a smooth puree. Transfer to a large bowl. Add the chickpea flour, salt, and caraway seeds, if using, and stir well to form a smooth, thick batter. Add the florets and turn to coat with the marinade. Cover and let marinate at room temperature, turning occasionally, for 1 hour.

3.   Coat 4 to 5 thick metal skewers with a little oil. Thread the florets on the skewers.

4.   To cook the veggies on a barbecue grill, prepare a charcoal fire, letting the coals burn until they are covered with gray ash and medium-hot. Position the rack about 6 inches above the coals and lightly coat with oil. Grill until the florets start to brown on the edges, 8 to 10 minutes. Alternatively, to cook the veggies in a conventional oven, preheat the broiler for 5 minutes. Lay the skewers on top of a shallow baking pan so both ends of the skewers rest on the rim of the pan. Broil 6 inches away from the heat source, turning occasionally, until the florets start to brown on the edges, about 15 minutes total.

5.   You have two choices for serving: Lay the skewers attractively on a warm decorative platter; or nestle the tandoori florets on a lettuce-lined serving platter. Surround with lime wedges and serve with the Tamarind Chutney and Fresh Cilantro Chutney for dipping.

MIXED VEGETABLE-PANEER SEEKH | Paneer Sabji Shaslik

Be creative with your use of colorful seasonal vegetables. In this dish, you can use baby squash, corn on the cob, yams, eggplant, and more. Serve this as an hors d'oeuvre with the recommended chutney sauces or your favorite dips. Any leftovers can be tossed in a salad the next day for a delectable treat.

SERVES 8 AS AN APPETIZER OR 6 AS A CASUAL SIDE DISH

1 recipe Fresh Basic Paneer (page 221), or 8 ounces store-bought

1 tablespoon *garam masala* (pages 36–37), or store-bought

2 teaspoons ground cumin

2 teaspoons minced fresh ginger

2 teaspoons salt

1 teaspoon cayenne

1 cup white button mushrooms

5 pearl onions, peeled

1 small yellow bell pepper, cored and cut into large chunks

1 small red bell pepper, cored and cut into large chunks

1/2 cup plain yogurt

1/2 cup heavy whipping cream

2 tablespoons chickpea flour, or corn starch

1 lime or lemon, cut into wedges

Sweet Chutney Sauce (page 130), for serving

Hot Green Chutney Sauce (page 130), for serving

1. Cut the *paneer* into 1-inch chunks; you should have about 8 pieces. Gently prick the sides with a fork and set aside. In a large bowl, combine the *garam masala*, cumin, ginger, salt, and cayenne and mix well. Add the *paneer* to the bowl, along with the mushrooms, pearl onions, and bell peppers. Toss well to coat with the spice mixture. Cover and set aside for 10 minutes at room temperature.

2. In a small bowl, combine the yogurt, cream, and chickpea flour and whisk until smooth. Add to the bowl containing the *paneer* and vegetables. Mix and turn to coat the pieces evenly. Cover and refrigerate, turning several times, for 1 hour.

3. To cook on a barbecue grill, prepare a charcoal fire, letting the coals burn until they are covered with gray ash and medium-hot. Position the rack about 6 inches above the coals and lightly coat with oil. Thread the cheese and vegetables in a colorful pattern on lightly oiled bamboo or metal skewers. Grill, turning occasionally, until lightly golden, 6 to 8 minutes total. Alternatively, to cook in a conventional oven, preheat the broiler for 10 minutes. Place the skewers on a broiler pan and place the pan 4 inches from the heat source. Broil, turning once or twice, until lightly golden on all sides, 6 to 8 minutes total.

4. Arrange the skewers on an old-fashioned brass or copper platter and serve surrounded by lime wedges, with the Sweet Chutney Sauce and Hot Green Chutney Sauce on the side.

DAL, RASAM, AND MULLIGATAWNY SOUPS

Narm-Garm

As a youngster, when I felt ill, nothing made me feel better than a steaming bowl of my mother's lentil *rasam* soup, scented with *kari* leaves, spiked with black pepper, and finished with our much-loved, sweet, fresh fluffy coconut. That, plus flaky wedges of *paratha*, spread with *desi ghee*, was mother's idea of the perfect comfort food. Unfortunately, my mother's visits from India and my colds rarely coincide. Today, in California, I make *rasam* and its close cousin, *sambar*, almost everyday. You could say that these soups are India's answer to the West's chicken soup, they're so digestible and healthful.

Preparing Indian soups is almost as easy as opening a can of soup, with the right ingredients on hand, such as cooked legumes and homemade spice mixtures. And these soups are nearly always low in calories and fat, not to mention cost. Their wonderful variety—hot or cold, light or hearty, mild or fiery, sweet or sour—makes them easily adaptable to the American kitchen.

Dals, Indian legume-based soups, are an expression of India's national culinary identity and have been staples for centuries, feeding everyone from infants to the elderly. In fact, a baby's first solid food is mushy *dal,* rice, and *desi ghee. Dal* is eaten by all types of people, from the farmer to the warrior, from the poor to the royal. When Shah Jahan, who built the Taj Mahal, was overthrown and imprisoned by his ruthless son, Aurangzeb, he was asked what he wanted to eat. "*Dal!*" replied Shah Jahan quickly. "*Dal!*" the son exclaimed in contempt. "Oh! Even in prison, royal tastes persist!"

There is no "stock" or "broth" in Indian gastronomic conversation, nor are there recipes for last week's carrots, mushrooms, and celery to be boiled and reused. *Dal* is the broth. Meat stock, if used at all, is prepared fresh for a particular dish. The soups correspond to four regional styles: the *shorbas* of the north are robust and chunky; the southern Indian *rasams,* on the other hand, are smooth pureed soups—legumes and vegetables combine with fragrant spices and herbs for a wonderful texture; the eastern *dalnas* are velvety soups made of *dal,* leafy vegetables, and spicy seasonings. The *kadhis* and *saars* of western India are herbal and pleasingly spiced broths—my recipe for Indian-Style Spicy Tomato Soup (page 372) features a mélange of tomatoes, ginger, garlic, and cilantro.

Indian soups have no season; they can be warm and comforting in winter or refreshing in summer, and most can be enjoyed year-round. A thoughtful cook can select a soup to suit any meal, any guest or child, and any occasion.

WARM MANGO SOUP | Aam Rasa

When I was writing this book, now and then at the dinner table my husband and sons would propose some ingredients and ask me to create recipes for them. Mango *lassi* is a standard in our house, and they suggested, "How about a savory yogurt-mango consommé for cold weather?" I came up with this simple concoction: raisins, mango, and yogurt add up to a rich-tasting, elegant, flavorful, soothing soup that is quick and easy to make. They approved of this dynamic combination the very first time.

In this and other recipes in the book, I recommend you use Indian canned Alphonso mango pulp (pages 52–53). If you must resort to fresh mangoes, select good-quality fruit; they should smell floral and fruity at the stem end and should not be fibrous, or you may have to strain the pulp. You can serve this soup with croutons and even a spoonful of cream, but do try it by itself, since it is simply delicious.

SERVES 6 TO 8 AS A FIRST COURSE

1/4 cup *desi ghee* (pages 47–48), or unsalted butter

1 teaspoon yellow or brown mustard seeds

2 tablespoons dark raisins

1/2 cup finely chopped yellow onion

1/4 cup loosely packed chopped cilantro

2 cups plain yogurt

One 30-ounce can (about 3 1/3 cups) Alphonso mango pulp (pages 52–53), or 4 large ripe mangoes, peeled, fruit cut from pits, and pureed in a blender

2 teaspoons sugar

1 teaspoon salt

Have a spatter screen ready before you continue. Heat the *desi ghee* in a heavy large saucepan over medium-high heat. Add the mustard seeds, immediately cover with the spatter screen, and cook until the seeds stop popping, about 30 seconds. Reduce the heat to medium, add the raisins, and stir until plump, about 30 seconds. Add the onion and cook, stirring, until the onion is very soft, about 4 minutes. Add the cilantro and stir for a few seconds. In a mixing bowl, whisk together the yogurt and mango pulp and stir into the pan. Add the sugar and salt and stir. Bring to a gentle boil, stirring occasionally, cover, reduce the heat, and simmer until heated through. When the soup is ready, taste and adjust the salt and sugar to focus the flavors, depending on the type of mango used. Ladle the soup into warm soup bowls and serve.

MAKE AHEAD Refrigerate, covered, for up to 1 day. Thin, if necessary, with a few tablespoons of water or mango pulp to the desired consistency. Reheat over medium heat before serving.

KERALA MUSSEL CHOWDER | Mussel Molee

Gorgeous green-lip mussels—sweet, flavorful, plump pillows nestled in their shells—loll in this mellow vegetable-laden soup. These mussels are larger, firmer, and meatier than the regular ones. Serve it before a not-too-rich main course, such as Fragrant Mixed Vegetable Pilaf with Cashews (pages 98–99), plus Garlicky Dal Stew (page 383) and Mango-Macadamia Raita (page 206).

SERVES 4

1 pound fresh mussels, preferably New Zealand green

2 tablespoons vegetable oil

1 teaspoon yellow or brown mustard seeds

20 *kari* leaves (page 28) (optional), or cilantro

1 cup finely chopped yellow onion

4 cloves garlic, minced

1 tablespoon minced fresh ginger

2 teaspoons ground coriander

1 teaspoon freshly ground black pepper

1/2 teaspoon cayenne

1/2 teaspoon ground fenugreek

1 cup chopped ripe tomatoes, or canned diced tomatoes

1/2 cup chopped green bell pepper

1 cup water

1 1/2 teaspoons salt

1 cup Fresh Coconut Milk (page 308), or canned unsweetened coconut milk

2 limes, cut into wedges

1. Rinse the mussels well and remove any stringy "beards" trailing from between the mussel shells. Set aside in a bowl.

2. Have a spatter screen ready before you continue. Heat the oil in a heavy large saucepan over medium-high heat. Add the mustard seeds, immediately cover with the spatter screen, and cook until the seeds stop popping, about 30 seconds. Add the *kari* leaves, if using, and the onion, garlic, and ginger. Cook, stirring, until the onion starts to brown at the edges, 4 to 5 minutes. Reduce the heat, add the coriander, pepper, cayenne, and fenugreek and stir for a few seconds until fragrant. Add the mussels and cook, stirring occasionally, for 3 minutes. Add the tomatoes and bell pepper and cook, stirring occasionally, until softened, 3 to 4 minutes.

3. Add the water and salt, cover, and simmer, stirring occasionally, until the mussels have opened, 7 to 8 minutes. Stir in the coconut milk and cook, uncovered, until very hot. Discard any mussels that do not open. Ladle into warm soup bowls, and pass lime wedges for everyone to squeeze into the soup, as they like.

SOOTHING DAL SOUP | Dal

This dish is made with *toovar dal*, or yellow lentils, one of the staples of Indian cooking. Yellow split peas, more commonly available in America, can be substituted. While *dal* is sometimes served as an accompaniment to bread, rice, and curries, this recipe is a soup to be enjoyed on its own. If you have never eaten lentils before, this mild and delicious dish makes for a good introduction.

SERVES 5 TO 6 AS A FIRST COURSE, OR 4 AS A LIGHT MAIN DISH

3 cups cooked Basic Dal–Stove-Top Method (page 383)

2 tablespoons *desi ghee* (pages 47–48), or vegetable oil

1 teaspoon yellow or brown mustard seeds

1 teaspoon cumin seeds

1/4 teaspoon turmeric

A big pinch asafetida

2 to 3 fresh green serrano or jalapeñno chilis, stemmed and slit lengthwise

2 cups water

1/2 tablespoon salt

2 tablespoons freshly squeezed lime juice

Chopped fresh cilantro

1. Whisk the hot Basic Dal. Set aside.

2. Have a spatter screen ready before you continue. Heat the *desi ghee* in a large heavy saucepan over medium-high heat. Add the mustard seeds and cumin seeds, immediately cover with the spatter screen, and cook until the seeds stop popping, about 30 seconds. Reduce the heat to medium and add the turmeric, asafetida, and chilis. Cook, stirring, until the chili skins blister, about 30 seconds.

3. Add the pureed *dal,* water, and salt to the saucepan. Bring to a boil, stirring occasionally. Reduce the heat, cover, and simmer, stirring occasionally, until the soup is slightly thick, about 15 minutes. Just before serving, add the lime juice, give the soup a good stir, and then ladle it into bowls. Garnish with cilantro and serve.

MAKE AHEAD Refrigerate, covered, for up to 5 days. This soup freezes beautifully for up to 6 weeks.

CHICKEN MULLIGATAWNY WITH MIXED VEGETABLES | Milagu Thunny

The term *mulligatawny* comes from the Tamil words *milagu,* meaning "pepper," and *thunny,* meaning "water," and was coined by the British to designate a lentil consommé, or *rasam.* The luxurious addition of cream and chicken turns this soup into a hearty special-occasion dish.

SERVES 8 AS A FIRST COURSE, 4 TO 6 AS A MAIN DISH

3 tablespoons vegetable oil

1 cup finely chopped yellow onion

6 cloves garlic, roughly chopped

2-inch piece fresh ginger, crushed

4-inch cinnamon stick, broken

2 teaspoons ground coriander

1 teaspoon ground cumin

1 teaspoon black peppercorns, lightly crushed

3/4 teaspoon ground fennel

1 medium 2 1/2- to 3-pound chicken, preferably free-range, skinned and cut into pieces

1 pound ripe tomatoes, finely diced, or one 14-ounce can diced tomatoes

2 medium fennel bulbs, trimmed and thinly sliced

3/4 cup 1-inch cauliflower florets

3/4 cup chopped green beans

1 cup thinly sliced carrots

1 cup dried pink lentils, *toovar dal* (yellow lentils), or yellow split peas, picked clean

8 cups chicken broth, vegetable broth, or water

1 tablespoon sugar

2 teaspoons salt

Juice of 1 lime

1/2 cup heavy whipping cream

Fresh cilantro sprigs

1. Heat the oil in a large heavy saucepan over medium-high heat. Add the onion and cook, stirring, for about 2 minutes. Add the garlic and ginger and cook, stirring, until the onion starts to brown, about 3 minutes. Add the cinnamon, coriander, cumin, peppercorns, and fennel, and stir until aromatic, about 30 seconds. Add the chicken pieces and sear until the pieces brown in places and the meat is no longer pink, 3 to 4 minutes per side. Stir in the tomatoes, fennel, cauliflower, green beans, carrots, and lentils. Add the broth and mix well. Bring to a boil, reduce the heat, cover, and simmer until the chicken is tender, 25 to 30 minutes. Uncover, and using a slotted spoon, transfer 1 cup of the vegetables and lentils to a bowl and set aside. Transfer the chicken pieces to a plate and set aside to cool. Pass the remaining soup through a strainer, pressing on the solids to extract as much puree as possible. Discard the solids. Pull the meat from the bone and reserve.

2. Season the soup with the sugar, salt, and lime juice. Stir in the cream and reserved chicken meat and the cup of vegetables and lentils. Cook over low heat until piping hot. Serve the soup in warm bowls, garnished with cilantro sprigs.

RHUBARB RASAM SOUP | Nuge Kai Rasam

Rasam is one of southern India's best-known soups. Tart and spicy, it is traditionally flavored with tamarind and sugar. Here I add rhubarb—not a traditional Indian ingredient—for its lovely color and natural astringency. As you turn these pages, you'll find more versions of this healthful soup, which many Indians believe helps to ward off colds. Choose any to suit the season, mood, or occasion. To keep the preparation of *rasam* simple, I mix up basic Rasam Powder (page 38) and always keep some on hand.

SERVES 4 AS A FIRST COURSE

2 tender and firm pink rhubarb stalks

1^1/$_2$ tablespoons *desi ghee* (pages 47–48), or vegetable oil

^{1}/$_2$ teaspoon yellow or brown mustard seeds

^{1}/$_2$ teaspoon cumin seeds

1^1/$_2$ tablespoons Rasam Powder (page 38), or store-bought

^{1}/$_4$ teaspoon turmeric

^{1}/$_4$ teaspoon freshly ground black pepper

10 *kari* leaves (page 28) (optional), or cilantro

1 teaspoon tamarind concentrate, dissolved in ^{1}/$_2$ cup water

1^1/$_4$ tablespoons jaggery (pages 51–52), raw sugar, or light brown sugar

1 teaspoon salt

1^1/$_2$ cups cooked pink lentils (page 43)

3^1/$_2$ cups water

Chopped cilantro, for garnish

Freshly grated coconut (page 307), or frozen, defrosted unsweetened coconut, for garnish

1. Rinse the rhubarb and pat it dry. Trim away any leaves, then cut the stalks into 1-inch matchsticks to make about 1 cup.

2. Have a spatter screen ready before you continue. Heat the *desi ghee* in a medium heavy saucepan over medium-high heat. Add the mustard seeds and cumin seeds, immediately cover with the spatter screen, and cook until the seeds stop popping, about 30 seconds. Add the Rasam Powder, turmeric, pepper, and *kari* leaves and stir until aromatic, about 30 seconds. Add the tamarind liquid, jaggery, and salt. Bring to a boil, reduce the heat, and simmer until the raw tamarind smell dissipates, 4 to 5 minutes. Add the lentils, rhubarb, and water, bring to a boil, and simmer until the flavors blend and the soup is slightly thick, 15 to 20 minutes. Transfer to a tureen and garnish with about a tablespoon each of cilantro and coconut. Serve hot.

LENTIL RASAM SOUP WITH ORANGE JUICE | Bele Rasam

In this recipe, I've used fresh-squeezed orange juice in place of the traditional tamarind-sugar seasoning. The sweet-tangy flavor of oranges blends well with and complements the lentils and freshly ground spices. I've used three kinds of lentils here for a variety of textures, but for convenience, you can use 1 1/2 cups of just one type. Delightfully herbal, spicy, and citrusy, this soup is loaded with nutrients. A bowl of *rasam* is a soothing way to start off a meal, but this soup is also substantial enough to be a vegetarian main course. Accompany with cooked brown rice and/or wheat flatbread to round out the meal. Add a quick vegetable side dish for a complete, balanced, low-calorie meatless dinner. For a formal meal, serve it with any fish entree.

SERVES 4 AS A LIGHT MAIN COURSE

1 1/2 tablespoons vegetable oil

1/2 teaspoon yellow or brown mustard seeds

10 *kari* leaves (page 28) (optional), or cilantro

1/4 teaspoon turmeric

Rasam Thickening Powder (recipe follows), or 1/3 cup Rasam Powder (page 38), or store-bought

1 medium ripe tomato, chopped, or 1 cup canned diced tomatoes

1 1/4 teaspoons salt

1/2 cup cooked *toovar dal* (yellow lentils, page 44)

1/2 cup cooked pink lentils (page 43)

1/2 cup cooked *mung dal* (yellow split mung beans, page 43)

2 1/2 cups water

1 tablespoon freshly grated coconut (page 307), or frozen, defrosted unsweetened coconut

1/4 cup fresh orange juice

1. Have a spatter screen ready before you continue. Heat the oil in a heavy medium saucepan over medium-high heat. Add the mustard seeds, immediately cover with the spatter screen, and cook until the seeds stop popping, about 30 seconds. Toss in the kari leaves, if using, and the turmeric and cook, stirring, for a few seconds until the leaves crisp. Stir in the Rasam Thickening Powder and cook, stirring, until aromatic, about 30 seconds. Add the tomato and salt and cook, stirring occasionally, until softened, about 5 minutes. Add the *toovar dal*, lentils, *mung dal*, water, and coconut. Bring to a boil, reduce the heat, cover, and simmer until the flavors meld and the *rasam* is slightly thick, 15 to 20 minutes. Transfer to a tureen and stir in the orange juice.

MAKE AHEAD Refrigerate, covered, for up to 4 days. Reheat gently.

RASAM THICKENING POWDER

MAKES ABOUT ⅓ CUP

1 tablespoon *chana dal* (split chickpeas)
(pages 42–43)

1 tablespoon coriander seeds

2 teaspoons long-grain white rice

1 teaspoon cumin seeds

1 teaspoon black peppercorns

2 small dried hot red chilis, such as chiles de
arbol or cayennes, stemmed

10 *kari* leaves (page 28) (optional), or cilantro

In a large heavy skillet, combine the *chana dal*, coriander seeds, rice, cumin seeds, peppercorns, chilis, and *kari* leaves. Toast over medium heat, stirring frequently, until the seeds are aromatic and darken a shade, 5 to 6 minutes. Let the spice mixture cool slightly, then transfer to a coffee mill or spice grinder and grind to a fine powder, in small batches, if necessary. Use as instructed in the recipe above, or cool completely, pour into an airtight glass jar, cover, and store at room temperature, away from direct light, for up to 1 month.

INDIAN-STYLE SPICY TOMATO SOUP | Tomato Saar

The rustic *saars* of western India are herb-scented and lightly spiced consommés, perfect every-day fare. On a cold evening, try this soup infused with flecked garlic and ginger; stir-frying the garlic and ginger in oil humbles it to a mellow sweetness. Serve topped with zesty croutons or alongside multigrain bread.

SERVES 6 AS A FIRST COURSE

1 1/2 pounds (3 to 4 medium-large) ripe tomatoes, or 4 cups canned diced tomatoes

2 tablespoons peanut or vegetable oil

1/2 teaspoon yellow or brown mustard seeds

1 teaspoon cumin seeds

2 tablespoons minced garlic

2 teaspoons grated fresh ginger

1 teaspoon cayenne

1/4 teaspoon turmeric

2 tablespoons jaggery (pages 51–52), raw sugar, or light-brown sugar

1 1/4 teaspoons salt

2 1/2 cups water

Minced fresh cilantro

1. Blanch the tomatoes in boiling water for 2 minutes to loosen the skins, then plunge them into cold water. When cool enough to handle, peel, core, and chop the tomatoes to make 4 cups. Set aside. (Skip this step if using canned tomatoes.)

2. Have a spatter screen ready before you continue. Heat the oil in a large heavy saucepan over medium-high heat. Add the mustard seeds and cumin seeds, immediately cover with the spatter screen, and cook until the seeds stop popping, about 30 seconds. Add the garlic and ginger and cook, stirring, until the garlic is lightly golden, 2 to 3 minutes. Add the cayenne and turmeric and stir for a few seconds. Add the tomatoes, jaggery, and salt and cook, stirring occasionally, until the tomatoes are softened, about 5 minutes.

3. Add the water and bring to a boil. Reduce the heat to low, cover, and simmer until the soup is fragrant, 15 to 20 minutes. Serve hot, garnished with a sprinkling of cilantro.

BUTTERMILK KADHI SOUP WITH KARI LEAVES | Kadhi

This is one of the most distinctive soups in the state of Gujarat, in western India. The interplay of ginger, garlic, and chilis with tangy, nutty buttermilk makes for a delicious soup. Once the ginger-garlic paste has sweetened with the *kadhi*, this soup is ready. The fenugreek seeds are essential, as they add a special touch, balancing the flavors and enhancing visual appeal.

SERVES 4 AS A LIGHT MAIN COURSE

1-inch piece fresh ginger

3 large cloves garlic

1 to 2 fresh green serrano or jalapeño chilis, stemmed

1/2 teaspoon cumin seeds

2 1/2 tablespoons chickpea flour

1 cup water

2 cups buttermilk

1 teaspoon salt

1 teaspoon sugar

2 tablespoons vegetable oil

1/2 teaspoon yellow or brown mustard seeds

1 teaspoon fenugreek seeds

1 teaspoon coriander seeds

1/4 teaspoon turmeric

15 *kari* leaves (page 28) (optional), or cilantro

1. Using a mortar and pestle or a food processor, pulverize the ginger, garlic, chilis, and cumin seeds to a coarse-textured paste, paying close attention to breaking up the chili. Set the paste aside.

2. In a heavy medium saucepan, combine the chickpea flour and 1/2 cup of the water and whisk until smooth. Stir in the remaining 1/2 cup of water and the buttermilk, salt, sugar, and ginger-garlic paste. Bring the soup to a bare simmer over medium heat, stirring constantly. Simmer, uncovered, for 6 to 8 minutes. Taste and adjust the salt and sugar— salt to brighten and focus the flavors and sugar to smooth any tart or rough edges in the buttermilk. Remove from the heat and transfer to a heated serving pot.

3. Have a spatter screen ready before you continue. Heat the oil in a small skillet over medium-high heat. Add the mustard seeds, fenugreek seeds, and coriander seeds, immediately cover with the spatter screen, and cook until the mustard seeds stop popping, about 30 seconds. Add the turmeric and *kari* leaves, if using, and stir for a few seconds until the leaves are crisp. Pour the seasoned oil over the soup and serve hot in individual bowls.

CHILL CHASERS: BEAN AND LENTIL SAMBARS AND STEWS

Hari Bhari Dal

One of my earliest childhood memories is of eating *sambar*, the fragrant soup-stew of southern India. My mother would mound steaming basmati rice on a plate, then pour on some hot *sambar*, velvety smooth and creamy, with soft lentils. Next she added just a little aromatic *desi ghee*, our beloved clarified butter. The *desi ghee* melted slowly, gently trickling down the hill of rice. Mother carefully mixed the rice and soup, then, with her delicate fingers, fed me this light and healthful fare. When I was old enough to eat the *sambar* myself, she would sit with me and enliven mealtimes by reading to me the classic stories of Indian folklore.

Even now, on damp, chilly evenings, I like nothing better than a steaming bowl of robust bean stew or my favorite *sambar*, accompanied by buttery grain-rich rolls and a hot drink. Bay Area winters bring back memories of the rainy season in India, when the cold seemed to penetrate the walls of the house. While my brother and sister and I curled up under a quilt, my mother made us wonderful winter stews. Of course, nippy nights always produced big appetites, and the aromas of herbs and spices wafting from the kitchen made us even hungrier.

Although the traditional Indian meal consists of small portions of a variety of dishes, some of these richly flavored stews are substantial one-dish affairs. Examples include Hearty Pheasant Lentil Stew with Wilted Greens (pages 387–388) and Dal with Chapati Pasta and Spinach (pages 397–398). These days, I like them for other reasons, too: they're easy to prepare for casual, relaxed family meals.

Legumes—pink or green lentils, yellow split peas, pink pintos, deep-purple kidney beans, creamy chickpeas, and even speckled fresh cranberry beans—form the basis of my favorite stews and curries. Their meaty flavors marry naturally with all kinds of seasonings, poultry, and other vegetables. Best of all, their satisfying earthiness invites experimentation. Their affinity for spices—cumin, cloves, and coriander—is almost infinite. And they make a perfect foil for aromatics, from garlic to shallots, ginger to chilis.

Dried peas, lentils, and beans are richer in protein than any other plant food; when paired with grains, seeds, nuts, dairy products, or a little meat, they provide all the essential amino acids. I mix two or three varieties of legumes when I cook stews, for maximum nutrition. These rich-tasting dishes are just one indication of the versatility of fresh and dried beans, lentils, and split peas.

As in most developing countries, vegetables, grains, and legumes are the focus of everyday eating in rural India. Legumes are known as "nature's broom" because of their high dietary fiber. They contain no cholesterol and only a trace of fat (of the polyunsaturated variety). Besides, they are highly affordable. Legumes are a staple of the Indian diet and make the best comfort food.

What Is Dal?

I'm sure it is quite mind-boggling to walk through an Indian specialty market for the first time and see the vast display of glistening pink, yellow, green, and black legumes. Although the word *dal* is sometimes used to refer to a specific type of legume, it also serves as a generic term for all dried, split, hulled, and skinned legumes. The dishes cooked with these legumes are also termed *dal*.

PUTTING ON THE PRESSURE

Using a pressure cooker reduces the cooking time for legumes by half. Twice a week, I cook up an assortment of lentils and beans to keep in the refrigerator. They're then ready to be whisked together into a stew at a moment's notice.

Pressure cookers vary in size and other details, so be sure to follow the manufacturer's directions. The recipes in this chapter were tested in a 6-quart cooker. Whatever size you use, the contents should not reach higher than halfway up the sides of the pot. Cover and cook at full pressure over high heat for 10 to 15 minutes. Some beans have a tendency to froth and clog the vent; adding a teaspoon of vegetable oil per cup of dried beans will help prevent this. If the vents do get clogged, don't panic; turn off the heat and set the cooker on a cold burner to allow it to depressurize on its own (this is always the best way to depressurize the cooker and to to save it from wear and tear), or, if you're in a hurry, carefully place it in a sink and run cold water over it. Tilt the weight and release the pressure gradually. Reseal the pressure cooker to finish cooking the legumes, if necessary. You may also continue cooking them uncovered on the stovetop.

Cooking legumes this way is even more efficient when you use the special stacking containers sold in Indian stores. A three-layer stand will fit comfortably in a 6-quart pressure cooker. Each legume variety sits in its own container with its cooking liquid, and additional water in the bottom of the cooker provides the pressurized steam that cooks them quickly. Place dried chickpeas and other large beans in the cooker by themselves, since their cooking time is different from other legumes.

The cooking time and proportions for several popular legumes are given below. Consult the chart on page 379 for other varieties suitable for pressure-cooking.

BUYING, STORING, AND COOKING

Buy beans where there's a lot of turnover, since those that stay on the shelf for more than 4 to 6 months will be so dried out they won't cook evenly. When buying beans, especially in bulk, choose plump-looking, whole beans. Discard any that are broken, moldy, shriveled, or spotted. Sort through them, discarding any pebbles or bits of debris. Store sorted beans in an airtight container in a cool, dry place for up to a year, or better yet, refrigerate.

Cooking time depends on the age of the legumes. Older beans can take twice as long to cook as new-crop beans. Small lentils and beans cook faster than larger beans; split beans cook fastest. To see if the legume is fully cooked, fish one from the pot and press it between your thumb and finger, or eat it. If it is thoroughly soft, it is done; cook further if there is a hard core. Add water, if necessary, then cook some more and test again.

Cooking Legumes

The chart below contains the basic information you need to cook the legumes (split peas, lentils, and beans) called for in this chapter and throughout this book.

Legume Know-How

* Soaking *dals* (lentils, split and skinned chickpeas, and beans) is not mandatory, but larger beans, such as black pinto, dried lima, and chickpeas, must be soaked. Soaking helps the beans cook more evenly.

* Turmeric and minced ginger should be used in cooking legumes, especially the larger varieties, as it helps break down the protein and makes them easier to digest.

* Jaggery (pages 51–52) is best in stews, because it melds beautifully; if unavailable, use raw sugar; turbinado or light-brown sugar also makes a good substitute.

Dried Legumes	Soaking Time for Stove-Top Cooking (Hours)	Water for Cooking (Cups)	Stove-Top Cooking (Minutes)	Pressure Cooking (Minutes)	Approximate Yield After Cooking (Cups)
$^1/_2$ cup black-eyed peas	4	$1^1/_2$	30	15	$1^1/_2$
$^1/_2$ cup brown lentils	—	$1^1/_2$	45	12	$1^1/_4$
$^1/_2$ cup masoor dal (pink lentils)	—	$1^1/_4$	22	8	1
1 cup chickpeas	8	4	$2^1/_2$–3 hours	25	$2^1/_2$
1 cup chana dal (split chickpeas)	—	2	50	12	$2^1/_4$
$^1/_2$ cup kidney beans	8	$1^1/_2$	$1^1/_2$ hours	20	$1^1/_2$
$^1/_2$ cup lima beans	8	1	20	12	$1^1/_2$
$^1/_2$ cup whole mung beans	4	$1^1/_2$	20–30	—	$1^1/_2$
$^1/_4$ cup mung dal (yellow split mung beans)	—	1	20	8	1
1 cup toovar dal (yellow lentils), or split peas (yellow or green)	—	2	32	10	$2^1/_2$

Taming the Musical Fruit

A word about flatulence: Legumes contain complex sugars called oligosaccharides, which are indigestible by humans. Bacteria in the intestinal tract consume the sugars, emitting gas as a byproduct. For centuries, cooks have tried dozens of procedures to prevent gas, but with limited success. However, there are ways to deal with it.

First, eat beans frequently; nutritionists tell us we should anyway. People who consume legumes regularly seem to have less discomfort. Start with small quantities, then gradually increase the serving size. If you are just starting to add legumes to your diet, mung *dal* is one of the most easily digestible varieties.

Second, discard the water in which you have soaked the legumes and replace it with fresh water for cooking. Some of the oligosaccharides are released into the soaking water. Some of the protein and vitamins also leach into the water, but the loss is minimal—1 to 3 percent.

Finally, drink plenty of liquids while eating beans. Fluids help in the digestion of beans. Some people cook legumes with baking soda in an attempt to reduce flatulence, but this does little but destroy the B vitamins and toughen the beans. The only time baking soda is worth adding is when the beans are soaked and cooked in extremely hard water.

SPROUTS (MATKI)

Sprouts offer an attractive alternative to dry legumes and are an important part of the Indian diet. They add distinctive flavor, texture, and color to dishes. One way of dealing with the oligosaccharide (flatulence) problem is to turn dry legumes into sprouts. The sprouting process consumes most of the oligosaccharides and boosts the levels of vitamins B, C, and E. The legume's starches turn to sugar, making them easily digestible and nutritious, with a crisp texture and fresh nutty taste. Try them raw in salads, *chaats*, and vegetable dishes. You can also stir them into soups for extra crunch, or sprinkle them over pilafs. Once you understand their qualities, you can use them in foods as freely as you use parsley. Mung beans, chickpeas, brown lentils, fenugreek, and sunflower seeds are particularly suited for sprouting. Most sprouts are low in calories, and all are good sources of vitamin C. Bland and crisp, sprouts can be used raw or steam-cooked.

DIRECTIONS FOR SPROUTING LEGUMES

1. You do not need any fancy sprouting containers to grow sprouts at home. It's very easy. Pick clean $1/2$ cup dried legumes of your choice. Wash in several changes of water, and then add enough water to cover them by at least 2 inches. Soak 20 to 24 hours. Drain and rinse the beans. Transfer to a colander or wicker basket lined with cheesecloth. Cover loosely with a damp muslin or cheesecloth. Place in a warm, dark place in the pantry. (If the place is cool, the legumes will take a little longer to sprout.)

2. Sprinkle some water on the cheesecloth once or twice per day, especially in warm weather, to keep the beans moist. The beans should start to sprout within 2 to 3 days. Sprouts are mature when the tails are $1/3$ to $1/2$ inch long. Remove any beans that have not sprouted. Store in a covered container up to 4 days in the refrigerator. In order to enjoy the maximum nutritional value, use within 2 days.

SPROUT-GROWING CHART

Dry Legumes, 1 cup each	Growing Time	Harvest Size	Approx. Yield	Flavor
whole mung beans	3 to 5 days	$1/2$ to $1 1/2$ inches	3 to 4 cups	pleasant, crunchy
brown lentils	2 to 4 days	$1/2$ to $3/4$ inch	3 to 4 cups	fresh taste, slightly starchy when raw
chickpeas	3 to 5 days	$1/3$ to $1/2$ inch	1 $1/2$ cups	sweet, full–bodied, distinctive taste

BASIC DAL—STOVE-TOP METHOD

This is the most basic method for cooking *dal*. I've used *toovar dal*—glossy (not oily), smooth, and rich lentils—since it forms the base for many recipes. *Toovar dal* is prized in much of India. Other varieties of *dal* can be cooked the same way; consult the table (page 379) for the amount of water and cooking time. For a small quantity, you may easily halve the recipe.

When I was in India, every morning a pot of *dal* was cooked in a pressure cooker, to be turned into *sambars*, *rasams*, or *dal* soups or stews; occasionally, when I needed a substantial brunch, my mother placed steaming hot *dal* in a bowl, drizzled it with sesame oil, seasoned it with her heirloom spice blend, salt, and cilantro, topped it with chopped tomatoes, and served it with hot *chapati* or *paratha*. In my American kitchen, I combine the *dal* puree in a food processor with herbs, spices, and a variety of flours to make a nutritious dough for daily bread.

MAKES 5 CUPS OF PUREE

2 cups *toovar dal* (yellow lentils), or yellow split peas

4 cups water

2 teaspoons oil (optional)

1. Sift through the lentils and remove any debris. Using a colander, wash in several changes of running tap water. Transfer the lentils to a large saucepan and add the water, plus the oil, if desired. Bring to a boil. Reduce the heat to medium, cover (partially at first, until the foam settles, then snugly), and cook until the lentils are tender and start to fall apart (adding more water if necessary), 30 to 40 minutes. Turn off the heat and let the lentils stand, covered, for 5 minutes. Use an immersion blender to coarsely puree the *dal*, or use a whisk (legumes mash easily when warm). Use the lentils in recipes or store.

MAKE AHEAD The cooked *dal* can be stored, covered, in the refrigerator for up to 4 days or frozen for up to 1 month.

VARIATION

Microwave Method

A microwave oven cooks small portions of dried legumes fairly quickly. Use small quantities of *dal* (roughly 1 cup), as cooking large quantities in this manner is not advisable. Add the water (3 cups water for 1 cup *dal*) and cook on high power in a large microwave-safe container, uncovered, stirring once or twice midway, for 25 to 35 minutes.

GARLICKY DAL STEW | Bele Saaru

This soup-stew is a staple in my house; I cook it almost every other day. It is truly a wonderful, comforting accompaniment, scented with cilantro leaves, tangy tamarind, and lively garlic and tomatoes. This light stew makes a lovely meal paired with toasted wheat dinner rolls, though small cups of it can easily be served as a prelude to a menu of Dakshin Fenugreek-Marinated Salmon Braised in Coconut Milk (pages 319–320), Fragrant Mixed Vegetable Pilaf with Cashews (pages 98–99), and Spicy-Sweet Green Mango Relish (page 197).

SERVES 4 TO 6 AS AN ACCOMPANIMENT OR SIDE DISH

1 1/2 tablespoons vegetable oil

1/2 teaspoon yellow or brown mustard seeds

1/2 teaspoon cumin seeds

3 dried hot red chilis, such as cayennes or chiles de arbol, or fewer to taste, stemmed and broken into rough pieces

5 large cloves garlic, minced

2 teaspoons salt

1 1/2 tablespoons Rasam Powder (page 38), or store-bought

1/4 teaspoon turmeric

1/4 teaspoon cayenne

1 1/2 cups diced ripe tomatoes, or canned diced tomatoes

1 tablespoon light-brown sugar, jaggery (pages 51–52), or raw sugar

1/2 teaspoon tamarind concentrate, dissolved in 1/2 cup water

2 1/2 cups water

3 cups cooked Basic Dal–Stove-Top Method (page 382)

Chopped fresh cilantro

1.   Have a spatter screen ready before you continue. Heat the oil in a heavy medium skillet over medium-high heat. Add the mustard and cumin seeds, immediately cover with the spatter screen, and cook until the seeds stop popping, about 30 seconds. Add the chilis and garlic and cook, stirring, until the garlic starts to brown, about 2 minutes. Add the salt, *Rasam* Powder, turmeric, and cayenne and stir until fragrant, about 30 seconds. Add the tomatoes and sugar and cook, stirring, until softened, about 6 minutes.

2.   Add the tamarind liquid to the skillet and bring to a boil. Reduce the heat and simmer until the raw tamarind smell disappears, about 5 minutes. Stir in the water and Basic Dal and cook, partially covered, stirring occasionally, for 15 to 20 minutes. Taste and adjust the seasonings, if necessary. The soup-stew should have a medium-thick consistency. Transfer to a large tureen and cover. When ready to serve, ladle into warm soup bowls. Strew each serving generously with cilantro.

> MAKE AHEAD The soup-stew can be made several hours ahead and set aside at cool room temperature, or stored, covered, in the refrigerator for up to 3 days.

PINK LENTIL AND MUNG DAL STEW WITH LEEKS

| Erullihu Rasavangi

The bright flavors of this simple, homey stew are easy to savor. This is a spicier version of the preceding soup-stew, made with leeks, a specialty of southern India. Kohlrabi, chayote, eggplants, summer squash, or jicama can all be used in this recipe. It is wonderful as a first course or even as a light main dish.

SERVES 6 AS AN ACCOMPANIMENT OR SIDE DISH

1 tablespoon coriander seeds

20 *kari* leaves (page 28) (optional)

2 tablespoons dried unsweetened flaked coconut

1/8 teaspoon asafetida

1/2 pound (2 to 3) leeks

2 tablespoons vegetable oil

1/2 teaspoon yellow or brown mustard seeds

1/2 teaspoon cumin seeds

1/4 teaspoon turmeric

2 dried hot red chilis, such as cayennes or chiles de arbol, stemmed and broken into rough pieces

1 1/2 cups diced ripe tomatoes, or canned diced tomatoes

1/2 teaspoon tamarind concentrate, dissolved in 1/2 cup water

1 1/2 tablespoons light-brown sugar, jaggery (pages 51–52), or raw sugar

2 cups cooked *masoor dal* (pink lentils) (page 43)

1 cup cooked mung *dal* (yellow split mung beans) (page 43)

2 cups water

2 teaspoons Sambar Powder (pages 37–38), or store-bought

1 1/2 teaspoons salt

Melted *desi ghee* (pages 47–48), or unsalted butter, for serving

Chopped cilantro, for garnish

1. Heat a small skillet over medium heat. Add the coriander seeds and 10 of the *kari* leaves, if using, and toast, stirring frequently, until the seeds are aromatic, 3 to 4 minutes. Add the coconut and asafetida and toast, stirring, until the coconut is toasty smelling and light golden, about 2 minutes. Cool slightly. Transfer to a spice grinder or coffee mill and grind to a fine powder. Set aside.

2. Trim off and discard the roots and dark green ends of the leeks. Wash the leeks to remove any sand and grit: Without breaking them, gently split the leeks apart lengthwise. Swish them repeatedly in a pan of cold water or hold them under the faucet to remove the grit. Chop into 1/2-inch pieces (you should have about 2 cups) and set aside.

3. Have a spatter screen ready before you continue. Heat the oil in a large skillet over medium-high heat. Add the mustard and cumin seeds, immediately cover with the spatter screen, and cook until the seeds stop popping, about 30 seconds. Add the turmeric, chilis, and remaining 10 *kari* leaves and stir for a few seconds. Add the leeks and tomatoes and cook, stirring, until softened, about 5 minutes. Add the tamarind liquid and sugar, bring to a boil, and cook 5 minutes more. Add the *masoor dal*, mung *dal*, water, Sambar Powder, ground spice mixture, and salt. Bring to a boil. Reduce the heat and simmer until the mixture is medium-thick and the flavors meld, 15 to 20 minutes. Transfer to a large tureen and cover. When ready to serve, ladle into warm soup bowls, drizzle with a little *desi ghee* (this traditional touch makes it special), and sprinkle with cilantro.

CREAMED KIDNEY BEANS AND LENTILS | Makhani Dal

This is a comforting and stimulating dish—legumes scented with complex seasonings and served in a cream sauce. The sauce is spiked with garlic, flecked with fresh hot green chilis, scented with cilantro, and gleaming with a hint of rust-red tomato paste.

You may have tasted this popular dish at Indian restaurants, where it's usually made with whole *urad* (whole black gram beans). My recipe is rather robust. The wholesome flavors of kidney beans and brown lentils combine well with the myriad ingredients. Traditionally, this dish is cooked in the dying embers of a tandoor for twenty hours or more, but it comes out just as fragrant and velvety when simmered on top of the stove.

SERVES 4 TO 6 AS AN ACCOMPANIMENT OR SIDE DISH

1/2 cup dried red kidney beans, picked over

1/2 cup brown lentils, picked over

2 1/2 cups water

1 tablespoon *desi ghee* (pages 47–48), or unsalted butter

1/2 cup minced yellow onion

1/2 tablespoon minced fresh ginger

1/2 tablespoon crushed garlic

2 fresh green serrano or jalapeño chilis, stemmed and minced

1 teaspoon ground coriander

1/2 teaspoon ground cumin

1/4 teaspoon freshly ground black pepper

1/4 cup tomato paste

1/2 teaspoon salt, or to taste

1/4 cup whole or low-fat (2%) milk

1/4 cup heavy whipping cream

1 tablespoon minced cilantro, for garnish

1.   Wash the kidney beans in several changes of water. Place in a pan and add water to cover by at least 2 inches. Let soak for 8 hours or overnight.

2.   Drain and rinse the beans. Rinse the lentils and combine them with the kidney beans in a large heavy saucepan. Add the water and bring to a boil. Reduce the heat to medium, cover (partially at first, until the foam settles, then snugly), and cook until the beans and lentils are tender but still hold their shape, about 40 minutes. Remove from the heat and let stand, covered, for 5 minutes.

3.   Heat the *desi ghee* in a heavy large saucepan over medium-high heat. Add the onion and cook, stirring, for 2 to 3 minutes. Add the ginger, garlic, and chilis and cook, stirring, until the onion just starts to brown, about 3 minutes. Add the coriander, cumin, and pepper, stir for a few seconds, add the tomato paste, and cook, stirring constantly, for 5 minutes. Add the cooked beans and lentils, salt, and milk. Bring to a gentle boil, reduce the heat to low, cover, and cook until most of the liquid is absorbed, 6 to 8 minutes. Add the cream and cook until heated through. Transfer to a warm deep dish, garnish with cilantro, and serve.

SHORTCUTS

If time is of the essence, the lentils and beans may be cooked in a pressure cooker in step 2, though their texture won't be as nice. Put rinsed lentils and beans in a 4-quart pressure cooker along with 2 cups water (or you can use $2^{1}/_{2}$ cups legumes and 5 cups of water if you have a 6-quart pressure cooker). Cook according to your manufacturer's directions for 25 minutes.

You can substitute canned beans for the dried beans. Add the canned beans after cooking the lentils.

HEARTY PHEASANT-LENTIL STEW WITH WILTED GREENS | Dhansak

When you're going to be home all day long and want to fill the house with a tempting bouquet, try making this rich stew with subtle seasonings. Don't be put off by the long list of ingredients; it's well worth it. The flavors improve considerably the next day. Traditional *dhansak* is made with lamb or chicken, but I've tried this recipe with duck and pheasant, and their gamy flavors meld beautifully with accompanying ingredients and harmonize the dish. Usually as many as three to nine *dals* are cooked together, but you can use packaged mixed lentils, or include pink lentils and mung *dal* along with the others I've suggested.

The flavors are typical of Parsee cuisine; the Parsee community in India is known for its elaborate and distinctive meals. *Dhan* is Parsee for rice; *sak* is vegetables; *dhansak* is lentil-meat-vegetable stew eaten with brown rice. The brown rice is made by an unusual method. First, the rice is cooked with whole spices, plenty of crispy-golden fried onions, and caramelized sugar. This complete meal can be served for Sunday brunch with a *kachumber*, lamb kebabs, and chilled Indian beer. Game meat and the earthy flavors of beans and lentils also make me think of pinot noir.

SERVES 4 TO 6 AS AN ACCOMPANIMENT OR SIDE DISH

1/2 cup *toovar dal* (yellow lentils), or yellow split peas

1/2 cup dried baby lima beans

1 pheasant or Muscovy duck (about 3 pounds), skinned and cut into 6 to 8 pieces

1 cup diced (1-inch pieces) banana squash, or zucchini or yellow crookneck squash

1 cup peeled and sliced carrot

1 cup diced (1-inch pieces) Japanese eggplant

4 cups water

2-inch piece fresh ginger

5 large cloves garlic

3 tablespoons vegetable oil

1 cup thinly sliced yellow onion

2 teaspoons Sambar Powder (pages 37–38), or store-bought

1 1/2 teaspoons salt

1 teaspoon crushed red pepper flakes

1 teaspoon ground coriander

1/2 teaspoon ground cumin

1/2 teaspoon freshly ground black pepper

1/4 teaspoon ground cinnamon

1/4 teaspoon turmeric

1/8 teaspoon ground cloves

1 tablespoon light-brown sugar, jaggery (pages 51–52), or raw sugar

1 cup packed chopped spinach

1/4 cup loosely packed chopped cilantro

20 fresh mint leaves, coarsely chopped

1 cup chopped ripe tomatoes, or canned diced tomatoes

2 tablespoons freshly squeezed lime juice

1.   Rinse the lentils and beans in several changes of water. Place them in a large pot. Add the pheasant or duck, banana squash, carrot, eggplant, and water and bring to a boil. Reduce the heat to medium-low and skim off the grayish foam that rises during the first few minutes of simmering. Cover partially and simmer until the lima beans are tender, 40 to 45 minutes.

2.   While the meat is cooking, combine the ginger and garlic in a blender. Add 3 to 4 tablespoons water and blend to a smooth puree. Transfer to a small bowl and set aside.

3. Heat the oil in a large sauté pan over medium heat. Add the onion and cook, stirring often, until softened, about 5 minutes. Add the ginger-garlic paste and cook, stirring, until the onion is deep golden, about 6 minutes more. Add the Sambar Powder, salt, red pepper flakes, coriander, cumin, black pepper, cinnamon, turmeric, cloves, and sugar. Stir until aromatic, about 1 minute. Add the spinach, cilantro, mint, and tomatoes and cook, stirring, until the spinach wilts, about 4 minutes. Remove the meat from the pot and add it to the pan (you may also take the meat off the bone, if you prefer). Cook, stirring occasionally, until the flavors blend, about 5 minutes.

3.   Traditionally, the lentil-vegetable mixture is processed to a smooth puree. You can transfer the mixture to a blender or food processor, or use an immersion blender to puree the mixture in the pot. I like a heartier texture, so I prefer to simply mash the lentils and vegetables with the back of a large spoon while everything is still warm (they firm as they cool). Add the lentil mixture to the sauté pan, cover, and cook until the stew is very hot. Add the lime juice and stir to mix. Transfer to a heated serving dish and serve right away.

BASIC SAMBAR | Sambar/Kuzhambu

Sambar is an everyday dish in southern India, kind of a cross between soup and stew. This is a type you may have tasted at Indian restaurants, but hundreds of variations are prepared in Indian homes, each with distinctive flavors. A few of those variations can be found on the pages that follow. This dish is often paired with *dosa* and *idli* (pages 153–162).

For a truly authentic flavor, make this stew with *toovar dal*. I recommend the MTR brand of *sambar* powder, available in Indian markets, if you are too short on time to make your own. If you don't want to cut into a big head of cauliflower for just half a cup, you can substitute any number of vegetables, such as a small Japanese eggplant, zucchini, or even a small cucumber.

1 cup *toovar* dal (dried yellow lentils), or yellow split peas, rinsed

3 1/2 cups water

1 tablespoon vegetable oil

1/2 teaspoon yellow or brown mustard seeds

1/2 teaspoon cumin seeds

1/8 teaspoon turmeric

15 *kari* leaves (page 28) (optional)

2 to 4 dried hot red chilis, such as cayennes or chiles de arbol, stemmed and broken into rough pieces

1 cup chopped ripe tomatoes, or canned diced tomatoes

1/2 chopped (1/2-inch pieces) cauliflower

1/4 cup sliced carrot

1/4 cup green beans, cut into 1/2-inch lengths

1 tablespoon *Sambar* Powder (pages 37–38), or store-bought

1 1/4 teaspoons salt

1/4 teaspoon cayenne

1/4 teaspoon light-brown sugar, jaggery (pages 51–52), or raw sugar

2 tablespoons chopped cilantro, plus additional for garnish

1/2 teaspoon tamarind concentrate, dissolved in 1/2 cup water

1. Combine the *dal* and water in a large saucepan. Bring to a boil, reduce the heat to medium, and cook, partially covered, until the *dal* is soft, about 30 minutes (do not drain the liquid). Whisk to a coarse puree, cover, and set aside.

2. Have a spatter screen ready before you continue. Heat the oil in a large skillet over medium-high heat. Add the mustard and cumin seeds, immediately cover with the spatter screen, and cook until the seeds stop popping, about 30 seconds. Add the turmeric, *kari* leaves, if using, and chilis and stir for a few seconds until aromatic. Add the tomatoes, cauliflower, carrot, and green beans and cook, stirring, until the tomatoes are soft, about 5 minutes. Add the Sambar Powder, salt, cayenne, sugar, and cilantro and cook, stirring, for about 1 minute. Add the tamarind liquid and bring to a boil. Cover and simmer for 5 minutes. Add the *dal* puree, cover, and cook to a medium-thick consistency, 20 to 25 minutes. Transfer to a large tureen. Ladle into bowls; garnish with a sprinkling of cilantro.

> MAKE AHEAD *Sambar* may be cooked and stored in the refrigerator, covered, for up to 3 days in advance (in fact, it gets better with a little age). Just before serving, bring the *sambar* to a simmer over medium heat; serve sprinkled with chopped cilantro.

VARIATION

Sambar can be made with practically any vegetables you'd like: bell peppers, cucumbers, okra, potatoes, radishes, or any variety of eggplant.

PEARL ONION MYSORE SAMBAR | Vengaya Kuzhambu

Glistening caramelized pearl onions lend sweetness as well as visual appeal to this hearty soup-stew. The tangy richness of the spices and tamarind paired with the sweet coconut and earthy legumes is one of my favorite combinations.

In India, baby onions, called *sambar* onions, are used in this preparation, but American pearl onions make a fine substitute. *Sambars* get better with age; make this a day ahead if possible. Serve with *dosa* (page 155).

SERVES 4 AS AN ACCOMPANIMENT OR SIDE DISH

3/4 cup *toovar dal* (yellow lentils), or yellow split peas, rinsed

3 1/2 cups water

1 teaspoon plus 2 tablespoons vegetable oil

1 1/2 tablespoons coriander seeds

1/2 tablespoon plus 1/2 teaspoon cumin seeds

1/4 teaspoon fenugreek seeds

1 tablespoon *chana dal* (split chickpeas)

3 dried hot red chilis, such as cayennes or chiles de arbol, or fewer to taste, stemmed

12 pearl onions, peeled and left whole

1 teaspoon poppy seeds, preferably white

Pinch asafetida

1 tablespoon freshly grated coconut (page 307), or dried unsweetened flaked or defrosted frozen unsweetened coconut

1/2 teaspoon yellow or brown mustard seeds

1/8 teaspoon turmeric

10 *kari* leaves (page 28) (optional), or cilantro

1 teaspoon tamarind concentrate, dissolved in 1/2 cup water

1 tablespoon light brown sugar, jaggery (pages 51–52), or raw sugar

1 1/2 teaspoons salt

1/2 teaspoon cayenne

Cherry tomato halves, for garnish

Chopped fresh dill, for garnish

1. Combine the *dal* and 3 cups of the water in a large saucepan. Bring to a boil, reduce the heat to medium, and cook, partially covered, until the *dal* is soft, about 30 minutes (do not drain the liquid). Whisk to a coarse puree, cover, and set aside.

2. Heat 1 teaspoon of the oil in a small skillet over medium heat. Add the coriander seeds, 1/2 tablespoon cumin seeds, and the fenugreek seeds, *chana dal,* and chilis and toast, stirring frequently, until the seeds are aromatic, 3 to 4 minutes. Add 5 of the pearl onions and cook, stirring, until the onions start to brown, 4 to 5 minutes. Transfer to a bowl. Add the poppy seeds, asafetida, and coconut and cook, stirring, until the coconut is toasty smelling and light golden, about 2 minutes. Add to the bowl. Cool slightly and transfer to a blender. Add the remaining 1/2 cup of water and blend to a thick, pasty consistency, stopping from time to time to scrape down the sides of the container, if necessary. Set aside.

3. Have a spatter screen ready before you continue. Heat the remaining 2 tablespoons of oil in a large skillet over medium-high heat. Add the mustard and remaining 1/2 teaspoon cumin seeds, immediately cover with the spatter screen, and cook until the seeds stop popping, about 30 seconds. Add the turmeric, *kari* leaves, if using, and remaining 7 pearl onions and cook, stirring, until the onions start to brown in spots, about 4 minutes. Add the tamarind liquid and sugar and cook, stirring, until the raw tamarind smell disappears, 6 to 8 minutes. Add the *dal* puree, reserved spice paste, salt, and cayenne and bring to a boil. Cover and simmer until the *sambar* has thickened slightly, 20 to 25 minutes. Transfer to a heated serving dish. Garnish with cherry tomatoes and fresh dill and serve.

> MAKE AHEAD *Sambar* may be cooked and stored, covered, in the refrigerator for up to 3 days (in fact, it gets better with a little age). Just before serving, bring the *sambar* to a simmer over medium heat and add fresh cilantro or dill to liven up the flavors.

SHORTCUT

You may substitute 2 to 3 tablespoons Sambar Powder (pages 37–38, or store-bought) and skip step 2 altogether, although the flavors will not be the same.

BROCCOLI-CAULIFLOWER SAMBAR | Cauliflower Kuzhambu

When I first came to America almost two decades ago, cilantro was rarely available, but today it is offered in almost every grocery store. I am hopeful that *kari* leaves will find a niche in Western markets as well.

SERVES 4 TO 6 AS AN ACCOMPANIMENT OR SIDE DISH

1 1/2 cups 1-inch cauliflower florets with stems

1 1/2 cups 1-inch broccoli florets with stems

1 cup chopped ripe tomatoes, or canned diced tomatoes

2 cups water

3 cups cooked pink lentils (page 43)

2 teaspoons freshly grated coconut (page 307), or defrosted frozen unsweetened coconut

1 tablespoon Sambar Powder (pages 37–38), or store-bought

2 teaspoons ground coriander

1 1/2 teaspoons salt

1/8 teaspoon freshly ground black pepper

1/2 cup Fresh Coconut Milk (page 308), or canned unsweetened coconut milk

1 1/2 tablespoons vegetable oil

1/2 teaspoon yellow or brown mustard seeds

1/4 cup thinly sliced yellow onion

1/8 teaspoon asafetida

1/4 teaspoon turmeric

1. Combine the cauliflower, broccoli, tomato, water, and lentils in a heavy medium saucepan. Add the coconut, Sambar Powder, coriander, salt, and pepper and stir to mix. Bring the mixture to a boil, reduce the heat, cover, and simmer, stirring occasionally, for 12 to 15 minutes. Stir in the coconut milk and cook until heated through, 4 to 5 minutes. Remove from the heat and transfer to a heated serving dish.

2. Have a spatter screen ready before you continue. Heat the oil in a small skillet over medium-high heat. Add the mustard seeds, immediately cover with the spatter screen, and cook until the seeds stop popping, about 30 seconds. Add the onion, asafetida, and turmeric and cook, stirring, until the onion starts to brown on the edges, 3 to 4 minutes. Remove from the heat.

3. Pour the oil seasoning, scraping the spice seeds with a rubber spatula, over the vegetable and lentil mixture. Stir gently and carry to the table.

> MAKE AHEAD The recipe can be prepared through step 1, without the addition of coconut milk, cooled, and stored, covered, in the refrigerator for up to 4 days. Reheat gently and add the coconut milk. If it's too thick, add a little water. Taste and adjust the salt. Prepare the oil seasoning and finish as directed.

CLASSIC PUNE-STYLE FRAGRANT STEW | Saadi Aamti

Aamti is the Maharashtrian equivalent of southern Indian *sambar*. It is so beloved in Mumbai and Pune that it is indispensable at daily meals. The nutty flavors come from a slightly sweet, sesame-laced *goda masala* (pages 40–41), typical of Maharashtra State. Serve with *chapati* (pages 63–64), Almond-Stuffed Pasilla Chili (pages 264–265), Celery Root Kachumber (page 217), Spicy Lassi with Oil Seasoning (page 427), and Konkan Shrimp Rice (pages 102–103) for a hearty meal.

SERVES 4 TO 6 AS AN ACCOMPANIMENT OR SIDE DISH

1 tablespoon vegetable oil

1/2 teaspoon yellow or brown mustard seeds

1/8 teaspoon asafetida

1/8 teaspoon turmeric

10 *kari* leaves (optional) (page 28), or cilantro

1/2 cup finely chopped yellow onion

1 teaspoon freshly grated coconut (page 307), or dried unsweetened flaked or defrosted frozen unsweetened coconut

1/2 teaspoon cayenne

1/2 tablespoon light-brown sugar, jaggery (pages 51–52), or raw sugar

1/2 teaspoon tamarind concentrate dissolved in 1/2 cup water

2 1/2 cups Basic Dal–Stove-Top Method (page 382)

2 1/2 tablespoons *goda masala* (pages 40–41), or store-bought

1 1/2 teaspoons salt

2 1/2 cups water

Beautiful sprigs cilantro

1. Have a spatter screen ready before you continue. Heat the oil in a large skillet over medium-high heat. Add the mustard seeds, immediately cover with the spatter screen, and cook until the seeds stop popping, about 30 seconds. Add the asafetida, turmeric, *kari* leaves, and onion and cook, stirring, until the onion starts to brown on the edges, about 3 minutes. Add the coconut, cayenne, and sugar and cook, stirring, until fragrant, about 30 seconds. Add the tamarind liquid and cook, stirring occasionally, until the raw tamarind smell disappears, 6 to 8 minutes.

2. Add the pureed lentils, *goda masala,* salt, and water and bring to a boil. Cover and simmer, stirring occasionally, until the *aamti* has thickened slightly, 20 to 25 minutes. Transfer to a heated serving dish, garnish with cilantro sprigs, and serve.

VARIATION

This dish can be prepared with diced tomatoes, potatoes, yams, and eggplant as well. Add them along with the coconut and cook, stirring, for a few minutes to soften.

FRESH CRANBERRY BEAN AND PURPLE POTATO STEW

| Dali Ambat

Shelling beans takes center stage during the fall; fresh favas, butter beans, and baby limas show up in display baskets. One of the most eye-catching is cranberry beans. Plump, with specks and streaks of burgundy, these luxuriously handsome beans combine with rich cashews and spicy red chilis to make a terrific spread for company. Pair with Chicken Breasts in Korma Sauce (pages 270–271) and Street-Style Buttermilk Balloon Bread (pages 82–83), and finish the meal with a rich dessert such as Toasted Cream-of-Wheat Halvah with Orange Juice (page 418).

Choose cranberry beans that are well filled out. Store unwashed in a plastic bag in the refrigerator, for 2 to 3 days. Shell them just before cooking.

SERVES 4 TO 6 AS AN ACCOMPANIMENT OR SIDE DISH

1¹/4 pounds fresh cranberry beans

10 whole roasted salted or unsalted cashews

2 large cloves garlic

¹/2-inch piece fresh ginger

1¹/2 cups water

1¹/2 tablespoons vegetable oil

2 dried hot red chilis, such as cayennes or chiles de arbol, stemmed

1 teaspoon ground coriander

¹/2 teaspoon ground cumin

¹/4 teaspoon freshly ground black pepper

1¹/2 cups (1-inch pieces) diced purple potatoes, or new potatoes

¹/2 teaspoon tamarind concentrate, dissolved in ¹/2 cup water

1 teaspoon salt, or to taste

Chopped fresh cilantro

1. To shell the cranberry beans, pull down on the string and press the pod seam with your thumb. Split open the seam and remove the beans. You should have about 2 cups. Rinse and set aside.

2. Combine the cashews, garlic, and ginger in a blender or food processor. Add ¹/4 cup of the water and blend to a smooth puree. Set aside.

3. Heat the oil in a heavy saucepan over medium heat. Add the chilis, coriander, cumin, and pepper and cook, stirring, for 30 seconds. Add the beans and potatoes and cook, stirring, for 2 to 3 minutes more. Stir in the cashew-garlic paste and cook, stirring, until the raw garlic smell dissipates, 3 to 4 minutes. Add the tamarind liquid, remaining 1¹/4 cups of water, and the salt, bring to a boil, reduce the heat, and cook, covered, until the beans and potatoes are tender and still hold their shape, about 15 minutes. Transfer to a heated serving dish and garnish with cilantro.

Fresh cranberry beans can be very hard to find. As with most bean dishes, you may use any beans you like or can find easily, including fresh or frozen lima beans, mealy-textured black-eyed peas, or the chic favas. You may also presoak and cook dried cranberry beans, if you have the time to spare.

CHICKPEAS SIMMERED IN TOMATO-GINGER SAUCE

| Pindi Chole/Channa Masala

The caramel flavor of onion is the highlight of this classic dish, where it is blended with lush tomatoes and the sweetness of garlic. You can use the sauce as a base for roasted vegetables, cook other large beans in it, or slip in fried fish. Sometimes tea bags are added to this dish during the cooking to create its characteristic dark color. I prefer natural colors steeped from the spices.

This stew is typically served on street corners, where it is cooked on a large (2 x 3–foot) griddle with a shallow well in the center for stir-frying; then paired with Street-Style Buttermilk Balloon Bread (pages 82–83). You may also serve it with buttered sourdough bread or over cooked Chinese noodles.

SERVES 6 TO 8 AS AN ACCOMPANIMENT OR SIDE DISH

3 tablespoons vegetable oil

2 cups coarsely chopped yellow onion

6 large cloves garlic, crushed

2-inch piece fresh ginger, crushed

1 1/2 teaspoons ground coriander

1 teaspoon ground cumin

1 teaspoon cayenne

1/2 teaspoon ground cloves

1 1/2 teaspoons ground pomegranate seeds (page 32) (optional)

3 cups coarsely chopped ripe tomatoes, or canned diced tomatoes

1/2 cup packed cilantro sprigs, plus additional for garnish

1 cup water

2 tablespoons *desi ghee* (pages 47–48), or unsalted butter

1/4 teaspoon turmeric

Two 15-ounce cans chickpeas, drained

1 teaspoon salt

1 tablespoon freshly squeezed lime juice, or 2 teaspoons mango powder *(amchur)* (page 29)

1 medium-size red or white onion, peeled and thinly sliced, for serving

1 lime or lemon cut into wedges, for serving

1. Heat the oil in a heavy large skillet over medium-high heat. Add the onion, garlic, and ginger and cook, stirring, until the onion starts to brown, 4 to 5 minutes. Add the coriander, cumin, cayenne, cloves, and ground pomegranate seeds, if using, and cook, stirring, for a few seconds until fragrant. Add the tomatoes and cilantro, reduce the heat to medium, and cook, stirring occasionally, until the tomato is softened, about 6 minutes. Cool slightly and transfer to a blender or food processor. Add 1/4 cup of the water and process until smooth. Set aside.

2. Heat the *desi ghee* in a heavy large saucepan over medium heat. Add the turmeric and onion-spice puree. Cook, stirring constantly, until fragrant, 2 to 3 minutes. Add the chickpeas, salt, and remaining 3/4 cup of water, raise the heat, and bring to a boil. Reduce the heat to low, cover, and simmer until the sauce is thick, 15 to 20 minutes. The curry will concentrate and turn into an earthy red, thickish sauce, similar to a medium-thick spaghetti sauce. Stir in the lime juice and cook 2 minutes more. Serve in individual bowls, garnished with cilantro sprigs. Offer slices of onion and lime wedges at the table.

> MAKE AHEAD Prepare through step 1 and refrigerate, covered, for up to 4 days, or freeze in an airtight container for up to a month. The entire dish can be prepared and refrigerated for up to 2 to 3 days; reheat over low heat and add cilantro to liven the flavors.

DAL WITH CHAPATI PASTA AND SPINACH | Dal Dhokli

Every region in the subcontinent has its own pasta dish. *Dal dhokli* is my favorite Indian soul food—a comforting pot of slightly chewy *chapati* dough, *dal*, and spinach, simmered with satisfying spicy flavors.

When we were experiencing rolling blackouts in California in 2002 and I told my mother in India about it, she was quite surprised. She thought in California something like that would be as rare as snow. When I was growing up in India, blackouts were the norm. Two or three days a week, during the day and sometimes night, the electricity was turned off to limit consumption. We were quite used to it and prepared for it. My father always replenished the batteries in the flashlights. My grandmother kept the lanterns ready; she had a half-dozen of them. Once a week, she went through her morning ritual of preparing the lanterns. Gently, with her fragile hands, she removed the glass from each one and polished it sparklingly clean with a muslin cloth dipped in vinegar. Then, she refilled the lanterns with kerosene. Even if the wick had not been used, she would trim the front end and pour a few drops of kerosene on it. When she was done, she placed the lanterns in a safe place, ready to use.

During the power shortage, my mother never liked to spend time in the kitchen, so she planned some quick-fix meals as a backup. One of my favorite dishes was this Indian-style pasta, cooked with lentils and fragrant spices. First, she made a zesty mustard-infused oil in a large, heavy pot. Then she added lentils, more spices, greens, and water. She rolled out the *chapati* dough, cut it into diamonds, transferred the dough to the pot, and let the whole dish simmer gently. This was a meal in itself. We enjoyed the lovely dish together. (I might add, with tablespoonfuls of *desi ghee*.) In a way, Mother used the rolling blackouts as an opportunity to bring the whole family together in one place to share thoughts, jokes, and stories. For us children, there was no better time. And the centerpiece on the table was none other than grandmother's luminous lantern.

MAKES 5 MAIN DISH SERVINGS

1/2 recipe *chapati* dough (pages 63–64, prepared through step 2)

3 tablespoons vegetable oil

1 teaspoon yellow or brown mustard seeds

1/4 teaspoon turmeric

1/4 cup *toovar dal* (yellow lentils), or yellow split peas, rinsed

4 cups water

2 teaspoons Hot and Fragrant Curry Powder (page 35), or store-bought

1 1/4 teaspoons salt

1 teaspoon cayenne

2 cups lightly packed chopped fresh spinach leaves and tender stems

Melted *desi ghee* (pages 47–48), or unsalted butter, for serving

1. Lightly oil your hands, place the *chapati* dough onto a work surface, and knead for a few minutes until the dough is smooth. Divide the dough into 4 equal portions; roll each portion between your palms to form into a smooth ball, flatten slightly, put on a plate, and cover.

2. Have a spatter screen ready before you continue. Heat the oil in a large heavy saucepan over medium-high heat. Add the mustard seeds, immediately cover with the spatter screen, and cook until the seeds stop popping, about 30 seconds. Add the turmeric and stir for a few seconds until fragrant. Add the *dal* and water and bring to a boil.

3. While the mixture is coming to a boil, place a portion of the dough on a floured surface and roll out to $1/8$ inch thick, dusting with flour as necessary. With a sharp knife, cut the dough into 1-inch diamond shapes. Lift the diamonds with your hands and drop carefully into the simmering lentil mixture. Combine and reroll the dough scraps and cut again. Repeat with the remaining dough.

4. Add the curry powder, salt, cayenne, and spinach to the saucepan and cook, uncovered and stirring occasionally, for about 5 minutes. Reduce the heat to low, cover, and cook, stirring, until most of the liquid is absorbed and the lentils are fully cooked and soft, about 25 minutes. (If the lentils have been presoaked, they will be tender in 15 to 20 minutes.) There should be very little liquid in the finished entrée. Turn off the heat and let stand, covered, for 5 minutes. Spoon the stew into deep plates and serve piping hot with *desi ghee*.

MIXED SPROUTS STEW | Matki Usal

Use a combination of homegrown sprouts—lentil and mung bean, fenugreek and chickpea, or wheat berry and mung bean—or buy packaged mixed sprouts at the supermarket. When you cook sprouts, you should cook them as lightly as possible to preserve the nutrients. My mother used to add diced potato to this stew dish, for variation. This makes a lovely side dish with *poori* (pages 80–81) or any of the suggested colorful *poori* variations (pages 80–82).

SERVES 4 AS AN ACCOMPANIMENT OR SIDE DISH

2 tablespoons vegetable oil

1 teaspoon yellow or brown mustard seeds

1/2 teaspoon cumin seeds

1 cup finely chopped yellow onion

3 large cloves garlic, minced

1/4 teaspoon turmeric

1 cup chopped ripe tomatoes, or canned diced tomatoes

3/4 cup mixed sprouts (see headnote)

2 teaspoons My Mother's Heirloom Spice Blend (pages 39–40), or Hot Fragrant Curry Powder (page 35), or store-bought curry powder

1 teaspoon salt

1/2 to 1 teaspoon cayenne

2 cups water

Thinly sliced scallion (both green and white parts), for garnish

2 tablespoons freshly grated coconut (page 307), or defrosted frozen unsweetened coconut, for garnish (optional)

1. Have a spatter screen ready before you continue. Heat the oil in a large skillet over medium-high heat. Add the mustard and cumin seeds, immediately cover with the spatter screen, and cook until the seeds stop popping, about 30 seconds. Add the onion, garlic, and turmeric and cook, stirring, until the onion just starts to brown at the edges, about 4 minutes. Add the tomatoes and sprouts and stir until well mixed. Add the heirloom spice blend, salt, and cayenne and cook, stirring, until fragrant, about 30 seconds.

2. Add the water, bring to a boil, reduce the heat to low, cover, and simmer until the sprouts are tender, 18 to 20 minutes. Remove from the heat and let stand, covered, for 5 minutes. Transfer to a heated serving dish and garnish with scallions and coconut, if desired.

STEWED KABOCHA SQUASH WITH MUNG BEANS | Kumbala Usili

Kabocha is a hybrid squash popular in Japan and also increasingly gaining favor with American chefs. It is most readily available from late fall into spring. Select one that seems heavy for its size, with dull and thick skin and hard bumpy blemishes, without soft spots. The flesh of *kabocha* squash is a vibrant orange color that matches its sweet taste, which reminds me of similar squashes cooked with legumes in India. *Kabocha* can be replaced in this recipe with one of its fellow winter squashes, such as acorn or butternut. Gently seasoned, this stew is lovely accompanied with Aromatic Tomato Rice (pages 100–101) and Mumbai Fish Steamed in Banana Leaves (pages 330–331).

SERVES 4 TO 6 AS AN ACCOMPANIMENT OR SIDE DISH

2 pounds *kabocha* squash

4 teaspoons vegetable or canola oil

1/2 cup chopped yellow onion

6 large cloves garlic, minced

2 fresh green serrano or jalapeño chilis, stemmed and minced

1/4 teaspoon turmeric

1/2 cup whole mung beans, or French green lentils

2 tablespoons light-brown sugar, jaggery (pages 51–52), or raw sugar

1/2 teaspoon tamarind concentrate, dissolved in 1 cup water

3 cups water

2 teaspoons salt

2 tablespoons chopped fresh chives, for garnish

1. Peel the squash with a vegetable peeler. Cut in half and remove the seeds; when halving the *kabocha*, place the knife just off center, so you don't have to hack through the tough stem-end. Chop the flesh; you will need 4 heaping cups of squash. Cover and set aside.

2. Heat the oil in a medium heavy saucepan over medium-high heat. Add the onion, garlic, chili, and turmeric and cook, stirring, until the onion starts to brown, about 4 minutes. Add the mung beans and squash and cook, stirring, for 2 to 3 minutes. Add the sugar, tamarind liquid, water, and salt and bring to a boil. Cover, reduce the heat to medium, and cook until the beans are tender but still hold their shape, 20 to 25 minutes. Add a little more water if needed to give the mixture a stewlike consistency. Taste for salt, sprinkle with chives, and it is ready to ladle into warm bowls.

MAKE AHEAD Store the finished dish, covered, in the refrigerator for 4 to 5 days.

GRANDMOTHER'S PUMPKIN GREENS AND LENTIL STEW

| Kumbala Soppu

One particular childhood recollection of mine is inspired by yearly visits to my grandparents' farmhouse. Those wonderful afternoons, eating my grandmother's leafy greens–lentil stew with *jawar roti*, became cheerful memories.

From the front door of Grandma's house, I could see straight to the garden beyond. Pumpkins galore rambled through the other vegetables, trailing along the fence and climbing up the arches and trellises; they nestled between the walkway and a stone-rimmed pond in which blue and pink lotuses floated. The moist earth smelled sweetly of hay. There were miniature pumpkins that would fit into my palm, and others so large and heavy they'd certainly be blue-ribbon winners at an American county fair.

I would help Grandma cut young pumpkin leaves to make this dish. Grandma always offered the first big gourd to the goddess. Afterward, her fragile hands wielding a small sharp knife with ease, she cracked it open with her sickle and peeled off the skin. Next she grated the pumpkin meat, preparing to turn it into numerous concoctions. Grandma entertained with cleverness and ferocity. She loved nothing better than to be cooking and talking about food with her peers. One of the tastiest of her communal dishes was an easy pumpkin-seed snack. She coated the seeds with butter, then sprinkled them with salt and minced garlic. Finally, they were toasted until they exuded a nutty aroma. Then everyone nibbled, and the happy conversation went on and on. When I toast and eat pumpkin seeds today, it's enough to take me back to girlhood. I like to sprinkle Grandma's pumpkin-seed snack over this stew. Serve alongside Rustic Punjab Cornmeal Flatbread (pages 70–71) or any crusty bread.

Growing pumpkins (and thus pumpkin greens) is easy. Buy seeds at a nursery (or even let the kids save some seeds from this year's jack-o'-lantern) and plant according to package directions. Water the young creeper as you would any plant, and watch it trail in the garden. To select pumpkin greens, snip off the young leaves with their tender stems near the end of the creeper.

3 tablespoons peanut or vegetable oil

3 small shallots, finely chopped

1 to 2 fresh green serrano or jalapeño chilis, stemmed and minced

6 ounces pumpkin greens with tender stems, finely chopped

1/3 cup *toovar dal* (yellow lentils), or yellow split peas, rinsed

2 cups water

3/4 teaspoon salt

Melted *desi ghee* (pages 47–48), or unsalted butter, for serving

1. Heat the oil in a heavy medium saucepan over medium heat. Add the shallots and cook, stirring, until softened but not brown, about 2 minutes. Stir in the chilis and cook, stirring, for 1 minute more. Add the greens and cook, stirring constantly, until fragrant, about 2 minutes.

2. Add the *toovar dal* and water and bring to a boil. Reduce the heat to low, cover, and simmer until the lentils are tender but still hold their shape, 25 to 30 minutes. Add the salt. There will be a little liquid in the finished dish. Let stand, covered, for 5 minutes. Ladle into bowls and drizzle with *desi ghee* for a classic touch.

VARIATION

If pumpkin greens are unavailable, substitute any of the widely available leafy greens, such as red or green Swiss chard, sorrel, chicory, kale, collards, spinach, or turnip greens.

A SWEET NOTE: DESSERTS

Samapti-ek Mithas ke Saath

I remember the grand Hindu feast known as Diwali; the name means "rows of lamps" or "the festival of lights." To celebrate, my mother ornamented the entire house with garlands of fresh mango leaves and marigolds. Before dawn and at dusk, she lit traditional earthenware lamps filled with *desi ghee* in the doorways, windows sills, and garden. Each morning and evening I bedecked the entrance of our home with bright patterns called *rangoli,* made from rice flour, colorful powders, and glitter. One of the main features of the festival is the worship of Laxmi, the goddess of fortune, beauty, prosperity, and wealth. Merchants and businesses close old accounts and start the new year by revamping their stores and offering prayers to the goddess. The major attractions for us kids were the firecrackers, special foods, gifts, and entertainment. Mother hired professional *halvais*, or sweets-makers, to make snacks and sweets. They set up a makeshift wood-burning stove in the backyard. In a short amount of time they made elaborate desserts and snacks with their seemingly heat-resistant hands. The sweets of every shape, flavor, and hue were as dazzling to the eye as the display of fireworks. My sister and I would pack these sweets and snacks neatly in baskets and distribute them to friends and neighbors.

In India, children are bribed with sweets, and gods are placated with them. Sweets are offered as a token of friendship, an expression of love, and proof of hospitality. Sweets are also prepared as gifts for graduations, weddings, festivals, or to celebrate the birth of a child.

It's only recently that Indian restaurants in the United States have helped their unusual desserts become popular with Western customers. At the request of my dedicated students, readers, and other Indian food lovers, I've included recipes for traditional desserts made with a simple dairy base, nuts, vegetables, fruits, and grains.

When I'm in India I get a hankering for the sweets made with *khoa;* fresh milk is cooked down until all of the water evaporates, leaving a creamy, fudgelike mass. *Khoa* is tedious to make but gives an extraordinary richness and smoothness of texture to desserts. In India *khoa* can be purchased ready-made, but in the United States we have to resort to using dry milk powder.

The desserts I've chosen to include are authentic indulgences for both adults and children, to be savored and enjoyed. May they leave all cravings fulfilled.

MAKING KHOA

Khoa, or *mawa,* is a fudgelike soft dough, made by cooking milk slowly until all of its water content evaporates. Here is a method for those of you who are interested in making it. Use whole milk or half-and-half (not traditional, but it takes much less time), and bring it to a boil in a heavy skillet or any wide-mouthed heavy pan, then reduce the heat to medium and simmer, stirring and scraping the pan occasionally with a wide wooden spatula. As it cooks down, first it will resemble heavy cream, then a thick paste; continue to cook until it forms a thick mass and starts to pull away from the sides of the pan. This takes about an hour if using whole milk, 40 minutes if using half-and-half. Remove from the heat. As it cools, the *khoa* will firm to a fudgelike consistency. If not using immediately, cover and refrigerate for up to 2 weeks, or freeze for 6 months. Makes about $3/4$ cup *khoa* if you start with 1 quart whole milk, or 1 cup if you start with 1 quart half-and-half.

CARDAMOM-SCENTED FUDGE CONFECTION | Peda

Here is a great recipe using *khoa*.

3/4 to 1 cup *khoa* (see above)

1/2 cup sugar

5 green cardamom pods, seeds removed and ground

Sliced nuts, toasted (page 208), for topping (optional)

In a heavy medium saucepan, combine the *khoa*, sugar, and cardamom. Set over medium heat and cook, stirring constantly, until the sugar has completely dissolved and the fudge pulls away from the sides of the pan into a soft ball, 12 to 15 minutes. Spread the fudge evenly on a serving plate to a thickness of 1/4 inch. Sprinkle with your choice of toasted, sliced nuts, if desired. Cut into 1-inch bars and serve. Store in the refrigerator, covered, for up to 1 week, but bring to room temperature before serving.

MANGO MOUSSE | Aam Ice Cream

This is the best way I know to create a simple, yet truly satisfying mousse. I fold in a little cream to give the mousse some body, but not enough to detract from the fresh fruit flavor. For a special Valentine's Day dinner, stir a little rum into the cream. Occasionally, I take the liberty of serving this mousse on tart shells; it's simple but makes an elegant-looking dessert. You can also serve it as Mango Mousse Pie; chill the mousse in two 8-inch baked pie crusts.

SERVES 4 TO 6, OR MAKES 12 INDIVIDUAL TARTS

2 cups canned Alphonso mango pulp (pages 52–53)

1/2 cup plain or lemon-flavored yogurt

1 envelope (1/4 ounce) unflavored gelatin

1 cup heavy whipping cream

1/2 cup confectioner's sugar

12 homemade or prepared individual tart shells (optional)

3 cups chopped fruit, such as mango, pineapple, strawberries, and nectarines, for garnish

Fresh mint leaves, for garnish

1. Chill a medium glass bowl for several hours in the refrigerator.

2. In a mixing bowl, add the mango pulp and yogurt and beat with a spoon until well combined. Set aside.

3. Place the gelatin in a small saucepan and sprinkle with 3 tablespoons water. Set aside to soften a few minutes. Cook over low heat, stirring frequently, until dissolved, 2 to 3 minutes. Immediately stir the gelatin into the mango mixture.

4. Add the cream to the chilled bowl (cream stiffens faster in a chilled bowl). Using a handheld electric mixer, beat the cream on medium speed until it holds luscious soft peaks, about 4 minutes. Gradually beat in the sugar, a tablespoon at a time. Taste and adjust the sugar to your liking. Gently fold the cream into the yogurt-mango mixture. Divide the mousse into 4 to 6 dessert cups or sundae dishes, or the 12 individual tart shells, if using. Cover loosely with saran wrap to prevent the top from drying out. Refrigerate until set, at least 4 hours.

5. Just before serving, set the cups or tarts out on dessert plates and spoon a few tablespoons of chopped fruit around each cup or tart. Garnish with mint leaves and serve.

VARIATION

To make mango pulp from fresh mangoes, start with 2 large (1 1/2 to 2 pounds total) ripe mangoes. Wash and wipe the mangoes thoroughly. Cut off the stem end of each mango. Using a sharp knife, slice the mango lengthwise on either side of the flat pit, into 2 pieces, each about 1/2 inch thick. Cut the flesh of each half, making a fine crisscross pattern. Turn each half inside out and cut the fruit from the skin. Peel the remaining skin and cut the fruit into chunks. Transfer to a food processor or blender. Pulse a few times to make a smooth puree. You should have 2 cups of pulp. Strain the puree if it is fibrous.

PISTACHIO ICE CREAM | Pista Kulfi

Indian ice cream is based on milk and sugar, concentrated by boiling. This intense liquid gives *kulfi* a delicate, caramelized taste. Flavorings such as cardamom, saffron, and pistachio add to the richness. In India, street vendors with wooden carts sell *kulfi* set in conical metal molds, which are kept cool in a large earthenware pot.

Kulfi was traditionally made with boiled-down milk spiked with sugar, until sweetened condensed milk and evaporated milk became commonly available. It's easy to make at home, and you don't need an ice cream maker to do it. You can easily double or triple the recipe for a crowd.

SERVES 6 TO 8

1 cup shelled, roasted unsalted pistachios

One 14-ounce can sweetened condensed milk

One 12-ounce can evaporated milk

1 cup heavy whipping cream

2 teaspoons rose water

Chopped mixed fruit, such as mango, papaya, strawberries, and banana, for serving

Edible rose petals, for garnish (optional)

1. Place the pistachios in a blender and process until finely powdered. Add the condensed milk, evaporated milk, and cream and process until smooth. Add the rose water and pulse once or twice. Pour into 6 to 8 individual dessert cups, a pudding mold, or a rectangular dish. Freeze overnight or until set.

2. Just before serving, let the ice cream soften for a few minutes in the refrigerator. If serving from individual dessert cups, top each with about 1/2 cup chopped fruit, garnish, and carry right to the table. If using a pudding mold or dish, slice into serving portions or scoop into large balls, transfer to serving bowls, add 1/2 cup chopped fruit to each serving, garnish, and serve.

MAKE AHEAD Once the *kulfi* sets, cover tightly with plastic wrap and freeze for up to 3 months.

Mango Kulfi

Add 1 cup mango pulp (canned or fresh, see pages 52–53 and 406) along with the milks and cream and continue with the recipe, omitting the rose water. If you prefer to use the pistachios, reduce to 1/2 cup.

Cardamom-Scented Kulfi

Add the crushed seeds from 5 green cardamom pods to the milks, and cream and process in the blender, omitting the nuts. Continue with the recipe.

Saffron Kulfi

Soak 1/2 teaspoon lightly toasted and crushed saffron threads in the evaporated milk for 15 to 20 minutes, then proceed with the recipe, with or without the nuts and omitting the rose water.

Kulfi Pops

To make individual pops for children, divide the milk mixture among paper cups or cones (cut an 8-inch square of waxed paper, fold into a triangle, then roll one end toward other angle to form a cone, and seal tightly with tape). Freeze until the *kulfi* is thick but not fully set, 1 to 1 1/2 hours. Push an ice cream stick into each container. Freeze until firm, about 2 hours longer. Peel off the paper and serve. To store, seal the *kulfi*, still in cups or cones, in large resealable plastic bags for up to 3 months.

FLUFFY YOGURT CHEESE | Shrikhand

I love this for its delicious texture. Unlike most desserts, this one uses yogurt, making it lighter, fresher, and more satisfying. Appropriately, its name, *shrikhand*, translates as "ambrosia of the gods." Homemade yogurt cheese forms the basis of this classic, creamy and luscious

Maharashtrian dessert. It is traditionally served at family get-togethers, after a meal composed of *poori* (pages 80–81) and Yukon Gold Potatoes with Zesty Seasoning (page 236–237). *Charoli* nuts are sprinkled on top before serving; from time to time they are available at Indian groceries. Of late I serve *shrikhand* topped with crushed praline or with chopped fresh fruit on the side; the lively flavors complement the creamy dessert nicely. Pistachios also add a nice touch.

My sons' friends love this dessert. You too can turn this into a charming treat for your children; make colorful layers in tall stemmed glasses. Use plenty of fresh fruit and green and/or red cubes of gelatin, then add the *shrikhand,* repeat the layers if you like, and top with crushed praline or peanuts.

MAKES ABOUT 1 1/2 CUPS, SERVES 3 TO 4

4 cups (one 32-ounce container) plain yogurt

1/4 teaspoon saffron threads

1 to 2 tablespoons very hot milk

1/2 cup sugar

4 green cardamom pods, seeds removed and ground

1/4 cup shelled, roasted unsalted pistachios

1. To make yogurt cheese, line a colander with a double thickness of cheesecloth. Spoon the yogurt into the cloth, gather the four corners, and tie with a string. Hang it above the sink to drain for 12 to 15 hours, or overnight. (In the summer, place it in a strainer set over a bowl in the refrigerator.) You may save the whey (drained liquid) for soups or rice, or use it as a fertilizer on houseplants.

2. Toast the saffron threads in a small skillet over low heat, stirring occasionally, until brittle, 2 to 3 minutes. Transfer to a small mortar and pestle and crush (or use a rolling pin or spoon and crush on a work surface). Place the crushed saffron in a small bowl and add the hot milk.

3. Transfer the yogurt cheese to a mixing bowl. Add the sugar and the saffron mixture and beat with a fork until the mixture is light and fluffy and the sugar has dissolved, 3 to 4 minutes. Fold in the cardamom. The mixture should resemble whipped cream cheese. Refrigerate until well chilled, about 4 hours. To serve, scoop into goblets or sundae dishes and top with pistachios.

MAKE AHEAD Refrigerate, covered, for up to 4 days.

BENGAL DAINTY CHEESE CAKES IN CREAM SAUCE | Ras Malai

Ras malai is one of the glories of Indian confectionery; you'll agree if you've tasted the dessert on a visit to a good Indian restaurant. Bengal's greatest contribution to the food heritage of India is a magnificent spectrum of sweets made from *paneer*. *Rasgulla, ras malai, cham cham, anarkali, sandesh,* crisp *sweet samosa* (called *rajbhog*)—the list of mouthwatering delicacies is endless, and guests in Bengal are always welcomed with these sweets. Though *ras malai* can be made with ricotta cheese, it will lack the distinctiveness that *paneer* brings to the plate.

Rasgulla—paneer balls poached in sugar syrup—was first created in 1868. Several decades later, the *paneer* balls were flattened into petite cakes and cooked gently in syrup, then soaked in a milk sauce. To make this sauce, milk was slowly cooked until reduced to a third of its original volume; as a result, the natural milk sugars browned, making it soft, sensuous, and seductively sweet. The dessert was commercially marketed as *ras malai,* which translates simply as "creamed syrup." It has been popular ever since.

SERVES 6 TO 8

3 cups whole or low-fat (2%) milk

1/2 cup heavy whipping cream

2 1/2 tablespoons plus 1 cup sugar

3 green cardamom pods, seeds removed and crushed

1 1/2 cups water

1 recipe Fresh Basic Paneer (pages 221–222), or 8 ounces store-bought

1/4 teaspoon unbleached all-purpose flour

Saffron threads, for garnish (optional)

1.   Bring the milk to a boil, stirring occasionally, in a heavy large skillet. Reduce the heat to medium and cook, stirring regularly, until the milk is reduced to a third of its original volume, about 45 minutes. Add the cream and continue to cook, stirring, until very thick, 10 to 12 minutes. Add the 2 1/2 tablespoons of sugar and the crushed cardamom seeds and cook, stirring, for 5 minutes more. Turn off the heat and set aside.

2.   Combine the remaining 1 cup of sugar and the water in a wide skillet. Bring to a boil and cook, stirring regularly. Reduce the heat to medium and simmer, uncovered, until the mixture is reduced to a third of its original volume, 20 to 25 minutes. Cool a teaspoon of the syrup and taste; it should be pleasantly sweet but not watery. Continue to cook for a few minutes if necessary.

3. While the sugar syrup is cooking, crumble the *paneer* on a clean work surface. Press with paper towels to remove any excess moisture. Divide the *paneer* into 2 portions and spread one with the heel and palm of your hand across the work surface. Gather it with a spatula and repeat the process 5 or 6 times, or until the *paneer* is smooth and without any trace of graininess. Be sure to knead the *paneer* thoroughly; the more you knead, the lighter and fluffier it will be. Repeat with the remaining portion of *paneer*. Knead all of the *paneer* into a ball. Rinse your hands and wipe them dry; scoop about 2 teaspoons of the *paneer* at a time and shape into a smooth 1-inch ball between your palms. Flatten to a 1/4-inch thickness. You should have about 24 *paneer* cakes.

4. Heat the sugar syrup over medium heat. Add the flour to the syrup and stir. Add 8 to 10 *paneer* cakes (or as many as will fit in a single layer, allowing enough space for turning). Bring to a simmer and cook for 5 minutes. The *paneer* cakes should swell to almost double their original size at this time; the flour accelerates the swelling process. You may notice a little foam at the top, which is perfectly okay. Turn the *paneer* cakes with a slotted spoon and simmer until firm, 4 to 5 minutes more. Transfer the cakes to a 3-quart serving casserole. Repeat with the remaining *paneer* cakes and add to the casserole. Scrape the remaining syrup over the cakes in the casserole.

5. Pour the cream sauce over the *paneer* cakes. Turn the cakes gently with a slotted spoon so that the cream incorporates with the syrup. Cover and chill overnight. To serve, place 3 to 4 cakes in each bowl or deep plate and spoon the sauce over the top. Sprinkle each serving with a few strands of saffron threads, if desired, and serve.

MAKE AHEAD The sugar syrup can be refrigerated, covered, for up to 5 days. The cream sauce and *paneer* can be made in advance and refrigerated, covered, for up to 3 days. The finished dish can be assembled and refrigerated, covered, for up to 2 days.

CAKEY BALLS IN ROSE-SCENTED WARM SYRUP | Gulab Jamun

Small, gleaming, sensuous, cakey balls, occasionally draped with gold or silver leaf, float in rose-perfumed syrup. These golden beauties are my weakness, and I'm sure they'll turn out to be yours too.

Even with dry milk and without gold leaf, *gulab jamun* makes a lovely special-dinner grand finale. I like to serve this popular restaurant dessert slightly warm; the cakey balls become nice and plump after reheating. If you have leftover syrup after the *jamuns* are all eaten, as is often the case in our home, then cut a few slices of bread neatly into quarters, deep-fry to golden perfection, and add to the syrup.

MAKES 50 MEDIUM BALLS, 10 TO 12 SERVINGS

2^1/4 cups sugar

2 cups water

6 green cardamom pods, seeds removed and pulverized

1 tablespoon rose water

2 cups Carnation nonfat dry milk

1/2 cup unbleached all-purpose flour

1 teaspoon baking powder

1 cup heavy whipping cream

Vegetable oil for frying

Edible rose petals, for garnish (optional)

1. Combine the sugar and water in a large saucepan. Bring to a boil, stirring, until the sugar dissolves. Reduce the heat to medium and simmer, uncovered, until the volume is reduced by a third, 20 to 25 minutes. Cool a teaspoon of the syrup and taste; it should be pleasantly sweet but not watery. Continue to cook for a few more minutes if necessary. Turn off the heat and stir in the cardamom and rose water.

2. In the bowl of a food processor, combine the dry milk, flour, and baking powder and pulse twice to mix. Add the cream and process until crumbly. With the machine running, gradually add a tablespoon of water through the feed tube. Process until the dough begins to clean the sides of the bowl. (Alternatively, to mix by hand: combine the dry milk, flour, and baking powder in a large mixing bowl. Gradually pour in the cream and mix until crumbly. Add a tablespoon of water and knead into a smooth, pliable dough.) Form the dough into a smooth ball, cover, and set aside.

3. Fill a wok or saucepan with oil to a depth of 2 to 2^1/$_2$ inches, set over medium heat, and heat the oil to 225°F to 250°F on a candy thermometer. The oil should be only moderately hot, because the balls have to cook very gradually. Pinch off portions of dough and roll between your hands, applying pressure, into smooth balls about 1 inch in diameter. Working in batches, carefully slip 8 to 10 balls at a time (or as many as can fit in the pan in single layer) into the hot oil. After about 30 seconds, using a slotted spoon, stir them gently so they brown evenly (do not stir them immediately, or they may break). Fry until golden brown all over, 4 to 5 minutes in all. Remove with a slotted spoon, drain briefly over the oil, and add to the sugar syrup. Continue frying with the remaining dough; if the dough starts to dry out and crumble or develop cracks while being shaped into balls, then transfer to the food processor and reprocess with a few tablespoons of water or milk.

4. Cool completely, cover, and let the balls soak for at least 3 to 4 hours before serving. Scoop 3 to 4 balls into individual dessert bowls and spoon 2 to 3 tablespoons of syrup on top. Garnish with rose petals, if desired, and serve.

> MAKE AHEAD Refrigerate, covered, for up to 5 days. Serve warm or at room temperature. To rewarm in the microwave, heat in individual bowls for 20 to 30 seconds.

CREAMY RICE PUDDING | Kheer/Payasam

Indian rice pudding is a creamy stove-top dessert, rather than a custardy baked one. As the pudding simmers, the rice and milk meld to a comforting creaminess. Rose water adds a nice dimension to the pudding's gentle sweetness. Rice pudding is at its most delectable when it is somewhat warm. A dessert wine such as La Famiglia di Robert Mondavi Moscato Bianco will amplify the flavors of the *kheer* beautifully.

SERVES 6 TO 8

1/2 cup basmati rice, jasmine rice, or other long-grain white rice

8 cups whole or low-fat (2%) milk (use whole milk for a creamier texture)

1 cup sugar

1/4 cup roughly chopped cashews

1 tablespoon rose water

1. Rinse the rice in several changes of water; drain well. Combine the rice and milk in a heavy medium saucepan. Bring to a boil over medium-high heat, stirring constantly. Reduce the heat to medium and cook, uncovered, stirring occasionally, until the rice is tender, about 15 minutes. Stir in the sugar and cashews and continue to simmer, stirring occasionally, until the pudding is thick and reduced by half (it should look no thicker than heavy cream), 25 to 30 minutes. Remove from the heat and stir in the rose water. The pudding will thicken as it cools. Serve warm or chilled, in individual bowls.

VARIATION

Stir in some fresh chopped nectarine or mango while the pudding is still warm.

MAKE AHEAD You may prepare this dessert in advance and store it in the refrigerator, covered, for up to 2 days. The cold pudding thickens, so stir in enough milk to soften it before serving.

VERMICELLI PUDDING WITH FRESH BERRIES | Semiya Payasam/Kheer

As a child I recall watching fresh vermicelli, as fine as hair, being made by hand. It was rolled on wooden equipment that resembled a seesaw. A person sat on one end rolling a small piece of wheat-flour dough; as the delicate strands rolled down from both ends of the wooden plank, another person sitting on the floor gently draped the strands on rows of rods placed in a neat zigzag pattern, and the strands were sun-dried. My mother browned the dried vermicelli in *desi ghee* to make this classic *kheer*, which added a deep, rich nuttiness. Vermicelli making has a come a long way. Dried ready-made, preroasted packages, not to mention ones flavored with saffron, are available at many Indian markets. Making it a breeze to fix. Serve this dish as a mid-day snack or a satisfying dessert. It is quick to assemble for a crowd.

SERVES 6

3 tablespoons *desi ghee* (pages 47–48), or unsalted butter

2 cups preroasted Indian-style vermicelli, crushed
into fine pieces (this makes it easier to stir-
fry)

3^1/$_2$ cups whole or low-fat (2%) milk

2/3 cup sugar

6 green cardamom pods

1 cup fresh berries, such as raspberries, blueber-
ries, or blackberries

1. Melt the *desi ghee* or butter in a heavy 2-quart saucepan over medium heat. Add the vermicelli and cook, stirring, until aromatic, about 5 minutes; don't worry if some pieces are not browned. It browns quickly, so watch closely. (If you are using Italian-style vermicelli pasta from the supermarket, stir-fry until lightly browned for at least 6 to 8 minutes.)

2. Add the milk and sugar and cook, stirring occasionally, until thick and creamy, 12 to 15 minutes. (If you are using Italian-style vermicelli pasta use 4^1/$_2$ cups of milk.) While the *kheer* is cooking, remove the cardamom seeds from the pods and pulverize them with a mortar and pestle. Stir the crushed seeds into the *kheer* and remove the pan from the heat. Cool slightly. Serve warm or chilled in small bowls with a sprinkling of berries.

VARIATION

The consistency of this pudding is quite nice with low-fat milk, but if you prefer a very rich pudding, you can replace 1 cup of the milk with heavy cream.

MAKE AHEAD You may prepare this in advance and store it in the refrigerator, covered, for up to 2 days. The cold pudding thickens, so stir in enough milk to soften it.

VELVETY PISTACHIO AND CHAYOTE PUDDING | Sime Badnekai Payasam

In India, chayote is used in a number of vegetable preparations and along with legumes to make stews, as well as in desserts. Americans fail to appreciate chayote simply because they do not yet understand its delicacies. There is nothing more satisfying than the silkiness of a perfectly cooked *payasam* at the end of a spicy meal. It is delicious warm or chilled.

SERVES 8 TO 10

1¹/₂ pounds (3 medium) chayotes

2 cups whole or low-fat (2%) milk

¹/₄ cup shelled, roasted salted or unsalted pistachios

2 cups heavy whipping cream

2 tablespoons *desi ghee* (pages 47–48)

³/₄ cup sugar

Freshly grated nutmeg

1.   Wash and wipe the chayotes, then cut them in half through the stem end and use a small knife or spoon to wedge out the pit from each piece. Using a hand grater (the fine holes of a hand grater result in a fine, fluffy texture, which I prefer; the larger holes create a coarse texture), grate the chayote. Measure 2 cups and set aside.

2.   Heat 1 cup of the milk in a small saucepan until hot; add the pistachios and soak for 30 minutes.

3.   Combine the remaining 1 cup of milk and the cream in a heavy medium saucepan. Bring to a gentle boil, then reduce the heat to medium and cook, stirring often to prevent burning, until reduced by half, about 30 minutes. Turn off the heat.

4.   In a heavy medium skillet, melt the *desi ghee* over medium-high heat. Add the grated chayote and cook, stirring, until aromatic, 5 to 6 minutes. Remove from the heat and cool slightly. Transfer to a blender or food processor, add the pistachios along with the soaking milk, and process into a coarse puree.

5.   Add the chayote puree to the cream mixture. Add the sugar, mix well, and simmer over medium heat, stirring occasionally, until very thick, 12 to 15 minutes. Remove from the heat. Serve warm, at room temperature, or chilled, in stemmed glasses with a sprinkling of nutmeg.

MAKE AHEAD Refrigerate, covered, for up to 3 days. Before serving, stir in a little milk to soften.

BEET PUDDING | Beet ki Kheer

This is an irresistible combination to serve any time of the day. Shredded beets, milk, sugar, and cardamom are simmered on the stove-top to a soothing creaminess. Add just enough sugar to bring out the natural sweetness of the beets. Though it sounds similar to the previous recipe, here the technique is different (because the beets are not stir-fried in *desi ghee*). Traditionally, this dessert is cooked down to an almost a fudgelike consistency, then patted on a plate and cut into bars, I like to serve it like a pudding instead. Dress it up with silver leaf *(varq)* for an elegant yet easy garnish. Flavorless and odorless, relatively inexpensive edible silver leaf and moderately priced gold leaf can be purchased at gourmet, baking, and cake-decorating shops and Indian markets. The leaves are sold in packages of a dozen, each between two tissue papers.

SERVES 6 TO 8

4 to 5 medium beets

1 cup whole or low-fat (2%) milk

2 cups heavy whipping cream

1/3 cup sugar

5 green cardamom pods, seeds removed and crushed

2 to 3 squares silver leaf, for garnish (optional)

1. Wash, wipe, and peel the beets. Using a hand grater (the fine holes of a hand grater result in a fine, fluffy texture, which I prefer; the larger holes create a coarse texture), grate the beets. Measure 3 cups and set aside.

2. Combine the beets, milk, and cream in a heavy medium saucepan. Bring to a boil, then reduce the heat to medium and cook, stirring often to prevent burning, and scraping the milk solids from the sides of the pan into the pudding, until thick, about 20 minutes. Stir in the sugar and cardamom and cook, stirring, until very thick, 10 to 15 minutes more. Transfer to a warm serving bowl.

3. See page 54 for directions for transferring the silver leaf garnish to the top of the pudding, if desired. Serve warm, at room temperature, or chilled, in decorative dessert cups.

MAKE AHEAD You may prepare this in advance and store it in the refrigerator, covered, for up to 4 days. Before serving, stir in a little milk to soften it.

TOASTED CREAM-OF-WHEAT HALVAH WITH ORANGE JUICE

| Kesari Bhat/Sheera

This halvah, popular from the snowcapped north to the sun-drenched south of India, has a wonderful moistness soaked into its fluffy texture. It is offered to the deities in temples throughout India.

In this recipe, I've transformed halvah into a personal culinary statement by using fruit juice. The orange juice gives an unexpected twist and a nice undertone of orange flavor. This is a quick and delicious halvah to make for any occasion, but if you want to dress it up, top the dessert with a spoonful of cream, either plain or whipped, or a scoop of vanilla ice cream.

MAKES ABOUT 3 CUPS, SERVES 6

1/4 cup *desi ghee* (pages 47–48)

1 1/2 cups quick-cooking cream of wheat, or Indian semolina (sooji, page 46)

3/4 cup sugar

3 cups orange juice, preferably freshly squeezed

2 tablespoons dark raisins or dried cranberries

1 tablespoon cashew pieces

Sliced peaches, mango, pineapple, papaya, or other seasonal fruits

1. Melt the *desi ghee* in a heavy medium saucepan over medium heat. Add the cream of wheat and cook, stirring regularly and taking care not to brown, until the mixture is aromatic and the grains look pleasantly plump, about 5 minutes. (If you're using the Indian *sooji,* cook for at least 8 to 10 minutes, until the *sooji* is toasty and you begin to smell the nutty flavor.) Add the sugar, followed by orange juice, stirring constantly to make sure there are no lumps. At this point the mixture may spatter a bit, so be careful and adjust the heat as necessary. Bring the mixture to a gentle boil, then reduce the heat to low. Add the raisins and cashews and mix well. Cover and cook until all of the liquid is absorbed and the halvah is fluffy, 5 to 6 minutes. Turn off the heat. Let the halvah rest, covered, for 5 minutes.

2. Just before serving, spoon the halvah into individual custard cups or a decorative mold. For a lovely presentation, place a serving plate upside down on top of the decorative mold. Invert the mold over the plate, holding both securely, and let the halvah drop down onto the serving plate. Top each serving with fresh fruit and serve hot, warm, or at room temperature. I like this dessert best when it is warm; it loses its fluffy texture as it cools.

MAKE AHEAD Refrigerate, covered, for up to 4 days. Just rewarm it before serving to restore all the unctuous goodness. If it looks dry, sprinkle it with a few tablespoons of orange juice or water.

VARIATION

This recipe welcomes a variety of adaptations: Stir in a mashed ripe banana just before serving; omit the orange juice and cook in water or milk; the cashews easily can be omitted.

BANANA FUDGE HALVAH | Kele ka Halwa

The idea of cooked banana had never appealed to me until a recent trip to India, when I first tasted banana halvah prepared by my sister-in-law, Keertilata. I liked it very much, and have been using her recipe ever since. These days, I deliberately set bananas aside to make this dessert. It is slightly soft and chewy, and denser than American fudge.

MAKES TEN 2-INCH DIAMONDS, 5 SERVINGS

2 medium ripe bananas

1/2 cup plus 2 tablespoons sugar

3 tablespoons *desi ghee* (pages 47–48)

3 green cardamom pods, seeds removed and ground

2 tablespoons sliced almonds

1. Peel the bananas and mash them to measure 1 cup.

2. Combine the banana, sugar, and *desi ghee* in a heavy medium sauté pan or skillet. Cook over medium-high heat, stirring constantly with a wooden spoon, until the sugar melts. Reduce the heat to medium and continue cooking, stirring and adjusting the heat as necessary so it does not burn; begin stirring more rapidly as the mixture colors to light brown and starts to form into a glazed mass and the *desi ghee* starts to separate, about 15 minutes. Add the ground cardamom, mix well, and remove from the heat.

3. Pour the mixture quickly (it hardens promptly, especially in winter) onto a serving platter or dinner plate and spread out evenly to a 1/4-inch thickness. Sprinkle with the almonds and pat them in lightly so the halvah is neatly studded. Let cool to room temperature. To serve, cut into 2-inch diamonds. Store at cool room temperature up to 3 days, or refrigerate in summer, in a loosely covered container.

INDIAN-STYLE BAKED FLAKY DOUGHNUTS | Baked Balushahi

Here's my spin on India's flaky *balushahi*. The original is deep-fried in *desi ghee;* this one is baked to a light and tender, but rich, flaky pastry. Kids will love the homey flavors, and it's great for school lunches. It can be made several days ahead, and it travels well too. Serve one or two on the side with crème brulée or vanilla ice cream.

MAKES ABOUT 24, SERVES 10 TO 12

2 cups unbleached all-purpose flour

1 teaspoon baking soda

Pinch salt

1/2 cup melted *desi ghee* (pages 47–48)

1/2 cup plain yogurt

3 cups sugar

3 cups water

1. In the bowl of a food processor, combine the flour, baking soda, and salt and pulse twice to mix. Add the *desi ghee* and pulse until crumbly. With the machine running, gradually add the yogurt through the feed tube. Process until the dough comes together into a ball and begins to clean the sides of the bowl—avoid overprocessing. (Alternatively, you may make the dough by hand: combine the flour, baking soda, and salt in a large mixing bowl. Make a well in the center. Drizzle in the *desi ghee* and rub it in with your fingertips until it is fully incorporated and the mixture resembles fresh bread crumbs. Gradually add the yogurt and continue mixing with your fingertips until the dough holds together.) Form the dough into a smooth ball. Cover and let rest for 1 hour.

2. Meanwhile, dissolve the sugar in the water in a saucepan and bring to a boil. Simmer, stirring occasionally, until the syrup is slightly thick, about 25 minutes. Set aside.

3. Position a rack in the center of the oven and preheat the oven to 400°F.

4. Place the dough on a work surface and knead briefly. Divide into 24 walnut-size portions. Roll each portion between your palms to form a smooth ball, flatten slightly to form a small disc, and place the discs on a cookie sheet 1 inch apart. (You can make them prettier by crimping the edges.) Bake for about 15 minutes, until lightly golden.

5. Place the freshly baked doughnuts in a single layer in a large baking dish (using more than one dish if necessary). Pour the syrup over the doughnuts and let soak for 1 hour. (If the sugar syrup is still hot, you need to soak for just 30 minutes.) Cool and serve, or transfer to a container and store between wax paper or parchment at cool room temperature for up to 4 days.

FULL MOON COOKIES | Nankhatai

When we first came to Ohio two decades ago, I always made sure that a supply of *nankhatai* was available in the cookie jar for my little boys and their friends; they often called them "full moon cookies," for their whitish color. Since then I've called them that myself.

From western India, this baked biscuit (as it is called in India) is almost white, and rich, but delicate and mildly sweet. *Nankhatai* complement many sorbets and ice creams; they are also wonderful on their own. My favorite way to eat these cookies is accompanied with jasmine tea or dipped in strong coffee.

MAKES 16

1 1/4 cups unbleached all-purpose flour

1/8 teaspoon baking soda

1/8 teaspoon salt

2/3 cup *desi ghee* (pages 47–48)

1/2 cup sugar

4 green cardamom pods, seeds removed and crushed (optional)

1. Position a rack in the center of the oven and preheat the oven to 350°F.

2. In a large mixing bowl, combine the flour, soda, and salt and set aside.

3. Melt the *desi ghee* in a small saucepan over low heat. Add the sugar and stir to dissolve, 2 to 3 minutes. Remove from the heat and combine with the dry ingredients in the mixing bowl. Add the cardamom seeds, if using, and mix thoroughly with a wooden spoon. (Some of my friends also add a few drops of yellow food coloring here.) When the dough is just cool enough to handle, mix with your fingers until it holds together; it should resemble mashed potatoes. Knead into a smooth ball. While it is still warm, divide it into 16 walnut-size portions. Roll each portion between your palms to form a smooth ball, flatten slightly, and place the discs on a cookie sheet 1 inch apart. Bake 15 to 20 minutes, or until the bottoms are lightly colored. Cool on a wire rack. Serve or store, covered, at room temperature for up to 1 week.

TOASTED CHICKPEA FLOUR CANDY BALLS | Besan Laddu

When I was growing up, there were hardly any stores that sold goodies in India; most of the snacks and sweets were freshly made at home and stored in large stainless steel containers. This is my grandmother's recipe, and one of my very favorite after-school treats. Imagine toasted chickpea flour, rich with *desi ghee* and the scent of cardamom. The result is what I'd call a near perfect balance of tastes. Serve anytime in moderation.

MAKES ABOUT FIFTEEN 1 1/2- TO 2-INCH CANDY BALLS

2 cups chickpea flour

1 cup *desi ghee* (pages 47–48)

2 cups sugar

5 green cardamom pods, seeds removed and pulverized

1 tablespoon dark raisins (optional)

1. Place the chickpea flour in a heavy medium sauté pan over medium-low heat. Toast, stirring constantly, while adding the *desi ghee* a tablespoon at a time. Cook, stirring, until the flour is aromatic, turns lightly reddish and golden, looks sticky, and feels very soft (somewhat like the consistency of mashed potatoes), 25 to 30 minutes. (This technique is crucial; the end result should have a nice toasty taste rather than a raw flour flavor.)

2. Remove the pan from the heat and immediately stir in the sugar, cardamom, and raisins, if using. Mix thoroughly and let cool slightly. When the mixture is just cool enough to handle, with the help of a large spoon (or a small ice-cream scoop), scoop some of the mixture into your palm and press it to form a candy ball about the size of a golf ball. If you wait too long to form the balls and the mixture cools completely, the *desi ghee* will harden and you'll have difficulty shaping them. You may coat your palms with *desi ghee* for easier shaping of the balls.

MAKE AHEAD Store, covered, at room temperature for up to 2 weeks.

THIRST QUENCHERS:
COLD AND HOT DRINKS

Pyas ki Tripti

When I look back on my childhood summers in India, I recall a panorama of tall mango trees, full of luscious, bright-yellow fruits. Some branches were so heavy with ripe mangoes that they almost touched the ground. The most prized and the finest of the 1,500 varieties available is the Alphonso mango, grown widely in Konkan, a narrow band of coastal area extending three hundred miles south of Mumbai. The region's soil and humid climate are believed to contribute to the mango's unique taste and flavor. Pleasantly plump and brilliantly orange-red, Alphonso mangoes have an exquisite flavor reminiscent of nectarine, pineapple, and rose water, with a melting, fiber-free texture. Though they were introduced to Europeans by a seventeenth-century Portuguese traveler named Alphonso (hence the name), the Alphonso variety isn't available fresh in the United States.

The Alphonso is so wonderful, in fact, that it's worth buying the canned puree at Indian groceries; there are several good brands, Ratna and Gulsitan among them, that I routinely use as substitutes for fresh mango.

This chapter starts with the famous Mango Lassi (page 425). Yogurt and buttermilk make pleasantly tart, creamy-textured refreshers. Buttermilk *lassis* are made in three varieties. The salty version, served especially in hot summer months to replace body salt lost from sweating, stimulates digestion and keeps the body cool. The sweet variety is served on special occasions and at family gatherings, but it is easy enough to prepare on short notice for unexpected guests. Then there is the spicy kind, served at marriage banquets, where it provides a nice balance to the numerous sweets that are served.

Every region of India boasts a variety of tea. Indians start the day with a hot cup of *chai*, tea flavored with various individual spices, or even a blend called Spiced Tea Mix (page 430). A common sight in Kashmir is the samovar, a Russian-style metal teapot. Children take steaming samovars to their parents working in the fields. Boat owners keep them in the slender vessels that cross the canals. Shopkeepers huddle around them, hunched over clusters of coal, puffing on the *hookah* (a tall water pipe that takes special musky tobacco). Inside the samovar is one kind or another of strongly brewed and flavored tea—either a salty variety made with cream or a delicately flavored sweet green tea called *kahava*, enriched with honey, spices, almonds, and saffron.

More than half of India's tea comes from the most beautiful region of India, the northeastern hill state of Assam. Darjeeling, a hill resort and major tea-growing center, straddles a ridge in the Himalayas. The dominant strain grown there is orange pekoe. Much like the grapes used in fine wines, tea is sensitive to soil and weather. It varies greatly in flavor and bouquet from location to location, and even from season to season, within the same valley or on the same mountain. As a result, tea is almost always blended to produce a consistent taste.

The southern state of Karnataka is carpeted with lush coffee plantations, hence coffee is most popular in southern India. Coffee beans are freshly roasted, ground, and filtered using special straining equipment. In true southern Indian style, the coffee arrives steaming hot in a stainless steel or glass container, its aromas captive under an inverted small steel bowl, which you have to lift to release the brew. If you travel by train, you'll be amazed to see vendors pouring hot coffee in flamboyant sweeping motions between tall glasses at a height of 2 to 3 feet, creating a creamy froth as well as any luxurious espresso machine and without spilling a drop.

MANGO LASSI | Aam Lassi

The mango season in India is unfortunately short (April through June), so my father would place an order for several baskets of Alphonso mangoes ahead of time, and my mother made sure we ate fresh fruit every morning for breakfast. For meals, the flesh was cut off from the pit and mixed with clotted cream, a little sugar, and nutmeg. The leftover pulp was then turned into *lassi* to drink any time of the day. I'd enjoy fine mangoes to my heart's content each summer.

This luscious beverage is best made with canned Alphonso mango pulp; if you can lay your hands on fresh Alphonso mangoes, the *lassi* is divine. Try it with other mango varieties when they are plentiful.

MAKES 5 1/2 CUPS, SERVES 6

5 green cardamom pods, seeds removed and pulverized

3 1/3 cups (one 30-ounce can) canned Alphonso mango pulp, or 4 large ripe mangoes, pureed (see note below)

1 1/2 cups plain yogurt or buttermilk

1/4 cup sugar

1/2 cup water

In a blender, combine the cardamom, mango pulp, yogurt (or buttermilk), sugar, and water. Blend until the sugar is dissolved and the mixture is smooth and slightly frothy; you may have to do this in two batches. Taste and add water or yogurt if you think it is too thick to drink. Pour in tall, slender glasses and serve.

VARIATION

For a special occasion, stir in about 1/4 cup of light Puerto Rican rum per serving.

NOTE To puree fresh mangoes: Rinse and wipe the mangoes thoroughly. Cut off the stem end of each mango. Using a sharp knife, slice the mango lengthwise on either side of the flat pit, into 2 pieces, each about 1/2 inch thick. Cut the flesh of each half, making a fine crisscross pattern. Turn each half inside out and cut the fruit from the skin. Peel the remaining skin and cut the fruit into chunks. You should have about 4 cups of mango. Puree in a blender. Makes about 3 1/3 cups of puree.

ROSE-ACCENTED SWEET BUTTERMILK LASSI | Meetha Lassi

This is the sweet *lassi* served occasionally at Indian restaurants. Store-bought buttermilk adds the right tartness. Delicately perfumed rose water is wonderful and, yes, a touch exotic.

MAKES ABOUT 5 CUPS, SERVES 4 TO 6

4 green cardamom pods, seeds removed and pulverized

4 cups buttermilk

3/4 cup water

1/4 cup sugar, or to taste

1/4 teaspoon salt

2 teaspoons rose water

Crushed ice

In a blender, combine the cardamom, buttermilk, water, sugar, salt, and rose water. Whirl until the sugar is dissolved and the drink is frothy. Divide about a cup of crushed ice among four tall 10- to 12-ounce glasses and pour in the *lassi*.

SALTY LASSI WITH FRESH MINT | Lassi

This is just the right drink for warm weather, after working in the garden or shopping. Like yogurt, buttermilk is common to all regions of India and is served as a health drink. This *lassi* is valued in the tropics, especially in the villages, as an appetite stimulant. Freshly ground cumin adds a nice touch. Northern Indians also add freshly milled black pepper. The *kala namak*, or "black salt," gives the *lassi* a smoky, earthy finish. If you're not familiar with the flavor of black salt, start with just a pinch at first. For an additional tang, rub the rims of 4 martini glasses with a lime wedge, then dip them in a dish of coarse salt. Refrigerate the glasses, if desired, before serving.

MAKES ABOUT 4 CUPS, SERVES 3 TO 4

3 cups buttermilk

1/2 cup water

8 to 10 fresh mint leaves

1 teaspoon sugar

1/2 teaspoon ground cumin

1/2 teaspoon salt

1/4 teaspoon *kala namak* (black salt, page 54) (optional)

In a blender, combine the buttermilk, water, mint, sugar, cumin, salt, and *kala namak*, if using. Whirl until the sugar is dissolved and the mint is minced. Taste and adjust the salt and sugar—salt to brighten and focus the flavors, sugar to smooth any tart or rough edges in the buttermilk. Do not strain the lassi. Pour into mugs or glasses and serve.

SPICY LASSI WITH OIL SEASONING | Mattha

If you're drawn to the spark of fresh hot chili, then try this refresher. Though this Maharashtrian recipe is similar to the previous *lassi* in some ways, it is laced with spiced oil seasoning for a unique finish. Oil seasoning in a drink? You'll be surprised at the novel flavors. In northern cuisine, cinnamon sticks and whole cloves float in this drink. It is usually made with very sour, thin buttermilk in large clay pots and served at weddings. *Mattha* is believed to be good for digestion. Serve with Lucknow Mixed Vegetable Biryani (pages 121–122) and a bowl of baby greens. Finish with Beet Pudding (page 417).

MAKES 3 1/2 CUPS, SERVES 4

1 tablespoon vegetable oil	2 teaspoons sugar
1/2 teaspoon mustard seeds	1/2 teaspoon ground cumin
1 fresh green serrano or jalapeño chili, stemmed	1/4 teaspoon salt
2 teaspoons fresh grated ginger	2 1/2 cups buttermilk
5 sprigs cilantro	1/2 cup water

1. Have a spatter screen ready before you continue. Heat the oil in a small skillet over medium-high heat. Add the mustard seeds, immediately cover with the spatter screen, and cook until the seeds stop popping, about 30 seconds. Remove from the heat and let cool.

2. In a blender, combine the chili, ginger, cilantro, sugar, cumin, salt, buttermilk, and water. Whirl until the chili is minced and the sugar dissolved. Taste and adjust the salt to brighten and focus the flavors. Transfer to a pitcher. Pour the oil seasoning over the *lassi*, scraping the pan with a spatula, and stir well. Pour into mugs or glasses and serve.

GREEN COCONUT–WATER COOLER | Vasanthaneer

The water of tender young coconuts is *the* prized drink in India, known for its many nutrients. You'll find vendors selling green coconuts along the beaches, street corners, and even near hospitals for its curative properties—it helps to restore energy to weakened bodies recovering from illness. In the United States, young coconuts are occasionally sold in specialty produce markets and in large Asian markets. They are available in two forms: one has a spongy, cream-colored husk, sculpted to a point on top and with a flat bottom; the other is green, and you'll need a professional to cut it, since it is very hard. Green coconuts are very different in appearance from the more widely available hard, brown coconuts, and they spoil easily when not refrigerated. You may find young coconut water packaged in pouches, sold in the frozen foods section of large Asian food markets. It comes in cans, too, but the canned variety is sweetened with sugar and not as fresh tasting. Most green coconuts contain a little less than a cup of water.

MAKES ABOUT 4 CUPS, SERVES 3 TO 4

Coconut water from 4 green coconuts (see headnote)

2 tablespoons honey

1/4 cup loosely packed fresh mint leaves, plus additional for garnish

3 tablespoons freshly squeezed lime juice

Lime or lemon slices, for garnish

1. In a blender, combine the coconut water, honey, mint, and lime juice and whirl until the honey is dissolved and the mint is minced. Cover and refrigerate for at least 2 but no more than 4 hours.

2. Taste and add more honey if you prefer. Whirl briefly until combined and pour into old-fashioned mugs or glasses. Float a slice of lime or lemon on top, decorate with mint leaves, and serve. For a rustic look, serve in empty green coconut shells.

AUTHENTIC INDIAN TEA | Chai

Of all traditional beverages, warm tea *(garam chai)* is the finest, for there's nothing that says "India" so well as a hot, sweet, spicy cup of milk tea. This is the real *chai*, and every morning I start my day with this comforting, sizzling, gingery tea. Brands like Indian Brooke Bond or Tea India (available in Indian markets) make a full-bodied, bright reddish-brown brew with a lovely malty taste. Darjeeling tea, from the foothills of the Himalayan mountains, makes a paler brew; the mountain altitude and gentle misting rains produce a unique, full-bodied, but light flavor with a subtly lingering aroma reminiscent of sweet muscatel wine and black currant. In the summer, I occasionally make Darjeeling tea without milk, serving it chilled over ice. Sliced lemon is good, but milk would bury its unique qualities. For a rich taste, use equal parts Assam and Darjeeling tea. If you're using tea bags, you may have to add an extra bag for a stronger brew, according to your preference.

MAKES 4 CUPS

2 cups water

6 teaspoons raw sugar, or regular granulated sugar

2 cups whole or low-fat (2%) milk

1/2-inch piece fresh ginger, crushed

4 heaping teaspoons leaf tea, such as Indian Brooke Bond, Tea India, Assam, or orange pekoe, or 4 or 5 Lipton tea bags

1. Heat the water in a medium saucepan over medium-high heat until very hot but not boiling. Add the sugar. Heat the milk in another saucepan over medium heat until very hot, but not boiling. Set aside.

2. Add the ginger to the hot water and bring to a boil. Add the leaf tea or bags and boil for 30 seconds. Add the hot milk, bring to a boil again, reduce the heat, and simmer for 2 minutes. Turn off the heat, cover, and let the *chai* steep for 3 to 4 minutes. Strain the tea into a heated teapot or individual cups and serve.

SPICED TEA MIX | Chai Masala

This spice blend is the perfect complement to either hot or cold orange pekoe or Assam tea. For iced tea, add a little crushed dried basil along with this *masala*, for a more fragrant herbal aroma. Use 1/2 teaspoon (for 1 cup) of this blend when you make your next cup of *chai* (page 429).

MAKES A SCANT 1/3 CUP

2 tablespoons green cardamom pods

1 teaspoon fennel seeds

12 whole cloves

1 tablespoon ground ginger

2 teaspoons ground cinnamon

1. In a small skillet over medium heat, toast the cardamom pods, stirring frequently, until the pods are plump and start to color in places (some pods may even crack open), about 4 minutes. Let cool slightly.

2. Transfer the cardamom pods to a coffee mill and grind to a fine powder. Transfer to a small bowl. Add the fennel seeds and cloves to the coffee mill and grind to a fine powder. Add the ginger and cinnamon and whirl for a few seconds until well mixed. Transfer to the bowl and mix thoroughly with the cardamom.

3. Let cool completely. Pour into an airtight glass jar, cover, and store at room temperature, away from direct light, for up to 2 months, or in the refrigerator for up to 6 months.

MYSORE COFFEE | Kaape

Southern Indians brew strong filtered coffee, and to give it a light, airy froth, they pour it back and forth between pots several times before serving. To get a similar effect, hold the mug of coffee high over a small bowl and pour the coffee several times. In southern India, coffee beans are sold freshly roasted. Nescafe crystals or any French roasted beans (ground for espresso) will yield robust brew.

2 cups water

6 teaspoons raw sugar, or regular granulated
    sugar

2 cups low-fat (2%) milk, or whole milk for a
    creamier texture

4 teaspoons Nescafe crystals

Heat the water in a medium saucepan over medium-high heat. Add the sugar and stir.
Heat the milk in another saucepan over medium heat until very hot. (If you wish, use a
hand mixer to beat the milk until foamy, 2 to 3 minutes.) Set aside. Bring the water to a
boil, add the milk, and boil for 30 seconds. Turn off the heat, add the coffee crystals, and
stir. Cover and let steep for 2 to 3 minutes before serving in individual mugs or cups.

PINEAPPLE SMOOTHIE | Ananas Sharbat

The arrival of Islam in the second millennium AD brought new types of sweet *sharbats* to India,
often colored and flavored with essences. The rich and nutty flavors of this simple and quick-
to-make refresher will likely get you hooked. Serve this smoothie as a prelude to an elegant dinner. It is also perfect for sipping on the porch on a warm spring or summer day.

MAKES ABOUT 5 CUPS, SERVES 4 TO 6

1/4 to 1/2 cup shelled, roasted salted or unsalted
    pistachios

4 cups pineapple juice

1 cup buttermilk

1/4 cup sour cream

1/4 cup sugar

Add the pistachios to a blender and process until finely powdered. Add the pineapple
juice, buttermilk, sour cream, and sugar and whirl until thoroughly mixed and frothy. Pour
into tall 10- to 12-ounce glasses and serve.

PERSIMMON LASSI | Persimmon Thandai

Twenty years ago, when I was leaving India to come to the United States, my mother advised me to adapt and make use of local ingredients. My experiments with the unknown have continued over the years. When I saw my first display of brilliant orange persimmons, I was immediately taken. The flagrant color suggested the tropical markets familiar to me. When I purchased the fruit for the first time, the grocer warned me to wait until it was soft; but it got so mushy that I got nervous when I came across its jellylike texture. Its spiced sweetness, however, tasted almost like honey. I was hooked, and now I savor them by the bagful.

Two types are commonly seen in markets during the fall. The nonastringent kind, the fuyu persimmon, resembles a bright orange, medium-sized tomato. When ripe, it is firm and has a red-orange skin and flesh, with a lovely flavor and texture reminiscent of cinnamon-scented apricots. The hachiya persimmon is large and round, with orange-red skin and a slightly elongated, pointed base. The fruit is quite soft when completely ripe and has a smooth, creamy texture and a tangy-sweet flavor.

MAKES ABOUT 4 CUPS, SERVES 4

2 large fuyu or other persimmons, pitted

2 cups buttermilk

1/2 cup fresh orange juice

1/2 cup water

4 teaspoons sugar, or to taste

1 cup crushed ice

Freshly grated nutmeg

I do not peel the persimmons, I leave the skin for texture, you may peel them if you wish. In a blender, combine the persimmons, buttermilk, orange juice, water, and sugar. Whirl until the sugar is dissolved. Divide ice among four stemmed glasses and pour in the *lassi*. Serve with a sprinkling of nutmeg.

MIXED-FRUIT INDIAN SUMMER COOLER | Phal Thandai

I enjoy the aromas, subtle flavors, and sensuality of tropical fruits. In this cooler, I like to add nuts for texture. This makes a very nutritious drink for after games or workouts. Buttermilk adds flavor; you may substitute soy milk, if you prefer, or leave it out and make a light all-fruit drink.

MAKES 5 CUPS, SERVES 3 TO 4

5 to 6 whole almonds

3 cups diced cantaloupe

2 cups diced ripe mango

1/2 cup pineapple chunks

1 1/2 cups buttermilk

1/2 cup sparkling or regular water

2 to 3 tablespoons honey

1/2-inch piece fresh ginger

6 standard ice cubes (optional)

Process the almonds in a blender until finely powdered. Add the cantaloupe, mango, pineapple, buttermilk, water, honey, and ginger and whirl until the mixture is frothy. Serve in tall slender glasses, with ice, if desired.

MAKE AHEAD Blend as directed, transfer to a pitcher (without the ice), and refrigerate for up to 4 hours. Before serving, whirl in a blender with ice.

INDIAN BREATH MINTS

Mukhashudhi

My grandmother had a miniature box shaped like a peacock. She always kept roasted fennel seeds, *ajwain* seeds, a few green cardamom pods, and whole cloves in the tiny compartments of the box. She tucked the box neatly at one end of her sari and took it everywhere she went. As a child, I always loved to open the box and simply look inside. She would persuade me to chew some of the seeds. Now I am the beneficiary of the lovely box. My mother kept a similar box in her purse, which contained a toasted spice mix. Now I always carry a small container of cardamom and fennel seeds in my purse. I shared this with my students, and one of them now takes cardamom pods to work every day and chews on the seeds after meals.

Raw or toasted fennel seeds and the seeds of green cardamom pods are chewed after meals in India to freshen breath and aid digestion. In Indian homes, stimulants or breath mints are prepared along with the meal and served right after dessert. The offering might be a simple serving of dry-roasted, salted, or candied fennel seeds or an elaborate preparation—fennel seeds mixed with other spices, sesame seeds, and flaked coconut and flavored with saffron. Shredded betel nut, also known as *supari*, contains enzymes that help in digestion and may be added to the mix as well.

These days you can also buy these mixtures prepackaged in Indian markets. Nevertheless, I'd like to share with you some of the quick and simple recipes that my mother made so often.

My grandmother's valuable tip: fresh mint leaves chewed daily serve as an effective oral antiseptic.

ROASTED FENNEL SEED STIMULANT | Hurdid Badishep

On your way out of most Indian restaurants you'll see a bowl of salted or candied fennel seeds, sometimes mixed with shredded coconut. This refresher is served after meals to aid digestion, because fennel seeds are believed to relieve hunger, stimulate the organs of digestion, disinfect the breath, and strengthen the teeth. You must try this simple recipe and keep it handy, much as you would chewing gum. In this recipe, turmeric is added to heighten the color of the fennel seeds. Serve half a teaspoon or more to each guest to chew on after meals.

MAKES ¹/₂ CUP

¹/₂ cup fennel seeds, picked through and cleaned
    of debris

1 teaspoon sea salt, or kosher salt

¹/₄ teaspoon turmeric

1 tablespoon water

1. Place the fennel seeds on a dinner plate or cookie sheet. Sprinkle with the salt and turmeric and mix well. Sprinkle with the water and mix, stirring until all of the seeds are well moistened with water. Spread in single layer and allow the seeds to air dry for 1 to 2 hours.

2. In a heavy medium skillet over medium heat, roast the seeds, stirring regularly, until toasty smelling, dry, and crisp, about 12 minutes. The seeds will take on a beautiful tinge of yellow from the turmeric at this point. Turn off the heat and cool thoroughly. Transfer to an airtight container, cover, and store for up to 2 months.

SESAME-AJWAIN STIMULANT WITH LIME JUICE | Til-Owa Supari

Fennel seeds are India's breath mints; their clean licorice taste freshens the breath. Here, I have also added *ajwain* seeds, which help with digestion, and sesame, which adds color and crunch to the mix. Spiked with fresh lime juice, this stimulant is my favorite—I always keep a jar of it at home to offer to guests after meals.

MAKES A HEAPING 1/2 CUP

1/4 cup fennel seeds, picked through and cleaned
of debris

1/4 cup white sesame seeds

2 tablespoons *ajwain* seeds (page 20)

1 teaspoon sea salt, or kosher salt

1/4 teaspoon turmeric

1 tablespoon water

1 tablespoon freshly squeezed lime juice

1. On a dinner plate or cookie sheet, combine the fennel seeds, sesame seeds, and *ajwain* seeds. Sprinkle with the salt and turmeric and mix well. Sprinkle with the water and lime juice and mix, stirring, until all of the seeds are well moistened. Spread the seeds in a single layer and allow them to air-dry for 1 to 2 hours.

2. In a heavy medium skillet over medium heat, roast the seeds, stirring regularly, until toasty smelling, dry, and crisp, about 15 minutes. The seeds will take on a beautiful tinge of yellow from the turmeric at this point. Turn off the heat and cool thoroughly. Transfer to an airtight container, cover, and store for up to 2 months.

SOURCES

Indian markets can seem intimidating at first; don't be afraid to ask the grocers for help. Spices and legumes play a prominent part in Indian cuisine, and at a good market they will be bountiful, fresh, and inexpensive. Many Indian markets carry a huge assortment of well-priced basmati rice, chutneys, pickles, *pappadams,* snacks, tamarind concentrate, canned Alphonso mango pulp (Ratna and several other brands), and nuts. Most offer dry goods, a selection of fresh produce, and refrigerated and frozen foods such as *samosa* and vegetarian as well as nonvegetarian entrees. On weekends you might find desserts, freshly baked *samosa,* and other snacks. Fresh *kari* leaves are available at many Indian markets as well.

For a list of Indian markets in your state or city, visit www.littleindia.us/search/grocery.html. Two good online sources for Indian ingredients are Namaste (www.namaste.com or (866) 438-4642) and Indian Foods Company (www.indianfoodsco.com).

Bombay Spice House
1036 University Avenue
Berkeley, CA 94702
(510) 845-5200
Alphonso mango pulp, *desi ghee,* tea, *sev,* flours, legumes, fresh *kari* leaves, saffron

Bombay Bazaar
548 Valencia Street
San Francisco, CA 94110
(415) 621-1717
Alphonso mango pulp, *desi ghee, poha, sooji,* varieties of *pappadam,* spice blends, pickles, chutneys, tea, various sev, hot-mix, Kwality and Real Ice Creams (saffron, pistachios, mango, litchi), flours, legumes, pressure cookers, *kadais, tavas*

Certified Foods, Inc.
1055 Montague Avenue
San Leandro, CA 94577
(510) 483-1177
http://www.certifiedfoods.com
Chapati flour, chick pea flour *(besan),* rice flour

Coconut Hill
554 South Murphy Avenue
Sunnyvale, CA 94086
(408) 738-8837
Specialize in products from Kerala such as *kodampuli,* frozen fish, *appam* pans, *puttu* steamer

Cosmos Indian Store
2910 Southwest Oakley, Suite B
Topeka, KA 66614
(785) 228-3900
(785) 228-3902
http://www.cosmosindianstore.com
Fresh Indian vegetables, spices, goat
   meat, fish

Everest Groceries
208 New Churchman's Road
New Castle, DE 19720
(302) 323-1080
Spices, dry goods

Foods of India
21 Lexington Avenue
New York, NY 10016
(212) 683-4419
Atta (chapati flour), Alphonso mango pulp,
   tea, *desi ghee*, legumes, fresh *kari* leaves

Hearth Kitchen Company
644 Danbury Road
Wilton, CT 06897
(800) 383-7818
http://www.hearthkitchen.com
HearthKit brick oven

India Bazaar
933 East University Drive
Tempe, AZ 85281
(480) 784-4442
Spices, snacks, legumes

Indian Groceries
105 Select Street
Scarborough, ON M1V 4A8
(416) 292-9444
Flours, legumes, spices

Indian Groceries & Spices
10633 West North Avenue
Milwaukee, WI 53226
(414) 771-3535
Spices, rice, flours

Kundan Foods
225 West 134th Street
Los Angeles, CA 90061
(888) 950-3375
http://www.qualityspices.com
Poha, churmura, sooji, legumes, spices,
   basmati rice, flours

Kalustyan's
123 Lexington Avenue
New York, NY 10016
(800) 352-3451
http://www.kalustyans.com
Flours, oils, *desi ghee*, nuts, *poha, churmura, sooji*, legumes, spices, fresh *kari*
   leaves, spices, white poppy seeds

Krishan Grocery
9132 Rothbury Drive, Goshen Plaza
Gaithersburg, MD 20879
(301) 208-3579
Spices, legumes, basmati rice, flours

Maharishi Ayurveda Products
International, Inc.
1068 Elkton Drive
Colorado Springs, CO 80907
(800) 810-1118
good quality *desi ghee*, rose petal conserve, mango chutney, ginger preserve, teas

Morton & Bassett Spices
32 Pamaron Way
Novato, CA 94949
(415) 883-8530
http://www.mortonbassett.com
Whole spices, organic spices

Orchard Nursery and Florist
4010 Mount Diablo Boulevard
Lafayette, CA 94549
(925) 284-4474
http://www.orchardnursery.com
Curry *(kari)* leaf plants

Penzeys Spices
19300 West Janacek Court
P. O. Box 924
Brookfield, WI 53008
(800) 741-7787
http://www.penzeys.com
Spices, including black and green cardamom, black and regular cumin,
white poppy seeds

Santos Spice Product
1188 Montague Street
San Leandro, CA 94577
(510) 357-0277
Alphonso mango pulp, spices, white
poppy seeds, *churmura, poha, sooji,*
varieties of *pappadam*, tea, *sev,* hot
mix, oils and *desi ghee,* Kwality and
Real Ice Creams (saffron, pistachios,
mango, litchi), flours, legumes, pressure cookers, *kadais, tavas*

Shiva Groceries
6560 Dixie Highway
Fairfield, OH 45014
(513) 874-1221
Spices, legumes, frozen *naan*

Taj Mahal Grocery
4936 East Busch Boulevard
Temple Terrace, FL 33617
(813) 987-9755
Legumes, spices

Vik Distributors
1321 7th Street
Berkeley, CA 94710
(510) 558-8515
(510) 644-4412
Tandoors (clay and stainless steel), pots
and pans, flours, fresh *kari* leaves,
poha, sooji, and *chaat* made fresh
daily, Indian beers and wines

INDEX

aalu gedde dosa, 163
aalu gedde palya, 236–237
aalu gedde rassa, 254–255
aam, described, 52–53
aam bhareli murg, 345–346
aam chatni, 185
aam ice cream, 405–406
aam lassi, 425
aam raita, 206
aam rasa, 364–365
aamtekai chatni, 188
adrak. See ginger
ajwain, described, 20
ajwaini machchi, 357–358
ajwain-marinated whole tandoori fish, 357–358
allspice, described, 19
almond-laced saffron *naan,* 86
almonds
    lamb maharaja with caramelized onion and, fragrant, 350–351
    pasilla chilis stuffed with, 264–265
aloo paratha, 78–79
aloo raita, 210–211
alu bukhara kofte, 277
amchur. See mango powder
amotik, 318–319
ananas sharbat, 431
ananas upinkai, 196
anardana. See pomegranate seed
anasphal/badiyan. See star anise
aniseed, described, 19–20
appetizers. *See* starters
apple relish, with jaggery, *Paschim* zesty, 181
apricots
    chicken breast stuffed with cranberries and, 278–279
    figs and, in delicate nutty sauce, 256–257
    pear-apricot chutney with almonds, 187
    sauce, lamb chops in, 285
    yogurt gravy with mint and, Moghul lamb *biryani,* 118
arati kai koora, 242

Arborio rice, risotto with *dal,* spicy Udupi-style, 110–112
arhar dal/toovar dal/toor dal (yellow lentils), described, 44
aromatic(s), 10–12
    ginger-garlic paste, 11
    onion, 10
    tomato puree, 11–12
aromatic *garam masala,* recipe, 36–37
aromatic tomato rice, 100–101
asafetida, described, 20–21
astringent (nippy) taste, sources of, 7
atta (*chapati* flour), described, 45, 60
authentic Indian tea, 429
avalaki/poha/pohe, 167–168
ayala porichathu/tareli tava machchi, 326–327

badam-jodambe kari, 256–257
baingan bharata, 238–239
baked *balushahi,* 420
baked fish, Kashmir *dum*-style, 322
balance
    curry preparation, 5–6
    menu composition, 14–15
    nutrition, 6–7
balushahi, baked, 420
banana
    fudge halvah with, 419
    peach chutney with, 186
    tamarind chutney with, 182
banana leaf
    fish steamed in, Mumbai, 330–331
    scallops roasted in, Malabar, 314–315
basil, described, 21
basmati rice, 91–125
    basic recipe, 96
    biryani, 114–125
        cooking tips for, 114–115
        lamb, Moghul, 116–118
        mahimahi, 120
        scallop, spiked with coconut, 118–119
        vegetable, Lucknow mixed *biryani,* 121–123
    chutney rice, 178

coconut rice with fresh green chilis, 107
cooking methods, 95
cooking tips for, 94–95
culture and, 91–93
cumin-scented rice, 99
fresh fenugreek rice, 97
fresh green lentils with, 105–106
fresh mint rice, 97
lemon rice, 108
pilaf with vegetables, spicy, 112–113
rice preparation, 93–94
shrimp rice, Konkan, 102–103
sweet rice, 106
tamarind rice, 109
tomato rice, aromatic, 100–101
vegetable pilaf with cashews, fragrant mixed, 98–99
yogurt rice, 103–104
batter, for *idli* and *dosa,* 155
bay leaf, described, 21
beans. *See also* legumes
    green beans *poriyal,* 240
    toasty Mysore cream of wheat with carrots and, 165–166
beet(s)
    kachumber, with orange, red and golden, 216
    poori, 82
    pudding, 417
beet *ki kheer,* 417
belan (rolling pin), described, 56
bele rasam, 370
bele saaru, 383
bell pepper
    glazed skillet *paneer* with mushroom and, 227
    poriyal, 241
    yellow, *poori,* 82
bellulli pachadi, 211
Benal fish, seared, in tangy mustard sauce, 325–326
Bengal dainty cheese cakes in cream sauce, 410–411
besan (chickpea flour), described, 45–46
besan laddu, 422

beverages, 423–433
   buttermilk *lassi,* rose-accented
      sweet, 426
   coffee, Mysore, 430–431
   described, 423–424
   green coconut - water cooler,
      428–429
   mango *lassi,* 425
   persimmon *lassi,* 432
   pineapple smoothie, 431
   salty *lassi* with fresh mint, 426–427
   spicy *lassi* with oil seasoning, 427
   summer cooler, mixed-fruit, 433
   tea
      authentic Indian, authentic,
        429
      spiced mix, 430
bhatura
   described, 59
   recipe, 82–83
bhelpuri, 129
bhendi kurkure/tali hui bhindi, 147
bhoona, curry preparation, 4–5
biryani, 114–125
   chicken *biryani* with wild rice,
      124–125
   cooking tips for, 114–115
   lamb, Moghul, 116–118
   mahimahi, 120
   scallop, spiked with coconut,
      118–119
   vegetable, Lucknow mixed *biryani,*
      121–123
bitter melon, home-style, 250
bitter taste, sources of, 7
black pepper, brussels sprouts stir-fry
      with sesame, peppery,
      234
black salt, described, 54
blenders, 153–154
boatman's crab curry, 311
Bombay (Mumbai), seafood, 302
boondi raita, Punjab, 214
boti kabab/reshmi mamsa, 352–353
breads, 57–90
   buttermilk balloon bread, street-
      style, 82–83
   flatbreads, 60–79
      cardamom-scented sweet *dal-*
        stuffed flatbread, 72–73
      cornmeal flatbread, rustic
        Punjab, 70–71
      Kashmir *roti,* 68–69
      multigrain with spinach, 66–67

paratha
   flaky cilantro-laced, 76–77
   flaky cumin-scented, 74–75
   potato-stuffed savory, 78–79
   tips for, 60–62
   whole-wheat, 63–65
flour, 60
naan, 84–90
   master recipe, 84–85
   rose-flavored with silver leaf,
      89–90
   sourdough starter, 87–88
   variations, 85–86
puffy breads, 80–82
types of, 58–59
breakfast. *See also* casual fare
   with beaten rice, nutritious
      Mumbai, 167–168
   described, 154
breath mints, 435–437
   roasted fennel seed stimulant, 436
   sesame-*ajwain* stimulant with lime
      juice, 437
broccoli
   cauliflower and, Mangalore curry,
      251
   cauliflower *sambar,* 392
   tandoori, cauliflower and, 361
brown lentils (*saabat masoor*),
      described, 44
brussels sprouts, stir-fry with sesame,
      peppery, 234
butter chicken, 274–275
butter (clarified). *See also* oil
   curry preparation, 3, 4
   described, 46–47
   preparation of, 47–48
buttermilk
   balloon bread, street-style, 82–83
   kahdi soup with *kari* leaves, 373
   lassi, rose-accented sweet, 426

cabbage *kachumber,* with peas, 218
cabbage rolls, stuffed with *uppuma,*
      166
cakey balls, in rose-scented warm
      syrup, 412–413
calamari, hot-sour Goa, 318–319
calamari, lobster and, bathed in aro-
      matics, Cochin, 317–318
Calcutta (Kolkata), seafood, 305
candy balls, toasted chickpea flour,
      422

caramelized onion
   lamb maharaja with caramelized
      onion and, fragrant,
      350–351
   pearl onion Mysore *sambar,*
      390–391
caraway, described, 21
carbohydrates, balance in, 6–7
cardamom, described, 21–22
cardamom-scented fudge confection,
      405
cardamom-scented sweet *dal*-stuffed
      flatbread, 72–73
carrot
   raita, with toasted walnuts, 208–209
   toasty Mysore cream of wheat with
      beans and, 165–166
   tomato-carrot chutney, ruby-red, 180
cashew, *paneer* steaks honey sauce and,
      228
cashew-lime sweet pickle, 195
casual fare, 153–169
   breakfast with beaten rice, nutri-
      tious Mumbai, 167–168
   cream of wheat with carrots and
      beans, toasty Mysore,
      165–166
   crepes
      easy potato, 163
      quick semolina, 162
      savory mixed-flour, 164
   idli cakes
      steamed, 156–157
      steamed cream-of-wheat,
        158–159
   pancakes, pineapple-speckled
      crusty, 161
   pearl tapioca cakes, 169
   pearl tapioca pilaf, classic, 168–169
   rice crepes, paper-thin crispy,
      159–160
catfish, coastal Kerala, with tomatoes,
      321–322
cauliflower
   broccoli and, Mangalore curry, 251
   broccoli *sambar,* 392
   ghassi, 251
   tandoori, broccoli and, 361
celery root *kachumber,* with fresh dill,
      217
chaat, 127–140
   chutney sauce
      hot green, 130–131
      sweet, 130

dumplings bathed in savory yogurt sauce, 136–137
Gujarat stuffed pastry with savory topping, 138–140
mango-cucumber, quick, for steamed fish, 332
mung dal, savory, 139–140
papaya-kiwi with pistachios, 140
papdi chaat, 135
poori
　crispy puffy, 131–132
　filled with zesty tamarind sauce, 132–133
poori canapé
　crowned with yogurt topping, classic, 135
　with savory topping, classic, 134
roadside combo with chutney garnishes, 129
chaat masala, recipe, 41–42
chai, 429
chai masala, 430
chakra pongal, 106
chana dal (split peas), described, 42–43
channa, paneer, 222
channa masala/pindi chole, 395–396
chapati, 60–65
　described, 45, 58, 60
　tips for, 60–62
　whole-wheat flatbreads, 63–65
chapati pasta, *dal* with spinach and, 397–398
chawal ka atta (rice flour), described, 46
cheese, potato-chutney-cheese bake, 178. *See also paneer*
cheese cakes, in cream sauce, Bengal dainty, 410–411
Chettinad corn simmered with tangy tamarind, 247–248
chicken, 267–284. *See also* duck; poultry
　biryani with wild rice, 124–125
　breasts in *korma* sauce, 270–271
　breast stuffed with apricots and cranberries, 278–279
　butter sauce, 274–275
　with *khada masala,* pan-fried *paneer* and, 224
　kofta curry in ruby-red grapefruit juice, Kandahar, 276–277
　Mangalore, with sweet, toasty garlic, 282–283
　pan-roasted cilantro-mint marinated, 284
　stew with summer vegetables, 280

tandoori, 340–341
　chicken *tikka, kandahari,* 349
　cuts for, 337
　seared *tikka,* 344–345
　spinach-crusted, 342–343
tikka masala, 272–274, 345
vegetarianism, 267–268
xacuti sauce, Goa, 281–282
chicken *mulligatawny,* with mixed vegetables, 368
chickpea(s)
　described, 43
　green mango *kachumber* and, warm, 215
　simmered in tomato-ginger sauce, 395–396
chickpea flour
　described, 45–46
　toasted, candy balls, 422
chili(s)
　described, 22–24
　eggplant with masala, chili- and garlic-stuffed roasted, 238–239
　green, tips on, 12
　pasilla chilis, almond-stuffed, 264–265
chili-lime pickles, 194
chitranaam, 108
chivda, 151
chole (chickpeas/garbanzo beans), described, 43
chundo, 197
chutney, 171–191. *See also* pickles
　apple relish with jaggery, Paschim zesty, 181
　banana and peach chutney, 186
　chutney powder
　　dal-rice, 191
　　pecan-peanut, 190
　cilantro-lemony green garlic, 175
　cilantro-mint-onion chutney/dip, fresh, 177–178
　cilantro with coconut, fresh, 175
　cilantro with peanuts, fresh, 174–175
　coconut chutney with zesty oil seasoning, 179
　cranberry-tangerine chutney, hot and sweet, 189
　described, 172–173
　garnishes, roadside combo with, 129
　green tomato-sesame chutney, 183–184

green tomato-tomatillo chutney, 184
　ingredients for, 174
　kumquat chutney with figs, spicy-sweet, 188
　mango chutney with pecans, sweet spiced, 185
　mint chutney with garlic, fresh, 176–177
　mortar and pestle preparation, 176
　pear-apricot chutney with almonds, 187
　potato-chutney-cheese bake, 178
　tamarind chutney with banana, 182
　tamarind-cilantro-mint chutney, fresh, 178
　tomato-carrot chutney, ruby-red, 180
　zucchini chutney with fresh dill, 184
chutney powder
　dal-rice, 191
　pecan-peanut, 190
chutney rice, 178
chutney sauce
　hot green, 130–131
　sweet, 130
cilantro
　chicken, pan-roasted cilantro-mint marinated, 284
　curry preparation, 6
　described, 24
　tips on, 12
cilantro chutney
　with coconut, 175
　lemony green garlic, 175
　with peanuts, 174–175
cilantro-garlicky *naan,* 86
cilantro-laced *paratha,* 76–77
cilantro-mint-onion chutney, fresh, 177–178
cilantro-mint-tamarind chutney, 178
cinnamon, described, 24–25
citrus-curry sauce, mango and kumquat with, Queen's, 248–249
clams, fragrant steamed Goa, 313–314
clarified butter
　curry preparation, 3, 4
　described, 46–47
　preparation of, 47–48
classic *poori* canapé
　crowned with yogurt topping, 135
　with savory topping, 134
classic pork *vindaloo,* 298–299

classic Pune-style fragrant stew, 393

clove, described, 25

coastal Kerala catfish with tomatoes, 321–322

Cochin lobster and calamari bathed in aromatics, 317–318

cocktail *samosa*, 149

coconut
  cracking and grating of, 307
  described, 305–306
  fresh cilantro chutney with, 175
  green coconut - water cooler, 428–429
  scallop *biryani* spiked with, 118–119
  tips on, 12

coconut chutney, with zesty oil seasoning, 179

coconut milk
  curry preparation, 5
  recipe for, 308
  salmon, Dakshin fenugreek-marinated, braised in, 319–320

coconut rice with fresh green chilis, 107

coconut sauce, Goa fish in fragrant, 328–329

cocum, described, 50–51

codwa pandi kari, 297

coffee, Mysore, 430–431

color, curry preparation, 6

cookies, full moon, 421

cookware, 56

cooler, mixed-fruit summer cooler, 433

Coorg-style pork stew, 297

coriander leaves, described, 24

coriander seed, described, 25–26

corn, simmered with tangy tamarind, Chettinad, 247–248

Cornish game hen, stuffed with mango tandoori, 345–346

cornmeal flatbread, rustic Punjab, 70–71

corn-zucchini *raita*, 209

crab curry
  boatman's, 311
  Konkan, 309–310

cranberry
  chicken breast stuffed with apricots and, 278–279
  pineapple, pickled, cranberry-studded, 196

cranberry bean, fresh, and purple potato stew, 394–395

cranberry-tangerine chutney, hot and sweet, 189

cream, curry preparation, 5

creamed kidney beans and lentils, 385–386

cream of wheat
  with carrots and beans, toasty Mysore, 165–166
  halvah, toasted, with orange juice, 418–419
  idli cakes, steamed, 158–159

cream sauce, cheese cakes in, Bengal dainty, 410–411

creamy rice pudding, 414

crepes
  easy potato, 163
  quick semolina, 162
  savory mixed-flour, 164

crisp okra with *chaat masala*, 147

crispy *pakora*, 144–146

crispy puffy *poori*, 131–132
  filled with zesty tamarind sauce, 132–133

crispy rice crepes, paper-thin, 159–160

cucumber, *raita* with radish, 207

cucumber *kachumber*, with fresh dill, 217

cucumber-mango *chaat*, quick, for steamed fish, 332

cumin, curry preparation, 3

cumin-scented *paratha*, 74–75

cumin-scented rice, 99

cumin seed, described, 26

curry
  defined, 2
  preparation of, 3–6
  varieties of, 2

curry leaf. *See kari* (curry) leaf

curry powder, hot and fragrant, recipe, 35

daanyacha koot (peanuts, crushed and roasted), described, 53

dahi, 204–205

dahi bhaat/masaru anna, 103–104

dahi bhalla/dahi wada, 136–137

dahi ka channa, 205

Dakshin fenugreek-marinated salmon braised in coconut milk, 319–320

Dakshini meen kari, 319–320

dal, 2. *See also* legumes
  term of, 377

dalchini. See cinnamon

dal dhokli, 397–398

dali ambat, 394–395

dal-rice chutney powder, 191

dal soup, soothing, 367

dal with *chapati* pasta and spinach, 397–398

delicate mango sauce crowned with *paneer*, 222–223

denji kari, 311

desi ghee (clarified butter). *See also* oil
  curry preparation, 3, 4
  described, 46–47
  preparation of, 47–48

desserts, 403–422
  banana fudge halvah, 419
  beet pudding, 417
  cakey balls in rose-scented warm syrup, 412–413
  candy balls, toasted chickpea flour, 422
  cheese cakes in cream sauce, Bengal dainty, 410–411
  cookies, full moon, 421
  cream-of-wheat halvah, toasted, with orange juice, 418–419
  doughnuts, Indian-style baked flaky, 420
  fudge confection, cardamom-scented, 405
  ice cream
    mango *kulfi*, 407–408
    pistachio, 407–408
  khoa (mawa), 404–405
  mousse, mango, 405–406
  pistachio and *chayote* pudding, velvety, 416
  rice pudding, creamy, 414
  vermicelli pudding with fresh berries, 415
  yogurt cheese, fluffy, 408–409

dhan dar ne colmi no patio, 312–313

dhansak, 387–388

dhokla bread, steamed instant, 150

dill (fresh)
  celery root *kachumber* with, 217
  zucchini chutney with, 184

dining, 12–15
  dining tables, 13
  with fingers, 12–13
  menu composition, 14–15
  place setting, 13–14

dining tables, dining, 13

doi maach, 332–333
dosa
    batter for, 155
    easy potato crepes, 163
    paper-thin crispy rice crepes, 159–160
    quick semolina crepes, 162
doughnuts, Indian-style baked flaky, 420
drinks. *See* beverages
duck, 294–296. *See also* chicken; poultry
    breast with crusty turnip and rutabaga, Kashmir, 294–295
    legs with subtle spinach sauce, 295–296
dumplings, bathed in savory yogurt sauce, 136–137

easy potato crepes, 163
eggplant
    with masala, chili- and garlic-stuffed roasted, 238–239
    peanut-stuffed old-fashioned, 262
    zucchini and, with pecans, skillet-seared zesty, 233
eggs, 267, 299–300
    skillet egg masala, 299–300
elaichi. See cardamom
eratchi ularthiyathu, 291
erullihu rasavangi, 384–385
essence, described, 51

fats, balance in, 6
fennel-scented Kashmir lamb, 286–287
fennel seed
    breath mint, roasted, 436
    described, 26
fenugreek leaf, described, 27
fenugreek rice, fresh, 97
fenugreek seed, described, 27
figs, apricots and, in delicate nutty sauce, 256–257
fingers, dining with, 12–13
fish. *See also* shellfish
    baked, Kashmir *dum*-style, 322
    Bengal fish, seared, in tangy mustard sauce, 325–326
    catfish, coastal Kerala, with tomatoes, 321–322
    fried fragrant, 326–327

Goa, in fragrant coconut sauce, 328–329
    halibut, Malvan, simmered in green sauce, 322–323
    kingfish in spinach gravy, 226
    mahimahi *biryani,* 120
    mahimahi fillets with shallots, tangy, 324
    molee, 321–322
    pan-roasted Bengal, with raisins, 332–333
    salmon, Dakshin fenugreek-marinated, braised in coconut milk, 319–320
    steamed in banana leaves, Mumbai, 330–331
    sturgeon fillet, Kashmir-style, with *kohlrabi,* 329–330
    tandoori
        ajwain-marinated whole, 357–358
        shrimp, jumbo Bengal, 359
        zucchini with, Seekh, 360
flaky cilantro-laced *paratha,* 76–77
flaky cumin-scented *paratha,* 74–75
flatbreads, 60–79
    cardamom-scented sweet *dal*-stuffed flatbread, 72–73
    cornmeal flatbread, rustic Punjab, 70–71
    Kashmir roti, 68–69
    multigrain with spinach, 66–67
    paratha
        flaky cilantro-laced, 76–77
        flaky cumin-scented, 74–75
        potato-stuffed savory, 78–79
    tips for, 60–62
    whole-wheat, 63–65
flatulence, legumes, 380
flavored clarified butter, preparation of, 48
flavors, of India, 6–12
flours, 45–46
    breads, 60
    chapati flour, 45
    chickpea flour, 45–46
    rice flour, 46
fluffy yogurt cheese, 408–409
fragrant *dum*-style lamb with mushrooms, 292–293
fragrant fish fry, 326–327
fragrant lamb maharaja with almonds and caramelized onion, 350–351

fragrant masala powder, tomato rice, aromatic, 101
fragrant mixed vegetable pilaf with cashews, 98–99
fragrant spinach sauce, roasted *paneer* in, 225–226
fragrant steamed Goa clams, 313–314
fresh cilantro chutney
    with coconut, 175
    with mint and onion, 177–178
    with peanuts, 174–175
fresh dill
    celery root *kachumber* with, 217
    zucchini chutney with, 184
fresh fenugreek rice, 97
fresh green chilis, coconut rice with, 107
fresh green lentils with rice, 105–106
fresh masala powder, tamarind rice, 110
fresh mint chutney, with garlic, 176–177
fresh mint rice, 97
fruit and vegetable *navratna korma,* 271
frying, flatbreads, 61
fudge confection, cardamom-scented, 405
full moon cookies, 421

gadhapun, curry preparation, 5
gajar raita, 208–209
game hen, Cornish, stuffed with mango tandoori, 345–346
garam masala
    aromatic, recipe, 36–37
    recipe, 36–37
garbanzo beans/chickpeas *(chole),* described, 43
garlic. *See also* ginger-garlic paste
    chicken, Mangalore, with sweet, toasty garlic, 282–283
    eggplant with masala, chili- and garlic-stuffed roasted, 238–239
    fresh mint chutney with, 176–177
    garlicky *dal* stew, 383
    ginger-garlic paste, 11
    green, lemony cilantro chutney, 175
    squash with, sweet-spiced, 235
garlicky *dal* stew, 383
garlic *naan,* 85
garlic *raita,* 211
garnishes, curry preparation, 6

gedde kootu, 244
geography. *See* regional cuisines
ghirdi, 164
ginger, described, 27–28
ginger-garlic paste
    aromatics, 11
    curry preparation, 4
glazed skillet *paneer,* with mushroom
    and bell pepper, 227
Goa, seafood, 303
Goa chicken *xacuti,* 281–282
Goa fish in fragrant coconut sauce,
    328–329
Goan *pomfret caldeen,* 328–329
goda masala. See Pune-style sesame-
    laced powder *(goda*
    masala)
gogji bathak, 294–295
golden *paneer kofta* in aromatic spinach
    sauce, 258–259
golden yellow beet *poori,* 82
gold leaf, described, 54
gol gappa, 131–132
Grandma's tamarind-laced potato
    curry, 254–255
Grandmother's pumpkin greens and
    lentil stew, 401–402
grapefruit juice, chicken *kofta* curry in,
    Kandahar, 276–277
gravy
    apricot yogurt gravy with mint,
        Moghul lamb *biryani,* 118
    sweet-scented tomato gravy, mixed
        vegetable *biryani,*
        Lucknow, 123
green beans
    poriyal, 240
    yams and, in aromatic velvety
        sauce, 246
green chilis
    described, 23
    fresh, coconut rice with, 107
    tips on, 12
green chutney sauce, hot, 130–131
green coconut - water cooler, 428–429
green garlic, lemony cilantro chutney,
    175
green lentils, fresh, with rice, 105–106
green mango
    beet *kachumber* with orange, red
        and golden, 216
    kachumber, and chickpea, warm,
        215
    relish, spicy-sweet, 197

green papaya, meat tenderizer, 337
greens, mixed, with toasted pecans,
    257–258
green sauce, halibut, Malvan, sim-
    mered in, 322–323
green tomato, with masala, chili- and
    garlic-stuffed roasted,
    239
green tomato-sesame chutney,
    183–184
green tomato-tomatillo chutney, 184
griddle, described, 56
grilling tips, outdoor, 339. *See also* tan-
    doori foods
grinders, 153–154
grinding, of spices, 8–10
ground lamb, sweet-scented
    Hyderabad, 289–290
ground spices, curry preparation, 4, 5
Gujarat stuffed pastry with savory top-
    ping, 138–140
gulab jamun, 412–413
gur (jaggery), described, 51–52. *See also*
    jaggery *(gur)*

haldi. See turmeric
halibut, Malvan, simmered in green
    sauce, 322–323
halvah
    banana fudge, 419
    cream-of-wheat, toasted, with
        orange juice, 418–419
handi gosht khusk purdah, 292–293
hara dhania chatni, 174–175
hara tamatar bharata, 239
hari methi. See fenugreek leaf
heirloom spice blend, my mother's
    (kala masla/kari khar),
    recipe, 39–40
herbs. *See* spices; specific herbs and
    spices
hing. See asafetida
homemade yogurt, 204–205
homemade yogurt cheese, 205
home-style bitter melon, 250
honey sauce, *paneer* steaks cashew
    and, 228
hot and fragrant curry powder *(kari*
    pudi), recipe, 35
hot green chutney sauce, 130–131
hot-sour Goa calamari, 318–319
huli anna powder, Udupi-style risotto,
    spicy, with *dal,* 112

hurdid badishep, 436
Hyderabadi kheema, 289–290

ice cream, pistachio, 407–408
idli, batter for, 155
idli cakes
    steamed, 156–157
    steamed cream-of-wheat, 158–159
imli (tamarind), described, 54–55
imli chatni, 182
Indian breath mints, 435–437
    roasted fennel seed stimulant, 436
    sesame-*ajwain* stimulant with lime
        juice, 437
Indian markets, sources for, 439–442
Indian-style baked flaky doughnuts,
    420
Indian-style spicy tomato soup, 372
Indian tea, authentic, 429
ingredients, Indian market sources for,
    439–442
instant steamed *dhokla* bread, 150

jaggery *(gur)*
    apple relish with, Paschim zesty,
        181
    curry preparation, 6
    described, 51–52
    stews, 379
jaiphal/javitri. See nutmeg/mace
jardaloo ma gosht, 285
jardalu chatni, 187
jasmine rice, tomato rice, aromatic,
    100–101
jeera. See cumin seed
jeera rice, 99
jhinge ka tikka, 359

kaape, 430–431
kababchini. See allspice
kabocha squash, with mung beans
    stew, 400
kachumbers, 215–218. *See also* raitas;
    yogurt
    beet with orange, red and golden,
        216
    cabbage with peas, 218
    celery root with fresh dill, 217
    chickpea and green mango, warm,
        215
    described, 203

kadai, described, 56
kadai ande, 299–300
kadai murg pasandey, 284
kadai paneer, 227
kadhi, 2, 373
kadi patta. See kari (curry) leaf
kaikari ishtew, 280
Kakori, 353
Kakori kebab, 354–355
kala masla/kari khar. See heirloom spice
    blend
kala namak (black salt), described, 54
kali mirch. See peppercorn
kalonji. See nigella seed
kandahari chicken *tikka*, 349
kari (curry) leaf
    buttermilk *kahdi* soup with, 373
    described, 28–29
kari khar. See heirloom spice blend, my
    mother's *(kala
    masla/kari khar)*
kari pudi. See curry powder
karnataka chatni pudi, 191
karonda chatni, 189
Karwar, seafood, 303
Karwar oyster skillet roast, 316
Kashmir, seafood, 302
Kashmir chilis, described, 23–24
Kashmir duck breast with crusty turnip
    and rutabaga,
    294–295
Kashmir *dum*-style baked fish, 322
Kashmir mushrooms braised in tomato
    sauce, 253–254
Kashmir *roti*, 68–69
Kashmir-style sturgeon fillet with
    kohlrabi, 329–330
kele ka halwa, 419
Kerala, seafood, 304
Kerala mussel chowder, 366
Kerala-style aromatic lamb, 291
kesar. See saffron
kesari bhat/sheera, 418–419
khada masala, pan-fried *paneer* and
    chicken with, 224
khamiri naan, 87–88
khara bhat/uppuma, 165–166
khasta kachori, 138–140
khasta paratha, 76–77
kheema naan, 86
kheer/payasam, 414
kheer/semiya payaam, 415
khoa (mawa), 353
    preparation of, 404–405

khobri chatni, 179
khus khus. See poppy seed
kidney beans
    described, 44
    lentils and, creamed, 385–386
kingfish, in spinach gravy, 226
kitchen equipment, 55–56, 153–154,
    336
kiwi-papaya *chaat*, with pistachios, 140
kofta, 2
    mixed vegetable, in cream sauce,
        260–261
    paneer, in aromatic spinach sauce,
        golden, 258–259
kofta curry
    chicken, in ruby-red grapefruit
        juice, Kandahar, 276–277
    cooking techniques, 232
    plum-stuffed, 277
kohlrabi, sturgeon fillet, Kashmir-style,
    with, 329–330
Kolkata (Calcutta), seafood, 305
kolmi bhaat, 102–103
konju koonthal ularthiyathu, 317–318
Konkan crab curry, 309–310
Konkan shrimp rice, 102–103
kootu, cooking techniques, 232
kori ghassi, 282–283
korma, 2
    cooking techniques, 232
    lamb, 288–289
korma sauce, chicken breasts in,
    270–271
kulfi, 407–408
kumbala palya, 235
kumbala soppu, 401–402
kumbala usili, 400
kumquat, mango and, with subtle cit-
    rus-curry sauce,
    Queen's, 248–249
kumquat chutney, with figs, spicy-
    sweet, 188
kurli masala, 309–310
kuzhambu, 388–389

lamb, 285–293
    chops in golden apricot sauce, 285
    dum-style, fragrant, with mush-
        rooms, 292–293
    fennel-scented Kashmir, 286–287
    ground, sweet-scented Hyderabad,
        289–290
    Kerala-style aromatic, 291

korma, 288–289
Moghul *biryani*, 116–118
samosa, fragrant, 148–149
tandoori
    cuts for, 337
    kebabs, Oudh-style, 354–355
    maharaja with almonds and
        caramelized onion, fra-
        grant, 350–351
    rolls with lentils, 356–357
    tikka with saffron sauce,
        352–353
lassi, 426–427
lauki chatni, 184
leeks, pink lentil and *mung dal* stew
    with, 384–385
legumes. *See also* beans; *sambars* and
    stews
    cooking methods, 382
    described, 42–45
        chana dal (split peas), 42–43
        chole (chickpeas/garbanzo
            beans), 43
        masoor dal (pink lentils), 43
        mung dal (yellow split mung
            beans), 43
        pardesi dal (split peas), 43
        rajma (kidney beans), 44
        saabat masoor (brown lentils), 44
        sabaat mung (mung beans), 44
        sime avarekai (lima beans), 44
        toovar dal/toor dal/arhar dal
            (yellow lentils), 44
        urad dal (white split gram
            beans), 44
    flatulence, 380
    purchase, storage, and cooking,
        378–379
    sprouts, 380
    tips on, 379
lemon rice, 108
lemony green garlic-cilantro chutney,
    175
lentil *rasam* soup, with orange juice, 370
lentils
    fresh green, with rice, 105–106
    kidney beans and, creamed,
        385–386
    pink, and *mung dal* stew with leeks,
        384–385
    pumpkin greens and lentil stew,
        Grandmother's, 401–402
    squash boats, filled with, 263–264
    tandoori lamb rolls with, 356–357

lima beans, described, 44
limbekai upinkai, 193–194
lime(s)
    cashew-lime sweet pickle, 195
    chile-lime pickles, 194
    described, 52
    meat tenderizer, 337
    pickled, my mother's heirloom,
        193–194
    tips on, 12
lime juice
    curry preparation, 5
    sesame-*ajwain* stimulant with,
        437
lobster, calamari and, bathed in aro-
        matics, Cochin, 317–318
long-grain white rice, risotto with *dal,*
        spicy Udupi-style,
        110–112
Lucknow, 353, 354
Lucknowi *tehri biryani,* 121–123
lush yogurt rice, 103–104

macadamia nuts, mango-macadamia
        raita, 206
mace. *See* nutmeg/mace
machchi biryani, 120
mahimahi *biryani,* 120
mahimahi fillets, with shallots, tangy,
        324
makhani dal, 385–386
makhmale kofte, 258–259
makkai ki roti, 70–71
makkai-lauki raita, 209
Malabar *karimeen pollichathu,* 314–315
Malabar scallops roasted in banana
        leaf, 314–315
Malvan halibut simmered in green
        sauce, 322–323
Malvan region, seafood, 302
Mangalore, seafood, 304
Mangalore chicken with sweet, toasty
        garlic, 282–283
mango
    beet *kachumber* with orange, red
        and golden, 216
    chaat, with cucumber, quick, for
        steamed fish, 332
    chutney, with pecans, sweet spiced,
        185
    described, 52–53
    kulfi, 407–408
    kumquat and, with subtle citrus-

    curry sauce, Queen's,
        248–249
lassi, 425
mousse, 405–406
raita, with macadamia, 206
relish, green, spicy-sweet, 197
sauce, crowned with *paneer,* deli-
        cate, 222–223
soup, warm, 364–365
tandoori Cornish game hen stuffed
        with, 345–346
mango powder, described, 29
marinades, tandoor, 338
markets, sources for, 439–442
martsawangan korma, 288–289
marvai biryani, 118–119
masala, 2
    chicken *tikka masala,* 272–274
    curry preparation, 3
    eggplant with, chili- and garlic-
        stuffed roasted, 238–239
    green tomato with, chili- and garlic-
        stuffed roasted, 239
    zucchini with, chili- and garlic-
        stuffed roasted, 239
masala bhaat, 112–113
masala papad, 143
masala powder
    fragrant, tomato rice, aromatic, 101
    fresh, tamarind rice, 110
masaru anna/dahi bhaat, 103–104
masoor dal (pink lentils), described, 43
matki
    described, 380
    methods for, 381
matki usal, 399
mattha, 427
mawa (khoa), preparation of, 404–405
meats. *See also* chicken; duck; eggs
    curry preparation, 4
    cuts for tandoori cooking, 337
    lamb
        biryani, Moghul, 116–118
        chops in golden apricot sauce,
        285
        dum-style, fragrant, with mush-
        rooms, 292–293
        fennel-scented Kashmir,
        286–287
        ground, sweet-scented
        Hyderabad, 289–290
        Kerala-style aromatic, 291
        korma, 288–289
        tandoori

kebabs, Oudh-style, 354–355
maharaja with almonds and
    caramelized onion, fra-
    grant, 350–351
rolls with lentils, 356–357
tikka with saffron sauce,
    352–353
pork
    stew, Coorg-style, 297
    vindaloo, classic, 298–299
vegetarianism, 267–268
meen vevichathu, 324
meetha chatni, 130
meetha lassi, 426
melon, bitter, home-style, 250
menu composition, 14–15
methi chawal, 97
methi dana. See fenugreek seed
microwave cooking, legumes, 382
milagu thunny, 368
mint, chicken, pan-roasted cilantro-
    mint marinated, 284
mint chutney, with garlic, fresh,
    176–177
mint *naan,* 86
mint rice, fresh, 97
mint-tamarind-cilantro chutney, 178
mirch. See chili(s)
mixed-fruit summer cooler, 433
mixed greens, with toasted pecans,
    257–258
mixed sprouts stew, 399
mixed vegetables
    biryani, Lucknow, 121–123
    chicken *mulligatawny* with, 368
    kofta in cream sauce, 260–261
    kootu, 245
    paneer Seekh, tandoori, 362
moderation, in eating, 6
Moghul lamb *biryani,* 116–118
mokka jonna kulambu, 247–248
monji gada, 329–330
mortar and pestle
    chutney preparation, 176
    spice grinding, 8–10
moru kootu, 245
mousse, mango, 405–406
Mughalai Gosht *biryani,* 116–118
mulligatawny, with mixed vegetables,
    368
multigrain flatbread with spinach, 66–67
Mumbai (Bombay), seafood, 302
Mumbai breakfast with beaten rice,
    nutritious, 167–168

Mumbai fish steamed in banana leaves, 330–331

mung beans
    described, 43, 44
    kabocha squash stew with, 400
    savory, 139–140
    stew, pink lentils and, with leeks, 384–385

murg daraanpur, 278–279
murg kandahari kofte, 276–277
murg korma, 270–271
murg makhani, 274–275
murg tikka masala, 272–274, 345

mushrooms
    braised in tomato sauce, Kashmir, 253–254
    glazed skillet *paneer* with bell pepper and, 227
    lamb, *dum*-style, fragrant, with, 292–293

mussel chowder, Kerala, 366
mustard sauce, seared Bengal fish in, 325–326
mustard seed, described, 29–30
my mother's heirloom pickled limes, 193–194
my mother's heirloom spice blend *(kala masla/kari khar),* recipe, 39–40
Mysore coffee, 430–431

naan, 84–90
    described, 59
    master recipe, 84–85
    rose-flavored with silver leaf, 89–90
    sourdough starter, 87–88
    variations, 85–86
namak (salt), described, 54
nankhatai, 421
nigella seed, described, 30
nimbu (lime), described, 52
nippy (astringent) taste, sources of, 7
nuge kai rasam, 369
nutmeg/mace, described, 30–31
nutrition, balance in, 6–7
nutritious Mumbai breakfast with beaten rice, 167–168
nuts, toasting of, 208

oil. *See also desi ghee* (clarified butter)
    curry preparation, 3, 4
    described, 49

whole spice Bengal seasoning (panch puran), 50
okra
    with *chaat masala,* crisp, 147
    sautéed in tumeric-tinted yogurt, 252
onion(s)
    aromatics, 10
    caramelized, lamb maharaja with caramelized onion and, fragrant, 350–351
    curry preparation, 4, 5
    pearl onion Mysore *sambar,* 390–391
onion - red pepper flakes *naan,* 86
orange juice
    cream-of-wheat halvah, toasted, with, 418–419
    lentil *rasam* soup with, 370
Oudh-style tandoori lamb kebabs, 354–355
outdoor grilling tips, 339
oven, preheating of, 12
oyster skillet roast, Karwar, 316

pachadi, 212
padolkai doni, 263–264
pakora, crispy, 144–146
palak bathak, 295–296
palak paneer, 225–226
palak poori, 81
palak raita, 213
palak tangdi, 342–343
palak thepla, 66–67
pancakes, pineapple-speckled crusty, 161
Panchamrit, 181
panch puran (whole spice Bengal seasoning), recipe for, 50
panchranga pulao, 98–99
paneer, 219–228
    basic fresh, 221–222
    described, 219–220
    glazed skillet *paneer* with mushroom and bell pepper, 227
    kingfish in spinach gravy, 226
    mango sauce crowned with, delicate, 222–223
    mixed vegetable-*paneer* Seekh, tandoori, 362
    pan-fried, and chicken with *khada masala,* 224

roasted, in fragrant spinach sauce, 225–226
    steaks with honey sauce and cashew, 228
    tandoori lamb rolls with, 357
paneer kofta, in aromatic spinach sauce, golden, 258–259
paneer naan, 86
paneer sabji shaslik, 362
pan-fried *paneer,* and chicken with *khada masala,* 224
pani puri, 132–133
pan-roasted Bengal fish with raisins, 332–333
pan-roasted cilantro-mint marinated chicken, 284
papaya, green, meat tenderizer, 337
papaya-kiwi *chaat,* with pistachios, 140
papdi chaat, 135
paper-thin crispy rice crepes, 159–160
pappadam, crispy, 142–143
paratha
    flaky cilantro-laced, 76–77
    flaky cumin-scented, 74–75
    potato-stuffed savory, 78–79
paratha, described, 58–59
pardesi dal (split peas), described, 43
pardesi saunf. See aniseed
Parsee shrimp in sweet-hot-sour curry, 312–313
pasilla chilis, almond-stuffed, 264–265
pasta, *chapati* pasta, *dal* with spinach and, 397–398
patrani machchi, 330–331
pawakkai kari, 250
payasam/kheer, 414
peaches, banana and peach chutney, 186
peanuts
    crushed and roasted, described, 53
    eggplant, peanut-stuffed old-fashioned, 262
    fresh cilantro chutney with, 174–175
    greens, mixed, with deep-fried, 258
    pecan-peanut chutney powder, 190
pear-apricot chutney, with almonds, 187
pearl onion Mysore *sambar,* 390–391
pearl tapioca, 53
pearl tapioca cakes, 169
pearl tapioca pilaf, classic, 168–169
peas, cabbage *kachumber* with, 218
pecan-peanut chutney powder, 190

pecans
  greens, mixed, with toasted, 257–258
  sweet spiced mango chutney with, 185
  zucchini and eggplant with, skillet-seared zesty, 233
peppercorn
  brussels sprouts stir-fry with sesame, peppery, 234
  described, 31
peppery brussels sprouts stir-fry with sesame, 234
persimmon *lassi,* 432
persimmon *thandai,* 432
phal chaat, 140
phal thandai, 433
pheasant-lentil stew, with wilted greens, 387–388
phulka, whole-wheat flatbreads, 65
pickles, 192–200. *See also* chutney
  cashew-lime sweet pickle, 195
  chile-lime pickles, 194
  green mango relish, spicy-sweet, 197
  limes, my mother's heirloom, 193–194
  pineapple, cranberry-studded, 196
  shrimp, coastal, 198–199
  vegetables with zesty seasoning, 199–200
pilaf
  pearl tapioca pilaf, classic, 168–169
  vegetable, with cashews, fragrant mixed, 98–99
  with vegetables, spicy, 112–113
pindi chole/channa masala, 395–396
pineapple
  crusty pancakes speckled with, 161
  meat tenderizer, 337
  pickled, cranberry-studded, 196
  smoothie, 431
pink lentils
  described, 43
  mung dal stew and, with leeks, 384–385
pistachios
  chayote pudding and, velvety, 416
  ice cream, 407–408
  kiwi-papaya *chaat* with, 140
pista kulfi, 407–408
place setting, dining, 13–14
plantain, braised with tamarind, 242
plum-stuffed *kofta,* 277

poha/pohe/avalaki, 167–168
pomegranate juice, turkey tandoori with, 348–349
pomegranate seed, described, 32
poori
  crispy puffy, 131–132
    filled with zesty tamarind sauce, 132–133
  described, 59
  master recipes, 80–82
poori canapé
  crowned with yogurt topping, classic, 135
  with savory topping, classic, 134
poppy seed, described, 31–32
poriyals, cooking techniques, 232
pork, 297–299
  stew, Coorg-style, 297
  vindaloo, classic, 298–299
potato(es)
  crepes, easy, 163
  curry, tamarind-laced, Grandma's, 254–255
  potato-chutney-cheese bake, 178
  potato-stuffed savory *paratha,* 78–79
  purple potato, cranberry bean stew and, fresh, 394–395
  rogan josh, 287
  samosa, spiced, 149
  yam-potato *raita,* 210–211
  Yukon gold, with zesty seasoning, 236–237
potpourri, 19
poultry. *See also* chicken; duck
  Cornish game hen stuffed with mango tandoori, 345–346
  quail tandoori, with tropical fruits, 347–348
  turkey, with pomegranate juice, tandoori, 348–349
powdered nuts and seeds, curry preparation, 5
prawn Balchao, 198–199
preheating, of oven, 12
presentation, curry preparation, 6
pressure cooking, *sambars* and stews, 377–378
protein, balance in, 6
pudina chatni, 176–177, 177–178
puffed rice nibble, with dried fruits and nuts, 151
puffy breads, 80–82

puliyodharai, 109
pumpkin greens, and lentil stew, Grandmother's, 401–402
Pune-style fragrant stew, classic, 393
Pune-style sesame-laced powder *(goda masala),* recipe, 40–41
pungent taste, sources of, 7
Punjab *boondi raita,* 214
puran poli/holige, 72–73
purple potato, cranberry bean stew and, fresh, 394–395

quail tandoori, with tropical fruits, 347–348
Queen's mango and kumquat with subtle citrus-curry sauce, 248–249
quick and easy yams in herb sauce, 244
quick semolina crepes, 162

radishes, cucumber and radish *raita,* 207
raitas, 206–214. *See also kachumbers;* yogurt
  boondi raita, Punjab, 214
  carrot *raita* with toasted walnuts, 208–209
  corn-zucchini *raita,* 209
  cucumber and radish *raita,* 207
  described, 202–203
  garlic *raita,* 211
  mango-macadamia *raita,* 206
  scallion-spinach *raita* with sesame seed, 213
  yam-potato *raita,* 210–211
  zucchini *raita,* roasted, 212
rajma (kidney beans), described, 44
ran maharaja, 350–351
rasam, 2
rasam powder, recipe, 38
rasam soup
  lentil *rasam* soup with orange juice, 370
  rhubarb *rasam* soup, 369
  thickening powder, 371
ras malai, 410–411
rava dosa, 162
rava masala dosa, 162
raw (turbinado) sugar, described, 52
red chilis, described, 23
red wines. *See* wines

regional cuisines
Indian cuisine, 269
seafood, 302–305
reshmi mamsa/boti kabab, 352–353
rhubarb *rasam* soup, 369
rice. *See* Arborio rice; basmati rice;
biryani; jasmine rice;
long-grain white rice;
wild rice
rice crepes, paper-thin crispy, 159–160
rice flour *(chawal ka atta),* described, 46
rice nibble, puffed, with dried fruits and
nuts, 151
rice pudding, creamy, 414
risotto with *dal,* spicy Udupi-style,
110–112
roadside combo with chutney garnishes, 129
roasted fennel seed stimulant, 436
roasted *paneer,* in fragrant spinach
sauce, 225–226
roasted zucchini *raita,* 212
rogani dhingri, 253–254
rogan josh, 286–287
rolling pin, described, 56
rose-accented sweet buttermilk *lassi,*
426
rose-flavored *naan* with silver leaf,
89–90
rose-scented warm syrup, cakey balls
in, 412–413
roti
Kashmir *roti,* 68–69
whole-wheat flatbreads, 65
ruby-red tomato-carrot chutney, 180
ruh (essence), described, 51
rustic Punjab cornmeal flatbread,
70–71
rutabaga
duck breast with crusty turnip and,
Kashmir, 294–295
in silken yogurt, 243
rutabaga kootu, 243

saabat masoor (brown lentils),
described, 44
saadi aamti, 393
saag, 257–258
saar, 2
sabaat mung (mung beans), described,
44
sabji malai kofta, 260–261
saboodana khichdi, 168–169

sabudana (pearl tapioca), 53
sada chawal (basmati rice), basic
recipe, 96
sada paneer, 221–222
sada paratha, 74–75
saffron
described, 32
tandoori lamb *tikka* with, 352–353
saffron *naan,* almond-laced, 86
sago vadai, 169
salmon, Dakshin fenugreek-marinated,
braised in coconut milk,
319–320
salt, 7
curry preparation, 6
described, 54
salty *lassi* with fresh mint, 426–427
sambar powder, recipe, 37–38
sambars and stews, 375–402. *See also*
legumes; soups
basic recipe, 388–389
broccoli-cauliflower *sambar,* 392
chickpeas simmered in tomato-ginger sauce, 395–396
cooking methods, 382
cranberry bean, fresh, and purple
potato stew, 394–395
dal with *chapati* pasta and spinach,
397–398
flatulence, 380
garlicky *dal* stew, 383
kabocha squash with mung beans,
400
kidney beans and lentils, creamed,
385–386
legume purchase, storage, and
cooking, 378–379
lentil, pink, and *mung dal* stew with
leeks, 384–385
pearl onion Mysore *sambar,*
390–391
pheasant-lentil stew, with wilted
greens, 387–388
pressure cooking, 377–378
pumpkin greens and lentil stew,
Grandmother's, 401–402
Pune-style fragrant stew, classic,
393
sprouts, 380–381
sprouts stew, mixed, 399
samosa
cocktail, 149
fragrant lamb, 148–149
spiced potato, 149

sasam, 248–249
saunf. See fennel seed
sautéed vegetables, cooking techniques, 230
savory mixed-flour crepes, 164
savory *mung dal,* 139–140
savory yogurt sauce, dumplings bathed
in, 136–137
scallion-spinach *raita,* with sesame
seed, 213
scallops
biryani, spiked with coconut,
118–119
roasted in banana leaf, Malabar,
314–315
seafood, 301–333. *See also* fish; shellfish; specific fish and
shellfish
coconut, 305–308
geography, 302–305
seared Bengal fish in tangy mustard
sauce, 325–326
seared chicken *tikka,* 344–345
seasoned cooked vegetables, cooking
techniques, 230–231
seasonings, curry preparation, 5–6
semiya payaam/kheer, 415
semolina crepes, quick, 162
semolina *(sooji),* described, 46. *See also*
flours
sesame-*ajwain* stimulant, with lime
juice, 437
sesame-laced powder *(goda masala),*
Pune-style, recipe, 40–41
sesame seed(s)
brussels sprouts stir-fry with, peppery, 234
described, 32–33
green tomato-sesame chutney,
183–184
sev puri, 134
shami kabab, 356–357
sheera/kesari bhat, 418–419
sheer mal, 89–90
shellfish. *See also* fish
calamari, hot-sour Goa, 318–319
clams, fragrant steamed Goa,
313–314
crab curry, boatman's, 311
crab curry, Konkan, 309–310
lobster and calamari bathed in aromatics, Cochin, 317–318
mussel chowder, Kerala, 366
oyster skillet roast, Karwar, 316

shellfish *(cont.)*

shrimp in sweet-hot-sour curry, Parsee, 312–313

shrimp rice, Konkan, 102–103

tandoori, shrimp, jumbo Bengal, 359

shorshay baata maach, 325–326

shrikhand, 408–409

shrimp

pickled, coastal, 198–199

in sweet-hot-sour curry, Parsee, 312–313

tandoori, jumbo Bengal, 359

shrimp rice, Konkan, 102–103

shukto, cooking techniques, 232

silver leaf

described, 54

rose-flavored *naan* with, 89–90

sime avarekai (lima beans), described, 44

sime badnekai payasam, 416

siya jeera. See caraway

skillet egg masala, 299–300

skillet-seared zesty zucchini and eggplant with pecans, 233

small plates. *See chaat*

smoothie, pineapple, 431

snacks. *See chaat*

sooji (semolina), described, 46. *See also* flours

soothing *dal* soup, 367

soups, 363–373. *See also sambars and* stews

buttermilk *kahdi* soup with *kari* leaves, 373

chicken *mulligatawny,* with mixed vegetables, 368

dal soup, soothing, 367

described, 363–364

mango soup, warm, 364–365

mussel chowder, Kerala, 366

rasam

lentil *rasam* soup with orange juice, 370

rhubarb *rasam* soup, 369

thickening powder, 371

tomato, Indian-style spicy, 372

sourdough starter, *naan* with, 87–88

sour taste, sources of, 7

sowthekai pachadi, 207

spice blends, 34–42

chaat masala, 41–42

curry powder *(kari pudi),* 35

garam masala, 36–37

heirloom spice blend, my mother's

(kala masla / kari khar), 39–40

Pune-style sesame-laced powder *(goda masala),* 40–41

rasam powder, 38

sambar powder, 37–38

tandoori spice mix *(tandoori chatpata masala),* 34

spice box, 55–56

spiced potato *samosa,* 149

spiced tea mix, 430

spice mix, curry preparation, 3

spices, 17–33

ajwain, 20

allspice, 19

aniseed, 19–20

asafetida, 20–21

basil, 21

bay leaf, 21

caraway, 21

cardamom, 21–22

chilis, 22–24

cilantro, 24

cinnamon, 24–25

clove, 25

coriander seed, 25–26

cumin seed, 26

curry leaf, 28–29

defined, 18

fennel seed, 26

fenugreek leaf, 27

fenugreek seed, 27

ginger, 27–28

grinding of, 8–10

mango powder, 29

mustard seed, 29–30

nigella seed, 30

nutmeg/mace, 30–31

peppercorn, 31

pomegranate seed, 32

poppy seed, 31–32

purchasing of, 18–19

saffron, 32

sesame seed, 32–33

star anise, 33

toasting of, 4, 7–8, 9

turmeric, 33

whole, 14

spicy Indian lamb burger, 355

spicy *lassi* with oil seasoning, 427

spicy pilaf with vegetables, 112–113

spicy-sweet green mango relish, 197

spicy-sweet kumquat chutney, with figs, 188

spicy Udupi-style risotto with *dal,* 110–112

spinach

dal with *chapati* pasta and, 397–398

duck legs with subtle spinach sauce, 295–296

greens, mixed, with toasted pecans, 257–258

multigrain flatbread with, 66–67

paneer kofta in aromatic spinach sauce, golden, 258–259

scallion-spinach *raita,* with sesame seed, 213

spinach-crusted tandoori chicken, 342–343

spinach gravy, kingfish in, 226

spinach *poori,* 81

spinach sauce, roasted *paneer* in fragrant, 225–226

split chickpeas *(chana dal),* described, 42–43

split peas *(pardesi dal),* described, 43

sprouts

described, 380

methods for, 381

sprouts stew, mixed, 399

squash, sweet-spiced, with garlic, 235

squash boats, filled with lentils, 263–264

star anise, described, 33

starters, 141–151

cocktail *samosa,* 149

lamb *samosa,* fragrant, 148–149

masala papad, 143

okra with *chaat masala,* crisp, 147

pakora, crispy, 144–146

pappadam, crispy, 142–143

puffed rice nibble with dried fruits and nuts, 151

spiced potato *samosa,* 149

steamed *dhokla* bread, instant, 150

steamed cream-of-wheat *idli* cakes, 158–159

steamed *dhokla* bread, instant, 150

steamed *idli* cakes, 156–157

stews. *See sambars and stews*

stir-fry

cooking techniques, 230

curry preparation, 4–5

street-style buttermilk balloon bread, 82–83

stuffed vegetables, cooking techniques, 232

sturgeon fillet, Kashmir-style, with *kohlrabi,* 329–330

sugar, curry preparation, 6
sukha dhania. See coriander seed
sukke kalwas, 316
summer cooler, mixed-fruit, 433
sweet chutney sauce, 130
sweet rice, 106
sweet-scented Hyderabad ground
　　　　lamb, 289–290
sweet-scented tomato gravy, mixed
　　　　vegetable *biryani,*
　　　　Lucknow, 123
sweet-spiced mango chutney, with
　　　　pecans, 185
sweet-spiced squash with garlic, 235
sweet taste, sources of, 7

tables, dining, 13
tadka, curry preparation, 3–4
tali hui bhindi/bhendi kurkure, 147
tamarind
　　　　corn simmered with tangy,
　　　　　　　Chettinad, 247–248
　　　　described, 54–55
　　　　lobster and calamari bathed in aro-
　　　　　　　matics, Cochin, 317–318
　　　　meat tenderizer, 338
　　　　plantain braised with, 242
tamarind chutney, with banana, 182
tamarind-cilantro-mint chutney, 178
tamarind rice, 109
tamarind sauce, crispy puffy *poori* filled
　　　　with, 132–133
tamatar makhani gravy, *lucknowi tehri*
　　　　biryani, 123
tandoori bater, 347–348
tandoori chatpata masala. See tandoori
　　　　spice mix
tandoori foods, 335–362
　　　　chicken, 340–341
　　　　　　　seared *tikka,* 344–345
　　　　　　　spinach-crusted, 342–343
　　　　　　　tikka, kandahari, 349
　　　　Cornish game hen stuffed with
　　　　　　　mango, 345–346
　　　　described, 335–336
　　　　fish
　　　　　　　ajwain-marinated whole,
　　　　　　　　　357–358
　　　　　　　shrimp, jumbo Bengal, 359
　　　　　　　zucchini with, Seekh, 360
　　　　lamb
　　　　　　　kebabs, Oudh-style, 354–355
　　　　　　　maharaja with almonds and

caramelized onion, fra-
　　　　grant, 350–351
rolls, with lentils, 356–357
tikka with saffron sauce,
　　　　352–353
marinades, 338
meat cuts for, 337
outdoor grilling tips, 339
quail with tropical fruits, 347–348
tenderizers, 336–338
turkey with pomegranate juice,
　　　　348–349
vegetables
　　　　cauliflower and broccoli, 361
　　　　mixed vegetable-*paneer* Seekh,
　　　　　　　362
tandoori masala gobi, 361
tandoori murg, 340–341
tandoori spice mix, tangy *(tandoori
　　　　chatpata masala),* recipe,
　　　　34
tandoori teetar, 348–349
tandoori tikka, 344–345
tangerines, cranberry-tangerine chut-
　　　　ney, hot and sweet, 189
tangy mahimahi fillets with shallots, 324
tangy tandoori spice mix *(tandoori chat-
　　　　pata masala),* recipe, 34
tapioca cakes, pearl, 169
tapioca pilaf, pearl, classic, 168–169
tareli tava machchi/ayala porichathu,
　　　　326–327
tarkari chatni, 180
tarkari kari, 246
tarkari upinkai, 199–200
tastes, of India, 6–12
tava (griddle), described, 56
tavai baingan, 233
tavai tilwala pattagobi, 234
tea, spiced mix, 430
tej patta. See bay leaf
tenderizers, recommended, 336–338
thakkali sadam, 100–101
theeka chatni, 130–131
thickeners
　　　　curry preparation, 5
　　　　power, *rasam* soup, 371
thirsts quenches. *See* beverages
til. See sesame seed
til-owa supari, 437
tisryo, 313–314
toasted chickpea flour candy balls, 422
toasting
　　　　of nuts, 208

of spices, 4, 7–8, 9
toasty Mysore cream of wheat, with
　　　　carrots and beans,
　　　　165–166
tokku, 195
tomatillo, green tomato-tomatillo chut-
　　　　ney, 184
tomato(es)
　　　　carrot chutney with, ruby-red, 180
　　　　catfish, coastal Kerala, with,
　　　　　　　321–322
　　　　curry preparation, 4–5
　　　　garlic and, 11
　　　　ginger sauce with, chickpeas sim-
　　　　　　　mered in, 395–396
　　　　gravy, sweet-scented, mixed veg-
　　　　　　　etable *biryani,* Lucknow,
　　　　　　　123
　　　　green tomato-sesame chutney,
　　　　　　　183–184
　　　　green tomato with masala, chili-
　　　　　　　and garlic-stuffed roast-
　　　　　　　ed, 239
　　　　poori, 82
　　　　puree, aromatics, 11–12
　　　　rice, aromatic, 100–101
　　　　saar, 372
　　　　sauce, mushrooms braised in,
　　　　　　　Kashmir, 253–254
　　　　soup, Indian-style spicy, 372
toovar dal/toor dal/arhar dal (yellow
　　　　lentils), described, 44
tulsi. See basil
tumbidu mensinkai, 264–265
tumeric, pan-roasted Bengal fish with
　　　　raisins, 332–333
turbinado (raw) sugar, described, 52
turkey, with pomegranate juice, tan-
　　　　doori, 348–349
turmeric, described, 33
turnip, duck breast with crusty rutaba-
　　　　ga and, Kashmir,
　　　　294–295

udupi dosa, 159–160
Udupi-style risotto, spicy, with *dal,*
　　　　110–112
U.S. Food and Drug Administration
　　　　(FDA), 49
uppuma/khara bhat, 165–166
urad dal (white split gram beans),
　　　　described, 44
uttappam, pineapple, 161

varq (silver and gold leaf), described, 54
vasanthaneer, 428–429
vegetables, 229–265
    apricots and figs in delicate nutty
        sauce, 256–257
    bell pepper *poriyal,* 241
    biryani, Lucknow mixed,
        121–123
    bitter melon, home-style, 250
    broccoli-cauliflower Mangalore
        curry, 251
    brussels sprouts stir-fry with
        sesame, peppery, 234
    chicken stew with, 280
    cooking techniques, 230–232
        kofta curries, 232
        kootu, korma, and shukto, 232
        poriyals, 232
        sautéed and stir-fry dishes, 230
        seasoned cooked dishes,
            230–231
        stuffed vegetables, 232
    corn simmered with tangy
        tamarind, Chettinad,
        247–248
    eggplant, peanut-stuffed old-fash-
        ioned, 262
    eggplant with masala, chili- and
        garlic-stuffed roasted,
        238–239
    fruit and vegetable *navratna korma,*
        271
    green beans *poriyal,* 240
    greens, mixed, with toasted pecans,
        257–258
    mango and kumquat with subtle
        citrus-curry sauce,
        Queen's, 248–249
    mixed vegetable *kofta* in cream
        sauce, 260–261
    mixed vegetable *kootu,* 245
    mixed vegetables, chicken *mulli-*
        gatawny with, 368
    mushrooms braised in tomato
        sauce, Kashmir,
        253–254
    okra, sautéed in tumeric-tinted
        yogurt, 252
    paneer kofta in aromatic spinach
        sauce, golden, 258–259
    pasilla chilis, almond-stuffed,
        264–265
    pickled, with zesty seasoning,
        199–200

    pilaf with cashews, fragrant mixed,
        98–99
    plantain braised with tamarind, 242
    potato curry, tamarind-laced,
        Grandma's, 254–255
    potatoes, Yukon gold, with zesty
        seasoning, 236–237
    potato *rogan josh,* 287
    rutabaga in silken yogurt, 243
    squash, sweet-spiced, with garlic,
        235
    squash boats, filled with lentils,
        263–264
    tandoori
        cauliflower and broccoli, 361
        mixed vegetable-*paneer* Seekh,
            362
        zucchini, fish Seekh with, 360
    yams, quick and easy, in herb
        sauce, 244
    yams and green beans in aromatic
        velvety sauce, 246
    zucchini and eggplant with pecans,
        skillet-seared zesty,
        233
    zucchini with masala, chili- and
        garlic-stuffed roasted,
        239
vegetarianism, 267–268
velvety pistachio and chayote pudding,
    416
vendakkai mor thalippu, 252
vengaya kuzhambu, 390–391
ven pongal, 105–106
vermicelli pudding, with fresh berries,
    415
vinegar, meat tenderizer, 338
vitamins, sprouts *(matki),* 380

walnuts, carrot *raita* with toasted,
    208–209
warm mango soup, 364–365
water, curry preparation, 4–5
white split gram beans *(urad dal),*
    described, 44
whole spice Bengal seasoning *(panch*
    puran), recipe for, 50
whole spices, 14
whole-wheat flatbreads, 63–65
wild rice, chicken *biryani* and,
    124–125
wilted greens, pheasant-lentil stew
    with, 387–388

wines, suggestions for, 237, 275
wok, described, 56

xacuti sauce, chicken, Goa, 281–282

yams
    green beans and, in aromatic vel-
        vety sauce, 246
    potato *raita* with, 210–211
    quick and easy, in herb sauce, 244
yellow beet *poori,* 82
yellow bell peppers *poori,* 82
yellow lentils *(toovar dal / toor dal / arhar*
    dal), described, 44
yellow split mung beans *(mung dal),*
    described, 43
yenkai badnekai, 262
yogurt, 201–202. *See also kachumbers;*
    raitas
    apricot gravy with mint and,
        Moghul lamb *biryani,*
        118
    curry preparation, 5
    meat tenderizer, 337
    okra, sautéed in tumeric-tinted
        yogurt, 252
    raitas, 203
    rutabaga in silken, 243
    sauce, savory, dumplings bathed in,
        136–137
yogurt cheese
    curry preparation, 5
    fluffy, 408–409
    homemade, 205
yogurt rice, 103–104
Yukon gold potatoes with zesty season-
    ing, 236–237

zesty seasoning, pickled vegetables
    with, 199–200
zucchini
    chutney, with fresh dill, 184
    eggplant and, with pecans, skillet-
        seared zesty, 233
    raita
        corn-zucchini *raita,* 209
        roasted, 212
    roasted with masala, chili- and gar-
        lic-stuffed, 239
    tandoori, fish Seekh with, 360
zucchini *bharata,* 239